HOLT
LITERATURE AND LANGUAGE ARTS

Introductory Course

Kylene Beers
Carol Jago
Deborah Appleman
Leila Christenbury
Sara Kajder
Linda Rief

Senior Program Consultants for English Language Development

Robin Scarcella
Mabel Rivera
Héctor Rivera

Mastering the California Standards
Reading, Writing, Listening, Speaking

HOLT, RINEHART AND WINSTON

Program Authors

Kylene Beers is the senior program author for *Holt Literature and Language Arts*. A former middle school teacher, she is now Senior Reading Advisor to Secondary Schools for Teachers College Reading and Writing Project at Columbia University. She is the author of *When Kids Can't Read: What Teachers Can Do* and co-editor (with Linda Rief and Robert E. Probst) of *Adolescent Literacy: Turning Promise into Practice*. The former editor of the National Council of Teachers of English (NCTE) literacy journal *Voices from the Middle*, Dr. Beers assumed the NCTE presidency in 2008. With articles in *English Journal, Journal of Adolescent and Adult Literacy, School Library Journal, Middle Matters,* and *Voices from the Middle,* she speaks both nationally and internationally as a recognized authority on struggling readers. Dr. Beers has served on the review boards of *English Journal, The ALAN Review,* the Special Interest Group on Adolescent Literature of the International Reading Association, and the Assembly on Literature for Adolescents of the NCTE. She is the 2001 recipient of the Richard W. Halley Award given by NCTE for outstanding contributions to middle school literacy.

Carol Jago is a teacher with thirty-two years of experience at Santa Monica High School in California. The author of nine books on education, she continues to share her experiences as a writer and as a speaker at conferences and seminars across the country. Her wide and varied experience in standards assessment and secondary education in general has made her a sought-after speaker. As an author, Ms. Jago also works closely with Heinemann Publishers and with the National Council of Teachers of English. Her long-time association with NCTE led to her June 2007 election to a four-year term on the council's board. During that term she will serve for one year as president of the council. She is also active with the California Association of Teachers of English (CATE) and has edited CATE's scholarly journal *California English* since 1996. Ms. Jago served on the planning committees for the 2009 NAEP Reading Framework and the 2011 NAEP Writing Framework.

Deborah Appleman is professor and chair of educational studies and director of the Summer Writing Program at Carleton College in Northfield, Minnesota. Dr. Appleman's primary research interests include adolescent response to literature, multicultural literature, and the teaching of literary theory in high school. With a team of classroom teachers, she co-edited *Braided Lives,* a multicultural literature anthology. In addition to many articles and book chapters, she is the author of *Critical Encounters in High School English: Teaching Literary Theory to Adolescents* and co-author of *Teaching Literature to Adolescents*. Her most recent book, *Reading for Themselves,* explores the use of extracurricular book clubs to encourage adolescents to read for pleasure. Dr. Appleman was a high school English teacher, working in both urban and suburban schools. She is a frequent national speaker and consultant and continues to work weekly in high schools with students and teachers.

Leila Christenbury is a former high school English teacher and currently professor of English education at Virginia Commonwealth University, Richmond. The former editor of *English Journal,* she is the author of ten books, including *Writing on Demand, Making the Journey,* and *Retracing the Journey: Teaching and Learning in an American High School*. Past president of the National Council of Teachers of English, Dr. Christenbury is also a former member of the steering committee of the National Assessment

PROGRAM AUTHORS **continued**

of Educational Progress (NAEP). A recipient of the Rewey Belle Inglis Award for Outstanding Woman in English Teaching, Dr. Christenbury is a frequent speaker on issues of English teaching and learning and has been interviewed and quoted on CNN and in the *New York Times, USA Today, Washington Post, Chicago Tribune,* and *US News & World Report.*

 **Sara Kajder,** author of *Bringing the Outside In: Visual Ways to Engage Reluctant Readers* and *The Tech-Savvy English Classroom,* is an assistant professor at Virginia Polytechnic Institute and State University (Virginia Tech). She has served as co-chair of NCTE's Conference on English Education (CEE) Technology Commission and of the Society for Information Technology and Teacher Education (SITE) English Education Committee. Dr. Kajder is the recipient of the first SITE

National Technology Leadership Fellowship in English Education; she is a former English and language arts teacher for high school and middle school.

 **Linda Rief** has been a classroom teacher for twenty-five years. She is author of *The Writer's-Reader's Notebook, Inside the Writer's-Reader's Notebook, Seeking Diversity, 100 Quickwrites,* and *Vision and Voice* as well as the co-editor (with Kylene Beers and Robert E. Probst) of *Adolescent Literacy: Turning Promise into Practice.* Ms. Rief has written numerous chapters and journal articles, and she co-edited the first five years of *Voices from the Middle.* During the summer she teaches graduate courses at the University of New Hampshire and Northeastern University. She is a national and international consultant on adolescent literacy issues.

Program Consultants

 **Robin Scarcella** is a professor at the University of California at Irvine, where she also directs the Program in Academic English/English as a Second Language. She has a Ph.D. in linguistics from the University of Southern California and an M.A. in education/second language acquisition from Stanford University. She has taught all grade levels. She has been active in shaping policies affecting language assessment, instruction, and teacher professional development. In the last four years, she has spoken to over ten thousand teachers and administrators. She has written over thirty scholarly articles that appear in such journals as the *TESOL Quarterly* and *Brain and Language.* Her most recent publication is *Accelerating Academic English: A Focus on the English Learner.*

 Mabel Rivera is a research assistant professor at the Texas Institute for Measurement, Evaluation, and Statistics at the University of Houston. Her current research interests include the education of and prevention of reading difficulties in English-language learners. In addition, Dr. Rivera is involved in local and national service activities for preparing school personnel to teach students with special needs.

 Héctor H. Rivera is an assistant professor at Southern Methodist University, School of Education and Human Development. Dr. Rivera is also the director of the SMU Professional Development/ ESL Supplemental Certification Program for Math

and Science Teachers of At-Risk Middle and High School LEP Newcomer Adolescents. This federally funded program develops, delivers, and evaluates professional development for educators who work with at-risk newcomer adolescent students. Dr. Rivera is also collaborating on school reform projects in Guatemala and with the Institute of Arctic Education in Greenland.

Marilyn Astore is a former teacher, principal, and county office assistant superintendent with over 20 years of classroom experience and over 40 years in the field of education. In her role as chair of both the California Curriculum Commission and its Reading/Language Arts/English Language Development Subject Matter Committees, she worked with other commissioners to advise the California State Board of Education on the adoption of curricular and instructional materials. She has taught teacher education classes at California State University, Sacramento; the University of San Diego; and the University of California, Davis, University Extension. Ms. Astore presents and consults on K–12 reading issues and intervention for older struggling readers.

Isabel L. Beck is professor of education and senior scientist at the University of Pittsburgh. Dr. Beck has conducted extensive research on vocabulary and comprehension and has published well over one hundred articles and several books, including *Improving Comprehension with Questioning the Author* (with Margaret McKeown) and *Bringing Words to Life: Robust Vocabulary Instruction* (with Margaret McKeown and Linda Kucan). Dr. Beck's numerous national awards include the Oscar S. Causey Award for outstanding research from the National Reading Conference and the William S. Gray Award from the International Reading Association for lifetime contributions to the field of reading research and practice.

Margaret G. McKeown is a senior scientist at the University of Pittsburgh's Learning Research and Development Center. Her research in reading comprehension and vocabulary has been published extensively in outlets for both research and practitioner audiences. Recognition of her work includes the International Reading Association's (IRA) Dissertation of the Year Award and a National Academy of Education Spencer Fellowship. Before her career in research, Dr. McKeown taught elementary school.

Amy Benjamin is a veteran teacher, literacy coach, consultant, and researcher in secondary-level literacy instruction. She has been recognized for excellence in teaching from the New York State English Council, Union College, and Tufts University. Ms. Benjamin is the author of several books about reading comprehension, writing instruction, grammar, and differentiation. Her most recent book (with Tom Oliva) is *Engaging Grammar: Practical Advice for Real Classrooms,* published by the National Council of Teachers of English. Ms. Benjamin has had a long association and leadership role with the NCTE's Assembly for the Teaching of English Grammar (ATEG).

Sandra Carsten has over thirty-seven years of experience as a teacher and administrator in the Fresno Unified School District. She has been a leader in curriculum, instruction, and professional development and has supervised national grants. As an assistant superintendent for curriculum

PROGRAM CONSULTANTS continued

and instruction, she implemented standards-based programs, benchmark assessments, and protocols for monitoring student achievement. In addition, Ms. Carsten served for five years as the director of the Association of California School Administrators.

 Eric Cooper is the president of the National Urban Alliance for Effective Education (NUA) and co-founder of the Urban Partnership for Literacy with the IRA. He currently works with the NCTE to support improvements in urban education and collaborates with the Council of the Great City Schools. In line with his educational mission to support the improvement of education for urban and minority students, Dr. Cooper writes, lectures, and produces educational documentaries and talk shows to provide advocacy for children who live in disadvantaged circumstances.

 **Harvey Daniels** is a former college professor and classroom teacher, working in urban and suburban Chicago schools. Known for his pioneering work on student book clubs, Dr. Daniels is author and co-author of many books, including *Literature Circles: Voice and Choice in Book Clubs and Reading Groups* and *Best Practice: Today's Standards for Teaching and Learning in America's Schools.*

 **Judith L. Irvin** taught middle school for several years before entering her career as a university professor. She now teaches courses in curriculum and instructional leadership and literacy at Florida State University. Dr. Irvin's many publications include *Reading and the High School Student: Strategies to Enhance Literacy* and *Integrating Literacy and*

Learning in the Content Area Classroom. Her latest book, *Taking Action: A Leadership Model for Improving Adolescent Literacy,* is the result of a Carnegie-funded project and is published by the Association for Supervision and Curriculum Development.

 Patrick Schwarz is professor of special education and chair of the Diversity in Learning and Development department for National-Louis University, Chicago, Illinois. He is author of *From Disability to Possibility* and *You're Welcome* (co-written with Paula Kluth), texts that have inspired teachers worldwide to reconceptualize inclusion to help all children. Other books co-written with Paula Kluth include *Just Give Him the Whale* and *Inclusion Bootcamp.* Dr. Schwarz also presents and consults worldwide through Creative Culture Consulting.

 Marianne Steverson is currently president and COO of the educational services company known as Smar^{2}tel Learning Links. She has forty-two years of diversified experience in the public school sector and private educational therapy practice. She coordinates the company's in-school professional development for teachers of reading. She also manages the development of new products and methodologies. Her areas of specialization include teaching students who speak African American Vernacular English and teaching struggling readers.

Critical Reviewers

Program Advisors

Contents in Brief

 Chapter Standards Focus

Mastering the Standards Reading • Writing • Listening • Speaking

CHAPTER

Setting and Plot

"You never find yourself until you face the truth." —**Pearl Bailey**

What Do You Think? How can discovering a tough truth help you gain a better understanding of who you are as a person?

 California Standards

Word Analysis, Fluency, and Systematic Vocabulary Development
1.4 Monitor expository text for unknown words or words with novel meanings by using word, sentence, and paragraph clues to determine meaning.

Reading Comprehension (Focus on Informational Materials)
2.4 Clarify an understanding of texts by creating outlines, logical notes, summaries, or reports.

Literary Response and Analysis
3.3 Analyze the influence of setting on the problem and its resolution.

Writing Applications (Genres and Their Characteristics)
2.1 Write narratives:
   a. Establish and develop a plot and setting and present a point of view that is appropriate to the stories.
   b. Include sensory details and concrete language to develop plot and character.
   c. Use a range of narrative devices (e.g., dialogue, suspense).

CHAPTER 2

Character

"Always do right; this will gratify some people and astonish the rest."
—Mark Twain

What Do You Think? How do you know what the right thing to do is? What do you think motivates people to "do right"?

California Standards

Word Analysis, Fluency, and Systematic Vocabulary Development
1.5 Understand and explain "shades of meaning" in related words (e.g., *softly* and *quietly*).

Reading Comprehension (Focus on Informational Materials)
2.2 Analyze text that uses the compare-and-contrast organizational pattern.

Literary Response and Analysis
3.2 Analyze the effect of the qualities of the character (e.g., courage or cowardice, ambition or laziness) on the plot and the resolution of the conflict.

Writing Applications (Genres and Their Characteristics)
2.2 Write expository compositions (e.g., description, explanation, comparison and contrast, problem and solution):
  a. State the thesis or purpose.
  b. Explain the situation.
  c. Follow an organizational pattern appropriate to the type of composition.
  d. Offer persuasive evidence to validate arguments and conclusions as needed.

Theme

"In every conceivable manner, the family is link to our past, bridge to our future."
—Alex Haley

What Do You Think? How do the people you consider family help you find your place in the world?

 California Standards

Word Analysis, Fluency, and Systematic Vocabulary Development
1.3 Recognize the origins and meanings of frequently used foreign words in English and use these words accurately in speaking and writing.

Reading Comprehension (Focus on Informational Materials)
2.5 Follow multiple-step instructions for preparing applications (e.g., for a public library card, bank savings account, sports club, league membership).

Literary Response and Analysis
3.2 Analyze the effect of the qualities of the character (e.g., courage or cowardice, ambition or laziness) on the plot and the resolution of the conflict.
3.6 Identify and analyze features of themes conveyed through characters, actions, and images.

Writing Applications (Genres and Their Characteristics)
2.2 Write expository compositions (e.g., description, explanation, comparison and contrast, problem and solution):
   a. State the thesis or purpose.
   b. Explain the situation.
   c. Follow an organizational pattern appropriate to the type of composition.
   d. Offer persuasive evidence to validate arguments and conclusions as needed.

CHAPTER 4

Forms of Fiction

"We need to travel that road of danger and laughter, of mystery and understanding, which has always been the road of stories."
—**Joseph Bruchac**

What Do You Think? In what ways are stories an important part of your life?

California Standards

Word Analysis, Fluency, and Systematic Vocabulary Development
1.2 Identify and interpret figurative language and words with multiple meanings.

Reading Comprehension (Focus on Informational Materials)
2.1 Identify the structural features of popular media (e.g., newspapers, magazines, online information) and use the features to obtain information.

Literary Response and Analysis
3.1 Identify the forms of fiction and describe the major characteristics of each form.

3.6 Identify and analyze features of themes conveyed through characters, actions, and images.

Writing Applications (Genres and Their Characteristics)
2.2 Write expository compositions (e.g., description, explanation, comparison and contrast, problem and solution):
  a. State the thesis or purpose.
  b. Explain the situation.
  c. Follow an organizational pattern appropriate to the type of composition.
  d. Offer persuasive evidence to validate arguments and conclusions as needed.

CHAPTER 5

Elements of Poetry

"The best and most beautiful things in the world cannot be seen or even touched—they must be felt with the heart." —**Helen Keller**

What Do You Think? How can poetry help us appreciate "the best and most beautiful things in the world"?

California Standards

Word Analysis, Fluency, and Systematic Vocabulary Development
1.2 Identify and interpret figurative language and words with multiple meanings.

Literary Response and Analysis
3.4 Define how tone or meaning is conveyed in poetry through word choice, figurative language, sentence structure, line length, punctuation, rhythm, repetition, and rhyme.

Writing Applications (Genres and Their Characteristics)
2.2 Write expository compositions (e.g., description, explanation, comparison and contrast, problem and solution):
   a. State the thesis or purpose.
   b. Explain the situation.
   c. Follow an organizational pattern appropriate to the type of composition.
   d. Offer persuasive evidence to validate arguments and conclusions as needed.

CHAPTER 6

Biography and Autobiography

"The biggest adventure you can ever take is to live the life of your dreams."

—Oprah Winfrey

What Do You Think?   In what ways is life an adventure? How can you make your dreams in life come true?

 California Standards

Word Analysis, Fluency, and Systematic Vocabulary Development
1.4 Monitor expository text for unknown words or words with novel meanings by using word, sentence, and paragraph clues to determine meaning.

Reading Comprehension (Focus on Informational Materials)
2.3 Connect and clarify main ideas by identifying their relationships to other sources and related topics.

Literary Response and Analysis
3.5 Identify the speaker and recognize the difference between first- and third-person narration (e.g., autobiography compared with biography).

3.7 Explain the effects of common literary devices (e.g., symbolism, imagery, metaphor) in a variety of fictional and nonfictional texts.

Writing Applications (Genres and Their Characteristics)
2.3 Write research reports:
   a. Pose relevant questions with a scope narrow enough to be thoroughly covered.
   b. Support the main idea or ideas with facts, details, examples, and explanations from multiple authoritative sources (e.g., speakers, periodicals, online information searches).
   c. Include a bibliography.

Comparing Texts

Informational Text Focus

Expository Critique: Persuasive Texts and Media

"How wonderful it is that nobody need wait a single moment before starting to improve the world." —**Anne Frank**

What Do You Think? What actions can individuals take to improve the world?

California Standards

Reading Comprehension (Focus on Informational Materials)

2.6 Determine the adequacy and appropriateness of the evidence for an author's conclusions.

2.7 Make reasonable assertions about a text through accurate, supporting citations.

2.8 Note instances of unsupported inferences, fallacious reasoning, persuasion, and propaganda in text.

Writing Applications (Genres and Their Characteristics)

2.5 Write persuasive compositions:
  a. State a clear position on a proposition or proposal.
  b. Support the position with organized and relevant evidence.
  c. Anticipate and address reader concerns and counterarguments.

Jamie Rodgers

Literary Criticism

"Fiction is Truth in another shape." —**Leigh Hunt**

What Do You Think? How does fiction express truths about our lives?

 California Standards

Word Analysis, Fluency, and Systematic Vocabulary Development
1.2 Identify and interpret figurative language and words with multiple meanings.

Literary Response and Analysis
3.8 Critique the credibility of characterization and the degree to which a plot is contrived or realistic (e.g., compare use of fact and fantasy in historical fiction).

Writing Applications (Genres and Their Characteristics)
2.4 Write responses to literature:
   a. Develop an interpretation exhibiting careful reading, understanding, and insight.
   b. Organize the interpretation around several clear ideas, premises, or images.
   c. Develop and justify the interpretation through sustained use of examples and textual evidence.

Skills, Standards, and Features

![] LITERARY SKILLS

![] READING SKILLS FOR LITERARY TEXTS

SKILLS, STANDARDS, AND FEATURES continued

READING SKILLS FOR INFORMATIONAL TEXTS

VOCABULARY SKILLS
ACADEMIC VOCABULARY

LANGUAGE COACH

VOCABULARY DEVELOPMENT

WORKSHOPS
WRITING WORKSHOPS

PREPARING FOR TIMED WRITING

LISTENING AND SPEAKING WORKSHOPS

SKILLS, STANDARDS, AND FEATURES continued

MEDIA WORKSHOPS

FEATURES

LITERARY PERSPECTIVES

CROSS CURRICULAR LINKS

GRAMMAR LINKS

STANDARDS REVIEW

Selections by Genre

FICTION
SHORT STORIES

SELECTIONS BY GENRE continued

NOVELLA

NOVEL EXCERPTS

MYTHS/FOLK TALES/LEGENDS

GRAPHIC STORY

PLAYS

POETRY

SELECTIONS BY GENRE continued

English–Language Arts Content Standards
Grade 6

READING

 1.0 Word Analysis, Fluency, and Systematic Vocabulary Development

Students use their knowledge of word origins and word relationships, as well as historical and literary context clues, to determine the meaning of specialized vocabulary and to understand the precise meaning of grade-level-appropriate words.

WORD RECOGNITION

1.1 Read aloud narrative and expository text fluently and accurately and with appropriate pacing, intonation, and expression. **Chapters 5, 6**

VOCABULARY AND CONCEPT DEVELOPMENT

1.2 Identify and interpret figurative language and words with multiple meanings. **Chapters 2, 4, 5, 6, 8**

1.3 Recognize the origins and meanings of frequently used foreign words in English and use these words accurately in speaking and writing. **Chapters 1, 3**

1.4 Monitor expository text for unknown words or words with novel meanings by using word, sentence, and paragraph clues to determine meaning. **Chapters 1, 3, 6**

1.5 Understand and explain "shades of meaning" in related words (e.g., *softly* and *quietly*). **Chapter 2**

 2.0 Reading Comprehension (Focus on Informational Materials)

Students read and understand grade-level-appropriate material. They describe and connect the essential ideas, arguments, and perspectives of the text by using their knowledge of text structure, organization, and purpose. The selections in *Recommended Literature: Kindergarten Through Grade Twelve* illustrate the quality and complexity of the materials to be read by students. In addition, by grade eight, students read one million words annually on their own, including a good representation of grade-level-appropriate narrative and expository text (e.g., classic and contemporary literature, magazines, newspapers, online information). In grade six, students continue to make progress toward this goal.

STRUCTURAL FEATURES OF INFORMATIONAL MATERIALS

2.1 Identify the structural features of popular media (e.g., newspapers, magazines, online information) and use the features to obtain information. **Chapter 4**

2.2 Analyze text that uses the compare-and-contrast organizational pattern. **Chapter 2**

COMPREHENSION AND ANALYSIS OF GRADE-LEVEL-APPROPRIATE TEXT

2.3 Connect and clarify main ideas by identifying their relationships to other sources and related topics. **Chapter 6**

2.4 Clarify an understanding of texts by creating outlines, logical notes, summaries, or reports. **Chapter 1**

2.5 Follow multiple-step instructions for preparing applications (e.g., for a public library card, bank savings account, sports club, league membership). **Chapter 3**

EXPOSITORY CRITIQUE

2.6 Determine the adequacy and appropriateness of the evidence for an author's conclusions. **Chapter 7**

2.7 Make reasonable assertions about a text through accurate, supporting citations. **Chapter 7**

2.8 Note instances of unsupported inferences, fallacious reasoning, persuasion, and propaganda in text. **Chapter 7**

3.0 Literary Response and Analysis

Students read and respond to historically or culturally significant works of literature that reflect and enhance their studies of history and social science. They clarify the ideas and connect them to other literary works. The selections in *Recommended Literature: Kindergarten Through Grade Twelve* illustrate the quality and complexity of the materials to be read by students.

STRUCTURAL FEATURES OF LITERATURE

3.1 Identify the forms of fiction and describe the major characteristics of each form. **Chapter 4**

NARRATIVE ANALYSIS OF GRADE-LEVEL-APPROPRIATE TEXT

3.2 Analyze the effect of the qualities of the character (e.g., courage or cowardice, ambition or laziness) on the plot and the resolution of the conflict. **Chapters 2, 3**

3.3 Analyze the influence of setting on the problem and its resolution. **Chapter 1**

3.4 Define how tone or meaning is conveyed in poetry through word choice, figurative language, sentence structure, line length, punctuation, rhythm, repetition, and rhyme. **Chapter 5**

3.5 Identify the speaker and recognize the difference between first- and third-person narration (e.g., autobiography compared with biography). **Chapter 6**

3.6 Identify and analyze features of themes conveyed through characters, actions, and images. **Chapters 3, 4**

3.7 Explain the effects of common literary devices (e.g., symbolism, imagery, metaphor) in a variety of fictional and nonfictional texts. **Chapter 6**

LITERARY CRITICISM

3.8 Critique the credibility of characterization and the degree to which a plot is contrived or realistic (e.g., compare use of fact and fantasy in historical fiction). **Chapter 8**

ENGLISH–LANGUAGE ARTS CONTENT STANDARDS continued

WRITING

 1.0 Writing Strategies
Students write clear, coherent, and focused essays. The writing exhibits students' awareness of the audience and purpose. Essays contain formal introductions, supporting evidence, and conclusions. Students progress through the stages of the writing process as needed.

ORGANIZATION AND FOCUS

1.1 Choose the form of writing (e.g., personal letter, letter to the editor, review, poem, report, narrative) that best suits the intended purpose. **Chapter 7**

1.2 Create multiple-paragraph expository compositions:
  a. Engage the interest of the reader and state a clear purpose.
  b. Develop the topic with supporting details and precise verbs, nouns, and adjectives to paint a visual image in the mind of the reader.
  c. Conclude with a detailed summary linked to the purpose of the composition.
Chapters 2, 3, 6

1.3 Use a variety of effective and coherent organizational patterns, including comparison and contrast; organization by categories; and arrangement by spatial order, order of importance, or climactic order. **Chapters 1, 3, 4, 5, 8**

RESEARCH AND TECHNOLOGY

1.4 Use organizational features of electronic text (e.g., bulletin boards, databases, keyword searches, e-mail addresses) to locate information. **Chapter 4**

1.5 Compose documents with appropriate formatting by using word-processing skills and principles of design (e.g., margins, tabs, spacing, columns, page orientation). **Chapter 2**

EVALUATION AND REVISION

1.6 Revise writing to improve the organization and consistency of ideas within and between paragraphs. **Chapters 4, 7, 8**

 2.0 Writing Applications (Genres and Their Characteristics)
Students write narrative, expository, persuasive, and descriptive texts of at least 500 to 700 words in each genre. Student writing demonstrates a command of standard American English and the research, organizational, and drafting strategies outlined in Writing Standard 1.0.

Using the writing strategies of grade six outlined in Writing Standard 1.0, students:

2.1 Write narratives:
  a. Establish and develop a plot and setting and present a point of view that is appropriate to the stories.
  b. Include sensory details and concrete language to develop plot and character.
  c. Use a range of narrative devices (e.g., dialogue, suspense).
Chapter 1

2.2 Write expository compositions (e.g., description, explanation, comparison and contrast, problem and solution):

a. State the thesis or purpose.
b. Explain the situation.
c. Follow an organizational pattern appropriate to the type of composition.
d. Offer persuasive evidence to validate arguments and conclusions as needed.

Chapters 2, 3, 4, 5

2.3 Write research reports:

a. Pose relevant questions with a scope narrow enough to be thoroughly covered.
b. Support the main idea or ideas with facts, details, examples, and explanations from multiple authoritative sources (e.g., speakers, periodicals, online information searches).
c. Include a bibliography.

Chapter 6

2.4 Write responses to literature:

a. Develop an interpretation exhibiting careful reading, understanding, and insight.
b. Organize the interpretation around several clear ideas, premises, or images.
c. Develop and justify the interpretation through sustained use of examples and textual evidence.

Chapter 8

2.5 Write persuasive compositions:

a. State a clear position on a proposition or proposal.
b. Support the position with organized and relevant evidence.
c. Anticipate and address reader concerns and counterarguments.

Chapter 7

WRITTEN AND ORAL ENGLISH LANGUAGE CONVENTIONS

The standards for written and oral English language conventions have been placed between those for writing and for listening and speaking because these conventions are essential to both sets of skills.

 1.0 Written and Oral English Language Conventions

Students write and speak with a command of standard English conventions appropriate to this grade level.

SENTENCE STRUCTURE

1.1 Use simple, compound, and compound-complex sentences; use effective coordination and subordination of ideas to express complete thoughts. *Warriner's Handbook Introductory Course* **Chapters 3, 4, 12, 16**

GRAMMAR

1.2 Identify and properly use indefinite pronouns and present perfect, past perfect, and future perfect verb tenses; ensure that verbs agree with compound subjects. *Warriner's Handbook Introductory Course* **Chapters 2, 6, 7**

PUNCTUATION

1.3 Use colons after the salutation in business letters, semicolons to connect independent clauses, and commas when linking two clauses with a conjunction in compound sentences. *Warriner's Handbook Introductory Course* **Chapter 12**

ENGLISH–LANGUAGE ARTS CONTENT STANDARDS continued

CAPITALIZATION

1.4 Use correct capitalization. *Warriner's Handbook Introductory Course* **Chapter 11**

SPELLING

1.5 Spell frequently misspelled words correctly (e.g., *their, they're, there*). *Warriner's Handbook Introductory Course* **Chapter 14**

LISTENING AND SPEAKING

 1.0 Listening and Speaking Strategies

Students deliver focused, coherent presentations that convey ideas clearly and relate to the background and interests of the audience. They evaluate the content of oral communication.

COMPREHENSION

1.1 Relate the speaker's verbal communication (e.g., word choice, pitch, feeling, tone) to the nonverbal message (e.g., posture, gesture). **Chapters 2, 3, 7**

1.2 Identify the tone, mood, and emotion conveyed in the oral communication. **Chapter 8**

1.3 Restate and execute multiple-step oral instructions and directions. **Chapter 2**

ORGANIZATION AND DELIVERY OF ORAL COMMUNICATION

1.4 Select a focus, an organizational structure, and a point of view, matching the purpose, message, occasion, and vocal modulation to the audience. **Chapters 2, 7**

1.5 Emphasize salient points to assist the listener in following the main ideas and concepts. **Chapters 3, 6**

1.6 Support opinions with detailed evidence and with visual or media displays that use appropriate technology. **Chapter 6**

1.7 Use effective rate, volume, pitch, and tone and align nonverbal elements to sustain audience interest and attention. **Chapters 1, 8**

ANALYSIS AND EVALUATION OF ORAL AND MEDIA COMMUNICATIONS

1.8 Analyze the use of rhetorical devices (e.g., cadence, repetitive patterns, use of onomatopoeia) for intent and effect. **Chapter 7**

1.9 Identify persuasive and propaganda techniques used in television and identify false and misleading information. **Chapter 5**

2.0 Speaking Applications (Genres and Their Characteristics)

Students deliver well-organized formal presentations employing traditional rhetorical strategies (e.g., narration, exposition, persuasion, description). Student speaking demonstrates a command of standard American English and the organizational and delivery strategies outlined in Listening and Speaking Standard 1.0.

Using the speaking strategies of grade six outlined in Listening and Speaking Standard 1.0, students:

2.1 Deliver narrative presentations:

a. Establish a context, plot, and point of view.
b. Include sensory details and concrete language to develop the plot and character.
c. Use a range of narrative devices (e.g., dialogue, tension, or suspense).

Chapter 1

2.2 Deliver informative presentations:

a. Pose relevant questions sufficiently limited in scope to be completely and thoroughly answered.
b. Develop the topic with facts, details, examples, and explanations from multiple authoritative sources (e.g., speakers, periodicals, online information).

Chapter 6

2.3 Deliver oral responses to literature:

a. Develop an interpretation exhibiting careful reading, understanding, and insight.
b. Organize the selected interpretation around several clear ideas, premises, or images.
c. Develop and justify the selected interpretation through sustained use of examples and textual evidence.

Chapter 8

2.4 Deliver persuasive presentations:

a. Provide a clear statement of the position.
b. Include relevant evidence.
c. Offer a logical sequence of information.
d. Engage the listener and foster acceptance of the proposition or proposal.

Chapter 7

2.5 Deliver presentations on problems and solutions:

a. Theorize on the causes and effects of each problem and establish connections between the defined problem and at least one solution.
b. Offer persuasive evidence to validate the definition of the problem and the proposed solutions.

Chapter 3

Why Be a Reader/Writer?

by **Kylene Beers**

You've heard this story before, haven't you?

Once upon a time there were three bears— Mama Bear, Papa Bear, and Baby Bear.

Goldilocks "visits" the Bear home while the family is out. She destroys their place while searching for the food, chair, and bed that are *just right* for her. When the Bear family returns, Goldie runs off without even an "I'm-so-sorry" apology.

The Bears are left to clean up everything— end of story.

What Is the Message?

Isn't this an odd story to tell young children? Is it trying to teach them that

- children can be more trouble than bears?
- we must lock the door when we leave the house?
- sometimes people might do things they know are wrong?

The message I like most is that we are all searching for the things that are *just right* for us. While I don't like the way Goldilocks went about getting what she wanted, I do understand her need to find the food, the chair, and the bed that were *just right*.

Goldilocks wanted things that fit her needs. Interestingly, as she grows and changes, those needs will change. She'll outgrow the *just right* chair, and the *too big* chair will fit *just right*.

The *Just Right* Reading / Writing Experience

When you read and write, you're often looking for the *just right* experience that fits your needs. *Holt Literature and Language Arts* gives you many opportunities to find out how a book is *just right* for you.

Using the Standards to Set the Standard

Sometimes we need lessons to help us accomplish all the things a skilled reader can do. This book is designed to help you master the skills you need to be a strong reader *and* writer. The California standards are your tour guide. They will lead you through this book, helping you learn the literacy skills you'll need for this year, for your remaining years in school, and for all your life as a member of society.

Everyone who worked on this book—the people who chose the reading selections, the people who wrote the activities, the people who chose the artwork—continually asked themselves, "How do we create a book that not only meets the California standards but also *sets* the standard when it comes to helping students become readers and writers?" We think that, as you read through this book, you'll find that we answered that question by providing you with

- interesting selections to read
- powerful models to help you learn to write
- many opportunities to practice new skills
- specific information about each standard— so that you will always know what is expected of you
- the kinds of topics and art that middle-schoolers have told us interest them

In this book, then, you'll get practice in all kinds of language skills.

- You will read a variety of material, from ads to odes, from stories to Web pages.
- You will learn better ways to speak, listen, and write.
- You will understand more, sound better, and be more confident about what you know and understand.

There are many reasons to be a skillful reader and an effective writer—good grades, passing tests, getting into college. The best reason—the *just right* reason—has to do with reading and writing to discover more about yourself and the world you live in.

So, let what you read and write this year act as a *mirror* that shows you more about yourself or a *window* that shows you worlds beyond where you live.

Whichever you do, you'll be discovering the reason that is *just right* for you.

Kylene Beers

Senior Author
Holt Literature and Language Arts

How to Use Your Textbook

Getting to know a new textbook is like getting to know a new video game. In each case, you have to figure out how the game or book is structured, as well as understand its rules. If you understand the structure of your book, you can be successful from the start.

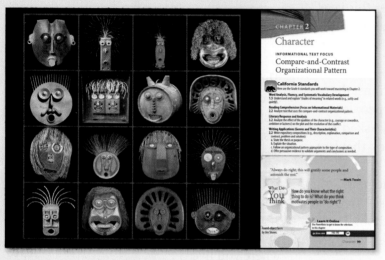

Chapter Opener

What is the focus of each chapter, or section of the book? What does the image suggest about what the chapter will cover? On the right, you'll see a bold heading that says "Plot and Setting" or "Character." These are the **literary skills** you will study in the chapter. Also in bold type is the **Informational Text Focus** for the chapter. These are the skills you use to read informational texts such as a newspaper or Web site. Keep the **What Do You Think?** question in mind as you go through the chapter. Your answers may even surprise you.

Literary Skills Focus

Like a set of rules or a map, the **Literary Skills Focus** shows you how literary elements work in stories and poems, helping you navigate through selections more easily. The Literary Skills Focus will help you get to your destination— understanding and enjoying the selections.

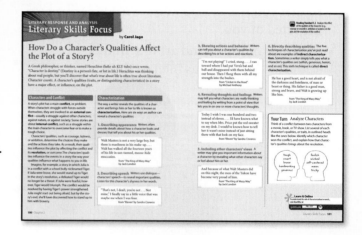

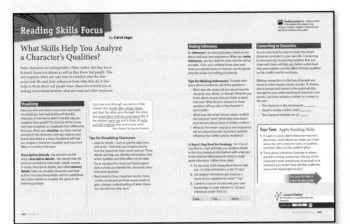

Reading Skills Focus

Your mind is working all the time as you read, even if you're not aware of it. Still, all readers, even very good ones, sometimes don't understand what they've read. **Reading Skills Focus** gives you the skills to help you improve your reading.

Reading Model

You tend to do things more quickly and easily if you have a model to follow. The **Reading Model** enhances your learning by demonstrating the literary and reading skills that you will practice in the chapter.

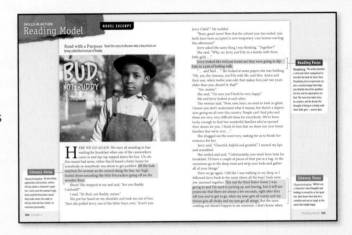

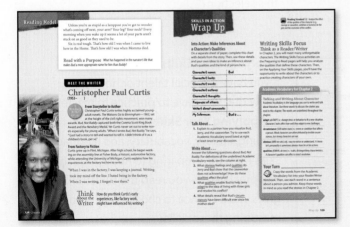

Wrap Up

Think of **Wrap Up** as a bridge that gives you a chance to practice the skills on which the chapter will focus. It also introduces you to the **Academic Vocabulary** you will study in the chapter: the language of school, business, and standardized tests. To be successful in school, you'll need to understand and use academic language.

How to Use Your Textbook

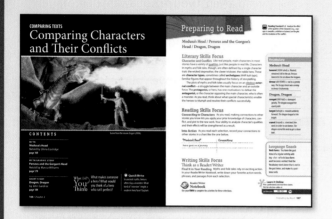

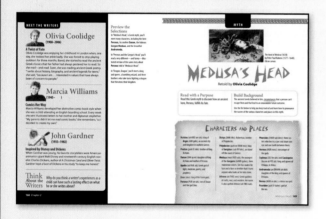

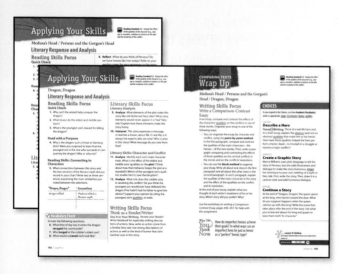

Literary Selection Pages

Preparing to Read

If you have ever done something complicated, you know that things go more smoothly with some preparation. It is the same with reading. The **Preparing to Read** page gives you a boost by presenting the literary, reading, and writing skills you will learn about and use as you read the selection. The list of **Vocabulary** words gives the words you need to know for reading both the selection and beyond the selection. **Language Coach** explains the inner workings of English—like looking at the inside of a clock.

Selection

Meet the Writer gives you all kinds of interesting facts about the authors who wrote the selections in this book. **Build Background** provides information you sometimes need when a selection deals with unfamiliar times, places, and situations. **Preview the Selection** presents the selection's main character and hints at what is to come. **Read with a Purpose** helps you set a goal for your reading. It helps you answer the question, "What is the point of this selection?"

Applying Your Skills

If you have a special talent or hobby, you know that you have to practice to master it. In **Applying Your Skills,** you will apply the reading, literary, vocabulary, and language skills from the Preparing to Read page that you practiced as you read the selection. This gives you a chance to check on how you are mastering these skills.

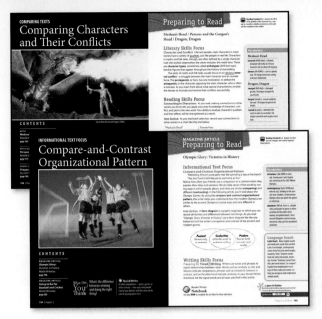

Comparing Texts

You probably compare people, places, and things all the time, such as a favorite singer's new songs with her previous album. In **Comparing Texts,** you will compare different works—sometimes by the same author, sometimes by different authors—that have something in common.

Informational Text Focus

When you read a Web site or follow a technical manual, you are reading informational text. The skills you use in this type of reading are different from the ones you use for literary text. **Informational Text Focus** helps you gain the skills that will enable you to be a more successful reader in daily life and on standardized tests.

Standards Review

Do you dread test-taking time? Do you struggle over reading the passage and then choosing the correct answer? **Standards Review** can reduce your "guesses" and give you the practice you need to feel more confident during testing.

Writing Workshop

Does a blank piece of paper send shivers up your spine? **The Writing Workshop** will help you tackle the page. It takes you step-by-step through developing an effective piece of writing. Models, annotations, graphic organizers, and charts take the "What now?" out of writing for different purposes and audiences.

Preparing for Timed Writing

What is your idea of a nightmare? Maybe it is trying to respond to a writing prompt. **Preparing for Timed Writing** helps you practice for on-demand, or timed, writing so that you can realize your dreams of success.

CHAPTER 1

Setting and Plot

INFORMATIONAL TEXT FOCUS

Notes, Outlines, and Summaries

California Standards

Here are the Grade 6 standards you will work toward mastering in Chapter 1.

Word Analysis, Fluency, and Systematic Vocabulary Development
1.4 Monitor expository text for unknown words or words with novel meanings by using word, sentence, and paragraph clues to determine meaning.

Reading Comprehension (Focus on Informational Materials)
2.4 Clarify an understanding of texts by creating outlines, logical notes, summaries, or reports.

Literary Response and Analysis
3.3 Analyze the influence of setting on the problem and its resolution.

Writing Applications (Genres and Their Characteristics)
2.1 Write narratives:
   a. Establish and develop a plot and setting and present a point of view that is appropriate to the stories.
   b. Include sensory details and concrete language to develop plot and character.
   c. Use a range of narrative devices (e.g., dialogue, suspense).

"You never find yourself until you face the truth."
—**Pearl Bailey**

What Do
You
Think

How can discovering a tough truth help you gain a better understanding of who you are as a person?

Learn It Online
Use the interactive graphic organizers online to help you take notes:

| go.hrw.com | H6-3 | Go |

Literary Skills Focus

by **Linda Rief**

What Are Setting and Plot?

Everybody has stories: your great-grandfather's survival of a submarine attack during World War II; your neighbor's rescue of three hikers stranded on a mountain in a blizzard; an embarrassing moment in class last year. The more vividly a storyteller describes what happened—the plot—and where and when it happened—the setting—the better the listeners or readers can imagine and experience the story.

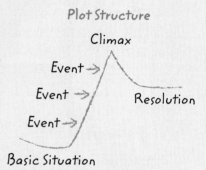

Setting

The **setting** is where (the place) and when (the time) the action of a story takes place. Some stories could take place almost anywhere, but sometimes setting is so essential to a plot that the story could not possibly take place anywhere else. The setting can **influence,** or affect, a story in several ways:

1. Setting can influence the story's problem and its resolution. In many stories the characters are in an **external conflict** with the setting, as when a character is lost in a blizzard or struggles to survive on a deserted island. If the character triumphs over the problem posed by the setting, the story has a happy resolution. If the setting is more powerful than the character, the story's resolution can be tragic.

2. Setting can give a story a sense of reality. Vivid **details** can make a setting seem very real to you, helping you imagine how people live, what they eat, how they dress, and where they work.

3. Setting can create atmosphere. Writers often use setting to create an **atmosphere,** or mood: creepy, peaceful, joyous, threatening.

Plot

"What happened?" When you answer this question about a story, you're describing the **plot**—the series of related events that make up the story. A plot usually has four key parts. The diagram above will help you visualize a plot's structure.

1. Basic situation Most plots begin with a setup of the story's **basic situation.** You learn what you need to know to follow the story as it unfolds. The basic situation answers these questions:

- Who is the main character?
- What does the main character want?
- What stands in the character's way? In other words, what is his or her **problem,** or conflict?

Conflict is the struggle that makes a story interesting and keeps you reading to see what happens next. There are two main types of conflict:

- In an **external conflict** the main character struggles against a force *outside* the character. The main character might clash with another character or with a situation, such as a dangerous ice storm or a badly damaged spaceship.

- An **internal conflict** takes place within a character. This kind of conflict comes from a struggle *inside* the character—to overcome fear, for example, or to exercise self-control.

Think about this story opener, which presents a character named Margot facing two **problems**—one with other characters and the other with the **setting,** her rain-soaked alien environment:

> It had been raining for seven years; thousands upon thousands of days compounded and filled from one end to the other with rain. . . .
>
> Margot stood apart from them, from these children who could never remember a time when there wasn't rain and rain and rain.
>
> from "All Summer in a Day" by Ray Bradbury

2. Complications If a story's conflict could be resolved easily, there wouldn't be much of a story. That's why writers introduce **complications** to the plot. Complications are **additional problems** that arise and prevent the main character from resolving the conflict.

> "Oh, but," Margot whispered, her eyes helpless. "But this is the day, the scientists predict, they say, they know, the sun . . ."
>
> "All a joke!" said the boy, and seized her roughly. "Hey everyone, let's put her in a closet before teacher comes!"
>
> from "All Summer in a Day" by Ray Bradbury

3. Climax A strong plot pulls you in and moves you along toward the **climax,** the most exciting part of the story. In the climax you find out how the conflict will be resolved, or worked out.

> The Moose took the ball and cradled it in his right hand. So far, so good. He hadn't fumbled. . . .
>
> He ran a couple of steps and looked out in front and said aloud, "Whoa!"
>
> Where had all those tacklers come from?
>
> from "Just Once" by Thomas J. Dygard

4. Resolution The final part of the plot, in which events are wrapped up and the story comes to a conclusion, is the **resolution**. Here the main character's **problem** is solved—sometimes happily, sometimes not. What does the sentence below reveal about the story's resolution?

> The Moose glanced at the coach, took another deep breath, and said, "Never again."
>
> from "Just Once" by Thomas J. Dygard

Your Turn Analyze Setting and Plot

1. Identify a story in which setting plays a crucial role. Try to think of a story in which a character struggles with a setting that threatens his or her life. Then, analyze how the setting influences the problem and its resolution.

2. Trace the plot of a book, movie, or short story you know well by filling out a plot diagram like the one on page 4.

Learn It Online
Try the *PowerNotes* version of this lesson on:

go.hrw.com   H6-5   **Go**

Reading Skills Focus

What Skills Help You Analyze Setting and Plot?

Good readers know what to do when asked to analyze setting and plot. They think about the story they read by sequencing important events, retelling the plot, and summarizing. As you practice using these reading skills, they are likely to become a habit—a very good habit for understanding and enjoying literature.

Sequencing

Sequence is the order of events in a story. Most stories are written in chronological order, or logical time order, as when a writer tells what happened in the course of a day. As you read, watch for words and phrases such as *later* and *earlier in the day*. They signal when events occur and are clues to help you in sequencing the plot.

Tips for Sequencing When you review a story, ask yourself these questions:

- What are the story's key events?
- When did each event happen?
- Did one event cause another event to happen? How do you know?

Using a Sequence Chart Show the order of events in a story by filling in a chart like this:

> Sequence
> 1. Describe the first important event.
> 2. Describe the second important event.
> 3. Describe the third important event.

Keep adding events in order until the story's end.

Retelling

Have you ever stopped after reading a difficult part of a story to think about what you just read? If you've tried to describe what just happened in order to check your understanding, then you've used a strategy called **retelling.** Retelling helps you identify the sequence of events in a story and understand how those events are connected. Retelling can also help you identify and analyze the way the setting influences, or affects, the plot.

Tips for Retelling a Story

- As you read, pause for a moment when something important in the story occurs or when you feel confused about what you just read.
- Then, review in your mind what just happened in the story, re-reading the passage if necessary.
- Finally, describe the events in your own words. You might write down your retellings in your *Reader/Writer Notebook*.

Use this **retelling sheet** to help you successfully retell the plot of any story:

Retelling Sheet

1. Basic situation

Begin with the **title** and **author** of the story. Then, identify the setting—where and when the story takes place. Tell the **characters' names,** and explain how the characters are connected to one another. Explain what the main character wants to do.

2. Conflict

What is the main character's **conflict,** or problem? In other words, what is keeping the main character from getting what he or she wants? How does the setting add to the problem?

3. Complications

Describe the **main events**—what happens as characters try to solve the conflict and roadblocks develop.

4. Climax

Describe the **climax,** the most suspenseful moment, when you discover either how the main character will overcome the conflict or how the main character will be defeated.

5. Resolution

Tell what happens **after the climax.** How does the story end? How does the setting influence the resolution?

When you've finished a written retelling of a story, you can also add a personal response—your own thoughts and feelings about the story.

Using Time-Order Words A retelling should provide a clear and interesting presentation of a story. Avoid linking the events with a string of *and*s. There is nothing as boring as an account of a story in which "and" and "and then" are repeated over and over. Here are some good **time-order words** to use instead:

then	*additionally*	*last*
after that	*following that*	*first*
next	*as a result*	*finally*

Summarizing

You can summarize any piece of writing, fiction or nonfiction. When you **summarize** a short story, you restate its main events in your own words. Summarizing is similar to retelling, but it involves identifying only the *most important* characters, events, and details. A good summary is shorter than a retelling and much shorter than the original story, since it includes only those key events that make up the plot and show the influence of the setting on the problem and the problem's resolution.

Tips for Summarizing a Short Story

- Every few paragraphs, stop and try to restate in a sentence or two what the author wrote.
- When you're finished, go back and delete any details that don't seem crucial to the plot.
- Try to make your summary one page long at most. Sometimes you can summarize an entire short story in a single paragraph.

Your Turn Apply Reading Skills

1. Explain why identifying the sequence of events in a plot is necessary for understanding a story.
2. Retell a favorite story. Then, summarize the story, including the influence of the setting, in a paragraph or two.

Now go to the Skills in Action: Reading Model

Learn It Online
Find interactive graphic organizers to help you with sequencing and other reading skills at:

go.hrw.com | H6-7 | **Go**

Read with a Purpose   Read this story
to see how Priscilla handles the bullies at her school.

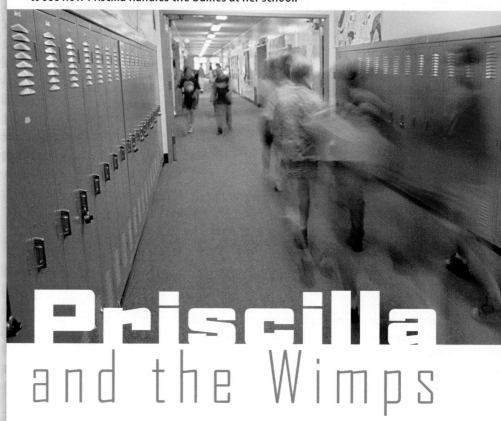

Priscilla
and the Wimps

by **Richard Peck**

Literary Focus

Setting The first sentence
reveals that the story is set in a
school. The time period is not as
obvious, but as you read further,
look for details that signal that the
story takes place before you were
born. (It was written in the late
1970s.)

L isten, there was a time when you couldn't even go to
the *rest room* in this school without a pass. And I'm not
talking about those little pink tickets made out by some
teacher. I'm talking about a pass that could cost anywhere up to
a buck, sold by Monk Klutter.

Not that Mighty Monk ever touched money, not in public.
The gang he ran, which ran the school for him, was his collection agency. They were Klutter's Kobras, a name spelled out in
nailheads on six well-known black plastic windbreakers.

Monk's threads were more . . . subtle. A pile-lined suede battle
jacket with lizard-skin flaps over tailored Levis and a pair of

ostrich-skin boots, brassed-toed and suitable for kicking people around. One of his Kobras did nothing all day but walk a half step behind Monk, carrying a fitted bag with Monk's gym shoes, a roll of restroom passes, a cashbox, and a switchblade that Monk gave himself manicures with at lunch over at the Kobras' table.

Speaking of lunch, there were a few cases of advanced malnutrition among the newer kids. The ones who were a little slow in handing over a cut of their lunch money and were therefore barred from the cafeteria. Monk ran a tight ship.

I admit it. I'm five foot five, and when the Kobras slithered by, with or without Monk, I shrank. I admit this, too: I paid up on a regular basis. And I might add: so would you.

This school was old Monk's Garden of Eden.[1] Unfortunately for him, there was a serpent in it. The reason Monk didn't recognize trouble when it was staring him in the face is that the serpent in the Kobras' Eden was a girl.

Practically every guy in school could show you his scars. Fang marks from Kobras, you might say. And they were all highly visible in the shower room: lumps, lacerations,[2] blue bruises, you name it. But girls usually got off with a warning.

Except there was this one girl named Priscilla Roseberry. Picture a girl named Priscilla Roseberry, and you'll be light years off. Priscilla was, hands down, the largest student in our particular institution of learning. I'm not talking fat. I'm talking big. Even beautiful, in a bionic[3] way. Priscilla wasn't inclined toward organized crime. Otherwise, she could have put together a gang that would turn Klutter's Kobras into garter snakes.

Priscilla was basically a loner except she had one friend. A little guy named Melvin Detweiler. You talk about The Odd Couple. Melvin's one of the smallest guys above midget status ever seen. A really nice guy, but, you know—little. They even had lockers next to each other, in the same bank as mine. I don't know what they had going. I'm not saying this was a romance. After all, people deserve their privacy.

---

1. **Garden of Eden:** In the Bible, the paradise where Adam and Eve first lived.
2. **lacerations** (las uh RAY shuhnz): cuts.
3. **bionic** (by AHN ihk): having artificial body parts; in science fiction, bionic parts give people superhuman strength or other powers.

Reading Model

Reading Focus

Sequencing Pay attention to the order of events in the story. Peck uses the phrase *Until one winter day* to signal the timing of a new event that changes the relationship between Priscilla and the Kobras. Watch for the sequence of events that follows.

Reading Focus

Retelling This is an important event in the story. Retell important events in your own words to make sure you understand what happened. For example: "Priscilla puts her books away and then chops the Kobra's hand, breaking his grip on Melvin. Afterward, the hallway is really quiet because no one had ever hit a Kobra before."

Priscilla was sort of above everything, if you'll pardon the pun.[4] And very calm, as only the very big can be. If there was anybody who didn't notice Klutter's Kobras, it was Priscilla.

Until one winter day after school when we were all grabbing our coats out of our lockers. And hurrying, since Klutter's Kobras made sweeps of the halls for after-school shakedowns.

Anyway, up to Melvin's locker swaggers one of the Kobras. Never mind his name. Gang members don't need names. They've got group identity. He reaches down and grabs little Melvin by the neck and slams his head against his locker door. The sound of skull against steel rippled all the way down the locker row, speeding the crowds on their way.

"Okay, let's see your pass," snarls the Kobra.

"A pass for what this time?" Melvin asks, probably still dazed.

"Let's call it a pass for very short people," says the Kobra, "a dwarf tax." He wheezes a little Kobra chuckle at his own wittiness. And already he's reaching for Melvin's wallet with the hand that isn't circling Melvin's windpipe. All this time, of course, Melvin and the Kobra are standing in Priscilla's big shadow.

She's taking her time shoving her books into her locker and pulling on a very large-size coat. Then, quicker than the eye, she brings the side of her enormous hand down in a chop that breaks the Kobra's hold on Melvin's throat. You could hear a pin drop in that hallway. Nobody'd ever laid a finger on a Kobra, let alone a hand the size of Priscilla's.

Then Priscilla, who hardly ever says anything to anybody except Melvin, says to the Kobra, "Who's your leader, wimp?"

This practically blows the Kobra away. First he's chopped by a girl, and now she's acting like she doesn't know Monk Klutter, the Head Honcho of the World. He's so amazed, he tells her. "Monk Klutter."

"Never heard of him," Priscilla mentions. "Send him to see me." The Kobra just backs away from her like the whole situation is too big for him, which it is.

---

4. **pun:** humorous play on words, often involving two meanings of the same word or phrase.

Pretty soon Monk himself slides up. He jerks his head once, and his Kobras slither off down the hall. He's going to handle this interesting case personally. "Who is it around here doesn't know Monk Klutter?"

He's standing inches from Priscilla, but since he'd have to look up at her, he doesn't. "Never heard of him," says Priscilla.

Monk's not happy with this answer, but by now he's spotted Melvin, who's grown smaller in spite of himself. Monk breaks his own rule by reaching for Melvin with his own hands. "Kid," he says, "you're going to have to educate your girl friend."

His hands never quite make it to Melvin. In a move of pure poetry Priscilla has Monk in a hammerlock. His neck's popping like gunfire, and his head's bowed under the immense weight of her forearm. His suede jacket's peeling back, showing pile.

Priscilla's behind him in another easy motion. And with a single mighty thrust forward, frog-marches Monk into her own locker. It's incredible. His ostrich-skin boots click once in the air. And suddenly he's gone, neatly wedged into the locker, a perfect fit. Priscilla bangs the door shut, twirls the lock, and strolls out of school. Melvin goes with her, of course, trotting along below her shoulder. The last stragglers leave quietly.

Well, this is where fate, an even bigger force than Priscilla, steps in. It snows all that night, a blizzard. The whole town ices up. And school closes for a week.

Read with a Purpose   How does Priscilla deal with the bullies in this story? How else could she have handled them?

Literary Focus

Plot   The **climax** is the story's most suspenseful moment, when you find out how the problem, or conflict, will be resolved. This story's climax is a confrontation between Monk and Priscilla.

Reading Focus

Summarizing   Remember that summarizing involves identifying only the key events. This paragraph can easily be summarized in one sentence: "Priscilla shoves Monk into her locker, locks him in, and then leaves with Melvin."

Literary Focus

Setting   These sentences suggest how the **setting** influences the resolution of the conflict, or problem. You can predict that Monk might be trapped in the locker for a while.

Analyzing Visuals

Connecting to the Text
Which of Priscilla's character traits, as described in the story, do you see in this photograph?

Richard Peck
(1934–   )

Newbery Medal WINNER

Taught by His Students

As a high school English teacher, Richard Peck became familiar with the reading habits of his teenage students: "It was my students who taught me to be a writer, though I had been hired to teach them. They taught me that a novel must entertain first before it can be anything else."

Although Peck liked his students and found their lives fascinating, he eventually decided the classroom wasn't the best place for him. He wanted to write young adult fiction—novels for readers around his students' ages. He has written more than thirty-two books to date, all of them on a typewriter. Before he left teaching, however, he learned about far more than his audience's taste in stories; he also learned about the problems that young people face both inside and outside of school. His books have been praised for dealing with such problems bravely and realistically.

Asking Honest Questions

Peck writes about tough topics, such as peer pressure, censorship, and death. He says that a goal of his writing is to "ask honest questions about serious issues." Although the answers to such questions aren't always pleasant, dealing with serious issues is a part of growing up. Peck hopes that his books help young people do just that. In his young adult novels he hopes that "the reader meets a worthy young character who takes one step nearer maturity, and he or she takes that step independently."

"A novel is never an answer; it's always a question."

Think About the Writer

Peck wants his writing to "ask honest questions about serious issues." In his story "Priscilla and the Wimps," what questions does he raise about bullying?

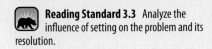

Reading Standard 3.3 Analyze the influence of setting on the problem and its resolution.

Into Action: Sequencing

Draw and complete a diagram like this one to trace the sequence of events in "Priscilla and the Wimps":

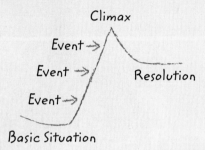

Talk About . . .

1. Retell your favorite part of "Priscilla and the Wimps" to a partner. Then, explain why you liked the story. In your explanation, try to use each Academic Vocabulary word listed on the right at least once.

Write About . . .

Answer the following questions about "Priscilla and the Wimps." For definitions of the underlined Academic Vocabulary words, see the column on the right.

2. What is the <u>major</u> conflict in the story? What is the <u>influence</u> of the setting on this conflict?

3. How does Priscilla <u>interact</u> with Melvin, with other students who are not Kobras, and with the Kobras?

4. What does Priscilla <u>achieve</u> for all students when she defeats Monk?

Writing Skills Focus
Think as a Reader/Writer

In Chapter 1, the Writing Skills Focus activities explain how writers create interesting plots and memorable settings. You'll have a chance to write about these methods and practice them yourself.

Academic Vocabulary for Chapter 1

Talking and Writing About Setting and Plot

Academic Vocabulary is the language you use to write and talk about literature. Use these words to discuss the stories you read in this chapter. The words are underlined throughout the chapter.

achieve (uh CHEEV) *v.:* succeed in getting a good result or in doing something you want. *The main character's struggle to achieve something produces the conflict in a story.*

influence (IHN flu uhns) *n.:* ability or power to affect thought, behavior, or development. *The setting of a story often has a strong influence on the plot.*

interact (ihn tuhr AKT) *v.:* talk to and deal with others. *Problems can develop when characters who don't get along interact.*

major (MAY juhr) *adj.:* very large and important, especially compared with other things of a similar kind. *The major event in a story is the climax.*

Your Turn

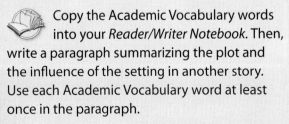

Copy the Academic Vocabulary words into your *Reader/Writer Notebook*. Then, write a paragraph summarizing the plot and the influence of the setting in another story. Use each Academic Vocabulary word at least once in the paragraph.

JUST ONCE

by **Thomas J. Dygard**

Black Shirts (1974) by Leroy Neiman.

What Do **You** Think?

How can achieving something you think you want turn out unexpectedly?

QuickWrite

Write about some of your dreams or goals in your *Reader/Writer Notebook*. Choose one, and explain what would be the best thing about achieving it.

Reader/Writer
Notebook
Use your **RWN** to complete the
activities for this selection.

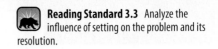
Reading Standard 3.3 Analyze the influence of setting on the problem and its resolution.

Literary Skills Focus

Plot and Setting Most **plots** are built on these bare bones: The **basic situation** tells who the main characters are and defines their **problem,** or conflict—a struggle, or clash, between opposing characters or opposing forces. **Complications** arise as the characters <u>interact</u>, taking steps to overcome the conflict. As the story builds to a **climax,** the peak of the action, you see where the story is going. The **resolution** tells how the problem is solved.

In this story a high school football player has a dream he wants to <u>achieve</u>. His campaign to make his dream come true creates a **conflict.** As you read, think about how the **setting**—when and where the story takes place—influences the story's conflict and resolution.

Reading Skills Focus

Retelling You can use **retelling** to help you recall and understand the <u>major</u> events in a story. Retelling will also help focus your awareness of the main character's problems.

Into Action Use a **retelling** chart like this one to trace the main characters' problems:

Who or what is in conflict?	Describe what's happening
The Moose has a conflict, or problem, with his coach.	The Moose wants to carry the ball, but his coach won't let him because Moose is a lineman.

Writing Skills Focus

Think as a Reader/Writer

Find It in Your Reading Much of what you learn about the Moose, the main character in "Just Once," is provided by the narrator, the voice telling the story. As you read, record what the narrator reveals about the Moose and what the Moose wants. How does this information help you fully understand the problem the Moose faces?

Language Coach
Parts of Speech You will probably use the word *influence* often as you discuss the stories in this chapter. *Influence* can be a noun or a verb:

1. The setting had a strong *influence* (noun) on the story's resolution.
2. The setting strongly *influences* (verb) the story's resolution.

Read Standard 3.3 at the top of this page. In that sentence, is *influence* a noun or a verb?

Learn It Online
There's more to learn about words. Visit:

| go.hrw.com | H6-15 | Go |

Thomas J. Dygard
(1931–1996)

"I'm Not a Writer. I'm a Rewriter."

For Thomas J. Dygard, writing and editing newspaper articles was a full-time job, but writing novels was what he loved most. Dygard wrote seventeen novels, all related to sports, for young people. Despite his years of working with words, he said he always considered writing a challenge.

Dygard worked as a reporter and bureau chief for the Associated Press, a news agency. He published his first novel, *Running Scared*, in 1977 and continued to publish one book a year until 1986.

> "My mistakes in my writing are so common that I'd bet I've thrown more pieces of paper in a wastebasket than any person alive. I'm not a writer. I'm a rewriter. As for having learned it all, I know that I haven't, and I also know that I never will."

Think About the Writer Dygard had to rewrite his stories repeatedly to get them right. How do you improve *your* writing?

Build Background

In this story you'll read about a talented football player who is part of his team's offensive line. In football the offensive linemen block for other players and do not carry the ball themselves. Although the job they do is important, it isn't always a position that gets much attention. During running plays the offensive linemen try to clear the way for a running back to carry the ball and gain yards. The running back often gets the glory, while the linemen are the "unsung heroes."

Preview the Selection

In "Just Once" you'll meet **the Moose,** the nickname of the high school senior Bryan Jefferson Crawford. The Moose is a lineman on the Bedford City Bears high school football team. You'll also meet **Coach Buford Williams** and the Moose's teammates, **Jerry Dixon, Dan Blevins,** and **Larry Hinden**—all of whom have their own ideas about what the Moose's role on the team should be.

JUST ONCE

by **Thomas J. Dygard**

Everybody liked the Moose. To his father and mother he was Bryan—as in Bryan Jefferson Crawford—but to everyone at Bedford City High he was the Moose. He was large and strong, as you might imagine from his nickname, and he was pretty fast on his feet—sort of nimble, you might say—considering his size. He didn't have a pretty face but he had a quick and easy smile—"sweet," some of the teachers called it; "nice," others said. But on the football field, the Moose was neither sweet nor nice. He was just strong and fast and a little bit devastating as the left tackle of the Bedford City Bears. When the Moose blocked somebody, he stayed blocked. When the Moose was called on to open a hole in the line for one of the Bears' runners, the hole more often than not resembled an open garage door.

Now in his senior season, the Moose had twice been named to the all-conference team and was considered a cinch for all-state. He spent a lot of his spare time, when he wasn't in a classroom or on the football field, reading letters from colleges eager to have the Moose pursue higher education—and football—at their institution.

But the Moose had a hang-up.

He didn't go public with his hang-up until the sixth game of the season. But, looking back, most of his teammates agreed that probably the Moose had been nurturing the hang-up secretly for two years or more.

The Moose wanted to carry the ball. Ⓐ

For sure, the Moose was not the first interior lineman in the history of football, or even the history of Bedford City High, who banged heads up front and wore bruises like badges of honor—and dreamed of racing down the field with the ball to the end zone[1] while everybody in the bleachers screamed his name.

But most linemen, it seems, are able to stifle the urge. The idea may pop into

1. **end zone:** area between the goal line and the end line (the line marking the boundary of the playing area) at each end of a football field.

Ⓐ **Read and Discuss** What has the narrator told you about the Moose and what he wants?

Vocabulary **devastating** (DEHV uh stay tihng) *adj.*: causing great damage.
nurturing (NUR chuhr ihng) *v.*: keeping alive.

their minds from time to time, but in their hearts they know they can't run fast enough, they know they can't do that fancy dancing to elude tacklers, they know they aren't trained to read blocks. They know that their strengths and talents are best utilized in the line. Football is, after all, a team sport, and everyone plays the position where he most helps the team. And so these linemen, or most of them, go back to banging heads without saying the first word about the dream that flickered through their minds.

Not so with the Moose. **B**

That sixth game, when the Moose's hang-up first came into public view, had ended with the Moose truly in all his glory as the Bears' left tackle. Yes, glory—but uncheered and sort of anonymous. The Bears were trailing 21–17 and had the ball on Mitchell High's five-yard line, fourth down,[2] with time running out. The rule in such a situation is simple—the best back carries the ball behind the best blocker—and it is a rule seldom violated by those in control of their faculties.[3] The Bears, of course, followed the rule. That meant Jerry Dixon running behind the Moose's blocking. With the snap of the ball, the Moose knocked down one lineman, bumped another one aside, and charged forward to flatten an approaching linebacker. Jerry did a little jig behind the Moose and then ran into the end zone, virtually untouched, to win the game.

After circling in the end zone a moment while the cheers echoed through the night, Jerry did run across and hug the Moose, that's true. Jerry knew who had made the touchdown possible.

But it wasn't the Moose's name that everybody was shouting. The fans in the bleachers were cheering Jerry Dixon.

It was probably at that precise moment that the Moose decided to go public. **C**

In the dressing room, Coach Buford Williams was making his rounds among the cheering players and came to a halt in front of the Moose. "It was your great blocking that did it," he said.

"I want to carry the ball," the Moose said.

Coach Williams was already turning away and taking a step toward the next player due an accolade[4] when his brain registered the fact that the Moose had said something strange. He was expecting the Moose to say, "Aw, gee, thanks, Coach." That was what the Moose always said when the coach issued a compliment. But the Moose had said something else. The coach turned back to the Moose, a look of disbelief on his face. "What did you say?"

"I want to carry the ball."

Coach Williams was good at quick recoveries, as any high school football coach

---

2. **fourth down:** In football the team holding the ball is allowed four downs, or attempts, to carry the ball forward at least ten yards.

3. **faculties:** mental powers.

4. **accolade** (AK uh layd): something said or done to express praise.

B **Read and Discuss** How is the Moose's dream of carrying the ball similar to and different from the thoughts of the other linemen?

C **Literary Focus** **Plot** What is the main problem, or conflict, in this story?

Vocabulary **anonymous** (uh NAHN uh muhs) *adj.*: unknown; unidentified.

had better be. He gave a tolerant smile and a little nod and said, "You keep right on blocking, son." **D**

This time Coach Williams made good on his turn and moved away from the Moose.

The following week's practice and the next Friday's game passed without further incident. After all, the game was a road game over at Cartwright High, thirty-five miles away. The Moose wanted to carry the ball in front of the Bedford City fans.

Then the Moose went to work.

He caught up with the coach on the way to the practice field on Wednesday.

"Remember," he said, leaning forward and down a little to get his face in the coach's face, "I said I want to carry the ball."

Coach Williams must have been thinking about something else because it took him a minute to look up into the Moose's face, and even then he didn't say anything.

"I meant it," the Moose said.

"Meant what?"

"I want to run the ball."

"Oh," Coach Williams said. Yes, he remembered. "Son, you're a great left tackle, a great blocker. Let's leave it that way." **E**

The Moose let the remaining days of the

D Read and Discuss What does the coach think of the Moose's request? How can you tell?

E Reading Focus Retelling What conflict is happening between the Moose and his coach? Retell this part of the story in your own words.

Vocabulary **tolerant** (TAHL uhr uhnt) *adj.*: patient; accepting of others.

practice week and then the game on Friday night against Edgewood High pass while he reviewed strategies. The review led him to Dan Blevins, the Bears' quarterback. If the signal caller would join in, maybe Coach Williams would listen.

"Yeah, I heard," Dan said. "But, look, what about Joe Wright at guard, Bill Slocum at right tackle, even Herbie Watson at center. They might all want to carry the ball. What are we going to do—take turns? It doesn't work that way."

So much for Dan Blevins.

The Moose found that most of the players in the backfield agreed with Dan. They couldn't see any reason why the Moose should carry the ball, especially in place of themselves. Even Jerry Dixon, who owed a lot of his glory to the Moose's blocking, gaped in disbelief at the Moose's idea. The Moose, however, got some support from his fellow linemen. Maybe they had dreams of their own, and saw value in a precedent.[5]

As the days went by, the word spread— not just on the practice field and in the corridors of Bedford City High, but all around town. The players by now were openly taking sides. Some thought it a jolly

> The players by now were openly taking sides. Some thought it a jolly good idea that the Moose carry the ball.

good idea that the Moose carry the ball. Others, like Dan Blevins, held to the purist[6] line—a left tackle plays left tackle, a ball carrier carries the ball, and that's it.

Around town, the vote wasn't even close. Everyone wanted the Moose to carry the ball. **F**

"Look, son," Coach Williams said to the Moose on the practice field the Thursday before the Benton Heights game, "this has gone far enough. Fun is fun. A joke is a joke. But let's drop it."

"Just once," the Moose pleaded.

Coach Williams looked at the Moose and didn't answer.

The Moose didn't know what that meant.

The Benton Heights Tigers were duck soup for the Bears, as everyone knew they would be. The Bears scored in their first three possessions and led 28–0 at the half. The hapless[7] Tigers had yet to cross the fifty-yard line under their own steam.

All the Bears, of course, were enjoying the way the game was going, as were the Bedford City fans jamming the bleachers.

Coach Williams looked irritated when the crowd on a couple of occasions broke into a chant: "Give the Moose the ball! Give the Moose the ball!" **G**

---

5. **precedent** (PREHS uh duhnt): action or statement that can serve as an example.

6. **purist** (PYUR ihst): someone who insists that rules be followed strictly.

7. **hapless:** unlucky.

F **Read and Discuss** Why might the townspeople care about the Moose's dream of carrying the ball?

G **Reading Focus** Retelling What's happening on the field and in the bleachers? Retell this section.

On the field, the Moose did not know whether to grin at hearing his name shouted by the crowd or to frown because the sound of his name was irritating the coach. Was the crowd going to talk Coach Williams into putting the Moose in the backfield? Probably not; Coach Williams didn't bow to that kind of pressure. Was the coach going to refuse to give the ball to the Moose just to show the crowd—and the Moose and the rest of the players—who was boss? The Moose feared so. **H**

In his time on the sideline, when the defensive unit was on the field, the Moose, of course, said nothing to Coach Williams. He knew better than to break the coach's concentration during a game—even a run-away victory—with a comment on any subject at all, much less his desire to carry the ball. As a matter of fact, the Moose was careful to stay out of the coach's line of vision, especially when the crowd was chanting "Give the Moose the ball!"

By the end of the third quarter the Bears were leading 42–0.

Coach Williams had been feeding substitutes into the game since halftime, but the Bears kept marching on. And now, in the opening minutes of the fourth quarter, the Moose and his teammates were standing on the Tigers' five-yard line, about to pile on another touchdown.

The Moose saw his substitute, Larry Hinden, getting a slap on the behind and then running onto the field. The Moose turned to leave.

Then he heard Larry tell the referee, "Hinden for Holbrook."

Holbrook? Chad Holbrook, the fullback?

Chad gave the coach a funny look and jogged off the field.

Larry joined the huddle and said, "Coach says the Moose at fullback and give him the ball." **I**

Dan Blevins said, "Really?"

"Really."

The Moose was giving his grin— "sweet," some of the teachers called it; "nice," others said.

"I want to do an end run," the Moose said. **J**

Dan looked at the sky a moment, then said, "What does it matter?"

The quarterback took the snap from center, moved back and to his right while turning, and extended the ball to the Moose.

The Moose took the ball and cradled it in his right hand. So far, so good. He hadn't fumbled. Probably both Coach Williams and Dan were surprised.

He ran a couple of steps and looked out in front and said aloud, "Whoa!"

Where had all those tacklers come from?

The whole world seemed to be peopled with players in red jerseys—the red of the Benton Heights Tigers. They all were looking straight at the Moose and advancing toward him. They looked very determined, and not

---

H Read and Discuss What's going on at the game? What does the Moose think about the crowd's actions?

I Literary Focus Setting How has the setting influenced the coach's decision to let the Moose carry the ball?

J Literary Focus Plot How is the Moose complicating the situation here?

friendly at all. And there were so many of them. The Moose had faced tough guys in the line, but usually one at a time, or maybe two. But this—five or six. And all of them heading for him. **(K)**

The Moose screeched to a halt, whirled, and ran the other way.

Dan Blevins blocked somebody in a red jersey breaking through the middle of the line, and the Moose wanted to stop running and thank him. But he kept going.

His reverse had caught the Tigers' defenders going the wrong way, and the field in front of the Moose looked open. But his blockers were going the wrong way, too. Maybe that was why the field looked so open. What did it matter, though, with the field clear in front of him? This was going to be a cakewalk;[8] the Moose was going to score a touchdown.

Then, again—"Whoa!"

Players with red jerseys were beginning to fill the empty space—a lot of them. And they were all running toward the Moose. They were kind of low, with their arms spread, as if they wanted to hit him hard and then grab him. **(L)**

A picture of Jerry Dixon dancing his little jig and wriggling between tacklers flashed through the Moose's mind. How did Jerry do that? Well, no time to ponder that one right now.

The Moose lowered his shoulder and thundered ahead, into the cloud of red jerseys. Something hit his left thigh. It hurt. Then

something pounded his hip, then his shoulder. They both hurt. Somebody was hanging on to him and was a terrible drag. How could he run with somebody hanging on to him? He knew he was going down, but maybe he was across the goal. He hit the ground hard, with somebody coming down on top of him, right on the small of his back.

The Moose couldn't move. They had him pinned. Wasn't the referee supposed to get these guys off?

Finally the load was gone and the Moose, still holding the ball, got to his knees and one hand, then stood.

He heard the screaming of the crowd, and he saw the scoreboard blinking.

He had scored.

His teammates were slapping him on the shoulder pads and laughing and shouting.

The Moose grinned, but he had a strange and distant look in his eyes.

He jogged to the sideline, the roars of the crowd still ringing in his ears.

"OK, son?" Coach Williams asked.

The Moose was puffing. He took a couple of deep breaths. He relived for a moment the first sight of a half dozen players in red jerseys, all with one target—him. He saw again the menacing horde of red jerseys that had risen up just when he'd thought he had clear sailing to the goal. They all zeroed in on him, the Moose, alone.

The Moose glanced at the coach, took another deep breath, and said, "Never again." **(M)**

---

8. cakewalk: easy job.

(K) | Read and Discuss | Do you think the Moose will succeed? Why or why not?

(L) | Literary Focus | **Plot** What new complications may prevent the Moose from reaching his goal?

(M) | Read and Discuss | The Moose finally realized his dream. Why does he tell the coach, "Never again"?

Vocabulary **ponder** (PAHN duhr) *v.*: think over carefully.

Applying Your Skills

Just Once
Literary Response and Analysis

Reading Skills Focus
Quick Check

1. How does the Moose let his coach know what he wants?
2. How do others feel about the Moose's wish to carry the ball?
3. What happens when the Moose finally gets his chance?

Read with a Purpose

4. What does the Moose learn after he <u>achieves</u> his dream? How does reality turn out to be different from his dream?

Reading Skills: Retelling

5. Review the chart you filled in, and add a column showing how each conflict is resolved.

Who or what is in conflict?	Describe what's happening	How is the conflict resolved?
The Moose has a conflict, or problem with his coach.	The Moose wants to carry the ball, but his coach won't let him because Moose is a lineman.	The coach finally gives in, but running the ball isn't like the Moose thought it would be.

Literary Skills Focus
Literary Analysis

6. **Connect** Is this a story only athletic people—especially boys—can appreciate, or does it have something to say to everyone? Explain.
7. **Infer** Describe the **conflict** the Moose faces when the crowd chants, "Give the Moose the ball!" What does he want to <u>achieve</u>? What prevents him from getting what he wants?

Literary Skills: Plot and Setting

8. **Analyze** This story takes place over the course of several games and practice days. How does the **setting** influence the Moose's approach to his problem? How does the setting influence the story's **climax** and **resolution?**
9. **Analyze** Could this story take place in another setting? Explain why or why not.

Literary Skills Review: Theme

10. **Evaluate** The **theme** is the <u>major</u> message a story reveals about life. What is this story's theme, or underlying message? Is it the same lesson that the Moose learns? Explain.

Writing Skills Focus
Think as a Reader/Writer

Use It in Your Writing Review your notes about the Moose. Then, develop a character who faces a problem, and place him or her in a specific setting. You might want to involve your character in a struggle against nature.

 What Do You Think Now

How do you think the Moose would feel about the expression "Be careful what you wish for—you may get it"?

Just Once

Vocabulary Development

Context Clues

If you walked into class and an unfamiliar person was at your teacher's desk, what would you assume? You'd probably assume that he or she was a substitute teacher. Even without knowing this person's name, you'd be able to infer, or make a guess about, who he or she was. You can do the same thing with words. You can look at the words and sentences around them—their **context**—and make an accurate guess about what they mean.

Your Turn

In the following paragraph, each Vocabulary word appears in italics and has at least one **context clue** that will help you determine its meaning. Copy the paragraph, and circle the clues that help you understand each word's meaning.

> devastating
> nurturing
> anonymous
> tolerant
> ponder

> The coach read aloud the *anonymous* note, wondering who had written it: "Please take some time to *ponder* our request carefully. You may think that it would have a *devastating* effect, but we're sure it won't ruin the sports program. It's time to be *tolerant* and fair. After all, we've been *nurturing* our dreams for months. Please let girls try out for the team."

Language Coach

Suffixes A **suffix** is a letter or group of letters added to the end of a word to create a different meaning. Adding different suffixes to the same root word can alter that word's part of speech. For example, adding different suffixes to the word *pray* results in different parts of speech: *prayer, praying, prayerful.* Try adding suffixes to these words so that they may be used as different parts of speech.

1. obey
2. pay
3. try
4. fry

Use a dictionary to help you if necessary.

Academic Vocabulary

Write About . . .

Write a short paragraph explaining what the Moose did to <u>achieve</u> his goal. Provide examples of how the Moose chose to <u>interact</u> with Coach Williams. Was the Moose's approach effective, or should he have made a <u>major</u> change to the way he tried to persuade his coach? Use the underlined Academic Vocabulary words in your paragraph.

Learn It Online
For more on context clues, visit *WordSharp* at:

go.hrw.com   H6-24   Go

Grammar Link
Common and Proper Nouns

What part of speech is the word *once* in the title "Just Once"? It's a **noun**—a word used to name a person, place, thing, or idea.

Persons	Moose, Jerry Dixon, Coach Buford Williams, Dan Blevins
Places	Mitchell High School, practice field, dressing room
Things	football, red jerseys
Ideas	hang-up, badge of honor, talents

A **common noun** is a general name for a person, place, thing, or idea, while a **proper noun** names a particular one. A proper noun begins with a capital letter, while a common noun is not capitalized.

Common Noun	**Proper Noun**
school	Mitchell High School
coach	Buford Williams
teammate	Dan Blevins

Your Turn

In the sentences that follow, underline the common nouns, and circle the proper nouns.

1. Moose is a high school athlete.
2. He plays left tackle for the Bears' football team but dreams of carrying the ball.
3. The boy is rebuffed when he tells Coach Williams of his dream.
4. His fellow teammate Dan Blevins disagrees with Moose.
5. Despite everything, Moose finally gets his chance in a game against the Benton Heights Tigers.

CHOICES

As you respond to the Choices, use these **Academic Vocabulary** words as appropriate: achieve, influence, interact, major.

REVIEW
Write a Summary

TechFocus Create a sportscast of the Bears-versus-Tigers game. First, write a **summary** of what happened. Use details in the story to answer *who, what, when, where, why,* and *how* questions. Be sure to empahsize the setting's influence on the game's action and outcome. Then, practice reading your report for a broadcast. Tape the reading, and play it for your class.

CONNECT
Write About a Conflict

Timed └Writing Write about a time when you faced a **conflict** between doing what you wanted and doing what was best for a group or team, such as your family, friends, or an organization. Include important details, and end with an explanation of what you learned.

EXTEND
Draw a Life Map

People want different things at different times in their lives. Draw a "life map" as a kind of road or journey, showing a person at one end and the person's goal at the other end. Draw some of the forces that person might have to overcome along the way. Then, write a paragraph explaining your map. (It does not have to be a map of the life *you* want.)

Learn It Online
Learn more about this story with the Internet links available at:

go.hrw.com   H6-25   Go

Preparing to Read

All Summer in a Day

by **Ray Bradbury**

What Do **You** Think

What truths about ourselves can we learn in extreme, dangerous, or unusual situations?

QuickWrite

What kinds of environments or situations lift your spirits? What kinds of environments or situations bring out the worst in you? Write an explanation of how you think the settings we find ourselves in affect our moods, thoughts, and actions.

Reader/Writer Notebook

Use your **RWN** to complete the activities for this selection.

Literary Skills Focus

Setting The **plot** is the series of events that make up a story, and the **setting** is the time and place in which the story occurs. In some stories the setting plays a <u>major</u> role in what the characters do and how the action unfolds. As you read this science fiction story, think about the importance of setting. How does the setting shape the action and the problems the characters face? If you changed any of the details of the setting, how would the story be affected?

Reading Skills Focus

Sequencing The **sequence** is the order of events in a story. Placing the story events in the correct sequence is important for understanding how a story develops and what happens at key moments in the plot.

Into Action To keep track of the order of the main events in this story, use a sequence chart like the one below. Number each event, and describe it briefly. Add as many rows to the chart as you need.

Sequence Chart: "All Summer in a Day"

1. The children are waiting for the rain to stop.

2.

TechFocus Research the atmosphere of a planet in our solar system other than Earth or Venus. What equipment and protection would be necessary for people to be able to live there?

Writing Skills Focus
Think as a Reader/Writer

Find It in Your Reading Pay attention to the unusual words and phrases Bradbury uses to describe the setting, such as "concussion of storms." List these descriptive images in your *Reader/Writer Notebook*.

Vocabulary

frail (frayl) *adj.:* not very strong; easily broken. *The girl was small and frail.*

vital (VY tuhl) *adj.:* necessary for life; very important. *It was vital that everyone see the sun.*

consequence (KAHN suh kwehns) *n.:* of value; importance. *Their teacher realized that the day was of great consequence.*

surged (surjd) *v.:* moved forward, as if in a wave. *The children surged toward the door, eager to escape.*

savored (SAY vuhrd) *v.:* delighted in. *The children savored the chance to play outside.*

Language Coach

Dialogue The words that characters in a story speak are called **dialogue.** Bradbury brings this story to life with carefully crafted dialogue that moves events forward and reveals the feelings and motivations of the characters. There are no long conversations, but the dialogue is full of emotion. In your *Reader/Writer Notebook*, write down examples of dialogue that powerfully reveals the feelings of the characters.

Learn It Online
For a preview of this story, see the video introduction at:

go.hrw.com   H6-27   **Go**

Ray Bradbury
(1920–   )

Space-Age Storyteller

Ray Bradbury has been called the world's greatest science fiction writer. He once described himself more simply: "I am a storyteller. That's all I've ever tried to be." Although Bradbury's stories are often set in outer space, his characters and their emotions are human and down-to-earth. Through this connection of the imagined and the real, Bradbury's fiction challenges the reader to question where we might be headed and what we might learn about ourselves.

Imagine the Future

In his fiction, Bradbury encourages his readers to try to imagine the wonders the future will hold:

> "Everything confronting us in the next thirty years will be science-fictional, that is, impossible a few years ago. The things you are doing right now, if you had told anyone you'd be doing them when you were children, they would have laughed you out of school. . . . "

Think About the Writer What can imaginative tales like science fiction stories teach us about ourselves and our lives?

Build Background

"All Summer in a Day" takes place on the planet Venus in a future world where "rocket men and women," as Bradbury calls them, have come to live and set up a colony. Bradbury's description of Venus and its weather patterns is entirely fictional. As the second planet from the sun in our solar system, Venus is actually very hot and dry—and has no liquid water.

Bradbury wrote this story in 1959, during a period (roughly 1957–1975) when the space race between the United States and the Soviet Union was in full swing. The two countries were in competition to see who would reach the moon first and who would go the farthest to make space travel a reality. Nine years after this story was written, the United States made the first moon landing, and many people thought it would not be long before spaceships made it to Mars and other planets.

Preview the Selection

On the planet Venus—as imagined by Bradbury—the sun appears for only two hours every seven years. A class of nine-year-olds, especially one student named **Margot,** eagerly awaits a brief glimpse of the sun.

All Summer in a Day

by **Ray Bradbury**

"Ready."

"Ready."

"Now?"

"Soon."

"Do the scientists really know? Will it happen today, will it?"

"Look, look; see for yourself!"

The children pressed to each other like so many roses, so many weeds, intermixed, peering out for a look at the hidden sun.

It rained.

It had been raining for seven years; thousands upon thousands of days compounded and filled from one end to the other with rain, with the drum and gush of water, with the sweet crystal fall of showers and the concussion[1] of storms so heavy they were tidal waves come over the islands. A thousand forests had been crushed under the rain and grown up a thousand times to be crushed again. And this was the way life was forever on the planet Venus, and this

was the schoolroom of the children of the rocket men and women who had come to a raining world to set up civilization and live out their lives. **Ⓐ**

"It's stopping, it's stopping!"

"Yes, yes!"

Margot stood apart from them, from these children who could never remember a time when there wasn't rain and rain and rain. They were all nine years old, and if there had been a day, seven years ago, when the sun came out for an hour and showed its face to the stunned world, they could not recall. Sometimes, at night, she heard them stir, in remembrance, and she knew they were dreaming and remembering gold or a yellow crayon or a coin large enough to buy the world with. She knew they thought they remembered a warmness, like a blushing in the face, in the body, in the arms and legs and trembling hands. But then they always awoke to the tatting drum, the endless shaking down of clear bead necklaces upon the roof, the walk, the gardens, the forests, and their dreams were gone. **Ⓑ**

---

1. **concussion** (kuhn KUHSH uhn): violent shaking or shock.

Ⓐ **Literary Focus** Setting What is the major influence of this setting so far? Which details suggest this?

Ⓑ **Literary Focus** Setting What change in the setting does Margot think the other children might be remembering?

All day yesterday they had read in class about the sun. About how like a lemon it was, and how hot. And they had written small stories or essays or poems about it.

I think the sun is a flower
That blooms for just one hour.

That was Margot's poem, read in a quiet voice in the still classroom while the rain was falling outside.

"Aw, you didn't write that!" protested one of the boys.

"I did," said Margot. "*I did.*"

"William!" said the teacher.

But that was yesterday. Now the rain was slackening,[2] and the children were crushed in the great thick windows.

"Where's teacher?"

"She'll be back."

"She'd better hurry; we'll miss it!"

They turned on themselves like a feverish wheel, all tumbling spokes.

Margot stood alone. She was a very frail girl who looked as if she had been lost in the rain for years and the rain had washed out the blue from her eyes and the red from her mouth and the yellow from her hair. She was an old photograph dusted from an album, whitened away, and if she spoke at all her voice would be a ghost. Now she stood, separate, staring at the rain and the loud wet world beyond the huge glass.

"What're *you* looking at?" said William.

Margot said nothing.

"Speak when you're spoken to." He gave her a shove. But she did not move; rather she let herself be moved only by him and nothing else.

They edged away from her; they would not look at her. She felt them go away. And this was because she would play no games with them in the echoing tunnels of the underground city. If they tagged her and ran, she stood blinking after them and did not follow. When the class sang songs about happiness and life and games, her lips barely moved. Only when they sang about the sun and the summer did her lips move as she watched the drenched windows. **C**

And then, of course, the biggest crime of all was that she had come here only five years ago from Earth, and she remembered the sun and the way the sun was and the sky was when she was four in Ohio. And they, they had been on Venus all their lives, and they had been only two years old when last the sun came out and had long since forgotten the color and heat of it and the way it really was. But Margot remembered.

"It's like a penny," she said once, eyes closed.

"No, it's not!" the children cried.

"It's like a fire," she said, "in the stove."

"You're lying; you don't remember!" cried the children.

But she remembered and stood quietly apart from all of them and watched the patterning windows. And once, a month ago, she had refused to shower in the school shower rooms, had clutched her hands to her ears and over her head, screaming the water mustn't touch her head. So after that, dimly, dimly, she sensed it, she was

---

2. **slackening** (SLAK uh nihng): lessening; slowing.

C [Read and Discuss] What does this scene suggest about how the other children view Margot?

Vocabulary   frail (frayl) *adj.*: not very strong; easily broken.

different, and they knew her difference and kept away.

There was talk that her father and mother were taking her back to Earth next year; it seemed vital to her that they do so, though it would mean the loss of thousands of dollars to her family. And so, the children hated her for all these reasons of big and little consequence. They hated her pale snow face, her waiting silence, her thinness, and her possible future.

"Get away!" The boy gave her another push. "What're you waiting for?"

Then, for the first time, she turned and looked at him. And what she was waiting for was in her eyes.

"Well, don't wait around here!" cried the boy savagely. "You won't see nothing!"

Her lips moved.

"Nothing!" he cried. "It was all a joke, wasn't it?" He turned to the other children. "Nothing's happening today. Is it?"

They all blinked at him and then, understanding, laughed and shook their heads. "Nothing, nothing!"

"Oh, but," Margot whispered, her eyes helpless. "But this is the day, the scientists predict, they say, they know, the sun . . ."

"All a joke!" said the boy, and seized her roughly. "Hey everyone, let's put her in a closet before teacher comes!"

D Literary Focus **Setting** What kind of setting does Margot remember? How is it different from the story's setting?

E Read and Discuss What is the author explaining here?

Vocabulary **vital** (VY tuhl) *adj.*: necessary for life; very important.
consequence (KAHN suh kwehns) *n.*: of value; importance.

Life on Venus?

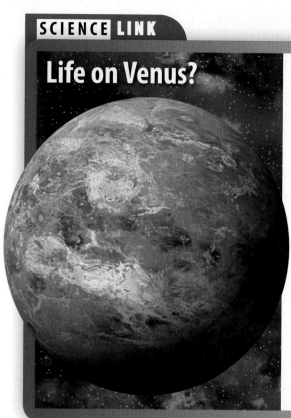

We don't know whether there's life on Venus. We can be pretty sure, though, that Ray Bradbury's science fiction vision of a rain-drenched Venus is more fiction than science.

Venus is the second planet from the Sun. Mercury is closer to the Sun, but Venus is hotter than Mercury because its atmosphere is full of thick clouds of sulfuric acid strong enough to etch metal and burn through flesh. These clouds trap the sun's rays and increase the temperature to more than 800°F.

It's too hot to rain on Venus, but scientists think its thick clouds might contain areas of lower temperatures where microscopic forms of life could exist. It's possible that small microbes are responsible for the types of gases in Venus's clouds. Could there be some form of life on Venus? Researchers will keep looking.

Ask Yourself

If life were found on Venus, how might people react?

"No," said Margot, falling back.

They surged about her, caught her up and bore her, protesting, and then pleading, and then crying, back into a tunnel, a room, a closet, where they slammed and locked the door. They stood looking at the door and saw it tremble from her beating and throwing herself against it. They heard her muffled cries. Then, smiling, they turned and went out and back down the tunnel, just as the teacher arrived. **F**

"Ready, children?" She glanced at her watch.

"Yes!" said everyone.

"Are we all here?"

"Yes!" **G**

The rain slackened still more.

They crowded to the huge door.

The rain stopped.

It was as if, in the midst of a film concerning an avalanche, a tornado, a hurricane, a volcanic eruption, something had, first, gone wrong with the sound apparatus, thus muffling and finally cutting off all noise, all of the blasts and repercussions and thunders, and then, second, ripped the film from the projector and inserted in its place a peaceful tropical slide which did not move or tremor. The world ground to a standstill. The silence was so immense and unbelievable that you felt your ears had been stuffed or you had lost your hearing altogether. The children put their

---

F Read and Discuss How do the children seem to feel about what they've done to Margot?

G Reading Focus Sequencing Who is present at this point? Where is Margot now?

Vocabulary **surged** (surjd) v.: moved forward, as if in a wave.

hands to their ears. They stood apart. The door slid back and the smell of the silent, waiting world came in to them.

The sun came out.

It was the color of flaming bronze and it was very large. And the sky around it was a blazing blue tile color. And the jungle burned with sunlight as the children, released from their spell, rushed out, yelling, into the springtime.

"Now, don't go too far," called the teacher after them. "You've only two hours, you know. You wouldn't want to get caught out!"

But they were running and turning their faces up to the sky and feeling the sun on their cheeks like a warm iron; they were taking off their jackets and letting the sun burn their arms.

"Oh, it's better than the sun lamps, isn't it?"

"Much, much better!"

They stopped running and stood in the great jungle that covered Venus, that grew and never stopped growing, tumultuously,[3] even as you watched it. It was a nest of octopuses, clustering up great arms of fleshlike weed, wavering, flowering in this brief spring. It was the color of rubber and ash, this jungle, from the many years without sun. It was the color of stones and white cheeses and ink, and it was the color of the moon.

The children lay out, laughing, on the jungle mattress and heard it sigh and squeak under them, resilient[4] and alive. They ran among the trees, they slipped and fell, they pushed each other, they played hide-and-seek and tag, but most of all they squinted at the

---

3. **tumultuously** (too MUHL choo uhs lee): wildly; violently.
4. **resilient** (rih ZIHL yuhnt): springy, quick to recover.

Radiance by Simon Cook.

Analyzing Visuals   Connecting to the Text
How does this image of the sun capture the change in the story's setting that occurs when the sun comes out?

All Summer in a Day   **33**

sun until tears ran down their faces; they put their hands up to that yellowness and that amazing blueness and they breathed of the fresh, fresh air and listened and listened to the silence which suspended them in a blessed sea of no sound and no motion. They looked at everything and savored everything. Then, wildly, like animals escaped from their caves, they ran and ran in shouting circles. They ran for an hour and did not stop running. **H**

And then—

In the midst of their running, one of the girls wailed.

Everyone stopped.

The girl, standing in the open, held out her hand.

"Oh, look, look," she said, trembling.

They came slowly to look at her opened palm.

In the center of it, cupped and huge, was a single raindrop.

She began to cry, looking at it.

They glanced quietly at the sky.

"Oh. Oh."

A few cold drops fell on their noses and their cheeks and their mouths. The sun faded behind a stir of mist. A wind blew cool around them. They turned and started to walk back toward the underground house, their hands at their sides, their smiles vanishing away. **I**

A boom of thunder startled them, and like leaves before a new hurricane, they tumbled upon each other and ran. Lightning struck ten miles away, five miles away, a mile, a half-mile. The sky darkened into midnight in a flash.

They stood in the doorway of the underground for a moment until it was raining hard. Then they closed the door and heard the gigantic sound of the rain falling in tons and avalanches, everywhere and forever.

"Will it be seven more years?"

"Yes. Seven."

Then one of them gave a little cry.

"Margot!"

"What?"

"She's still in the closet where we locked her."

"Margot."

They stood as if someone had driven them, like so many stakes, into the floor. They looked at each other and then looked away. They glanced out at the world that was raining now and raining and raining steadily. They could not meet each other's glances. Their faces were solemn and pale. They looked at their hands and feet, their faces down.

"Margot."

One of the girls said, "Well . . . ?"

No one moved.

"Go on," whispered the girl.

They walked slowly down the hall in the sound of cold rain. They turned through the doorway to the room in the sound of the storm and thunder, lightning on their faces, blue and terrible. They walked over to the closet door slowly and stood by it.

Behind the closet door was only silence.

They unlocked the door, even more slowly, and let Margot out. **J**

H [Read and Discuss] Why might Bradbury compare the children to animals?

I [Reading Focus] Sequencing How much time has passed since the children went outside? How do you know?

J [Read and Discuss] What does this say about Margot's classmates?

Vocabulary **savored** (SAY vuhrd) *v*.: delighted in.

Applying Your Skills

All Summer in a Day

Literary Response and Analysis

Reading Skills Focus
Quick Check

1. Why are the children so excited at the beginning of the story?
2. What does Margot remember that the other children do not?
3. What happens while Margot is in the closet?

Read with a Purpose

4. How do the children in this story react to the long-awaited event? Does their behavior surprise you? Explain.

Reading Skills: Sequencing

5. Review your chart for "All Summer in a Day." Now, create a chart like the one below that focuses on the sequence of events from Margot's perspective. Compare and contrast the two charts. Mark with a star the event that causes the two sequences to begin to differ. How does this event change the "summer day" for Margot? for the other children?

   Sequence Chart: Margot's Day

   1. Margot is in the classroom with the other children, waiting for the rain to stop.

   2.

Literary Skills Focus
Literary Analysis

6. **Interpret** Differences between people often cause **conflicts,** or clashes. What causes the conflict between Margot and the other children? Why does she keep to herself?

7. **Analyze** Why would the children lock Margot in the closet when they know how much the sun means to her? How might this experience affect both Margot and the children who mistreated her?

Literary Skills: Setting

8. **Interpret/Evaluate** What do you think the title of Bradbury's story means? What is the influence of the setting on this title?

9. **Analyze** How does the **setting** of this story influence the **plot,** including the conflict and **resolution**? Would there be a story if Bradbury's Venus had less extreme weather? Explain.

Literary Skills Review: Character

10. **Infer/Evaluate** From what you know of her character, how do you think Margot will react when she is let out of the closet? Should Bradbury have described what happens next, or do you like the story as it is? Explain.

Writing Skills Focus
Think as a Reader/Writer

Use It in Your Writing Use precise language to write a description of a memorable experience in which you faced extreme weather.

What Do You Think Now If you were living on Bradbury's Venus, how might the setting influence you? What truths about yourself might you learn?

Applying Your Skills

All Summer in a Day

Vocabulary Development
Context Clues

When you're reading, you can often determine the meaning of an unknown word by looking at its **context**—the words and sentences surrounding the unfamiliar word. Sometimes **context clues** appear in the same sentence as the unfamiliar word. Other times the clues appear before or even after the sentence containing the unfamiliar word. Look at how the underlined context clues help you understand the meaning of *muffling* in the following sentence from the story:

"It was as if, in the midst of a film concerning an avalanche, a tornado, a hurricane, a volcanic eruption, <u>something had, first, gone wrong with the sound apparatus</u>, thus **muffling** and <u>finally cutting off all noise</u>. . . ."

The clues help you guess that the author uses *muffling* to indicate that the noise was decreasing. In fact, the word means "making less intense."

Your Turn

Find the place in the story where each Vocabulary word is used: *frail, vital, consequence, surged,* and *savored.* For each word, write down any context clues you find in the story. Remember to look for clues in sentences coming before and after the sentences in which the words are used. Are there any words for which you can't find context clues?

Language Coach

Dialogue Bradbury does not always identify *who* is speaking in his dialogue. You know a different person is speaking when dialogue begins on a new line:

"*Now?*"

"*Soon.*"

When Bradbury wants to be sure we know who is speaking, he includes a **speaker tag**—the name or description of the speaker:

"*Aw, you didn't write that!*"
  protested one of the boys.
"*I did,*" *said Margot.* "*I did.*"

Think about the dialogue above that lacks speaker tags. Who might be speaking? Re-reading the beginning of the story may help you decide.

Academic Vocabulary

Talk About . . .

With a partner, discuss the <u>major</u> event in "All Summer in a Day." Did the event likely create more conflict between Margot and the children, or do you think they will <u>interact</u> with her in more positive ways in the future? Use the underlined Academic Vocabulary words in your discussion.

Learn It Online
Sharpen your word skills with *WordSharp* at:

go.hrw.com | H6-36 | Go

Grammar Link
Pronouns: Make It Specific

Have you ever listened to someone repeat the same thing over and over instead of getting to some new point? If so, you were probably bored and found it difficult to keep listening. You're lucky that English is full of **pronouns**—words that are used in place of nouns and, sometimes, other pronouns. Without pronouns, people would have to repeat themselves every time they spoke. For example, look at the following repetitive sentence:

> **The girl said that the girl's parents were taking the girl back to Earth next year.**

Pronouns shorten this sentence, making it much easier to read (and listen to):

> **The girl said her parents were taking her back to Earth next year.**

Your Turn

Rewrite each of the following sentences by replacing any repeated nouns with pronouns.

1. Margot had come to Venus when Margot was four years old.
2. The sun was a stranger to the children because the sun was always hidden by rain clouds.
3. The children grabbed Margot, and the children pushed Margo into the closet.
4. The teacher told the teacher's students that the teacher did not want the teacher's students to go far.
5. The boys and girls were sorry about what the boys and girls had done to Margot.

CHOICES

As you respond to the Choices, use these **Academic Vocabulary** words as appropriate: achieve, influence, interact, major.

REVIEW
Diagram a Plot
Partner Work Fill out a diagram like this one, showing the plot of "All Summer in a Day":

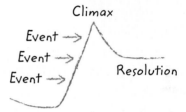

Setting and basic situation (main character and his or her problem)

CONNECT
Write a Movie Proposal
TechFocus Create a movie proposal about people living in a colony on the real Venus. Use Internet resources to learn what conditions on Venus are like. Describe the set designs and special effects that you would need for the movie. What will be the story's major conflict?

EXTEND
Write a Persuasive Letter
Timed Writing Imagine that you're one of Margot's classmates and it's the day after the sun came out. Write a persuasive letter urging your classmates to change their attitudes toward Margot. End by suggesting what all of you should do to make up for your actions.

Learn It Online
Research background information on this story using the Internet links available at:

go.hrw.com   H6-37   Go

Preparing to Read

The Bracelet

by **Yoshiko Uchida**

To School (1945) by Hisako Hibi.
Gift of Ibuki Hibi Lee, Japanese
American National Museum
(96.601.50).

 What Do You Think

What truths can we learn about ourselves when we can't control the things that change in our lives?

 QuickTalk

What story can you think of in which painful historical events are used to teach us never to repeat mistakes? With a partner, discuss at least two examples.

Reader/Writer Notebook

Use your **RWN** to complete the activities for this selection.

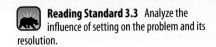

Reading Standard 3.3 Analyze the influence of setting on the problem and its resolution.

Literary Skills Focus

Setting and Conflict Stories occur in a particular time and place—the story's **setting.** In some stories the setting is part of, or even the cause of, the main character's **conflict,** or problem. As you read, note how this story starts out in one setting and moves to another, quite different setting. Think about the <u>influence</u> these settings have on the conflict and its resolution.

Literary Perspectives Use the literary perspective described on page 41 as you read this story.

Reading Skills Focus

Summarizing When you **summarize** a story, you briefly retell the main ideas and important events in your own words.

Into Action As you read "The Bracelet," use a chart like this one to list the main ideas and events that a summary would include.

"The Bracelet"
Setting: _____
Main Characters: _____
Conflict: _____
Sequence of Main Events:
  1. _____
  2. _____
Resolution (Ending): _____

Writing Skills Focus
Think as a Reader/Writer

Find It in Your Reading In each of the story's settings the author uses contrast to show how the place has changed or is different than imagined. Create a "T" chart in your *Reader/Writer Notebook*. On one side, record how each setting once was or how Ruri imagined it would be. On the other side, note how each place has changed or how it looks in reality.

Vocabulary

evacuated (ih VAK yoo ayt uhd) *v.:* removed from an area. *In 1942, Japanese Americans were evacuated from the West Coast.*

interned (ihn TURND) *v.:* imprisoned or confined. *Ruri's father was interned in a prisoner-of-war camp.*

thrust (thruhst) *v.:* shoved; pushed. *Laurie thrust the bracelet into Ruri's hand.*

forsaken (fawr SAY kuhn) *adj.:* abandoned. *The garden looked as forsaken as Ruri felt when she had to leave home.*

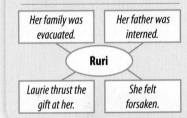

Language Coach

Words Borrowed from Other Languages

When people speaking different languages interact, they often borrow one another's words. American English has been borrowing words from other languages for centuries. Can you think of any words that have been borrowed from the Japanese language?

 Learn It Online

Use our online graphic organizers to help you as you read:

| go.hrw.com | H6-39 | Go |

Yoshiko Uchida
(1921–1992)

Writing to Keep It from Happening Again

Yoshiko Uchida was in her last year of college when the United States entered World War II. Like most people of Japanese descent on the West Coast, Uchida and her family were uprooted by the government and forced to go to an internment camp. She and her family lived at Tanforan Racetrack, in horse stall 40. Uchida later gave the same "address" to the fictional family in her short story "The Bracelet." Uchida said that in writing about the internment camps, she tried to give readers a sense of the courage and strength that enabled most Japanese Americans to endure this tragedy:

> "I always ask the children why they think I wrote *Journey to Topaz* and *Journey Home*, in which I tell of the wartime experiences of the Japanese Americans. . . . I continue the discussion until finally one of them will say, 'You wrote those books so it won't ever happen again.'"

Think About the Writer

Why do you think Uchida feels it is important that people not forget the Japanese internment?

Build Background

Shortly after the United States entered World War II to fight against Japan after the attack on Pearl Harbor, more than 110,000 people of Japanese ancestry who were living in the United States were interned—forced to move to guarded camps. Most were American citizens who had been born here and had done nothing wrong. Nevertheless, the U.S. government feared that they might give support to Japan. When they were finally allowed to leave the internment camps after the war, many Japanese Americans found that other people had taken over their homes and businesses. In 1989, the U.S. government issued a formal apology to Japanese Americans for the injustice that had been done to them.

Preview the Selection

When **Ruri** and **her family** have to move to an internment camp simply because they are of Japanese descent, Ruri's best friend, **Laurie,** gives her a bracelet as a going-away gift.

The Bracelet

by **Yoshiko Uchida**

Mama, is it time to go?" I hadn't planned to cry, but the tears came suddenly, and I wiped them away with the back of my hand. I didn't want my older sister to see me crying.

"It's almost time, Ruri," my mother said gently. Her face was filled with a kind of sadness I had never seen before.

I looked around at my empty room. The clothes that Mama always told me to hang up in the closet, the junk piled on my dresser, the old rag doll I could never bear to part with— they were all gone. There was nothing left in my room, and there was nothing left in the rest of the house. The rugs and furniture were gone, the pictures and drapes were down, and the closets and cupboards were empty. The house was like a gift box after the nice thing inside was gone; just a lot of nothingness.

It was almost time to leave our home, but we weren't moving to a nicer house or to a new town. It was April 21, 1942. The United States and Japan were at war, and every Japanese person on the West Coast was being evacuated by the government to a concentration camp. Mama, my sister Keiko, and I were being sent from our home, and out of Berkeley, and eventually out of California. **Ⓐ**

The doorbell rang, and I ran to answer it before my sister could. I thought maybe by some miracle a messenger from the government might be standing there, tall and proper and buttoned into a uniform, come to tell us it was all a terrible mistake, that we

Literary Perspectives

Historical Perspective We focus on the life of an author for a biographical perspective, but the historical perspective broadens our focus. It asks us to consider the world at the time the story was written. What important historical events shape the author's thinking? What evidence of those events is in the text? How is the story tied to the historical period in which it is set? Could the story have happened in any other time or place?

Ⓐ **Read and Discuss** What have you learned so far about the characters' situation?

Vocabulary **evacuated** (ih VAK yoo ayt uhd) *v.*: removed from an area.

Analyzing Visuals

Connecting to the Text
How does this photograph and picture of a bracelet affect your understanding of this story's time period?

wouldn't have to leave after all. Or maybe the messenger would have a telegram from Papa, who was interned in a prisoner-of-war camp in Montana because he had worked for a Japanese business firm. **B**

The FBI had come to pick up Papa and hundreds of other Japanese community leaders on the very day that Japanese planes had bombed Pearl Harbor. The government thought they were dangerous enemy aliens. If it weren't so sad, it would have been funny. Papa could no more be dangerous than the mayor of our city, and he was every bit as loyal to the United States. He had lived here since 1917. **C**

When I opened the door, it wasn't a messenger from anywhere. It was my best friend, Laurie Madison, from next door. She was

B **Reading Focus** **Summarizing** What has happened so far? Who is the main character?

C **Read and Discuss** What have you learned from this paragraph about people going to internment camps?

Vocabulary **interned** (ihn TURND) *v.*: imprisoned or confined.

holding a package wrapped up like a birthday present, but she wasn't wearing her party dress, and her face drooped like a wilted tulip.

"Hi," she said. "I came to say goodbye."

She thrust the present at me and told me it was something to take to camp. "It's a bracelet," she said before I could open the package. "Put it on so you won't have to pack it." She knew I didn't have one inch of space left in my suitcase. We had been instructed to take only what we could carry into camp, and Mama had told us that we could each take only two suitcases.

"Then how are we ever going to pack the dishes and blankets and sheets they've told us to bring with us?" Keiko worried.

"I don't really know," Mama said, and she simply began packing those big impossible things into an enormous duffel bag—along with umbrellas, boots, a kettle, hot plate, and flashlight.

"Who's going to carry that huge sack?" I asked.

But Mama didn't worry about things like that. "Someone will help us," she said. "Don't worry." So I didn't.

Laurie wanted me to open her package and put on the bracelet before she left. It was a thin gold chain with a heart dangling on it. She helped me put it on, and I told her I'd never take it off, ever.

"Well, goodbye then," Laurie said awkwardly. "Come home soon."

"I will," I said, although I didn't know if I would ever get back to Berkeley again.   **D**

I watched Laurie go down the block, her long blond pigtails bouncing as she walked. I wondered who would be sitting in my desk at Lincoln Junior High now that I was gone. Laurie kept turning and waving, even walking backward for a while, until she got to the corner. I didn't want to watch anymore, and I slammed the door shut.   **E**

The next time the doorbell rang, it was Mrs. Simpson, our other neighbor. She was going to drive us to the Congregational Church, which was the Civil Control Station where all the Japanese of Berkeley were supposed to report.

It was time to go. "Come on, Ruri. Get your things," my sister called to me.

It was a warm day, but I put on a sweater and my coat so I wouldn't have to carry them, and I picked up my two suitcases. Each one had a tag with my name and our family number on it. Every Japanese family had to register and get a number. We were Family Number 13453.

Mama was taking one last look around our house. She was going from room to room, as though she were trying to take a mental picture of the house she had lived in for fifteen years, so she would never forget it.   **F**

I saw her take a long last look at the garden that Papa loved. The irises beside the fish pond were just beginning to bloom. If Papa had been home, he would have cut the first iris blossom and brought it inside to Mama. "This one is for you," he would have

---

D **Reading Focus** **Summarizing** In one or two sentences, tell what has happened since Laurie came to the door.

E **Read and Discuss** What emotions do you think Laurie and Ruri are feeling here?

F **Read and Discuss** What does Ruri think her mother is doing when she looks at the empty rooms?

Vocabulary **thrust** (thruhst) *v.*: shoved; pushed.

said. And Mama would have smiled and said, "Thank you, Papa San"[1] and put it in her favorite cut-glass vase.

But the garden looked shabby and forsaken now that Papa was gone and Mama was too busy to take care of it. It looked the way I felt, sort of empty and lonely and abandoned. **Ⓖ**

When Mrs. Simpson took us to the Civil Control Station, I felt even worse. I was scared, and for a minute I thought I was going to lose my breakfast right in front of everybody. There must have been over a thousand Japanese people gathered at the church. Some were old and some were young. Some were talking and laughing, and some were crying. I guess everybody else was scared too. No one knew exactly what was going to happen to us. We just knew we were being taken to the Tanforan Racetracks, which the army had turned into a camp for the Japanese. There were fourteen other camps like ours along the West Coast.

What scared me most were the soldiers standing at the doorway of the church hall. They were carrying guns with mounted bayonets. I wondered if they thought we would try to run away and whether they'd shoot us or come after us with their bayonets if we did. **Ⓗ**

A long line of buses waited to take us to camp. There were trucks, too, for our baggage. And Mama was right; some men

---

1. **San** (sahn): Japanese term added to names to indicate respect.

were there to help us load our duffel bag. When it was time to board the buses, I sat with Keiko, and Mama sat behind us. The bus went down Grove Street and passed the small Japanese food store where Mama used to order her bean-curd cakes and pickled radish. The windows were all boarded up, but there was a sign still hanging on the door that read, "We are loyal Americans."

The crazy thing about the whole evacuation was that we were all loyal Americans. Most of us were citizens because we had been born here. But our parents, who had come from Japan, couldn't become citizens because there was a law that prevented any Asian from becoming a citizen. Now everybody with a Japanese face was being shipped off to concentration camps.

"It's stupid," Keiko muttered as we saw the racetrack looming up beside the highway. "If there were any Japanese spies around, they'd have gone back to Japan long ago."

"I'll say," I agreed. My sister was in high school and she ought to know, I thought.

When the bus turned into Tanforan, there were more armed guards at the gate, and I saw barbed wire strung around the entire grounds. I felt as though I were going into a prison, but I hadn't done anything wrong. **Ⓘ**

We streamed off the buses and poured into a huge room, where doctors looked down our throats and peeled back our eyelids to see if we had any diseases. Then we

---

Ⓖ Literary Focus Setting What feelings are evoked by this description of the setting? How do these feelings help you understand Ruri's experiences at this point in the plot?

Ⓗ Read and Discuss What is your impression of the events the author is describing here?

Ⓘ Read and Discuss How does the treatment of the Japanese Americans and the appearance of Tanforan cause Ruri to feel like a prisoner?

Vocabulary forsaken (fawr SAY kuhn) *adj.*: abandoned.

4. Uchida
august 20, 1942

Analyzing Visuals   **Connecting to the Text**   How does this scene of an internment camp compare with the picture in your mind of the camp where Ruri and her family lived?

were given our housing assignments. The man in charge gave Mama a slip of paper. We were in Barrack 16, Apartment 40.

"Mama!" I said. "We're going to live in an apartment!" The only apartment I had ever seen was the one my piano teacher lived in. It was in an enormous building in San Francisco, with an elevator and thick-carpeted hallways. I thought how wonderful it would be to have our own elevator. A house was all right, but an apartment seemed elegant and special.

We walked down the racetrack, looking for Barrack 16. Mr. Noma, a friend of Papa's, helped us carry our bags. I was so busy looking around I slipped and almost fell on the muddy track. Army barracks had been built everywhere, all around the racetrack and even in the center oval.

Mr. Noma pointed beyond the track toward the horse stables. "I think your barrack is out there."

He was right. We came to a long stable that had once housed the horses of Tanforan, and we climbed up the wide ramp. Each stall had a number painted on it, and when we got to 40, Mr. Noma pushed open the door.

"Well, here it is," he said, "Apartment 40."

The stall was narrow and empty and dark. There were two small windows on each side of the door. Three folded army cots were on the dust-covered floor, and one light bulb dangled from the ceiling. That was all. This was our apartment, and it still smelled of horses.

Mama looked at my sister and then at me. "It won't be so bad when we fix it up," she began. "I'll ask Mrs. Simpson to send me some material for curtains. I could make some cushions too, and . . . well . . ." She stopped. She couldn't think of anything more to say. **J**

Mr. Noma said he'd go get some mattresses for us. "I'd better hurry before they're all gone." He rushed off. I think he wanted to leave so that he wouldn't have to see Mama cry. But he needn't have run off, because Mama didn't cry. She just went out to borrow a broom and began sweeping out the dust and dirt. "Will you girls set up the cots?" she asked.

It was only after we'd put up the last cot that I noticed my bracelet was gone. "I've

> "Those are things we can carry in our hearts and take with us no matter where we are sent."

lost Laurie's bracelet!" I screamed. "My bracelet's gone!"

We looked all over the stall and even down the ramp. I wanted to run back down the track and go over every inch of ground we'd walked on, but it was getting dark and Mama wouldn't let me.

I thought of what I'd promised Laurie. I wasn't ever going to take the bracelet off, not even when I went to take a shower. And now I had lost it on my very first day in camp. I wanted to cry.

I kept looking for it all the time we were in Tanforan. I didn't stop looking until the day we were sent to another camp, called Topaz, in the middle of a desert in Utah. And then I gave up. **K**

But Mama told me never mind. She said I didn't need a bracelet to remember Laurie, just as I didn't need anything to remember Papa or our home in Berkeley or all the people and things we loved and had left behind.

"Those are things we can carry in our hearts and take with us no matter where we are sent," she said. **L**

And I guess she was right. I've never forgotten Laurie, even now. **M**

J Read and Discuss How do the family's living arrangements contrast with Ruri's idea of an apartment?

K Reading Focus Summarizing In two or three sentences, state what has happened since Ruri said goodbye to Laurie.

L Literary Focus Conflict Has Ruri's conflict been resolved? If so, how?

M Read and Discuss What does the conversation between Mama and Ruri teach Ruri?

Applying Your Skills

Reading Standard 3.3 Analyze the influence of setting on the problem and its resolution.

The Bracelet
Literary Response and Analysis

Reading Skills Focus
Quick Check

1. Why does Ruri's family have to leave home?
2. Why does Laurie give Ruri a bracelet?
3. What were the barracks used for before Ruri and her family went to live there?

Read with a Purpose

4. What lesson does Ruri learn?

Reading Skills: Summarizing

5. Review and revise the chart that you filled in as you read the story. Be sure to add notes on the resolution, or ending. Now, use that chart to help you write a paragraph that summarizes the plot of this story.

Literary Skills Focus
Literary Analysis

6. **Infer** How do you think being forced to live in Apartment 40 makes Ruri and her family feel?
7. **Extend** Discuss the different ways experiences like Ruri's might affect the people involved. How might they deal with life in the future, and how might they interact with people who are different from them?
8. **Literary Perspectives** What does the fact that the United States and Japan are at war tell you about Ruri's family being sent away? What does the story show you about how people react under extreme circumstances?

Literary Skills: Setting and Conflict

9. **Analyze** The plot centers on a major **conflict** that goes far beyond the characters in the story. Ruri's family is on one side of this conflict. Who or what is on the other side? Explain whether this conflict is resolved.
10. **Analyze** This story's plot can be reduced to this: Laurie gives Ruri a bracelet as a going-away present. Ruri loses it. How do the larger **setting** (the United States during World War II) and the two specific settings in the story (Ruri's home and the internment camp) affect the plot?

Literary Skills Review: Point of View

11. **Evaluate** In the **first-person point of view,** the narrator tells the story, using the personal pronoun *I*. Why do you think the writer tells this story from Ruri's first-person point of view? What can Ruri tell you that no other character can tell you? What does Ruri *not* know?

Writing Skills Focus
Think as a Reader/Writer

Use It in Your Writing Review your "T" chart. Then, write a brief description of a place, using contrasting details, such as *new/shabby*. Include a contrast between how you imagined the place to be and how it really appears.

 What Do You Think Now?

What truths do you think "The Bracelet" reveals about fairness and about a family enduring difficult and unexpected changes?

Applying Your Skills

The Bracelet

Vocabulary Development
Word Origins

Many of the words we use today can be traced to Latin or Old English, the language used in England from the 400s until around the 1100s.

Your Turn

From the Vocabulary words at right, choose the word that correctly completes each sentence below. Then, use each word in a sentence that shows you know its meaning.

> evacuated
> interned
> thrust
> forsaken

1. The Old English word *forsacan,* meaning "to oppose," is related to the word _____.

2. The Latin word *trudere,* meaning "to push," is related to the word _____.

3. The Latin word *internus,* meaning "inward," is related to the word _____.

4. The Latin verb *vacuare,* meaning "to make empty," is the basis of the word _____.

Language Coach

Words Borrowed from Other Languages In the past century a number of Japanese words entered the English language. Use a dictionary to find out what each of the Japanese words in the box means. Then, fill in the blanks in the sentences that follow. Use context clues to find the words that fit best. What other Japanese words can you think of that have entered the English language?

kimono	(kih MOH noh)
futon	(FOO tahn)
karaoke	(kahr ee OH kee)
sayonara	(sah yoh NAH rah)
origami	(awr uh GAH mee)

1. My cousin enjoyed sleeping on a _____ so much, she said, "_____" to her mattress.

2. I brought my friend a beautiful silk _____ for her birthday.

Academic Vocabulary

Talk About . . .
If you were Ruri, what would you do so that you could again <u>interact</u> in positive ways with non-Japanese Americans? How would you <u>achieve</u> peace of mind and get over resentment caused by how you and your family were treated?

Learn It Online
Uncover more about this story with these links:

go.hrw.com | H6-48 | **Go**

Grammar Link

Adjectives

An **adjective** is a word that is used to modify a noun or a pronoun. To **modify** a word means to describe the word or to make its meaning more definite. An adjective modifies a noun or pronoun by adding information about *what kind, which one, how many,* or *how much.*

What Kind ?	Which One or Ones?	How Many or How Much?
sad face	**other** stable	**all** Japanese
empty room	**those** barracks	**one** bracelet
tall messenger	**next** garden	**many** soldiers

Adjectives usually come before the words they modify. Sometimes, however, an adjective comes *after* the word it modifies.

> Laurie is sad. (The predicate adjective *sad* modifies *Laurie.*)
> Mama, upset and confused, stopped talking. (The adjectives *upset* and *confused* modify the noun *Mama.*)

Note: The words *a, an,* and *the* are a special kind of adjective called **articles.**

Your Turn

Identify the adjectives and words they modify in the sentences below. Do not include *a, an,* or *the.*

1. Ruri wiped salty tears from her face.
2. The old rag doll was gone.
3. We weren't moving to a nicer house.
4. She was my best friend.
5. A long line of buses waited for us.

CHOICES

As you respond to the Choices, use these **Academic Vocabulary** words as appropriate: achieve, create, interact, major.

REVIEW

Write a Blog Entry

TechFocus Imagine you are Ruri. Write a blog entry about your experiences in the camp so that your friends from school can know about your life there. Describe what happens to you after you leave Berkeley and what happened to the bracelet Laurie gave you. Be sure to describe the setting and its effects on you.

CONNECT

Write from Another Point of View

Ruri's mother tells her that we don't need things to remind us of people and places; we carry them in our hearts. Suppose that this story had been told from the point of view of Ruri's mother. Rewrite the scene between Ruri and Laurie near the beginning of the story, telling it from the perspective of Ruri's mother.

EXTEND

Write to Persuade Voters

Timed Writing Imagine that you are running for senator from your state shortly after World War II is over. Write a short persuasive speech that will convince voters that American citizens should never again be sent to internment camps if they have done nothing wrong. Be sure to explain your reasoning.

Learn It Online
There's more to this story than meets the eye. Expand your view at this site:

go.hrw.com | H6-49 | **Go**

Comparing and Contrasting Plot and Setting

CONTENTS

What Do You Think

How can we prove to others, as well as ourselves, what we can achieve?

🕐 **QuickTalk**

Think of movies or stories in which characters' abilities are tested. What challenges do we face when we try to show others and ourselves what we can do?

Preparing to Read

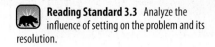
The Southpaw / Concha

Literary Skills Focus

Plot and Setting The **plot** of a story consists of a series of events. The **setting** is the time and place in which these events occur. Sometimes the setting plays an essential role in a story by influencing the **conflict,** or problem, and its **resolution,** or how the conflict is solved. Other times, the story could be set in almost any time or place—the setting doesn't shape the plot, or the writer hasn't described the setting at all. As you read, think about the way the setting does—or does not—influence the problem the main character faces in each story.

Reading Skills Focus

Summarizing When you **summarize** a story, you tell about its main events and details in your own words. Summarizing can help you identify the major elements of the plot and the setting's influence on it.

Into Action As you read, record the main elements of each story in a chart like the one below.

Title and Author: "The Southpaw" by Judith Viorst

Setting:

Main Characters:

Conflict or Problem:

Sequence of Main Events:
1.
2.
[etc.]

Resolution:

Writing Skills Focus
Think as a Reader/Writer

Find It in Your Reading What makes these stories realistic? As you read, record in your *Reader/Writer Notebook* details of the plot or setting that seem real to you.

 **Reader/Writer Notebook**

Use your **RWN** to complete the activities for these selections.

Language Coach
Homophones Which Vocabulary word above is a **homophone**—a word that sounds like another word but has a different meaning? How do you spell the word it sounds like?

Learn It Online
Organize your thoughts! Use one of the interactive graphic organizers at:

go.hrw.com   H6-51   **Go**

Courtesy of the author.

Judith Viorst
(1931–   )

Laughing at the Ups and Downs
When she was only seven years old, Judith Viorst decided that she wanted to be a writer. At first she wrote about "deadly serious things." Later, she found success in writing humorously about the ups and downs of everyday life. Viorst once explained her approach to successfully writing about young people this way: "Kids need to encounter kids like themselves—kids who can sometimes be crabby and fresh and rebellious, kids who talk back and disobey, tell fibs and get into trouble, and are nonetheless still likable and redeemable."

Mary Helen Ponce
(1938–   )

From a Latina Perspective
Like the characters in "Concha," Mary Helen Ponce grew up in Pacoima, California, in a Mexican American community. Many of her stories are based on her own life. "I chose to write of a loving family that, throughout the journey, is sustained by bonds of mutual love and respect," she says. Today, Ponce often speaks and writes of the problems of women, especially of Latina women whose contributions to the American Southwest have been forgotten by history.

Think About the Writers
Both writers create stories that resemble real life. What can we gain from reading realistic fiction?

Preview the Selections
"The Southpaw" takes an unusual form. It's told completely through notes written back and forth between two friends—**Janet** and **Richard.**

In "Concha," the narrator is a character in the story. So is her brother **Joey** and several friends: **Mundo,** a boy; **Beto,** another boy; **Virgie,** a girl; and, of course, **Concha,** the girl whose name is the title of the story.

THE SOUTHPAW

by **Judith Viorst**

Read with a Purpose
As you read, note how this writer brings two characters and a situation to life just by reproducing notes that are passed back and forth.

Build Background
This story was written before the days of computer and wireless technology, so the characters communicate through handwritten notes on whatever scraps of paper are handy. The focus of their notes is a baseball team that Richard plays for and manages. When the story was written, it was almost unthinkable for a girl to play on a boy's team.

Dear Richard,
Don't invite me to your birthday party because I'm not coming. And give back the Disneyland sweatshirt I said you could wear. If I'm not good enough to play on your team, I'm not good enough to be friends with.
Your former friend,
Janet
P.S. I hope when you go to the dentist he finds 20 cavities.

Dear Janet,
Here is your stupid Disneyland sweatshirt, if that's how you're going to be. I want my comic books now—finished or not. No girl has ever played on the Mapes Street baseball team, and as long as I'm captain, no girl ever will.
Your former friend,
Richard
P.S. I hope when you go for your checkup you need a tetanus shot.

1. **The Southpaw:** The title is a sports slang term for a left-handed person, especially a left-handed pitcher in baseball.

A [Read and Discuss] What situation has the author set up in these two notes?

Dear Richard,
I'm changing my goldfish's name from Richard to Stanley. Don't count on my vote for class president next year. Just because I'm a member of the ballet club doesn't mean I'm not a terrific ballplayer.
Your former friend,
Janet
P.S. I see you lost your first game 28-0.

Dear Janet,
I'm not saving anymore seats for you on the bus. For all I care you can stand the whole way to school. Why don't you just forget about baseball and learn something nice like knitting?
Your former friend,
Richard
P.S. Wait until Wednesday.

Dear Richard,
My father said I could call someone to go with us for a ride and hot-fudge sundaes. In case you didn't notice, I didn't call you.
Your former friend,
Janet
P.S. I see you lost your second game, 34-0.

Dear Janet,
Remember when I took the laces out of my blue-and-white sneakers and gave them to you? I want them back.
Your former friend,
Richard
P.S. Wait until Friday.

Dear Richard,
Congratulations on your unbroken record. Eight straight losses, wow: I understand you're the laughing stock of New Jersey.
Your former friend,
Janet
P.S. Why don't you and your team forget about baseball and learn something nice like knitting maybe? **B**

B **Literary Focus** Setting What clue about where the story takes place does Janet provide in this note?

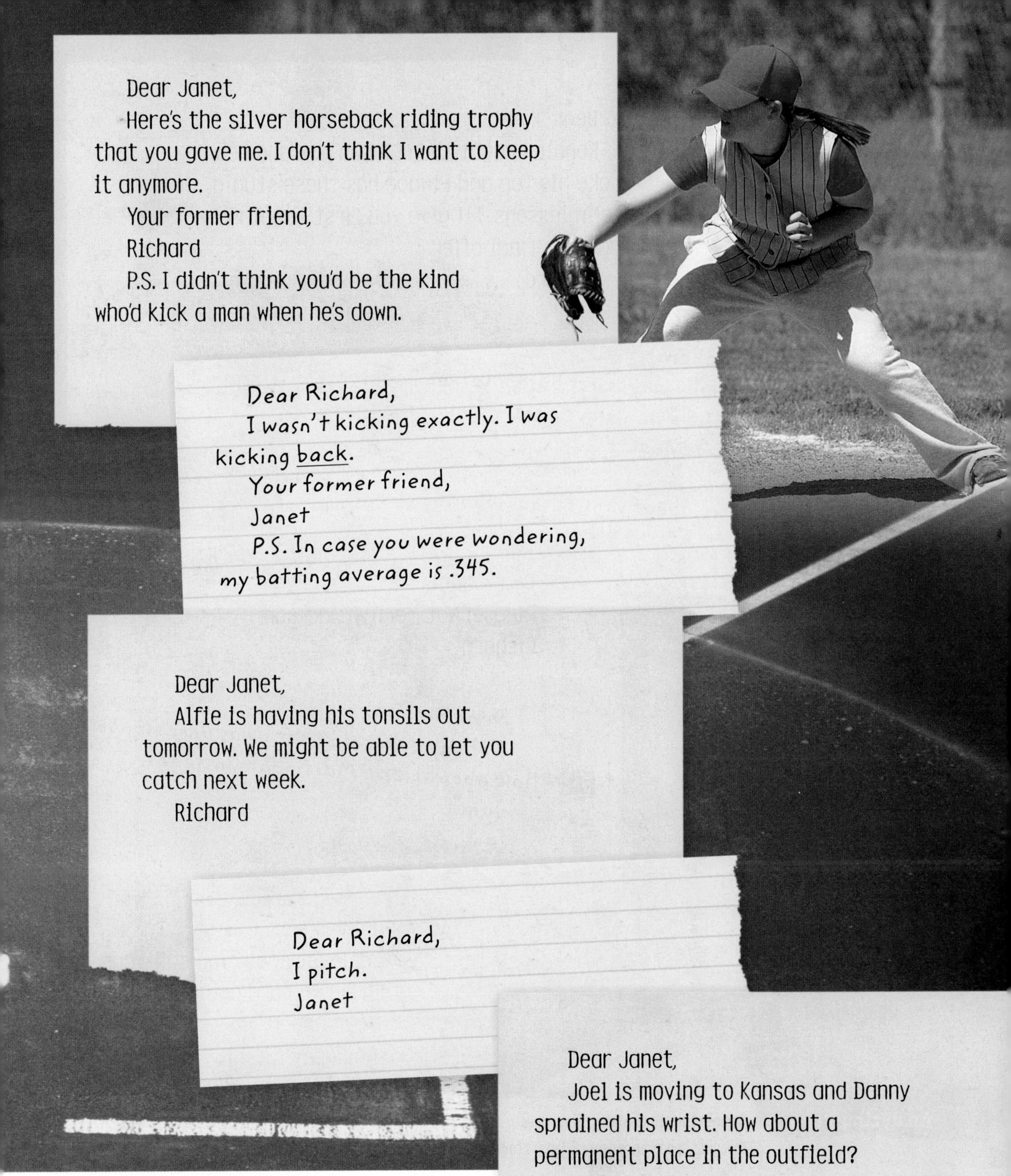

Dear Janet,
Here's the silver horseback riding trophy that you gave me. I don't think I want to keep it anymore.
Your former friend,
Richard
P.S. I didn't think you'd be the kind who'd kick a man when he's down.

Dear Richard,
I wasn't kicking exactly. I was kicking <u>back</u>.
Your former friend,
Janet
P.S. In case you were wondering, my batting average is .345.

Dear Janet,
Alfie is having his tonsils out tomorrow. We might be able to let you catch next week.
Richard

Dear Richard,
I pitch.
Janet

Dear Janet,
Joel is moving to Kansas and Danny sprained his wrist. How about a permanent place in the outfield?
Richard

C

C **Reading Focus** Summarizing In your own words, explain what has happened in the last three notes.

Dear Richard,
I pitch.
Janet   **D**

Dear Janet,
Ronnie caught the chicken pox and Leo broke his toe and Elwood has these stupid violin lessons. I'll give you first base, and that's my final offer.
Richard

Dear Richard,
Susan Reilly plays first base, Marilyn Jackson catches, Ethel Kahn plays center field, I pitch. It's a package deal.
Janet
P.S. Sorry about your 12-game losing streak.

Dear Janet,
Please! Not Marilyn Jackson.
Richard

Dear Richard,
Nobody ever said that I was unreasonable. How about Lizzie Martindale instead?
Janet

Dear Janet,
At least could you call your goldfish Richard again?
Your friend,
Richard   **E**

Analyzing Visuals   **Connecting to the Text** How does this girl's appearance express Janet's conflict?

D **Read and Discuss** What's Janet doing by sending the same note again?

E **Literary Focus** Plot How is the conflict resolved finally? What has each side given up?

Applying Your Skills

Reading Standard 3.3 Analyze the influence of setting on the problem and its resolution.

The Southpaw
Literary Response and Analysis

Reading Skills Focus
Quick Check

1. Why does Janet demand that Richard give back her Disneyland sweatshirt?
2. Why does Richard offer to let Janet catch?
3. Why does Janet refuse Richard's offer to catch, play in the outfield, and play first base?

Read with a Purpose

4. How does the author show what each character's personality is like? What do you learn about Janet and Richard's relationship from their notes? To answer, think about what their writing notes back and forth tells you about their true feelings for each other.

Reading Skills: Summarizing

5. Use the information in the chart you filled in as you read to write a paragraph **summarizing** the story. Then, compare your summary to that of a partner. Did you include the same information in your summaries? Why or why not?

6. **Compare and Contrast** What's similar about the way Richard and Janet write to each other? Of the two, who do you think is better at reaching a way to work out their problem? Why?

Literary Skills Focus
Literary Analysis

7. **Extend** Try reversing the situation in this story. What judgments would the girls make about the boys? How do those judgments, or prejudices, cause conflicts?

8. **Evaluate** If this story had been written in a typical short story format, would it have been more or less effective? Explain. In what ways would a more typical version be different from the form of this story?

Literary Skills: Setting and Plot

9. **Analyze** Explain the **conflict,** or problem, in the story. How does this story demonstrate that being stubborn and close-minded can get in the way of a good friendship?

10. **Infer** Although the author provides very little information about the story's **setting,** what clues do the notes contain about where the events take place, what the characters do, and how they live?

11. **Analyze** Could this story be set in any time or place? Explain. How might a different **setting** influence the problem and its resolution?

Writing Skills Focus
Think as a Reader/Writer

Use It in Your Writing Write the next two notes that Janet and Richard might send to each other. Be sure to include realistic events and details that bring the situation to life.

Concha

by **Mary Helen Ponce**

Read with a Purpose
Read this story to decide if you agree that Concha holds "first place for bravery."

Preparing to Read for this selection is on page 51.

Build Background
This writer is known for mixing Spanish and English in her stories, so you'll find many Spanish words in italic type here. If you read closely, you'll also find that most of the Spanish words are explained in context. For example, in the first sentence the narrator says that as children she and her brother Joey "were left alone to find ways *para divertirnos*." If you do not know what this Spanish phrase means, you can find the meaning in the next part of the sentence: "to keep ourselves busy."

While growing up in the small barrio of Pacoima, my younger brother Joey and I were left alone to find ways *para divertirnos*, to keep ourselves busy—and out of our mother's way. One way in which we whiled away long summer days was by making pea shooters. These were made from a hollow reed which we first cleaned with a piece of wire. We then collected berries from *los pirules,* the pepper trees that lined our driveway. Once we amassed enough dry berries we put them in our mouths and spat them out at each other through the pea shooter. **Ⓐ**

The berries had a terrible taste—they were even said to be poison! I was most careful not to swallow them. We selected only the hard, firm peas. The soft ones, we knew, would get mushy, crumble in our mouths and force us to gag—and lose a fight. During an important battle a short pause could spell defeat. Oftentimes while playing with Joey I watched closely. When he appeared to gag I dashed back to the pepper tree to load up on ammunition. I pelted him without mercy until he begged me to stop. **Ⓑ**

"No more. Ya no," Joey cried as he bent over to spit berries. "No more!"

"Ha, ha I got you now." I spat berries at Joey until, exhausted, we called a truce and slumped onto a wooden bench.

In fall our game came to a halt—the trees dried up; the berries fell to the ground. This was a sign for us to begin other games.

Ⓐ **Literary Focus** Setting What have you learned so far about the story's setting?

Ⓑ **Literary Focus** Plot What conflict have the children created for themselves? Why is it important not to lose a battle?

Our games were seasonal. During early spring we made whistles from the long blades of grass that grew in the open field behind our house. In winter we made dams, forts, and canals from the soft mud that was our street. We tied burnt matchsticks together with string. These were our men. We positioned them along the forts (camouflaged with small branches). We also played kick the can, but our most challenging game was playing with red ants.

The ants were of the common variety: red, round and treacherous. They invaded our yard and the *llano* every summer. We always knew where ants could be found, *donde habia hormigas*. We liked to build mud and grass forts smack in the middle of ant territory. The ants were the enemy, the matchstickmen the heroes, or good guys.

Playing with ants was a real challenge! While placing our men in battle positions we timed it so as not to get bitten. We delighted in beating the ants at their own game. **C**

Sometimes we got really brave and picked up ants with a stick, then twirled the stick around until the ants got dizzy-drunk (or so we thought)—and fell to the ground. We made ridges of dirt and pushed the ants inside, covered them with dirt and made bets as to how long it would take them to dig their way out.

Concha, my best friend and neighbor, was quite timid at school. She avoided all rough games such as kickball and Red Rover. When it came to playing with ants, however, Concha held first place for bravery. She could stand with her feet atop an anthill for the longest time! We stood trembling as ants

C **Reading Focus** Summarizing In two sentences, tell what you have learned about the children's games.

Vocabulary **treacherous** (TREHCH uhr uhs) *adj.*: dangerous.
timid (TIHM ihd) *adj.*: shy; lacking self-confidence.

Analyzing Visuals **Connecting to the Text**
What sort of game are these two boys playing? In what ways might it be similar to events in this story?

crawled up our shoes, then quickly stomped our feet to scare them off. But Concha never lost her nerve. **D**

One time we decided to have an ant contest. The prize was a candy bar—a Sugar Daddy sucker. We first found an anthill, lined up, then took turns standing beside the anthill while the juicy red ants climbed over our shoes. We dared not move—but when the first ant moved towards our ankles we stomped away, our Oxfords making swirls of dust that allowed us to retreat to the sidelines. But not Concha. She remained in place as big red ants crept up her shoes. One, five, ten! We stood and counted, holding our breath as the ants continued to climb. Fifteen, twenty! Twenty ants were crawling over Concha! **E**

"*Ujule*, she sure ain't scared," cried Mundo in a hushed voice. "*No le tiene miedo a las hormigas.*"

"Uhhhhh," answered Beto, his eyes wide.

". . . I mean for a girl," added Mundo as he poked Beto in the ribs. We knew Beto liked Concha—and always came to her rescue.

We stood and counted ants. We were so caught up in this feat that we failed to notice the twenty-first ant that climbed up the back

> We stood and counted, holding our breath as the ants continued to climb. Fifteen, twenty! Twenty ants were crawling over Concha!

of Concha's sock . . . and bit her!

"Ay, ay, ay," screeched Concha.

"Gosh, she's gonna die," cried an alarmed Virgie as she helped stomp out ants. "She's gonna die!"

"She's too stupid to die," laughed Mundo, busy brushing ants off his feet. "She's too stupid."

"But sometimes people die when ants bite them," insisted Virgie, her face pale. "They gets real sick."

"The ants will probably die," Mundo snickered, holding his stomach and laughing loudly. "Ah, ha, ha."

"Gosh you're mean," said a shocked Virgie, hands on hips. "You are so mean."

"Yeah, but I ain't stupid."

"Come on you guys, let's get her to the *mangera*," Beto cried as he reached out to Concha who by now had decided she would live. "Come on, let's take her to the faucet." **F**

We held Concha by the waist as she hobbled to the water faucet. Her cries were now mere whimpers as no grownup had come out to investigate. From experience

---

D **Read and Discuss** What's Concha able to do?

E **Literary Focus** **Plot** What problem does Concha face in this contest?

F **Literary Focus** **Plot** What conflicts do you identify among the various characters? Who is on Concha's side, and who is against her?

Vocabulary **feat** (feet) *n.*: accomplishment; daring act.
investigate (ihn VEHS tuh gayt) *v.*: look into; examine.

we knew that if a first cry did not bring someone to our aid we should stop crying—or go home.

We helped Concha to the faucet, turned it on and began to mix water with dirt. We knew the best remedy for insect bites was *lodo*. We applied mud to all bug stings to stop the swelling. Mud was especially good for wasp stings, the yellowjackets we so feared—and from which we ran away at top speed. Whenever bees came close we stood still until they flew away, but there were no set rules on how to get rid of *avispas*. We hit out at them, and tried to scare them off but the yellowjackets were fierce! In desperation we flung dirt at them, screamed and ran home. **G**

Not long after the ant incident Concha decided she was not about to run when a huge wasp broke up our game of jacks. She stood still, so still the wasp remained on her dark head for what seemed like hours. We stood and watched, thinking perhaps the wasp had mistaken Concha's curly hair for a bush! We watched—and waited.

"*Ujule*, she sure is brave," exclaimed Virgie as she sucked on a Popsicle. "She sure is brave."

"She's stupid," grunted Mundo, trying to be indifferent. "She's just a big show-off who thinks she's so big."

"So are you," began Virgie, backing off. "So are you."

"Yeah? Ya wanna make something outta it?"

"Let's go," interrupted Beto in his soft voice.

"*Ya vamonos.*" He smiled at Concha—who smiled back. **H**

In time the wasp flew away. Concha immediately began to brag about how a "real big wasp" sat on her hair for hours. She never mentioned the ant contest—nor the twenty-first ant that led her to *el lodo*.

G **Reading Focus** Summarizing What happens to Concha after the ant contest?

H **Literary Focus** Plot What conflict does Beto resolve? How does he do this?

Vocabulary **remedy** (REHM uh dee) *n.*: cure; solution.

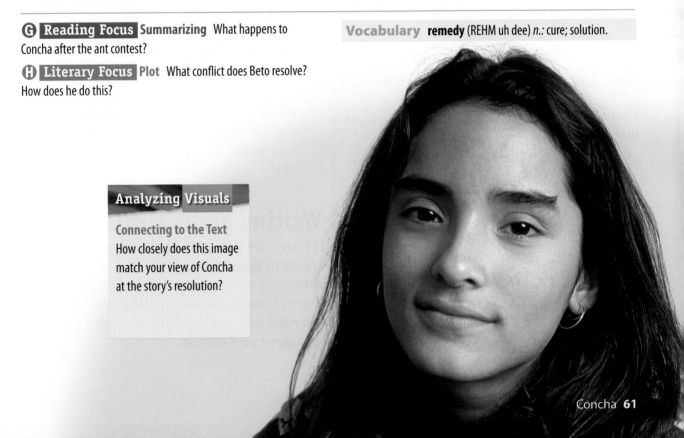

Analyzing Visuals

Connecting to the Text
How closely does this image match your view of Concha at the story's resolution?

Applying Your Skills

Concha

Literary Response and Analysis

Reading Skills Focus
Quick Check

1. Why does playing with the ants pose a "challenge" for the children?

2. How does Beto feel about Concha?

3. Why does Concha never mention the ant contest?

Read with a Purpose

4. Do you agree with the narrator that Concha is brave? Why or why not?

Reading Skills: Summarizing

5. Use the information in the chart you filled in as you read to write a paragraph **summarizing** the story. Then, discuss your summary with a partner. Have you included all the story's <u>major</u> events and details in your summary? Is there any information you should take out?

✓ Vocabulary Check

Match the Vocabulary words in the first column with their definitions in the second column.

6. **remedy**   a. shy
7. **investigate** b. cure
8. **treacherous** c. accomplishment
9. **timid**   d. look into
10. **feat**   e. dangerous

Literary Skills Focus
Literary Analysis

11. **Interpret** What do you think is Concha's reason for standing on the anthill and later letting the wasp sit in her hair?

12. **Extend** What seems to be Mundo's view of girls? How do you think this view accounts for the things he says in the story? Explain whether you think Mundo's attitude toward girls is common today.

Literary Skills: Plot and Setting

13. **Evaluate** Explain Concha's <u>major</u> **conflict,** or problem, in the story and the conflict's **resolution.** In your opinion, is the conflict interesting? Is the resolution satisfying? Why or why not?

14. **Identify** Describe the story's **setting.** What details does the author provide that help you visualize, or picture in your mind, the place where the events occur?

15. **Analyze** What is the setting's <u>influence</u> on the problem Concha faces and its resolution? How would the story be different if the setting were changed? For example, how might a girl prove she is brave if she lives in a big city?

Writing Skills Focus
Think as a Reader/Writer

Use It in Your Writing Write a brief paragraph explaining whether you think the events and setting in "Concha" are realistic. Use examples from the notes you took in your *Reader/Writer Notebook* to support your opinion.

Reading Standard 3.3 Analyze the influence of setting on the problem and its resolution.

The Southpaw / Concha

Writing Skills Focus
Write a Comparison-Contrast Essay

Write an essay comparing and contrasting the plot and setting in "The Southpaw" and "Concha." You can organize your essay in one of two ways:

1. Write two paragraphs, one for each selection. In your first paragraph, write about "The Southpaw," analyzing the conflict, the resolution, and the <u>influence</u> of the setting on the plot. In your second paragraph, present the same information for "Concha." Then, wrap up your essay with a final paragraph in which you analyze the main ways the selections are alike and different and explain what you learned from reading them.

2. Write three paragraphs—one on the conflict in both selections, one on the resolution in both selections, and one on the <u>influence</u> of the setting on the plot in both selections. Conclude your essay with a paragraph that sums up how the two selections are alike and different and what you learned from them.

Use the workshop on writing a comparison-contrast essay, pages 450–458, for help with this assignment.

What Do **You Think Now** What truths do the characters in these stories discover about themselves and their friends?

CHOICES

As you respond to the Choices, use these **Academic Vocabulary** words as appropriate: <u>achieve</u>, <u>influence</u>, <u>interact</u>, and <u>major</u>.

REVIEW
Write an Essay

Timed ⌐Writing Think of a movie or another story (not one in this chapter) in which the setting plays a <u>major</u> role. Write an essay in which you analyze the <u>influence</u> of the setting on the problem and its resolution. You might want to conclude by explaining how the story would change if the setting were different.

CONNECT
Write a Story in Letters

TechFocus Work with a partner to create a "collaborative story" (a story written with another person) in the form of e-mail or text messages sent back and forth between two characters. Show through the messages that your characters are having a conflict over something. Be sure you resolve the conflict by the end of your story.

EXTEND
Draw a Comic Strip

Create a comic strip of at least three panels showing an interaction between a male and a female character in one of these stories. Your comic strip should have a concept, or idea, behind it, such as "Boys and girls don't always speak the same language."

Notes, Outlines, and Summaries

CONTENTS

What Do
You
Think

Facing the truth can mean admitting mistakes. How can coming to terms with mistakes help you overcome them?

QuickWrite

Think of a time when you faced unfair treatment. Briefly describe the situation and what you found unfair about it. Were you offered an apology? If so, did it help? Explain how you dealt with your feelings of injustice.

Reading Standard 2.4 Clarify an understanding of texts by creating outlines, **logical notes,** summaries, or reports.

Wartime Mistakes, Peacetime Apologies

Informational Text Focus

Taking Notes "The Bracelet" (page 41) is fiction, but it is based on real historical events. Some of those events are explained in the following article. You'll learn the facts about Executive Order 9066 and its effects on one real-life Japanese American woman. As you read the article, you'll take **notes** to help you clarify your understanding of the text.

Into Action To take logical, detailed notes, get some notecards and follow these steps:

1. Read through the selection once to find the main ideas, or most important points.
2. Make one card for each main idea.
3. Re-read the selection, and take notes about each main idea. List essential details about them in your own words, or use quotation marks around the author's words. Your notecards will look like this:

> Main Idea
> • supporting detail
> • supporting detail
> • supporting detail
> • supporting detail

The supporting details you choose to include should answer key questions about the main idea, such as *who? what? when? where? why?* and *how?*

Writing Skills Focus

Preparing for Timed Writing As you read "Wartime Mistakes, Peacetime Apologies," look at the model cards that appear with the selection and write down the missing word or words in your *Reader/Writer Notebook*. Work with one idea at a time.

Reader/Writer Notebook

Use your **RWN** to complete the activities for this selection.

Vocabulary

prescribe (prih SKRYB) *v.:* define officially. *Governments often prescribe new laws during wartime.*

discretion (dihs KREHSH uhn) *n.:* authority to make decisions. *Executive orders are within the president's discretion.*

compensation (kahm puhn SAY shuhn) *n.:* payment given to make up for a loss or injury. *Internees received financial compensation in 1990.*

rectify (REHK tuh fy) *v.:* correct. *It may be difficult to rectify the mistakes of the past.*

Language Coach

Word Parts A **suffix** is a word part attached to the end of a word or root. Knowing suffixes may help you determine a word's part of speech. For instance, the suffix *–fy* means "make or form into." It turns a word into an action word—a verb. Even if you didn't know the exact meaning of *rectify*, the suffix would tell you that the word is probably a verb. What two vocabulary words above share the same suffix?

Learn It Online

Practice taking notes with the interactive Reading Workshop on:

| go.hrw.com | H6-65 | Go |

WARTIME MISTAKES,
Peacetime Apologies

by Nancy Day, from *Cobblestone Magazine*

Read with a Purpose
Read the following article to discover what happened to many Japanese Americans during and after World War II—and who was responsible.

O n March 13, 1942, Yoshiko Imamoto opened her door to face three FBI agents. They let her pack a nightgown and a Bible, then took her to jail while they "checked into a few things." Imamoto had lived in America for twenty-four years. She was a teacher and had done nothing wrong. But a month earlier, President Franklin D. Roosevelt had issued Executive Order 9066, which drastically changed the lives of Imamoto and more than 120,000 other people of Japanese ancestry living in the United States. **Ⓐ**

When Japan bombed Pearl Harbor on December 7, 1941, Japanese Americans were caught in the middle. They felt like Americans but looked like the enemy. Neighbors and co-workers eyed them suspiciously. Then Executive Order 9066, issued on February 19, 1942, authorized the exclusion of "any or all persons" from any areas the military chose. The word "Japanese" was never used, but the order was designed to allow the military to force Japanese Americans living near the coast to leave their homes for the duration of the war. Some were allowed to move inland, but most, like Yoshiko Imamoto, were herded into prisonlike camps. **Ⓑ**

Ⓐ Informational Focus Taking Notes Which model notecard relates to the main idea of the first paragraph?

Ⓑ Informational Focus Taking Notes Remember to answer key questions—such as *when?*—about the main ideas. What dates are given in this paragraph?

Yoshiko Imamoto
- On _____ (when?), the FBI arrested her with no warning.
- 24-year U.S. resident
- teacher
- had broken no laws

Pearl Harbor
- 12/7/1941
- Japan attacked U.S.
- Japanese Americans felt _____ (how?).
- They were treated _____ (how? by whom?).

Executive Order 9066
- issued by President Franklin D. Roosevelt
- affected _____ (how many?) people
- issued _____ (when?)
- allowed _____ (what?)
- never used _____ (what word?)
- Only _____ (who?) were moved.
- Most were moved _____ (where?).

Analyzing Visuals

Connecting to the Text
If you were taking notes about this image, what would you write down about the expression on this toddler's face? How does the expression reflect the emotions people must have felt when forced to go to internment camps?

I hereby authorize and direct the Secretary of War, and the Military Commanders whom he may from time to time designate, whenever he or any designated Commander deems such action necessary or desirable, to prescribe military areas in such places and of such extent as he or the appropriate Military Commander may determine, from which any or all persons may be excluded, and with respect to which, the right of any person to enter, remain in, or leave shall be subject to whatever restrictions the Secretary of War or the appropriate Military Commander may impose in his discretion.

—**President Franklin D. Roosevelt,** excerpt from Executive Order 9066, 1942

Vocabulary **prescribe** (prih SKRYB) *v.:* define officially. **discretion** (dihs KREHSH uhn) *n.:* authority to make decisions.

After the war, Japanese Americans tried to start over. They had lost their jobs, their property, and their pride. Some used the Japanese American Evacuation Claims Act of 1948 to get compensation for property they had lost. But it was not until the late 1960s that cries for redress—compensation for all they had suffered—began to emerge.

In 1976, Executive Order 9066 was officially ended by President Gerald Ford. Four years later, President Jimmy Carter signed a bill that created the Commission on Wartime Relocation and Internment of Civilians (CWRIC) to investigate the relocation of Japanese Americans. The CWRIC concluded that Executive Order 9066 was "not justified by military necessity" but was the result of "race prejudice, war hysteria, and a failure of political leadership." In 1983, the commission recommended to Congress that each surviving Japanese American evacuee be given a payment of twenty thousand dollars and an apology. **C**

A bill to authorize the payments was introduced in the House of Representatives in 1983 but met resistance. Intensive lobbying[1] by Japanese Americans was met by arguments that the government had acted legally and appropriately at the time.

---

1. **lobbying** (LAHB ee ihng): activity aimed at influencing public officials.

C | Read and Discuss | What did the commission recognize about Executive Order 9066?

Vocabulary **compensation** (kahm puhn SAY shuhn) *n.*: payment given to make up for a loss or injury.

After the War
- Japanese Americans had lost _____ (what?).
- _____ (what?) was used by some Japanese Americans to claim payment for lost property.
- _____ (what?) began in the late 1960s.

9066 Ended—Investigation Begun
- _____ (who?) ended 9066 in _____ (when?).
- _____ (who?) authorized CWRIC _____ (to do what?).
- CWRIC recommended _____ (what?).

Repayment
- Bill introduced in House of Representatives in 1983.
- supported by Japanese Americans
- Opponents argued that _____ (what?).

Analyzing Visuals

Connecting to the Text
If you were taking notes about this image, how would you describe what the people pictured here with President Reagan felt about the passing of the Civil Liberties Act? How do you know?

A monetary sum and words alone cannot restore lost years or erase painful memories; neither can they fully convey our Nation's resolve to rectify injustice and to uphold the rights of individuals. We can never fully right the wrongs of the past. But we can take a clear stand for justice and recognize that serious injustices were done to Japanese Americans during World War II.

—President George H. W. Bush,
excerpt from letter accompanying redress checks, 1990

Vocabulary **rectify** (REHK tuh fy) *v.:* correct.

Meanwhile, three men who had long since served their jail sentences for refusing to comply with curfew[2] or relocation orders filed suit[3] to challenge the government's actions. The court ruled that the government had had no legal basis for detaining Japanese Americans.

The rulings increased pressure to provide redress. In 1988, Congress approved the final version of the redress bill, which became known as the Civil Liberties Act. It was signed by President Ronald Reagan on August 10, 1988. Two years later, Congress funded the payments. **D**

In 1990, at the age of ninety-three, Yoshiko Imamoto opened her door not to FBI agents, but to a small brown envelope containing a check for twenty thousand dollars and an apology from President George Bush. It had taken almost fifty years and the actions of four presidents, but the government had made redress and apologized for its mistakes. **E**

---

2. **curfew** (KUR fyoo): Shortly before the relocation began, the head of the Western Defense Command, Lt. Gen. John DeWitt, set a curfew. Between 8:00 P.M. and 6:00 A.M. each day, "all persons of Japanese ancestry" had to remain indoors and off the streets.

3. **filed suit:** went to court in an attempt to recover something.

Read with a Purpose
How did the U.S. government recognize the injustices that Japanese Americans endured during World War II?

D Informational Focus Taking Notes Why should you add information to the Repayment card?

E Read and Discuss How does the information in this paragraph connect to the beginning of the selection? How does Yoshiko's story come full circle?

Court Ruling
- _____ (who?) took the government to court.
- The court decided _____ (what?).
- This ruling helped build support for _____ (what?).

Add to Repayment card:
- Congress approved repayment bill in 1988.
- called Civil Liberties Act
- signed by _____ (whom?) _____ (when?)
- Payments were sent _____ (when?).

Add to Yoshiko Imamoto card:
- in 1990, received _____ (what?)
- She was 93 years old.
- It had taken _____ (how long?).
- It had taken the work of four presidents.

Applying Your Skills

Reading Standard 2.4 Clarify an understanding of texts by creating outlines, **logical notes,** summaries, or reports.

Wartime Mistakes, Peacetime Apologies

Standards Review

Informational Text and Vocabulary

1. From your **note taking,** you can conclude that Yoshiko Imamoto came to the United States when she was
   A a young woman.
   B a mother with a young child.
   C a baby.
   D a child.

2. Which sentence *best* **summarizes,** or captures the main ideas of, Executive Order 9066?
   A Military commanders must follow instructions given by the secretary of war.
   B When an area is put under military control, all civilians in that area must be evacuated.
   C The military may set aside areas and decide who enters, stays in, or leaves those areas.
   D Japanese Americans must leave California.

3. Discussion of a redress bill caused conflict between
   A Japanese Americans and people who felt that the government had acted legally.
   B Japanese American members of Congress and other elected officials.
   C people who had been evacuated and those who were veterans of World War II.
   D Congress and the Supreme Court.

4. Which of the following answers is something or someone that you can *prescribe?*
   A Japanese Americans
   B a new rule
   C 1990
   D the police

5. When people are granted *discretion,* they have
   A the power to imprison someone.
   B the authority to make decisions.
   C the freedom to leave a country.
   D the right to a fair trial.

6. *Compensation* is usually
   A illegal.
   B misunderstood.
   C financial.
   D unwanted.

7. Which of the following words is *most* similar in meaning to *rectify?*
   A destroy
   B examine
   C finish
   D fix

Writing Skills Focus

Timed └Writing Use your **notes** to answer the following questions: What was the Commission on Wartime Relocation and Internment of Civilians? What did its investigation achieve?

What Do You Think Now

What kinds of reactions might the survivors of internment have had to the government's apology and repayment?

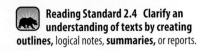
What a Character: Iwao Takamoto and His Toons

Informational Text Focus

Outlining An **outline** is a good way to organize and better understand your notes about factual writing. Remember that when you take notes, you determine and record the **main ideas** and the **details** that support them. Once you've taken your notes, you can organize the main ideas in an outline like this one for the beginning of "What a Character":

> I. Takamoto's Internment (First Main Idea)
> A. Takamoto and his family sent to Manzanar Internment Camp (Detail supporting point I)
>   1. After the bombing of Pearl Harbor, Japanese Americans were sent to internment camps (Detail supporting point A)

Summarizing A **summary** is a brief restatement of the main ideas in a text. Creating summaries of informational materials will help you grasp the meaning of a text. Summaries are especially useful if you are doing research from a number of sources because they will help you recognize ways in which one source differs from another. Follow these tips when you are summarizing:
- A summary is much shorter than the original text and includes only the most important points. In nonfiction, these are the **main ideas** and **key supporting details.**
- Stop at the end of each paragraph to restate in a sentence what the author wrote. This will help you find main ideas and details.
- If you have already completed an outline, look at the first two levels of information (I, II, . . . and A, B, . . .). These are the main ideas and important details you'll probably want to include in your summary.

Writing Skills Focus
Preparing for Timed ⌐Writing Writers of informational materials use headings that suggest main ideas and organize their writing. As you read "What a Character," pay attention to how it is organized.

Reader/Writer
Notebook
Use your **RWN** to complete the activities for this selection.

Vocabulary

apprentice (uh PREHN tihs) *n.*: beginner; someone who is just starting to learn a craft or job. *Takamoto was an apprentice to Disney's animators.*

instrumental (ihn struh MEHN tuhl) *adj.*: helping to make something happen. *Takamoto was instrumental in Hanna-Barbera's success.*

legacy (LEHG uh see) *n.*: something handed down or left for others. *Takamoto's legacy for cartoon fans includes many memorable characters.*

Language Coach
Puns A pun (or play on words) often suggests multiple meanings of a word. For example, the title of this article contains a pun. "What a Character" refers both to the subject of the article, Iwao Takamoto (a character is a memorable, unique, or funny person), and to his cartoon characters.

Identify and explain the pun in the following quotation about Takamoto: "His admirers are still drawing lessons from his spirited ways."

Learn It Online
Do pictures and animation help you learn? Try the *PowerNotes* lesson on:
go.hrw.com | H6-73 | Go

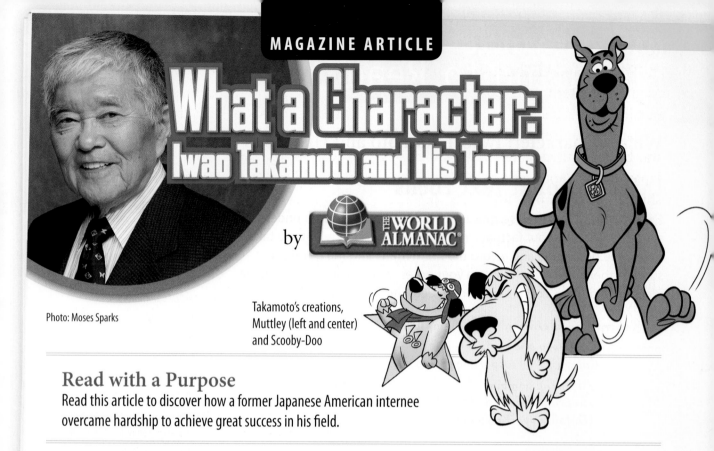

What a Character: Iwao Takamoto and His Toons

by THE WORLD ALMANAC

Photo: Moses Sparks

Takamoto's creations,
Muttley (left and center)
and Scooby-Doo

Read with a Purpose
Read this article to discover how a former Japanese American internee overcame hardship to achieve great success in his field.

Animated cartoons—or toons, as many call them today—aren't just for children any more. Books, magazines, and Web sites are devoted to cartoon trivia, and famous cartoon characters are everywhere in popular culture: on T-shirts, lunch boxes, toys, bedsheets, pajamas, fast foods, and practically any other kind of product you can name. Most of us know certain cartoon characters, but what do we know about the real people behind the toons—the writers, producers, directors, and, perhaps most importantly, the artists who bring these beloved characters to life? Here's the story of one of those artists, a name from the cartoon world everyone should know: Iwao Takamoto, the animator.

A Journey Begins in Manzanar

You'd never think that a Japanese internment camp near Los Angeles in the early 1940s and a cartoon canine by the name of Scooby-Doo could possibly have any connection to each other, but they do. The connection is animator Iwao Takamoto. His name may not be a household word, but many of his creations are. Takamoto's journey from an internment camp to the world of animation makes for a unique story of creative success. **Ⓐ**

Takamoto, a Japanese American, was born in Los Angeles in 1925. By age 15, he had graduated ahead of his high school class. His promising future was put on hold when the Japanese bombed Pearl Harbor

Ⓐ **Read and Discuss** What is the author's purpose here?

in 1941. He and his family were forced into Manzanar Internment Camp, in the desert outside Los Angeles.

Japan had been declared an enemy of war by the United States. Thousands of Japanese and Japanese Americans were shuttled into camps, supposedly for their and the country's protection. But out of bad situations, good sometimes comes, and this was true for Takamoto. While in Manzanar, the teenage Takamoto met some former Hollywood art directors who were interned with him. The men saw his sketches of scenes in the camp and encouraged him to draw. They gave him valuable informal training in illustration.

An Animated Life Ⓑ

In order to escape the camp, Takamoto agreed to become a laborer, picking fruit in Idaho. But it was his drawing talent that freed him in the end. Just two months before the end of World War II, Takamoto contacted Disney Studios and landed an interview. He was not even fully aware of what Disney was or how large it was. Asked to bring his portfolio, he went to a corner store and bought sketchpads and pencils. He had no portfolio of work to show; he had been doing farm labor.

Over a weekend he filled two sketchpads with images, everything he liked to draw "from knights to cowboys." He got a job at Disney Studios on the spot. He became an apprentice, training under famous animators of the day during a Golden Age of animation.

At Disney, Takamoto had the chance to work on cartoon shorts and longer films. In the 1950s, he worked on popular Disney animated films such as *Cinderella, Peter Pan, Lady and the Tramp,* and *Sleeping Beauty.* He learned his craft at Disney but eventually realized that he could go no further there. In 1961, he took what he learned to Hanna-Barbera Studios, a company that was energizing TV cartoons with such creations as *Huckleberry Hound, Top Cat, The Yogi Bear Show,* and *The Flintstones.*

Takamoto at Disney

For the next 40 years, Takamoto designed for Hanna-Barbera, taking a hand in virtually everything, even licensed products and theme park rides. He brought such characters as Secret Squirrel and Atom Ant to life. Later, he was instrumental in launching *Josie and the Pussy Cats* and other successful cartoons. Ⓒ

Ⓑ **Informational Focus** Outlining What features of this article hint at its main ideas? How can they help you create an outline?

Ⓒ **Informational Focus** Summarizing Summarize this short paragraph in one sentence.

Vocabulary **apprentice** (uh PREHN tihs) *n.*: beginner; someone who is just starting to learn a craft or job.
instrumental (ihn struh MEHN tuhl) *adj.*: helping to make something happen.

Crazy Canine Characters

Takamoto's legacy includes characters of all kinds. But his four-legged creations are his most memorable. There is Astro, the family dog on *The Jetsons;* the perpetually wheezing pooch Muttley of *The Wacky Races;* and the unforgettable Scooby-Doo of *Scooby-Doo, Where Are You?* a big dog who solves mysteries despite being afraid of practically everything.

By design, the animator made Scooby's appearance all wrong. Takamoto called Scooby-Doo a Great Dane, but most of the details of the cartoon dog's appearance were in fact the *opposite* of that breed's characteristics. "There was a lady that bred Great Danes," he said. "She showed me some pictures and talked about the important points of a Great Dane, like a straight back, straight legs, small chin and such. I decided to go the opposite and give him a hump back, bowed legs, big chin and such. Even his color was wrong."

Takamoto had an inventive sense of humor. Even nonsense inspired him. The name Scooby-Doo, for instance, came from a playful refrain[1] in the Frank Sinatra song "Strangers in the Night." Sinatra sings the phrase "scooby-dooby-do" as if it means something. **D**

Creative Recognition

For Scooby-Doo and other beloved and distinctive creations, Takamoto won the Windsor McKay Lifetime Achievement Award by the International Animated Film Association in 1996. The Japanese American National Museum honored him in 2001, and the Animation Guild gave him their Golden Award in 2005. **E**

Takamoto died in 2007 at age 81, but his admirers are still drawing lessons from his spirited ways. Imprisonment in a Japanese internment camp seemed to place his future in doubt, but it ended up putting him on the road to a lasting success. He went from a world of grim reality to a world of fantasy and imagination in a few short years. His death was a contradiction, too. He died of heart failure, but those who knew him say that, above all, he was full of heart. And that heart lives on in his beloved creations. **F**

> 1. **refrain** (rih FRAYN): phrase or verse repeated during a song.

Read with a Purpose

What did you find most surprising or inspiring about the story of Iwao Takamoto?

D | Read and Discuss | How did Takamoto approach the creation of cartoons, including *Scooby-Doo*?

E | Informational Focus | Outlining What main idea in this paragraph would you include as a main point in your outline?

F | Read and Discuss | How do the author's words "[the] Japanese internment camp seemed to place his future in doubt, but it ended up putting him on the road to a lasting success" sum up Takamoto's life as it is presented here?

Vocabulary **legacy** (LEHG uh see) *n.:* something handed down or left for others.

What a Character: Iwao Takamoto and His Toons

Standards Review

Informational Text and Vocabulary

1. The writer *most likely* lists characters Takamoto created because

A they show that cartoons are underappreciated.

B they explain the process of animation.

C they demonstrate Takamoto's importance.

D they reveal facts about Takamoto's life in an internment camp.

2. Suppose that an **outline** of this article lists these main ideas:

I. Takamoto's internment

II. Takamoto's animation career

III.

IV. Recognition of Takamoto's achievements

Which **main idea** belongs in the blank space at number III?

A Takamoto and Frank Sinatra

B Takamoto's picking fruit in Idaho

C Takamoto's canine characters

D Takamoto's sketches of cowboys

3. Suppose that an **outline** of this article includes the main heading "Takamoto's animation career." Which of these details does *not* support that main idea?

A Takamoto landed an interview with Disney.

B At Disney, Takamoto worked on cartoon shorts and popular animated films.

C Takamoto graduated early from high school.

D Takamoto worked at Hanna-Barbera for forty years.

4. Which of the following words is *most* similar in meaning to *instrumental*?

A brave

B useless

C incorrect

D important

5. A *legacy* is *always* something that is

A handed down to others.

B animated.

C kept for oneself.

D thrown away.

6. An *apprentice* is

A the head of a company.

B a type of animator.

C a prisoner.

D a beginner.

Writing Skills Focus

Timed ⌐Writing Write a **summary** of "What a Character." If you've completed an outline, use it to determine the <u>major</u> points you want to include in the summary and the order in which you should present them.

What Do **You** **Think** **Now** According to this article, Takamoto was "freed" by his talent. What does his success say about overcoming injustice?

Writing Workshop

Fictional Narrative

Write with a Purpose

Use your imagination to come up with a great idea for a fictional narrative. Your **purpose** is to entertain your readers. Your **audience** can be your friends, your classmates, or a larger group of people.

A Good Fictional Narrative

- centers on a conflict, or problem that a character has to solve
- includes a series of related events in climactic order that keeps readers in suspense
- provides a detailed setting
- presents an appropriate point of view
- uses dialogue and action to develop the plot
- includes sensory details and concrete language
- ends with a resolution of the conflict

Reader/Writer Notebook

Use your **RWN** to complete the activities for this workshop.

Think as a Reader/Writer

Reading the short stories, or fictional narratives, in this chapter introduced you to the techniques some writers use. Before you write your own fictional narrative, read this excerpt from the short story "The Bracelet" (page 41) by Yoshiko Uchida. Notice how the author introduces the main character and reveals the conflict.

"Mama, is it time to go?" I hadn't planned to cry, but the tears came suddenly, and I wiped them away with the back of my hand. I didn't want my older sister to see me crying.

— The author establishes right away that the narrator, Ruri, is facing a difficult conflict.

"It's almost time, Ruri," my mother said gently. Her face was filled with a kind of sadness I had never seen before.

I looked around at my empty room. The clothes that Mama always told me to hang up in the closet, the junk piled on my dresser, the old rag doll I could never bear to part with—they were all gone. There was nothing left in my room, and there was nothing left in the rest of the house. The rugs and furniture were gone, the pictures and drapes were down, and the closets and cupboards were empty. The house was like a gift box after the nice thing inside was gone; just a lot of nothingness.

— Specific details describe the setting.

It was almost time to leave our home, but we weren't moving to a nicer house or to a new town. It was April 21, 1942. The United States and Japan were at war, and every Japanese person on the West Coast was being evacuated by the government to a concentration camp. Mama, my sister Keiko, and I were being sent from our home, and out of Berkeley, and eventually out of California.

— Additional details further define the setting and describe an external conflict, war between the United States and Japan.

Think About the Professional Model

With a partner, discuss the following questions about the model:

1. How is Ruri's conflict linked to the external conflict of war?
2. How do details about the setting help you understand Ruri's feelings?

Writing Standard 1.3 Use a variety of effective and coherent organizational patterns, including comparison and contrast; organization by categories; and arrangement by spatial order, order of importance, or **climactic order.** **2.1** Write narratives: a. Establish and develop a plot and setting and present a point of view that is appropriate to the stories. b. Include sensory details and concrete language to develop plot and character. c. Use a range of narrative devices (e.g., dialogue, suspense).

Prewriting

Choose a Story Idea

When you write a fictional narrative, you can draw on your own experience, or you can let your imagination run wild. Ideas for short stories often begin with the question "What if?": What if your best friend won millions of dollars? What if your teacher could read people's minds? Think about whether your story will center on characters, setting, or conflict. The Idea Starters in the margin might help you choose an idea for your story.

Identify Characters and Conflict

Once you have a basic story idea, define your **characters** and the problem, or **conflict,** they will face. What kinds of characters appeal to you? (Think of favorite characters from books, TV, and movies.) Perhaps you want to base your main character on an actual historical figure. Be sure to make your characters and conflict realistic so that readers will believe your character would face the kind of conflict you've described in your story.

Plan Your Setting

In some stories the **setting**—where and when the action takes place—plays as big a role as the characters. The setting provides the background for your fictional narrative, but setting can also help create the problem, or conflict. The chart below shows one writer's plan for a story's setting. Create your own chart to brainstorm details about your story's setting.

Setting	Details
Place: Where does the story take place?	The story takes place in a small village near the Arctic Circle.
Time: When does it take place, and how much time passes during the story?	The story takes place in modern times, and one week passes during the story.
How does the setting influence the conflict and characters?	A scientist studying climate change is stranded when the ice pack he is on unexpectedly breaks apart and drifts away from land.

Idea Starters

- a personal experience
- a news story that would make a good fictional narrative
- an interesting person who could be a model for your main character
- a particular problem that the characters would have to overcome
- a "what if" situation

Your Turn _____

Get Started Take notes in your **RWN** about your story idea and conflict. Then, write answers to these questions about your main character:

- How does the character act?
- How does the character look?
- What does the character think?
- What does the character say?
- How do other characters react to the main character?

Learn It Online
Try using an interactive graphic organizer at:

| go.hrw.com | H6-79 | Go |

Think About Purpose and Audience

The **purpose** in writing a fictional narrative is usually to entertain. That doesn't mean the story has to be funny. It can be scary, thrilling, mysterious, tragic, or hilarious. Whichever direction your story takes, you want to keep your reader wondering what will happen next.

Who are your readers? Think about the **audience** you want to reach. Are they people you know? If so, what kind of plot would interest them? What types of characters would they relate to? What background information would you need to provide? If you want to reach a larger audience, people you don't know, what general assumptions can you make? What do most people find interesting? Try to imagine the people you are writing for, and keep them in mind as you draft your fictional narrative.

Develop the Plot

Your story's **plot**—the things that happen in the story—should have four main elements: the **conflict;** the **complications** that arise as characters deal with the conflict; the **climax,** or point of highest drama; and the **resolution,** which shows how the conflict is resolved. You can visualize these four elements in a diagram that shows the typical "shape" of a story.

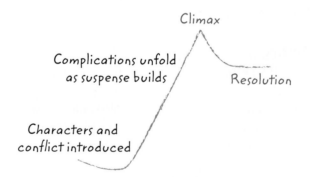

Your Turn

Plan Your Plot As you plan your fictional narrative, place events in **climactic order,** a dramatic arrangement of events in which the climax delivers the biggest emotional punch. Climactic order usually means that the events occur in time order. This type of organizational pattern will give your story **coherence.** That is, the events will be connected in a way that makes sense. Climactic order can also help you create **suspense,** or the anxious curiosity readers feel about what will happen next in a story. Make sure your climax isn't predictable. Instead, try to keep your readers guessing, but be sure to develop the plot in a believable way.

Drafting

Present a Point of View

All fictional narratives have a **narrator,** someone who tells the story. If the story is told by a character involved in the events, it is told from a **first-person point of view.** The narrator refers to himself or herself with first-person pronouns (*I, me, my, mine*), and readers know only what that character sees, hears, and thinks. When the narrator is someone outside the story, the story is told from a **third-person point of view** and uses third-person pronouns (*he, she, they, them*). With this point of view, readers might be told the thoughts and feelings of all the characters, or readers may be limited to seeing the story from only one character's point of view. Present a point of view that is appropriate for your story.

Use Dialogue, Sensory Details, and Concrete Language

Dialogue, what the characters say to each other, tells readers what the characters are like. Dialogue can also be used as a narrative device to describe plot events, help create suspense or tension, describe setting, or explain the story's resolution. Look back at the excerpt from "The Bracelet," and notice the power of dialogue in the very first line of the story: "Mama, is it time to go?" Uchida uses that bit of dialogue to connect the reader to the story's plot, setting, and conflict.

Include **sensory details** and **concrete language** in your fictional narrative to develop your plot and characters. Sensory details describe what you can see, hear, taste, feel, and smell. Concrete language consists of words and phrases that are precise and specific. Use such details and language to *show,* not tell, your readers what is happening and to make characters and events vivid in the minds of your readers.

● **Writer's Tip**

To choose the point of view that is most appropriate for your fictional narrative, think about your purpose. If you want to draw your reader into the heart and mind of a particular character who faces a problem, you'll probably want to use the first-person point of view. If you want to explore the thoughts and feelings of several characters as they interact, you will want to use the third-person point of view. Whichever point of view you choose, use it consistently throughout your story.

Grammar Link Punctuating Dialogue

Note how these rules for punctuating dialogue are used in the examples from "The Bracelet."

- Put quotation marks before and after a speaker's exact words, and place punctuation marks such as commas, question marks, and periods inside the closing quotation mark.

"Mama, is it time to go**?"**

- Use a speaker tag, such as *she said,* to identify who is speaking. If a speaker tag comes before a quotation, put a comma after the tag; if a speaker tag comes in the middle of a quotation, put commas before and after the tag; and if a speaker tag comes at the end of a sentence, put a comma or other appropriate punctuation at the end of the quotation (inside the quotation mark), and put a period at the end of the speaker tag.

"It's almost time, Ruri," **my mother said gently.**

Your Turn _____

Write Your Draft Use the notes you made about your story's plot and setting to write a draft of your story. Also think about the following:

- Which point of view will you use?
- How will you use dialogue to move the story along?

Peer Review

Work with a peer to review each other's drafts. Answer each question in this chart to decide where and how your fictional narratives can be improved. As you discuss your stories, be sure to take notes about each other's suggestions. You can refer to your notes as you revise your drafts.

Evaluating and Revising

Now that you've written your draft, you can go back and make improvements by answering the questions below. The tips in the middle column will help you evaluate your short story. The right column suggests techniques you can use to revise your draft.

Fictional Narrative: Guidelines for Content and Organization

Evaluation Question	Tip	Revision Technique
1. Have you established a vivid setting?	**Put a check mark** next to details about the setting.	**Add** details about time and place, if needed.
2. Do the characters seem real?	**Highlight** character details, description, and dialogue.	**Elaborate** as needed by adding sensory details, concrete language, and dialogue.
3. Is the problem, or conflict, of the story clear?	**Underline** the conflict.	If necessary, **add** sentences that describe the problem the characters face.
4. Are events arranged in climactic order and clearly connected? Does the plot keep readers in suspense?	**Number each event.** Check that events are in the correct order. **Bracket** words or sentences that help create suspense.	**Reorganize** events if necessary. **Add** details to tie events together and to heighten suspense. **Cut or rearrange** details that reveal plot developments too soon.
5. Is the point of view appropriate, clear, and consistent?	**Circle** pronouns that establish the point of view in the opening paragraphs.	**Cut** pronouns or details that shift the point of view.
6. Is the conflict resolved? Does the story's resolution make sense?	**Draw a star** next to the story's climax and resolution.	**Add** a climax, or high point, if necessary. **Add** details to show how the conflict is resolved.

Read this student's draft and the comments about it as a model for revising your own fictional narrative.

Apples in the Snow
by Jane Caflisch, Kensington Intermediate

Little Bear longed to become the sacred medicine man of the tribe.

The elders thought it unwise for him to become the medicine man. They said that he was too wild and young. But Little Bear persisted. Finally, the elders said, "Go out into the hills. If you can find apples in the snow, it will be a sign that the Great Spirit wills you to become our medicine man."

Little Bear fasted all day. Then he set out into the hills. He climbed and searched to no avail for that day and the next. He stopped often to pray to Mon-o-La, the earth, and to the Great Spirit.

← The opening sentence introduces the main **character** and hints at the **conflict** he faces.

← The second paragraph establishes the **conflict** between Little Bear and the elders and the setting's influence on the problem. **Dialogue** is used to reveal the elders' test for Little Bear.

← The third paragraph outlines a **series of events** set in motion by the elders' test for Little Bear.

MINI-LESSON ▶ **How to Use Dialogue as a Narrative Device**

Jane's first paragraph lacks vital information. She decides to develop a dialogue between Little Bear and his father to tell us more about these characters and their relationship. Dialogue is an excellent device for adding information about characters and for advancing the action of the plot.

Jane's Draft

Little Bear longed to become the sacred medicine man of the tribe.

Jane's Revision of Paragraph One

Little Bear longed to become the sacred medicine man of the tribe. "Father, I have passed all tests for a young warrior in the Cherokee nation," Little Bear said humbly. "But I seek more challenge—more responsibility. I want to be our tribe's sacred medicine man."

"Little Bear," his father replied, "you have my permission to address the elders. Since you are only fourteen, they will surely reject your petition."

Your Turn _____

Use Dialogue Read your draft and think about the following:

- Have you developed your characters and plot thoroughly?
- Are there places where you can add dialogue to help develop characters and move the plot forward?

Student Draft *continues*

A **setting** within the main character's dream is described. →

Then, on the third night, Little Bear had a dream. He dreamed that he was standing by a golden apple tree. Around it the snow had melted. Then from inside the tree came a musical voice. "Come pick my apples. I grow them for you, for you, for you...." Little Bear awoke. He tried to think of what the dream meant. While he thought, he walked up the hill.

The story reaches a **climax** as the main character achieves his goal. →

Thinking and walking, he soon reached the top. There he began to pray. When he opened his eyes, there was the golden apple tree of his dream. He waited for the voice to come, but when it did not, he decided that it had spoken in his dream and that was enough. So he picked the apples and started down the mountain, thanking the goodness of the spirits. When he turned to look at the tree, it was gone.

The conflict is **resolved.** →

When he reached his village, there was great feasting. The elders told him that the golden tree was the tree of Mon-o-La. So Little Bear became Snow Child and assumed the role of the tribe's sacred medicine man.

MINI-LESSON ▷ **How to Create an Effective Conclusion**

In Jane's draft the feasting occurs before the elders accept Little Bear as the tribe's medicine man. Jane decides to revise her conclusion to improve the organization of the ideas within the paragraph and to give her story a more powerful ending. Rearranging the order of events and giving more details about the elders' decision will leave readers with a lasting image.

Jane's Draft

When he reached his village, there was great feasting. The elders told him that the golden tree was the tree of Mon-o-La. So Little Bear became Snow Child and assumed the role of the tribe's sacred medicine man.

Jane's Revision of the Last Paragraph

> When Little Bear reached the village, he humbly presented the golden apple to the elders. Smiling broadly, the chief elder raised the apple high above his head and proclaimed Little Bear the tribe's sacred medicine man: "You are now Snow Child." The entire village feasted in honor of Snow Child, their new sacred medicine man.

Your Turn _____

Add Drama to Your Conclusion With a partner, review your conclusion. Does it wrap up the action of the story in a dramatic way? What could you add to your conclusion to make your story more powerful?

Proofreading and Publishing

Proofreading

After you revise your fictional narrative, you should make sure your final version is free of any errors in spelling, punctuation, and sentence structure. Proofread, or edit, your writing carefully, using proofreading marks to make the necessary corrections.

Grammar Link Using Participial Phrases

Participial phrases provide action and movement in writing. Because a participle is a verb form that is being used as an adjective to describe something, it is an excellent way to add variety to your sentences. When used at the beginning of a sentence, a participle or series of participles is separated from the main clause by a comma.

Jane uses several participles in her story, but she forgot to separate the one below with a comma. She found the error in her proofreading.

> **Jane's Draft:** Thinking and walking he soon reached the top.

> **Jane's Revision:** Thinking and walking[,] he soon reached the top.

Jane also used a participle phrase at the end of a sentence, but she remembered to use a comma there.

> So he picked the apples and started down the mountain[,] thanking the
>
> goodness of the spirit.

Publishing

Think of creative ways to share your story. Consider the following:

- Present it to your class as a dramatic presentation.
- Turn it into a graphic novel, with illustrations and speech balloons for dialogue.

Reflect on the Process Thinking about how you wrote your fictional narrative will help you create other forms of writing. In your **RWN,** write a short response to the following questions:

1. What was the most challenging aspect of coming up with a story idea? Explain.
2. What techniques helped you plan your plot? What might you do differently next time?
3. How did you use dialogue to advance the plot? to describe the setting? to develop characters?

⬤ Proofreading Tip

There are three main areas to focus on when proofreading: spelling, punctuation, and sentence structure. It makes sense to focus on just one area at a time while proofreading. Ask two peers to help you, assigning each person just one area to check.

Your Turn _____

Use Pronouns Clearly As you proofread your fictional narrative, make sure all of your pronouns have clear antecedents. Ask yourself, "Could this pronoun refer to more than one character?" Revise any unclear references you find.

Scoring Rubric

You can use the rubric below to evaluate your fictional narrative.

	Fictional Narrative	Organization and Focus	Sentence Structure	Conventions
4	• Provides a *thoroughly developed* plot line (with: 1) beginning conflict, 2) rising action, 3) climax, 4) resolution, 5) point of view), characters, and a *definite* setting. • Includes *appropriate* strategies (e.g., dialogue and suspense).	• *Clearly* addresses all of the writing task. • Demonstrates a *clear* understanding of purpose and audience. • Maintains a *consistent* point of view and *smooth* transitions. • Includes a *clearly presented* central idea with *relevant* details.	• Includes sentence *variety* (e.g. simple, complex, compound-complex).	• Contains *few, if any,* errors in the conventions of the English language (grammar, punctuation, capitalization, spelling). These errors do **not** interfere with the reader's understanding of the writing.
3	• Provides an *adequately developed* plot line (with: 1) beginning conflict ,2) rising action, 3) climax, 4) resolution, 5) point of view), characters, and a *definite* setting. • Includes *appropriate* strategies (e.g., dialogue and suspense).	• Addresses *most* of the writing task. • Demonstrates a *general* understanding of purpose and audience. • Maintains a *mostly consistent* point of view and *relatively smooth* transitions. • *Presents* a central idea with *relevant* details.	• Includes *some* sentence *variety* (e.g. simple, complex, compound-complex).	• Contains *some errors* in the conventions of the English language (grammar, punctuation, capitalization, spelling). These errors do **not** interfere with the reader's understanding of the writing.
2	• Provides a *minimally developed* plot line, characters, and a setting. • *Attempts* to use strategies but with *minimal* effectiveness (e.g., dialogue and suspense).	• Addresses *some* of the writing task. • Demonstrates *little* understanding of purpose and audience. • Maintains an *inconsistent* point of view and *awkward* transitions that do not unify important ideas. • *Suggests* a central idea with *limited* details.	• Includes *little* sentence *variety*.	• Contains *several errors* in the conventions of the English language (grammar, punctuation, capitalization, spelling). These errors **may** interfere with the reader's understanding of the writing.
1	• *Lacks* a developed plot line. • *Fails* to use strategies (e.g., dialogue and suspense).	• Addresses *only one* part of the writing task. • Demonstrates *no* understanding of purpose and audience. • *Lacks* a point of view and transitions that unify important ideas. • *Lacks* a central idea but may contain *marginally related* details.	• Includes *no* sentence *variety*.	• Contains *serious errors* in the conventions of the English language (grammar, punctuation, capitalization, spelling). These errors interfere with the reader's understanding of the writing.

Preparing for Timed ⏱ Writing

Fictional Narrative

When responding to an on-demand fictional narrative prompt, use the models you have read, what you've learned from writing your own short story, the rubric on page 86, and the steps below.

> **Writing Standard 2.1** Write narratives: a. Establish and develop a plot and setting and present a point of view that is appropriate to the stories. b. Include sensory details and concrete language to develop plot and character. c. Use a range of narrative devices (e.g., dialogue, suspense).

Writing Prompt

Imagine a boy or girl your age who wants to play a team sport but whose parents are against it. Write an entertaining short story for your classmates about the events that occur as the boy or girl tries to overcome this conflict. Establish a vivid setting, and use sensory details, concrete language, and dialogue to develop a believable plot and characters.

Study the Prompt

Begin by reading the prompt carefully. Circle any specific information in the prompt that you'll need to include in your response. Your **main character** is a boy or girl your age. The **conflict** is provided for you: The main character's parents don't want him or her to play a team sport. Your **purpose** is to entertain, and your **audience** is your classmates. The prompt also instructs you to develop characters and **setting** with **details** and **dialogue.**

Tip: *Spend about five minutes studying the prompt.*

Plan Your Response

Here are some quick tips to help you plan your response:

- Write down who your main character will be.
- Write down the conflict, main events, climax, and resolution.
- Write down where and when the story takes place. How might this setting influence the plot?
- Decide whether you'll use a first-person narrative or a third-person narrative.

Tip: *Spend about ten minutes planning your response.*

Respond to the Prompt

Using the notes you just made, draft your fictional narrative. Follow these guidelines:

- In the opening of your story, grab your readers' attention by creating suspense or showing your characters in action.
- Use sensory details and concrete language to develop your plot, characters, and setting. Remember to use realistic dialogue.
- Tell how the conflict was resolved and how the characters were changed or affected by the conflict.

As you write, remember to use words that are appropriate for your characters and the story—not too formal. Write as neatly as you can. If your short story can't be read easily, it won't be scored.

Tip: *Spend about twenty minutes writing your draft.*

Improve Your Response

Revising Go back over the key aspects of the prompt. Did you explain the conflict? Did you describe the setting? Are your characters and conclusion believable?

Proofreading Take a few minutes to proofread your story to correct errors in grammar, spelling, punctuation, and capitalization. Make sure all your edits are neat, and erase any stray marks.

Checking Your Final Copy Before you turn your story in, read it one more time to catch any errors you may have missed. You'll be glad that you took the extra time for one final review.

Tip: *Save ten minutes to improve your paper.*

Delivering a Narrative Presentation

Speak with a Purpose

Deliver a narrative presentation. Practice telling the story, and then present it to your class.

Think as a Reader/Writer Whether you are writing a short story or delivering a narrative presentation, you should develop a story around a clearly defined problem that is resolved at the end. To sustain your audience's interest in this problem, you can use a range of devices: sensory details and concrete language, dialogue, and suspense. When you present a story orally, you can also use your voice, face, and movements to hold your audience's attention and convey your points.

Plan Your Presentation

Match the Story to the Audience

To choose a story to tell, first consider your **audience, purpose,** and **occasion.** Ask yourself: *Who will listen to my narrative? What effect do I want to have on my audience? When and where will I present my narrative?* Answering these questions will help you choose the right **message** and an appropriate story. Write down the **plot** events in a time line. The **organizational structure** of most stories will be time order. However, your audience, purpose, and occasion may determine how you arrange events.

Establish a Context and a Point of View

An introduction will help prepare listeners to understand your oral narrative. In your introduction, establish the **context** of the narrative, telling listeners any important information about the **setting.** Then, identify the **point of view** from which you will tell the story. For example, one of the characters may tell the story, or a narrator who is outside of the story may tell what happens.

Develop Plot and Character

Use **sensory details** and **concrete language** to develop your plot and characters and bring them to life. Sensory details appeal to the senses—describing sights, sounds, smells, tastes, or sensations. Concrete language, or specific words, gives your audience an exact mental image of what you are describing. Include **dialogue,** or what characters say to each other, to move the plot forward and show what your characters are like. As you develop your plot, remember to build **suspense.** Save some important details to reveal right before the story's climax, or high point, or scatter hints throughout your story to sustain your audience's interest.

Reader/Writer Notebook

Use your **RWN** to complete the activities for this workshop.

Listening and Speaking Standard
1.7 Use effective rate, volume, pitch, and tone and align nonverbal elements to sustain audience interest and attention. **2.1** Deliver narrative presentations: a. Establish a context, plot, and point of view. b. Include sensory details and concrete language to develop the plot and character. c. Use a range of narrative devices (e.g., dialogue, tension, or suspense).

Deliver Your Short Story

Use Verbal Elements

Delivering an oral narrative means more than just talking. You can convey character by adjusting your voice to re-create the characters' speech and to communicate a different personality for each character. You can also convey the overall feeling of an oral communication, or its **tone,** through the sound of your voice as well as through your choice of words. Use these verbal elements, or techniques, to help you create character and sustain your audience's interest and attention:

- **Rate** refers to the speed at which you speak. Consider where you should slow down or speed up in your narrative to show emotions or to reflect the pace at which plot events occur.
- **Volume** refers to how loudly or softly you speak. Change your volume to convey different characters or to express emotions.
- **Pitch** refers to the high or low sounds of your voice. Vary your pitch to suit your characters and to show emotions.

Use Nonverbal Elements

Nonverbal communication, or body language, helps you relate to your audience and communicate your message when you speak. Make **eye contact** with your audience to hold your listeners' attention. Use **facial expressions** and gestures to help you convey character and emotions and to emphasize points. Make sure your nonverbal elements, or techniques, are aligned with your verbal ones so that your body language matches your voice. That way, you will communicate your ideas effectively to your audience.

Rehearse and Present

To help you remember all of the elements of your oral narrative, add delivery notes to your time line. Write down notes about your introduction, the devices you will use to develop your plot and characters, and the verbal and nonverbal techniques you will include. Then, practice delivering your narrative. If possible, make a video or an audio recording of your practice session, and carefully evaluate your presentation. If you don't have access to an audio recorder or a video camera, practice in front of a mirror. When you're ready, deliver your narrative to the class.

A Good Short Story Presentation

- has an appealing story line that suits the audience, purpose, and occasion
- establishes a context, plot, and point of view
- presents a clear conflict and a suspenseful plot
- use sensory language, concrete details, and dialogue to develop plot and character
- sustains the audience's interest through the use of effective verbal and nonverbal elements

⬤ Speaking Tip

Using interesting verbal techniques does not mean you should forget to enunciate every word clearly. Always speak slowly, clearly, and loudly enough so that audience members in the back can hear and understand you.

Literary Skills Review

Setting and Plot   **Directions:** Read the following story. Then, answer each question that follows.

The Path Through the Cemetery

by **Leonard Q. Ross**

Ivan was a timid little man—so timid that the villagers called him "Pigeon" or mocked him with the title "Ivan the Terrible." Every night Ivan stopped in at the saloon which was on the edge of the village cemetery. Ivan never crossed the cemetery to get to his lonely shack on the other side. That path would save many minutes, but he had never taken it—not even in the full light of noon.

Late one winter's night, when bitter wind and snow beat against the saloon, the customers took up the familiar mockery. "Ivan's mother was scared by a canary when she carried him." "Ivan the Terrible—Ivan the Terribly Timid One."

Ivan's sickly protest only fed their taunts, and they jeered cruelly when the young Cossack lieutenant flung his horrid challenge at their quarry.

"You are a pigeon, Ivan. You'll walk all around the cemetery in this cold—but you dare not cross it."

Ivan murmured, "The cemetery is nothing to cross, Lieutenant. It is nothing but earth, like all the other earth."

The lieutenant cried, "A challenge, then! Cross the cemetery tonight, Ivan, and I'll give you five rubles—five gold rubles!"

Perhaps it was the vodka. Perhaps it was the temptation of the five gold rubles. No one ever knew why Ivan, moistening his lips, said suddenly: "Yes, Lieutenant, I'll cross the cemetery!"

The saloon echoed with their disbelief. The lieutenant winked to the men and unbuckled his saber. "Here, Ivan. When you get to the center of the cemetery, in front of the biggest tomb, stick the saber into the ground. In the morning we shall go there. And if the saber is in the ground—five gold rubles to you!"

Ivan took the saber. The men drank a toast: "To Ivan the Terrible!" They roared with laughter.

The wind howled around Ivan as he closed the door of the saloon behind him. The cold was knife-sharp. He buttoned his long coat and crossed the dirt road. He could hear the lieutenant's voice, louder than the rest, yelling after him, "Five rubles, pigeon! If you live!"

Ivan pushed the cemetery gate open. He walked fast. "Earth, just earth . . . like any other earth." But the darkness was a massive dread. "Five gold rubles . . ." The wind was cruel and the saber was like ice in his hands. Ivan shivered under the long, thick coat and broke into a limping run.

He recognized the large tomb. He must have sobbed—that was the sound that was drowned in the wind. And he knelt, cold and terrified, and drove the saber through the crust into the hard ground. With all his strength, he pushed it down to the hilt. It was done. The cemetery . . . the challenge . . . five gold rubles.

Ivan started to rise from his knees. But he could not move. Something held him. Something gripped him in an unyield-ing and implacable hold. Ivan tugged and lurched and pulled—gasping in his panic, shaken by a monstrous fear. But something held Ivan. He cried out in terror, then made senseless gurgling noises.

They found Ivan, next morning, on the ground in front of the tomb that was in the center of the cemetery. He was frozen to death. The look on his face was not that of a frozen man, but of a man killed by some nameless horror. And the lieutenant's saber was in the ground where Ivan had pounded it—through the dragging folds of his long coat.

---

1. How does the setting help create the *main* problem in the selection?
   A The dark of night prevents Ivan from seeing his way.
   B The freezing weather makes Ivan want to get home quickly.
   C The saloon's customers tease Ivan cruelly.
   D The cemetery terrifies Ivan.

2. Which of the following weather-related issues is *most* important to the resolution of the main problem?
   A Ivan must run through the cemetery.
   B Ivan wears a long and heavy coat.
   C The saber feels like ice in his hand.
   D The loud wind covers Ivan's sobs.

3. Which of the following elements of setting does *not* influence the selection?
   A the dirt road
   B the weather
   C the time of year
   D the cemetery path

4. Which of the following places *most* influences the resolution of the main problem?
   A the cemetery gate
   B the saloon
   C the large tomb
   D Ivan's shack

Timed Writing
5. How does the story's setting influence the problem and its resolution? Use details from the story to support your answer.

Informational Skills Review

Note Taking, Outlining, Summarizing   **Directions:** Read the following selection. Then, read and respond to the questions that follow.

Celebrating the Quinceañera by **Mara Rockliff**

You stand at the back of the church between your parents and godparents, your knees shaking. You feel special, and a bit awkward, in your first formal dress and your tiara. Your honor court has walked up the aisle ahead of you: fourteen girls in pastel dresses, fourteen boys in tuxedos. With you and your escort there are fifteen couples—one for each year of your life. The long months of planning and preparation have finally ended. Your quinceañera has begun.

The quinceañera (keen say ah NYEH ruh, from the Spanish words *quince,* "fifteen," and *años,* "years") is a rite of passage celebrated by Mexicans and Mexican Americans. People believe that the tradition can be traced back to the Aztec culture, in which girls commonly married at the age of fifteen. Today a girl's quinceañera marks her coming of age. It means she is ready to take on adult privileges and responsibilities.

The most important part of your quinceañera is the *misa de acción de gracias,* the thanksgiving Mass. You slowly walk up the aisle to the front of the church. You kneel, placing a bouquet of fifteen roses on the altar to thank the Virgin Mary for bringing you to this important day. A birthstone ring glitters on your finger, and a religious medal hangs from your neck, inscribed with your name and today's date—special gifts from adult relatives or friends of the family. The priest will bless your medal during the Mass.

Next comes a sermon, followed by prayers and readings from the Bible. You recite your speech, and the service ends. Then the photographer rushes over, and you pose for an endless series of photographs with your family and friends.

But the quinceañera celebration has just begun, for the fiesta is still to come. You enter to the sound of music, a traditional mariachi band or a DJ playing current hits. You dance in turn with your father, your grandfathers, your escort. You and your honor court perform a group dance that you have rehearsed. Then everyone joins in the dancing.

You're almost too excited to eat, but the food is wonderful. There's your favorite— chicken in mole sauce, made from chilies and unsweetened chocolate. The tables are covered with everything from tamales and corn soup to an elaborately decorated cake.

Later, as everyone watches, your father removes the flat shoes you have worn all day and replaces them with a pair of high heels. In your parents' eyes you are no longer a child. They'll treat you differently from now on, and they'll expect you to act more like an adult as well.

Among your many gifts, one stands out: the last doll. It's not a toy for you to play with, of course; it's a symbol of the child-

hood you're leaving behind. If you have a younger sister, you might present it to her. You look around at the people who have watched you grow up. You see tears in many eyes. The quinceañera is a tradition many centuries old, but for you it will happen only once.

1. A report on this article would state that its main idea is
   A the quinceañera tradition is losing its importance.
   B the quinceañera happens only once in a girl's life.
   C young people rehearse quinceañera dances for months.
   D the quinceañera is a celebration of a girl's passage into adulthood.

2. Here is the beginning of an outline of "Celebrating the Quinceañera."

   I. Introduction
   II. Tradition
   III. Events of the day
       A.
       B. photographs
       C. fiesta

   Which of the following items belongs in the blank space at number III.A.?
   A definition of *quinceañera*
   B thanksgiving Mass
   C speech
   D dancing

3. Which of the following details would be *most* important to include in notes taken on this article?
   A last doll—symbol of leaving childhood
   B chiles and unsweetened chocolate in mole sauce
   C girls in honor court wear light-colored dresses
   D a DJ plays current music

4. An outline of this article might have a main heading called "Tradition." Which following detail does *not* support that main idea?
   A importance of the number fifteen
   B Aztec girls married at age fifteen
   C "rite of passage"
   D honor court performs group dance

Timed Writing

5. Suppose you were **summarizing** this article. Re-read the third and fourth paragraphs. Then, list four events from the quinceañera ceremony you would include in your summary. List the events in the order they take place.

Vocabulary Skills Review

Reading Standard 1.4 Monitor expository text for unknown words or words with novel meanings by using word, sentence, and paragraph clues to determine meaning.

Context Clues

Directions: Use context clues to determine the meaning of the italicized words in each of the following sentences.

1. I could tell by looking at the ruined buildings that this earthquake was *devastating*.
   - A destructive
   - B interesting
   - C fulfilling
   - D disappointing

2. After the fire alarm sounded, the residents were *evacuated* from the building for their safety.
   - A watched
   - B hidden
   - C removed
   - D thrown

3. The *tolerant* dog calmly let the kittens run up and down his back.
   - A tired
   - B patient
   - C confused
   - D slow-moving

4. I knew Stella was no friend of mine when I saw how much she *savored* my defeat.
   - A regretted
   - B copied
   - C delighted in
   - D discussed

5. From the sagging porch to the broken windows, the house showed that it had been *forsaken* long ago.
   - A repaired
   - B abandoned
   - C loved
   - D decorated

6. The new game show demanded rapid responses, so contestants had no time to *ponder* their answers.
   - A think over
   - B recover
   - C regret
   - D shout

7. As soon as the doors opened, the crowd *surged* into the store, crowded the aisles, and looked for bargains.
   - A yelled
   - B sneaked
   - C walked slowly
   - D moved forward suddenly

Academic Vocabulary

Directions: Use context clues to determine the meaning of the italicized Academic Vocabulary word in the sentence below.

8. She never made things from clay before, so creating the bowl was a *major* feat.
   - A simple
   - B precise
   - C important
   - D artistic

Writing Skills Review

Short Story   **Directions:** Read this paragraph from a fictional narrative. Then, answer each question.

Writing Standard 2.1 Write narratives: a. Establish and develop a plot and setting and present a point of view that is appropriate to the stories. b. Include sensory details and concrete language to develop plot and character. c. Use a range of narrative devices (e.g., dialogue, suspense).

Flat Out of Luck

Mrs. Fiona McNulty was late. She smashed her wig onto her head, pulled up the suspenders on her overalls, crammed her feet into the openings of her oversized shoes, grabbed her bag of tricks, and raced out the door to her small car. "Oops," she thought to herself, "I should have had that tire checked. It looks low. I don't have time to check it now. I'll do it on the way home from the birthday party."

Fifteen minutes later, in the middle of the five o'clock rush-hour traffic jam, Mrs. McNulty felt the tire go flat. She braced herself and moved as quickly as she could to the side of the road. She turned off the motor and climbed out of her car. "Great! What do I do now?" she thought. Mrs. McNulty was already late for her appearance at a child's birthday party as JoJo the Juggling Clown.

1. What words did the writer use to establish the setting?
   - **A** "crammed her feet into the openings of her oversized shoes"
   - **B** "in the middle of the five o'clock rush-hour traffic jam"
   - **C** "braced herself and moved as quickly as she could"
   - **D** "should have had that tire checked"

2. If the writer wanted to add sensory details to the story, which of the following sentences would it be *best* to include?
   - **A** The birthday party was at a house across town.
   - **B** She had to hurry if she wanted to be on time.
   - **C** She couldn't call anyone because she had left her cell phone at home.
   - **D** Passersby stared at the clown in a red wig, baggy overalls, and oversized shoes.

3. Why did the writer put the sentence "Great! What do I do now?" in quotation marks?
   - **A** It contains the character's exact words.
   - **B** It is the title of the story.
   - **C** It is the story's conflict.
   - **D** It creates suspense.

4. Why did the writer identify the character first as Mrs. Fiona McNulty and later as JoJo the Juggling Clown?
   - **A** to reveal that Mrs. McNulty is not a real person
   - **B** to clarify that the character changed her clothing in the car
   - **C** to create suspense by describing Mrs. McNulty's strange clothing before revealing that it is a clown's costume
   - **D** to cause the reader to feel sympathetic toward Mrs. McNulty

Read On

For Independent Reading

Fiction

Nothing but the Truth

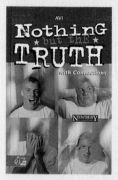

Philip Molloy is suspended when he defies school policy by humming along to the national anthem. He *says* he is humming to be patriotic. That's only part of the story, however: He really wants to irritate his English teacher, because Philip made a D in her class and it kept him off the track team. Philip's deception turns a minor infraction into a media circus in Avi's popular novel *Nothing but the Truth*.

Life As We Knew It

Imagine your life as the earth changes drastically overnight. An asteroid has knocked the moon from its orbit, causing gigantic tsunamis, worldwide earthquakes, and violent volcanoes, whose ash blots out the sun. In Susan Beth Pfeffer's novel *Life As We Knew It*, fifteen-year-old Miranda keeps a journal as summer turns into arctic winter and her family survives on stockpiled supplies. Follow Miranda's story as she struggles to hold on to her most precious resource—hope.

Regarding the Sink

When a clogged cafeteria sink stinks up Geyser Creek Middle School, Sam N's sixth-grade class knows who can help—Florence Waters, the famous designer of the school's fountain. The problem is that Waters can't come to Geyser to create a new sink because she's gone missing. Kate Klise's *Regarding the Sink* leads the students on a quest to solve the mystery, a quest that takes them all the way to China.

Roughnecks

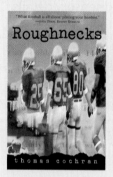

Once in a while you get a second chance. For Travis Cody, today is one of those times. His team, the Oil Camp Roughnecks, is facing the Pineview Pelicans for the state championship. Travis will have forty-eight minutes to redeem himself in a face-off with his rival, Jericho Grooms. In his debut novel set in southern Louisiana, Thomas Cochran takes us out on the gridiron and inside the mind of Travis Cody, who has one chance, one game, to prove he isn't a quitter.

Nonfiction

Through My Eyes

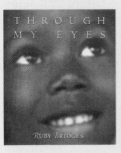

In *Through My Eyes,* Ruby Bridges tells what it was like to be the first African American student in an all-white elementary school. In this moving memoir, we see her confronting abuse and isolation with remarkable courage. Newspaper articles, photographs, and quotations from the time provide a deeper understanding of her struggle.

How We Lived: Invasion, War and Travel

As early people found new methods of transportation, they saw new and distant lands. To expand their own civilization, they often had to fight for the new land. *Invasion, War and Travel* traces more than ten thousand years of the development of travel, empires, and weapons and the ways each one influenced the other. John Haywood, editor of the How We Lived series, has included hundreds of maps, works of art, time lines, and photographs.

Here's Looking at Me: How Artists See Themselves

A self-portrait can sometimes tell you more about an artist than a detailed biography. In *Here's Looking at Me,* author Bob Raczka has chosen fourteen self-portraits by artists spanning some five hundred years. The reproductions are clear and in color, and Raczka's descriptions give you background into the artists' lives and history.

I Want to Be an Astronaut

Filled with facts about the history and future of space exploration, *I Want to Be an Astronaut* by Stephanie Maze launches you toward a career as an astronaut. This book will help you take the first steps necessary to make your dreams of traveling to the moon and beyond come true.

Learn It Online
Find study guides for *Nothing But the Truth* and *Roughnecks* at NovelWise on:

go.hrw.com | H6-97 | Go

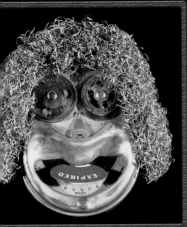

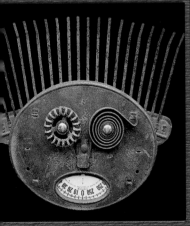

CHAPTER 2

Character

INFORMATIONAL TEXT FOCUS

Compare-and-Contrast Organizational Pattern

California Standards

Here are the Grade 6 standards you will work toward mastering in Chapter 2.

Word Analysis, Fluency, and Systematic Vocabulary Development
1.5 Understand and explain "shades of meaning" in related words (e.g., *softly* and *quietly*).

Reading Comprehension (Focus on Informational Materials)
2.2 Analyze text that uses the compare-and-contrast organizational pattern.

Literary Response and Analysis
3.2 Analyze the effect of the qualities of the character (e.g., courage or cowardice, ambition or laziness) on the plot and the resolution of the conflict.

Writing Applications (Genres and Their Characteristics)
2.2 Write expository compositions (e.g., description, explanation, comparison and contrast, problem and solution):
   a. State the thesis or purpose.
   b. Explain the situation.
   c. Follow an organizational pattern appropriate to the type of composition.
   d. Offer persuasive evidence to validate arguments and conclusions as needed.

"Always do right; this will gratify some people and astonish the rest."

—**Mark Twain**

What Do
You
Think

How do you know what the right thing to do is? What do you think motivates people to "do right"?

Found-object faces
by Jim Shores.

Learn It Online
Use *PowerNotes* to get to know the selections in this chapter:

go.hrw.com   H6-99   Go

Literary Skills Focus

by **Carol Jago**

How Do a Character's Qualities Affect the Plot of a Story?

A Greek philosopher, or thinker, named Heraclitus (hehr uh KLY tuhs) once wrote, "Character is destiny." (Destiny is a person's fate, or lot in life.) Heraclitus was thinking about real people, but you'll discover that what's true about life is often true about literature. Character *counts*. A character's qualities (traits, or distinguishing characteristics) in a story have a major effect, or influence, on the plot.

Characters and Conflict

A story's plot has a main **conflict,** or problem. When characters struggle with forces *outside* themselves, they are involved in an **external conflict**—usually a struggle against other characters, against nature, or against society. Some stories are about **internal conflict,** such as a struggle *within* the main character to overcome fear or to make a tough choice.

Characters' qualities, such as courage, laziness, or ambition, determine the choices they make and the actions they take. As a result, their qualities influence the plot by affecting the conflict and its **resolution,** or outcome. The characters' qualities influence the events in a story the way your qualities influence what happens to you in life.

Imagine, for example, a story in which Julia is in a conflict with a school bully nicknamed Tiger. If Julia were brave, she would stand up to Tiger. In the story's resolution, a defeated Tiger would no longer be a threat. If Julia were fearful, however, Tiger would triumph. The conflict would be resolved by having Tiger's power strengthened. Julia might start out being afraid, but by the story's end, she'll have discovered how to stand up to him with bravery.

Characterization

The way a writer reveals the qualities of a character and brings him or her to life is known as **characterization.** Here are six ways an author can reveal a character's qualities:

1. Describing appearance Writers often provide details about how a character looks and dresses that tell you about his or her qualities.

> Walt Masters is not a very large boy, but there is manliness in his make-up. . . . Walt has walked all the fourteen years of his life in sun-tanned, moose-hide moccasins.
>
> from "The King of Mazy May" by Jack London

2. Describing speech Writers use dialogue—characters' speech—to reveal important qualities. Listen for this character's shyness in her words.

> "That's not, I don't, you're not . . . Not mine," I finally say in a little voice that was maybe me when I was four.
>
> from "Eleven" by Sandra Cisneros

3. Showing actions and behavior Writers can tell you about a character's qualities by describing his or her actions and reactions.

> "I'm *not* playing!" I cried, stung. . . . I ran toward where I had put Vern's bat and ball and disappeared with them behind our house. Then I flung them with all my strength into the bushes.
>
> from "Cricket in the Road"
> by Michael Anthony

4. Revealing thoughts and feelings Writers may tell you what characters are *really* thinking and feeling by writing from a point of view that lets you in on one or more characters' thoughts.

> Today I wish I was one hundred and two instead of eleven. . . . I'd have known what to say when Mrs. Price put the red sweater on my desk. I would've known how to tell her it wasn't mine instead of just sitting there with that look on my face.
>
> from "Eleven" by Sandra Cisneros

5. Including other characters' views A writer may give you important information about a character by revealing what other characters say or feel about him or her.

> And because of what Walt Masters did on this night, the men of the Yukon have become very proud of him.
>
> from "The King of Mazy May"
> by Jack London

6. Directly describing qualities The five techniques of characterization you've just read about are examples of **indirect characterization.** Sometimes a writer simply tells you what a character's qualities are (selfish, generous, heroic, and so on). This sixth technique is called **direct characterization.**

> He has a good heart, and is not afraid of the darkness and loneliness, of man or beast or thing. His father is a good man, strong and brave, and Walt is growing up like him.
>
> from "The King of Mazy May"
> by Jack London

Your Turn Analyze Characters

Think of a conflict between two characters from a movie, book, or TV show. List several of each character's qualities, or traits, in outlined heads like the ones below. Identify which character won the conflict, and explain how that character's qualities bring about the resolution.

tough
smart
brave
hardworking
generous

foolish
wicked
self-centered
mean
tricky

Learn It Online
To understand the role of characterization in novels, visit *NovelWise* at:

go.hrw.com   H6-101   **Go**

Reading Skills Focus

by **Carol Jago**

What Skills Help You Analyze a Character's Qualities?

Some characters are unforgettable. Often readers feel they know fictional characters almost as well as they know real people. This only happens when you take time to visualize what the characters look like and draw inferences from what they do. It also helps to think about real people these characters remind you of, making connections between what you read and what you know.

Visualizing

Have you ever watched a movie that was based on a book you had read and found that the characters in the movie didn't look the way you imagined they would? The director of the movie may have imagined, or visualized, them differently from you. When you **visualize,** you form mental pictures of the characters, settings, objects, and events described in a story. Visualizing will help you analyze a character's qualities and trace their effect on events in the story.

Descriptive Details Pay attention to the story's **descriptive details**—the details that tell you how something looks, feels, smells, sounds, or tastes. Descriptive details, also called **sensory details,** help you visualize characters and their actions. Use your imagination and the underlined descriptive details to visualize the scene in the following passage:

> I put one arm through one sleeve of the sweater that <u>smells like cottage cheese</u>, and then the other arm through the other and <u>stand there with my arms apart</u> like if the sweater <u>hurts me</u> and it does, all <u>itchy and full of germs</u> that aren't even mine.
>
> from "Eleven" by Sandra Cisneros

Tips for Visualizing Characters

- Look for details—such as precise adjectives and verbs—that help you imagine exactly how the characters look, move, and act. These details will help you identify and analyze characters' qualities and their effect on the plot.

- Try to visualize the characters' facial expressions to help you identify the characters' emotions and reactions.

- Read aloud to hear characters' words. Focus on the mental picture those words create to gain a deeper understanding of *what* characters say and *how* they say it.

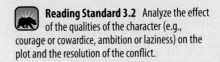

Reading Standard 3.2 Analyze the effect of the qualities of the character (e.g., courage or cowardice, ambition or laziness) on the plot and the resolution of the conflict.

Making Inferences

An **inference** is an educated guess based on evidence and your own experience. When you **make inferences,** you first look for clues that the author provides. Then, you combine those clues with what you already know so that you can recognize what the writer *isn't* telling you directly.

Tips for Making Inferences To make inferences about a character, ask these questions:

- What does the writer tell you about how the character acts, thinks, or dresses? What do you know about people who act, think, or dress that way? What do your answers to these questions tell you about the character's personality?
- What does the writer tell you about conflicts the character faces? What does your experience tell you about those or similar conflicts?
- What do the writer's and your own experience tell you about how the character's qualities influence the conflict and its resolution?

It Says/I Say/And So Strategy An It Says/I Say/And So chart will help you combine details in the story (external information) with what you know (internal information) in order to make good inferences. Follow these steps:

1. As you read, think about what the text tells you. List that information under "It Says."

2. List related information you know as a result of your experiences under "I Say."

3. Combine clues in the text with your own knowledge to make inferences. List your inferences under "And So."

It Says . . .	I Say . . .	And So . . .

Connecting to Characters

As you read, look for ways to relate the story's characters and plot to your own life. Connecting to characters by recognizing qualities that you share with them will help you better understand their personalities and the effect of those qualities on the conflict and its resolution.

Making connections to the lives of people you know, to other stories (novels, movies, TV shows), and to people and events in the world will also strengthen your understanding of characters and events. Use these sentence starters to connect to the text:

- This character is like me because _____.
- I faced a similar conflict when _____.
- This character reminds me of _____.

Your Turn Apply Reading Skills

1. If a girl in a story didn't follow her teacher's directions, what inferences might you make about the girl's character traits, or qualities, and their effect on the conflict? Why?

2. Think about a fictional character to whom you felt a strong connection. Did any of the character's traits remind you of yourself or of someone you know? How did that make the story more meaningful to you?

Now go to the Skills in Action: Reading Model

Learn It Online
Use *PowerNotes* as a visual aid to boost your learning at:

go.hrw.com   H6-103   **Go**

Read with a Purpose Read this story to discover why a boy insists on being called Bud instead of Buddy.

from
BUD, NOT BUDDY
by
Christopher Paul Curtis

HERE WE GO AGAIN. We were all standing in line waiting for breakfast when one of the caseworkers came in and *tap-tap-tap*ped down the line. Uh-oh, this meant bad news, either they'd found a foster home for somebody or somebody was about to get paddled. All the kids watched the woman as she moved along the line, her high-heeled shoes sounding like little firecrackers going off on the wooden floor.

Shoot! She stopped at me and said, "Are you Buddy Caldwell?"

I said, "It's Bud, not Buddy, ma'am."

She put her hand on my shoulder and took me out of line. Then she pulled Jerry, one of the littler boys, over. "Aren't you

Literary Focus

Characterization By describing appearance and actions, writers tell you about a character's qualities. Curtis uses the woman's high heels and the firecracker sound they make when she walks to tell you that she has a brisk, no-nonsense personality.

Jerry Clark?" He nodded.

"Boys, good news! Now that the school year has ended, you both have been accepted in new temporary-care homes starting this afternoon!"

Jerry asked the same thing I was thinking. "Together?"

She said, "Why, no. Jerry, you'll be in a family with three little girls . . ."

Jerry looked like he'd just found out they were going to dip him in a pot of boiling milk.

". . . and Bud . . ." She looked at some papers she was holding. "Oh, yes, the Amoses, you'll be with Mr. and Mrs. Amos and their son, who's twelve years old, that makes him just two years older than you, doesn't it, Bud?"

"Yes, ma'am."

She said, "I'm sure you'll both be very happy."

Me and Jerry looked at each other.

The woman said, "Now, now, boys, no need to look so glum. I know you don't understand what it means, but there's a depression going on all over this country. People can't find jobs and these are very, very difficult times for everybody. We've been lucky enough to find two wonderful families who've opened their doors for you. I think it's best that we show our new foster families that we're very . . ."

She dragged out the word very, waiting for us to finish her sentence for her.

Jerry said, "Cheerful, helpful and grateful." I moved my lips and mumbled.

She smiled and said, "Unfortunately, you won't have time for breakfast. I'll have a couple of pieces of fruit put in a bag. In the meantime go to the sleep room and strip your beds and gather all of your things."

Here we go again. I felt like I was walking in my sleep as I followed Jerry back to the room where all the boys' beds were jim-jammed together. This was the third foster home I was going to and I'm used to packing up and leaving, but it still surprises me that there are always a few seconds, right after they tell you you've got to go, when my nose gets all runny and my throat gets all choky and my eyes get all stingy. But the tears coming out doesn't happen to me anymore, I don't know when

Reading Focus

Visualizing The writer provides a vivid and clever comparison to describe the look on Jerry's face. Visualizing Jerry's expression creates a mental image that helps you identify two of his qualities: his fear and his dependence on Bud. The news has taken Jerry by surprise, and he dreads the thought of living in a family with three little girls—and no Bud.

Literary Focus

Characterization Writers use a character's own thoughts and feelings to reveal his or her qualities. Bud shows here that he is sensitive and not as tough as the name Bud might imply.

Reading Model

it first happened, but it seems like my eyes don't cry no more.

Jerry sat on his bed and I could tell that he was losing the fight not to cry. Tears were popping out of his eyes and slipping down his cheeks.

I sat down next to him and said, "I know being in a house with three girls sounds terrible, Jerry, but it's a lot better than being with a boy who's a couple of years older than you. I'm the one who's going to have problems. A older boy is going to want to fight, but those little girls are going to treat you real good. They're going to treat you like some kind of special pet or something."

Jerry said, "You really think so?"

I said, "I'd trade you in a minute. The worst thing that's going to happen to you is that they're going to make you play house a lot. They'll probably make you be the baby and will hug you and do this kind of junk to you." I tickled Jerry under his chin and said, "Ga-ga goo-goo, baby-waby."

Jerry couldn't help but smile. I said, "You're going to be great."

Jerry looked like he wasn't so scared anymore so I went over to my bed and started getting ready.

Even though it was me who was in a lot of trouble I couldn't help but feel sorry for Jerry. Not only because he was going to have to live around three girls, but also because being six is a real rough age to be at. Most folks think you start to be a real adult when you're fifteen or sixteen years old, but that's not true, it really starts when you're around six.

It's at six that grown folks don't think you're a cute little kid anymore, they talk to you and expect that you understand everything they mean. And you'd best understand too, if you aren't looking for some real trouble, 'cause it's around six that grown folks stop giving you little swats and taps and jump clean up to giving you slugs that'll knock you right down and have you seeing stars in the middle of the day. The first foster home I was in taught me that real quick.

Six is a bad time too 'cause that's when some real scary things start to happen to your body, it's around then that your teeth start coming a-loose in your mouth.

You wake up one morning and it seems like your tongue is the first one to notice that something strange is going on, 'cause

Analyzing Visuals

Connecting to the Text
How well do you think this photograph captures the internal conflict both Bud and Jerry are experiencing?

as soon as you get up there it is pushing and rubbing up against one of your front teeth and I'll be doggoned if that tooth isn't the littlest bit wiggly.

At first you think it's kind of funny, but the tooth keeps getting looser and looser and one day, in the middle of pushing the tooth back and forth and squinching your eyes shut, you pull it clean out. It's the scariest thing you can think of 'cause you lose control of your tongue at the same time and no matter how hard you try to stop it, it won't leave the new hole in your mouth alone, it keeps digging around in the spot where that tooth used to be. You tell some adult about what's happening but all they do is say it's normal. You can't be too sure, though, 'cause it shakes you up a whole lot more than grown folks think it does when perfectly good parts of your body commence to loosening up and falling off of you.

Reading Focus

Connecting to Characters
Relating to a character's qualities, feelings, or conflicts can help you read for deeper meaning. Think about ways that you can connect with Bud. Did you share some of Bud's thoughts when you were losing your "baby teeth"? Have you ever been reassured by an adult who didn't really seem to understand how you felt? Writers often use common human experiences to make their characters come to life for readers.

Unless you're as stupid as a lamppost you've got to wonder what's coming off next, your arm? Your leg? Your neck? Every morning when you wake up it seems a lot of your parts aren't stuck on as good as they used to be.

Six is real tough. That's how old I was when I came to live here in the Home. That's how old I was when Momma died.

Read with a Purpose   What has happened in the narrator's life that makes *Bud* a more appropriate name for him than *Buddy*?

MEET THE WRITER

Christopher Paul Curtis
(1953–   )

From Storyteller to Author

Christopher Paul Curtis writes highly acclaimed young-adult novels. *The Watsons Go to Birmingham—1963,* set at the height of the civil rights movement, won many awards. *Bud, Not Buddy* captured both the Coretta Scott King Book Award and the Newbery Medal. Yet Curtis never set out to write novels especially for young adults. "When I wrote *Bud, Not Buddy,*" he says, "I just had a story to tell and wanted to tell it. I didn't think of it as a children's book, per se."

From Factory to Fiction

Curtis grew up in Flint, Michigan. After high school, he began working on the assembly line at Fisher Body, a historic automotive factory, while attending the University of Michigan. Curtis explains how his experiences at the factory led him to write:

"When I was in the factory, I was keeping a journal. Writing took my mind off the line. I hated being in the factory. When I was writing, I forgot I was there."

Think About the Writer   How do you think Curtis's early experiences, like factory work, might have influenced his writing?

Wrap Up

Reading Standard 3.2 Analyze the effect of the qualities of the character (e.g., courage or cowardice, ambition or laziness) on the plot and the resolution of the conflict.

Into Action: Make Inferences About a Character's Qualities

On a separate sheet of paper, complete this chart with details from the story. Then, use these details and your own ideas to make an inference about Bud's qualities and the kind of person he is.

Character's name:	Bud
Character's looks:	
Character's words:	
Character's actions:	
Character's thoughts:	
Responses of others:	
Writer's direct comments:	
My Inference:	Bud is . . .

Talk About . . .

1. Explain to a partner how you visualize Bud, Jerry, and the caseworker. Try to use each Academic Vocabulary word listed at right at least once in your discussion.

Write About . . .

Answer the following questions about *Bud, Not Buddy*. For definitions of the underlined Academic Vocabulary words, see the column at right.

2. What obvious feelings and qualities do Jerry and Bud show that the caseworker does not acknowledge? How do these qualities affect the plot?

3. What qualities enable Bud to help Jerry adapt to the idea of living with three girls and resolve his conflict?

4. What details reveal that Bud's circumstances have been difficult ever since his mother died?

Writing Skills Focus
Think as a Reader/Writer

In Chapter 2, you will meet many unforgettable characters. The Writing Skills Focus activities on the Preparing to Read pages will help you analyze the qualities that define these characters. Then, on the Applying Your Skills pages, you'll have the opportunity to write about the characters or to practice creating characters of your own.

Academic Vocabulary for Chapter 2

Talking and Writing About Character

Academic Vocabulary is the language you use to write and talk about literature. Use these words to discuss the stories you read in this chapter. The words are underlined throughout the chapter.

adapt (uh DAPT) *v.*: change ideas or behavior to fit a new situation. *Characters' traits affect how well they adapt to new challenges.*

circumstance (SUR kuhm stans) *n.*: event or condition that affects a person. *Weak characters are often defeated by terrible circumstances, but strong characters are not.*

obvious (AHB vee uhs) *adj.*: easy to notice or understand. *A character's personality is sometimes obvious from his or her actions.*

qualities (KWAHL uh teez) *n.*: traits; distinguishing characteristics. *A character's qualities can affect a story's resolution.*

Your Turn

Copy the words from the Academic Vocabulary list into your *Reader/Writer Notebook*. Then, use each word in a sentence about a person you admire. Keep these words in mind as you read the stories in Chapter 2.

Preparing to Read

Eleven

by **Sandra Cisneros**

Cumpleaños de Lala y Tudi (Lala and Tudi's Birthday Party) by Carmen Lomas Garza.
Oil on canvas (36″ × 48″).

What Do **You** Think?

What can you learn about someone's character from how he or she acts in an embarrassing situation?

 QuickWrite

What is your definition of an "embarrassing moment"? Describe a situation at school that might embarrass a student your age.

Reader/Writer Notebook

Use your **RWN** to complete the activities for this selection.

Literary Skills Focus

Character and Point of View This story lets you into the mind of its main character, Rachel, who is also the narrator. Rachel uses the **first-person point of view,** speaking as "I." Because Rachel is telling the story herself, you'll only know what Rachel tells you. Her viewpoint will color what she tells you about herself, other characters, and events. As she tells her story, Rachel expresses her thoughts and feelings about her situation. As you read, think about how Rachel's attitudes and behavior affect the conflict and its resolution.

Reading Skills Focus

Making Inferences Writers seldom make everything <u>obvious</u> in a story. You must figure out some things by **making inferences:** combining clues in the text with what you know to make an educated guess. Making inferences helps you uncover a character's <u>qualities</u> and their effects on the plot.

Into Action Use a chart like this one to make at least two inferences about characters and events in "Eleven." An example is provided for you. Add rows to make inferences based on other details.

It Says . . . (in the story)	I Say . . . (what you know)	And So . . . (inference)
It's Rachel's birthday.	Birthdays are usually happy days that people look forward to.	Rachel must be excited about her birthday.

TechFocus As you read, imagine how Rachel would tell her story in a video diary. What would she say? How would she say it?

Writing Skills Focus

Think as a Reader/Writer

Find It in Your Reading In her narration, Rachel uses language that appeals to the senses and helps reveal her <u>qualities</u> and feelings: "My face all hot and spit coming out of my mouth because I can't stop the little animal noises from coming out of me." This image connects to sight, touch, and hearing. List other sensory details from this story in your *Reader/Writer Notebook.*

Vocabulary

rattling (RAT lihng) *v.* used as *adj.:* shaking and hitting together. *Rachel felt all the years of her life rattling inside her like coins in a metal box.*

raggedy (RAG uh dee) *adj.:* torn and in poor condition. *The sweater was worn and raggedy.*

invisible (ihn VIHZ uh buhl) *adj.:* not able to be seen. *Rachel wished that she could be invisible and disappear.*

Language Coach

Figurative Language In "Eleven," Rachel uses many descriptive comparisons to communicate how she feels on her birthday. When she says that growing older is "like an onion or like the rings inside a tree trunk," she is using similes, a type of figurative language. A **simile** is a comparison of unlike things that uses a word such as *like, as, than,* or *resembles.* Which of the Vocabulary example sentences above contains a simile?

Learn It Online
Strengthen your vocabulary with Word Watch at:

go.hrw.com | H6-111 | **Go**

Sandra Cisneros
(1954–)

Writing from Experience

Sandra Cisneros was born in Chicago, where she grew up speaking both Spanish and English. Although she sometimes had a hard time in school, she eventually became a teacher and a highly acclaimed writer. Today she lives in San Antonio, Texas. Her childhood experiences, her family, and her Mexican American heritage all find a place in her writing.

"Inside I'm Eleven"

In much of her writing, Cisneros explores the feeling of being shy and out-of-place. In this quotation, she describes what she sees when she looks back on her childhood:

> "When I think how I see myself, I would have to say at age eleven. I know I'm older on the outside, but inside I'm eleven. I'm the girl in the picture with the skinny arms and a crumpled shirt and crooked hair. I didn't like school because all they saw was the outside of me."

Think About the Writer What details convince you that Cisneros really *does* remember what being eleven is like?

Preview the Selection

On the day this story takes place, **Rachel,** the story's main character and narrator, is turning eleven years old. Rachel's birthday is complicated by a difficult circumstance at school.

Eleven

by **Sandra Cisneros**

What they don't understand about birthdays and what they never tell you is that when you're eleven, you're also ten, and nine, and eight, and seven, and six, and five, and four, and three, and two, and one. And when you wake up on your eleventh birthday you expect to feel eleven, but you don't. You open your eyes and everything's just like yesterday, only it's today. And you don't feel eleven at all. You feel like you're still ten. And you are—underneath the year that makes you eleven.

Like some days you might say something stupid, and that's the part of you that's still ten. Or maybe some days you might need to sit on your mama's lap because you're scared, and that's the part of you that's five. And maybe one day when you're all grown up maybe you will need to cry like if you're three, and that's okay. That's what I tell Mama when she's sad and needs to cry. Maybe she's feeling three. **A**

Because the way you grow old is kind of like an onion or like the rings inside a tree trunk or like my little wooden dolls that fit one inside the other, each year inside the next one. That's how being eleven years old is. **B**

You don't feel eleven. Not right away. It takes a few days, weeks even, sometimes even months before you say Eleven when they ask you. And you don't feel smart eleven, not until you're almost twelve. That's the way it is.

Only today I wish I didn't have only eleven years rattling inside me like pennies in a tin Band-Aid box. Today I wish I was one hundred and two instead of eleven because if I was one hundred and two I'd have known what to say when Mrs. Price put the red sweater on my desk. I would've known how to tell her it wasn't mine instead of just sitting there with that look on my face and nothing coming out of my mouth. **C**

A **Literary Focus** **Character and Point of View** What do you learn about the narrator from the thoughts and feelings she shares in this paragraph?

B **Read and Discuss** The author has given you a lot of information about what it means to be eleven. What point is she trying to make?

C **Literary Focus** **Character** What conflict does Rachel face? How does her behavior help create this conflict?

Vocabulary **rattling** (RAT lihng) *v.* used as *adj.:* shaking and hitting together.

"Whose is this?" Mrs. Price says, and she holds the red sweater up in the air for all the class to see. "Whose? It's been sitting in the coatroom for a month."

"Not mine," says everybody. "Not me."

"It has to belong to somebody," Mrs. Price keeps saying, but nobody can remember. It's an ugly sweater with red plastic buttons and a collar and sleeves all stretched out like you could use it for a jump-rope. It's maybe a thousand years old and even if it belonged to me I wouldn't say so.

Maybe because I'm skinny, maybe because she doesn't like me, that stupid Sylvia Saldívar says, "I think it belongs to Rachel." An ugly sweater like that, all raggedy and old, but Mrs. Price believes her. Mrs. Price takes the sweater and puts it right on my desk, but when I open my mouth nothing comes out. **D**

"That's not, I don't, you're not . . . Not mine," I finally say in a little voice that was maybe me when I was four. **E**

"Of course it's yours," Mrs. Price says. "I remember you wearing it once." Because she's older and the teacher, she's right and I'm not.

Not mine, not mine, not mine, but Mrs. Price is already turning to page thirty-two, and math problem number four. I don't know why but all of a sudden I'm feeling sick inside, like the part of me that's three wants to come out of my eyes, only I squeeze them shut tight and bite down on my teeth real hard and try to remember today I am eleven, eleven. Mama is making a cake for me for tonight, and when Papa comes home everybody will sing Happy birthday, happy birthday to you. **F**

But when the sick feeling goes away and I open my eyes, the red sweater's still sitting there like a big red mountain. I move the red sweater to the corner of my desk with my ruler. I move my pencil and books and eraser as far from it as possible. I even move my chair a little to the right. Not mine, not mine, not mine.

In my head I'm thinking how long till lunchtime, how long till I can take the red sweater and throw it over the schoolyard fence, or leave it hanging on a parking meter, or bunch it up into a little ball and toss it in the alley. Except when math period ends Mrs. Price says loud and in front of everybody, "Now, Rachel, that's enough," because she sees I've shoved the red sweater to the tippy-tip corner of my desk and it's hanging all over the edge like a waterfall, but I don't care.

> But when the sick feeling goes away and I open my eyes, the red sweater's still sitting there like a big red mountain.

D **Reading Focus** Making Inferences What details in the story suggest why Rachel feels so strongly about the sweater?

E **Literary Focus** Character and Point of View What do the narrator's description of herself and her speech in this and the previous paragraph tell you about her qualities?

F **Read and Discuss** How do Rachel's thoughts here support the inference you made about her strong feelings?

Vocabulary raggedy (RAG uh dee) *adj.*: torn and in poor condition.

Portrait of a Girl by Rosa Ibarra.

Analyzing Visuals   **Connecting to the Text**   What qualities does this girl seem to share with Rachel?

"Rachel," Mrs. Price says. She says it like she's getting mad. "You put that sweater on right now and no more nonsense."

"But it's not—"

"Now!" Mrs. Price says.

This is when I wish I wasn't eleven, because all the years inside of me—ten, nine, eight, seven, six, five, four, three, two, and one—are pushing at the back of my eyes when I put one arm through one sleeve of the sweater that smells like cottage cheese, and then the other arm through the other and stand there with my arms apart like if the sweater hurts me and it does, all itchy and full of germs that aren't even mine.

That's when everything I've been holding in since this morning, since when Mrs. Price put the sweater on my desk, finally lets go, and all of a sudden I'm crying in front of everybody. I wish I was invisible but I'm not. I'm eleven and it's my birthday today and I'm crying like I'm three in front of everybody. I put my head down on the desk and bury my face in my stupid clown-sweater arms. My face all hot and spit coming out of my mouth because I can't stop the little animal noises from coming out of me, until there aren't any more tears left in my eyes, and it's just my body shaking like when you have the hiccups and my whole head hurts like when you drink milk too fast.

But the worst part is right before the bell rings for lunch. That stupid Phyllis Lopez, who is even dumber than Sylvia Saldívar, says she remembers the red sweater is hers! I take it off right away and give it to her, only Mrs. Price pretends like everything's okay. **G**

Today I'm eleven. There's a cake Mama's making for tonight, and when Papa comes home from work we'll eat it. There'll be candles and presents and everybody will sing Happy birthday, happy birthday to you, Rachel, only it's too late. **H**

I'm eleven today. I'm eleven, ten, nine, eight, seven, six, five, four, three, two, and one, but I wish I was one hundred and two. I wish I was anything but eleven, because I want today to be far away already, far away like a runaway balloon, like a tiny *o* in the sky, so tiny-tiny you have to close your eyes to see it. **I**

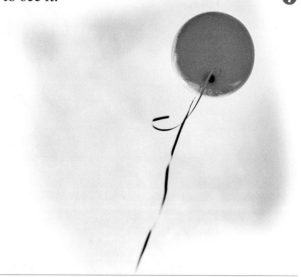

G Read and Discuss How does this situation connect with the inference you made about Rachel's feelings?

H Reading Focus Making Inferences What does Rachel mean by "it's too late"? Make an inference from clues in the story and your thoughts about how you might feel in a similar situation.

I Read and Discuss How has this birthday ended up for Rachel?

Vocabulary invisible (ihn VIHZ uh buhl) *adj.*: not able to be seen.

Applying Your Skills

Reading Standard 3.2 Analyze the effect of the qualities of the character (e.g., courage or cowardice, ambition or laziness) on the plot and the resolution of the conflict.

Eleven
Literary Response and Analysis

Reading Skills Focus
Quick Check

1. What does Mrs. Price put on Rachel's desk?
2. What mistake has Mrs. Price made?

Read with a Purpose

3. What happens to Rachel that upsets her so much in class? How does this event affect her feelings about her eleventh birthday?

Reading Skills: Making Inferences

4. How do you think Rachel gets along with the other students? How does she feel about herself? Review your It Says/I Say/And So chart to answer both questions and to identify Rachel's qualities. (Look for other details to add under "It Says.")

It Says . . . (in the story)	I Say . . . (what you know)	And So . . . (inference)
Rachel calls Sylvia "stupid."		
Rachel calls herself "skinny."		

Literary Skills Focus
Literary Analysis

5. **Interpret** Rachel says that "when you're eleven, you're also ten, and nine," and so on. What does she mean?

6. **Infer** What assumptions does Mrs. Price seem to make about Rachel? Why didn't Rachel just refuse to put on the sweater?

Literary Skills: Character and Point of View

7. **Analyze** Identify Rachel's major qualities. How does she reveal these qualities through her thoughts and feelings as well as her actions? If the story were told from the **point of view** of Phyllis Lopez or Mrs. Price, what might you *not* learn about Rachel?

8. **Analyze** What **external conflict** does Rachel face? How is this problem also an **internal conflict**?

9. **Interpret** Explain how Rachel's qualities affect the conflict and its **resolution.** How do her reactions make the situation worse?

Literary Skills Review: Setting

10. **Interpret** What is the role of **setting** in this story? Explain whether or not this story could take place somewhere else.

Writing Skills Focus
Think as a Reader/Writer
Use It in Your Writing Using sensory details to reveal characters' qualities, write a paragraph about an imaginary embarrassing situation.

What Do You Think Now

Explain whether you think Rachel did "the right thing" in an embarrassing situation. What could she have done differently?

Reading Standard 1.2 Identify and interpret figurative language and words with multiple meanings. **1.5** Understand and explain "shades of meaning" in related words (e.g., *softly* and *quietly*).

Vocabulary Development

Shades of Meaning

Writers choose words based on their **shades of meaning** and their **connotations.** A word's **connotations** are the feelings and ideas that we associate with the word. For example, Rachel calls the red sweater "ugly." Someone who didn't hate the sweater might say it was "plain" or "unattractive." *Unattractive* means "not pretty or pleasing." *Ugly* is a much stronger word. It suggests the sweater is disgusting or repulsive, as the word has very negative connotations.

Your Turn

rattling
raggedy
invisible

Here are some words that mean more or less the same thing as *raggedy* (which Rachel uses to describe the sweater): *old, tattered, torn, shabby,* and *scruffy.* All the words have different shades of meaning, and none has a positive connotation when applied to a sweater. Some of the words, however, are more negative than others. Put these words in order, starting with the one that seems the *least* negative and ending with the one that seems the *most* negative. Include *raggedy* in the list.

For each remaining Vocabulary word (*rattling, invisible*), identify three or four synonyms—words with similar meanings. Then, list the words in order of their shades of meaning and their connotations, from least negative to most negative. Use a thesaurus or a dictionary to help you find synonyms for each Vocabulary word.

Language Coach

Figurative Language Read this simile from "Eleven":

"But when the sick feeling goes away and I open my eyes, the red sweater's still sitting there *like a big red mountain*."

Remember that a **simile** is a comparison of unlike things that uses a comparing word such as *like, as, than,* or *resembles.* A **metaphor** is another example of figurative language, but unlike a simile, it compares unlike things without using any comparison words. A metaphor says that something *is* something else: The ugly red sweater is a mountain, casting its shadow of disappointment over my birthday. Come up with four of your own figurative descriptions of the sweater in "Eleven." Write two of them as similes and two as metaphors.

Academic Vocabulary

Talk About . . .

With a partner, discuss the <u>circumstance</u> that makes Rachel feel as if her birthday is ruined. What makes it <u>obvious</u> that Mrs. Price has a particular view of Rachel? Use the underlined Academic Vocabulary words in your discussion.

Grammar Link

Adjective Phrases: Adding Word Power

Just as one person working alone can accomplish only so much, one word working alone has its limitations. The adjective *large* can tell you that a cat is big, but what does *large* really mean? Adjectives like *large* or *small* don't pack a lot of power. They don't tell you *how* large or *how* small something is or *what* it looks like. That's why we need adjective phrases. An **adjective phrase** is a group of words that, like an adjective, describes (or modifies) a noun or a pronoun. Adjective phrases add power to descriptions by answering questions like these.

What kind?	Which one?
How many?	How much?

An adjective phrase can tell you much more about the "large" cat:

EXAMPLE   a large cat *with a fluffy striped tail as long as my arm*

Your Turn

Using your imagination, add more details to the nouns below by inserting an adjective phrase to expand on each adjective in italics.

1. *lonely* dog
2. *hungry* shark
3. *broken* chair
4. *tall* tree

Writing Application   Go back to the work you did for the Writing Skills Focus on page 117, and add adjective phrases to make your description of an embarrassing moment even more vivid.

CHOICES

As you respond to the Choices, use these **Academic Vocabulary** words as appropriate: <u>adapt</u>, <u>circumstance</u>, <u>obvious</u>, <u>qualities</u>.

REVIEW
Write a Scene

Partner Work   With a partner, list <u>qualities</u> that characterize either Phyllis Lopez or Mrs. Price. Start your list by making inferences based on clues in the story, but use your imagination to develop the character and add qualities to your list. Then, choose one scene in the story, and rewrite it from that character's point of view. The character should serve as the narrator, speaking as "I." Be sure to show how the character's qualities affect plot events and the resolution of the conflict.

CONNECT
Describe a Birthday

Timed ⌞Writing   What's *your* idea of a memorable birthday? Based on your own experiences or just on your imagination, describe your idea of the best, worst, most unusual, or funniest birthday. Use sensory details to describe this birthday.

EXTEND
Create a Video Diary

TechFocus   Work with a partner to <u>adapt</u> this story as an entry in Rachel's video diary. Write a script, and film the diary entry in one take. Be sure to capture Rachel's <u>qualities</u> and voice.

Learn It Online
Describe a birthday through a digital story. Find out how online at:

go.hrw.com   H6-119   **Go**

THE
KING
OF
MAZY
MAY

by **Jack London**

Reader/Writer Notebook

Use your **RWN** to complete the activities for this selection.

Reading Standard 3.2 Analyze the effect of the qualities of the character (e.g., courage or cowardice, ambition or laziness) on the plot and the resolution of the conflict.

Literary Skills Focus

Character and Motivation When we talk about a character's **motivation,** we're referring to the reasons for his or her actions. The main character's <u>qualities</u> and motivation drive the plot because they influence his or her choices and actions. This adventure story, like most such stories, focuses on an **external conflict**—in this case, a struggle between the main character, fourteen-year-old Walt Masters, and a group of men who want something that isn't theirs. As you read, think about the effect of Walt's qualities and motivation on the conflict's **resolution,** or outcome. How does Walt's determination and courage influence what happens?

Reading Skills Focus

Visualizing When you read, **visualizing,** or picturing in your mind, can bring a story to life by making characters and events seem real to you. Visualizing makes things clear. As a result, it can help you recognize a character's <u>qualities</u> and their effect on the plot.

Into Action In your *Reader/Writer Notebook,* draw a concept map like this one, and record descriptions that help you visualize Walt and events in the plot.

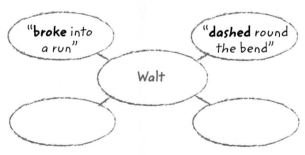

Writing Skills Focus

Think as a Reader/Writer

Find It in Your Reading Writers can help you visualize characters and events by using descriptive language. Strong verbs often help you see the action that takes place in a story. Record examples of this story's precise verbs in your *Reader/Writer Notebook.*

Vocabulary

endured (ehn DURD) *v.:* withstood or held up under. *The dogs endured months of freezing weather.*

claim (klaym) *n.:* piece of land a prospector takes as his or her own. *Walt had to help the old man protect his claim.*

adjoining (uh JOY nihng) *adj.:* next to. *His claim was the one adjoining Walt's.*

stampede (stam PEED) *n.:* sudden rush. *A stampede of people arrived in search of gold.*

Language Coach

Multiple-Meaning Words Some words have several, often related, meanings. For example, the word *endured* means "withstood" in this story, but it can also mean "continued existing; lasted." Which other Vocabulary word from the list above is a multiple-meaning word?

Learn It Online
Watch a video introduction to this story at:
go.hrw.com   H6-121   **Go**

Jack London
(1876–1916)

Seeking Adventure

Jack London grew up very poor in Oakland, California, and worked in a factory as a young man. When he was seventeen, he worked on a seal-hunting ship, which gave him a taste for travel and adventure. Later, he tried a life of hitching rides on trains, which eventually landed him in jail for thirty days. Determined to turn his life around, London studied hard, read a great deal, and began to write seriously.

The "Gold Mine" of Success

In 1897, London went to the Yukon Territory in Canada to witness the Gold Rush. This trip would turn out to be a "gold mine" of ideas he would draw on for the rest of his life. London became one of the most popular writers in the United States. As his stories were translated into many languages, his popularity expanded all over the world.

London died young, at age forty. While his life was short, he had always expressed a desire to live his life to the fullest.

> "I would rather be a superb meteor, every atom of me in magnificent glow, than a sleepy and permanent planet."

Think About the Writer

What does the quotation reveal about London's character and his qualities?

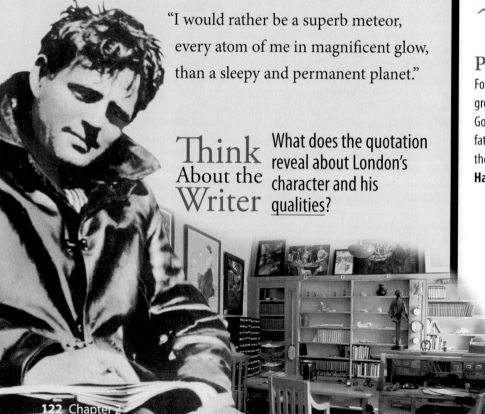

Build Background

Gold Rush This story is set on the Mazy May Creek in the Klondike, an area in the Yukon Territory of Canada. This is where the Yukon Gold Rush took place, starting at the very end of the nineteenth century. Thousands of people headed for this treacherous region of northern Canada to seek their fortune by "staking claims," or marking and claiming spots where they found gold. In this story, newcomers are trying to "jump claims," meaning they are trying to steal the rights to the gold in specific areas from those who have already claimed the land.

Preview the Selection

Fourteen-year-old **Walt Masters** has grown up along the Yukon during the Gold Rush. <u>Circumstances</u> cause Walt's father to leave him alone to look after their claim and their neighbor **Loren Hall's** claim.

Read with a Purpose Read this story to learn how a young man takes a big risk to help out a friend during the Klondike Gold Rush.

THE KING OF MAZY MAY

by **Jack London**

Walt Masters is not a very large boy, but there is manliness in his make-up, and he himself, although he does not know a great deal that most boys know, knows much that other boys do not know.

He has never seen a train of cars nor an elevator in his life, and for that matter he has never once looked upon a cornfield, a plow, a cow, or even a chicken. He has never had a pair of shoes on his feet, nor gone to a picnic or a party, nor talked to a girl. But he has seen the sun at midnight, watched the ice jams on one of the mightiest of rivers, and played beneath the northern lights, the one white child in thousands of square miles of frozen wilderness.

Walt has walked all the fourteen years of his life in sun-tanned, moose-hide moccasins, and he can go to the Indian camps and "talk big" with the men, and trade calico and beads with them for their precious furs.

A **Literary Focus** **Character** From the way London describes him at the beginning of the story, what kind of person would you say Walt is?

He can make bread without baking powder, yeast, or hops, shoot a moose at three hundred yards, and drive the wild wolf dogs fifty miles a day on the packed trail.

Last of all, he has a good heart, and is not afraid of the darkness and loneliness, of man or beast or thing. His father is a good man, strong and brave, and Walt is growing up like him. **B**

Walt was born a thousand miles or so down the Yukon, in a trading post below the Ramparts. After his mother died, his father and he came on up the river, step by step, from camp to camp, till now they are settled down on the Mazy May Creek in the Klondike country. Last year they and several others had spent much toil and time on the Mazy May, and endured great hardships; the creek, in turn, was just beginning to show up its richness and to reward them for their heavy labor. But with the news of their discoveries, strange men began to come and go through the short days and long nights, and many unjust things they did to the men who had worked so long upon the creek. **C**

Si Hartman had gone away on a moose hunt, to return and find new stakes driven and his claim jumped. George Lukens and his brother had lost their claims in a like

> Walt Masters's father had recorded his claim at the start, so Walt had nothing to fear.

manner, having delayed too long on the way to Dawson to record them. In short, it was the old story, and quite a number of the earnest, industrious prospectors had suffered similar losses.

But Walt Masters's father had recorded his claim at the start, so Walt had nothing to fear now that his father had gone on a short trip up the White River prospecting for quartz. Walt was well able to stay by himself in the cabin, cook his three meals a day, and look after things. Not only did he look after his father's claim, but he had agreed to keep an eye on the adjoining one of Loren Hall, who had started for Dawson to record it.

Loren Hall was an old man, and he had no dogs, so he had to travel very slowly. After he had been gone some time, word came up the river that he had broken through the ice at Rosebud Creek, and frozen his feet so badly that he would not be able to travel for a couple of weeks. Then Walt Masters received the news that old Loren was nearly all right again, and about to move on afoot for Dawson as fast as a weakened man could.

Walt was worried, however; the claim was liable to be jumped at any moment

---

B **Reading Focus** **Visualizing** How do you picture Walt at this point in the story?

C **Read and Discuss** What is the author setting up here? What seems to be the problem?

Vocabulary **endured** (ehn DURD) *v.*: withstood or held up under.
claim (klaym) *n.*: piece of land a prospector takes as his or her own.
adjoining (uh JOY nihng) *adj.*: next to.

because of this delay, and a fresh stampede had started in on the Mazy May. He did not like the looks of the newcomers, and one day, when five of them came by with crack dog teams and the lightest of camping outfits, he could see that they were prepared to make speed, and resolved to keep an eye on them. So he locked up the cabin and followed them, being at the same time careful to remain hidden.

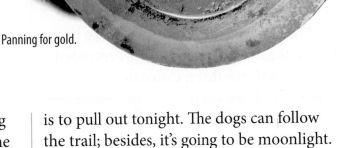

Panning for gold.

He had not watched them long before he was sure that they were professional stampeders, bent on jumping all the claims in sight. Walt crept along the snow at the rim of the creek and saw them change many stakes, destroy old ones, and set up new ones. **D**

In the afternoon, with Walt always trailing on their heels, they came back down the creek, unharnessed their dogs, and went into camp within two claims of his cabin. When he saw them make preparations to cook, he hurried home to get something to eat himself, and then hurried back. He crept so close that he could hear them talking quite plainly, and by pushing the underbrush aside he could catch occasional glimpses of them. They had finished eating and were smoking around the fire.

"The creek is all right, boys," a large, black-bearded man, evidently the leader, said, "and I think the best thing we can do is to pull out tonight. The dogs can follow the trail; besides, it's going to be moonlight. What say you?"

"But it's going to be beastly cold," objected one of the party. "It's forty below zero now."

"An' sure, can't ye keep warm by jumpin' off the sleds an' runnin' after the dogs?" cried an Irishman. "An' who wouldn't? The creek's as rich as a United States mint! Faith, it's an ilegant chanst to be gettin' a run fer yer money! An' if ye don't run, it's mebbe you'll not get the money at all, at all."

"That's it," said the leader. "If we can get to Dawson and record, we're rich men; and there is no telling who's been sneaking along in our tracks, watching us, and perhaps now off to give the alarm. The thing for us to do is to rest the dogs a bit, and then hit the trail as hard as we can. What do you say?" **E**

D Literary Focus Motivation Why does Walt start following the newcomers? How are his fears about them confirmed?

E Literary Focus External Conflict What external conflicts do the men around the campfire assume they will face?

Vocabulary **stampede** (stam PEED) *n.*: sudden rush.

The King of Mazy May **125**

Evidently the men had agreed with their leader, for Walt Masters could hear nothing but the rattle of the tin dishes which were being washed. Peering out cautiously, he could see the leader studying a piece of paper. Walt knew what it was at a glance—a list of all the unrecorded claims on Mazy May. Any man could get these lists by applying to the gold commissioner at Dawson.

"Thirty-two," the leader said lifting his face to the men. "Thirty-two isn't recorded, and this is thirty-three. Come on; let's take a look at it. I saw somebody had been working on it when we came up this morning."

Three of the men went with him, leaving one to remain in camp. Walt crept carefully after them till they came to Loren Hall's shaft. One of the men went down and built a fire on the bottom to thaw out the frozen gravel, while the others built another fire on the dump and melted water in a couple of gold pans. This they poured into a piece of canvas stretched between two logs, used by Loren Hall in which to wash his gold.

In a short time a couple of buckets of dirt were sent up by the man in the shaft, and Walt could see the others grouped anxiously about their leader as he proceeded to wash it. When this was finished, they stared at the broad streak of black sand and yellow gold grains on the bottom of the pan, and one of them called excitedly for the man who had remained in camp to come. Loren Hall had struck it rich and his claim was not yet recorded. It was plain that they were going to jump it. **F**

Walt lay in the snow, thinking rapidly. He was only a boy, but in the face of the threatened injustice to old lame Loren Hall he felt that he must do something. He waited and watched, with his mind made up, till he saw the men begin to square up new stakes. Then he crawled away till out of hearing, and broke into a run for the camp of the stampeders. Walt's father had taken their own dogs with him prospecting, and the boy knew how impossible it was for him to undertake the seventy miles to Dawson without the aid of dogs. **G**

Gaining the camp, he picked out, with an experienced eye, the easiest running sled and started to harness up the stampeders' dogs. There were three teams of six each, and from these he chose ten of the best. Realizing how necessary it was to have a good head dog, he strove to discover a leader amongst them; but he had little time in which to do it, for he could hear the voices of the returning men. By the time the team was in shape and everything ready, the claim-

> He was only a boy, but in the face of the threatened injustice to old lame Loren Hall he felt that he must do something.

F **Read and Discuss** What does Walt learn here? Why didn't Loren record his claim as Walt's father had?

G **Literary Focus** **Character** How does the writer show you that Walt is not "only a boy"? What qualities does Walt display?

Yukon Gold Rush

Gold rush is the term used to describe a great number of people "rushing" to a place where gold is discovered. The greatest gold rush in American history began with the discovery of gold at Sutter's Mill, California, on January 24, 1848. Almost fifty years later, gold was discovered in the Klondike region of Canada's Yukon Territory. On August 17, 1896, George W. Carmack found a large amount of gold in a creek he named the Bonanza.

Word that gold had been discovered in the Yukon did not reach the United States until July 1897. However, the news created a rush of thousands of people heading north on horseback. The thousands of unexpected visitors caused a famine in the region, and many of those hoping to find gold did not survive.

Some of the first people to arrive were able to stake their claims and mine a rich vein of gold. Others could not find a claim or did not find gold in their claims. Some of these people continued on to find gold in Alaska. Others, unable to endure the difficulties, returned empty-handed to the United States.

By 1928, more than $200 million worth of gold had been mined from the area. Several working mines continue to operate in the Yukon today.

The Granger Collection, New York.

Ask Yourself

Why do you think so many people risked their lives to look for gold?

---

jumpers came into sight in an open place not more than a hundred yards from the trail, which ran down the bed of the creek. They cried out to Walt, but instead of giving heed to them, he grabbed up one of their fur sleeping robes, which lay loosely in the snow, and leaped upon the sled. **(H)**

"Mush! Hi! Mush on!" he cried to the animals, snapping the keen-lashed whip among them.

The dogs sprang against the yoke straps, and the sled jerked under way so suddenly as to almost throw him off. Then it curved into the creek, poising perilously on the runner. He was almost breathless with suspense, when it finally righted with a bound and sprang ahead again. The creek bank was high and he could not see the men, although he could hear the cries of the men and knew they were running to cut him off.

(H) Literary Focus Motivation Why does Walt take the men's sled? What is he planning to do?

Analyzing Visuals

Connecting to the Text
Why is this snow sculpture a fitting illustration for this story? What aspects of Walt's conflict does it show?

He did not dare to think what would happen if they caught him; he just clung to the sled, his heart beating wildly, and watched the snow rim of the bank above him.

Suddenly, over this snow rim came the flying body of the Irishman, who had leaped straight for the sled in a desperate attempt to capture it; but he was an instant too late. Striking on the very rear of it, he was thrown from his feet, backward, into the snow. Yet, with the quickness of a cat,

he had clutched the end of the sled with one hand, turned over, and was dragging behind on his breast, swearing at the boy and threatening all kinds of terrible things if he did not stop the dogs; but Walt cracked him sharply across the knuckles with the butt of the dog whip till he let go. **❶**

It was eight miles from Walt's claim to the Yukon—eight very crooked miles, for the creek wound back and forth like a snake, "tying knots in itself," as George Lukens

---

❶ **Reading Focus** **Visualizing** How does picturing Walt and the Irishman at this point help you identify their <u>qualities</u>?

said. And because it was so crooked the dogs could not get up their best speed, while the sled ground heavily on its side against the curves, now to the right, now to the left. **J**

Travelers who had come up and down the Mazy May on foot, with packs on their backs, had declined to go round all the bends, and instead had made shortcuts across the narrow necks of creek bottom. Two of his pursuers had gone back to harness the remaining dogs, but the others took advantage of these shortcuts, running on foot, and before he knew it they had almost overtaken him.

"Halt!" they cried after him. "Stop, or we'll shoot!"

But Walt only yelled the harder at the dogs, and dashed round the bend with a couple of revolver bullets singing after him. At the next bend they had drawn up closer still, and the bullets struck uncomfortably near to him but at this point the Mazy May straightened out and ran for half a mile as the crow flies. Here the dogs stretched out in their long wolf swing, and the stampeders, quickly winded, slowed down and waited for their own sled to come up. **K**

Looking over his shoulder, Walt reasoned that they had not given up the chase

for good, and that they would soon be after him again. So he wrapped the fur robe about him to shut out the stinging air, and lay flat on the empty sled, encouraging the dogs, as he well knew how.

At last, twisting abruptly between two river islands, he came upon the mighty Yukon sweeping grandly to the north. He could not see from bank to bank, and in the quick-falling twilight it loomed a great white sea of frozen stillness. There was not a sound, save the breathing of the dogs, and the churn of the steel-shod sled.

> There was not a sound, save the breathing of the dogs, and the churn of the steel-shod sled.

No snow had fallen for several weeks, and the traffic had packed the main river trail till it was hard and glassy as glare ice. Over this the sled flew along, and the dogs kept the trail fairly well, although Walt quickly discovered that he had made a mistake in choosing the leader. As they were driven in single file, without reins, he had to guide them by his voice, and it was evident the head dog had never learned the meaning of "gee" and "haw." He hugged the inside of the curves too closely, often forcing his comrades behind him into the soft snow, while several times he thus capsized the sled. **L**

There was no wind, but the speed at which he traveled created a bitter blast, and with the

---

J **Literary Focus** External Conflict What makes Walt's struggle more difficult in this paragraph?

K **Literary Focus** Character The stampeders threaten to shoot Walt. What qualities does he display by continuing in spite of their threats?

L **Read and Discuss** Which of Walt's decisions is slowing him down and putting him in danger?

thermometer down to forty below, this bit through fur and flesh to the very bones. Aware that if he remained constantly upon the sled he would freeze to death, and knowing the practice of Arctic travelers, Walt shortened up one of the lashing thongs, and whenever he felt chilled, seized hold of it, jumped off, and ran behind till warmth was restored. Then he would climb on and rest till the process had to be repeated.

Looking back he could see the sled of his pursuers, drawn by eight dogs, rising and falling over the ice hummocks[1] like a boat in a seaway. The Irishman and the black-bearded leader were with it, taking turns in running and riding.

Night fell, and in the blackness of the first hour or so, Walt toiled desperately with his dogs. On account of the poor lead dog, they were constantly floundering off the beaten track into the soft snow, and the sled was as often riding on its side or top as it was in the proper way. This work and strain tried his strength sorely. Had he not been in such haste he could have avoided much of it, but he feared the stampeders would creep up in the darkness and overtake him. However, he could hear them yelling to their dogs, and knew from the sounds that they were coming up very slowly.

When the moon rose he was off Sixty Mile, and Dawson was only fifty miles away. He was almost exhausted, and breathed a sigh of relief as he climbed on the sled again. Looking back, he saw his enemies

had crawled up within four hundred yards. At this space they remained, a black speck of motion on the white river breast. Strive as they would, they could not shorten this distance, and strive as he would, he could not increase it.

He had now discovered the proper lead dog, and he knew he could easily run away from them if he could only change the bad leader for the good one. But this was impossible, for a moment's delay, at the speed they were running, would bring the men behind upon him. **Ⓜ**

When he got off the mouth of Rosebud Creek, just as he was topping a rise, the report of a gun and the ping of a bullet on

Analyzing Visuals

Connecting to the Text
What role do dogs like these play in the resolution of Walt's conflict?

1. **ice hummocks** (YS HUHM uhks): small ice hills.

Ⓜ **Read and Discuss** What are the advantages and disadvantages of stopping to replace the lead dog?

the ice beside him told him that they were this time shooting at him with a rifle. And from then on, as he cleared the summit of each ice jam, he stretched flat on the leaping sled till the rifle shot from the rear warned him that he was safe till the next ice jam was reached.

Now it is very hard to lie on a moving sled, jumping and plunging and yawing[2]

---

2. **yawing** (YAW ihng): turning from a straight course.

like a boat before the wind, and to shoot through the deceiving moonlight at an object four hundred yards away on another moving sled performing equally wild antics. So it is not to be wondered at that the black-bearded leader did not hit him.

After several hours of this, during which, perhaps, a score of bullets had struck about him, their ammunition began to give out and their fire slackened. They took greater care, and shot at him at the

N Reading Focus **Visualizing** How does the author's language help you picture this plot event and understand why the men could not hit Walt?

most favorable opportunities. He was also leaving them behind, the distance slowly increasing to six hundred yards.

Lifting clear on the crest of a great jam off Indian River, Walt Masters met with his first accident. A bullet sang past his ears, and struck the bad lead dog.

The poor brute plunged in a heap, with the rest of the team on top of him.

Like a flash Walt was by the leader. Cutting the traces with his hunting knife, he dragged the dying animal to one side and straightened out the team. **O**

He glanced back. The other sled was coming up like an express train. With half the dogs still over their traces, he cried, "Mush on!" and leaped upon the sled just as the pursuers dashed abreast of him.

The Irishman was just preparing to spring for him—they were so sure they had him that they did not shoot—when Walt turned fiercely upon them with his whip.

He struck at their faces, and men must save their faces with their hands. So there was no shooting just then. Before they could recover from the hot rain of blows, Walt reached out from his sled, catching their wheel dog by the forelegs in mid spring, and throwing him heavily. This snarled the

> The other sled was coming up like an express train. With half the dogs still over their traces, he cried, "Mush on!"

team, capsizing the sled and tangling his enemies up beautifully.

Away Walt flew, the runners of his sled fairly screaming as they bounded over the frozen surface. And what had seemed an accident proved to be a blessing in disguise. The proper lead dog was now to the fore, and he stretched low and whined with joy as he jerked his comrades along. **P**

By the time he reached Ainslie's Creek, seventeen miles from Dawson, Walt had left his pursuers, a tiny speck, far behind. At Monte Cristo Island he could no longer see them. And at Swede Creek, just as daylight was silvering the pines, he ran plump into the camp of old Loren Hall.

Almost as quick as it takes to tell it, Loren had his sleeping-furs rolled up, and had joined Walt on the sled. They permitted the dogs to travel more slowly, as there was no sign of the chase in the rear, and just as they pulled up at the gold commissioner's office in Dawson, Walt, who had kept his eyes open to the last, fell asleep. **Q**

And because of what Walt Masters did on this night, the men of the Yukon have become very proud of him, and always speak of him now as the King of Mazy May.

O **Literary Focus** Character and Motivation Why doesn't Walt have any difficulty leaving the wounded animal?

P **Read and Discuss** How does the dog team adapt to having a new leader?

Q **Literary Focus** Character Why does Walt wait until now to close his eyes? What qualities does this action reveal?

Applying Your Skills

Reading Standard 3.2 Analyze the effect of the qualities of the character (e.g., courage or cowardice, ambition or laziness) on the plot and the resolution of the conflict.

The King of Mazy May

Literary Response and Analysis

Reading Skills Focus

Quick Check

1. Why is Walt looking after the claims alone?
2. Does Loren Hall get to make his claim official? Why or why not?
3. Why is Walt called the King of Mazy May?

Read with a Purpose

4. What does Walt risk to help his neighbor?

Reading Skills: Visualizing

5. Review the concept map you filled in as you read. Which descriptions helped you picture Walt and plot events most vividly in your mind? Why? How did these descriptions help you identify Walt's <u>qualities</u>?

Literary Skills Focus

Literary Analysis

6. **Interpret** Why do you think the stampeders try to stake other people's claims? Why don't they find their own place to stake a claim?
7. **Evaluate** Explain whether you think Walt did the right thing by taking the newcomers' dogs. Are there any <u>circumstances</u> in which people might be justified in taking something that's not theirs? Discuss.

Literary Skills: Character and Motivation

8. **Analyze** How does the writer **characterize** Walt's pursuers? What kind of men are they? What <u>qualities</u> do they share?

9. **Analyze** What is Walt's **motivation** for entering into an **external conflict** with the stampeders? Does he remain committed to his decision to reach Dawson before his pursuers do, or does he show any signs of doubt or regret? Explain.
10. **Analyze** Identify Walt's character traits. How do these <u>qualities</u> drive the plot of the story? Would there have been a story if Walt had not been the kind of person he is? Explain.
11. **Analyze** What obstacles does Walt face in his **conflict** with the stampeders? What **motivates** him to overcome these problems?

Literary Skills Review: Suspense

12. **Analyze** **Suspense** is the curiosity and worry you feel about what will happen next in a story. How does London create suspense in this adventure tale?

Writing Skills Focus

Think as a Reader/Writer

Use It in Your Writing What powerful verbs did you notice in the story? Write a paragraph describing an action that might take place in a short story of your own. Use precise verbs to help your readers visualize the characters and the event.

What Do **You Think Now** How did the story affect your ideas about injustice? Would you take action, as Walt did, to make sure justice was done? Explain.

Applying Your Skills

The King of Mazy May

Vocabulary Development

Words with Multiple Meanings

Multiple-meaning words are words with more than one meaning. When you look up a multiple-meaning word in a dictionary, you'll find a numbered list of definitions, often for different parts of speech, as in this example:

> **alarm** (uh LAHRM) *n.* **1.** a piece of equipment that makes a noise to warn people of danger **2.** a feeling of fear that something bad might happen **3.** a warning about something bad or dangerous that is happening   *v.* **1.** make someone feel worried or frightened

If you come across a multiple-meaning word in a sentence and you're not sure which meaning is the one intended, figure out what part of speech the word is. Is it a noun, a verb, or an adjective? Look at its **context,** the words around it, to see if you can determine its part of speech. If you're still confused, review the definitions listed in a dictionary. Then, choose the meaning that fits best in the sentence.

Here is a sentence from "The King of Mazy May." Which definitions of *record* and *alarm* fit best in this context?

> If we can get to Dawson and *record*, we're rich men; and there is no telling who's been sneaking along in our tracks, watching us, and perhaps now off to give the *alarm*.

Your Turn

Two of the words in the list at right have multiple meanings and can be used as different parts of speech. Identify these words. For each word, write two sentences that show two different meanings of the word. Use a dictionary for help.

> endured
> claim
> adjoining
> stampede

Language Coach

Multiple-Meaning Words Read the following sentence, and look for context clues that tell you which meaning of the word is being used.

Walt climbed the hill until he was *topping* the rise.

Ask yourself: "Does the word *topping* describe an action or a thing?"

Academic Vocabulary

Talk About ...
How does Walt's ability to <u>adapt</u> to a variety of <u>circumstances</u> help him survive? Use the underlined Academic Vocabulary words in your discussion.

Learn It Online
Focus on vocabulary. Visit *WordSharp* at:
go.hrw.com   H6-134   **Go**

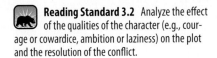

Reading Standard 3.2 Analyze the effect of the qualities of the character (e.g., courage or cowardice, ambition or laziness) on the plot and the resolution of the conflict.

Grammar Link
Verbs That Are Hard to Tackle

Some verbs are predictable. They don't make tricky moves or zigzag back and forth. For that reason we call them **regular verbs.** The **past tense** and **past participle** of a regular verb are formed by adding *–d* or *–ed*. Some other verbs are more troublesome, though. Just as you think you might pin them down, they take a crazy turn and get away. These are **irregular verbs.** These verbs are unpredictable, so you just have to memorize their different forms.

Here are some irregular verbs from "The King of Mazy May":

Base Form	Past	Past Participle
see	saw	(have) seen
drive	drove	(have) driven
run	ran	(have) run
know	knew	(have) known

Your Turn

In the following sentences, find the incorrect verb forms, and replace them with the correct forms.

1. Walt had saw the claim jumpers.
2. He drived the sled as fast as he could.
3. Walt known Loren Hall would travel slowly.
4. He suggested they ran after the dogs to keep warm.

CHOICES

As you respond to the Choices, use these **Academic Vocabulary** words as appropriate: adapt, circumstance, obvious, qualities.

REVIEW
Write a Newspaper Article

Write a newspaper article about Walt's achievement. Describe the main events, explain Walt's motivation, and tell which of his strongest qualities led to the conflict's successful resolution. Be sure to answer the *Who? What? When? Where? Why?* and *How?* questions. Include quotations from Walt, his father, and Loren Hall, and use vivid language. Start with an attention-grabbing headline.

CONNECT
Write a Thank-You Letter

Timed └Writing Imagine that you are Loren Hall. Write a letter in which you express your gratitude to Walt, mentioning key qualities of his character that helped him carry out his amazing deed under dangerous circumstances.

EXTEND
Present a Story to an Audience

TechFocus Imagine that you are Walt and you are speaking to a local group about your experience. Write a speech explaining your actions and describing the things you had to do to adapt to difficult circumstances. Use visuals, such as slides of the area in winter or a videotape of dogsled racing, to illustrate your presentation. Deliver your presentation to your class, acting as Walt.

CRICKET IN THE ROAD

by **Michael Anthony**

Cricket, Sri Lanka (1998) by Andrew Macara.

What Do You Think?

What is the best way to resolve a conflict with friends?

QuickWrite

Write about how you settle conflicts that arise during a game that you play regularly with friends or family. How does the game affect your relationships?

Reader/Writer Notebook

Use your **RWN** to complete the activities for this selection.

Literary Skills Focus

Character and Conflict Characters in stories have qualities—courage or cruelty, for instance—just as people do in real life. What happens in a story depends on the way the characters respond to a **conflict.** There are two basic kinds of conflict. **External conflict** is a struggle between a character and an outside force, such as a rival or an earthquake. **Internal conflict** is a struggle in a character's mind or heart. A character might struggle with shyness, for example, or fear or jealousy.

Literary Perspectives Apply the literary perspective described on page 139 as you read this story.

Reading Skills Focus

Connecting to Characters When you read, **making connections** can deepen your understanding of characters' <u>qualities</u> and conflicts. You may connect the characters and plot events to your own life, to other literature, or to people and events in the world.

Into Action Use a chart like this one to make connections as you read "Cricket in the Road." Some examples are filled in for you.

I can connect	To myself or my friends	To other stories	To situations in the world
The narrator	He is young like me. He is also a boy, like me.	He is tired of rain, like the children in "All Summer in a Day."	I have seen pictures of terrible storms in the Caribbean.

Writing Skills Focus
Think as a Reader/Writer

Find It in Your Reading As you read, locate words, phrases, and sentences that make the storms seem threatening or scary. Write them in your *Reader/Writer Notebook*.

Selo

sweeping with all their **tumult** upon us

torrents of rain

disliked the **downpour** and was afraid of the storm

I stood there, **depressed** about the rain, and then I put Vern's bat and ball underneath the house and went indoors.

Language Coach

Word Families Many words are related—that is, they share a **root**, or base, word. Which word above is related to the word *torrential*?

Learn It Online
Study words in a new way with Word Watch at:

| go.hrw.com | H6-137 | Go |

Michael Anthony
(1930–   )

From Trinidad to England

Like Selo, the main character in "Cricket in the Road," Michael Anthony grew up in Mayaro, Trinidad. He went to a technical school, after which he worked at a foundry, or metal-casting factory. Wanting to be a journalist, Michael Anthony left Trinidad for England in his early twenties, hoping to improve his chances of pursuing a newspaper career. He eventually went to work for the Reuters News Agency. While in England, he married a woman from Trinidad. Anthony moved his family to Brazil for two years before returning to Trinidad in 1970.

A Major Caribbean Writer

Over the course of his career, Michael Anthony has published more than twenty travel books, novels, and books of short stories, and has become a major Caribbean writer. His first novel—*The Games Were Coming*—was published in 1963. The images from his life in Trinidad play an important role in his writing. In the poem "Tree of My Dreams," which recalls his childhood in Mayaro, Anthony observes:

> "The words I weave in memory's name,
>
> I weave. It is the truth."

Think About the Writer

How do you think a writer's childhood home influences what he or she writes about?

Build Background

Trinidad and Tobago   The Caribbean island of Trinidad, where "Cricket in the Road" is set, is just off the coast of Venezuela. Together with the island of Tobago, Trinidad forms a country that has been independent since 1962. Before that, Trinidad and Tobago formed a British colony.

Cricket   The game of cricket is similar to baseball. Its modern form originated in England and spread to many of the British colonies, where it is still popular today.

Preview the Selection

During the rainy season in Trinidad, a boy named **Selo** tries to play cricket with his friends **Vern** and **Amy,** but they are interrupted by a fierce storm.

CRICKET IN THE ROAD

by **Michael Anthony**

In the rainy season we got few chances to play cricket in the road, for whenever we were at the game, the rains came down, chasing us into the yard again. That was the way it was in Mayaro in the rainy season. The skies were always overcast, and over the sea the rain clouds hung low and gray and scowling, and the winds blew in and whipped angrily through the palms. And when the winds were strongest and raging, the low-hanging clouds would become dense and black, and the sea would roar, and the torrents of rain would come sweeping with all their tumult upon us. **(A)**

We had just run in from the rain. Amy and Vern from next door were in good spirits and laughing, for oddly enough they seemed to enjoy the downpour as much as playing cricket in the road. Amy was in our

yard, giggling and pretending to drink the falling rain, with her face all wet and her clothes drenched, and Vern, who was sheltering under the eaves,[1] excitedly jumped out to join her. "Rain, rain, go to Spain," they shouted. And presently their mother, who must have heard the noise and knew,

---

1. **eaves:** lower edges of a roof extending beyond the sides of a building.

(A) Literary Perspectives Author's Techniques How does the writer create a vivid sense of place in this opening paragraph? What is most effective about the author's technique?

Vocabulary **torrents** (TAWR uhnts) *n.:* rushing streams of water.
tumult (TOO muhlt) *n.:* violent disturbance.
downpour (DOWN pawr) *n.:* great amount of rain that falls in a short time.

Literary Perspectives

The following perspective will help you think about the author's techniques used in "Cricket in the Road."

Analyzing an Author's Techniques Writers of fiction use literary tools such as figurative language, imagery, and characterization to help convey the mood, tone, and theme of a work. When you're reading a text from this perspective, you don't need to consider such "ouside the text" factors as the writer's biography or historical or current events. Instead, you focus on exactly what's there in the text: the writer's language. Read closely to keep track of—and appreciate— how the writer uses certain techniques to create literary effects. These effects are what help give the work a theme or message about life. As you read, notice the questions at the bottom of the pages, which will guide you in using this perspective.

appeared from next door, and Vern and Amy vanished through the hedge.

I stood there, depressed about the rain, and then I put Vern's bat and ball underneath the house and went indoors. "Stupes!" I said to myself. I had been batting when the rains came down. It was only when *I* was batting that the rains came down! I wiped my feet so I wouldn't soil the sheets and went up on the bed. I was sitting, sad, and wishing that the rain would really go away—go to Spain, as Vern said—when my heart seemed to jump out of me. A deafening peal[2] of thunder struck across the sky. **B**

Quickly I closed the window. The rain hammered awfully on the rooftop, and I kept tense for the thunder which I knew would break again and for the unearthly flashes of lightning.

Secretly I was afraid of the violent weather. I was afraid of the rain, and of the thunder and the lightning that came with them, and of the sea beating against the headlands,[3] and of the storm winds, and

> THE RAIN HAMMERED AWFULLY ON THE ROOFTOP, AND I KEPT TENSE FOR THE THUNDER WHICH I KNEW WOULD BREAK AGAIN.

of everything being so deathlike when the rains were gone. I started again at another flash of lightning, and before I had recovered from this, yet another terrifying peal of thunder hit the air. I screamed. I heard my mother running into the room. Thunder struck again, and I dashed under the bed. **C**

"Selo! Selo! First bat!" Vern shouted from the road. The rains had ceased and the sun had come out, but I was not quite recovered yet. I brought myself reluctantly to look out from the front door, and there was Vern, grinning and impatient and beckoning to me. **D**

"First bat," he said. And as if noting my indifference, he looked toward Amy, who was just coming out to play. "Who second bat?" he said.

"Me!" I said.

"Me!" shouted Amy almost at the same time.

"Amy second bat," Vern said.

"No, I said 'Me' first," I protested.

Vern grew impatient while Amy and I argued. Then an idea seemed to strike him. He took out a penny from his pocket. "Toss for it," he said. "What you want?" **E**

"Heads," I called.

---

2. **peal:** loud, prolonged sound.
3. **headlands** (HEHD luhndz): points of land extending into a body of water.

B | Literary Focus | Character and Conflict   What external conflict is Selo facing?

C | Reading Focus | Connecting to Characters   Do you have any fears you'd rather your friends didn't know about?

D | Read and Discuss | How do you think the narrator, who is so scared, feels when he sees Vern grinning and ready to play?

E | Literary Perspectives | Author's Techniques   How does the writer show the tension between Selo and Vern and Amy? Do you think their interactions are presented realistically? Explain.

Vocabulary   depressed (diH PREST) *adj.*: very sad.

Analyzing Visuals

Connecting to the Text
How does this picture help you understand the game at the center of this story's conflict?

"Tail," cried Amy. "Tail bound to come!" The coin went up in the air, fell down and overturned, showing tail.

"I'm *not* playing!" I cried, stung. And as that did not seem to disturb enough, I ran toward where I had put Vern's bat and ball and disappeared with them behind our house. Then I flung them with all my strength into the bushes. **F**

When I came back to the front of the house, Vern was standing there dumbfounded. "Selo, where's the bat and ball?" he said.

I was fuming. "I don't know about *any* bat and ball!"

"Tell on him," Amy cried. "He throw them away."

Vern's mouth twisted into a forced smile. "What's an old bat and ball," he said.

But as he walked out of the yard, I saw tears glinting from the corners of his eyes. **G**

For the rest of that rainy season, we never played cricket in the road again. Sometimes the rains ceased and the sun came out brightly, and I heard the voices

F **Literary Focus** Character and Conflict Why does Selo respond to the conflict by throwing the bat and ball into the bushes? What character qualities are revealed by this behavior?

G **Literary Focus** Character and Conflict How has the conflict between the children increased? How do Amy and Vern each respond as a result?

puzzled me how it could be so. For often I had made up my mind I would be brave, but when the thunder cracked I always dashed under the bed. **①**

It was the beginning of the new year when I saw Vern and Amy again. The rainy season was, happily, long past, and the day was hot and bright, and as I walked toward home I saw that I was walking toward Vern and Amy just about to start cricket in the road. My heart thumped violently. They looked strange and new, as if they had gone away, far, and did not want to come back anymore. They did not notice me until I came up quite near, and then I saw Amy start, her face all lit up. **①**

"Vern—" she cried, "Vern look— look Selo!"

Embarrassed, I looked at the ground and at the trees, and at the orange sky, and I was so happy I did not know what to say. Vern stared at me, a strange grin on his face. He was ripping the cellophane paper off a brand new bat. **①**

"Selo, here—*you* first bat," he said gleefully. **①**

And I cried as though it were raining and I was afraid. **①**

of Amy and Vern on the other side of the fence. At such times I would go out into the road and whistle to myself, hoping they would hear me and come out, but they never did, and I knew they were still very angry and would never forgive me. **①**

And so the rainy season went on. And it was as fearful as ever with the thunder and lightning and waves roaring in the bay, and the strong winds. But the people who talked of all this said that was the way Mayaro was, and they laughed about it. And sometimes when through the rain and even thunder I heard Vern's voice on the other side of the fence, shouting "Rain, rain, go to Spain," it

---

① **Reading Focus** **Connecting to Characters** If you or someone you know has ever been in an argument that lasted a long time, how did you feel?

① **Literary Focus** **Character and Conflict** What is Selo's internal conflict in this paragraph?

① **Read and Discuss** Why do you think Vern and Amy "looked strange and new" to Selo?

① **Reading Focus** **Connecting to Characters** Would you be happy if you were Selo? Why?

① **Literary Focus** **Character and Conflict** When Vern gets a new bat, he lets Selo use it first. Why do you think he does it? What words would you use to describe the qualities Vern shows?

① **Read and Discuss** What does the narrator mean when he says, "And I cried as though it were raining and I was afraid"?

Reading Standard 3.2 Analyze the effect of the qualities of the character (e.g., courage or cowardice, ambition or laziness) on the plot and the resolution of the conflict.

Cricket in the Road

Literary Response and Analysis

Reading Skills Focus
Quick Check

1. How does Selo react to the storm?
2. What does Selo do with Vern's bat and ball?
3. How do Vern and Amy behave toward Selo at the end of the story?

Read with a Purpose

4. How real did the relationship of these three friends seem to you? What did you think of the way they resolved their conflict?

Reading Skills: Connecting to Characters

5. Circle the connections in your chart that were most helpful in strengthening your understanding of the characters and plot. What did you learn from these connections?

I can connect	To myself or my friends	To other stories	To situations in the world
The narrator	He is young like me. He is also a boy, like me.	He is tired of rain, like the children in "All Summer in a Day."	⭕ I have seen pictures of terrible storms in the Caribbean.

Literary Skills Focus
Literary Analysis

6. **Interpret** What do you think Selo learns from his conflict with his friends? Explain whether you think he will let such a <u>circumstance</u> occur again.

7. **Literary Perspectives** Which of the author's techniques do you think most helped make this story successful? Consider the imagery that describes the storm, the descriptions of the characters' interactions, the dialogue, and the "voice" of Selo, the first-person narrator.

Literary Skills: Character and Conflict

8. **Analyze** List all the **conflicts** you can find in the story, and identify whether each conflict is **external** or **internal.** Explain the <u>circumstance</u> that caused each conflict.

9. **Analyze** Identify Selo's and Vern's major <u>qualities</u>. Which of these traits contribute to the **conflict** between the children? Which help put an end to the conflict? How do each character's <u>qualities</u> bring about the **resolution** of his conflict?

Literary Skills Review: Setting

10. **Analyze** Describe the setting of the story—its time and place. How does the setting influence the conflict and its resolution?

Writing Skills Focus
Think as a Reader/Writer

Use It in Your Writing Review the notes about the storm you recorded in your *Reader/Writer Notebook*. Use precise details to describe a scene in which you are confronted by something you fear.

What Do **You Think Now** Do you think you might handle a conflict with a friend differently after reading this story? Why or why not?

Cricket in the Road

Vocabulary Development

Shades of Meaning

Read these two sentences and discuss the differences between them:

- The rain made Ben feel sad.
- The rain made Ben feel depressed.

Even though both sentences tell you how Ben feels about the rain, the second sentence suggests a deeper emotion than the first.

Recognizing different **shades of meaning** between words helps you pick the right word to use when you're writing. It also helps you understand the writer's meaning as you read.

Your Turn

Read each of the sentences below. Then, choose a word from the pair in parentheses to complete each sentence. Note: You may find that in some sentences either word could be used, depending on what is meant. Be prepared to explain why you chose each word.

torrents
tumult
downpour
depressed

1. We played in the (rain/downpour) until our mother told us to come inside.
2. We got drenched in the (rain/downpour) and had to run for shelter.
3. After the man lost his job, he was (depressed/sad) for a long time.
4. Mia was so (depressed/sad) after she finished the last book in the series that she cried.
5. (Drops/Torrents) of rain will not damage the wooden chair.
6. (Drops/Torrents) of rain began to fall, and I saw a woman dash for shelter.

Language Coach

Word Families In word families, related words can serve as different parts of speech. For example, *torrents* is a noun: The rain came down in *torrents*, causing a flood. The related word *torrential* is an adjective: *Torrential* rains caused a flood. You can find related words in a dictionary. Sometimes related words are listed at the end of a word's entry. Other times, related words have separate entries that appear near each other. List related words for the Vocabulary words *tumult* and *depressed*. Use a dictionary for help in creating your lists. Be sure to write down the part of speech of each related word.

Academic Vocabulary

Write About . . .

Write a paragraph explaining which character in the story you think underlines adapts the most to the other characters. How does this help resolve the conflict? What underlines circumstances do you think changed to make the characters come together again? Use the underlined Academic Vocabulary words in your paragraph.

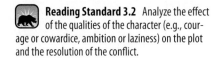

Reading Standard 3.2 Analyze the effect of the qualities of the character (e.g., courage or cowardice, ambition or laziness) on the plot and the resolution of the conflict.

Grammar Link
Adverbs: Make It Specific

If you enjoyed playing a sport and it rained every time it was your turn, how would you tell your friends? "It always rains when I want to play!" "It pours dreadfully hard." Words like *always* and *dreadfully* are adverbs that help you describe the situation more clearly. Just as adjectives are words that make the meaning of a noun or a pronoun more specific, an adverb makes the meaning of a verb, adjective, or another adverb more specific.

Adverbs answer the following questions:

Where?	How often?	To what extent?
When?	*or*	*or*
How?	How long?	How much?

EXAMPLES: We played cricket *outside*. (*Outside* modifies the verb *played* and tells *where*.)

The thunder was *terribly* loud. (*Terribly* modifies the adjective *loud* and tells *how much*.)

Your Turn _____

Read each of the sentences below, and identify the adverb and the word or words each modifies.

EXAMPLE: My heart thumped violently.

> violently—thumped

1. The winds whipped angrily through the palms.
2. I was sitting sadly on the bed.
3. Rain still poured beyond the window.
4. He slowly opened the door and let himself out.

CHOICES

As you respond to the Choices, use these **Academic Vocabulary** words as appropriate: adapt, circumstance, obvious, qualities.

REVIEW
Write a Reflective Essay
Timed ⌛ Writing Imagine that you are Selo one month after this story ends. Write a paragraph in which you discuss your conflict with Vern and Amy and its resolution. How do you think your reactions and behavior added to the conflict? If you could relive that time, what would you do differently? What is your view of the way Vern resolved the conflict? End by explaining what you have learned.

CONNECT
Write a Script
With a partner, write a script in which an older Selo tries to persuade his younger cousin to adapt to the rainy season and not be so afraid of storms. Act out the script, and alternate characters with your partner.

EXTEND
Take a Different Point of View
Group Discussion With a group of classmates, discuss what you think Vern and Amy were saying, doing, and thinking while they were not playing with Selo. Consider the circumstance that caused them to stop playing with Selo and their reactions when they saw him again in the beginning of the new year.

BLANCA FLOR

by **Angel Vigil**

What Do You Think?

When do people risk their lives to save another person?

QuickWrite

Think of true and fictional stories about rescuers. What kind of people are they? Why do they risk their lives to save others? Write down your ideas.

Reader/Writer
Notebook
Use your **RWN** to complete the
activities for this selection.

Reading Standard 3.2 Analyze the effect of the qualities of the character (e.g., courage or cowardice, ambition or laziness) on the plot and the resolution of the conflict.

Literary Skills Focus

Characterization The way writers reveal characters' <u>qualities</u>, or traits such as bravery or generosity or stubborness, is called **characterization.** Writers reveal their characters' qualities through the characters' appearance, speech, actions, thoughts, and feelings, and the responses of other characters. Sometimes writers also tell us directly what characters are like. In plays, like *Blanca Flor*, writers rely on dialogue, or conversation between characters, to tell us about characters' thoughts, feelings, and even their actions.

Stage directions—notes within parentheses or brackets that aren't read aloud in a performance—can provide information about characters' actions and reactions. The writer of this play also uses a narrator to tell us about the characters and events. As you read, think about how the characters' behavior drives the action in the play.

Literary Perspectives Apply the literary perspective described on page 149 as you read this play.

Reading Skills Focus

Visualizing When you read a play, try to **visualize,** or picture in your mind, the characters and plot events. You'll need to read all of the dialogue, stage directions, and narrator's parts to get the full experience of this play.

Into Action Use details from the dialogue, stage directions, and the narrator's descriptions to help you visualize the characters and their actions. Place the details in a chart as you read.

Juanito	
Blanca Flor	"young woman," "took out her brush and began to brush his hair," "cradled Juanito in her arms"

Writing Skills Focus
Think as a Reader/Writer

Find It in Your Reading Because *Blanca Flor* is a play, the story is told almost entirely through dialogue. As you read, note lines of dialogue that help you define the characters' <u>qualities</u>.

Vocabulary

valiant (VAL yuhnt) *adj.:* determined; brave. *Juanito made a valiant effort to help Blanca Flor.*

barren (BAR uhn) *adj.:* unable to bear crops or fruit. *Don Ricardo had a barren field.*

flourish (FLUR ihsh) *n.:* sweeping movement. *Don Ricardo left with a flourish.*

apprehensively (ap rih HEHN sihv lee) *adv.:* fearfully; uneasily. *Blanca Flor looked around apprehensively.*

Language Coach
Spanish Words in English
American English has been borrowing words from Spanish for a long time. Many of these words relate to foods, places, and animals. A *tortilla* (tawr TEE yuh), for example, is a flat Mexican bread made from cornmeal or flour. Look for other words in this play that come from Mexican culture.

Learn It Online
Preview this play by watching the video introduction at:

go.hrw.com   H6-147   **Go**

Angel Vigil

(1947–   )

A Family of Storytellers

Angel Vigil was born in New Mexico and was raised "in a large, traditional Hispanic extended family, with loving grandparents and plenty of aunts and cousins." Storytelling was an important part of his family life. In his book *The Corn Woman: Stories and Legends of the Hispanic Southwest,* Vigil explains how he was influenced by family stories:

> "I was amazed to discover that my living relatives were sources of folklore. . . . I felt it was my calling to do what I could to make sure that the rich oral tradition of my childhood would continue through my generation."

Vigil is an award-winning educator, author, and storyteller. Most of the legends and folk tales he retells—sometimes in the form of plays such as *Blanca Flor*—come from the Hispanic oral tradition. Vigil is also a performer and stage director and serves as chairman of the Fine and Performing Arts Department and director of drama at Colorado Academy in Denver.

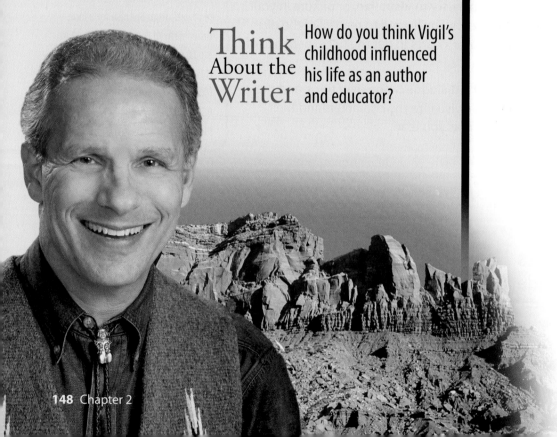

Think About the Writer How do you think Vigil's childhood influenced his life as an author and educator?

Build Background

Although *Blanca Flor* is based on a traditional European tale, the play also draws on Hispanic folklore. The mischievous little trickster known as a *duende* (DWEHN day) makes trouble for people in stories told throughout the Hispanic Southwest.

Preview the Selection

Blanca Flor tells the story of **Juanito,** a young man who leaves his parents, **Doña Arlette** and **Don Ramon,** to seek his fortune. After crossing paths with a mischievous creature called the **Duende,** Juanito meets a beautiful young woman named **Blanca Flor** and a man named **Don Ricardo.**

Read with a Purpose Read this play to discover what happens to a young man named Juanito when he leaves home to seek his fortune.

BLANCA FLOR

by **Angel Vigil**

Characters (in order of appearance)

The Narrator

Juanito, a young man

The Duende, a gnomelike, mischievous creature who lives in the forest

Blanca Flor, a young woman

Don[1] Ricardo, an evil man

Don Ramon, the father of Juanito

Doña[2] Arlette, the mother of Juanito

Two Doves, actors in costume

Scene 1.

In the Forest.

The Narrator. *Blanca Flor,* "White Flower." There never was a story with such a beautiful name as this story of Blanca Flor. At the beginning of our story, a young man named Juanito has left home to seek his fortune in the world. With the blessing of his parents to aid and protect him, he has begun what will be a fantastic adventure. At the beginning of his journey, he wanders into a forest and stops by a stream to rest and eat some of the tortillas his mother had packed for his journey. **Ⓐ**

---

1. **Don** (dahn): Spanish for "Sir" or "Mr."
2. **Doña** (DOH nyah): Spanish for "Lady" or "Madam."

Ⓐ Literary Perspectives **Archetypes** What literary archetype is presented by the narrator in the first paragraph? What other stories have you read that begin in a similar way?

Literary Perspectives

The following perspective will help you think about the characters and events in *Blanca Flor*.

Analyzing Archetypes No matter what culture or time period they are from, many stories share similar themes and characteristics. You're certain to recognize some familiar story elements in this play. These familiar features are called **archetypes** (AHR kuh typs) or **motifs** (moh TEEFS): patterns that appear again and again in literature. Why do so many stories share common elements? Perhaps it's because human beings everywhere share the same basic emotions and find satisfaction in the familiar but powerful ways certain stories play out.

Look for these archetypes: a son who is seeking his fortune; an enchanted forest; characters with magical powers; an evil curse; a powerful villain; transformations; events occurring in threes; magical objects. As you read, be sure to answer the Literary Perspectives questions at the bottom of this selection's pages.

[JUANITO *enters and walks around the stage as if looking for a comfortable place to rest. He finally decides upon a spot and sits down. He takes out a tortilla from his traveling bag and he begins to talk to himself.*] **Ⓑ**

Juanito. Whew! I'm hot. This river looks like a good spot to rest a while. I'm so tired. Maybe this journey wasn't such a good idea. Right now I could be home with *la familia* eating a good supper that *mamacita* cooked for us. But no, I'm out in the world seeking my fortune. So far I haven't found very much, and all I have to show for my efforts are two worn-out feet and a tired body . . . oh, and don't forget (*holding up a dried tortilla*) a dried-out tortilla . . . (*He quickly looks around as if startled.*) What was that? (*He listens intently and hears a sound again.*) There it is again. I know I heard something . . .

[*As* JUANITO *is talking,* THE DUENDE *enters, sneaking up behind him.*]

Juanito. Must be my imagination. I've been out in the woods too long. You know, if you're alone too long, your mind starts to play tricks on you. Just look at me. I'm talking to my tortilla and hearing things . . .
The Duende (*in a crackly voice*). Hello.
Juanito. Yikes! Who said that! (*He turns around quickly and is startled to see* THE DUENDE *behind him.*) Who are you?
The Duende (*with a mischievous twinkle in his eye*). Hello.

Juanito. Hello . . . who, who are you? And where did you come from?

[THE DUENDE *grabs the tortilla out of* JUANITO's *hand and begins to eat it. During the rest of the scene* THE DUENDE *continues to eat tortillas.*]

Juanito. Hey, that's my tortilla.
The Duende (*in a playful manner*). Thank you very much. Thank you very much.
Juanito (*to the audience*). He must be a forest Duende. I've heard of them. They're spirits who live in the wood and play tricks on humans. I better go along with him or he might hurt me. (*He offers* THE DUENDE *another tortilla.* THE DUENDE *takes the tortilla and begins to eat it, too.*) I hope he's not too hungry. If he eats all my tortillas, I won't have any left, and it'll be days before I get food again. I'll have to eat wild berries like an animal. (*He reaches for the tortilla and* THE DUENDE *hits his hand.*) Ouch, that hurt!
The Duende. Looking for work, eh?
Juanito. Now I know he's a Duende. He can read minds. **Ⓒ**
The Duende. No work here. Lost in the forest. No work here.
Juanito. I know that. We're in the middle of the forest. But I know there'll be work in the next town.
The Duende. Maybe work right here. Maybe.
Juanito. Really. Where?

[THE DUENDE *points to a path in the forest.* JUANITO *stands up and looks down the path.*]

Ⓑ Literary Focus Dialogue and Stage Directions How do you know these are stage directions? Who are they for, and what information do they provide?

Ⓒ Read and Discuss Why do you think the author has Juanito talk directly to the audience here?

Juanito. There's nothing down that path. I've been down that path and there is nothing there.

The Duende. Look again. Look again. Be careful. Be careful. (*He begins to walk off, carrying the bag of tortillas with him.*)

Juanito. Hey, don't leave yet. What type of work? And where? Who do I see? Hey, don't leave yet!

The Duende (THE DUENDE *stops and turns*). Be careful. Danger. Danger. (*He exits.*)

Juanito. Hey! That's my bag of tortillas. Oh, this is great. This is really going to sound good when I get back home. My tortillas? . . . Oh, they were stolen by a forest Duende. Not to worry . . . (*He yells in the direction of the departed* DUENDE.) And I'm not lost! . . . This is great. Lost and hungry and no work. I guess I'm never going to find my fortune in the world. But what did he mean about work . . . and be careful . . . and danger. I've been down that path and there was nothing there . . . I don't think there was anything there. Oh well, there is only one way to find out. It certainly can't get much worse than things are now, and maybe there is work there.

[JUANITO *exits, in the direction of the path* THE DUENDE *indicated.*] **Ⓓ**

Scene 2.
Farther in the Forest.

The Narrator. In spite of the Duende's warning, Juanito continued on the path of danger. As he came into a clearing, he came to a house and saw a young woman coming out of it. **Ⓔ**

[JUANITO *enters,* BLANCA FLOR *enters from the opposite side of the stage and stops, remaining at the opposite side of the stage.*]

Juanito. Where did this house come from? I was here just yesterday and there was no house here. I must really be lost and turned around. (*He sees the young woman and waves to her.*) Hey! Come here. Over here!

Analyzing Visuals **Connecting to the Text** How does this forest creature's expression reflect the Duende's character?

Ⓓ **Read and Discuss** What have you learned so far about Juanito and his circumstances?

Ⓔ **Reading Focus** **Visualizing** How does the playwright's use of a narrator help you visualize the action?

[BLANCA FLOR *runs to* JUANITO.]

Blanca Flor (*with fear in her voice*). How did you find this place? You must leave right away. The owner of this place is gone, but he will return soon. He leaves to do his work in the world, but he will return unexpectedly. If he finds you here, you'll never be able to leave. You must leave right away.

Juanito. Why? I haven't done anything.

Blanca Flor. Please, just leave. And hurry!

Juanito. Who are you? And why are you here?

Blanca Flor. I am Blanca Flor. My parents died long ago, and I am kept by this man to pay off their debts to him. I have to work day and night on his farm until I can be free. But he is mean, and he has kept prisoner others who have tried to free me. He makes them work until they die from exhaustion.

Juanito. Who would be so mean?

Blanca Flor. His name is Don Ricardo.

[DON RICARDO *enters, suddenly and with great force.*] **F**

Don Ricardo (*addressing* JUANITO). Why are you here! Didn't she tell you to leave!

Blanca Flor (*scared*). Don't hurt him. He is lost in the forest and got here by mistake. He was just leaving.

Don Ricardo. Let him answer for himself. Then I will decide what to do with him.

Juanito (*gathering all his courage*). Yes, she did tell me to leave. But . . . but I am in the world seeking my fortune and I am looking for work. Is there any work for me to do here?

Don Ricardo. Seeking your fortune! They always say that, don't they, Blanca Flor. Well, I will give you the same chance I have given others. For each of three days, I will give you a job. If in three days you have completed the jobs, then you may leave. If not, then you will work here with me until you are dead. What do you say, fortune-seeker?

Blanca Flor (*pulling* JUANITO *aside*). Do not say yes. You will never leave here alive. Run and try to escape.

Juanito. But what about you? You are more trapped than anybody.

Blanca Flor. That is not your worry. Just run and try to escape.

Juanito (*suddenly turning back to* DON RICARDO). I will do the work you ask.

Don Ricardo (*laughing*). Blanca Flor, it is always your fault they stay. They all think they will be able to set you free. Well, let's give this one his "fair" chance. (*To* JUANITO) Here is your first job. See that lake over there? Take this thimble (*he gives a thimble to* JUANITO) and use it to carry all the water in the lake to that field over there. **G**

Juanito. You want me to move a lake with a thimble?!

Don Ricardo. You wanted work, fortune-seeker. Well, this is your job. Have it finished by morning or your fate will be the same as all the others who tried to save poor Blanca Flor. (*He exits.*)

Juanito. What type of man is he? I have heard legends of evil men who keep people captive, and in my travels I heard many stories of young men seeking their fortunes who

---

F Literary Perspectives **Archetypes** What has happened so far in this scene that is familiar from other stories or plays? Explain whether you see more than one kind of archetype here.

G Literary Focus **Characterization** Why is Don Ricardo laughing? What does this reveal about the kind of person he is?

were never seen again, but I always thought they were just stories.

Blanca Flor. You have had the misfortune to get lost in a terrible part of the forest. Didn't anyone warn you to stay away from here?

Juanito. Yes . . . one person did. But I thought he was a forest Duende, and I didn't really believe him.

Blanca Flor. It was a forest Duende. In this part of the forest there are many creatures with magic. But my keeper, his magic is stronger than any of ours.

Juanito. Ours? . . . What do you mean, ours? Are you part of the magic of this forest?

Blanca Flor. Do not ask so many questions. The day is passing by, and soon it will be morning.

Juanito. Morning. I'm supposed to have moved the lake by then. I know this job is impossible, but while God is in his heaven there is a way. I will do this job. And when I am done, I will help you escape from here.

[JUANITO *and* BLANCA FLOR *exit.*] **H**

Scene 3.
The Next Morning.

JUANITO *and* BLANCA FLOR *enter. As* THE NARRATOR *speaks,* JUANITO *and* BLANCA FLOR *act out the scene as it is described.*

The Narrator. Juanito took the thimble and started to carry the water from the lake. He worked as hard as he could, but soon he began to realize that the job really was an impos-

> You want me to move a lake with a thimble?!

sible one, and he knew he was doomed. He sat down and began to cry because his luck had abandoned him and because his parents' blessings offered no protection in that evil place. Blanca Flor watched Juanito's **valiant** effort to move the water. As she watched him crying, her heart was touched, and she decided to use her powers to help him. She knew that it was very dangerous to use her powers to help Juanito and to cross Don Ricardo, but she felt it was finally time to end her own torment. As Juanito cried, Blanca Flor took out her brush and began to brush his hair. She cradled Juanito in her arms and her soothing comfort soon put him to sleep . . .

[*As soon as* JUANITO *is asleep,* BLANCA FLOR *gently puts his head down and leaves, taking the thimble with her.*]

The Narrator. When Juanito awoke, he frantically looked for the thimble and, not finding it, ran to the lake. When he reached the lake, he stood at its banks in amazement. All the water was gone. He looked over to the other part of the field, and there stood a lake where before there was nothing. He turned to look for Blanca Flor, but instead there was Don Ricardo.

[DON RICARDO *enters.*]

Don Ricardo (*in full force and very angry*). This must be the work of Blanca Flor, or else you have more power than I thought. I know Blanca Flor is too scared to ever use her pow-

---

ers against me, so as a test of your powers, tomorrow your next job will not be so easy. See that barren ground over on the side of the mountain? You are to clear that ground, plant seeds, grow wheat, harvest it, grind it, cook it, and have bread for me to eat before I return. You still have your life now, but I better have bread tomorrow. (*He exits, with a flourish.*) [JUANITO *exits.*]

Scene 4.
The Next Morning.

As THE NARRATOR *speaks,* JUANITO *and* BLANCA FLOR *enter and act out the scene as it is described.*

The Narrator. Immediately upon waking the next morning, Juanito tried to move the rocks in the field, but they were impossible to move because of their great size. Once again, Juanito knew that his efforts

were useless. He went over to the new lake and fell down in exhaustion. As he lay in the grass by the lake, Blanca Flor came to him once more and began to brush his hair. Soon, Juanito was asleep.

[BLANCA FLOR *exits.*]

The Narrator. As before, when he awoke, Juanito dashed to the field to make one last attempt to do his work. When he got there, he again stopped in amazement. The field was clear of rocks, and the land had been planted and harvested. As he turned around, there stood Blanca Flor.

[BLANCA FLOR *enters.*]

BLANCA FLOR (*She hands a loaf of bread to* JUANITO.) Give this to Don Ricardo.
Juanito. How did you do this?

---

1 **Literary Focus** **Characterization** The narrator tells you about Juanito's attempt to finish his work. What does this reveal about his character's qualities?

Vocabulary **barren** (BAR uhn) *adj.:* unable to bear crops or fruit.
flourish (FLUR ihsh) *n.:* sweeping movement.

[DON RICARDO *enters, quickly.*]

Don Ricardo. What do you have?
Juanito (*shaking with fear*). Just . . . just this loaf of bread. (*Giving the bread to* DON RICARDO) Here is the bread you asked for.
Don Ricardo (*very angry*). This is the work of Blanca Flor. This will not happen again. Tomorrow, your third job will be your final job, and even the powers of Blanca Flor will not help you this time! (*He exits.*)
Blanca Flor. Believe me, the third job will be impossible to do. It will be too difficult even for my powers. We must run from here if there is to be any chance of escaping his anger. He will kill you because I have helped you. Tonight I will come for you. Be ready to leave quickly as soon as I call for you.

[JUANITO *and* BLANCA FLOR *exit.*] **J**

Scene 5.
Later That Night.

On one side of the stage, JUANITO *sits waiting. On the other side,* BLANCA FLOR *is in her room grabbing her traveling bag. As she leaves her room, she turns and mimes spitting three times as* THE NARRATOR *describes the action.*

The Narrator. Late that night, as Juanito waited for her, Blanca Flor packed her belongings into a bag. Before she left the house, she went to the fireplace and spat three times into it.

[BLANCA FLOR *joins* JUANITO.]

Blanca Flor (*quietly calling*). Juanito . . . Juanito.
Juanito. Blanca Flor, is it time?
Blanca Flor. Yes. We must leave quickly, before he finds out I am gone, or it will be too late.
Juanito. Won't he know you are gone as soon as he calls for you?
Blanca Flor. Not right away. I've used my powers to fool him. But it won't last long. Let's go!

[JUANITO *and* BLANCA FLOR *exit.*]

The Narrator. When Don Ricardo heard the noise of Juanito and Blanca Flor leaving, he called out . . .
Don Ricardo (*from offstage*). Blanca Flor, are you there?
The Narrator. The spit she had left in the fireplace answered.
Blanca Flor (*from offstage*). Yes, I am here.
The Narrator. Later, Don Ricardo called out again.
Don Ricardo (*from offstage*). Blanca Flor, are you there?
The Narrator. For a second time, the spit she had left in the fireplace answered.
Blanca Flor (*from offstage*). Yes, I am here.
The Narrator. Still later, Don Ricardo called out again, a third time.
Don Ricardo (*from offstage*). Blanca Flor, are you there?
The Narrator. By this time, the fire had evaporated Blanca Flor's spit, and there was no answer. Don Ricardo knew that Blanca Flor was gone, and that she had run away with Juanito. He saddled his horse and gal-

J Read and Discuss | What has happened during the last two days?

Blanca Flor **155**

loped up the path to catch them before they escaped from his land. **(K)**

Scene 6.

In the Forest.

JUANITO *and* BLANCA FLOR *enter, running and out of breath.*

Juanito. Blanca Flor, we can rest now. We are free.

Blanca Flor. No, Juanito, we will not be free until we are beyond the borders of Don Ricardo's land. As long as we are on his land, his powers will work on us.

Juanito. How much farther?

Blanca Flor. Remember the river where you met The Duende? That river is the border. Across it we are free.

Juanito. That river is still really far. Let's rest here for a while.

Blanca Flor. No, he is already after us. We must keep going. I can hear the hooves of his horse.

Juanito (*he looks around desperately*). Where? How can that be?

Blanca Flor. He is really close. Juanito, come stand by me. Quickly!

Juanito (*still looking around*). I don't hear anything.

Blanca Flor (*grabbing him and pulling him to her*). Juanito! Now!

[*As* THE NARRATOR *describes the action,* JUANITO *and* BLANCA FLOR *act out the scene.* BLANCA FLOR *does not actually throw a brush. She mimes throwing the brush and the action.*]

The Narrator. Blanca Flor looked behind them and saw that Don Ricardo was getting closer. She reached into her bag, took her brush, and threw it behind her. The brush turned into a church by the side of the road. She then cast a spell on Juanito and turned him into a little old bell ringer. She turned herself into a statue outside the church. **(L)**

[DON RICARDO *enters, as if riding a horse.*]

Don Ricardo (*addressing the bell ringer* [JUANITO]). Bell ringer, have you seen two young people come this way recently? They would have been in a great hurry and out of breath.

Juanito (*in an old man's voice*). No . . . I don't think so. But maybe last week, two young boys came by. They stopped to pray in the church . . . Or was it two girls. I don't know. I am just an old bell ringer. Not many people actually come by this way at all. You're the first in a long time.

Don Ricardo. Bell ringer, if you are lying to me you will be sorry. (*He goes over to the statue* [BLANCA FLOR], *who is standing very still, as a statue. He examines the statue very closely and then addresses the bell ringer* [JUANITO].) Bell ringer, what saint is this a statue of? The face looks very familiar.

Juanito. I am an old bell ringer. I don't remember the names of all the saints. But I do know that the statue is very old and has been here a long time. Maybe Saint Theresa or Saint Bernadette.

Don Ricardo. Bell ringer, if you are lying, I will be back! (*He exits.*)

(K) Literary Focus Characterization What does this scene reveal about Blanca Flor?

(L) Reading Focus Visualizing Can you imagine the action occurring here? What details help you visualize the scene?

Juanito. Adiós, Señor!

[BLANCA FLOR *breaks her pose as a statue and goes to* JUANITO.]

Blanca Flor. Juanito, Juanito. The spell is over.
Juanito. What happened? I did hear the angry hooves of a horse being ridden hard.
Blanca Flor. We are safe for a while. But he will not give up, and we are not free yet.

[JUANITO *and* BLANCA FLOR *exit.*] **ⓜ**

Scene 7.
Farther into the Forest.

The Narrator. Blanca Flor and Juanito desperately continued their escape. As they finally stopped for a rest, they had their closest call yet.

[BLANCA FLOR *and* JUANITO *enter.*]

Juanito. Blanca Flor, please, let's rest just for a minute.
Blanca Flor. OK. We can rest here. I have not heard the hooves of his horse for a while now.
Juanito. What will he do if he catches us?
Blanca Flor. He will take us back. I will be watched more closely than ever, and you will—
Juanito (*sadly*). I know. Was there ever a time when you were free? Do you even remember your parents?

Blanca Flor. Yes. I have the most beautiful memories of my mother, our house, and our animals. Every day, my father would saddle the horses and together we would— **Ⓝ**
Juanito. Blanca Flor . . . I hear something.
Blanca Flor (*alarmed*). He's close. Very close.

[As THE NARRATOR *describes the action,* JUANITO *and* BLANCA FLOR *act out the scene.* BLANCA FLOR *does not actually throw a comb. She mimes throwing the comb and the action.*]

Analyzing Visuals **Connecting to the Text** What object in this picture holds Blanca Flor's power?

ⓜ Literary Focus Characterization What did you just find out about Blanca Flor's character?

Ⓝ Literary Focus Characterization Take a close look at this dialogue between Juanito and Blanca Flor. What does it tell you about what they think of each other?

Blanca Flor **157**

The Narrator. Blanca Flor quickly opened her bag and threw her comb behind her. Immediately the comb turned into a field of corn. This time she turned Juanito into a scarecrow, and she turned herself into a stalk of corn beside him.

[DON RICARDO *enters, as if riding a horse.*]

Don Ricardo. Where did they go? I still think that the bell ringer knew more than he was saying. They were just here. I could hear their scared little voices. Juanito will pay for this, and Blanca Flor will never have the chance to escape again . . . Now where did they go? Perhaps they are in this field of corn. It is strange to see a stalk of corn grow so close to a scarecrow. But this is a day for strange things. (*He exits.*)

Blanca Flor. Juanito, it is over again. Let's go. The river is not far. We are almost free.

[JUANITO *breaks his pose as a scarecrow and stretches and rubs his legs as* BLANCA FLOR *looks around* apprehensively.]

Juanito. Blanca Flor, that was close. We have to hurry now. The river is just through these trees. We can make it now for sure if we hurry.

The Narrator. But they spoke too soon. Don Ricardo had gotten suspicious about the field of corn and returned to it. When he saw Juanito and Blanca Flor he raced to catch them.

[DON RICARDO *enters suddenly and sees them.*]

Ⓞ **Read and Discuss** Is the escape plan a success?

Vocabulary **apprehensively** (ap rih HEHN sihv lee) *adv.*: fearfully; uneasily.

Don Ricardo. There you are. I knew something was wrong with that field of corn. Now you are mine.

[*As* THE NARRATOR *describes the action,* JUANITO *and* BLANCA FLOR *act out the scene.* BLANCA FLOR *does not actually throw a mirror. She mimes throwing the mirror and the action.*]

The Narrator. When Blanca Flor saw Don Ricardo, she reached into her bag and took out a mirror, the final object in the bag. She threw the mirror into the middle of the road. Instantly, the mirror became a large lake, its waters so smooth and still that it looked like a mirror as it reflected the sky and clouds. When Don Ricardo got to the lake, all he saw was two ducks, a male and a female, swimming peacefully in the middle of the lake. Suddenly, the ducks lifted off the lake and flew away. As they flew away, Don Ricardo knew that the ducks were Juanito and Blanca Flor, and that they were beyond his grasp. As they disappeared, he shouted one last curse.

[JUANITO *and* BLANCA FLOR *exit.*]

Don Ricardo. You may have escaped, Blanca Flor, but you will never have his love. I place a curse on both of you. The first person to embrace him will cause him to forget you forever! (*He exits.*) **Ⓞ**

Scene 8.
Near Juanito's Home.

BLANCA FLOR *and* JUANITO *enter.*

The Narrator. Disguised as ducks, Blanca Flor and Juanito flew safely away from that evil land and escaped from Don Ricardo. They finally arrived at Juanito's home, and using Blanca Flor's magical powers, they returned to their human selves.

Juanito. Blanca Flor, we are close to my home. Soon we will be finally safe forever. I will introduce you to my family, and we will begin our new life together . . . Blanca Flor, why do you look so sad? We have escaped the evil Don Ricardo, and soon we will be happy forever.

Blanca Flor. We have not escaped. His final curse will forever be over us.

Juanito. Remember, that curse will work only in his own land. You yourself told me that once we were beyond the borders of his land, his powers would have no hold on us.

Blanca Flor. His powers are very great, Juanito.

Juanito. Blanca Flor, you have never explained to me the source of your own powers. Are your powers also gone?

Blanca Flor. The powers have always been in the women of my family. That is why Don Ricardo would not let me leave. He was afraid that I would use my powers against him. I have never been away from that land, so I do not know about my powers in this new land.

Juanito. You will have no need for your powers here. Soon we will be with my family. Wait outside while I go and tell my family that I have returned from seeking my fortune, safe at last. Then I will tell them that the fortune I found was you.

Blanca Flor. Juanito, remember the curse.

Juanito. I am not afraid of any curse. Not with you here with me. All my dreams have come true. Come, let's go meet my family. **Ⓟ**

[JUANITO *and* BLANCA FLOR *exit.*]

Ⓟ Literary Focus **Characterization** What does this dialogue tell you about what Juanito thinks of his adventure now?

Analyzing Visuals

Connecting to the Text
What plot event in the play does this picture illustrate?

Scene 9.
At Juanito's Home.

DON RAMON *and* DOÑA ARLETTE *are sitting at home passing the time with idle talk.*

The Narrator. Juanito's parents had waited patiently for their son to return from seeking his fortune in the world. They did not know that his return home was only the beginning of another chapter of his great adventure.

Doña Arlette. Do you ever think we will hear from Juanito? It has been months since he left to seek his fortune in the world.

Don Ramon. We will hear word soon. I remember when I left home to seek my fortune in the world. Eventually, I found that the best thing to do was return home and make my fortune right here, with my *familia* at my side. Soon he will discover the same thing and you will have your son back.

Doña Arlette. It is easier for a father to know those things. A mother will never stop worrying about her children.

Don Ramon. I worry about the children just as much as you do. But there is no stopping children who want to grow up. He has our blessing and permission to go, and that will be what brings him back safe to us. Soon. You just wait.

[JUANITO *enters. His parents are overjoyed to see him.*]

Juanito. Mama! Papa! I am home.

Doña Arlette. *¡Mi 'jito!*[3]

Don Ramon. Juanito!

[*Overjoyed with seeing* JUANITO, *his parents rush and embrace him.*]   **Q**

Doña Arlette. God has answered my prayers. *Mi 'jito* has returned home safe.

Don Ramon. Juanito, come sit close to us and tell us all about your adventures in the world. What great adventures did you have?

Juanito. I had the greatest adventures. For the longest time I was unlucky and unable to find work but finally I . . . I . . .

Doña Arlette. What is it? Are you OK? Do you need some food?

Juanito. No, I'm OK. It's just that I was going to say something and I forgot what I was going to say.

Don Ramon. Don't worry. If it is truly important, it'll come back.

Juanito. No, I've definitely forgotten what I was going to say. Oh well, it probably wasn't important anyway.

Doña Arlette. Did you meet someone special? Did you bring a young woman back for us to meet?

Juanito. No, I didn't have those kind of adventures. Pretty much nothing happened, and then I finally decided that it was just best to come home.   **R**

Don Ramon (*to* DOÑA ARLETTE). See what I told you? That is exactly what I said would happen.

---

3. **mi 'jito** (mee HEE toh): contraction of *mi hijito,* Spanish for "my little son."

Q Read and Discuss When reading a play, you should pay close attention to stage directions. Why are these directions especially meaningful?

R Read and Discuss What does the conversation between Juanito and his mother tell you about Don Ricardo's curse?

Doña Arlette. Now that you are home, it is time to settle down and start your own family. You know our neighbor Don Emilio has a younger daughter who would make a very good wife. Perhaps we should go visit her family this Sunday.

Juanito. You know, that would probably be a good idea. I must admit that I was hoping I would find love on my adventures, but I have come home with no memories of love at all. Perhaps it is best to make my fortune right here, close to home.

Don Ramon (*to* DOÑA ARLETTE). See? That is exactly what I said would happen.

[*All exit.*] Ⓢ

SCENE 10.
Months Later at Juanito's Home.

The Narrator. Blanca Flor had seen the embrace and knew that the evil curse had been fulfilled. Brokenhearted, she traveled to a nearby village and lived there in hopes that one day the curse could be broken. The people of the village soon got to know Blanca Flor and came to respect her for the good person she was. One day, Blanca Flor heard news that a celebration was being held in honor of Juanito's return home. She immediately knew that this might be her one chance to break the curse. From the times when she had brushed Juanito's hair, she had kept a lock of his hair. She took one strand of his hair and made it into a dove. She then took one strand of her own hair and turned it into another dove. She took these two doves to Juanito's celebration as a present.

[JUANITO *and* DON RAMON *are sitting talking.*]

Don Ramon. Juanito, what was the most fantastic thing that happened on your adventures?

Juanito. Really, Father, nothing much at all happened. Sometimes I begin to have a memory of something, but it never becomes really clear. At night I have these dreams, but when I awake in the morning I cannot remember them. It must be some dream I keep trying to remember . . . or forget.

Don Ramon. I remember when I went into the world to seek my fortune. I was a young man like you . . .

[DOÑA ARLETTE *enters.*]

Doña Arlette. Juanito, there's a young woman here with a present for you.

Juanito. Who is it?

Doña Arlette. I don't really know her. She is the new young woman who just recently came to the village. The women of the church say she is constantly doing good works for the church and that she is a very good person. She has brought you a present to help celebrate your coming home safe.

Juanito. Sure. Let her come in.

[BLANCA FLOR *enters with the* TWO DOVES. *The* DOVES *are actors in costume.*]

Blanca Flor (*speaking to* JUANITO). Thank you for giving me the honor of presenting these doves as gifts to you.

Juanito. No. No. The honor is mine. Thank you. They are very beautiful.

Ⓢ [**Read and Discuss**] What is this conversation showing you?

Blanca Flor. They are special doves. They are singing doves.

Doña Arlette. I have never heard of singing doves before. Where did you get them?

Blanca Flor. They came from a special place. A place where all things have a magic power. There are no other doves like these in the world.

Don Ramon. Juanito, what a gift! Let's hear them sing!

Doña Arlette. Yes, let's hear them sing.

Blanca Flor. (*to* JUANITO). May they sing to you?

Juanito. Yes, of course. Let's hear their song.

[*Everyone sits to listen to the* DOVES' *song. As the* DOVES *begin to chant, their words begin to have a powerful effect on* JUANITO. *His memory of* BLANCA FLOR *returns to him.*]

Doves. Once there was a faraway land
A land of both good and evil powers.
A river flowed at the edge like a
         steady hand

And it was guarded by a Duende for
         all the hours.
Of all the beautiful things the land
         did hold
The most beautiful with the purest power
Was a young maiden, true and bold
Named Blanca Flor, the White Flower.   **T**

Juanito. I remember! The doves' song has made me remember. (*Going to* BLANCA FLOR) Blanca Flor, your love has broken the curse. Now I remember all that was struggling to come out. Mama, Papa, here is Blanca Flor, the love I found when I was seeking my fortune.

[JUANITO *and* BLANCA FLOR *embrace.*]

Don Ramon. This is going to be a really good story!

[*All exit, with* JUANITO *stopping to give* BLANCA FLOR *a big hug.*]   **U**

T **Reading Focus** **Visualizing** What images do you visualize when you read the song of the doves?

U **Read and Discuss** What was Blanca Flor's plan? How is the conflict resolved?

Applying Your Skills

Reading Standard 3.2 Analyze the effect of the qualities of the character (e.g., courage or cowardice, ambition or laziness) on the plot and the resolution of the conflict.

Blanca Flor

Literary Response and Analysis

Reading Skills Focus
Quick Check

1. Why does Juanito leave home?

2. How and why does Don Ricardo keep Blanca Flor captive on his farm?

3. Why does Juanito forget Blanca Flor when his parents embrace him?

Read with a Purpose

4. Do you think Juanito was successful in finding his fortune? Why or why not?

Reading Skills: Visualizing

5. Review the details in your chart. Then, add a row labeled "My View." For each character in your chart, write a sentence explaining how you pictured him or her.

Juanito	
Blanca Flor	"young woman," "took out her brush and began to brush his hair," "cradled Juanito in her arms"
My View	

Literary Skills Focus
Literary Analysis

6. **Interpret** Why didn't Blanca Flor escape from her captor before Juanito came to the forest?

7. **Literary Perspectives** The play's bare-bones plot could be summed up as "boy meets girl; boy loses girl; boy wins girl." Why can this plot be described as an archetype? Name one or more stories with a similar plot. Why is this plot so popular?

Literary Skills: Characterization

8. **Analyze** Choose two main characters from the play, and list two or three of each character's qualities (such as courage or ambition). Then, give examples of actions that illustrate these qualities.

9. **Analyze** Which character had the greatest effect on the plot and the resolution of the conflict? Cite examples from the play in your response.

Literary Skills Review: Suspense

10. **Evaluate** Suspense is the anxious curiosity readers feel about what is going to happen next in a story. Do you think the writer creates suspense in *Blanca Flor*, or do you think the play is predictable? Cite examples from the play to support your opinion.

Writing Skills Focus
Think as a Reader/Writer

Use It in Your Writing Review the dialogue you noted as you read *Blanca Flor*. How well did the dialogue capture the characters' qualities? Write a dialogue between two characters you invent. Be sure your dialogue conveys a strong sense of the personalities of both characters.

What Do You Think Now

Has *Blanca Flor* affected your view of rescuers—their qualities and motives? Explain.

Applying Your Skills

Reading Standard 1.5 Understand and explain "shades of meaning" in related words (e.g., *softly* and *quietly*). **1.3 Recognize the origins and meanings of frequently used foreign words in English and use these words accurately in** speaking and **writing.**

Blanca Flor

Vocabulary Development
Shades of Meaning

Synonyms are words that have similar meanings. *Journey* and *trip*, for example, mean about the same thing. As the example below shows, however, the two words have different **shades of meaning:**

> Juanito sets out on a *trip* to seek his fortune.
> Juanito sets out on a *journey* to seek his fortune.

Why is *journey* a better word to use than *trip* in this example? A trip is usually short, but a journey is usually long, and a person often has a significant experience on a journey.

Your Turn

Find two or three synonyms for each of the Vocabulary words listed at the right. (Use a thesaurus and a dictionary if you need help.) Then, find the place in the play where each Vocabulary word is used. Substitute each synonym for the Vocabulary word, and think about the synonym's shades of meaning. Does each synonym work as well as the Vocabulary word? Why or why not?

valiant
barren
flourish
apprehensively

Academic Vocabulary

Talk About . . .
With a partner, discuss how particular <u>circumstances</u> in the play bring out key <u>qualities</u> in the characters.

Language Coach

Spanish Words in English You can sometimes figure out the meaning of a Spanish word you don't know by thinking of English words that resemble it. (If Spanish is your first language, you can figure out the meanings of some English words in a similar way.)

Make a chart like the one below. Then, use an English dictionary that includes word origins to complete the chart with information about each word. Some information is given to help you begin.

Word	Spanish Origin/ Meaning	English Meaning	Sample Sentence
tortilla	*torta,* "a cake"	a thin, round cake of flour or cornmeal	Juanito ate the dried-out tortilla.
tornado	*tornar,* "to turn"	rapidly rotating column of air	
alligator			
armadillo			
bonanza			
cafeteria			
canyon			
chocolate			
mascara			
patio			

Learn It Online
Focus on synonyms and antonyms with *WordSharp*:

go.hrw.com   H6-164   **Go**

Grammar Link
Prepositional Phrases

A **prepositional phrase** is a word group that begins with a preposition and ends with a noun or pronoun. The noun or pronoun is called the **object of the preposition.** Look at the examples:

Preposition	Object of Preposition
He wanders **into**	a **forest.**
I'm talking **to**	the **tortilla** and hearing things.

When a preposition has two objects, and one or more is a pronoun, use the **objective** form of the pronoun—the form used for the object of a preposition. To make sure you use the right pronoun form, take one pronoun at a time without the other object, like this:

Choices	Don Ricardo gave the same chance to all the others and **I/me.**
Incorrect	Don Ricardo gave the same chance to **I.**
Correct	Don Ricardo gave the same chance to **me.**
	Don Ricardo gave the same chance **to all the others and me.**

Your Turn

Identify the preposition and object or objects in each of the following sentences. If a pronoun is the object, choose the correct pronoun form.

Example	He called out to Blanca Flor and I/me.
Answer	preposition: to; objects: Blanca Flor, me

1. My dog ran from the cat.
2. The woman spoke with Michelle and he/him.
3. The ship disappeared beyond the horizon.
4. I walked slowly behind she/her.

CHOICES

As you respond to the Choices, use these **Academic Vocabulary** words as appropriate: adapt, circumstance, obvious, qualities.

REVIEW
Write About a Character
Timed Writing If Blanca Flor had had different qualities, or character traits, how would the outcome of the play have been different? In a paragraph or two, explain how the plot would have changed if Blanca Flor had been less forceful, more shy, and more accepting of her fate.

CONNECT
Write a New Version
Retell the story of *Blanca Flor* as a short story with a contemporary setting and characters or as a graphic story with panels and word balloons. What parts of the story can you safely adapt while still keeping the same basic plot? Share your version with the class.

EXTEND
Present the Play
TechFocus Record a class performance of a scene from *Blanca Flor*. You will need a director and a stage manager, people to make costumes, and people to design and create scenery. Select actors for each role, and rehearse the play. Then, videotape the performance.

Learn It Online
Learn more about this play from the Internet links at:

go.hrw.com | H6-165 | **Go**

Comparing Characters and Their Conflicts

Scene from the movie *Eragon* (2006).

CONTENTS

What Do You Think?

What makes someone a hero? What would you think of a hero who isn't perfect?

QuickWrite
In ancient myths, heroes often slay a monster. What kind of "monster" might a modern hero face? Explain.

Preparing to Read

Reading Standard 3.2 Analyze the effect of the qualities of the character (e.g., courage or cowardice, ambition or laziness) on the plot and the resolution of the conflict.

Medusa's Head / Perseus and the Gorgon's Head / Dragon, Dragon

Literary Skills Focus

Character and Conflict Main characters in most stories have a variety of <u>qualities</u>, just like people in real life. Characters in myths and folk tales, though, are often defined by a single character trait: the wicked stepmother, the clever trickster, the noble hero. These are **character types,** sometimes called **archetypes** (AHR kuh typs), familiar figures that appear throughout the history of storytelling.

The plots of myths and folk tales usually focus on an <u>obvious</u> **external conflict**—a struggle between the main character and an outside force. The **protagonist,** or hero, has one motivation: to defeat the **antagonist,** or the character opposing the main character, who is often a monster. As you read, think about what special characteristics enable the heroes to triumph and resolve their conflicts successfully.

Reading Skills Focus

Connecting to Characters As you read, making connections to other stories you know lets you apply your prior knowledge of characters, conflict, and plot to the new work. Your ability to analyze characters' qualities and their effects will be strengthened as a result.

Into Action As you read each selection, record your connections to other stories in a chart like the one below.

"Medusa's Head"	Connections
hero goes on a journey	

Writing Skills Focus

Think as a Reader/Writer

Find It in Your Reading Myths and folk tales rely on exciting action. In your *Reader/Writer Notebook,* write down your favorite action words, phrases, and passages from each selection.

Reader/Writer Notebook

Use your **RWN** to complete the activities for these selections.

Language Coach

Verb Forms You form the past tense of a regular verb by adding *–d* or *–ed* to its base form: *work* becomes *worked.* Find the Vocabulary word above that is not in the past tense, and make it a past-tense verb.

Learn It Online

Hear a professional actor read these stories. Visit the selections online at:

go.hrw.com   H6-167   Go

Olivia Coolidge

(1908–2006)

A Twist of Fate

Olivia Coolidge was enjoying her childhood in London when, one day, she twisted her ankle badly. She was forced to stop playing outdoors for three months. Bored, she started to read the ancient Greek classics that her father had always pestered her to read. So she read—and read. Soon, she was reading ancient Greek poetry. "I write about history, biography, and ancient legends for teens," she said, "because I am . . . interested in values that have always been of concern to people."

Marcia Williams

(1945–   )

Comics Her Way

Marcia Williams developed her distinctive comic-book style when she was a child attending an English boarding school. Every week she sent illustrated letters to her mother and diplomat stepfather. "My parents didn't let me read comic books," she remembers, "so I decided to create my own."

John Gardner

(1933–1982)

Inspired by Disney and Dickens

When Gardner was young, his favorite storytellers were American animation giant Walt Disney and nineteenth-century English novelist Charles Dickens, author of *A Christmas Carol* and *Oliver Twist*. Gardner kept a bust of Dickens in his study "to keep me honest."

Think About the Writers

Why do you think a writer's experiences as a child can have such a lasting effect on what he or she writes about?

Preview the Selections

In "Medusa's Head," a Greek myth, you'll meet many characters, including the hero **Perseus,** his mother **Danae,** the hideous **Gorgon Medusa,** and the beautiful **Andromeda.**

In "Perseus and the Gorgon's Head," you'll read a very different—and funny—illustrated version of the same story about **Perseus** told in "Medusa's Head."

In "Dragon, Dragon," you'll meet a king and queen, a bumbling wizard, and three brothers who take turns fighting a dragon that threatens their kingdom.

The Head of Medusa (1618) by Peter Paul Rubens (1577–1640). Oil on canvas.

MEDUSA'S HEAD

Retold by **Olivia Coolidge**

Read with a Purpose
Read this Greek myth to discover how an ancient hero, Perseus, fulfills his fate.

Build Background
The ancient Greeks believed in fate, circumstances that a person can't escape from and that lead to an unavoidable future outcome.

Use the list below to help you keep track of and learn how to pronounce the names of the various characters and places in this myth.

CHARACTERS AND PLACES

Acrisios (uh KREE see ohs): king of **Argos** (AHR gohs), an ancient city and kingdom in southern Greece.

Proitos (proh EE tohs): brother of King Acrisios.

Danae (DAN ay ee): daughter of King Acrisios and mother of Perseus.

Apollo (uh PAHL oh): Greek god of light, medicine, poetry, and prophecy.

Zeus (zoos): king of the Greek gods.

Perseus (PUR see uhs): son of Danae and the god Zeus.

Dictys (DIHK tihs): fisherman, brother of Polydectes.

Polydectes (pahl ee DEHK teez): king of **Seriphos** (suh RY fuhs), an island off the coast of Greece.

Medusa (muh DOO suh): the youngest of the **Gorgons** (GAWR guhns), three monstrous sisters. She has snakes for hair and a face so terrible that it turns anyone who looks at her into stone.

Athene (uh THEE nee): Greek goddess of crafts, war, and wisdom. Her name is also spelled *Athena* (uh THEE nuh).

Phorcides (FAWR suh deez): three sisters who live in a cave and share one eye and one tooth between them.

Hermes (HUR meez): messenger of the gods.

Cepheus (SEE fee uhs) and **Cassiopeia** (kas ee oh PEE uh): king and queen of Ethiopa, in Africa.

Andromeda (an DRAHM uh duh): daughter of the king and queen of Ethiopia.

Nereus (NIHR ee uhs): a minor sea god.

Poseidon (puh SY duhn): god of the sea.

King Acrisios of Argos was a hard, selfish man. He hated his brother, Proitos, who later drove him from his kingdom, and he cared nothing for his daughter, Danae. His whole heart was set on having a son who should succeed him, but since many years went by and still he had only the one daughter, he sent a message to the oracle of Apollo[1] to ask whether he should have more children of his own. The answer of the oracle was terrible. Acrisios should have no son, but his daughter, Danae, would bear him a grandchild who should grow up to kill him. At these words Acrisios was beside himself with fear and rage. Swearing that Danae should never have a child to murder him, he had a room built underground and lined all through with brass. Thither[2] he conducted Danae and shut her up, bidding her spend the rest of her life alone. **Ⓐ**

It is possible to thwart the plans of mortal men, but never those of the gods. Zeus himself looked with pity on the unfortunate girl, and it is said he descended to her through the tiny hole that gave light and air to her chamber, pouring himself down into her lap in the form of a shower of gold.

When word came to the king from those who brought food and drink to his daughter that the girl was with child, Acrisios was angry and afraid. He would have liked best to murder both Danae and her infant son, Perseus, but he did not dare for fear of the gods' anger at so hideous a crime. He made, therefore, a great chest of wood with bands of brass about it. Shutting up the girl and her baby inside, he cast them into the sea, thinking that they would either drown or starve.

Again the gods came to the help of Danae, for they caused the planks of the chest to swell until they fitted tightly and let no water in. **Ⓑ**

The chest floated for some days and was cast up at last on an island. There Dictys, a fisherman, found it and took Danae to his brother, Polydectes, who was king of the island. Danae was made a servant in the palace, yet before many years had passed, both Dictys and Polydectes had fallen in love with the silent, golden-haired girl. She in her heart preferred Dictys, yet since his brother was king, she did not dare to make her choice. Therefore she hung always over Perseus, pretending that mother love left her no room for any other, and year after year a silent frown would cross Polydectes' face as he saw her caress the child. **Ⓒ**

At last, Perseus became a young man, handsome and strong beyond the common and a leader among the youths of the island, though he was but the son of a poor

---

1. **oracle** (AWR uh kuhl) **of Apollo:** priest or priestess of the god Apollo who foretold the future.
2. **thither:** old term meaning "over there."

Ⓐ Read and Discuss What have you learned about King Acrisios in this opening paragraph?

Ⓑ Literary Focus **Character and Conflict** What is the first external conflict that Perseus faces? What helps him overcome this conflict?

Ⓒ Read and Discuss What problem does Danae have?

Analyzing Visuals Connecting to the Text How does this image show the larger-than-life qualities of a hero like Perseus?

The Constellation of Perseus with the Head of Medusa by Alexander Mair.

servant. Then it seemed to Polydectes that if he could once get rid of Perseus, he could force Danae to become his wife, whether she would or not. Meanwhile, in order to lull the young man's suspicions, he pretended that he intended to marry a certain noble maiden and would collect a wedding gift for her. Now the custom was that this gift of the bridegroom to the bride was in part his own and in part put together from the marriage presents of his friends and relatives. All the young men, therefore, brought Polydectes a present, excepting Perseus, who was his servant's son and possessed nothing to bring. Then Polydectes said to the others, "This young man owes me more than any of you, since I took him in and brought him up in my own house, and yet he gives me nothing." **D**

Perseus answered in anger at the injustice of the charge, "I have nothing of my own, Polydectes, yet ask me what you will, and I will fetch it, for I owe you my life."

At this Polydectes smiled, for it was what he had intended, and he answered, "Fetch me, if this is your boast, the Gorgon's head." **E**

Now the Gorgons, who lived far off on the shores of the ocean, were three fearful sisters with hands of brass, wings of gold,

D **Literary Focus** Character and Conflict How do you think King Polydectes expects Perseus will react when he is criticized for bringing nothing?

E **Read and Discuss** What do you think is Polydectes' plan?

Medusa's Head **171**

and scales like a serpent. Two of them had scaly heads and tusks like the wild boar, but the third, Medusa, had the face of a beautiful woman with hair of writhing serpents, and so terrible was her expression that all who looked on it were immediately turned to stone. This much Perseus knew of the Gorgons, but of how to find or kill them, he had no idea. Nevertheless, he had given his promise, and though he saw now the satisfaction of King Polydectes, he was bound to keep his word. In his perplexity,[3] he prayed to the wise goddess Athene, who came to him in a vision and promised him her aid. **F**

"First, you must go," she said, "to the sisters Phorcides, who will tell you the way to the nymphs who guard the hat of darkness, the winged sandals, and the knapsack which can hold the Gorgon's head. Then I will give you a shield, and my brother Hermes will give you a sword, which shall be made of adamant, the hardest rock. For nothing else can kill the Gorgon, since so venomous is her blood that a mortal sword, when plunged in it, is eaten away. But when you come to the Gorgons, invisible in your hat of darkness, turn your eyes away from them and look only on their reflection in your gleaming shield.

3. **perplexity** (puhr PLEHK suh tee): puzzlement; confusion.

Thus you may kill the monster without yourself being turned to stone. Pass her sisters by, for they are immortal, but smite off the head of Medusa with the hair of writhing[4] snakes. Then put it in your knapsack and return, and I will be with you." **G**

The vision ended, and with the aid of Athene, Perseus set out on the long journey to seek the Phorcides. These live in a dim cavern in the far north, where nights and days are one and where the whole earth is

4. **writhing** (RYTH ihng): wriggling; moving about in a twisting way.

Study for Perseus and the Graiae (1880) by Sir Edward Burne-Jones.

Analyzing Visuals   **Connecting to the Text** What part of the plot does this painting illustrate? Does it match the scene as you imagined it? Why or why not?

F **Read and Discuss** What do you learn about the terrifying Gorgons in this section?

G **Reading Focus** **Connecting to Characters** Why are the gods and goddesses providing so much help to Perseus? What other stories can you name in which heroes are assisted by older or more powerful characters?

light. There sat the three old women mumbling to one another, crouched in a dim heap together, for they had but one eye and one tooth between them, which they passed from hand to hand. Perseus came quietly behind them, and as they fumbled for the eye, he put his strong, brown hand next to one of the long, yellow ones, so that the old crone thought that it was her sister's and put the eye into it. There was a high scream of anger when they discovered the theft, and much clawing and groping in the dim recesses[5] of the cavern. But they were helpless in their blindness and Perseus could laugh at them. At length, for the price of their eye, they told him how to reach the nymphs, and Perseus, laying the eye quickly in the hand of the nearest sister, fled as fast as he could before she could use it.

Again it was a far journey to the garden of the nymphs, where it is always sunshine and the trees bear golden apples. But the nymphs are friends of the wise gods and hate the monsters of darkness and the spirits of anger and despair. Therefore, they received Perseus with rejoicing and put the hat of darkness on his head, while on his feet they bound the golden, winged

> Here and there, a man who had looked on the terrible Medusa stood forever with horror on his face.

sandals, which are those Hermes wears when he runs down the slanting sunbeams or races along the pathways of the wind. Next, Perseus put on his back the silver sack with the gleaming tassels of gold, and flung across his shoulder the black-sheathed sword that was the gift of Hermes. On his left arm he fitted the shield that Athene gave, a gleaming silver shield like a mirror, plain without any marking. Then he sprang into the air and ran, invisible like the rushing wind, far out over the white-capped sea, across the yellow sands of the eastern desert, over strange streams and towering mountains, until at last he came to the shores of the distant ocean which flowed round all the world. **Ⓗ**

There was a gray gorge of stone by the ocean's edge, where lay Medusa and her sisters sleeping in the dim depths of the rock. All up and down the cleft, the stones took fantastic shapes of trees, beasts, birds, or serpents. Here and there, a man who had looked on the terrible Medusa stood forever with horror on his face. Far over the twilit gorge Perseus hovered invisible, while he loosened the pale, strange sword from its black sheath. Then, with his face turned away and eyes on the silver shield,

---

5. **recesses** (REE sehs ehz): inner places.

Ⓗ **Reading Focus** **Connecting to Characters** What other stories do you know in which a young hero or heroine is given special weapons or powers to help him or her against an enemy?

Vocabulary **hovered** (HUHV uhrd) v.: floated; remained still in the air.

he dropped, slow and silent as a falling leaf, down through the rocky cleft, twisting and turning past countless strange gray shapes, down from the bright sunlight into a chill, dim shadow echoing and reechoing with the dashing of waves on the tumbled rocks beneath. There on the heaped stones lay the Gorgons sleeping together in the dimness, and even as he looked on them in the shield, Perseus felt stiff with horror at the sight.

Two of the Gorgons lay sprawled together, shaped like women, yet scaled from head to foot as serpents are. Instead of hands they had gleaming claws like eagles, and their feet were dragons' feet. Skinny metallic wings like bats' wings hung from their shoulders. Their faces were neither snake nor woman, but part both, like faces in a nightmare. These two lay arm in arm and never stirred. Only the blue snakes still hissed and writhed round the pale, set face of Medusa, as though even in sleep she were troubled by an evil dream. She lay by herself, arms outstretched, face upwards, more beautiful and terrible than living man may bear. All the crimes and madnesses of the world rushed into Perseus' mind as he gazed at her image in the shield. Horror stiffened his arm as he hovered over her with his

Analyzing Visuals **Connecting to the Text** What are the most obvious of Medusa's qualities in this picture? How does the description of Medusa in the story compare with her appearance in this picture?

Medusa from "Perseus and the Gorgon" from *Jim Henson's the Storyteller: The Greek Myths* (1997).

sword uplifted. Then he shut his eyes to the vision and in the darkness struck. **Ⓘ**

There was a great cry and a hissing. Perseus groped for the head and seized it by the limp and snaky hair. Somehow he put it in his knapsack and was up and off, for at the dreadful scream the sister Gorgons had awakened. Now they were after him, their sharp claws grating against his silver shield. Perseus strained forward on the pathway of the wind like a runner, and behind him the two sisters came, smelling out the prey they could not see. Snakes darted from their girdles,[6] foam flew from their tusks, and the great wings beat the air. Yet the winged sandals were even swifter than they, and Perseus fled like the hunted deer with the speed of desperation. Presently the horrible noise grew faint behind him, the hissing of snakes and the sound of the bat wings died away. At last the Gorgons could smell him no longer and returned home unavenged. **Ⓙ**

By now, Perseus was over the Libyan desert, and as the blood from the horrible head touched the sand, it changed to serpents, from which the snakes of Africa are descended.

The storms of the Libyan desert blew against Perseus in clouds of eddying sand, until not even the divine sandals could hold him on his course. Far out to sea he was blown, and then north. Finally, whirled around the heavens like a cloud of mist, he alighted in the distant west, where the giant

Atlas held up on his shoulders the heavens from the earth. There the weary giant, crushed under the load of centuries, begged Perseus to show him Medusa's head. Perseus uncovered for him the dreadful thing, and Atlas was changed to the mighty mountain whose rocks rear up to reach the sky near the gateway to the Atlantic. Perseus himself, returning eastwards and still battling with the wind, was driven south to the land of Ethiopia, where King Cepheus reigned with his wife, Cassiopeia. **Ⓚ**

As Perseus came wheeling in like a gull from the ocean, he saw a strange sight. Far out to sea the water was troubled, seething and boiling as though stirred by a great force moving in its depths. Huge, sullen waves were starting far out and washing inland over sunken trees and flooded houses. Many miles of land were under water, and as he sped over them, he saw the muddy sea lapping around the foot of a black, upstanding rock. Here on a ledge above the water's edge stood a young girl chained by the arms, lips parted, eyes open and staring, face white as her linen garment. She might have been a statue, so still she stood, while the light breeze fluttered her dress and stirred her loosened hair. As Perseus looked at her and looked at the sea, the water began to boil again, and miles out a long gray scaly back of vast length lifted itself above the flood. At that, there was a shriek from a distant knoll where he could dimly see the forms of people, but

---

6. **girdles:** belts or sashes.

Ⓘ **Literary Focus** | **Character and Conflict** What qualities make Medusa a frightening, powerful foe that only a superhuman hero could defeat?

Ⓙ **Read and Discuss** What is Perseus's situation now?

Ⓚ **Read and Discuss** What two things have been created from Medusa's head so far?

the girl shrank a little and said nothing. Then Perseus, taking off the hat of darkness, alighted near the maiden to talk to her, and she, though nearly mad with terror, found words at last to tell him her tale. **L**

Her name was Andromeda, and she was the only child of the king and of his wife, Cassiopeia. Queen Cassiopeia was exceedingly beautiful, so that all people marveled at her. She herself was proud of her dark eyes, her white, slender fingers, and her long black hair, so proud that she had been heard to boast that she was fairer even than the sea nymphs, who are daughters of Nereus. At this, Nereus in wrath stirred up Poseidon, who came flooding in over the land, covering it far and wide. Not content with this, he sent a vast monster from the dark depths of the bottomless sea to ravage the whole coast of Ethiopia. When the unfortunate king and queen had sought the advice of the oracle on how to appease the god, they had been ordered to sacrifice their only daughter to the sea monster Poseidon had sent. Not daring for their people's sake to disobey, they had chained her to this rock, where she now awaited the beast who should devour her. **M**

Perseus comforted Andromeda as he stood by her on the rock, and she shrank closer against him while the great gray back writhed its half-mile length slowly towards the land. Then, bidding Andromeda hide her face, Perseus sprang once more into the air, unveiling the dreadful head of dead Medusa to the monster, which reared its dripping jaws yards high into the air. The mighty tail stiffened all of a sudden, the boiling of the water ceased, and only the gentle waves of the receding ocean lapped around a long, gray ridge of stone. Then Perseus freed Andromeda and restored her to her father and beautiful mother. Thereafter, with their consent, he married her amid scenes of tremendous rejoicing, and with his bride set sail at last for the kingdom of Polydectes. **N**

Polydectes had lost no time on the departure of Perseus. First he had begged Danae to become his wife, and then he had threatened her. Undoubtedly, he would have got his way by force if Danae had not fled in terror to Dictys. The two took refuge at the altar of a temple whence Polydectes did not dare drag them away. So matters stood when Perseus returned. Polydectes was enraged to see him, for he had hoped at least that Danae's most powerful protector would never return. But now, seeing him famous and with a king's daughter to wife, he could not contain himself. Openly he laughed at the tale of Perseus, saying that the hero had never killed the Gorgon, only pretended to, and that now he was claiming an honor he did not deserve. At this,

---

L **Literary Focus** **Character and Conflict** Compare Perseus's actions on his journey home with those on his mission to kill Medusa. Is it <u>obvious</u> why he stops to talk to the girl, or do you have to infer his motivation?

M **Literary Focus** **Character and Conflict** What causes the external conflict between Andromeda and the monster?

N **Literary Focus** **Character and Conflict** How are Perseus's reasons, or motivations, for challenging the sea monster different from his motivations for going after Medusa? What is the resolution of the conflict with the sea monster?

Vocabulary **devour** (dih VOWR) *v.*: eat in a greedy way.

Analyzing Visuals   **Connecting to the Text**   How is this creature similar to or different from your idea of what the sea monster in conflict with Andromeda looks like?

The Leviathan (1908) by Arthur Rackham.

Perseus, enraged by the insult and by reports of his mother's persecution, said to him, "You asked me for the Gorgon's head. Behold it!" And with that he lifted it high, and Polydectes became stone. **O**

Then Perseus left Dictys to be king of that island, but he himself went back to the Grecian mainland to seek out his grandfather, Acrisios, who was once again king of Argos. First, however, he gave back to the gods the gifts they had given him. Hermes took back the golden sandals and the hat of darkness, for both are his. But

Athene took Medusa's head, and she hung it on a fleece around her neck as part of her battle equipment, where it may be seen in statues and portraits of the warlike goddess.

Perseus took ship for Greece, but his fame had gone before him, and King Acrisios fled secretly from Argos in terror, since he remembered the prophecy and feared that Perseus had come to avenge the wrongs of Danae. The trembling old Acrisios took refuge in Larissa, where it happened the king was holding a great athletic contest in honor of his dead father. **P**

Heroes from all over Greece, among whom was Perseus, came to the games. As Perseus was competing at the discus throwing, he threw high into the air and far beyond the rest. A strong wind caught the discus as it spun, so that it left the course marked out for it and was carried into the stands. People scrambled away to right and left. Only Acrisios was not nimble enough. The heavy weight fell full on his foot and crushed his toes, and at that, the feeble old man, already weakened by his terrors, died from the shock. Thus the prophecy of Apollo was fulfilled at last; Acrisios was killed by his grandson. Then Perseus came into his kingdom, where he reigned with Andromeda long and happily. **O**

> "You asked me for the Gorgon's head. Behold it!"

Perseus with the Head of Medusa (1545–1554) by Benvenuto Cellini (1500–1571). Bronze sculpture.

O [Read and Discuss] What happens when Perseus reaches home?

P [Literary Focus] **Character and Conflict** At the end of the story, which of King Acrisios's qualities are different from those at the beginning? Which are the same?

O [Read and Discuss] What point does the writer make at the end?

Read with a Purpose
Note how this writer/artist takes a serious heroic myth and turns it into something funny.

Retold by **Marcia Williams**

A [Read and Discuss] How has the writer/artist set up the story for you?

B [Reading Focus] **Connecting to Characters** How is the conflict developing between Perseus, King Polydectes, and Danaë similar to and different from that in "Medusa's Head"?

C [Read and Discuss] Why is it intended to be a "deadly" mission?

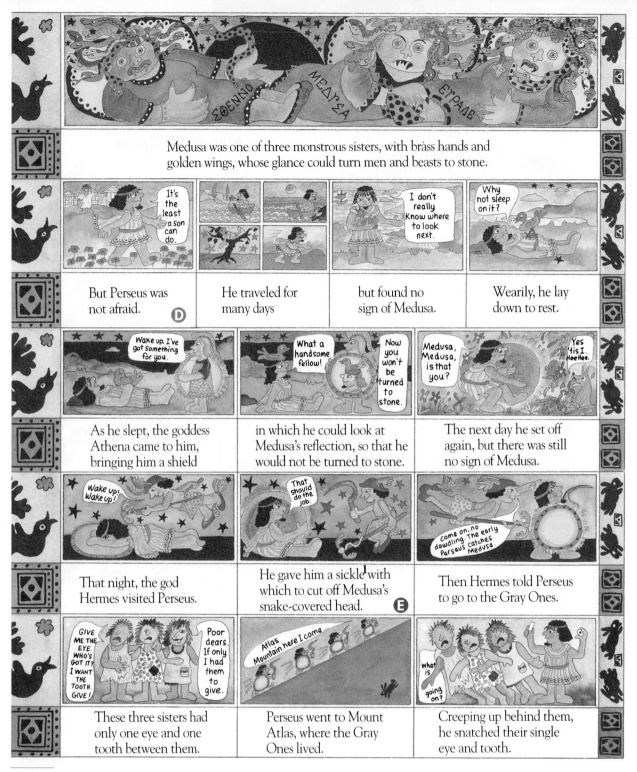

Medusa was one of three monstrous sisters, with brass hands and golden wings, whose glance could turn men and beasts to stone.

But Perseus was not afraid. **D**

He traveled for many days

but found no sign of Medusa.

Wearily, he lay down to rest.

As he slept, the goddess Athena came to him, bringing him a shield

in which he could look at Medusa's reflection, so that he would not be turned to stone.

The next day he set off again, but there was still no sign of Medusa.

That night, the god Hermes visited Perseus.

He gave him a sickle[1] with which to cut off Medusa's snake-covered head. **E**

Then Hermes told Perseus to go to the Gray Ones.

These three sisters had only one eye and one tooth between them.

Perseus went to Mount Atlas, where the Gray Ones lived.

Creeping up behind them, he snatched their single eye and tooth.

---

1. **sickle** (SIHK uhl): tool with a curved blade and a short handle.

D **Literary Focus** **Character and Conflict** What is the conflict in the story at this point? Which of Perseus's qualities have been revealed?

E **Read and Discuss** What roles do the shield and the sickle play in Perseus's mission?

H **Reading Focus** **Connecting to Characters** In "Medusa's Head" the scene in which Perseus kills Medusa is suspenseful and horrifying. How would you describe the way this plot event is handled here?

I **Read and Discuss** How have conflicts resolved for Perseus and his mother?

Applying Your Skills

Reading Standard 3.2 Analyze the effect of the qualities of the character (e.g., courage or cowardice, ambition or laziness) on the plot and the resolution of the conflict.

Medusa's Head / Perseus and the Gorgon's Head
Literary Response and Analysis

Reading Skills Focus
Quick Check

1. Why does King Polydectes send Perseus on such a dangerous mission?
2. Why is Medusa so dangerous?
3. How does Perseus help Andromeda?

Read with a Purpose

4. In each version of the story, how does Perseus fulfill his fate, or destiny? How are the authors' attitudes toward this story different?

Reading Skills: Connecting to Characters

5. Think about the connections you made between the two versions of the story in your chart for "Perseus and the Gorgon's Head." Do you think the two versions have more similarities or more differences? Explain.
6. Think about the connections to other stories you recorded in your chart for either selection. What have you learned from these connections about the qualities of heroes and the plots of heroic stories?

Literary Skills Focus
Literary Analysis

7. **Interpret** Why is Perseus a good example of a mythic hero? (Think about how he handles the challenges on his quest and how the gods help him.)

8. **Reflect** What do you think of Perseus? Do we have heroes like him today? Refer to your reading notes for your responses to the story.
9. **Evaluate** In "Medusa's Head," what kind of hero is Perseus? In "Perseus and the Gorgon's Head," how successfully does Marcia Williams adapt this heroic image in order to turn it upside down?
10. **Reflect** How does the myth of Perseus illustrate the idea that no one can escape fate? What do you think of the ancient Greek belief that everything that happens is decided in advance by fate?

Literary Skills: Character and Conflict

11. **Analyze** In both versions of the story, how does Perseus's character help set the story's conflicts in motion and keep them in motion?
12. **Infer** Could Perseus have resolved his conflicts without the help of the other characters? Explain your answer.

Writing Skills Focus
Think as a Reader/Writer

Use It in Your Writing Review the lists of action words you recorded. Now, try using similar words and descriptions to write your own action-packed scene.

Dragon, Dragon

by **John Gardner**

Read with a Purpose

Read "Dragon, Dragon" to learn what problem a king and his kingdom face and to discover who ends up solving the problem.

Preparing to Read for this selection is on page 167.

Build Background

A **parody** is a work that humorously imitates, or spoofs, the content or style of another work. This story is from John Gardner's first collection of stories for young readers, *Dragon, Dragon, and Other Tales* (1975). The book is a collection of fairy tale parodies—new and funny versions of traditional, old-fashioned tales.

There was once a king whose kingdom was plagued by a dragon. The king did not know which way to turn. The king's knights were all cowards who hid under their beds whenever the dragon came in sight, so they were of no use to the king at all. And the king's wizard could not help either because, being old, he had forgotten his magic spells. Nor could the wizard look up the spells that had slipped his mind, for he had unfortunately misplaced his wizard's book many years before. The king was at his wit's end. **A**

Every time there was a full moon, the dragon came out of his lair and ravaged the countryside. He frightened maidens and stopped up chimneys and broke store windows and set people's clocks back and made dogs bark until no one could hear himself think.

He tipped over fences and robbed graves and put frogs in people's drinking water and tore the last chapters out of novels and changed house numbers around.

He stole spark plugs out of people's cars and put firecrackers in people's cigars and stole the clappers from all the church bells and sprung every bear trap for miles around so the bears could wander wherever they pleased.

And to top it all off, he changed around all the roads in the kingdom so that people

---

A Read and Discuss | What has the author told you so far?

Vocabulary **ravaged** (RAV ihjd) *v.*: damaged greatly.

could not get anywhere except by starting out in the wrong direction.

"That," said the king in a fury, "is enough!" And he called a meeting of everyone in the kingdom.

Now it happened that there lived in the kingdom a wise old cobbler who had a wife and three sons. The cobbler and his family came to the king's meeting and stood way in back by the door, for the cobbler had a feeling that since he was nobody important, there had probably been some mistake, and no doubt the king had intended the meeting for everyone in the kingdom except his family and him.

"Ladies and gentlemen," said the king when everyone was present, "I've put up with that dragon as long as I can. He has got to be stopped." **C**

All the people whispered amongst themselves, and the king smiled, pleased with the impression he had made. **D**

B **Literary Focus** Character and Conflict What qualities are revealed by the dragon's actions? Explain how this dragon's character sets up the story's conflict.

C **Literary Focus** Character and Conflict How might the king's action here mark a new stage in the conflict?

D **Read and Discuss** How has the king changed his approach?

Analyzing Visuals **Connecting to the Text** How does this dragon resemble the dragon in the story?

Scene from the movie *Dragonheart* (1996).

But the wise cobbler said gloomily, "It's all very well to talk about it—but how are you going to do it?"

And now all the people smiled and winked as if to say, "Well, King, he's got you there!"

The king frowned.

"It's not that His Majesty hasn't tried," the queen spoke up loyally.

"Yes," said the king, "I've told my knights again and again that they ought to slay that dragon. But I can't *force* them to go. I'm not a tyrant."

"Why doesn't the wizard say a magic spell?" asked the cobbler.

"He's done the best he can," said the king.

The wizard blushed and everyone looked embarrassed. "I used to do all sorts of spells and chants when I was younger," the wizard explained. "But I've lost my spell book, and I begin to fear I'm losing my memory too. For instance, I've been trying for days to recall one spell I used to do. I forget, just now, what the deuce it was for. It went something like—

Bimble,
Wimble,
Cha, Cha
CHOOMPF!"

Suddenly, to everyone's surprise, the queen turned into a rosebush.

"Oh, dear," said the wizard.

"Now you've done it," groaned the king.

"Poor Mother," said the princess.

"I don't know what can have happened," the wizard said nervously, "but don't worry, I'll have her changed back in a jiffy." He shut his eyes and racked his brain for a spell that would change her back.

But the king said quickly, "You'd better leave well enough alone. If you change her into a rattlesnake, we'll have to chop off her head." **E**

Meanwhile the cobbler stood with his hands in his pockets, sighing at the waste of time. "About the dragon . . . ," he began.

"Oh, yes," said the king. "I'll tell you what I'll do. I'll give the princess's hand in marriage to anyone who can make the dragon stop."

"It's not enough," said the cobbler. "She's a nice enough girl, you understand. But how would an ordinary person support her? Also, what about those of us that are already married?"

"In that case," said the king, "I'll offer the princess's hand or half the kingdom or both—whichever is most convenient."

The cobbler scratched his chin and considered it. "It's not enough," he said at last. "It's a good enough kingdom, you understand, but it's too much responsibility."

"Take it or leave it," the king said.

"I'll leave it," said the cobbler. And he shrugged and went home. **F**

But the cobbler's eldest son thought the bargain was a good one, for the princess was very beautiful, and he liked the idea of having half the kingdom to run as he pleased.

E **Reading Focus** **Connecting to Characters** In what ways is this wizard similar to or different from wizards in other stories you know?

F **Literary Focus** **Character and Conflict** In what obvious ways are the king and the cobbler different from each other? How do their qualities affect the conflict?

So he said to the king, "I'll accept those terms, Your Majesty. By tomorrow morning the dragon will be slain." **G**

"Bless you!" cried the king.

"Hooray, hooray, hooray!" cried all the people, throwing their hats in the air.

The cobbler's eldest son beamed with pride, and the second eldest looked at him enviously. The youngest son said timidly, "Excuse me, Your Majesty, but don't you think the queen looks a little unwell? If I were you, I think I'd water her." **H**

"Good heavens," cried the king, glancing at the queen, who had been changed into a rosebush, "I'm glad you mentioned it!"

> "The old man is not as wise as I thought. If I say something like that to the dragon, he will eat me up in an instant."

Now the cobbler's eldest son was very clever and was known far and wide for how quickly he could multiply fractions in his head. He was perfectly sure he could slay the dragon by somehow or other playing a trick on him, and he didn't feel that he needed his wise old father's advice. But he thought it was only polite to ask, and so he went to his father, who was working as usual at his cobbler's bench, and said, "Well, Father, I'm off to slay the dragon. Have you any advice to give me?"

The cobbler thought a moment and replied, "When and if you come to the dragon's lair, recite the following poem.

Dragon, dragon, how do you do?
I've come from the king to murder you.

Say it very loudly and firmly, and the dragon will fall, God willing, at your feet."

"How curious!" said the eldest son. And he thought to himself, "The old man is not as wise as I thought. If I say something like that to the dragon, he will eat me up in an instant. The way to kill a dragon is to outfox him." And keeping his opinion to himself, the eldest son set forth on his quest. **I**

When he came at last to the dragon's lair, which was a cave, the eldest son slyly disguised himself as a peddler and knocked on the door and called out, "Hello there!"

"There's nobody home!" roared a voice.

The voice was as loud as an earthquake, and the eldest son's knees knocked together in terror.

"I don't come to trouble you," the eldest son said meekly. "I merely thought you might be interested in looking at some of our brushes. Or if you'd prefer," he added quickly, "I could leave our catalog with you and I could drop by again, say, early next week."

"I don't want any brushes," the voice roared, "and I especially don't want any brushes next week."

G [Read and Discuss] What does the eldest son think of the deal?

H [Read and Discuss] Why is the youngest son the only one not focused on the good news? What might he think of the deal?

I [Reading Focus] Connecting to Characters In what ways is the eldest son like and unlike a familiar character type? What ability does he plan to rely on to slay the dragon?

"Oh," said the eldest son. By now his knees were knocking together so badly that he had to sit down.

Suddenly a great shadow fell over him, and the eldest son looked up. It was the dragon. The eldest son drew his sword, but the dragon lunged and swallowed him in a single gulp, sword and all, and the eldest son found himself in the dark of the dragon's belly. "What a fool I was not to listen to my wise old father!" thought the eldest son. And he began to weep bitterly. **J**

"Well," sighed the king the next morning, "I see the dragon has not been slain yet."

"I'm just as glad, personally," said the princess, sprinkling the queen. "I would have had to marry that eldest son, and he had warts." **K**

Now the cobbler's middle son decided it was his turn to try. The middle son was very strong and was known far and wide for being able to lift up the corner of a church. He felt perfectly sure he could slay the dragon by simply laying into him, but he thought it would be only polite to ask his father's advice. So he went to his father and said to him, "Well, Father, I'm off to slay the dragon. Have you any advice for me?"

The cobbler told the middle son exactly what he'd told the eldest.

"When and if you come to the dragon's lair, recite the following poem.

J |Read and Discuss| How do things turn out for the cobbler's eldest son?

K |Read and Discuss| How does the princess feel about what happened to the cobbler's eldest son?

Vocabulary **lunged** (luhnjd) *v.*: moved suddenly forward.

Dragon, dragon, how do you do?
I've come from the king to murder you.

Say it very loudly and firmly, and the dragon will fall, God willing, at your feet."

"What an odd thing to say," thought the middle son. "The old man is not as wise as I thought. You have to take these dragons by surprise." But he kept his opinion to himself and set forth. **L**

When he came in sight of the dragon's lair, the middle son spurred his horse to a gallop and thundered into the entrance, swinging his sword with all his might.

But the dragon had seen him while he was still a long way off, and being very clever, the dragon had crawled up on top of the door so that when the son came charging in, he went under the dragon and on to the back of the cave and slammed into the wall. Then the dragon chuckled and got down off the door, taking his time, and strolled back to where the man and the horse lay unconscious from the terrific blow. Opening his mouth as if for a yawn, the dragon swallowed the middle son in a single gulp and put the horse in the freezer to eat another day.

"What a fool I was not to listen to my wise old father," thought the middle son when he came to in the dragon's belly. And he too began to weep bitterly. **M**

That night there was a full moon, and the dragon ravaged the countryside so terribly that several families moved to another kingdom.

"Well," sighed the king in the morning, "still no luck in this dragon business, I see."

"I'm just as glad, myself," said the princess, moving her mother, pot and all, to the window, where the sun could get at her. "The cobbler's middle son was a kind of humpback." **N**

Now the cobbler's youngest son saw that his turn had come. He was very upset and nervous, and he wished he had never been born. He was not clever, like his eldest brother, and he was not strong, like his second-eldest brother. He was a decent, honest boy who always minded his elders.

He borrowed a suit of armor from a friend of his who was a knight, and when the youngest son put the armor on, it was so heavy he could hardly walk. From another knight he borrowed a sword, and that was so heavy that the only way the youngest son could get it to the dragon's lair was to drag it along behind his horse like a plow.

When everything was in readiness, the youngest son went for a last conversation with his father.

"Father, have you any advice to give me?" he asked.

"Only this," said the cobbler. "When and if you come to the dragon's lair, recite the following poem.

Dragon, dragon, how do you do?
I've come from the king to murder you.

L **Literary Focus** Character and Conflict How is the middle son's approach to the conflict like his brother's?

M **Read and Discuss** How do things turn out for the middle son?

N **Read and Discuss** How do the princess's feelings about the middle son connect with what you already know about her?

Say it very loudly and firmly, and the dragon will fall, God willing, at your feet."

"Are you certain?" asked the youngest son uneasily.

"As certain as one can ever be in these matters," said the wise old cobbler.

And so the youngest son set forth on his quest. He traveled over hill and dale and at last came to the dragon's cave.

The dragon, who had seen the cobbler's youngest son while he was still a long way off, was seated up above the door, inside the cave, waiting and smiling to himself. But minutes passed and no one came thundering in. The dragon frowned, puzzled, and was tempted to peek out. However, reflecting that patience seldom goes unrewarded, the dragon kept his head up out of sight and went on waiting. At last, when he could stand it no longer, the dragon craned his neck and looked. There at the entrance of the cave stood a trembling young man in a suit of armor twice his size, struggling with a sword so heavy he could lift only one end of it at a time.

At the sight of the dragon, the cobbler's youngest son began to tremble so violently that his armor rattled like a house caving in. He heaved with all his might at the sword and got the handle up level with his chest, but even now the point was down in the dirt. As loudly and firmly as he could manage, the youngest son cried—

Dragon, dragon, how do you do?
I've come from the king to murder you.

Scene from the movie *Dragonslayer* (1981).

"What?" cried the dragon, flabbergasted. "You? *You?* Murder *Me???*" All at once he began to laugh, pointing at the little cobbler's son. "*He he he ho ha!*" he roared, shaking all over, and tears filled his eyes. "*He he he ho ho ho ha ha!*" laughed the dragon. He was laughing so hard he had to hang onto his sides, and he fell off the door and landed on his back, still laughing, kicking his legs helplessly, rolling from side to side, laughing and laughing and laughing.

The cobbler's son was annoyed. "I *do* come from the king to murder you," he said. "A person doesn't like to be laughed at for a thing like that."

O **Literary Focus** **Character and Conflict** The cobbler has given the same advice to all three sons. What's different about the conversation this time? What does this difference tell you about the youngest son's <u>qualities</u>?

P **Read and Discuss** What picture has the author created for you here?

Vocabulary **craned** (kraynd) *v.:* stretched (the neck) in order to see better.

"*He he he!*" wailed the dragon, almost sobbing, gasping for breath. "Of course not, poor dear boy! But really, *he he,* the *idea* of it, *ha ha ha!* And that simply *ridiculous poem!*" Tears streamed from the dragon's eyes, and he lay on his back perfectly helpless with laughter.

"It's a good poem," said the cobbler's youngest son loyally. "My father made it up." And growing angrier he shouted, "I want you to stop that laughing, or I'll—I'll—" But the dragon could not stop for the life of him. And suddenly, in a terrific rage, the cobbler's son began flopping the sword end over end in the direction of the dragon. Sweat ran off the youngest son's forehead, but he labored on, blistering mad, and at last, with one supreme heave, he had the sword standing on its handle a foot from the dragon's throat. Of its own weight the sword fell, slicing the dragon's head off.

"*He he ho huk,*" went the dragon—and then he lay dead. **Q**

The two older brothers crawled out and thanked their younger brother for saving their lives. "We have learned our lesson," they said.

Then the three brothers gathered all the treasures from the dragon's cave and tied them to the back end of the youngest brother's horse and tied the dragon's head on behind the treasures and started home. "I'm glad I listened to my father," the youngest son thought. "Now I'll be the richest man in the kingdom." **R**

There were hand-carved picture frames and silver spoons and boxes of jewels and chests of money and silver compasses and maps telling where there were more treasures buried when these ran out. There was also a curious old book with a picture of an owl on the cover, and inside, poems and odd sentences and recipes that seemed to make no sense.

When they reached the king's castle, the people all leaped for joy to see that the dragon was dead, and the princess ran out and kissed the youngest brother on the forehead, for secretly she had hoped it would be him.

"Well," said the king, "which half of the kingdom do you want?"

"My wizard's book!" exclaimed the wizard. "He's found my wizard's book!" He opened the book and ran his finger along under the words and then said in a loud voice, "Glmuzk, shkzmlp, blam!"

Instantly the queen stood before them in her natural shape, except she was soaking wet from being sprinkled too often. She glared at the king.

"Oh dear," said the king, hurrying toward the door. **S**

Q [Read and Discuss] How do things turn out for the youngest son?

R [Literary Focus] **Character and Conflict** What qualities enable the youngest son to adapt to the situation and slay the dragon? What does the cobbler's poem have to do with his son's conquest?

S [Read and Discuss] How do things turn out for the people of the kingdom?

Applying Your Skills

Reading Standard 3.2 Analyze the effect of the qualities of the character (e.g., courage or cowardice, ambition or laziness) on the plot and the resolution of the conflict.

Dragon, Dragon
Literary Response and Analysis

Reading Skills Focus
Quick Check

1. Why can't the wizard help conquer the dragon?
2. What lesson do the eldest and middle son learn?
3. What is the youngest son's reward for killing the dragon?

Read with a Purpose

4. Why is the dragon such a threat to the kingdom? Were you surprised to learn that the youngest son is the one who succeeds in conquering the dragon? Why or why not?

Reading Skills: Connecting to Characters

5. What connections between this story and the two versions of the Perseus myth did you record in your chart? Write two or three sentences explaining the main similarities you noted between the selections.

"Dragon, Dragon"	Connections
dragon killed	Medusa killed in Perseus myth

✔ Vocabulary Check

Answer the following questions:

6. What time of day was it when the dragon **ravaged** the countryside?
7. Who **lunged** at the cobbler's eldest son?
8. What would a **craned** neck look like?

Literary Skills Focus
Literary Analysis

9. **Analyze** What elements of the plot make this story like old-fashioned fairy tales? What story elements would never appear in a "real" fairy tale? Explain how these elements make the story funny.

10. **Interpret** This story expresses a message, or teaches a lesson, about life. In real life, is it always the experts who are wise? Who is wise in this story? What message do you take from that?

Literary Skills: Character and Conflict

11. **Analyze** Identify each son's main character traits. What is the effect of the eldest and middle sons' qualities on the **plot**? (Think about how their behavior keeps the plot at a standstill.) Which of the youngest son's qualities enable him to save the kingdom?

12. **Analyze** What role does the cobbler play in resolving the conflict? Do you think the youngest son would ever have defeated the dragon if he hadn't had his father to give him advice? Support your opinion by citing the youngest son's <u>qualities</u>, or traits.

Writing Skills Focus
Think as a Reader/Writer

Use It in Your Writing Review your *Reader/Writer Notebook* for especially striking descriptions of actions. Now, write an action scene from a familiar fairy tale. Use strong descriptions of actions as well as the kind of humor that John Gardner uses in this story.

Reading Standard 3.2 Analyze the effect of the qualities of the character (e.g., courage or cowardice, ambition or laziness) on the plot and the resolution of the conflict.

Medusa's Head / Perseus and the Gorgon's Head / Dragon, Dragon

Writing Skills Focus
Write a Comparison-Contrast Essay

In an essay, compare and contrast the effects of the characters' qualities on the conflicts in *two* of these stories. Organize your essay in one of the following ways:

- You can organize the essay by character and conflict, using the **point-by-point method.** In the first paragraph, compare and contrast the qualities of the main characters—the heroes—of the two stories. Then, write a paragraph comparing and contrasting the effects of those qualities on the central conflicts in the stories and on the conflicts' resolutions.

- You can use the **block method** to organize your essay. Write all about one story in the first paragraph and all about the other story in the second paragraph. In each paragraph, explain the qualities of the main character in the story and the effect of the qualities on the conflict and its resolution.

At the end of your essay, explain what you thought of each writer's treatment of his or her story. Which story did you prefer? Why?

Use the workshop on writing a Comparison-Contrast Essay, pages 450–458, for help with this assignment.

What Do **You Think Now** How do imperfect heroes achieve their goals? In what ways can an imperfect hero be just as heroic as a "perfect" heroic type?

CHOICES

As you respond to the Choices, use these **Academic Vocabulary** words as appropriate: adapt, circumstance, obvious, qualities.

REVIEW
Describe a Hero
Timed ⏱ Writing Think of a real-life hero and, in a short essay, explain the obvious (and not-so-obvious) qualities that make him or her heroic. How have these qualities helped the hero perform a heroic deed—to triumph in a struggle or resolve a major conflict?

CONNECT
Create a Graphic Story
Marcia Williams uses plain language to tell the story of Perseus, but she adds illustrations and dialogue to make the story humorous. Adapt her technique to your own retelling of a myth or fairy tale. First, write the story. Then, draw it in a cartoon style and add humorous dialogue.

EXTEND
Continue a Story
At the end of "Dragon, Dragon," the queen glares at the king, who hurries toward the door. What do you suppose happens when the queen catches up with the king? Write the scene that takes place *after* the end of the story. Use what you've learned about the king and queen to keep them both "in character."

Learn It Online
Investigate Internet links to learn more about these stories at:

go.hrw.com | H6-193 | **Go**

Compare-and-Contrast Organizational Pattern

CONTENTS

What Do **You** Think?

What's the difference between winning and doing the right thing?

⏱ **QuickWrite**

In what competitions—sports, games, or other contests—have you participated? Choose your favorite, and then describe its rules in a paragraph or two.

Reading Standard 2.2 Analyze text that uses the compare-and-contrast organizational pattern.

Olympic Glory: Victories in History

Informational Text Focus
Compare-and-Contrast Organizational Pattern

"Attending Allison's pool party was like spending a day at the beach."

"Yes, but Travis's birthday party was twice as fun."

Notice how often your friends use a comparison or a contrast when they express their ideas and opinions. We all make sense of the world by noting ways in which people, places, and ideas are similar **(comparing)** and different **(contrasting).** In the following article, you'll read about the Olympic Games. By using the **compare-and-contrast organizational pattern,** the writer helps you understand how the modern Olympics are similar to the ancient Olympics in some ways and very different in others.

Into Action   A **Venn diagram** is a graphic organizer in which you can record similarities and differences between two things. As you read "Olympic Glory: Victories in History," use a Venn diagram like the one below to track the writer's comparison and contrast of the ancient and modern games.

Ancient
Games only
in summer

Similarities
athletes want to
achieve victory

Modern
Games both
summer and
winter

Writing Skills Focus

Preparing for **Timed Writing**   Writers use words and phrases to signal relationships between ideas. Words such as *similarly, as, like,* and *likewise* indicate comparisons; phrases such as *instead of, however, in contrast,* and *on the other hand* indicate contrasts. In your *Reader/Writer Notebook,* list the signal words and phrases you find in this article.

Reader/Writer
Notebook
Use your **RWN** to complete the activities for these selections.

Vocabulary

victorious (vihk TAWR ee uhs) *adj.*: having won. *Sara Hughes was victorious in the 2002 Winter Olympics.*

contemporary (kuhn TEHM puh rehr ee) *adj.*: relating to the present time; modern. *Contemporary Olympics fans can watch the games on television.*

amateurs (AM uh churz) *n.*: people who participate in sports or other activities for fun rather than money; not professionals. *Since ancient Olympians earned money and prizes, they can't be considered amateurs.*

Language Coach

Latin Roots   Many English words and word parts come from ancient Latin. For example, *contemporary* comes from the Latin word *tempus,* meaning "time." *Amateur* comes from the Latin verb *amare,* meaning "to love." *Victorious* comes from the Latin word *vincere,* "to conquer." Explain how knowing the meanings of these Latin root words can help you recognize and understand related words.

Learn It Online
Need help understanding comparison and contrast? Check out the interactive Reading Workshop:

| go.hrw.com | H6-195 | Go |

OLYMPIC GLORY:
Victories in History

by **THE WORLD ALMANAC**

Read with a Purpose
Read this article to learn how times have both changed and stayed the same for the Olympic Games.

In Greece in 1896, a shepherd named Spyridon Louis ran a footrace from Marathon to Athens and became the first "marathon" champion of the modern Olympics. He ran the race in borrowed shoes. In the Olympic Games today and in the future, one would be hard-pressed to find athletes who have trouble finding footwear. Hoping to give their brands important public exposure, makers of specialized athletic shoes can't wait to give expensive shoes to Olympians for free.

However, modern Olympic athletes will always be like Louis in some important ways. Victorious runners will be asked how it feels to triumph, and they will sound like he did: "That hour was something unimaginable, and it still appears in my memory like a dream," Louis said forty years after his moment of glory. "Everybody was calling out my name and throwing their hats in the air." Crowds will always gather. Flags will unfurl. Athletes will triumph. Some elements of the Games change with time; others are eternal. **Ⓐ**

Exported from Greece
The very first Games were part of a Greek religious festival honoring Zeus, the "father" of Greek gods and goddesses. "They were a celebration of Hellenic culture,"[1] says David Potter, professor of Greek and Latin at the University of Michigan. Now, those gods and goddesses

---

1. **Hellenic** (heh LEHN ihk) **culture:** culture of the ancient Greeks during the period 776 B.C. to 323 B.C. Hellen was a mythological king believed to be the ancestor of all true Greeks.

Ⓐ **Informational Focus** **Compare and Contrast**
The writer begins this article by mentioning that even the modern Olympics have changed through time. What is the writer's point here? What features of the Olympics remain the same across time?

Vocabulary **victorious** (vihk TAWR ee uhs) *adj.:* having won.

are ancient myth, and the Games include athletes from all around the world, not just the Greek city-states of ancient times.

The ancient Olympics were held every four years in Olympia from 776 B.C. through A.D. 393—over one thousand years! The Games were revived in 1896 as international competitions. Today's Olympics are run by international committees rather than by Greek officials, and athletes gather in different host cities each time, not just in Olympia. Now, as in ancient times, says Potter, "The point in part is for people to come and represent who they are and where they're from."

Games for All Seasons

The ancient Games were summertime events. In the modern world, however, there are Winter Games as well. Like the ancient Games, the modern Summer and Winter Olympics are each held every four years, with the two alternating on even-numbered years. **B**

When the Olympics began in 776 B.C., they consisted of one footrace—covering a distance of 600 feet. In contrast, twenty-eight summer sports were set for the year 2008, and seven sports are scheduled for the 2010 Winter Games. "The range of sports has expanded enormously," says Potter. "The Olympians established a very

small canon[2] of sports initially. Now it appears to be an Olympian sport in itself to see what can be added each time." **C**

Ancient Olympians battled the Mediterranean heat, so to toughen up, they practiced in the sun. At the events, according to historians, they wore little or no clothing. Such a dress code would be shocking to modern sensibilities and a blow to manufacturers of sportswear and accessories—who, like shoemakers, make certain to place their products in the public eye during the Olympic Games. **D**

---

2. **canon** (KAN uhn): accepted body of rules, principles, or other norms. Here, the word refers to sports approved for the ancient Olympics.

B **Informational Focus** Compare and Contrast In terms of when they are held, how are the modern Olympics like the ancient ones? How are they different?

C **Informational Focus** Compare and Contrast What point of contrast is Potter making here?

D **Informational Focus** Compare and Contrast What has changed since the ancient Greek games?

Analyzing Visuals **Connecting to the Text** How does the attitude of the athletes in this illustration compare to the attitude of Olympic athletes in general?

Timeless Traditions

What has stayed the same in the Olympic Games between ancient and contemporary times? The motivation of the athletes is one enduring value. The hope of victory and the chance for fame propel an athlete's future, and there is "enormous economic benefit" for winning, says Potter. (In fact, the Greek word *athlete* means "one who competes for a prize.") In 516 B.C., Milo of Kroton wrestled his way into history and became the most famous Olympian of ancient times and the subject of legends. In 2002, Sarah Hughes figure-skated her way to a Gold Medal. One was a man from an ancient world; the other, a woman from our time. However, both stand in a long line of athletes who established Olympian fame and then fortune. Although contemporary athletes may not become the subjects of legends that last for centuries, they can end up temporarily "immortalized" on cereal boxes, in magazine and TV ads, on billboards, and on product labels. **E**

Amateurs and Other Myths

"A myth was promulgated[3] that these guys were amateurs," says Potter of the original Olympians. "But these guys were professionals. The people who go to the Games want to see the best possible performance." Now,

---

3. **promulgated** (PRAHM uhl gayt ihd): spread; made known.

E **Informational Focus** Compare and Contrast
According to the article, what do ancient and modern athletes have in common?

Vocabulary **contemporary** (kuhn TEHM puh rehr ee) *adj.:* relating to the present time; modern.
amateurs (AM uh churz) *n.:* people who participate in sports or other activities for fun rather than money; not professionals.

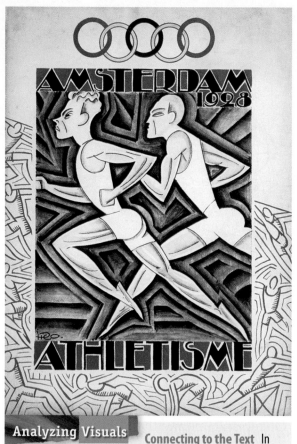

Analyzing Visuals **Connecting to the Text** In what way does the design of this poster for the 1928 Olympics reinforce the author's claim that the Olympics are timeless?

as in ancient times, people expect to witness the highest levels of athletic achievement at the Olympics. The athletes may not be professionals in the strict sense of the term—people of outstanding qualifications and experience hired and paid to perform—but they are true professionals in their level of achievement and commitment to their sport.

Another myth is that female Olympians like Hughes are something new. Ancient Olympia had a festival to honor Hera, the wife of Zeus, and in that festival unmarried girls ran footrace competitions. So women, too, have been holding the Olympic torch from the start. **F**

Carrying a Torch for the Olympics

In reality, though, no one has held the torch from the "start" of the Olympics in ancient times. The symbol of the Olympic torch wasn't introduced until 1928. Although the Greeks used torches in many of their religious festivals and kept a fire burning in honor of the god Prometheus during the ancient Olympic Games, there was no opening ceremony involving an Olympic torch. The Olympic torch ceremony—like the Olympic symbol of five interconnected rings—is actually a modern touch, a bit of dramatic staging. **G**

The main constant in the Olympics, says Potter, is the sense that the Games stand apart in time. "That weekend, for that weekend, the world would stop," he says. "You wanted to be there." Judging by the interest in today's Olympics, that old feeling remains. It's just that the audience has widened from those hundreds or thousands in attendance at the ancient Greek Olympic Games to the many millions of fascinated TV and Internet viewers around the world today.

Read with a Purpose In what main ways are the Olympics today still like the games that were held in ancient Greece?

F **Read and Discuss** What point is the writer making here about Olympic athletes?

G **Read and Discuss** What is this paragraph telling you about the Olympic torch?

Applying Your Skills

Reading Standard 2.2 Analyze text that uses the compare-and-contrast organizational pattern.

Olympic Glory: Victories in History

Standards Review

Informational Text and Vocabulary

1. Which of the following was an addition to the Olympic Games in modern times?

A crowds

B the Olympic torch

C footraces

D competition

2. Which of the following is a similarity between the Olympics of ancient and modern times?

A Winter Olympics

B sportswear and accessories

C fame and fortune

D Olympic rings symbol

3. The section "Timeless Traditions" in this article *mostly* deals with the

A rules of the original Olympic events.

B times when the Olympics were less popular.

C ways in which the Olympics have stayed the same.

D origin of the ancient games.

4. In which situation would reading an article using the **compare-and-contrast organizational pattern** be most helpful?

A You need to find out how life in China differs from life in the United States.

B You need to do research on Milo of Kroton.

C You need to find out why Jack London is considered a great American writer.

D You want to learn how a sport becomes an Olympic event.

5. *Victorious* is *most* similar in meaning to which of the following words?

A winning

B unsuccessful

C interesting

D cheating

6. The word that is *most* nearly the opposite of *contemporary* is

A athletic.

B separate.

C exciting.

D ancient.

7. When *amateurs* compete in a sport, they don't

A train regularly.

B earn money.

C have excellent skills.

D have any fans.

Writing Skills Focus

Timed └Writing Choose two things—dog breeds, kinds of cars, your favorite bands—and analyze their similarities and differences in an essay using the compare-and-contrast organizational pattern. Include phrases that signal when you're making a comparison or a contrast.

 What Do **You Think Now** Is it possible to be a "winner" and yet not have done the right thing? How might this happen in the Olympics?

Reading Standard 2.2 Analyze text that uses the compare-and-contrast organizational pattern.

Going to Bat for Baseball and Cricket

Informational Text Focus

Point-by-Point and Block Patterns When writers **compare** things, they look for similarities. When they **contrast** things, they look for differences. A writer who wants to explore two subjects that have important similarities and differences will use a **compare-and-contrast organizational pattern** that makes his or her points obvious to readers.

Writers generally arrange their ideas according to one of two compare-and-contrast organizational patterns: the point-by-point pattern and the block pattern. A writer using the **point-by-point pattern** moves back and forth between the subjects being compared, exploring each point for both subjects before moving to the next point. A writer using the **block pattern** covers all the points of comparison for the first subject and then all the points of comparison for the second subject. (See the charts below.)

Point-by-Point Pattern	
Point 1: teams	Baseball: two teams of nine players
	Cricket: two teams of eleven players
Point 2: field	Baseball: infield and outfield
	Cricket: the pitch and wickets

Block Pattern	
Subject 1: baseball	Point 1: teams; Point 2: field . . .
Subject 2: cricket	Point 1: teams; Point 2: field . . .

Writing Skills Focus

Preparing for **Timed Writing** The following article explains how baseball and cricket have much in common and yet have many differences. Pay attention to the features of each sport and where and how the features are presented in the article.

Reader/Writer
Notebook

Use your **RWN** to complete the activities for this selection.

Language Coach

Prefixes A **prefix** is a letter or group of letters added to the beginning of a word or a word part to create a new word. Each prefix has a specific meaning—sometimes more than one meaning. The first two Vocabulary words above have common prefixes: *com–*, meaning "together," and *pro–*, meaning "before," "moving forward," or "in support of." What other words do you know that begin with *com–* or *pro–*? What are their meanings?

Learn It Online
Use Word Watch to dig deeper into your understanding of words:

go.hrw.com	H6-202	Go

GOING TO BAT
for Baseball and Cricket

by  THE WORLD ALMANAC®

Read with a Purpose
Read to discover fascinating information about two popular sports.

Although there are other hugely popular American sports, such as football and basketball, baseball has a special place in Americans' hearts. In fact, baseball—which has been part of U.S. culture since the first recorded professional game in 1846—is often called "America's pastime." Not only Americans love the game: Baseball has proven to be a big hit from Canada to Latin America and from Japan to South Korea and Taiwan. Today it's played in more than one hundred countries.

Another famous sport played with bats and balls is a game from England called cricket—and it has nothing to do with the insect! Cricket is so near and dear to British culture that there's even a saying— "It's just not cricket"—to describe something that's unfair, wrong, or just not exactly what it should be. Cricket is a lot older than baseball—some say that a version of cricket was played hundreds of years ago, in the Middle Ages. Cricket is especially popular in the Commonwealth nations once ruled by Great Britain: Australia, India, parts of the Caribbean, Kenya, South Africa, and Zimbabwe. In all, cricket is played and enjoyed in more than 100 nations throughout the world. **A**

Both baseball and cricket involve a team that is fielding and another that is batting. Beyond that basic similarity, though, there is a world of difference between the two games. **B**

A Informational Focus Compare and Contrast
Which organizational pattern does the writer seem to be setting up in these first two paragraphs: block pattern or point-by-point pattern? What makes you think this?

B Read and Discuss What is the writer setting up for you in this paragraph?

The In(ning)s and Outs of Baseball

Baseball is a competition between two teams of nine players each (not including reserves).[1] Nine periods called *innings* make up a regular game. The game is played on an infield and an outfield. The *infield* is outlined by four flat *bases* laid out in a diamond shape, with the fourth base, known as *home plate,* at the bottom. Inside the diamond is a *pitcher's mound.* Beyond the diamond top is the *outfield.*

The person throwing the fist-sized ball from the mound is the *pitcher.* An opposing player, known as the *batter,* stands next to home plate and attempts to hit the ball with a rounded, narrow wooden bat. Behind the batter is the *catcher.* The pitcher aims for the *strike zone,* the area over home plate between the batter's shoulders and knees. If the ball goes through the strike zone without bouncing and the batter misses, the pitch is a *strike.*

One batter is up at a time. If the pitcher accidentally hits the batter with the ball, the batter gets to advance to first base. Pitchers try to avoid that, so batters do not need to wear protective pads, as some sports players do. They do, however, wear helmets. After all, some of those baseballs come at them pretty fast—sometimes more than 100 miles per hour in professional games! **C**

---

1. **reserves** (rih ZURVZ): players on a team who back up the starters or come into the game for special situations.

A batter's goal is to run the bases, so he or she tries to hit the ball toward an area of the field that is not well guarded. Generally, batters hit the ball in a forceful, aggressive way, using all their might. After hitting the ball, the batter has to drop the bat immediately and run for the bases. Players move around the bases counterclockwise, scoring for each runner who reaches home plate. If the batter has hit the ball forcefully *and* far—maybe even "hitting it out of the ballpark"—he or she may have scored a *home run,* meaning that the batter will be able to make it all the way around the bases without getting tagged "out." (An *out* occurs when a runner is tagged while not on base, though an out can also be called when three strikes are thrown or when a fielder catches a batted ball.) **D**

Because each team gets three outs per inning and those outs can take a while to pile up, the pace of a baseball game can be slow. Most professional games are over in three to three and a half hours, but sometimes a game will go into extra innings. The longest such game in the more modern history of baseball lasted twenty-five innings—a little over eight hours! Even a nine-inning game can last four and a half hours or more. Still, time spent playing doesn't necessarily equal points. Scores in baseball games tend to be low—often in the single digits. The highest number of runs ever scored in a single baseball game

---

C Read and Discuss You've been given a lot of information. What does the writer want you to learn from it?

D Informational Focus Compare and Contrast So far in this section, the writer has been telling you only about the rules of baseball and nothing about cricket. Why?

Vocabulary **competition** (kahm puh TIHSH uhn) *n.:* contest; struggle to see who is better.
protective (pruh TEHK tihv) *adj.:* preventing injury.
aggressive (uh GREHS ihv) *adj.:* ready to attack.

Analyzing Visuals

Connecting to the Text
What similarities and differences between the batter and the batsman described in the article do you see in these photographs?

was 49, way back in 1922, when the Chicago Cubs defeated the Philadelphia Phillies with a final score of 26–23. **E**

What's a Wicket in Cricket?

Cricket is played by two teams of eleven players each on an elliptical, or oval-shaped, field. The center of the field is the *pitch,* a rectangle marked at each end by white lines called *popping creases,* or just *creases.* Beyond each crease is a *wicket:* three wooden stumps topped by two cross pieces. The *bowler* (not pitcher) stands behind a wicket. He or she runs up to the crease from behind the wicket and then releases the ball—which most often bounces at least once—toward an opposing player known as the *batsman.* **F**

Teams are divided into bowling and batting sides. The bowling team has all eleven of its players on the field—one is the bowler, another is the *wicket keeper,* and the rest play various fielding positions. A cricket match is very long, and it is divided up into *overs.* Each *over* consists of the bowler delivering the ball to a batsman six times in a row. After the sixth bowl, the bowler rotates to take a fielding position, and another member of the team takes his or her place.

E **Informational Focus** Compare and Contrast
What was the topic of the section you just read? Is this article organized mostly in a point-by-point pattern or a block pattern?

F **Informational Focus** Compare and Contrast
How many players are on each team in cricket? in baseball? Where in the article did you find each of these facts?

The batting team has only two batsmen on the field at a time, each standing on opposite ends of the field near a wicket. The batsman who is chosen to receive the ball from the bowler is called the *striker;* the other batsman is the *nonstriker,* who stands near the bowler's end of the field. The bats used in cricket are wide and flat, and a batsman's goal is to keep the ball away from the wicket. When the striker hits the ball into the field, he or she may run across the pitch still holding the bat and change places with the nonstriker. A *run* is scored each time a batsman reaches the opposite crease. Batsmen have to watch out, though. Bowlers are allowed to hit batsmen, so batsmen cover up with protective pads. It can get dangerous on the cricket field!   **G**

There are at least ten ways that an *out,* also called a *dismissal,* can be declared against a batsman in cricket. (One way is to break the wicket!) When all ten batsmen from each side have been declared "out" once, an *innings* (the *s* is no mistake) has been completed. Generally, a cricket match of one innings takes place in one day and lasts up to six or even eight hours! (Some cricket matches can take place over three to five days.) In a typical cricket match, the two teams can make hundreds of runs, and scores can be in the triple digits.   **H**

The differences between baseball and cricket could fill a book. In fact, both games have very detailed rule books that you can find online. These rule books point to what is perhaps the biggest similarity the games share: their emphasis on good sportsmanship, on playing fairly and "by the rules." Just don't let the presence of a bat and a ball in both sports fool you. It's just not cricket to confuse the two games!   **I**

Read with a Purpose What did you learn about either baseball or cricket that you didn't know before?

G **Informational Focus** **Compare and Contrast**
How do cricket bats differ from baseball bats?

H **Read and Discuss** Now what is the author talking about? What do the high scores tell you about the game?

I **Read and Discuss** What is the main point the author is trying to make about baseball and cricket? If you have never played either cricket or baseball, what's to be gained from reading this article?

Applying Your Skills

Going to Bat for Baseball and Cricket

Standards Review

Informational Text and Vocabulary

1. Which of the following statements is true of baseball?

   A Each team gets nine outs per game.

   B Batters wear only protective pads, not helmets.

   C The pitcher stands on a mound.

   D Scores tend to be high, often more than one hundred runs.

2. This article was written *mainly* to

   A name different sports around the world.

   B persuade people to play baseball more often.

   C prove that cricket is the best sport.

   D explain the differences between baseball and cricket.

3. In cricket, the two batsmen stand

   A on top of each wicket.

   B on opposite ends of the field.

   C next to the bowler.

   D next to each other.

4. To compare and contrast baseball and cricket, this writer *mainly* uses which organizational pattern?

   A chronological pattern

   B point-by-point pattern

   C block pattern

   D cause-and-effect pattern

5. Any type of game that involves *competition* involves

   A bats and balls.

   B a playing field.

   C winners and losers.

   D players from around the world.

6. How can you tell if a baseball player is playing in an *aggressive* way?

   A He drops the bat.

   B He swings the bat hard.

   C He wears pads.

   D He declares another player "out."

7. One kind of *protective* equipment is a

   A pitch.

   B helmet.

   C bowler.

   D wicket.

Writing Skills Focus

Timed └Writing Compare and contrast two games you know well by explaining two ways in which they are similar and two ways in which they are different. Present the similarities and differences using the point-by-point organizational pattern.

What Do You Think Now?

Why do competitive sports like baseball and cricket have strict rules? What would organized sports be like without such rules?

Writing Workshop

"How-to" Explanation

Write with a Purpose

Write a "how-to" explanation that teaches readers how to do something or make something. Your **audience** is other students your age. Your **purpose** is to explain each step so clearly that your audience can easily follow your directions.

Reader/Writer Notebook

Use your **RWN** to complete the activities for this workshop.

Think as a Reader/Writer

Before you write your "how-to" explanation, read this excerpt from Paula Morrow's "Making a Flying Fish," published in *FACES* magazine. The article explains how to make a *koinobori*, a fish that is made of cloth or strong paper. The *koinobori* is attached to a pole in the gardens of many Japanese families to honor their children.

> You can make your own *koinobori* and fly it from a pole or hang it from your window on May 5. In that way, you can share Children's Day with the boys and girls of Japan.
>
> You need an 18- by 30-inch piece of lightweight cloth (cotton, rayon, or nylon), fabric paints or felt-tip markers, a needle and thread, scissors, a narrow plastic headband, and string.
>
> First, choose a piece of cloth with a bright, colorful pattern or decorate it yourself with felt-tip markers. Fold the fabric in half lengthwise, with the bright side on the inside. Sew a seam 1/2 inch from the long (30-inch) edge, making a sleeve.
>
> On one end of the sleeve, make a 1-inch-wide hem by turning the right side of the fabric over the wrong side. Then, sew the hem, leaving three 1-inch-wide openings about 5 inches apart.

← The introduction states a **clear purpose,** why you would want to make a *koinobori*.

← All the necessary **materials** are listed.

← Words like *First* help readers know the **order** of steps to follow.

← The author is very **precise** about the size and placement of the openings.

Think About the Professional Model

With a partner, discuss the following questions about the model:

1. Which step can you picture most clearly in your mind? Why?
2. The magazine article included an illustration of the step described in the last paragraph. Is the step clear without the illustration? Why or why not?

Writing Standard 1.2 Create multiple-paragraph expository compositions: a. Engage the interest of the reader and state a clear purpose. b. Develop the topic with supporting details and precise verbs, nouns, and adjectives to paint a visual image in the mind of the reader. c. Conclude with a detailed summary linked to the purpose of the composition. **1.5 Compose documents with appropriate formatting by using word-processing skills and principles of design (e.g., margins, tabs, spacing, columns, page orientation). 2.2 Write expository** compositions (e.g., description, **explanation,** comparison and contrast, problem and solution): a. State the thesis or purpose. b. Explain the situation. c. Follow an organizational pattern appropriate to the type of composition. d. Offer persuasive evidence to validate arguments and conclusions as needed.

Prewriting

Choose a Topic

To choose a topic for your "how-to" explanation, follow the rule successful writers live by: Write about what you know. Brainstorm a list of products that you have made or processes that you know how to complete. The Idea Starters in the margin at right might be helpful.

As you narrow your list of ideas, make a chart like the one below to help you evaluate the topics. You can see which topic would be best for this student by examining his answers to the questions.

Idea Starters
- something you have built or made at home
- a school project
- your favorite recipe
- handicrafts you can make
- tasks that relate to your favorite hobby or pastime

Topic	Have I made this or done this before, and do I know the process well?	Does this process have a manageable number of steps (between three and five)?
How to make a paper swan	yes	No—it has more than five steps.
How to instant message	yes	Yes—it has about four steps.
How to build a soapbox car	Not really—I helped my older brother make it.	No—this probably takes more than five steps.
How to remove a bicycle wheel with quick-release hubs	yes	No—there are really only two steps.

Choose an Organizational Pattern

One of the most important parts of writing an effective "how-to" explanation is presenting the steps in the proper order. This structure gives the explanation coherence—that is, the parts fit together in a way that makes sense to the reader. When a "how-to" explanation lacks coherence, readers can become very frustrated. Most "how-to" explanations are written in **chronological order,** or the order in which steps should be carried out.

To think of the steps in chronological order, imagine making the product or completing the process. What do you do first, next, and last? As you picture each step, write it down. Then, look over your steps and add anything you left out.

Your Turn

Get Started In your **RWN,** list the steps required to make your product or complete your process. Be sure to number the steps in correct **chronological order.** Your explanation should follow this chronological order.

Learn It Online
See how one writer develops a how-to essay at:

go.hrw.com H6-209   Go

Writing Tip

Think about specific details you can use to describe your steps and materials list. Ask questions such as *when? where? what kind? which one? how?* and *how much?* Write down these specific details in your **RWN** so you will remember to be precise as you write your draft.

List the Materials

Once you have decided on the steps and their correct order, look them over to see what **materials** are required. List the materials, thinking carefully about everything needed to make the product or complete the process. Be **precise** in how you describe materials. For example, "a two-inch length of black yarn" is more precise than merely "yarn." Double-check the list when you complete it. If you leave something out of your materials list, your readers will not be able to follow your directions successfully.

Now decide where you want to place the list of materials within your explanation. Most "how-to" explanations include the materials list at the beginning, separate from the steps. However, as you saw in "Making a Flying Fish," the materials can also be presented in paragraph form.

Consider Purpose and Audience

Since your **purpose** is to teach someone how to do or make something, make sure you can successfully complete this process yourself. You are acting as an expert on the process, so you need to be confident that your instructions are accurate and complete. As you select your final topic, also remember that your **audience** is other students your age. Try to choose something they will *want* to do or make, and think about how specific you'll need to be in describing the steps and materials.

Organize Your Ideas

Use a planning chart like the one below to organize your ideas. This chart has been completed for the Student Draft on pages 213–214.

Planning Chart for "How to Instant Message"

Purpose statement	Explain how to use instant messaging
Materials list	None (understood that computer or other IM device will be needed)
Steps in order	1. Get registered. 2. Sign on. 3. Fill the buddy list. 4. Select a buddy, type a message, and click "send."
Restatement of purpose	You are instantly connected with buddies.

Your Turn _____

Create a Planning Chart Use a planning chart to organize your ideas for your own "how-to" explanation. Be sure to include all the **materials** that will be needed and to use **precise language** to describe materials and steps.

Drafting

Get Your Readers' Attention

As you start to write your draft, think of a way to draw the reader into your "how-to" explanation. One way to engage the reader is to begin with a question. For example, if you were going to explain how to make a spicy soup, you could begin with a question like "Do you want to beat the winter blahs?" Then you could state your purpose: "This recipe will show you how to make a chill-chasing soup with ingredients found in most kitchens." You can refer to the Writer's Framework at right as you write your draft.

A "How-to" Explanation Framework
Introduction
• Attention-grabbing opener and purpose statement
Body
• Materials list, if any
• Step 1 (with precise language)
• Step 2 (with precise language) and so on . . .
Conclusion
• Summary of steps and restatement of purpose

Present Steps Clearly and Use Transitions

One way to present the steps of your process is to describe one step per paragraph. Another way is to use a numbered list. Both techniques offer visual cues that you are presenting new steps.

You can also make your steps clear and focused by connecting them with transitions. "How-to" explanations most often use chronological and spatial transitions.

- **Chronological transitions,** such as *first, second, after, next, then, finally,* and *last,* answer the question "In what order?"

- **Spatial transitions,** such as *inside, outside, above, below, into,* and *out of,* answer the question "Where?"

Grammar Link Punctuating Words in a Series

When you write a "how-to" explanation, you may present steps or list materials in a series. A **series** consists of three or more items written one after another. Study the following example from "Making a Flying Fish," and be sure to follow the rules for punctuating a series when you write your draft.

> "You need an 18- by 30-inch piece of lightweight cloth (cotton, rayon, or nylon), fabric paints or felt-tip markers, a needle and thread, scissors, a narrow plastic headband, and string."

Use commas to separate three or more items in a series.

● Writing Tip

Remember that your conclusion should **summarize the thesis, restating the reason** for making the product or completing the process.

Your Turn _____

Write Your Draft Follow your plan and the framework to write a draft of your "how-to" explanation. Remember to think about the following:

- How will you get your readers' attention?
- What **transitions** can you use to make your steps clear?

Peer Review

Have a partner read your explanation to see how confident he or she feels about being able to complete the process. Take notes about any questions your partner has. Then, serve as your partner's reviewer. Use this chart to locate where and how your draft can be improved.

Evaluating and Revising

Once you've written your draft, you'll want to go back through and look for ways to improve your "how-to" explanation. The chart below will help you identify ways to revise your draft.

"How-to" Explanation: Guidelines for Content and Organization

Evaluation Question	Tip	Revision Technique
1. Does the introduction grab the readers' attention and state why they would want to complete this process? Does it state a clear purpose?	**Put an asterisk** next to the statement of the reason readers would want to complete the process. **Put brackets** around the statement of purpose.	If needed, **add** a more powerful statement of the reason. **Add** a statement of purpose.
2. Are all of the required materials listed?	**Circle** all the materials needed, if any.	**Add** any materials that have been left out.
3. Are the steps of the process in the correct order?	**Write a number** next to each step in the margin of the paper.	To improve coherence, **rearrange** the steps so they are in the correct order. To make the order clear, number each step or part or put each step in its own paragraph.
4. Do you use transitional words to make the organization of your process clear?	Use a **colored highlighter** to mark chronological transitions such as *first, second, after, next, last*. Use a different colored highlighter to mark spatial transitions such as *inside, outside, above, below,* and *into*.	**Add** chronological and spatial transitions where needed.
5. Is each step described with precise language?	**Underline** precise verbs, nouns, and adjectives.	If necessary, **elaborate** on the steps by adding precise words.
6. Does the conclusion restate the reason for completing the process?	**Put a star** beside the sentence that restates the reason.	**Add** a sentence that restates the reason, if necessary.

Read this student draft, and notice the comments on its strengths as well as suggestions on how the draft could be improved.

Student Draft

How to Instant Message
by Christopher Cultrara, Queen of Peace Elementary School

Today, people use many different forms of communication, from letters to e-mail. Instant messaging is quickly becoming a favorite of people of all ages. In this essay I'll explain how to get started on instant messaging.

The first thing you need to do is get registered and get a screen name. Most people use a common instant messaging engine, so that's where you should start. Go to the instant messaging Web site and click on the "get a new screen name" link. Next, fill in all of the information that's requested. Then, enter the screen name you want to use, and enter a password. Your screen name and password can be anything you want. I always write my password and screen name in a safe place in case I forget them. Finally, click on "submit" to submit all of the information. You should then have your screen name and be able to sign on.

← The **introduction** makes general comments about instant messaging.

← Steps of the process are in **chronological order,** and Christopher uses clear **chronological order** words.

← Christopher adds a personal note of advice.

MINI-LESSON ▶ How to Introduce a "How-to" Essay

The introduction of a "how-to" essay should explain why the topic is interesting or important and should connect the **audience** to the task. Your introduction should help a reader answer, "Why do I need to know this?"

Christopher begins his essay by mentioning the widespread interest in instant messaging and then tells his readers that he will describe how to use instant messaging. A clear explanation of *why* readers might want to use instant messaging would make his introduction more effective.

Christopher's Revision of Paragraph One

~~Today, people use many different forms of communication, from letters to e-mail.~~ Instant messaging is quickly becoming a favorite of people of all ages. ~~In this essay, I'll explain how to get started on instant messaging.~~

I use this fun and simple form of communication every day. I stay in contact with everyone and never miss important events or parties anymore. If you are looking for a quick way to stay in immediate contact with your family and friends, then instant messaging is for you. Read this essay; then get ready for flying fingers!

Your Turn _____

Introduce Your "How-to" Essay Read your draft to make sure your introduction connects the audience to the task. Ask yourself these questions:

- Have I explained why the topic is interesting?
- Have I suggested a possible connection for the reader?

"How-to" Explanation

> Now you need to fill your buddy list. To get your buddy list, you must sign on using your screen name. Once you are signed on and your buddy list comes up, you can begin to enter your friends' screen names. Insert them into your buddy list by typing them in under "new buddy."
>
> Once you get some specific names in your list, you can arrange them into groups, such as "friends" or "family." You can also make up new groups and call them anything you want.
>
> Now that you are set up, instant messaging itself is very simple. Just click on the buddy you want to instant message. That will display the instant message window. Type in your message and hit "send." That's all there is to it. You and your "buddies" are connected in an instant! Enjoy!

Specific details and **precise examples** help readers "visualize" the steps.

The conclusion **restates** why readers would want to complete this process.

MINI-LESSON > **How to Add Personal Advice**

A "how-to" essay can be dry and impersonal if the writer does not include advice or tips throughout. When Christopher revised his paper, he decided to add some personal advice based on his own experience.

Christopher's Draft of Paragraph Three

> Now you need to fill your buddy list. To get your buddy list, you must sign on using your screen name. Once you are signed on and your buddy list comes up, you can begin to enter your friends' screen names. Insert them into your buddy list by typing them in under "new buddy."

Christopher's Revision of Paragraph Three

> Now you need to fill your buddy list. To get your buddy list, you must sign on using your screen name. Once you are signed on and your buddy list comes up, you can begin to enter your friends' screen names. Insert them into your buddy list by typing them in under "new buddy." *When you're sending a message, be careful to select your intended buddy. I once sent a message to an entire group of friends, and I meant to send it only to my brother—extremely embarrassing!*

Your Turn

Add Personal Advice Re-read your "how-to" explanation, looking for places where you can add personal advice or experience that is specific and helpful. Add at least one tip or experience that could help your reader be more successful with the task.

Designing Your Writing

Formatting Your Writing

Formatting is how text is arranged. Formatting can make a big difference in how your explanation looks and how easy it is to follow. Arrange your information in different ways by adjusting *spacing, margins,* and *columns.*

- **Spacing** is the distance between lines of text. In **single-spaced text,** the lines are close together. Books, newspapers, and magazines are typically single-spaced. **Double-spaced text** has a full space between lines of text. Double-spacing your classroom papers allows you to make corrections or your teacher to write comments on the page more easily.

- **Margins** are the spaces above, below, to the left, and to the right of the text on the page. Most word-processing programs automatically set the margins of a new page, but they will allow you to set each margin separately. Pages with very small margins, like Example A, can be difficult to read and nearly impossible to write comments on. Pages with

Example A

Example B

larger margins, like Example B, look better and are easier to read. On an 8½- x 11-inch piece of paper, a standard margin is about an inch on each side of the text.

- **Columns** are the sections of text that run vertically, side-by-side on a page. Most word-processing programs allow you to format your text in columns. Two-column text takes up less space than single-column text. If you wanted to publish a class set of "how-to" explanations on saving natural resources, you might use double columns to save paper, as shown in Example C.

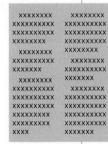

Example C

Reflect on the Process
Thinking about how you wrote your "how-to" explanation will help you with other types of writing. In your **RWN,** write a short response to each of the following questions:

1. Which step in the process was hardest for you to explain? How did you think through this problem?

2. How did creating a materials list cause you to think differently about using descriptions and explanations in your writing?

3. What writing skill that you learned in this workshop could you use in other types of writing?

Scoring Rubric

You can use the rubric below to evaluate your "how-to" explanation.

	Expository Writing	Organization and Focus	Sentence Structure	Conventions
4	• Focuses *consistently* on a process appropriate to the prompt. • Offers a *thoughtful, creative* explanation of the process. • Explains each step of the assigned process *thoroughly*.	• *Clearly* addresses all parts of the writing task. • Demonstrates a *clear* understanding of purpose and audience. • Shows *effective* step-by-step organization throughout, with *smooth* transitions. • Includes a *clearly presented* purpose with *relevant* details.	• Includes sentence *variety* (e.g., simple, complex, compound-complex).	• Contains *few, if any,* errors in the conventions of the English language (grammar, punctuation, capitalization, spelling). These errors do **not** interfere with the reader's understanding of the writing.
3	• Focuses on an appropriate process, with *minor* distractions. • Offers a *mostly thoughtful* explanation of the process. • Explains the process *adequately*, with a mixture of general and specific instructions.	• Addresses most of the writing task. • Demonstrates a *general* understanding of purpose and audience. • Shows *effective* step-by-step organization, with *minor* lapses. • Presents the purpose with *mostly relevant* details.	• Includes some sentence *variety* (e.g., simple, complex, compound-complex).	• Contains *some errors* in the conventions of the English language (grammar, punctuation, capitalization, spelling). These errors do **not** interfere with the reader's understanding of the writing.
2	• Includes some *loosely related* material that *distracts* from the writer's how-to focus. • Offers a *routine, predictable* explanation of the process. • Explains the process with *uneven* elaboration.	• Addresses *some* of the writing task. • Demonstrates *little* understanding of purpose and audience. • Shows *some* organization with *noticeable* gaps in presentation of the process. • Suggests a purpose with *limited* details.	• Includes *little* sentence variety.	• Contains *several errors* in the conventions of the English language (grammar, punctuation, capitalization, spelling). These errors **may** interfere with the reader's understanding of the writing.
1	• Shows *little awareness* of the topic and process. • Offers an *unclear* and *confusing* explanation. • Develops the explanation in only a *minimal* way, if at all.	• Addresses *only one* or *no* part of the writing task. • Demonstrates *no* understanding of purpose and audience. • Lacks organization. • Lacks a purpose, but may contain marginally related details.	• Includes *no* sentence variety.	• Contains *serious errors* in the conventions of the English language (grammar, punctuation, capitalization, spelling). These errors *interfere* with the reader's understanding of the writing.

Preparing for Timed Writing

"How-to" Explanation

When responding to an on-demand prompt for a "how-to" explanation, use the models you have read, what you've learned from writing your own "how-to" explanation, the rubric on page 216, and the steps below.

> **Writing Standard 2.2 Write expository compositions (e.g., description, explanation, comparison and contrast, problem and solution): a. State the thesis or purpose. b. Explain the situation. c. Follow an organizational pattern appropriate to the type of composition. d. Offer persuasive evidence to validate arguments and conclusions as needed.**

Writing Prompt

Your younger sister would like to borrow your cell phone, but she doesn't know how to use it. Write a "how-to" explanation that teaches students your age or younger how to use a cell phone. Use precise language, and present the steps in chronological order.

Study the Prompt

Begin by reading the prompt carefully. Notice that your **purpose** is to teach someone how to use a cell phone. Your **audience** includes students your age or younger. The prompt also instructs you to use **precise language** and to organize the steps in **chronological order.**

Tip: Spend about five minutes studying the prompt.

Plan Your Response

Once you have a solid grasp of what the prompt is requiring you to write,

- write down the topic of your explanation
- consider why you are writing and what your audience will need explained most carefully
- write the steps of your explanation in chronological order (the order in which the steps are completed)
- review your steps and make a list of anything that will be needed to complete the task.

Tip: Spend about ten minutes planning your response.

Respond to the Prompt

Using the notes you've just made, draft your essay. Follow these guidelines:

- In the opening, engage readers, give them a purpose and clear understanding of what you are explaining, and tell them why they should want to complete the task.
- In the body, list any materials needed to complete the task, and use precise language to present the steps in chronological order.
- In the conclusion, summarize the steps and restate the reason for completing the task.

As you are writing, be sure to use words that are appropriate for your audience. Your tone should not be too informal. Write as neatly as you can. If your essay can't be read easily, it won't be scored.

Tip: Spend about twenty minutes writing your draft.

Improve Your Response

Revising Go back over the key aspects of the explanation. Did you explain why readers would want to do or make what you are explaining? Did you organize your explanation clearly and provide steps in chronological order?

Proofreading Take a few minutes to proofread your work to correct errors in grammar, spelling, punctuation, and capitalization. Make sure all your edits are neat, and erase any stray marks.

Checking Your Final Copy Before you turn in your explanation, read it one more time to catch any errors you may have missed.

Tip: Save five or ten minutes to improve your essay.

Listening & Speaking Workshop

Following Oral Instructions and Directions

Think as a Reader/Writer The ability to write clear instructions is a very important skill. Likewise, being able to follow multiple-step oral instructions is a skill you need for life.

Do you sometimes find it hard to follow spoken instructions? Maybe you "tune out" for a moment, only to realize later that you have missed an important step. You can improve your ability to follow instructions and directions given aloud by learning to listen effectively and with care.

Listen to Instructions

Listen for Cues

Good listeners do much more than hear a speaker; they really listen. *Hearing* means being able to detect sounds. *Listening* means getting meaning from sounds that are heard. Listening is an active process. An active listener thinks while listening, trying to interpret the main points. The best listeners are able to pick up on cues from the speaker that help them follow the speaker's ideas. These include

- **verbal cues:** spoken hints, including how the words are said.
- **nonverbal cues:** unspoken hints, such as movements, facial expressions, and gestures.

Focus and Take Notes

Good listeners also **focus** on the speaker and avoid distractions. One way to maintain your focus is to **take notes** on what the speaker is saying. Jot down key words and phrases, and note any questions that occur to you. If the speaker asks for questions, you can check your notes for points that you missed or did not understand.

As you ask a question, follow these guidelines:

- Wait until the speaker pauses before you ask a question.
- Ask in a clear, loud voice; do not mumble.
- Ask specific questions that show you have been listening.

Reader/Writer Notebook

Use your **RWN** to complete the activities for this workshop.

Repeat After Me

Use your notes to restate the instructions in your own words. First, check that you have gotten each of the steps. Then, be sure that you have enough details to understand how to execute the instructions. Repeat them out loud so you can evaluate your own understanding. Finally, read your restatement back to the speaker and ask him or her to check it. Here are one speaker's instructions and a listener's restatement of them.

Instructions:	To lock a bicycle securely, you need a U-lock and a cable. Place your bike next to a bike ring or a narrow pole. Open the U-lock and put it around the pole and the bike frame. Do not close the U-lock yet. First, attach one end of the cable to one side of the U-lock. Then, pass the cable through your front wheel, pulling the free end all the way through. Next, pass the cable through the back wheel. Finally, attach the free end of the cable to the other side of the U-lock and lock it.
Restatement:	Use a U-lock to secure the bike frame to a pole. Then, pass a cable through both wheels and attach each end to a different side of the U-lock. Close the lock.

Follow Geographic Directions

Geographic directions are a specific kind of instructions that tell the way to a certain place. It is important to pay attention to verbal and nonverbal cues when listening to geographic directions. If possible, take notes, ask questions, and restate the directions out loud to the person giving them. Look at the directions below and a listener's restatement.

Directions:	The trail starts just behind the lodge. Start by following the trail for about three miles. When the trail forks, bear left. When you reach the logging road, turn right. Stay on the logging road for about four miles. Just before you reach the summit, look for the sign for the Three Pines Trail on the right. Finally, take the Three Pines Trail back to the lodge.
Restatement:	Take the trail that starts behind the lodge for three miles, then bear left at the fork. Turn right on the logging road and follow it for four miles. Take the Three Pines Trail to the right and follow it to the lodge.

A Good Listener

- looks directly at the speaker and stays focused on what he or she is saying
- actively thinks while listening, interpreting the main points
- takes notes that include the key ideas and that pose questions
- uses restatement to check understanding

Listening Tip

Note taking can help you focus on the speaker's main points. Pay attention to verbal and nonverbal cues such as the following:

Verbal Cues

- words such as *first, next, last,* and *in conclusion.*
- repetition of important ideas.
- emphasis on important information, such as speaking more loudly or stressing certain words.

Nonverbal Cues

- "body language," or movements and facial expressions that show the speaker's mood or attitude.
- demonstrating the activity or using hand movements to emphasize important parts.
- facial expressions that ask for questions or encourage the listener's participation.

Literary Skills Review

Character   **Directions:** Read the following excerpt from a novel. Then, read and respond to the questions that follow.

from Julie of the Wolves by **Jean Craighead George**

Miyax stared hard at the regal black wolf, hoping to catch his eye. She must somehow tell him that she was starving and ask him for food. This could be done, she knew, for her father, an Eskimo[1] hunter, had done so. One year he had camped near a wolf den while on a hunt. When a month had passed and her father had seen no game, he told the leader of the wolves that he was hungry and needed food. The next night the wolf called him from far away and her father went to him and found a freshly killed caribou. Unfortunately, Miyax's father never explained to her how he had told the wolf of his needs. And not long afterward he paddled his kayak into the Bering Sea to hunt for seal, and he never returned.

She had been watching the wolves for two days, trying to discern which of their sounds and movements expressed good will and friendship. Most animals had such signals. The little Arctic ground squirrels flicked their tails sideways to notify others of their kind that they were friendly. By imitating this signal with her forefinger, Miyax had lured many a squirrel to her hand. If she could discover such a gesture for the wolves, she would be able to make friends with them and share their food, like a bird or a fox.

Propped on her elbows with her chin in her fists, she stared at the black wolf, trying to catch his eye. She had chosen him because he was much larger than the others, and because he walked like her father, Kapugen, with his head high and his chest out. The black wolf also possessed wisdom, she had observed. The pack looked to him when the wind carried strange scents or the birds cried nervously. If he was alarmed, they were alarmed. If he was calm, they were calm.

Long minutes passed, and the black wolf did not look at her. He had ignored her since she first came upon them, two sleeps ago. True, she moved slowly and quietly, so as not to alarm him; yet she did wish he would see the kindness in her eyes. Many animals could tell the difference between hostile hunters and friendly people by merely looking at them. But the big black wolf would not even glance her way.

A bird stretched in the grass. The wolf looked at it. A flower twisted in

---

1. **Eskimo** (EHS kuh moh): outdated term for the various groups of native peoples of Arctic Circle regions such as Canada, Alaska, and Greenland. Many native peoples, such as the Inuit, find the term offensive.

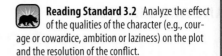

Reading Standard 3.2 Analyze the effect of the qualities of the character (e.g., courage or cowardice, ambition or laziness) on the plot and the resolution of the conflict.

the wind. He glanced at that. Then the breeze rippled the wolverine ruff on Miyax's parka and it glistened in the light. He did not look at that. She waited. Patience with the ways of nature had been instilled in her by her father. And so she knew better than to move or shout. Yet she must get food or die. Her hands shook slightly and she swallowed hard to keep calm.

1. Miyax can *best* be described as
   A careless.
   B patient.
   C shy.
   D funny.

2. Which of the following adjectives *best* describe Miyax's actions in the selection?
   A hurried and scared
   B graceful and smooth
   C calm and steady
   D hesitant and fumbling

3. In this excerpt from *Julie of the Wolves*, the author uses all of the following methods of characterization *except*
   A revealing thoughts.
   B quoting speech.
   C directly naming a character's qualities.
   D describing actions.

4. All of the following qualities are characteristic of the black wolf *except* being
   A leader of the pack.
   B quick to attack.
   C wise.
   D responsive to small changes that occur.

5. Which of these sentences from the excerpt reveals how Miyax feels about her situation?
   A "Propped on her elbows with her chin in her fists, she stared at the black wolf, trying to catch his eye."
   B "The black wolf also possessed wisdom, she had observed."
   C "Patience with the ways of nature had been instilled in her by her father."
   D "Her hands shook slightly and she swallowed hard to keep calm."

Timed Writing

6. Miyax must befriend the wolves in order to win her struggle to survive—her conflict. How do you think her qualities might affect the resolution of her conflict?

Informational Skills Review

Comparison / Contrast   **Directions:** Read the following selection. Then, read and respond to the questions that follow.

from All I Really Need to Know I Learned in Kindergarten by **Robert Fulghum**

This is my neighbor. Nice lady. Coming out her front door, on her way to work and in her "looking good" mode. She's locking the door now and picking up her daily luggage: purse, lunch bag, gym bag for aerobics, and the garbage bucket to take out. She turns, sees me, gives me the big, smiling Hello, and takes three steps across her front porch. And goes "AAAAAAAAGGGGGGGGG-HHHHHHHHH!!!!" *(That's a direct quote.)* At about the level of a fire engine at full cry. Spider web! She has walked full force into a spider web. And the pressing question, of course: Just where is the spider *now?*

She flings her baggage in all directions. And at the same time does a high-kick, jitter-bug sort of dance—like a mating stork in crazed heat. Clutches at her face and hair and goes "AAAAAAAGGGGG-GGHHHHHHHHHH!!!!!" at a new level of intensity. Tries opening the front door without unlocking it. Tries again. Breaks key in the lock. Runs around the house headed for the back door. Doppler effect[1] of "AAAAAGGGHHHHaaggh . . ."

Now a different view of this scene. Here is the spider. Rather ordinary, medium gray, middle-aged lady spider. She's been up since before dawn working on her web, and all is well. Nice day, no wind, dew point just right to keep things sticky. She's out checking the moorings and thinking about the little gnats she'd like for breakfast. Feeling good. Ready for action. All of a sudden everything breaks loose—earthquake, tornado, volcano. The web is torn loose and is wrapped around a frenzied moving haystack, and a huge piece of raw-but-painted meat is making a sound the spider never heard before: "AAAAAAAG-GGGGGGGGGHHHHHHHHHH!!!!!!" It's too big to wrap up and eat later, and it's moving too much to hold down. Jump for it? Hang on and hope? Dig in?

Human being. She has caught a human being. And the pressing question is, of course: Where is it going, and what will it do when it gets there?

The neighbor lady thinks the spider is about the size of a lobster and has big rub-

---

1. **Doppler effect:** change in the pitch of a sound, produced when the source of the sound moves toward or away from the listener.

ber lips and poisonous fangs. The neighbor lady will probably strip to the skin and take a full shower and shampoo just to make sure it's gone—and then put on a whole new outfit to make certain she is not inhabited.

The spider? Well, if she survives all this, she will really have something to talk about—the one that got away that was THIS BIG. "And you should have seen the JAWS on the thing!"

1. What does the writer compare and contrast in this essay?

   A a jitterbug and a stork

   B people and spiders

   C a spider web and a front porch

   D an earthquake and a tornado

2. What pattern does the writer use to organize his essay?

   A block method

   B point-by-point method

   C chronological order

   D cause-and-effect pattern

3. Both the human and the spider start out feeling

   A scared.

   B hungry.

   C good.

   D sleepy.

4. The human and the spider are both

   A very old.

   B male.

   C very young.

   D female.

5. Which of the following statements about the spider is *most* accurate?

   A The spider thinks of the human as meat.

   B The spider thinks of the human as a friend.

   C The spider screams.

   D The spider bites the human.

6. Which of the following statements about the human is *most* accurate?

   A The human thinks of the spider as meat.

   B The human thinks the spider is as big as a lobster.

   C The human thinks the spider got away.

   D The human thinks the spider is cute.

Timed Writing

7. According to the writer, what will the human do after the encounter with the spider? What will the spider do?

Vocabulary Skills Review

Shades of Meaning and Synonyms   Directions:
Choose the word or words that best complete each sentence.

1. A *stampede* is a

  A dance.

  B mark.

  C rush.

  D wind.

2. The *most* negative word is

  A sad.

  B unhappy.

  C depressed.

  D down.

3. The *best* word to use to describe a torn pair of jeans in bad condition is

  A old.

  B worn.

  C split.

  D raggedy.

4. The *strongest* word to use to describe the effect of a severe storm is

  A tumult.

  B disorder.

  C disturbance.

  D upset.

5. For a prospector, a *claim* is

  A a horse.

  B land.

  C a promise.

  D a crime.

6. If you are *invisible,* you cannot be

  A beaten.

  B heard.

  C seen.

  D captured.

7. *Adjoining* classrooms are

  A side by side.

  B across from one another.

  C on separate floors.

  D half the size of regular classrooms.

Academic Vocabulary

Directions: Choose the word that is closest in meaning to the italicized Academic Vocabulary word.

8. An *obvious* mistake is

  A big.

  B unimportant.

  C noticeable.

  D intentional.

Writing Skills Review

Writing Standard 2.2 Write expository compositions (e.g., description, **explanation**, comparison and contrast, problem and solution).

"How-to" Explanation
Directions: Read the following paragraph from a draft of a student's "how-to" paper. Then, answer each question.

Easy and Fun Zesty Bagels

(1) Evenly spread 1 tablespoon of spaghetti sauce over the face of each bagel. (2) First, you will need to cut the six plain bagels in half and place the halves on a cookie sheet. (3) Then, sprinkle ¼ cup chopped black olives, 6 finely chopped mushrooms, and 1 cup grated Parmesan cheese evenly over the sauce. (4) Place the cookie sheet in a preheated oven and bake for 15–20 minutes. (5) When the bagels are done, remove them from the oven and let them cool for 5 minutes.

1. If you were revising the paragraph above to put the instructions in chronological order, which sentence would you move?

   A 2

   B 3

   C 4

   D 5

2. If the writer wanted to add precise language to the paragraph, which of the following sentences would be appropriate?

   A You may add other toppings.

   B Your family will enjoy them.

   C Preheat the oven to 350 degrees.

   D Prepare the bagels.

3. If the writer wanted to add a transitional word to the beginning of sentence 5, which of the following would make the most sense?

   A However,

   B Meanwhile,

   C Since

   D Finally,

4. Which of these would you suggest the writer add to the recipe to make the instructions more helpful?

   A A list of ingredients to have ready

   B The number of times he or she has made these bagels

   C A definition of *zesty*

   D A quotation from someone who enjoys eating these bagels

5. If you were listening to, rather than reading, the instructions and were jotting down notes, which of the following would *best* summarize the last step?

   A Remove from oven, and cool 5 min.

   B Wash dishes.

   C Sprinkle olives, mushrooms, and Parmesan.

   D Pour sauce.

Read On

For Independent Reading

Fiction

Julie of the Wolves

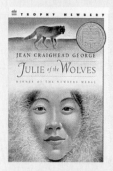

In Jean Craighead George's Newbery Award–winning novel *Julie of the Wolves*, a thirteen-year-old Inuit girl named Miyax runs away from home and gets lost on the frozen, treeless wilderness of the vast Alaskan tundra. Miyax is menaced by a host of dangers until a pack of wolves gradually accepts her as one of their own.

Perseus

In acclaimed author Geraldine McCaughrean's *Perseus,* you'll follow the teenage Perseus as he struggles with his fate that the oracles foretold. His seemingly impossible and deadly task is to kill the hideous, snake-haired Medusa to save his mother from marrying an evil king. In McCaughrean's retelling, the classic myth of Perseus becomes a coming-of-age story about an adventurous and lovesick young man.

Dealing with Dragons

When people were polite, they called her "strong-minded." When angry, they said she was "as stubborn as a pig." Cimorene, the hard-headed princess, runs away from her family's boring castle and is taken in by a powerful and good-hearted dragon. Throughout Patricia C. Wrede's *Dealing with Dragons,* you'll find contemporary dialogue woven into several familiar fairy tales that have been tweaked to create laugh-out-loud humor.

PaperQuake

San Francisco isn't the place to be if you're terrified of earthquakes, as Violet Jackstone is. Besides being frightened by the ground's tremors and teased mercilessly by her two popular sisters, she is frail and sickly and still called Baby. As her family renovates an old house, Violet finds mysterious letters and diaries that describe a girl very much like her. The girl, named V, lived nearly one hundred years ago, just before the deadly 1906 earthquake in San Francisco. *PaperQuake* is a popular time-travel mystery novel from author Kathryn Reiss.

Nonfiction

Changing Places

Homelessness is a problem that some people are uncomfortable discussing. In *Changing Places: A Kid's View of Shelter Living,* Margie Chalofsky, Glen Finland, and Judy Wallace give voice to eight homeless children. One of them, Roberto, bursts with pride when his mother finds a job. Another child, Anthony, is troubled by self-doubt and sadness. All tell stories of their own experiences—stories you will not soon forget.

Jesse Owens: Champion Athlete

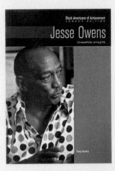

At the 1936 Olympic Games in Berlin, Jesse Owens, an African American athlete, undermined dictator Adolf Hitler's claim of German superiority. In *Jesse Owens: Champion Athlete,* Tony Gentry presents Owens from his youth in segregated Alabama, to his numerous athletic achievements, and to his death in 1980. High-quality black-and-white photographs help chronicle the career of this track-and-field great.

You Wouldn't Want to Be a Greek Athlete! Races You'd Rather Not Run

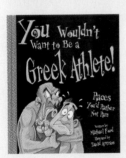

Imagine that you're living near Athens around 650 B.C. Your father sends you to a boarding school for athletes so that you can train for the Olympics. As you learn to compete in the pentathlon—racing and wrestling—you discover that life as an athlete in ancient Greece is not much fun. Michael Ford gives a humorous description, with well-researched facts, about why *You Wouldn't Want to Be a Greek Athlete!*

Gold Rush Dogs: And Other Favorite Dogs of the Last Frontier

Walt Frazier's life-and-death adventures and survival would have been impossible without the dogs of the Yukon. In *Gold Rush Dogs,* authors Claire Rudolf Murphy and Jane G. Haigh share action-filled stories of dogs who provided transportation, security, and companionship to the men, women, and children of the Alaska Gold Rush.

Learn It Online
Explore other novels and learn how to study them using *NovelWise* at:

go.hrw.com | H6-227 | Go

CHAPTER 3

Theme

INFORMATIONAL TEXT FOCUS
Following Multiple-Step Instructions

California Standards
Here are the Grade 6 standards you will work toward mastering in Chapter 3.

Word Analysis, Fluency, and Systematic Vocabulary Development
1.3 Recognize the origins and meanings of frequently used foreign words in English and use these words accurately in speaking and writing.

Reading Comprehension (Focus on Informational Materials)
2.5 Follow multiple-step instructions for preparing applications (e.g., for a public library card, bank savings account, sports club, league membership).

Literary Response and Analysis
3.2 Analyze the effect of the qualities of the character (e.g., courage or cowardice, ambition or laziness) on the plot and the resolution of the conflict.

3.6 Identify and analyze features of themes conveyed through characters, actions, and images.

Writing Applications (Genres and Their Characteristics)
2.2 Write expository compositions (e.g., description, explanation, comparison and contrast, problem and solution):
  a. State the thesis or purpose.
  b. Explain the situation.
  c. Follow an organizational pattern appropriate to the type of composition.
  d. Offer persuasive evidence to validate arguments and conclusions as needed.

"In every conceivable manner, the family is link to our past, bridge to our future."

—Alex Haley

What Do
You
Think

How do the people you consider family help you find your place in the world?

Learn It Online
Listen to the selections in this chapter online:

go.hrw.com   H6-229   Go

Literary Skills Focus

by **Linda Rief**

How Do Writers Convey Theme?

Do you have posters tacked to the walls of your room? If so, some of them may make statements about life—about friendship, or adventure, or goals. You probably put them on your walls to make a statement about your beliefs or values. Writers make similar statements through their stories' themes. They convey (make known) these themes through the characters, actions, and images in their stories.

Theme

"What does it all mean?" When we ask that question about a story, we're asking about its **theme**—an idea about life conveyed through the story's characters, actions, and images. A theme usually expresses an important truth about one of life's "big issues," such as love, revenge, or power.

Theme or Subject? The theme is not the same as the subject of a story. The **subject** is what the story is *about*; it can usually be stated in one or two words. The theme of a story is an idea, and it's best expressed as a complete sentence. This chart shows the difference between subject and theme.

Subject	Theme
growing up	Growing up means taking responsibility.
nature	Nature can be beautiful but deadly.
love	People will sometimes risk everything, even their lives, for love.

Theme and Characters Writers usually don't state themes directly. Instead, you have to read through the entire story, paying careful attention to all of its elements. One of the best places to look for features (parts or aspects) of the theme is in the thoughts or dialogue of the main character, especially if the character makes a sudden discovery near the end of a story. In "The All-American Slurp," the main character realizes that her non-Chinese friends are as confused by her culture as she is by theirs. This realization helps convey the story's theme.

> Then I caught my mother's eyes on me. She frowned and shook her head slightly, and I understood the message: The Gleasons were not used to Chinese ways, and they were just coping the best they could.
>
> from "The All-American Slurp"
> by Lensey Namioka

Theme and Actions A theme develops side-by-side with the actions in a story, but don't confuse a story's theme with its plot. Use what you know about plot and action to help you identify features of the theme. For example, an essential element of plot is conflict. Characters facing a conflict are forced to make a decision based on their beliefs or values. In "Ta-Na-E-Ka," the main character doesn't want to take part in an important ritual that's part of her heritage.

> I knew one thing. This particular Kaw Indian girl wasn't going to swallow a grasshopper no matter how hungry she got. And then I had an idea. Why hadn't I thought of it before? It would have saved nights of bad dreams about squooshy grasshoppers.
>
> I headed straight for my teacher's house.
>
> from "Ta-Na-E-Ka"
> by Mary Whitebird

The story shows us how Mary, the main character, gains a deeper understanding of her heritage. Her actions and the story's outcome convey a powerful theme about how people balance their individual needs with the needs of others.

Theme and Images Writers rely on descriptive language, in addition to characters and actions, to convey features of themes. They use **images**—language that appeals to our senses of sight, hearing, touch, taste, and smell—to provide clues about their stories' themes. For example, a writer may include images of violent weather, such as pounding rain, crashes of thunder, and flashes of lightning, to convey a theme related to anger or evil. The following image of a bird in flight suggests that the theme of "Aaron's Gift" relates to freedom and to a respect for all living things.

> But suddenly Pidge beat his wings in rhythm, and rose up, up over the roof of the nearest tenement, up over Second Avenue toward the park.
>
> from "Aaron's Gift"
> by Myron Levoy

Recurring Themes

Similar themes often appear in different stories, sometimes conveyed through similar characters, actions, or images. You've probably read more than one story that makes a statement about the horrors of war or the value of friendship, for example. Ideas that occur in stories from different times and cultures are called **recurring** or **universal themes.** Recurring themes are based on ideas that have been important to human beings in all times and places: love, death, family, loyalty, sacrifice.

Your Turn Analyze Theme

1. Use a chart like the one below to determine the theme of two of your favorite movies or stories. Then, for each theme, write two or three sentences explaining how the theme is conveyed through characters, actions, or images.

Work 1	Work 2
Subject:	Subject:
Theme:	Theme:

2. With a partner, think of some themes you have encountered more than once in books, movies, plays, and comics. What are the three most common recurring themes you can think of? Are these themes conveyed through recurring characters, actions, or images? Provide examples.

Learn It Online
Learn more about theme through *PowerNotes:*

go.hrw.com | H6-231 | **Go**

Reading Skills Focus

by **Kylene Beers**

What Skills Can Help You Identify and Analyze a Story's Theme?

A story's theme is a truth about life that the story conveys to readers. Identifying the theme can be a challenge, but if you begin by making generalizations about the story and think about cause-and-effect relationships, you may find that identifying a story's theme isn't as hard as it may seem.

Identifying the Theme

To identify a story's **theme,** you need to understand how theme differs from other elements in the story. Suppose a teacher asks three students to state the theme of "The Three Little Pigs." Consider these responses:

- The first student says, "There are three pigs. Each builds a house. A wolf blows two houses down." Is that the theme? No, that's the **plot.**

- The second student says, "There are three pigs. One is really lazy, one is a little lazy, and one isn't lazy at all." Is that the theme? No, that is a description of the **characters.**

- The third student says, "Doing things the easy way often isn't the best way." Is that the theme? Yes! It explains a truth about life.

Readers may identify different themes in a story or express the same theme in different words. There is no one way to state a story's theme, and stories can have more than one theme. What's important in identifying a theme is to make sure that it takes into account the whole story, not just part of it. You need to consider how each element of the story conveys a feature, or aspect, of the theme and how all those features contribute to the story's message.

Looking for Clues to Features of Themes Here are four ways to identify a story's theme.

1. **Think about what a character learns.** Pay attention to what characters and the narrator say and think to uncover clues about what characters discover. Their discovery will help you understand the writer's message.

2. **Think about how a character changes.** The changes that take place in characters may be revealed in their thoughts and words or in their actions. These changes often point to the writer's message.

3. **Consider the way in which the conflict is resolved.** The conflict's resolution and the way in which the characters' qualities and actions affect the resolution help convey the story's theme.

4. **Pay attention to images.** Images can convey information about characters, their actions, or important ideas. Keep track of images in a story, especially those that recur. What do they tell you about the author's central message?

Making Generalizations

A **generalization** is a broad, general conclusion that you draw from several examples or pieces of evidence. When you state a story's theme, you're actually making a kind of generalization about life and human experience. Here are tips that can help you use generalizations to make statements about a story's theme:

- Consider the characters' actions and the story's main events and conflicts.
- Observe what the characters have learned by the end.
- State the story's idea in a general way so that it applies not just to the story but also to situations in real life.

Look at "The Three Little Pigs" again.

Main Characters	Conflict/Actions	Observation
The three pigs and the wolf	The wolf wants to eat the pigs. Each pig builds a house, and the wolf blows the two weaker houses down.	**In the story:** Building a strong house keeps pigs safer than building a weak house. **Generalization from life:** Doing things the easy way isn't always best.

Notice that the generalization is based on what the pigs learn about their *specific* situations. Building weak houses is easier than building strong ones, but, in this story, building weak houses turns out to be a bad idea. From this observation, you can generalize that there are many situations in life when the easy way is not the best way.

Analyzing Cause and Effect

A story is made up of many different events. The first event is the **cause;** it makes something happen. What happens is called the **effect.** A story often follows a chain of causes and effects to its conclusion.

Tracing cause-and-effect relationships in a flowchart can help you see how characters' actions and decisions lead to the conflict's resolution. It can give you a clue to the story's theme, perhaps by showing how and why the main character changes or makes a discovery or why the conflict is resolved in a particular way.

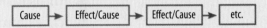

Cause → Effect/Cause → Effect/Cause → etc.

Your Turn Apply Reading Skills

1. Re-read a favorite story from an earlier chapter. Think about how the theme is conveyed through images and characters' thoughts, statements, and actions. Then, write your idea of the theme in a sentence.

2. Recall a recent important experience. Then, use it to make a generalization about life.

3. Think of a favorite folk tale or fairy tale from your childhood. Make a cause-and-effect flowchart of the tale's events. Then, use the chart to help you state the story's theme.

Now go to the Skills in Action: Reading Model

Learn It Online
Find tips on literature themes using *NovelWise:*

go.hrw.com   H6-233   **Go**

Build Background

Every year in the United States, millions of dogs are abandoned or born in the wild, without homes. This is a fictional account of one such puppy.

Read with a Purpose Read this short story to learn what happens in a family when a stray dog appears one day.

by **Cynthia Rylant**

In January, a puppy wandered onto the property of Mr. Amos Lacey and his wife, Mamie, and their daughter, Doris. Icicles hung three feet or more from the eaves of houses, snowdrifts swallowed up automobiles, and the birds were so fluffed up they looked comic.

The puppy had been abandoned, and it made its way down the road toward the Laceys' small house, its ears tucked, its tail between its legs, shivering.

Doris, whose school had been called off because of the snow, was out shoveling the cinder-block front steps when she spotted the pup on the road. She set down the shovel.

"Hey! Come on!" she called.

The puppy stopped in the road, wagging its tail timidly, trembling with shyness and cold.

Doris trudged through the yard, went up the shoveled drive and met the dog.

"Come on, pooch."

"Where did *that* come from?" Mrs. Lacey asked as soon as Doris put the dog down in the kitchen.

Mr. Lacey was at the table, cleaning his fingernails with his pocketknife. The snow was keeping him home from his job at the warehouse.

"I don't know where it came from," he said mildly, "but I know for sure where it's going."

Literary Focus

Theme The theme is the message about life that the author wants to convey in the story. Authors rarely state the theme directly. Through imagery describing the dog, this sentence provides clues to help you start determining what the theme might be.

Reading Focus

Identifying the Theme As you read, look for clues in characters' thoughts and words that can help you identify features of the theme. Write down statements that seem important, including characters' dialogue. In this sentence, you can see that Mr. Lacey does not plan to keep the dog.

Analyzing Visuals **Connecting to the Text** How does this photograph reflect Doris's feelings for the puppy and help convey the story's theme?

Doris hugged the puppy hard against her. She said nothing.

Because the roads would be too bad for travel for many days, Mr. Lacey couldn't get out to take the puppy to the pound in the city right away. He agreed to let it sleep in the basement, while Mrs. Lacey grudgingly let Doris feed it table scraps. The woman was sensitive about throwing out food.

By the looks of it, Doris figured the puppy was about six months old and on its way to being a big dog. She thought it might have some shepherd in it.

Four days passed and the puppy did not complain. It never cried in the night or howled at the wind. It didn't tear up everything in the basement. It wouldn't even follow Doris up the basement steps unless it was invited.

It was a good dog.

Several times Doris had opened the door in the kitchen that led to the basement, and the puppy had been there, all stretched out, on the top step. Doris knew it had wanted some company and that it had lain against the door, listening to the talk in the kitchen, smelling the food, being a part of things. It always wagged its tail, eyes all sleepy, when she found it there.

Reading Focus

Identifying the Theme As you look for clues about the story's theme, pay attention to statements made by the narrator. This description is about the dog, but notice that the dog is being described as though it were a person.

Even after a week had gone by, Doris didn't name the dog. She knew her parents wouldn't let her keep it, that her father made so little money any pets were out of the question, and that the pup would definitely go to the pound when the weather cleared.

Still, she tried talking to them about the dog at dinner one night.

"She's a good dog, isn't she?" Doris said, hoping one of them would agree with her.

Her parents glanced at each other and went on eating.

"She's not much trouble," Doris added. "I like her." She smiled at them, but they continued to ignore her.

"I figure she's real smart," Doris said to her mother. "I could teach her things."

Mrs. Lacey just shook her head and stuffed a forkful of sweet potato in her mouth. Doris fell silent, praying the weather would never clear.

But on Saturday, nine days after the dog had arrived, the sun was shining and the roads were plowed. Mr. Lacey opened up the trunk of his car and came into the house.

Doris was sitting alone in the living room, hugging a pillow and rocking back and forth on the edge of a chair. She was trying not to cry but she was not strong enough. Her face was wet and red, her eyes full of distress.

Mrs. Lacey looked into the room from the doorway.

"Mama," Doris said in a small voice. "Please."

Mrs. Lacey shook her head.

"You know we can't afford a dog, Doris. You try to act more grown-up about this."

Doris pressed her face into the pillow.

Outside, she heard the trunk of the car slam shut, one of the doors open and close, the old engine cough and choke and finally start up.

"Daddy," she whispered. "Please."

She heard the car travel down the road, and though it was early afternoon, she could do nothing but go to her bed. She cried herself to sleep, and her dreams were full of searching and searching for things lost.

It was nearly night when she finally woke up. Lying there, like stone, still exhausted, she wondered if she would ever in her life have anything. She stared at the wall for a while.

But she started feeling hungry, and she knew she'd have to make herself get out of bed and eat some dinner. She wanted not to go into the kitchen, past the basement door. She wanted not to face her parents.

But she rose up heavily.

Her parents were sitting at the table, dinner over, drinking coffee. They looked at her when she came in, but she kept her head down. No one spoke.

Doris made herself a glass of powdered milk and drank it all down. Then she picked up a cold biscuit and started out of the room.

"You'd better feed that mutt before it dies of starvation," Mr. Lacey said.

Doris turned around.

"What?"

"I said, you'd better feed your dog. I figure it's looking for you."

Doris put her hand to her mouth.

"You didn't take her?" she asked.

"Oh, I took her all right," her father answered. "Worst-looking place I've ever seen. Ten dogs to a cage. Smell was enough to knock you down. And they give an animal six days to live. Then they kill it with some kind of a shot."

Reading Focus

Identifying the Theme Pay attention to related ideas and images that keep appearing in a story; they can help convey the theme. Consider how this description echoes the earlier description of the dog lying against the door to the kitchen. The dog wanted something, too.

Analyzing Visuals **Connecting to the Text** How does this photograph relate to the story's resolution and reflect a feature of the story's theme?

Doris stared at her father.

"I wouldn't leave an *ant* in that place," he said. "So I brought the dog back."

Mrs. Lacey was smiling at him and shaking her head as if she would never, ever, understand him.

Mr. Lacey sipped his coffee.

"Well," he said, "are you going to feed it or not?"

Read with a Purpose How does the dog affect the relationship between Doris and her parents? How does the dog bring out the best in everyone?

MEET THE WRITER

Cynthia Rylant
(1954–   )

The Possibilities of Childhood

Cynthia Rylant spent part of her childhood living with her grandparents in West Virginia. Remembering them fondly, she says:

> "They lived life with strength . . . and a real sense of what it means to be devoted to and responsible for other people. The tone of my work reflects the way they spoke, the simplicity of their language, and, I hope, the depth of their own hearts."

Why does Rylant—winner of the Newbery Medal and other awards—like to write?

> "I like to show the way our lives are beautiful, breathtaking, in the smallest things. . . . I prefer writing about child characters because they have more possibilities. They can get away with more love, more anger, more fear than adult characters."

Think About the Writer Based on "Stray," how do you think Cynthia Rylant feels about children and pets?

SKILLS IN ACTION
Wrap Up

Reading Standard 3.6 Identify and analyze features of themes conveyed through characters, actions, and images.

Into Action: Making a Generalization to State the Theme

Use a table like the one below to make an observation about "Stray." (*Hint:* Decide what the main characters have learned.) Restate your observation as a generalization that applies to life.

Main Characters	Conflict/ Actions	Observations
Amos, Mamie, and Doris Lacey		In the story: In life:

Talk About . . .

1. Explain to a partner your idea of the theme of "Stray." (Remember that readers may state a theme in different ways.) Tell how features of this theme are conveyed through the characters, actions, and images in the story. Try to use each of the Academic Vocabulary words listed on the right at least once in your discussion.

Write About . . .

Answer the following questions about "Stray." For definitions of the underlined Academic Vocabulary words, see the column on the right.

2. How does the author <u>illustrate</u> the cruelty of abandoning pets?

3. How does the dog <u>communicate</u> that it wants to belong to the family? How does Doris communicate her pain over losing the dog?

4. How does Mr. Lacey's <u>attitude</u> toward the stray change after he visits the pound? Contrast Mr. Lacey's attitude before he visits the pound with his attitude after he visits the pound.

Writing Skills Focus
Think as a Reader/Writer

In Chapter 3, you will read more stories with powerful themes. The Writing Skills Focus activities will give you practice in developing characters and events that communicate truths about life.

Ta-Na-E-Ka

by **Mary Whitebird**

What Do **You Think?** Why is it important for elders to pass down traditions to the young?

QuickWrite
What family traditions do you know about? What can happen when a family member dislikes a tradition and chooses not to follow it?

Reader/Writer Notebook

Use your **RWN** to complete the activities for this selection.

Reading Standard 3.6 Identify and analyze features of themes conveyed through **characters, actions,** and images.

Literary Skills Focus

Theme and Character What happens in a story depends on the way the **characters** respond to conflict. Their responses—what they say and do, how they change, and what they learn—help convey features of the **theme,** or a truth about life expressed in the story. In the beginning of this story, Mary, the main character, communicates that she had nightmares about the difficult ritual she was about to face. As you read, think about how the writer conveys the story's theme through Mary's changing attitudes and her discovery at the end of the story.

Reading Skills Focus

Identifying the Theme Usually writers do not directly state a story's theme. Instead, characters' words and conflicts, in addition to how characters change and what they learn, provide clues to the theme. To identify the theme, you need to take into account all these features and determine what theme they convey.

Into Action Record notes in a chart like this one to help you identify the story's theme.

"Ta-Na-E-Ka"	Notes for Identifying the Theme
Comments by Characters	Mrs. Richardson: "All of us have rituals of one kind or another."
Conflicts	
How Characters Change/ What They Learn	

TechFocus As you read, think about this: If Mary, the main character, had had a laptop computer, what feelings and attitudes about Ta-Na-E-Ka might she have recorded?

Writing Skills Focus

Think as a Reader/Writer

Find It in Your Reading As you read, record in your *Reader/Writer Notebook* key thoughts of the **first-person narrator,** speaking as "I," who is also the main character. Consider how the use of the first person helps the writer communicate the theme.

Vocabulary

loftiest (LAWF tee ehst) *adj.:* noblest; highest. *The strength to withstand hardship was the loftiest virtue.*

shrewdest (SHROOD ihst) *adj.:* sharpest; most clever. *The shrewdest people survive the test.*

grimaced (GRIHM ihsd) *v.:* twisted the face to express pain, anger, or disgust. *Roger grimaced at the idea of eating bugs.*

gorging (GAWRJ ihng) *v.:* filling up; stuffing. *Since he was nervous, he was not gorging himself at dinner.*

audacity (aw DAS uh tee) *n.:* boldness; daring. *They were shocked at Mary's audacity.*

Language Coach

Comparatives and Superlatives
Comparatives are adjectives that compare two things: *better, faster.*
Superlatives are adjectives that compare three or more things: *best, fastest.*

In the Vocabulary box above, *loftiest* is a superlative. Which other word is too?

Positive	lofty
Comparative	loftier
Superlative	loftiest

Learn It Online
Watch a video introduction to this story at:

go.hrw.com   H6-241   Go

Mary Whitebird

Writing with a Pen Name

Some authors choose to write under a pen name, or made-up name, rather than their real name. That seems to be the case with the author of "Ta-Na-E-Ka." Little is known about Mary Whitebird, who may actually have been a male writer.

The author of "Ta-Na-E-Ka" is said to have based the pen name Mary Whitebird—as well as the first name of the main character of this story—on a Navajo girl he met. Like the main character in this story, the Navajo girl was trying to balance her place in the wider world with the Navajo customs of her family.

You've probably read other works by authors who use pen names, also known as pseudonyms (SOO duh nihmz). Two of the best-known pen names are Dr. Seuss, the name Theodor Seuss Geisel wrote under, and Lemony Snicket, the pen name of Daniel Handler. Writers who use a pen name of the opposite gender are actually following a literary tradition. The nineteenth-century English novelist Mary Anne Evans wrote under the famous pen name George Eliot.

Think About the Writer Why do you think the author of "Ta-Na-E-Ka" chose to use the name Mary Whitebird?

Build Background

This story refers to traditions of the American Indian group known as Kaw or Kansa. Both names are forms of a word that means "People of the South Wind." The Kaw originally lived along the river now known as the Kansas River.

IOWA
NEBRASKA
Missouri River
Kaw Homeland Kansas R.
Santa Fe Trail
KANSAS
Arkansas River
MO.
OKLAHOMA

Ta-Na-E-Ka is a rite of passage, which is a ritual or ceremony marking an important life transition—in this case, the transition from childhood to adulthood. Rites of passage exist in virtually every culture, marking such important events as birth, marriage, and other changes in social status—including death.

Preview the Selection

Mary and her cousin **Roger,** young Kaw Indians who live on a reservation, are both about to turn the important age of eleven. At this age, Kaw youth traditionally undergo a rite of passage into adulthood, a survival test called Ta-Na-E-Ka.

Ta-Na-E-Ka

by **Mary Whitebird**

As my birthday drew closer, I had awful nightmares about it. I was reaching the age at which all Kaw Indians had to participate in Ta-Na-E-Ka. Well, not all Kaws. Many of the younger families on the reservation were beginning to give up the old customs. But my grandfather, Amos Deer Leg, was devoted to tradition. He still wore handmade beaded moccasins instead of shoes and kept his iron-gray hair in tight braids. He could speak English, but he spoke it only with white men. With his family he used a Sioux dialect.[1]

Grandfather was one of the last living Indians (he died in 1953, when he was eighty-one) who actually fought against the U.S. Cavalry. Not only did he fight, he was wounded in a skirmish at Rose Creek—a famous encounter in which the celebrated Kaw chief Flat Nose lost his life. At the time, my grandfather was only eleven years old. **Ⓐ**

---

1. **Sioux** (soo) **dialect:** branch of the Sioux language, spoken by many Plains Indians.

Eleven was a magic word among the Kaws. It was the time of Ta-Na-E-Ka, the "flowering of adulthood." It was the age, my grandfather informed us hundreds of times, "when a boy could prove himself to be a warrior and a girl took the first steps to womanhood."

"I don't want to be a warrior," my cousin, Roger Deer Leg, confided to me. "I'm going to become an accountant."

"None of the other tribes make girls go through the endurance ritual," I complained to my mother.

"It won't be as bad as you think, Mary," my mother said, ignoring my protests. "Once you've gone through it, you'll certainly never forget it. You'll be proud." **Ⓑ**

I even complained to my teacher, Mrs. Richardson, feeling that, as a white woman, she would side with me.

She didn't. "All of us have rituals of one kind or another," Mrs. Richardson said. "And look at it this way: How many girls have the opportunity to compete on equal terms with boys? Don't look down on your heritage."

Ⓐ **Read and Discuss** What is the narrator's <u>attitude</u> toward her approaching birthday? How does the information about Amos Deer Leg and the idea of tradition relate to Mary's birthday?

Ⓑ **Reading Focus** Identifying the Theme What theme does the statement made by Mary's mother suggest? How does her <u>attitude</u> toward the ritual contrast with Mary's?

Heritage, indeed! I had no intention of living on a reservation for the rest of my life. I was a good student. I loved school. My fantasies were about knights in armor and fair ladies in flowing gowns being saved from dragons. It never once occurred to me that being an Indian was exciting. **C**

But I've always thought that the Kaw were the originators of the women's liberation movement. No other Indian tribe—and I've spent half a lifetime researching the subject—treated women more "equally" than the Kaw. Unlike most of the subtribes of the Sioux Nation, the Kaw allowed men and women to eat together. And hundreds of years before we were "acculturated,"[2] a Kaw woman had the right to refuse a prospective husband even if her father arranged the match.

The wisest women (generally wisdom was equated with age) often sat in tribal councils. Furthermore, most Kaw legends revolve around "Good Woman," a kind of supersquaw, a Joan of Arc[3] of the high plains. Good Woman led Kaw warriors into battle after battle, from which they always seemed to emerge victorious.

And girls as well as boys were required to undergo Ta-Na-E-Ka.

---

2. **acculturated** (uh KUHL chuh rayt ihd): adapted to a new or different culture.
3. **Joan of Arc** (1412–1431): French heroine who led her country's army to victory over the English in 1429.

The actual ceremony varied from tribe to tribe, but since the Indians' life on the plains was dedicated to survival, Ta-Na-E-Ka was a test of survival. **D**

"Endurance is the loftiest virtue of the Indian," my grandfather explained. "To survive, we must endure. When I was a boy, Ta-Na-E-Ka was more than the mere symbol it is now. We were painted white with the juice of a sacred herb and sent naked into the wilderness without so much as a knife. We couldn't return until the white had worn off. It wouldn't wash off. It took almost eighteen days, and during that time we had to stay alive, trapping food, eating insects and roots and berries, and watching out for enemies. And we did have enemies—both the white soldiers and the Omaha warriors, who were always trying to capture Kaw boys and girls undergoing their endurance test. It was an exciting time."

"What happened if you couldn't make it?" Roger asked. He was born only three days after I was, and we were being trained for Ta-Na-E-Ka together. I was happy to know he was frightened, too.

"Many didn't return," Grandfather said. "Only the strongest and shrewdest. Mothers were not allowed to weep over those who didn't return. If a Kaw couldn't survive, he or she wasn't worth weeping over. It was our way."

C **Reading Focus** Identifying the Theme What does this paragraph suggest Mary might learn in the course of the story? What might this <u>convey</u> about the theme?

D **Read and Discuss** How does women's liberation connect to Kaw history and traditions? What does Mary think of this?

Vocabulary **loftiest** (LAWF tee ehst) *adj.:* noblest; highest.
shrewdest (SHROOD ihst) *adj.:* sharpest; most clever.

"What a lot of hooey," Roger whispered. "I'd give anything to get out of it."

"I don't see how we have any choice," I replied.

Roger gave my arm a little squeeze. "Well, it's only five days."

Five days! Maybe it was better than being painted white and sent out naked for eighteen days. But not much better.

We were to be sent, barefoot and in bathing suits, into the woods. Even our very traditional parents put their foot down when Grandfather suggested we go naked. For five days we'd have to live off the land, keeping warm as best we could, getting food where we could. It was May, but on the northernmost reaches of the Missouri River, the days were still chilly and the nights were fiercely cold.  **E**

Grandfather was in charge of the month's training for Ta-Na-E-Ka. One day he caught a grasshopper and demonstrated how to pull its legs and wings off in one flick of the fingers and how to swallow it.

I felt sick, and Roger turned green. "It's a darn good thing it's 1947," I told Roger teasingly. "You'd make a terrible warrior." Roger just grimaced.

I knew one thing. This particular Kaw Indian girl wasn't going to swallow a grasshopper no matter how hungry she got. And then I had an idea. Why hadn't I thought of it before? It would have saved nights of bad dreams about squooshy grasshoppers.

I headed straight for my teacher's house. "Mrs. Richardson," I said, "would you lend me five dollars?" **F**

"Five dollars!" she exclaimed. "What for?"

"You remember the ceremony I talked about?"

"Ta-Na-E-Ka. Of course. Your parents have written me and asked me to excuse you from school so you can participate in it."

"Well, I need some things for the ceremony," I replied, in a half-truth. "I don't want to ask my parents for the money."

"It's not a crime to borrow money, Mary. But how can you pay it back?"

"I'll baby-sit for you ten times."

E [Read and Discuss] How is the Ta-Na-E-Ka of Grandfather's time connected to the rite that Roger and Mary will experience? What does this show the elders about the children?

F [Read and Discuss] What do you think Mary is planning to do?

Vocabulary **grimaced** (GRIHM ihsd) *v.*: twisted the face to express pain, anger, or disgust.

"That's more than fair," she said, going to her purse and handing me a crisp, new five-dollar bill. I'd never had that much money at once.

"I'm happy to know the money's going to be put to a good use," Mrs. Richardson said.

A few days later the ritual began with a long speech from my grandfather about how we had reached the age of decision, how we now had to fend for ourselves and prove that we could survive the most horrendous of ordeals. All the friends and relatives who had gathered at our house for dinner made jokes about their own Ta-Na-E-Ka experiences. They all advised us to fill up now, since for the next five days we'd be gorging ourselves on crickets. Neither Roger nor I was very hungry. "I'll probably laugh about this when I'm an accountant," Roger said, trembling.

"Are you trembling?" I asked.

"What do you think?"

"I'm happy to know boys tremble, too," I said. **G**

At six the next morning, we kissed our parents and went off to the woods. "Which side do you want?" Roger asked. According to the rules, Roger and I would stake out "territories" in separate areas of the woods, and we weren't to communicate during the entire ordeal.

"I'll go toward the river, if it's OK with you," I said.

"Sure," Roger answered. "What difference does it make?"

To me, it made a lot of difference. There was a marina a few miles up the river, and there were boats moored there. At least, I hoped so. I figured that a boat was a better place to sleep than under a pile of leaves.

"Why do you keep holding your head?" Roger asked.

"Oh, nothing. Just nervous," I told him. Actually, I was afraid I'd lose the five-dollar bill, which I had tucked into my hair with a bobby pin. As we came to a fork in the trail, Roger shook my hand. "Good luck, Mary."

"N'ko-n'ta," I said. It was the Kaw word for "courage."

The sun was shining and it was warm, but my bare feet began to hurt immediately. I spied one of the berry bushes Grandfather had told us about. "You're lucky," he had said. "The berries are ripe in the spring, and they are delicious and nourishing." They were orange and fat, and I popped one into my mouth.

Argh! I spat it out. It was awful and bitter, and even grasshoppers were probably better tasting, although I never intended to find out.

G [Read and Discuss] How are Roger and Mary reacting to the Ta-Na-E-Ka stories?

Vocabulary **gorging** (GAWRJ ihng) *v.*: filling up; stuffing.

Remembering the Wind People

The Kaw people had a rich and proud history. They were known as the Wind People or the People of the South Wind. The Kaw Nation originally covered more than twenty million acres, from what is now Kansas into Missouri, Iowa, and Nebraska. Some familiar place names have their origin in Kaw words: *Wi-Tsi-Ta* became *Wichita* (Kansas), and *U-Moln-Holn* became *Omaha* (Nebraska).

The Kaw population, like that of many other American Indian groups, began to decline when Europeans arrived, bringing new diseases like smallpox and influenza with them. These illnesses were especially dangerous to American Indians, who had no immunity to the diseases. The Kaw's shrinking population grew even smaller after the nation was moved to a reservation in Oklahoma in 1872. The last pure-blooded member of the Kaw Nation, William Mehojah (left), died in 2000.

Ask Yourself
How does knowing what ultimately happened to the Kaw make this story of Kaw traditions more meaningful?

I sat down to rest my feet. A rabbit hopped out from under the berry bush. He nuzzled the berry I'd spat out and ate it. He picked another one and ate that, too. He liked them. He looked at me, twitching his nose. I watched a redheaded woodpecker bore into an elm tree, and I caught a glimpse of a civet cat[4] waddling through some twigs. All of a sudden I realized I was no longer frightened. Ta-Na-E-Ka might be more fun than I'd anticipated. I got up and headed toward the marina. **H**

4. **civet** (SIHV iht) **cat:** furry, spotted catlike mammal.

H Read and Discuss What is happening to Mary?

"Not one boat," I said to myself dejectedly. But the restaurant on the shore, Ernie's Riverside, was open. I walked in, feeling silly in my bathing suit. The man at the counter was big and tough-looking. He wore a sweat shirt with the words "Fort Sheridan, 1944," and he had only three fingers on one of his hands. He asked me what I wanted.

"A hamburger and a milkshake," I said, holding the five-dollar bill in my hand so he'd know I had money.

"That's a pretty heavy breakfast, honey," he murmured.

"That's what I always have for breakfast," I lied.

"Forty-five cents," he said, bringing me the food. (Back in 1947, hamburgers were twenty-five cents and milkshakes were twenty cents.)

"Delicious," I thought. "Better 'n grass-hoppers—and Grandfather never once mentioned that I couldn't eat hamburgers."

While I was eating, I had a grand idea. Why not sleep in the restaurant? I went to the ladies' room and made sure the window was unlocked. Then I went back outside and played along the riverbank, watching the water birds and trying to identify each one. I planned to look for a beaver dam the next day.

The restaurant closed at sunset, and I watched the three-fingered man drive away. Then I climbed in the unlocked window. There was a night light on, so I didn't turn on any lights. But there was a radio on the counter. I turned it on to a music program. It was warm in the restaurant, and I was hungry. I helped myself to a glass of milk and a piece of pie, intending to keep a list of what I'd eaten so I could leave money. I also planned to get up early, sneak out through the window, and head for the woods before the three-fingered man returned. I turned off the radio, wrapped myself in the man's apron, and in spite of the hardness of the floor, fell asleep. **❶**

"What the heck are you doing here, kid?"
It was the man's voice.

It was morning. I'd overslept. I was scared.

"Hold it, kid. I just wanna know what you're doing here. You lost? You must be from the reservation. Your folks must be worried sick about you. Do they have a phone?"

"Yes, yes," I answered. "But don't call them."

I was shivering. The man, who told me his name was Ernie, made me a cup of hot chocolate while I explained about Ta-Na-E-Ka.

"Darnedest thing I ever heard," he said, when I was through. "Lived next to the reservation all my life and this is the first I've heard of Ta-Na-whatever-you-call-it." He looked at me, all goose bumps in my bathing suit. "Pretty silly thing to do to a kid," he muttered.

That was just what I'd been thinking for months, but when Ernie said it, I became angry. "No, it isn't silly. It's a custom of the Kaw. We've been doing this for hundreds of years. My mother and my grandfather and everybody in my family went through this ceremony. It's why the Kaw are great warriors." **❿**

"OK, great warrior," Ernie chuckled, "suit yourself. And, if you want to stick around, it's OK with me." Ernie went to the broom closet and tossed me a bundle. "That's the lost-and-found closet," he said. "Stuff people left on boats. Maybe there's something to keep you warm."

The sweater fitted loosely, but it felt good. I felt good. And I'd found a new friend. Most important, I was surviving Ta-Na-E-Ka.

My grandfather had said the experience would be filled with adventure, and I was having my fill. And Grandfather had never said we couldn't accept hospitality.

---

❶ | Read and Discuss | Based on what you know about Grand-father, what might he think of Mary's actions?

❿ | Reading Focus | Identifying the Theme What theme does Mary's statement suggest?

I stayed at Ernie's Riverside for the entire period. In the mornings I went into the woods and watched the animals and picked flowers for each of the tables in Ernie's. I had never felt better. I was up early enough to watch the sun rise on the Missouri, and I went to bed after it set. I ate everything I wanted—insisting that Ernie take all my money for the food. "I'll keep this in trust for you, Mary," Ernie promised, "in case you are ever desperate for five dollars." (He did, too, but that's another story.)

I was sorry when the five days were over. I'd enjoyed every minute with Ernie. He taught me how to make western omelets and to make Chili Ernie Style (still one of my favorite dishes). And I told Ernie all about the legends of the Kaw. I hadn't realized I knew so much about my people. **K**

But Ta-Na-E-Ka was over, and as I approached my house at about nine-thirty in the evening, I became nervous all over again. What if Grandfather asked me about the berries and the grasshoppers? And my feet were hardly cut. I hadn't lost a pound and my hair was combed.

"They'll be so happy to see me," I told myself hopefully, "that they won't ask too many questions." **L**

I opened the door. My grandfather was

Malt Shop in Sequim by Pam Ingalls.

Analyzing Visuals **Connecting to the Text** What does Mary learn in a restaurant like this one that helps convey the story's theme?

in the front room. He was wearing the ceremonial beaded deerskin shirt which had belonged to *his* grandfather. "N'g'da'ma," he said. "Welcome back."

I embraced my parents warmly, letting go only when I saw my cousin Roger sprawled on the couch. His eyes were red

---

K **Reading Focus** **Identifying the Theme** How does telling Kaw legends illustrate another way that Mary is changing?

L **Read and Discuss** How might Mary's family react to seeing her? How do you think Roger is getting along?

and swollen. He'd lost weight. His feet were an unsightly mass of blood and blisters, and he was moaning: "I made it, see. I made it. I'm a warrior. A warrior."

My grandfather looked at me strangely. I was clean, obviously well fed, and radiantly healthy. My parents got the message. My uncle and aunt gazed at me with hostility.

Finally my grandfather asked, "What did you eat to keep you so well?"

I sucked in my breath and blurted out the truth: "Hamburgers and milkshakes."

"Hamburgers!" my grandfather growled.

"Milkshakes!" Roger moaned.

"You didn't say we had to eat grasshoppers," I said sheepishly.

"Tell us all about your Ta-Na-E-Ka," my grandfather commanded.

I told them everything, from borrowing the five dollars, to Ernie's kindness, to observing the beaver.

"That's not what I trained you for," my grandfather said sadly.

I stood up. "Grandfather, I learned that Ta-Na-E-Ka is important. I didn't think so during training. I was scared stiff of it. I handled it my way. And I learned I had nothing to be afraid of. There's no reason in 1947 to eat grasshoppers when you can eat a hamburger."

I was inwardly shocked at my own audacity. But I liked it. "Grandfather, I'll bet you never ate one of those rotten berries yourself."

Grandfather laughed! He laughed aloud! My mother and father and aunt and uncle were all dumbfounded. Grandfather never laughed. Never.

"Those berries—they are terrible," Grandfather admitted. "I could never swallow them. I found a dead deer on the first day of my Ta-Na-E-Ka—shot by a soldier, probably—and he kept my belly full for the entire period of the test!" **M**

Grandfather stopped laughing. "We should send you out again," he said.

I looked at Roger. "You're pretty smart, Mary," Roger groaned. "I'd never have thought of what you did."

"Accountants just have to be good at arithmetic," I said comfortingly. "I'm terrible at arithmetic."

Roger tried to smile but couldn't. My grandfather called me to him. "You should have done what your cousin did. But I think you are more alert to what is happening to our people today than we are. I think you would have passed the test under any circumstances, in any time. Somehow, you know how to exist in a world that wasn't made for Indians. I don't think you're going to have any trouble surviving." **N**

Grandfather wasn't entirely right. But I'll tell about that another time. **O**

M Read and Discuss How does Grandfather react to Mary's recounting of her Ta-Na-E-Ka? What is his attitude?

N Reading Focus Identifying the Theme What theme does Grandfather's experience reveal?

O Literary Focus Theme What message in this story could have meaning for your own life?

Vocabulary **audacity** (aw DAS uh tee) *n*.: boldness; daring.

Applying Your Skills

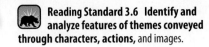
Ta-Na-E-Ka

Literary Response and Analysis

Reading Skills Focus
Quick Check

1. What is the purpose of Ta-Na-E-Ka?

2. How does Mary feel about her Kaw heritage at first? How does her <u>attitude</u> change?

Read with a Purpose

3. How do Roger's methods of survival differ from Mary's? Use examples from the story to <u>illustrate</u> your response.

Reading Skills: Identifying the Theme

4. Use the chart you completed while reading "Ta-Na-E-Ka" to help you identify the story's **theme.** Add the theme to your chart.

"Ta-Na-E-Ka"	Notes for Identifying the Theme
Comments by Characters	Mrs. Richardson: "All of us have rituals . . . ."
Conflicts	
How Characters Change/What They Learn	
Story's Theme	

Literary Skills Focus
Literary Analysis

5. **Infer** In addition to what Mary tells you about the Kaw, what Kaw values can you infer from what you learn about the Ta-Na-E-Ka?

6. **Evaluate** Did Mary pass the Ta-Na-E-Ka, or should she be sent out again? Explain.

7. **Connect** Mary's teacher tells her, "Don't look down on your heritage." Why do people sometimes fail to value their heritage?

Literary Skills: Theme and Character

8. **Analyze** Review the theme you recorded in your chart in response to question 4, and consider how this **theme** is <u>conveyed</u> through the **character** of Mary. How might this theme change if the story focused on Roger's experiences instead of Mary's?

Literary Skills Review: Character and Conflict

9. **Analyze/Evaluate** Explain which of Mary's **conflicts** are external and which are internal. Which of her qualities most affect the **resolution** of the story's conflicts? Why?

Writing Skills Focus
Think as a Reader/Writer
Use It in Your Writing Using Mary as an inspiration, think of a character, a conflict, and a theme. With this character as a **first-person narrator,** write a scene in which he or she changes or learns something. <u>Convey</u> your theme through what the narrator thinks, says, and does.

What Do **You Think Now** How has this story affected your <u>attitude</u> toward the value of knowledge and traditions that are passed down in families?

Applying Your Skills

Reading Standard 1.3 Recognize the origins and meanings of frequently used foreign words in English and use these words accurately in speaking and writing.

Ta-Na-E-Ka

Vocabulary Development

Word Origins

English is a rich language containing words of diverse origins. Many foreign words have entered the English language, and other English words, like the Vocabulary words below, come from languages that are no longer spoken.

Your Turn

loftiest
shrewdest
grimaced
gorging
audacity

Answer the following questions about the Vocabulary words listed at the right.

1. How are the definitions of *loftiest* and the Old Norse word *lopt*, meaning "upper room; air; sky," related?

2. What connection do you see between *shrewdest* and the Middle English word *schrewe*, meaning "evil or mean person"?

3. What probable connection do you see between *grimaced* and the Frankish word *grima*, meaning "mask"?

4. What connection do you see between *gorging* and *gurga*, a Late Latin word meaning "throat; narrow pass"?

5. How can you tell that *audacity* comes from the Latin word *audere*, meaning "to be bold"?

The words in the list below come from American Indian languages. Use the words to answer the questions that follow.

hickory	opossum or possum	skunk
moccasins	pecan	squash
moose	raccoon	succotash
muskrat	sequoia	woodchuck

Which of the items on the list

6. would you be most likely to put on your feet?
7. are animals?
8. are foods?
9. are types of trees?

Language Coach

Comparative and Superlative Adjectives The comparative forms of most short adjectives (one or two syllables) are formed by adding *–er* to the base word. The superlative forms of most short adjectives are formed by adding *–est*. If the word ends in *y*, change the *y* to *i* before adding *–er* or *–est*. Write the comparative and superlative forms of these words from "Ta-Na-E-Ka": *hungry, clean, lucky, silly*.

Academic Vocabulary

Talk About . . .
How can elders <u>communicate</u> the importance of tradition and help young people develop a positive <u>attitude</u> toward it?

Learn It Online
Use Word Watch to increase your word knowledge:

go.hrw.com | H6-252 | **Go**

Grammar Link
Adjective Phrases: Adding Word Power

Just as one person working alone can accomplish only so much, one word working alone has its limitations. The adjective *strong* can tell you that a girl is strong, but what does *strong* really mean? Adjectives like *strong* or *weak* don't pack a lot of power. They don't tell you how strong or how weak something is, or what it looks like. That's why you need adjective phrases. An **adjective phrase** is a group of words that, like an adjective, describes (or modifies) a noun or a pronoun. Adjective phrases add power to descriptions by answering questions like these:

What kind?	Which one?
How many?	How much?

An adjective phrase can tell you much more about the "strong" girl:

EXAMPLE a strong girl *with arms like steel and legs like tree trunks*

Your Turn

Use your imagination and add more details to the nouns below by joining an adjective phrase to each of the adjectives in italics.

1. *awful* nightmares
2. *magic* word
3. *big* man
4. *hard* floor

Writing Application Go back to the work you did for the Writing Skills Focus on page 251, and add adjective phrases to make your description of a character's transformation even more precise.

CHOICES

As you respond to the Choices, use these **Academic Vocabulary** words as appropriate: attitude, communicate, conveyed, illustrate.

REVIEW
Write Mary's Blog

TechFocus Imagine that you are Mary and you've taken your laptop along on your Ta-Na-E-Ka ritual. Write a daily blog in which you explain how you feel about what you are doing. Are you pleased? Do you feel guilty? Are you worried about what Roger will think of you? Explain how your attitude changes and what you learn. Be sure to convey the story's theme or themes through Mary's thoughts and experiences.

CONNECT
Compare Arguments

Timed └Writing This story deals with a conflict between an older generation and a younger one. What arguments do Mary's mother, grandfather, and teacher give in support of Ta-Na-E-Ka? What arguments do Mary and Roger give against it? Compare and contrast their arguments, and explain your own opinion.

EXTEND
Continue Mary's Story

Write a Story Grandfather says Mary will do well "in a world that wasn't made for Indians." Write a story about a conflict Mary faces as a teenager. The resolution should show why, as Mary hints, Grandfather was not "entirely right."

Learn It Online
Enhance your understanding of this story at:

go.hrw.com | H6-253 | Go

The All-American SLURP

by **Lensey Namioka**

What Do **You** Think?

What common ground can people find in their different cultural customs?

⏱ **QuickWrite**

Have you ever been embarrassed because you didn't know how you were supposed to behave in a new situation—at a party, at a new friend's house, in a foreign country? Write a few sentences about your experience.

Reader/Writer
Notebook
Use your **RWN** to complete the
activities for this selection.

Reading Standard 3.6 Identify and analyze features of themes conveyed through
characters, actions, and images.

Literary Skills Focus

Theme and Subject A story's theme is different from a story's subject. The **subject** of a story is what the story is about, and you can usually name it in a word or two. **Theme** is the meaning of the story, an idea
about life that the characters, actions, and images communicate to you.
As you read "The All-American Slurp," think about whether you've read
other stories or novels that have the same theme. Always try to connect
a story's theme to your own life. Also remember that no two readers will
state a theme in exactly the same way.

Reading Skills Focus

Making Generalizations A **generalization** is a broad conclusion
that is drawn from several examples or pieces of evidence. A statement
of a story's theme is a kind of generalization. From specific evidence
drawn from the characters, actions, and images in a story, you can make
a universal statement about life: "One person can make a difference" or
"There are no winners in war."

Into Action As you read, record notes about the characters' conflicts
and key actions in a chart like the one below. Then, make generalizations that apply to life based on these elements of the story.

Conflicts and Key Actions	Generalizations
The Lins aren't sure how to act during dinner at the Gleasons'. (1) They pull strings out of celery. (2) They set chairs at the buffet.	When you're not sure about another culture's customs, you may end up doing things that appear strange.

Writing Skills Focus
Think as a Reader/Writer

Find It in Your Reading *Onomatopoeia* (ahn uh maht uh PEE uh)
refers to words that sound like what they mean: *buzz, zip, clang*. Writers
use onomatopoeia to create images that appeal to our sense of hearing.
As you read, record in your *Reader/Writer Notebook* examples of images
that use onomatopoeia. Think about how the story's theme is
conveyed through these images.

Vocabulary

lavishly (LAV ihsh lee) *adv.*: abundantly; plentifully. *The table was
lavishly decorated.*

mortified (MAWR tuh fyd) *v.* used
as *adj.*: ashamed; embarrassed.
*Mortified by my family's mistakes, I
lost my appetite.*

spectacle (SPEHK tuh kuhl) *n.*:
strange or impressive sight. *The narrator fears that her brother is making
a spectacle of himself by eating too
noisily.*

acquainted (uh KWAYNT ihd) *v.*: be
familiar with. *Meg was acquainted
with many students in school.*

etiquette (EHT uh keht) *n.*: acceptable manners and behavior.
*Slurping is not proper etiquette in a
fancy restaurant.*

Language Coach

Word Forms You can change adjectives like *lavish* into adverbs by adding endings. When adding the suffix
—ly to most words, you don't change
the spelling of the word itself. For
words that end in *—y*, however, you
usually need to change the *y* to an *i*
before adding *—ly*. Add *—ly* to these
story words: *careful, helpful, pretty.*

 Learn It Online
Reinforce your learning of terms with Word Watch:

go.hrw.com	H6-255	Go

Lensey Namioka
(1929–   )

A Life on the Move

It's only natural for Lensey Namioka to write about young people trying to cope with the strange ways of a new culture, because she's spent so much of her own life adjusting to new people and places. Namioka was born in China, where her family moved around a lot when she was young. When she was a teenager, Namioka and her family immigrated to the United States, where they continued to move from place to place.

Namioka's Career

Before she began writing for young people, Lensey Namioka worked as a math teacher. Her realistic stories about teenagers today draw on her Chinese heritage and her experiences as a teacher. Namioka has also written adventure and mystery novels that are set in long-ago Japan and feature samurai warriors. These stories draw on her husband's Japanese heritage.

"Being on the move meant that I grew up with almost no toys. To amuse ourselves, my sisters and I made up stories."

Think About the Writer How might Namioka's experiences of moving so often have affected her life and writing?

Preview the Selection

This humorous story is told by a young Chinese girl, who, along with her family, has recently emigrated from China. The **narrator** and her family, the **Lins,** have some trouble adjusting to American food and table manners. However, the narrator learns an important lesson when the tables are turned.

Read with a Purpose Read this story to discover what sort of embarrassing but funny situations can develop when families encounter unfamiliar customs.

The All-American SLURP

by **Lensey Namioka**

The first time our family was invited out to dinner in America, we disgraced ourselves while eating celery. We had immigrated to this country from China, and during our early days here we had a hard time with American table manners. **A**

In China we never ate celery raw, or any other kind of vegetable raw. We always had to disinfect the vegetables in boiling water first. When we were presented with our first relish tray, the raw celery caught us unprepared. **B**

We had been invited to dinner by our neighbors, the Gleasons. After arriving at the house, we shook hands with our hosts and packed ourselves into a sofa. As our family of four sat stiffly in a row, my younger brother and I stole glances at our parents for a clue as to what to do next.

Mrs. Gleason offered the relish tray to Mother. The tray looked pretty, with its tiny red radishes, curly sticks of carrots, and long, slender stalks of pale-green celery. "Do try some of the celery, Mrs. Lin," she said. "It's from a local farmer, and it's sweet."

Mother picked up one of the green stalks, and Father followed suit. Then I picked up a stalk, and my brother did too. So there we sat, each with a stalk of celery in our right hand.

Mrs. Gleason kept smiling. "Would you like to try some of the dip, Mrs. Lin? It's my own recipe: sour cream and onion flakes, with a dash of Tabasco sauce."

Most Chinese don't care for dairy products, and in those days I wasn't even ready to drink fresh milk. Sour cream sounded perfectly revolting. Our family shook our heads in unison.

Mrs. Gleason went off with the relish tray to the other guests, and we carefully

---

A **Literary Focus** **Theme and Subject** Based on what you've read in the first paragraph, what do you think the subject of this story might be?

B **Read and Discuss** What has the author told you so far? What does the narrator mean when she says the family "disgraced" themselves?

watched to see what they did. Everyone seemed to eat the raw vegetables quite happily.

Mother took a bite of her celery. *Crunch.* "It's not bad!" she whispered.

Father took a bite of his celery. *Crunch.* "Yes, it is good," he said, looking surprised.

I took a bite, and then my brother. *Crunch, crunch.* It was more than good; it was delicious. Raw celery has a slight sparkle, a zingy taste that you don't get in cooked celery. When Mrs. Gleason came around with the relish tray, we each took another stalk of celery, except my brother. He took two.

There was only one problem: Long strings ran through the length of the stalk, and they got caught in my teeth. When I help my mother in the kitchen, I always pull the strings out before slicing celery.

I pulled the strings out of my stalk. *Z-z-zip, z-z-zip.* My brother followed suit. *Z-z-zip, z-z-zip, z-z-zip.* To my left, my parents were taking care of their own stalks. *Z-z-zip, z-z-zip, z-z-zip.*

Suddenly I realized that there was dead silence except for our zipping. Looking up, I saw that the eyes of everyone in the room were on our family. Mr. and Mrs. Gleason, their daughter Meg, who was my friend, and their neighbors the Badels—they were all staring at us as we busily pulled the strings of our celery. **C**

Father took a bite of his celery.

CRUNCH.

"Yes, it is good," he said.

That wasn't the end of it. Mrs. Gleason announced that dinner was served and invited us to the dining table. It was lavishly covered with platters of food, but we couldn't see any chairs around the table. So we helpfully carried over some dining chairs and sat down. All the other guests just stood there.

Mrs. Gleason bent down and whispered to us, "This is a buffet dinner. You help yourselves to some food and eat it in the living room."

Our family beat a retreat back to the sofa as if chased by enemy soldiers. For the rest of the evening, too mortified to go back to the dining table, I nursed a bit of potato salad on my plate. **D**

Next day, Meg and I got on the school bus together. I wasn't sure how she would feel about me after the spectacle our family made at the party. But she was just the same as usual, and the only reference she made to the party was, "Hope you and your folks got enough to eat last night. You certainly didn't take very much. Mom never tries to figure out how much food to prepare. She just puts everything on the table and hopes for the best."

I began to relax. The Gleasons' dinner party wasn't so different from a Chinese meal after all. My mother also puts everything on the table and hopes for the best.

C [Read and Discuss] What problem is created by the celery?

D [Read and Discuss] What is going on at this dinner party? What picture does the description of the family beating "a retreat back to the sofa as if chased by enemy soldiers" create in your mind?

Vocabulary **lavishly** (LAV ihsh lee) *adv.*: abundantly; plentifully.
mortified (MAWR tuh fyd) *v.* used as *adj.*: ashamed; embarrassed.
spectacle (SPEHK tuh kuhl) *n.*: strange or impressive sight.

Meg was the first friend I had made after we came to America. I eventually got acquainted with a few other kids in school, but Meg was still the only real friend I had.

My brother didn't have any problems making friends. He spent all his time with some boys who were teaching him baseball, and in no time he could speak English much faster than I could—not better, but faster.

I worried more about making mistakes, and I spoke carefully, making sure I could say everything right before opening my mouth. At least I had a better accent than my parents, who never really got rid of their Chinese accent, even years later. My parents had both studied English in school before coming to America, but what they had studied was mostly written English, not spoken.

Father's approach to English was a scientific one. Since Chinese verbs have no tense, he was fascinated by the way English verbs changed form according to whether they were in the present, past, perfect, pluperfect, future, or future perfect tense. He was always making diagrams of verbs and their inflections, and he looked for opportunities to show off his mastery of the pluperfect and future perfect tenses, his two favorites. "I shall have finished my project by Monday," he would say smugly.

Mother's approach was to memorize lists of polite phrases that would cover all possible social situations. She was constantly muttering things like "I'm fine, thank you. And you?" Once she accidentally stepped on someone's foot and hurriedly blurted,

"Oh, that's quite all right!" Embarrassed by her slip, she resolved to do better next time. So when someone stepped on *her* foot, she cried, "You're welcome!" **Ⓔ**

In our own different ways, we made progress in learning English. But I had another worry, and that was my appearance. My brother didn't have to worry, since Mother bought him blue jeans for school, and he dressed like all the other boys. But she insisted that girls had to wear skirts. By the time she saw that Meg and the other girls were wearing jeans, it was too late. My school clothes were bought already, and we didn't have money left to buy new outfits for me. We had too many other things to buy first, like furniture, pots, and pans.

The first time I visited Meg's house, she took me upstairs to her room, and I wound up trying on her clothes. We were pretty much the same size since Meg was shorter and thinner than average. Maybe that's how we became friends in the first place. Wearing Meg's jeans and T-shirt, I looked at myself in the mirror. I could almost pass for an American—from the back, anyway. At least the kids in school wouldn't stop and stare at me in the hallways, which was what they did when they saw me in my white

Analyzing Visuals **Connecting to the Text** What scene in the story does this photograph illustrate?

blouse and navy-blue skirt that went a couple of inches below the knees. **F**

When Meg came to my house, I invited her to try on my Chinese dresses, the ones with a high collar and slits up the sides. Meg's eyes were bright as she looked at herself in the mirror. She struck several sultry poses, and we nearly fell over laughing.

The dinner party at the Gleasons' didn't stop my growing friendship with Meg. Things were getting better for me in other ways too. Mother finally bought me some jeans at the end of the month, when Father got his paycheck. She wasn't in any hurry about buying them at first, until I worked on her. This is what I did. Since we didn't have a car in those days, I often ran down to the neighborhood store to pick up things for her. The groceries cost less at a big supermarket, but the closest one was many blocks away. One day, when she ran out of flour, I offered to borrow a bike from our neighbor's son and buy a ten-pound bag of flour at the big supermarket. I mounted the boy's bike and waved to Mother. "I'll be back in five minutes!"

Before I started pedaling, I heard her voice behind me. "You can't go out in public like that! People can see all the way up to your thighs!"

"I'm sorry," I said innocently. "I thought you were in a hurry to get the flour." For dinner we were going to have pot stickers (fried Chinese dumplings), and we needed a lot of flour.

"Couldn't you borrow a girl's bicycle?" complained Mother. "That way your skirt won't be pushed up."

"There aren't too many of those around," I said. "Almost all the girls wear jeans while

F [Read and Discuss] Now what problem is the narrator facing?

riding a bike, so they don't see any point buying a girl's bike." **G**

We didn't eat pot stickers that evening, and Mother was thoughtful. Next day we took the bus downtown and she bought me a pair of jeans. In the same week, my brother made the baseball team of his junior high school, Father started taking driving lessons, and Mother discovered rummage sales. We soon got all the furniture we needed, plus a dartboard and a 1,000-piece jigsaw puzzle. (Fourteen hours later, we discovered that it was a 999-piece jigsaw puzzle.) There was hope that the Lins might become a normal American family after all.

Then came our dinner at the Lakeview restaurant. The Lakeview was an expensive restaurant, one of those places where a head-waiter dressed in tails conducted you to your seat, and the only light came from candles and flaming desserts. In one corner of the room a lady harpist played tinkling melodies.

Father wanted to celebrate because he had just been promoted. He worked for an electronics company, and after his English started improving, his superiors decided to appoint him to a position more suited to his training. The promotion not only brought a higher salary but was also a tremendous boost to his pride.

Up to then we had eaten only in Chinese restaurants. Although my brother and I were becoming fond of hamburgers, my parents didn't care much for Western food, other than chow mein.

But this was a special occasion, and Father asked his co-workers to recommend a really elegant restaurant. So there we were at the Lakeview, stumbling after the head-waiter in the murky dining room.

At our table we were handed our menus, and they were so big that to read mine, I almost had to stand up again. But why bother? It was mostly in French, anyway.

Father, being an engineer, was always systematic. He took out a pocket French dictionary. "They told me that most of the items would be in French, so I came prepared." He even had a pocket flashlight the size of a marking pen. While Mother held the flashlight over the menu, he looked up the items that were in French.

"*Pâté en croûte,*" he muttered. "Let's see . . . *pâté* is paste . . . *croûte* is crust . . . hmmm . . . a paste in crust." **H**

The waiter stood looking patient. I squirmed and died at least fifty times.

At long last Father gave up. "Why don't we just order four complete dinners at random?" he suggested.

"Isn't that risky?" asked Mother. "The French eat some rather peculiar things, I've heard."

"A Chinese can eat anything a Frenchman can eat," Father declared.

The soup arrived in a plate. How do you get soup up from a plate? I glanced at the other diners, but the ones at the nearby tables were not on their soup course, while the more distant ones were invisible in the darkness.

G [Read and Discuss] What is the narrator trying to do now? What does this tell you about her?

H [Reading Focus] Generalizations What generalization can you make about Mr. Lin's approach to life in the United States?

Fortunately my parents had studied books on Western etiquette before they came to America. "Tilt your plate," whispered my mother. "It's easier to spoon the soup up that way."

She was right. Tilting the plate did the trick. But the etiquette book didn't say anything about what you did after the soup reached your lips. As any respectable Chinese knows, the correct way to eat your soup is to slurp. This helps to cool the liquid and prevent you from burning your lips. It also shows your appreciation.

We showed our appreciation. *Shloop*, went my father. *Shloop*, went my mother. *Shloop, shloop*, went my brother, who was the hungriest.

The lady harpist stopped playing to take a rest. And in the silence, our family's consumption of soup suddenly seemed unnaturally loud. You know how it sounds on a rocky beach when the tide goes out and the water drains from all those little pools? They go *shloop, shloop, shloop*. That was the Lin family eating soup.

At the next table a waiter was pouring wine. When a large *shloop* reached him, he froze. The bottle continued to pour, and red wine flooded the table top and into the lap of a customer. Even the customer didn't notice anything at first, being also

hypnotized by the *shloop, shloop, shloop.*

It was too much. "I need to go to the toilet," I mumbled, jumping to my feet. A waiter, sensing my urgency, quickly directed me to the ladies' room. **❶**

I splashed cold water on my burning face, and as I dried myself with a paper towel, I stared into the mirror. In this perfumed ladies' room, with its pink-and-silver wallpaper and marbled sinks, I looked completely out of place. What was I doing here? What was our family doing in the Lakeview restaurant? In America?

The door to the ladies' room opened. A woman came in and glanced curiously at me. I retreated into one of the toilet cubicles and latched the door.

Time passed—maybe half an hour, maybe an hour. Then I heard the door open again, and my mother's voice. "Are you in there? You're not sick, are you?"

There was real concern in her voice. A girl can't leave her family just because they slurp their soup. Besides, the toilet cubicle had a few drawbacks as a permanent residence. "I'm all right," I said, undoing the latch.

Mother didn't tell me how the rest of the dinner went, and I didn't want to know. In the weeks following, I managed to push the whole thing into the back of my mind, where it jumped out at me only a few times

SHLOOP, SHLOOP went my brother, who was the hungriest.

---

❶ Read and Discuss | Why does the narrator rush to the bathroom?

Vocabulary etiquette (EHT uh keht) *n.*: acceptable manners and behavior.

Analyzing Visuals

Connecting to the Text
What attitude does the girl in this photograph communicate? What qualities might she share with the narrator?

a day. Even now, I turn hot all over when I think of the Lakeview restaurant.

But by the time we had been in this country for three months, our family was definitely making progress toward becoming Americanized. I remember my parents' first PTA meeting. Father wore a neat suit and tie, and Mother put on her first pair of high heels. She stumbled only once. They met my homeroom teacher and beamed as she told them that I would make honor roll soon at the rate I was going. Of course Chinese etiquette forced Father to say that I was a very stupid girl and Mother to protest that the teacher was showing favoritism toward me. But I could tell they were both very proud. **J**

The day came when my parents announced that they wanted to give a dinner party. We had invited Chinese friends to eat with us before, but this dinner was going to be different. In addition to a Chinese American family, we were going to invite the Gleasons.

"Gee, I can hardly wait to have dinner at your house," Meg said to me. "I just *love* Chinese food."

That was a relief. Mother was a good cook, but I wasn't sure if people who ate sour cream would also eat chicken gizzards stewed in soy sauce.

Mother decided not to take a chance with chicken gizzards. Since we had Western guests, she set the table with large dinner plates, which we never used in Chinese meals. In fact we didn't use individual plates at all, but picked up food

J Read and Discuss | What have you learned so far about Chinese etiquette from this story?

The All-American Slurp **263**

from the platters in the middle of the table and brought it directly to our rice bowls. Following the practice of Chinese American restaurants, Mother also placed large serving spoons on the platters.

The dinner started well. Mrs. Gleason exclaimed at the beautifully arranged dishes of food: the colorful candied fruit in the sweet-and-sour pork dish, the noodle-thin shreds of chicken meat stir-fried with tiny peas, and the glistening pink prawns[1] in a ginger sauce.

At first I was too busy enjoying my food to notice how the guests were doing. But soon I remembered my duties. Sometimes guests were too polite to help themselves and you had to serve them with more food.

I glanced at Meg to see if she needed more food, and my eyes nearly popped out at the sight of her plate. It was piled with food: The sweet-and-sour meat pushed right against the chicken shreds, and the chicken sauce ran into the prawns. She had been taking food from a second dish before she finished eating her helping from the first!

Horrified, I turned to look at Mrs. Gleason. She was dumping rice out of her bowl and putting it on her dinner plate. Then she ladled prawns and gravy on top of the rice and mixed everything together, the way you mix sand, gravel, and cement to make concrete. **(K)**

I couldn't bear to look any longer, and I turned to Mr. Gleason. He was chasing a pea around his plate. Several times he got it to the edge, but when he tried to pick it up with his chopsticks, it rolled back toward the

---

1. **prawns:** large shrimps.

center of the plate again. Finally he put down his chopsticks and picked up the pea with his fingers. He really did! A grown man!

All of us, our family and the Chinese guests, stopped eating to watch the activities of the Gleasons. I wanted to giggle. Then I caught my mother's eyes on me. She frowned and shook her head slightly, and I understood the message: The Gleasons were not used to Chinese ways, and they were just coping the best they could. For some reason I thought of celery strings.

When the main courses were finished, Mother brought out a platter of fruit. "I hope you weren't expecting a sweet dessert," she said. "Since the Chinese don't eat dessert, I didn't think to prepare any."

"Oh, I couldn't possibly eat dessert!" cried Mrs. Gleason. "I'm simply stuffed!"

Meg had different ideas. When the table was cleared, she announced that she and I were going for a walk. "I don't know about you, but I feel like dessert," she told me, when we were outside. "Come on, there's a Dairy Queen down the street. I could use a big chocolate milkshake!"

Although I didn't really want anything more to eat, I insisted on paying for the milkshakes. After all, I was still hostess.

Meg got her large chocolate milkshake and I had a small one. Even so, she was finishing hers while I was only half done. Toward the end she pulled hard on her straws and went *shloop, shloop.*

"Do you always slurp when you eat a milkshake?" I asked, before I could stop myself.

Meg grinned. "Sure. All Americans slurp." **(L)**

(K) Literary Focus Theme and Subject How does the narrator's surprise relate to the subject of the story? to the theme?

(L) Literary Focus Theme and Subject What does this last line <u>convey</u> about the story's theme?

Applying Your Skills

Reading Standard 3.6 Identify and analyze features of themes conveyed through characters, actions, and images.

The All-American Slurp
Literary Response and Analysis

Reading Skills Focus
Quick Check

1. What American customs confuse the Lins when they eat at the Gleasons' house?
2. What "mistakes" do the Gleasons make when they have dinner at the Lins' home?

Read with a Purpose

3. How does the Lin family adapt to customs in the United States? How do you think they will adapt in the future?

Reading Skills: Making Generalizations

4. Review the chart you filled in while reading the story. Then add two rows. In the first, record what the narrator discovers through the conflicts and actions in the story. In the second, write down a generalization about life—the story's theme.

Conflicts and Key Actions	Generalizations
The Lins aren't sure how to act during dinner at the Gleasons'. (1) They pull strings out of celery. (2) They set chairs at the buffet.	When you're not sure about another culture's customs, you may end up doing things that appear strange.

What Narrator Discovers: _____

Final Generalization (Theme): _____

Literary Skills Focus
Literary Analysis

5. **Evaluate** Do you think the author makes the immigrant experience sound too easy, or does she present an accurate picture?

Literary Skills: Theme and Subject

6. **Analyze** State the subject of this story in a word or two. Meg's comment that "All Americans slurp" hints at the story's **theme.** What do you think that theme is? State the theme in a sentence or two and explain how it is conveyed through characters, actions, and images.

Literary Skills Review: Character

7. **Analyze** Think about the narrator's qualities and her situation as a girl. Why is it harder for the narrator to feel comfortable in the United States than it is for her brother? How do her qualities affect the plot?

Writing Skills Focus
Think as a Reader/Writer

Use It in Your Writing Write a scene that takes place during a meal. Use **images** containing onomatopoeia to <u>convey</u> features of your theme.

What Do You Think Now? How did this story affect your ideas about the things people have in common in spite of their different cultural customs?

Applying Your Skills

The All-American Slurp

Reading Standard 1.4 Monitor expository text for unknown words or words with novel meanings by using word, sentence, and paragraph clues to determine meaning.

Vocabulary Development

Context Clues

When you read, you can often determine the definitions of unknown words or words with novel meanings by using what you know about word parts and related words. You can also use word, sentence, and paragraph clues—also called **context clues**—which provide information that point to a word's meaning.

Unfamiliar Word	Using Context Clues
"The Lakeview was an expensive restaurant, one of those places where a head-waiter . . . *conducted* you to your seat . . ."	*conducted* I think this means the waiter took people to their seats. A conductor is someone who *leads* an orchestra. *Conducted* probably means *led*.

Your Turn

Complete each sentence, providing context clues to clarify the meaning of the word in italics. Then, write out the sentences, replacing the italicized words with blanks. Have a classmate fill in the correct words using the context clues in the sentences.

lavishly
mortified
spectacle
acquainted
etiquette

1. I noticed that the table was *lavishly* set with
   _____
   _____ .

2. *Mortified* by my brother's behavior, I _____
   _____

3. We were afraid that we created a *spectacle* because _____
   _____ .

4. Meg was *acquainted* with the new girl, but __
   _____
   _____ .

5. When you use proper *etiquette*, you _____
   _____
   _____ .

Language Coach

Word Forms Make adverbs by adding –*ly* to the words from the story shown in the box at right. Remember that when you add the suffix –*ly* to most words to form adverbs, you don't change the spelling of the word itself. However, for words that end in –*y*, you usually need to change the *y* to an *i* before adding –*ly*. Use a dictionary to check your spelling.

ready
real
polite
tremendous

Academic Vocabulary

Talk About . . .
How does the author use humor to illustrate that people from different cultures have similar feelings when they face unfamiliar situations?

Learn It Online
Use *WordSharp* to bolster language skills at:

go.hrw.com   H6-266   Go

Grammar Link

Understanding and Using Clauses

A **clause** is a group of words containing both a subject and a verb. Not all clauses, however, are identical. Some are called **independent clauses** because they have a subject and a verb and can stand alone as a complete sentence. Other types of clauses—called **subordinate clauses**—have a subject and a verb but don't make up a complete sentence. Here are some examples:

INDEPENDENT CLAUSE

     S   **V**
Mrs. Gleason offered the relish tray to Mother.

SUBORDINATE CLAUSE

   S V
As we sat stiffly

When an independent clause stands alone, it is called a sentence. (Usually the term *independent clause* is used only when such a clause is joined with another clause.) A subordinate clause must be joined with at least one independent clause to make a sentence and express a complete thought.

Your Turn

For each of the following items, decide if the italicized word group is an independent or subordinate clause.

1. I wasn't sure how she would feel about me *after the spectacle our family made at the party.*

2. *As I tried on Meg's jeans and T-shirt,* I looked at myself in the mirror.

3. In our own different ways, *we made progress in learning English.*

CHOICES

As you respond to the Choices, use these **Academic Vocabulary** words as appropriate: attitude, communicate, conveyed, illustrate.

REVIEW
Create a Poster

Group Activity In a group, compare the charts you filled in as you read the story. Did you record similar or different themes? How are features of your themes conveyed in the story? Create a poster for the story that communicates its themes in an attention-grabbing way.

CONNECT
Write an Essay

Timed └Writing In this story the narrator's friendship with Meg helps her discover new things and change her attitude about making mistakes. Think of a time when you made a new friend. What drew the two of you together? What made the friendship grow? What did you learn from your friend? Write a short essay that illustrates how important the friendship was.

EXTEND
Design a Helpful Web Site

TechFocus To help a newcomer from another culture feel more comfortable in your school, design a Web site of information, including a list of slang expressions, a description of currently popular things (foods, movies, music, TV shows, clothes), a map of your school, and tips on fun things to do in your town.

Learn It Online
Bring your essay to life with digital storytelling at:

go.hrw.com   H6-267   **Go**

Aaron's Gift

by **Myron Levoy**

What Do **You** Think

What is special about the gifts we receive from or give to the people who are important to us?

QuickWrite

Think about the best gift you have ever received from someone who means a lot to you. What made it such a good gift? Write down your thoughts.

Reader/Writer
Notebook
Use your **RWN** to complete the activities
for this selection.

Reading Standard 3.6 Identify and analyze features of themes conveyed through
characters, actions, and images.

Literary Skills Focus

Theme and Actions   The actions and events in a story form the
story's **plot;** the message is the story's **theme.** Writers often <u>commu-
nicate</u> theme through actions that happen more than once or that
seem to echo or repeat other actions. Actions that strongly affect the
way the plot unfolds, especially those that occur at the **climax** (the
moment when we know how the conflict will be resolved) often <u>convey</u>
the theme as well. As you read this story, think about how the writer
expresses his theme through present and past actions.

Literary Perspectives   Use the Analyzing Archetypes perspective
described on page 271 as you read this story.

Reading Skills Focus

Analyzing Cause and Effect   A story's **plot** consists of a series of
related actions and events. The first event in a plot **causes** something
else to happen—an **effect.** That effect, in turn, becomes the cause of
other events. Writers <u>express</u> their messages through the connections
between events. Analyzing the chain of causes and effects in a story can
help you discover the story's theme.

Into Action   Use a flowchart like the one below to record the chain of
causes and effects in this story. You'll use this information later to identify the story's theme.

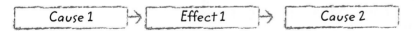

Cause 1 → Effect 1 → Cause 2

Writing Skills Focus
Think as a Reader/Writer

Find It in Your Reading   Writers <u>communicate</u> themes through
images, or language that appeals to the senses. A pigeon plays a crucial
role in this story. As you read, record in your *Reader/Writer Notebook*
images of the pigeon that seem particularly important to you. Think
about what the writer shares through these images.

Vocabulary

plunged (pluhnjd) *v.:* dived down
suddenly. *Aaron plunged and caught
the bird.*

thrashing (THRASH ihng) *n.:* movement from side to side in an uncontrolled way. *The bird was tired from
its thrashing.*

contented (kuhn TEHNT ihd) *adj.:*
happy or satisfied. *The bird was
contented when it was living with
Aaron.*

consoled (kuhn SOHLD) *v.:* comforted
when sad or disappointed. *She
couldn't be consoled after losing her
goat.*

Language Coach

Base Words   All of the Vocabulary
words above consist of a base word
to which an ending, or suffix, has
been added. Identify the base word
for each of the words. To which three
base words can both *–ed* and *–ing*
be added? Use a dictionary if you
need help.

Learn It Online
Elevate your vocabulary skills with Word Watch:

go.hrw.com   H6-269   **Go**

Myron Levoy

(1930–)

Inspired by an Author's Manuscript

When Myron Levoy was a teenager, he worked at the New York Public Library, and there he came across the original manuscript of the poem "Miniver Cheevy" by Edward Arlington Robinson. Levoy had just read the poem in school, and seeing it written in the author's own hand amazed him. He was inspired to become a writer himself.

Award-Winning Books

After deciding on his career, Myron Levoy wrote a popular book of short stories called *The Witch of Fourth Street*, along with many other books for children. He also wrote *Alan and Naomi*, a novel about two young people whose lives are changed by the effects of World War II. *Alan and Naomi* was named one of the "1969–1992 Best of the Best Books for Young Adults," and eventually a movie was based on it.

> "Seeing the poem before me in 'living' ink and paper, in that neat, tiny hand, was for me an epiphany. Such power, an entire world, on that one small sheet! It was absolute and final: yes, I would be a writer above all else!"

Think About the Writer Why was seeing a famous poem in the author's own handwriting so inspiring for Levoy?

Build Background

This story takes place in an immigrant neighborhood of New York City in the early 1900s. Aaron's grandmother is from Ukraine in Eastern Europe, a territory that was under the rule of Imperial Russia during the 1800s. Many Jewish people, like Aaron's grandmother, lived in the Ukraine at the time.

When Czar Alexander II died in 1881, the Jewish people were wrongly accused of his murder, and much violence was aimed at them. The Cossacks, a part of the Russian army famous for military skills and horsemanship, carried out the new czar's orders. As a result of state-sponsored violence against the Jewish people in Ukraine, many Jews moved to the United States, leaving their homeland behind.

Preview the Selection

In this selection, you will read about a young boy named **Aaron,** who finds a pigeon with a broken wing.

Aaron's Gift

by
Myron Levoy

Aaron Kandel had come to Tompkins Square Park to roller-skate, for the streets near Second Avenue were always too crowded with children and peddlers and old ladies and baby buggies. Though few children had bicycles in those days, almost every child owned a pair of roller skates. And Aaron was, it must be said, a Class A, triple-fantastic roller skater.

Aaron skated back and forth on the wide walkway of the park, pretending he was an aviator in an air race zooming around pylons, which were actually two lampposts. During his third lap around the racecourse, he noticed a pigeon on the grass, behaving very strangely. Aaron skated to the line of benches, then climbed over onto the lawn.

The pigeon was trying to fly, but all it could manage was to flutter and turn round and round in a large circle, as if it were performing a frenzied dance. The left wing was

only half open and was beating in a clumsy, jerking fashion; it was clearly broken.   **Ⓐ**

Luckily, Aaron hadn't eaten the cookies he'd stuffed into his pocket before he'd gone clacking down the three flights of

Literary Perspectives

Analyzing Archetypes In literary criticism, the word *archetype* (AHR kuh typ) refers to a pattern or "type" that we find again and again in literature. Certain plots, characters, symbols, and even themes that occur in a variety of literary works may be considered archetypal. Examples of archetypal plots include the heroic quest story and the story of the "underdog" hero who defeats a more powerful enemy. Archetypal themes cover the search for identity and the struggle for justice. Characters like the heroic youth, the wise elder, and the evil villain are also archetypal. These common story elements reflect ideas, concerns, and values that human beings from all times and places share. As you read, be sure to notice the questions in the text, which will guide you in using this perspective.

Ⓐ **Reading Focus** **Analyzing Cause and Effect**   What is the first important event in the story? What do you think might happen as a result of this event?

stairs from his apartment, his skates already on. He broke a cookie into small crumbs and tossed some toward the pigeon. "Here pidge, here pidge," he called. The pigeon spotted the cookie crumbs and, after a moment, stopped thrashing about. It folded its wings as best it could, but the broken wing still stuck half out. Then it strutted over to the crumbs, its head bobbing forth-back, forth-back, as if it were marching a little in front of the rest of the body—perfectly normal, except for that half-open wing which seemed to make the bird stagger sideways every so often.

The pigeon began eating the crumbs as Aaron quickly unbuttoned his shirt and pulled it off. Very slowly, he edged toward the bird, making little kissing sounds like the ones he heard his grandmother make when she fed the sparrows on the back fire escape.

Then suddenly Aaron plunged. The shirt, in both hands, came down like a torn parachute. The pigeon beat its wings, but Aaron held the shirt to the ground, and the bird couldn't escape. Aaron felt under the shirt, gently, and gently took hold of the wounded pigeon.

"Yes, yes, pidge," he said, very softly. "There's a good boy. Good pigeon, good."

The pigeon struggled in his hands, but little by little Aaron managed to soothe it. "Good boy, pidge. That's your new name. Pidge. I'm gonna take you home, Pidge. Yes, yes, *ssh*. Good boy. I'm gonna fix you up. Easy, Pidge, easy does it. Easy, boy." **Ⓑ**

Aaron squeezed through an opening between the row of benches and skated slowly out of the park, while holding the pigeon carefully with both hands as if it were one of his mother's rare, precious cups from the old country. How fast the pigeon's

---

Ⓑ | Read and Discuss | What is Aaron planning to do now?

Vocabulary **plunged** (pluhnjd) *v.*: dived down suddenly.

heart was beating! Was he afraid? Or did all pigeons' hearts beat fast?

It was fortunate that Aaron was an excellent skater, for he had to skate six blocks to his apartment, over broken pavement and sudden gratings and curbs and cobblestones. But when he reached home, he asked Noreen Callahan, who was playing on the stoop, to take off his skates for him. He would not chance going up three flights on roller skates this time.

"Is he sick?" asked Noreen.

"Broken wing," said Aaron. "I'm gonna fix him up and make him into a carrier pigeon or something."

"Can I watch?" asked Noreen.

"Watch what?"

"The operation. I'm gonna be a nurse when I grow up."

"OK," said Aaron. "You can even help. You can help hold him while I fix him up."

Aaron wasn't quite certain what his mother would say about his new-found pet, but he was pretty sure he knew what his grandmother would think. His grandmother had lived with them ever since his grandfather had died three years ago. And she fed the sparrows and jays and crows and robins on the back fire escape with every spare crumb she could find. In fact, Aaron noticed that she sometimes created crumbs where they didn't exist, by squeezing and tearing pieces of her breakfast roll when his mother wasn't looking.

Aaron didn't really understand his grandmother, for he often saw her by the window having long conversations with the birds,

telling them about her days as a little girl in the Ukraine.[1] And once he saw her take her mirror from her handbag and hold it out toward the birds. She told Aaron that she wanted them to see how beautiful they were. Very strange. But Aaron did know that she would love Pidge, because she loved everything.

To his surprise, his mother said he could keep the pigeon, temporarily, because it was sick, and we were all strangers in the land of Egypt, and it might not be bad for Aaron to have a pet. *Temporarily.*

The wing was surprisingly easy to fix, for the break showed clearly and Pidge was remarkably patient and still, as if he knew he was being helped. Or perhaps he was just exhausted from all the thrashing about he had done. Two Popsicle sticks served as splints, and strips from an old undershirt were used to tie them in place. Another strip held the wing to the bird's body.

Aaron's father arrived home and stared at the pigeon. Aaron waited for the expected storm. But instead, Mr. Kandel asked, "Who *did* this?"

"Me," said Aaron. "And Noreen Callahan."

"Sophie!" he called to his wife. "Did you see this! Ten years and it's better than Dr. Belasco could do. He's a genius!" Ⓒ

As the days passed, Aaron began training Pidge to be a carrier pigeon. He tied a little cardboard tube to Pidge's left leg and stuck tiny rolled-up sheets of paper with secret messages into it: THE ENEMY IS

---

1. **Ukraine** (yoo KRAYN): country in Eastern Europe that borders on Russia to the northeast.

Ⓒ [**Read and Discuss**] What does Aaron's family think of the pigeon? What is Aaron's father's attitude about the surgery?

Vocabulary thrashing (THRASH ihng) *n.*: movement from side to side in an uncontrolled way.

ATTACKING AT DAWN. Or: THE GUNS ARE HIDDEN IN THE TRUNK OF THE CAR. Or: VINCENT DeMARCO IS A BRITISH SPY. Then Aaron would set Pidge down at one end of the living room and put some popcorn at the other end. And Pidge would waddle slowly across the room, cooing softly, while the ends of his bandages trailed along the floor.

At the other end of the room, one of Aaron's friends would take out the message, stick a new one in, turn Pidge around, and aim him at the popcorn that Aaron put down on his side of the room.

And Pidge grew fat and contented on all the popcorn and crumbs and corn and crackers and Aaron's grandmother's breakfast rolls.

Analyzing Visuals **Connecting to the Text**
Which of Aaron's actions does this photograph reflect?

Aaron had told all the children about Pidge, but he only let his very best friends come up and play carrier-pigeon with him. But telling everyone had been a mistake. A group of older boys from down the block had a club—Aaron's mother called it a gang—and Aaron had longed to join as he had never longed for anything else. To be with them and share their secrets, the secrets of older boys. To be able to enter their clubhouse shack on the empty lot on the next street. To know the password and swear the secret oath. To belong. **D**

About a month after Aaron had brought the pigeon home, Carl, the gang leader, walked over to Aaron in the street and told him he could be a member if he'd bring the pigeon down to be the club mascot. Aaron couldn't believe it; he immediately raced home to get Pidge. But his mother told Aaron to stay away from those boys, or else. And Aaron, miserable, argued with his mother and pleaded and cried and coaxed. It was no use. Not with those boys. No.

Aaron's mother tried to change the subject. She told him that it would soon be his grandmother's sixtieth birthday, a very special birthday indeed, and all the family from Brooklyn and the East Side would be coming to their apartment for a dinner and celebration. Would Aaron try to build something or make something for Grandma? A present made with his own hands would be nice. A decorated box for her hairpins or a crayon picture for her room or anything he liked.

In a flash Aaron knew what to give her: Pidge! Pidge would be her present! Pidge

D **Literary Perspectives** Analyzing Archetypes
What common human desire is Aaron expressing?

Vocabulary contented (kuhn TEHNT ihd) *adj.*: happy or satisfied.

with his wing healed, who might be able to carry messages for her to the doctor or his Aunt Rachel or other people his grandmother seemed to go to a lot. It would be a surprise for everyone. And Pidge would make up for what had happened to Grandma when she'd been a little girl in the Ukraine, wherever that was. **E**

Often, in the evening, Aaron's grandmother would talk about the old days long ago in the Ukraine, in the same way that she talked to the birds on the back fire escape. She had lived in a village near a place called Kishinev with hundreds of other poor peasant families like her own. Things hadn't been too bad under someone called Czar Alexander the Second, whom Aaron always pictured as a tall handsome man in a gold uniform. But Alexander the Second was assassinated, and Alexander the Third, whom Aaron pictured as an ugly man in a black cape, became the Czar.[2] And the Jewish people of the Ukraine had no peace anymore.

One day, a thundering of horses was heard coming toward the village from the direction of Kishinev. *The Cossacks! The Cossacks!* someone had shouted. The czar's horsemen! Quickly, quickly, everyone in Aaron's grandmother's family had climbed down to the cellar through a little trap door hidden under a mat in the big central room of their shack. But his grandmother's pet goat, whom she'd loved as much as Aaron loved Pidge and more, had to be left above,

---

2. **Czar** (zahr): a male ruler of Russia before 1917.

because if it had made a sound in the cellar, they would never have lived to see the next morning. They all hid under the wood in the woodbin and waited, hardly breathing.

Suddenly, from above, they heard shouts and calls and screams at a distance. And then the noise was in their house. Boots pounding on the floor, and everything breaking and crashing overhead. The smell of smoke and the shouts of a dozen men.

The terror went on for an hour and then the sound of horses' hooves faded into the distance. They waited another hour to make sure, and then the father went up out of the cellar and the rest of the family followed. The door to the house had been torn from its hinges and every piece of furniture was broken. Every window, every dish, every stitch of clothing was totally destroyed, and one wall had been completely bashed in. And on the floor was the goat, lying quietly. Aaron's grandmother, who was just a little girl of eight at the time, had wept over the goat all day and all night and could not be consoled.

But they had been lucky. For other houses had been burned to the ground. And everywhere, not goats alone, nor sheep, but men and women and children lay quietly on the ground. The word for this sort of massacre, Aaron had learned, was *pogrom*. It had been a pogrom. And the men on the horses were Cossacks. Hated word. Cossacks.

And so Pidge would replace that goat of long ago. A pigeon on Second Avenue where no one needed trapdoors or secret escape passages or woodpiles to hide under.

E **Literary Focus** **Theme and Actions** Titles often communicate a story's theme. What clues do you have so far to the meaning of the title "Aaron's Gift"—and to the story's theme?

Vocabulary **consoled** (kuhn SOHLD) *v.*: comforted when sad or disappointed.

A pigeon for his grandmother's sixtieth birthday. *Oh wing, heal quickly so my grandmother can send you flying to everywhere she wants!* **F**

But a few days later, Aaron met Carl in the street again. And Carl told Aaron that there was going to be a meeting that afternoon in which a map was going to be drawn up to show where a secret treasure lay buried on the empty lot. "Bring the pigeon and you can come into the shack. We got a badge for you. A new kinda membership badge with a secret code on the back."

Aaron ran home, his heart pounding almost as fast as the pigeon's. He took Pidge in his hands and carried him out the door while his mother was busy in the kitchen making stuffed cabbage, his father's favorite dish. And by the time he reached the street, Aaron had decided to take the bandages off. Pidge would look like a real pigeon again, and none of the older boys would laugh or call him a bundle of rags. **G**

Gently, gently he removed the bandages and the splints and put them in his pocket in case he should need them again. But Pidge seemed to hold his wing properly in place.

When he reached the empty lot, Aaron walked up to the shack, then hesitated. Four bigger boys were there. After a moment, Carl came out and commanded Aaron to hand Pidge over.

"Be careful," said Aaron. "I just took the bandages off."

"Oh sure, don't worry," said Carl. By now Pidge was used to people holding him, and he remained calm in Carl's hands.

"OK," said Carl. "Give him the badge." And one of the older boys handed Aaron his badge with the code on the back. "Now light the fire," said Carl.

"What . . . what fire?" asked Aaron.

"The fire. You'll see," Carl answered.

"You didn't say nothing about a fire," said Aaron. "You didn't say nothing to—"

"Hey!" said Carl. "I'm the leader here. And you don't talk unless I tell you that you have p'mission. Light the fire, Al."

The boy named Al went out to the side of the shack, where some wood and cardboard and old newspapers had been piled into a huge mound. He struck a match and held it to the newspapers.

"OK," said Carl. "Let's get 'er good and hot. Blow on it. Everybody blow."

Aaron's eyes stung from the smoke, but he blew alongside the others, going from side to side as the smoke shifted toward them and away.

"Let's fan it," said Al.

In a few minutes, the fire was crackling and glowing with a bright yellow-orange flame.

"Get me the rope," said Carl.

One of the boys brought Carl some cord and Carl, without a word, wound it twice around the pigeon, so that its wings were tight against its body.

"What . . . what are you *doing!*" shouted Aaron. "You're hurting his wing!"

F Literary Perspectives **Analyzing Archetypes** Birds are common symbols in literature. What qualities do birds often symbolize? What might be the symbolism of Aaron's intended gift?

G Read and Discuss How is Aaron's situation changing? What does Aaron think of the gang's offer?

"Don't worry about his wing," said Carl. "We're gonna throw him into the fire. And when we do, we're gonna swear an oath of loyalty to—"

"No! *No!*" shouted Aaron, moving toward Carl.

"Grab him!" called Carl. "Don't let him get the pigeon!"

But Aaron had leaped right across the fire at Carl, taking him completely by surprise. He threw Carl back against the shack and hit out at his face with both fists. Carl slid down to the ground and the pigeon rolled out of his hands. Aaron scooped up the pigeon and ran, pretending he was on roller skates so that he would go faster and faster. And as he ran across the lot he pulled the cord off Pidge and tried to find a place, *any* place, to hide him. But the boys were on top of him, and the pigeon slipped from Aaron's hands.

"Get him!" shouted Carl.

Aaron thought of the worst, the most horrible thing he could shout at the boys. "Cossacks!" he screamed. "You're all Cossacks!"

Two boys held Aaron back while the others tried to catch the pigeon. Pidge flut-

H **Read and Discuss** What have you just found out? What might Aaron think of the gang now?

Analyzing Visuals **Connecting to the Text** What actions in the story does this photograph illustrate?

tered along the ground just out of reach, skittering one way and then the other. Then the boys came at him from two directions. But suddenly Pidge beat his wings in rhythm, and rose up, up over the roof of the nearest tenement, up over Second Avenue toward the park.

With the pigeon gone, the boys turned toward Aaron and tackled him to the ground and punched him and tore his clothes and punched him some more. Aaron twisted and turned and kicked and punched back, shouting "Cossacks! Cossacks!" And somehow the word gave him the strength to tear away from them. **❶**

When Aaron reached home, he tried to go past the kitchen quickly so his mother wouldn't see his bloody face and torn clothing. But it was no use; his father was home from work early that night and was seated in the living room. In a moment Aaron was surrounded by his mother, father, and grandmother, and in another moment he had told them everything that had happened, the words tumbling out between his broken sobs. Told them of the present he had planned, of the pigeon for a goat, of the gang, of the badge with the secret code on the back, of the shack, and the fire, and the pigeon's flight over the tenement roof.

And Aaron's grandmother kissed him and thanked him for his present which was even better than the pigeon.

"What present?" asked Aaron, trying to stop the series of sobs.

And his grandmother opened her pocketbook and handed Aaron her mirror and asked him to look. But all Aaron saw was his dirty, bruised face and his torn shirt.

Aaron thought he understood and then, again, he thought he didn't. How could she be so happy when there really was no present? And why pretend that there was? **❶**

Later that night, just before he fell asleep, Aaron tried to imagine what his grandmother might have done with the pigeon. She would have fed it, and she certainly would have talked to it, as she did to all the birds, and . . . and then she would have let it go free. Yes, of course. Pidge's flight to freedom must have been the gift that had made his grandmother so happy. Her goat has escaped from the Cossacks at last, Aaron thought, half dreaming. And he fell asleep with a smile.

---

❶ Reading Focus Analyzing Cause and Effect What caused Aaron to call the boys "Cossacks"? Why is that the worst word he can think of shouting?

❶ Literary Focus Theme and Actions What is Aaron's real gift to his grandmother? What theme is <u>conveyed</u> through this gift?

Applying Your Skills

Aaron's Gift

Literary Response and Analysis

Reading Skills Focus
Quick Check

1. What loss did Aaron's grandmother experience when she lived in Ukraine?

2. What do the other boys try to do with Pidge? How do Aaron's actions contrast with theirs?

Read with a Purpose

3. What does Aaron think was his gift to his grandmother? What does she consider his gift to be? How does she communicate this view?

Reading Skills: Analyzing Cause and Effect

4. Complete your cause-and-effect flowchart. Add a box labeled "Theme." Based on the actions and events in the story, what do you think is the story's theme? What final event especially conveys the theme?

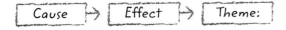

Literary Skills Focus
Literary Analysis

5. **Interpret** Explain Aaron's feelings for and attitude toward his grandmother. Why is he so determined to give Pidge to her?

6. **Literary Perspectives** Explain how each of these elements in the story might be considered archetypal: Aaron's rescue of the pigeon; the stories Aaron's grandmother tells; Aaron's desire to belong to a group; Aaron's stand against the gang; the pigeon's escape. What other archetypal elements did you note? How do these elements add to the story's power?

Literary Skills: Theme and Actions

7. **Compare** How does Aaron's experience with the gang echo his grandmother's experiences in Ukraine? How do both of these experiences convey the story's theme?

Literary Skills Review: Characterization

8. **Analyze** Writers bring characters to life through **characterization:** by describing how they talk, look, and act; by revealing their inner thoughts; and by showing how other characters react to them. How does the author make Aaron seem like a real person?

Writing Skills Focus
Think as a Reader/Writer
Use It in Your Writing Think of a message and a conflict involving an animal. Then, write a scene in which you use **images** of the animal to express your theme.

What Do You Think Now

Have your ideas about what makes a gift special changed? How special does Aaron's present seem to you? Explain.

Applying Your Skills

Aaron's Gift

Vocabulary Development
Words Borrowed from Other Languages

Words from Latin and Old English Many English words that we use today come from other languages, both past and present. The Vocabulary words in "Aaron's Gift" are related to words from Latin or Old English—languages that are no longer spoken.

Your Turn

| plunged |
| thrashing |
| contented |
| consoled |

From the Vocabulary list at the right, choose the word that correctly completes each sentence.

1. The Latin word *consolari*, meaning "comfort," is related to the word _____.
2. The Old English word *therscan*, meaning "to thresh," is related to the word _____.
3. The Latin word *contentus*, meaning "satisfied," is related to the word _____.
4. The Latin word *plumbum*, meaning "lead," is related to the word _____.

Words from Russian Many foreign words have come into the English language because of the more recent influence of immigrant cultures in English-speaking countries such as the United States. Some words in "Aaron's Gift," like *czar*, *Cossack*, and *pogrom*, came into the English language from Russian. So did the words below. Use a dictionary to identify the meaning of each word.

parka (PAHR kuh)	babushka (buh BOOSH kuh)
sable (SAY buhl)	steppe (stehp)

Your Turn

Complete each sentence below with the correct word from Russian at the bottom of the left-hand column. Use context clues to determine which word fits best.

5. Put on a _____ before you go out in this cold weather.
6. The _____ is a small animal with beautiful dark fur.
7. Grandma always wore a black _____ on her head when she went out in cold weather.
8. The Russian _____ is similar to the prairie or the plains in this country.

Language Coach
Base Words What other words can you make from the base words *plunge*, *thrash*, *content*, and *console*? With a partner, brainstorm words that can be formed from these base words. Identify the part of speech of each new word. Use a dictionary if you need help.

Academic Vocabulary

Write About . . .
Write a paragraph explaining how the author <u>communicates</u> the story's theme through the contrast between Aaron and the boys he calls "Cossacks."

For action-packed vocabulary lessons, visit:

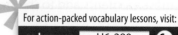

go.hrw.com   H6-280   **Go**

Grammar Link
Sentence Structures: Introducing Variety

If writers used the same sentence structures over and over, readers would become bored. So, writers use a variety of sentence types, such as these two:

SIMPLE SENTENCES **Simple sentences** are made up of only one **independent clause.** An independent clause is a group of words with a subject and a verb that expresses a complete thought and can stand alone as a complete sentence.

> S V
> **Aaron went** to the park.

Simple sentences may have more than one subject or more than one verb, or both. For example:

> S   S   S
> **Children, peddlers, and old ladies**
> V   V
> **walked and talked** along Second Avenue.

COMPOUND SENTENCES Unlike simple sentences, **compound sentences** always have two or more independent clauses. The clauses are joined by a comma and a connecting word such as *or, and,* or *but.* Each part of a compound sentence could stand alone as a separate sentence.

> S   V
> **Aaron rescued** the frightened pigeon, and
> S V
> **he bandaged** its broken wing.

Your Turn

Read each sentence and determine whether it is a simple sentence or a compound sentence.

1. Aaron squeezed through an opening between the row of benches.
2. The pigeon beat its wings, but Aaron held the shirt to the ground.

CHOICES

As you respond to the Choices, use these **Academic Vocabulary** words as appropriate: attitude, communicate, conveyed, illustrate.

REVIEW
Write a Thank-You Note

Timed └Writing Imagine that you are Aaron's grandmother. Write Aaron a thank-you note. Explain how you feel about his actions and tell him what message they convey. Be sure he understands what his real gift to you was.

CONNECT
Write a Persuasive Essay

One theme of the story is "People should show compassion to those who have suffered." Research an actual group of people in current times or the recent past that has suffered a devastating loss—perhaps through war, natural disaster, or social injustice. Write a persuasive essay describing how you think this group should be treated. What would be the best way to show kindness in the situation?

EXTEND
Deliver a Presentation

Group Project Work with a group to research how the pogroms affected Jews in Ukraine, or study how Jewish and Ukrainian immigration affected New York City in the early 1900s. Either project should help you understand the attitude of Aaron's grandmother. Present what you learn to the class.

Learn It Online
Add the sound of music to your story! Find out how at:

go.hrw.com H6-281 **Go**

Comparing Plot and Character

CONTENTS

What Do You Think?

If you were alone, without family or friends, what would you fear?

QuickWrite

Think of movies or stories in which characters face something terrifying or mysterious all alone. How do the characters react?

Preparing to Read

Reading Standard 3.2 Analyze the effect of the qualities of the character (e.g., courage or cowardice, ambition or laziness) on the plot and the resolution of the conflict.

In the Fog/The Hitchhiker

Literary Skills Focus

Plot and Character **Suspense** is the feeling of anxious curiosity about what will happen next. One technique writers use to create suspense is **foreshadowing**—the use of hints that suggest what is to come. As you read these two plays, think about how the characters' behavior affects their choices and actions and the plot as a whole. Note, too, how the playwrights build suspense, keeping you at the edge of your seat right until the end.

Reading Skills Focus

Analyzing Cause and Effect Most plots are made up of a chain of causes and effects. The first event **causes** something to happen, which is the **effect.** The effect, in turn, causes another event to happen, and so on. Analyzing cause-and-effect relationships as you read can help you understand how events and a character's qualities lead to the conflict's resolution. Sometimes, though, the causes of events aren't clear until the very end of a work.

Into Action As you read each play, fill in a flowchart like the one below for "In the Fog."

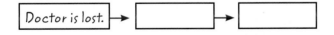

TechFocus These plays were written long before there were cell phones and GPS devices. Think about how the events of these plays might change if they took place today.

Writing Skills Focus
Think as a Reader/Writer

Find It in Your Reading As you read, note instances of foreshadowing that create suspense in the plays.

 Reader/Writer
Notebook
Use your **RWN** to complete the activities for these selections.

Vocabulary

In the Fog

indignant (ihn DIHG nuhnt) *adj.*: offended; angry. *The doctor was indignant that the men came to him.*

arrogant (AIR uh guhnt) *adj.*: unpleasantly proud. *The arrogant men are not afraid of the police.*

The Hitchhiker

coincidence (koh IHN suh duhns) *n.*: accidental happening of events that seem to be connected. *Is it a coincidence that Adams sees the man again?*

sinister (SIHN uh stuhr) *adj.*: creepy; threatening. *Why did the hitchhiker seem sinister?*

Language Coach

Compound Words Words formed from two separate words are called **compound words.** The word *hitchhiker* is an example of a compound word. It is formed from the words *hitch*—"to catch"—and *hiker*—"a walker." The word refers to someone who is traveling on foot but "catches" rides on vehicles. What other compound words can you think of?

Learn It Online
There's more to words than just definitions. Get the whole story on:

go.hrw.com | H6-283 | **Go**

Milton Geiger
(1907–1971)

Scripting for Stage and Screen

Milton Geiger made his living as a scriptwriter for radio, television, and theater. Trained as a pharmacist, he used his knowledge of medicine when writing his first successful script, which was about a small-town pharmacist. In fact, many of his scripts involve similar kinds of small-town characters: middle-aged medical professionals with quiet, wise personalities. Geiger wrote scripts for several popular television series, including *Perry Mason, Dragnet,* and *Night Gallery.*

Lucille Fletcher
(1912–2000)

Creating Suspense

Lucille Fletcher once shared her secret to writing convincing suspense stories: "You bury the secret, lead the reader down the path, put in false leads, and throughout the story remain completely logical." *The Hitchhiker* contains all of these elements, as well as a kernel of truth. The idea for the play originated during a drive to California. As Fletcher, a Brooklyn native, was leaving New York, she saw a strange man on the Brooklyn Bridge. The same stranger later appeared on the Pulaski Skyway in New Jersey. It's no accident, then, that the gray man who haunts Ronald Adams in *The Hitchhiker* appears on both of these bridges.

Think About the Writers

How do both authors draw on their experiences in their writing?

Build Background

In the 1930s and 1940s, Americans gathered around the radio the way we now gather around the television. Like television shows, radio shows came in many varieties: adventure series, detective stories, Westerns, comedies, and even soap operas (in fact, soap operas began on the radio). However, radio was different from television in important ways. Without pictures that showed what was happening, dialogue and sound effects had to tell the story and create mood. The rest was left to the listener's imagination.

The Hitchhiker is a popular and suspenseful radio play from the golden age of radio. As you read *The Hitchhiker,* use your imagination to "watch" the hair-raising events unfold.

Preview the Selections

In *In the Fog,* a **doctor** is lost on a Pennsylvania highway. When he stops to check a road sign, two strange men named **Eben** and **Zeke** arrive and ask for his help.

In *The Hitchhiker,* you will meet **Ronald Adams,** a man driving alone from New York to California, and the mysterious stranger he encounters: **the hitchhiker.**

IN THE FOG

by **Milton Geiger**

Read with a Purpose
Read to learn what happens when a doctor meets two strange men on a lonely highway.

CHARACTERS

| A Doctor | A Wounded Man | Eben |
| Zeke | A Gas Station Attendant | |

Sets: *A signpost on Pennsylvania Route 30. A rock or stump in the fog. A gas station pump.*

Night. At first we can only see fog drifting across a dark scene devoid of[1] detail. Then, out of the fog, there emerges toward us a white roadside signpost with a number

of white painted signboards pointing to right and to left. The marker is a Pennsylvania State Route—marked characteristically "PENNA-30." Now a light as from a far headlight sweeps the signs.

An automobile approaches. The car pulls up close. We hear the car door open and slam and a man's footsteps approaching on

---

1. **devoid** (dih VOYD) **of:** without.

the concrete. Now the signs are lit up again by a more localized, smaller source of light. The light grows stronger as the man, offstage, approaches. The DOCTOR enters, holding a flashlight before him. He scrutinizes[2] the road marker. He flashes his light up at the arrows. We see the legends on the markers. Pointing off right there are markers that read: York, Columbia, Lancaster; pointing left the signs read: Fayetteville, McConnellsburg, Pennsylvania Turnpike.

The DOCTOR's face is perplexed and annoyed as he turns his flashlight on a folded road map. He is a bit lost in the fog. Then his flashlight fails him. It goes out! **Ⓐ**

Doctor. Darn! (*He fumbles with the flashlight in the gloom. Then a voice is raised to him from offstage.*)
Eben (*offstage, strangely*). Turn around, mister. . . .

[*The DOCTOR turns sharply to stare offstage.*]

Zeke (*offstage*). You don't have to be afraid, mister. . . .

[*The DOCTOR sees two men slowly approaching out of the fog. One carries a*

---

2. **scrutinizes** (SKROO tuh nyz ihz): examines carefully.

---

lantern below his knees. The other holds a heavy rifle. Their features are utterly indistinct as they approach, and the rifleman holds up his gun with quiet threat.] **Ⓑ**

Eben. You don't have to be afraid.
Doctor (*more indignant than afraid*). So you say! Who are you, man?
Eben. We don't aim to hurt you none.
Doctor. That's reassuring. I'd like to know just what you mean by this? This gun business! Who *are* you?
Zeke (*mildly*). What's your trade, mister?
Doctor. I . . . I'm a doctor. Why?
Zeke (*to* EBEN). Doctor.
Eben (*nods; then to* DOCTOR). Yer the man we want.
Zeke. Ye'll do proper, we're thinkin'.
Eben. So ye'd better come along, mister.
Zeke. Aye.
Doctor. Why? Has—anyone been hurt?
Eben. It's for you to say if he's been hurt nigh to the finish.
Zeke. So we're askin' ye to come along, doctor. **Ⓒ**

[*The DOCTOR looks from one to another in indecision and puzzlement.*]
Eben. In the name o' mercy.
Zeke. Aye.
Doctor. I want you to understand—I'm not afraid of your gun! I'll go to your man

---

Ⓐ Literary Focus Plot Consider the stage directions you just read. Which details form pictures in your mind? How do these details create a sense of mystery and suspense?

Ⓑ Literary Focus Plot How does the fact that the men are not clearly visible add to the suspense?

Ⓒ Literary Focus Plot What details in this scene might foreshadow danger ahead?

Vocabulary **indignant** (ihn DIHG nuhnt) *adj.*: offended; angry.

all right. Naturally, I'm a doctor. But I demand to know who you are.  **D**
Zeke (*patiently*). Why not? Raise yer lantern, Eben. . . .
Eben (*tiredly*). Aye.

[EBEN *lifts his lantern. Its light falls on their faces now, and we see that they are terrifying. Matted beards, clotted with blood; crude head bandages, crusty with dirt and dry blood. Their hair, stringy and disheveled. Their faces are lean and hollow cheeked; their eyes sunken and tragic. The* DOCTOR *is shocked for a moment—then bursts out—*]

Doctor. Good heavens!—
Zeke. That's Eben; I'm Zeke.
Doctor. What's happened? Has there been an accident or . . . what? **E**
Zeke. Mischief's happened, stranger.
Eben. Mischief enough.
Doctor (*looks at rifle at his chest*). There's been gunplay—hasn't there?
Zeke (*mildly ironic*). Yer tellin' us there's been gunplay!
Doctor. And I'm telling you that I'm not at all frightened! It's my duty to report this, and report it I will!
Zeke. Aye, mister. You do that.
Doctor. You're arrogant about it now! You don't think you'll be caught and dealt

---

D **Literary Focus** Character What has the author conveyed about the doctor's qualities?

E **Read and Discuss** What do you think happened to Zeke and Eben? What makes you think so?

Vocabulary **arrogant** (AIR uh guhnt) *adj.:* unpleasantly proud.

with. But people are losing patience with you men. . . . You . . . you moonshiners![3] Running wild . . . a law unto yourselves . . . shooting up the countryside!

Zeke. Hear that, Eben? Moonshiners.

Eben. Mischief's happened, mister, we'll warrant[4] that. . . .

Doctor. And I don't like it!

Zeke. Can't say we like it better'n you do, mister. . . .

Eben (*strangely sad and remote*). What must be, must.

Zeke. There's no changin' or goin' back, and all 'at's left is the wishin' things were different. **F**

Eben. Aye.

Doctor. And while we talk, your wounded man lies bleeding, I suppose—worthless though he may be. Well? I'll have to get my instrument bag, you know. It's in the car.

[EBEN *and* ZEKE *part to let* DOCTOR *pass between them. The* DOCTOR *reenters, carrying his medical bag.*]

Doctor. I'm ready. Lead the way.

[EBEN *lifts his lantern a bit and goes first.* ZEKE *prods the* DOCTOR *ever so gently and apologetically but firmly with the rifle muzzle. The* DOCTOR *leaves.* ZEKE *strides off slowly after them.* **G**

A wounded man is lying against a section of stone fence. He, too, is bearded, though very young, and his shirt is dark with blood. He breathes but never stirs otherwise. EBEN *enters, followed by the* DOCTOR *and* ZEKE.] **H**

Zeke. Ain't stirred a mite since we left 'im.

Doctor. Let's have that lantern here!

(*The* DOCTOR *tears the man's shirt for better access to the wound. Softly*) Dreadful! Dreadful . . . !

Zeke's voice (*off scene*). Reckon it's bad in the chest like that, hey?

Doctor (*taking pulse*). His pulse is positively racing . . . ! How long has he been this way?

Zeke. A long time, mister. A long time. . . .

Doctor (*to* EBEN). You! Hand me my bag.

[EBEN *puts down lantern and hands bag to the* DOCTOR. *The* DOCTOR *opens bag and takes out a couple of retractors.*[5] ZEKE *holds lantern close now.*]

Doctor. Lend me a hand with these retractors. (*He works on the man.*) All right . . . when I tell you to draw back on the retractors—draw back.

Eben. Aye.

---

3. **moonshiners:** people who distill liquor illegally.
4. **warrant** (WAWR uhnt): declare positively.

5. **retractors** (rih TRAK tuhrz): surgical instruments for holding back the flesh at the edge of a wound.

F Literary Focus **Plot** Mystery helps create suspense. What mysterious, unexplained things do Zeke and Eben say?

G Reading Focus **Analyzing Cause and Effect** Why is the doctor going to help the wounded man?

H Read and Discuss Who do you think the injured person is? What do you think will happen to the doctor?

Zeke. How is 'e, mister?

Doctor (*preoccupied*). More retraction. Pull them a bit more. Hold it. . . .

Eben. Bad, ain't he?

Doctor. Bad enough. The bullet didn't touch any lung tissue far as I can see right now. There's some pneumothorax[6] though. All I can do now is plug the wound. There's some cotton and gauze wadding in my bag. Find it. . . .

[ZEKE *probes about silently in the bag and comes up with a small dark box of gauze.*]

Doctor. That's it. (*Works a moment in silence*) I've never seen anything quite like it.

Eben. Yer young, doctor. Lots o' things you've never seen.

Doctor. Adhesive tape!

[ZEKE *finds a roll of three-inch tape and hands it to the* DOCTOR, *who tears off long strips and slaps them on the dressing and pats and smooths them to the man's chest.*

EBEN *replaces equipment in* DOCTOR'*s bag and closes it with a hint of the finality*

to come. *A preview of dismissal, so to speak.*]

Doctor (*at length*). There. So much for that. Now then— (*takes man's shoulders*) give me a hand here.

Zeke (*quiet suspicion*). What fer?

Doctor. We've got to move this man.

Zeke. What fer?

Doctor (*stands; indignantly*). We've got to get him to a hospital for treatment; a thorough cleansing of the wound; irrigation.[7] I've done all I can for him here.

Zeke. I reckon he'll be all right 'thout no hospital.

Doctor. Do you realize how badly this man's hurt!

Eben. He won't bleed to death, will he?

Doctor. I don't think so—not with that plug and pressure dressing. But bleeding isn't the only danger we've got to—

Zeke (*interrupts*). All right, then. Much obliged to you. ❶

Doctor. This man's dangerously hurt!

Zeke. Reckon he'll pull through now, thanks to you.

Doctor. I'm glad you feel that way about it! But I'm going to report this to the ❿

> # WE NEVER MEANT A MITE O' HARM, I CAN TELL YE. IF WE KILLED, IT WAS NO WISH OF OURS.

---

6. **pneumothorax** (noo moh THAWR aks): air or gas in the chest cavity.

7. **irrigation:** here, flushing out a wound with water or other fluid.

❶ **Reading Focus** Analyzing Cause and Effect Why do you think Zeke and Eben do not want to take the man to the hospital?

❿ **Literary Focus** Character What qualities, or traits, does the doctor reveal in these lines of dialogue?

Pennsylvania State Police at the first telephone I reach!

Zeke. We ain't stoppin' ye, mister.

Eben. Fog is liftin', Zeke. Better be done with this, I say.

Zeke (*nods, sadly*). Aye. Ye can go now, mister . . . and thanks. (*Continues*) We never meant a mite o' harm, I can tell ye. If we killed, it was no wish of ours.

Eben. What's done is done. Aye.

Zeke. Ye can go now, stranger. . . . **Ⓚ**

[EBEN *hands* ZEKE *the* DOCTOR's *bag.* ZEKE *hands it gently to the* DOCTOR.]

Doctor. Very well. You haven't heard the last of this, though!

Zeke. That's the truth, mister. We've killed, aye; and we've been hurt for it. . . .

Eben. Hurt bad.

[*The* DOCTOR's *face is puckered with doubt and strange apprehension.*[8]]

> THAT'S THE TRUTH, MISTER. WE'VE KILLED, AYE; AND WE'VE BEEN HURT FOR IT.

Zeke. We're not alone, mister. We ain't the only ones. (*Sighs*) Ye can go now, doctor . . . and our thanks to ye. . . .

[*The* DOCTOR *leaves the other two, still gazing at them in strange enchantment and wonder and a touch of indignation.*] **Ⓛ**

Eben's voice. Thanks, mister. . . .

Zeke's voice. In the name o' mercy. . . . We thank you. . . .

Eben. In the name o' mercy.

Zeke. Thanks, mister. . . .

Eben. In the name o' kindness. . . .

[*The two men stand with their wounded comrade at their feet—like a group statue in the park. The fog thickens across the scene. Far off the long, sad wail of a locomotive whimpers in the dark.*] **Ⓜ**

The scene now shifts to a young ATTENDANT *standing in front of a gasoline pump taking a reading and recording it in a book as he prepares to close up. He turns as he hears the car approach on the gravel drive. The* DOCTOR *enters.*] **Ⓝ**

---

8. **apprehension** (ap rih HEHN shuhn): uneasiness; fearfulness.

Ⓚ Literary Focus **Plot** Has the doctor's conflict been resolved? Do Zeke and Eben feel that their problem has been resolved?

Ⓛ Read and Discuss Has the doctor's attitude toward Zeke and Eben changed? Do you think he has more sympathy for them than he did at first? Explain.

Ⓜ Literary Focus **Plot** How does this stage direction help you picture Zeke and Eben? How does it help create a mood of suspense?

Ⓝ Read and Discuss The doctor says he is going to report Zeke and Eben to the police. Do you think he will now? Why do you think Zeke and Eben seemed unconcerned about being reported?

Attendant (*pleasantly*). Good evening, sir. (*Nods off at car*) Care to pull 'er up to this pump, sir? Closing up.

Doctor (*impatiently*). No. Where's your telephone, please? I've just been held up!

Attendant. Pay station[9] inside, sir. . . .

Doctor. Thank you! (*The* DOCTOR *starts to go past the* ATTENDANT.)

9. **pay station:** pay telephone.

Attendant. Excuse me, sir. . . .

Doctor (*stops*). Eh, what is it, what is it?

Attendant. Uh . . . what sort of looking fellows were they?

Doctor. Oh—two big fellows with a rifle; faces and heads bandaged and smeared with dirt and blood. Friend of theirs with a gaping hole in his chest. I'm a doctor, so they forced me to attend him. Why?

Analyzing Visuals

Connecting to the Text
Which of the doctor's emotions does this picture convey?

Attendant. *Those* fellers, huh?

Doctor. Then you know about them!

Attendant. I guess so.

Doctor. They're armed and they're desperate!

Attendant. That was about two or three miles back, would you say?

Doctor (*fumbling in pocket*). Just about—I don't seem to have the change. I wonder if you'd spare me change for a quarter . . . ?

Attendant (*makes change from metal coin canister at his belt*). Certainly, sir. . . .

Doctor. What town was that back there, now?

Attendant (*dumps coins in other's hand*). There you are, sir.

Doctor (*impatient*). Yes, thank you. I say—what town was that back there, so I can tell the police?

Attendant. That was . . . Gettysburg, mister. . . .

Doctor. Gettysburg . . . ?

Attendant. Gettysburg and Gettysburg battlefield. . . . (*Looks off*) When it's light

---

O **Literary Focus** **Plot** How does the attendant react to the doctor's story? How does this reaction help sustain suspense?

and the fog's gone, you can see the gravestones. Meade's men . . . Pickett's men, Robert E. Lee's. . . .[10] **P**

[*The* DOCTOR *is looking off with the* ATTEN-DANT; *now he turns his head slowly to stare at the other man.*]

Attendant (*continues*). On nights like this—well—you're not the first those men've stopped . . . or the last. (*Nods off*) Fill 'er up, mister? **Q**

Doctor. Yes, fill 'er up. . . .

10. **Meade's men . . . Lee's:** The Battle of Gettysburg was a turning point in the American Civil War. On July 1–3, 1863, the Confederate forces, under Robert E. Lee, met the Union forces, under George Gordon Meade. The climax of the battle came when 15,000 Confederate soldiers, led by George Pickett, charged Cemetery Ridge and were repelled. The North suffered about 23,000 casualties; the South, about 20,000.

P **Read and Discuss** How does the information about Gettysburg connect with what the doctor has experienced?

Q **Literary Focus** **Plot** What important information does the attendant give the doctor?

Applying Your Skills

Reading Standard 3.2 Analyze the effect of the qualities of the character (e.g., courage or cowardice, ambition or laziness) on the plot and the resolution of the conflict.

In the Fog
Literary Response and Analysis

Reading Skills Focus
Quick Check

1. What does the doctor learn at the gas station about the area in which he is traveling?

Read with a Purpose

2. What can you can guess about the identity of the two strange men the doctor meets?

Reading Skills: Analyzing Cause and Effect

3. Review the flowchart you created as you read. Does what you learn in the play's resolution change any information in your chart? Make any necessary revisions. Then, add a box labeled "Effect on Me" to the end of your chart. Record your reactions to the story's ending.

Effect on Me:

✓ Vocabulary Check

Tell whether each statement is true or false.

4. An **indignant** person feels insulted and angry.
5. **Arrogant** people never brag about their skills.

Literary Skills Focus
Literary Analysis

6. **Interpret** What does Zeke mean when he says, "If we killed, it was no wish of ours"?

7. **Interpret** When the fog lifts, Eben and Zeke tell the doctor he can go. Find other references to the fog in the play. What do you think is the importance of the fog? Use details from the play to support your interpretation.

Literary Skills: Plot and Character

8. **Analyze** Think about the doctor's words and actions and the other characters' responses to him. What are the doctor's main qualities? How do his character traits affect the **plot** and the conflict's **resolution**? What might have happened, for example, if he had refused to go with the men?

9. **Analyze** How does the author create **suspense** in the play? Illustrate your response with examples. Explain which elements of suspense you think are the most effective in the play.

Writing Skills Focus
Think as a Reader/Writer

Use It in Your Writing Think of a situation in which a main character encounters a stranger. Then, turn this situation into a scene for a play. Use **foreshadowing** in your scene to create suspense.

THE HITCHHIKER

by **Lucille Fletcher**

> **Read with a Purpose**   Read this radio play to discover why a hitchhiker becomes such a frightening figure to Ronald Adams as he drives alone across the country.
> **Preparing to Read** for this selection is on page 283.

CHARACTERS

Ronald Adams	Henry	A Long-Distance Operator
His Mother	Henry's Wife	An Albuquerque Operator
The Gray Man	A Girl	A New York Operator
A Mechanic	A Telephone Operator	Mrs. Whitney

The time of the play is the early 1940s.

[Sound: *Automobile wheels humming over concrete road.* Music: *Something weird and shuddery.*]

Adams. I am in an auto camp[1] on Route Sixty-six just west of Gallup, New Mexico. If I tell it, perhaps it will help me. It will keep me from going mad. But I must tell this quickly. I am not mad now. I feel perfectly well, except that I am running a slight temperature. My name is Ronald Adams. I am thirty-six years of age, unmarried, tall, dark, with a black moustache. I drive a 1940 Ford V-8, license number 6V-7989. I was born in Brooklyn. All this I know. I know that I am at this moment perfectly sane. That it is not I who have gone mad—but something else—

---

1. **auto camp:** campground with places for drivers to park their cars.

something utterly beyond my control. But I must speak quickly. At any moment the link with life may break. This may be the last thing I ever tell on earth . . . the last night I ever see the stars. . . . **Ⓐ**

[Music: *In.*]

Adams. Six days ago I left Brooklyn, to drive to California. . . .

Mother. Goodbye, Son. Good luck to you, my boy. . . .

Adams. Goodbye, Mother. Here—give me a kiss, and then I'll go. . . .

Mother. I'll come out with you to the car.

Adams. No. It's raining. Stay here at the door. Hey—what is this? Tears? I thought you promised me you wouldn't cry.

Mother. I know, dear. I'm sorry. But I—do hate to see you go.

Adams. I'll be back. I'll only be on the Coast three months. **Ⓑ**

Mother. Oh, it isn't that. It's just—the trip. Ronald—I wish you weren't driving.

Adams. Oh—Mother. There you go again. People do it every day.

Mother. I know. But you'll be careful, won't you? Promise me you'll be extra careful. Don't fall asleep—or drive fast—or pick up any strangers on the road. . . .

Adams. Lord, no. You'd think I was still seventeen to hear you talk—

Mother. And wire me as soon as you get to Hollywood, won't you, Son?

Adams. Of course I will. Now don't you worry. There isn't anything going to happen. It's just eight days of perfectly simple driving on smooth, decent, civilized roads, with a hot dog or a hamburger stand every ten miles. . . . (*Fade*) **Ⓒ**

[Sound: *Auto hum.* Music: *In.*]

Adams. I was in excellent spirits. The drive ahead of me, even the loneliness, seemed like a lark.[2] But I reckoned without *him*. **Ⓓ**

[Music: *Changes to something weird and empty.*]

Adams. Crossing Brooklyn Bridge that morning in the rain, I saw a man leaning against the cables. He seemed to be waiting for a lift. There were spots of fresh rain on his shoulders. He was carrying a cheap overnight bag in one hand. He was thin, nondescript,[3] with a cap pulled down over his eyes. He stepped off the walk and if I hadn't swerved, I'd have hit him.

---

2. **lark:** good time; spree.
3. **nondescript** (NAHN duh skrihpt): without distinguishing characteristics; not memorable.

Ⓐ **Read and Discuss** What have you learned about Ronald Adams so far?

Ⓑ **Read and Discuss** When does this scene take place? How do you know?

Ⓒ **Literary Focus** Plot What details so far might foreshadow danger?

Ⓓ **Read and Discuss** Adams mentions "him," and the author puts the word in italics. What does that let you know about the character you haven't even met?

Analyzing Visuals **Connecting to the Text** How does this image reflect a plot event in the play and the play's eerie mood?

Tunnel on Pennsylvania Turnpike.

[Sound: *Terrific skidding.* Music: *In.*]

Adams. I would have forgotten him completely, except that just an hour later, while crossing the Pulaski Skyway[4] over the Jersey flats, I saw him again. At least, he looked like the same person. He was standing now, with one thumb pointing west. I couldn't figure out how he'd got there, but I thought probably one of those fast trucks had picked him up, beaten me to the Skyway, and let him

---

4. **Pulaski Skyway:** long-span bridge connecting the cities of Newark and Jersey City, New Jersey.

off. I didn't stop for him. Then—late that night, I saw him again.

[Music: *Changing.*]

Adams. It was on the new Pennsylvania Turnpike between Harrisburg and Pittsburgh. It's two hundred and sixty-five miles long, with a very high speed limit. I was just slowing down for one of the tunnels—when I saw him—standing under an arc light by the side of the road. I could see him quite distinctly. The bag, the cap, even the spots of fresh rain spattered over his shoulders. He hailed me this time. . . .

The Hitchhiker **297**

Voice (*very spooky and faint*). Hall-ooo. . . . (*Echo as through tunnel*) Hall-ooo . . . !

Adams. I stepped on the gas like a shot. That's lonely country through the Alleghenies,[5] and I had no intention of stopping. Besides, the coincidence, or whatever it was, gave me the willies.[6] I stopped at the next gas station. **Ⓔ**

[Sound: *Auto tires screeching to stop . . . horn honk.*]

Mechanic. Yes, sir.
Adams. Fill her up.
Mechanic. Certainly, sir. Check your oil, sir?
Adams. No, thanks.

...whatever it was, gave me the willies.

[Sound: *Gas being put into car . . . bell tinkle, etc.*]

Mechanic. Nice night, isn't it?
Adams. Yes. It—hasn't been raining here recently, has it?
Mechanic. Not a drop of rain all week.
Adams. Hm. I suppose that hasn't done your business any harm.

---

5. **Alleghenies** (al uh GAY neez): the Allegheny mountain range, a part of the Appalachian Mountains that runs through Pennsylvania, Maryland, West Virginia, and Virginia.

6. **willies:** feeling of nervousness; jitters.

Mechanic. Oh—people drive through here all kinds of weather. Mostly business, you know. There aren't many pleasure cars out on the Turnpike this season of the year.
Adams. I suppose not. (*Casually*) What about hitchhikers?
Mechanic (*half laughing*). Hitchhikers *here*?
Adams. What's the matter? Don't you ever see any?
Mechanic. Not much. If we did, it'd be a sight for sore eyes.
Adams. Why?
Mechanic. A guy'd be a fool who started out to hitch rides on this road. Look at it. It's two hundred and sixty-five miles long, there's practically no speed limit, and it's a straightaway. Now what car is going to stop to pick up a guy under those conditions? Would you stop?
Adams. No. (*Slowly, with puzzled emphasis*) Then you've never seen anybody?
Mechanic. Nope. Mebbe they get the lift before the Turnpike starts—I mean, you know just before the tollhouse—but then it'd be a mighty long ride. Most cars wouldn't want to pick up a guy for that long a ride. And you know—this is pretty lonesome country here—mountains, and woods. . . . You ain't seen anybody like that, have you? **Ⓕ**

Ⓔ **Reading Focus** **Analyzing Cause and Effect** What causes Adams to step on the gas and speed up?

Ⓕ **Literary Focus** **Plot** What does the mechanic tell Adams that adds to the mystery of the hitchhiker?

Vocabulary **coincidence** (koh IHN suh duhns) *n.*: accidental happening of events that seem to be connected.

Adams. No. (*Quickly*) Oh no, not at all. It was—just a—technical question.
Mechanic. I see. Well—that'll be just a dollar forty-nine—with the tax. . . . (*Fade*) **G**

[Sound: *Auto hum up.* Music: *Changing.*]

Adams. The thing gradually passed from my mind, as sheer coincidence. I had a good night's sleep in Pittsburgh. I did not think about the man all next day—until just outside Zanesville, Ohio, I saw him again.

[Music: *Dark, ominous note.*]

Adams. It was a bright sunshiny afternoon. The peaceful Ohio fields, brown with the autumn stubble, lay dreaming in the golden light. I was driving slowly, drinking it in, when the road suddenly ended in a detour. In front of the barrier, *he* was standing.

[Music: *In.*]

Adams. Let me explain about his appearance before I go on. I repeat. There was nothing sinister about him. He was as drab as a mud fence. Nor was his attitude menacing. He merely stood there, waiting, almost drooping a little, the cheap

---

G **Read and Discuss** What mood has been created by the conversation between Adams and the mechanic?

Vocabulary **sinister** (SIHN uh stuhr) *adj.*: creepy; threatening.

Urban legends united: Bigfoot meets an alien from a visiting UFO.

Urban Legends— Today's Scary Stories

The ancient Greeks were fascinated by tales about heroes and the frightening creatures they fought; people in medieval times looked out for dragons and vampires. These myths and legends, along with folk and fairy tales, are part of narrative folklore. Some of the tales reflect history; others teach moral lessons. Many exist simply to entertain—often by scaring us silly.

"Urban legends" are modern folk tales. Some of them, such as stories about alligators in sewers, seem almost believable. Some may be based on a small grain of truth. These word-of-mouth stories about everything from Bigfoot and crop circles to hauntings and hoaxes fly around today's world at the speed of the Internet.

Ask Yourself

How does this story about a mysterious hitchhiker resemble an urban legend?

overnight bag in his hand. He looked as though he had been waiting there for hours. Then he looked up. He hailed me. He started to walk forward.

Voice (*far-off*). Hall-ooo . . . Hall-ooo. . . .

Adams. I had stopped the car, of course, for the detour. And for a few moments, I couldn't seem to find the new road. I knew he must be thinking that I had stopped for him.

Voice (*closer*). Hall-ooo . . . Hallll . . . ooo. . . .

[Sound: *Gears jamming . . . sound of motor turning over hard . . . nervous accelerator.*]

Voice (*closer*). Halll . . . oooo. . . .

Adams (*panicky*). No. Not just now. Sorry. . . .

Voice (*closer*). Going to California?

[Sound: *Starter starting . . . gears jamming.*]

Adams (*as though sweating blood*). No. Not today. The other way. Going to New York. Sorry . . . sorry. . . .

[Sound: *Car starts with squeal of wheels on dirt . . . into auto hum.* Music: *In.*]

Adams. After I got the car back onto the road again, I felt like a fool. Yet the thought of picking him up, of having him sit beside me, was somehow unbearable. Yet, at the same time, I felt, more than ever, unspeakably alone. **H**

[Sound: *Auto hum up.*]

Adams. Hour after hour went by. The fields, the towns ticked off, one by one. The lights changed. I knew now that I was going to see him again. And though I dreaded the sight, I caught myself searching the side of the road, waiting for him to appear.

[Sound: *Auto hum up . . . car screeches to a halt . . . impatient honk two or three times . . . door being unbolted.*]

Sleepy Man's Voice. Yep? What is it? What do you want?

Adams (*breathless*). You sell sandwiches and pop here, don't you?

Voice (*cranky*). Yep. We do. In the daytime. But we're closed up now for the night.

Adams. I know. But—I was wondering if you could possibly let me have a cup of coffee—black coffee.

Voice. Not at this time of night, mister. My wife's the cook and she's in bed. Mebbe further down the road—at the Honeysuckle Rest. . . .

[Sound: *Door squeaking on hinges as though being closed.*]

Adams. No—no. Don't shut the door. (*Shakily*) Listen—just a minute ago, there was a man standing here—right beside this stand—a suspicious-looking man. . . . **I**

H **Literary Focus** **Character** In his description of his encounter with the hitchhiker, what does Adams reveal about himself?

I **Reading Focus** **Analyzing Cause and Effect** What do these lines suggest is Adams's real reason for stopping at the stand?

Woman's Voice (*from distance*). Hen-ry? Who is it, Hen-ry?

Henry. It's nobuddy, Mother. Just a feller thinks he wants a cup of coffee. Go back to bed.

Adams. I don't mean to disturb you. But you see, I was driving along—when I just happened to look—and there he was. . . .

Henry. What was he doing?

Adams. Nothing. He ran off—when I stopped the car.

Henry. Then what of it? That's nothing to wake a man in the middle of his sleep about. (*Sternly*) Young man, I've got a good mind to turn you over to the sheriff.

Adams. But—I—

Henry. You've been taking a nip, that's what you've been doing. And you haven't got anything better to do than to wake decent folk out of their hard-earned sleep. Get going. Go on.

Adams. But—he looked as though he were going to rob you.

Henry. I ain't got nothin' in this stand to lose. Now—on your way before I call out Sheriff Oakes. (*Fade*)

[Sound: *Auto hum up.*]

Adams. I got into the car again, and drove on slowly. I was beginning to hate the car. If I could have found a place to stop . . . to rest a little. But I was in the Ozark Mountains of Missouri now. The few resort places there were closed. Only an occasional log cabin, seemingly deserted, broke the monotony[7] of the wild wooded landscape. I *had* seen him at that roadside stand: I knew I would see him again— perhaps at the next turn of the road. I knew that when I saw him next, I would run him down. . . . **J**

[Sound: *Auto hum up.*]

Adams. But I did not see him again until late next afternoon. . . .
[Sound: *Of railroad warning signal at crossroads.*]

Adams. I had stopped the car at a sleepy little junction[8] just across the border into Oklahoma—to let a train pass by—when he appeared, across the tracks, leaning against a telephone pole.

[Sound: *Distant sound of train chugging . . . bell ringing steadily.*]

Adams (*very tense*). It was a perfectly airless, dry day. The red clay of Oklahoma was baking under the southwestern sun. Yet there were spots of fresh rain on his shoulders. I couldn't stand that. Without thinking, blindly, I started the car across the tracks.

[Sound: *Train chugging closer.*]

Adams. He didn't even look up at me. He was staring at the ground. I stepped on the gas hard, veering the wheel sharply toward him. I could hear the train in the distance now, but didn't care. Then something went wrong with the car. It stalled right on the tracks.

[Sound: *Train chugging closer. Above this, sound of car stalling.*]

Adams. The train was coming closer. I

---

7. **monotony** (muh NAHT uh ee): tiresome sameness.

8. **junction** (JUHNGK shuhn): point where two sets of railroad tracks join.

J Literary Focus **Character** What do Adams's thoughts and actions reveal about his character?

could hear its bell ringing, and the cry of its whistle. Still he stood there. And now—I knew that he was beckoning—beckoning me to my death.

[Sound: *Train chugging close. Whistle blows wildly. Then train rushes up and by with pistons going, etc.*]

Adams. Well—I frustrated him that time. The starter had worked at last. I managed to back up. But when the train passed, he was gone. I was all alone in the hot, dry afternoon. **Ⓚ**

[Sound: *Train retreating. Crickets begin to sing. Music: In.*]

Adams. After that, I knew I had to do something. I didn't know who this man was or what he wanted of me. I only knew that from now on, I must not let myself be alone on the road for one moment.

[Sound: *Auto hum up. Slow down. Stop. Door opening.*]
Adams. Hello, there. Like a ride?
Girl. What do you think? How far you going?
Adams. Amarillo . . . I'll take you to Amarillo.

Girl. Amarillo, Texas?
Adams. I'll drive you there.
Girl. Gee!

[Sound: *Door closed—car starts. Music: In.*]

Girl. Mind if I take off my shoes? My dogs[9] are killing me.
Adams. Go right ahead.
Girl. Gee, what a break this is. A swell car, a decent guy, and driving all the way to Amarillo. All I been getting so far is trucks.
Adams. Hitchhike much?
Girl. Sure. Only it's tough sometimes, in these great open spaces, to get the breaks.
Adams. I should think it would be. Though I'll bet if you get a good pickup in a fast car, you can get to places faster than—say, another person, in another car.
Girl. I don't get you.
Adams. Well, take me, for instance. Suppose I'm driving across the country, say, at a nice steady clip of about forty-five miles an hour. Couldn't a girl like you, just standing beside the road, waiting for lifts, beat me to town after town—provided she got picked up every time in a car doing

---
9. **dogs:** slang word for feet.

> Still he stood there. And now—I knew that he was beckoning—beckoning me to my death.

Ⓚ Literary Focus **Plot** What do you think will happen to Adams? What clues foreshadow his future?

from sixty-five to seventy miles an hour?

Girl. I dunno. Maybe she could and maybe she couldn't. What difference does it make?

Adams. Oh—no difference. It's just a—crazy idea I had sitting here in the car.

Girl (*laughing*). Imagine spending your time in a swell car thinking of things like that!

Adams. What would you do instead?

Girl (*admiringly*). What would I do? If I was a good-looking fellow like yourself? Why—I'd just *enjoy* myself—every minute of the time. I'd sit back, and relax, and if I saw a good-looking girl along the side of the road . . . (*Sharply*) Hey! Look out!

Adams (*breathlessly*). Did you see him too?

Girl. See who?

Adams. That man. Standing beside the barbed-wire fence.

Girl. I didn't see—anybody. There wasn't nothing but a bunch of steers—and the barbed-wire fence. What did you think you was doing? Trying to run into the barbed-wire fence?

Adams. There was a man there, I tell you . . . a thin, gray man, with an overnight bag in his hand. And I was trying to—run him down.

Girl. Run him down? You mean—kill him?

Adams. He's a sort of—phantom. I'm trying to get rid of him—or else prove that he's real. But (*desperately*) you say you didn't see him back there? You're sure?

Girl (*queerly*). I didn't see a soul. And as far as that's concerned, mister . . .

Adams. Watch for him the next time, then. Keep watching. Keep your eyes peeled on the road. He'll turn up again—maybe any minute now. (*Excitedly*) There. Look there—

[Sound: *Auto sharply veering and skidding.* GIRL *screams.* Sound: *Crash of car going into barbed-wire fence. Frightened lowing of steer.*]

> He's a sort of—phantom. I'm trying to get rid of him—or else prove that he's real.

Girl. How does this door work? I—I'm gettin' outta here.

Adams. Did you see him that time?

Girl (*sharply*). No. I didn't see him that time. And personally, mister, I don't expect never to see him. All I want to do is to go on living—and I don't see how I will very long driving with you—

Adams. I'm sorry. I—I don't know what came over me. (*Frightened*) Please—don't go. . . .

Girl. So if you'll excuse me, mister—

Adams. You can't go. Listen, how would you like to go to California? I'll drive you to California.

Girl. Seeing pink elephants[10] all the way? No thanks.

Adams (*desperately*). I could get you a job there. You wouldn't have to be a waitress. I have friends there—my name is Ronald Adams—you can check up.

---

10. **pink elephants:** imaginary objects seen by someone who is drunk or delirious.

[Sound: *Door opening.*]

Girl. Uhn-hunh. Thanks just the same.
Adams. Listen. Please. For just one minute. Maybe you think I am half cracked. But this man. You see, I've been seeing this man all the way across the country. He's been following me. And if you could only help me—stay with me—until I reach the Coast—
Girl. You know what I think you need, big boy? Not a girlfriend. Just a good dose of sleep. . . . There, I got it now.

[Sound: *Door opens . . . slams.*]

Adams. No. You can't go.
Girl (*screams*). Leave your hands offa me, do you hear! Leave your—
Adams. Come back here, please, come back.

[Sound: *Struggle . . . slap . . . footsteps running away on gravel . . . lowing of steer.*]

Adams. She ran from me, as though I were a monster. A few minutes later, I saw a passing truck pick her up. I knew then that I was utterly alone. **L**

[Sound: *Lowing of steer up.*]

Adams. I was in the heart of the great Texas prairies. There wasn't a car on the road after the truck went by. I tried to figure out what to do, how to get hold of myself. If I could find a place to rest. Or even, if I could sleep right here in the car for a few hours, along the side of the road. . . . I was getting my winter overcoat out of the back seat to use as a blanket (*Hall-ooo*) when I saw him coming toward me (*Hall-ooo*), emerging from the herd of moving steers. . . .
Voice. Hall-ooo . . . Hall-ooo. . . .

[Sound: *Auto starting violently . . . up to steady hum.* Music: *In.*]

Adams. I didn't wait for him to come any closer. Perhaps I should have spoken to him then, fought it out then and there. For now he began to be everywhere. Whenever I stopped, even for a moment—for gas, or oil, for a drink of pop, a cup of coffee, a sandwich—he was there.

[Music: *Faster.*] **M**

Adams. I saw him standing outside the auto camp in Amarillo that night, when I dared to slow down. He was sitting near the drinking fountain in a little camping spot just inside the border of New Mexico.

[Music: *Faster.*]

Adams. He was waiting for me outside the Navajo reservation, where I stopped to check my tires. I saw him in Albuquerque, where I bought twelve gallons of gas. . . . I was afraid now, afraid to stop. I began

---

L **Reading Focus** Analyzing Cause and Effect Why does Adams's passenger run from him as though he were a monster?

M **Literary Focus** Plot Why is the music getting faster now? What effect would this create?

The Hitchhiker **305**

to drive faster and faster. I was in lunar landscape now—the great arid mesa[11] country of New Mexico. I drove through it with the indifference of a fly crawling over the face of the moon.

[Music: *Faster.*]

Adams. But now he didn't even wait for me to stop. Unless I drove at eighty-five miles an hour over those endless roads—he waited for me at every other mile. I would see his figure, shadowless, flitting before me, still in its same attitude, over the cold and lifeless ground, flitting over dried-up rivers, over broken stones cast up by old glacial upheavals, flitting in the pure and cloudless air. . . . **N**

[Music: *Strikes sinister note of finality.*]

Adams. I was beside myself when I finally reached Gallup, New Mexico, this morning. There is an auto camp here—cold, almost deserted at this time of year. I went inside, and asked if there was a telephone. I had the feeling that if only I could speak to someone familiar, someone that I loved, I could pull myself together. **O**

[Sound: *Nickel put in slot.*]

---

11. **mesa** (MAY suh): elevated flat-topped land formation with steep sides.

Operator. Number, please?
Adams. Long distance.
Operator. Thank you.

[Sound: *Return of nickel; buzz.*]

Long Distance. This is long distance.
Adams. I'd like to put in a call to my home in Brooklyn, New York. I'm Ronald Adams. The number is Beechwood 2-0828.[12]
Long Distance. Thank you. What is your number?
Adams. 312.
Albuquerque Operator. Albuquerque.
Long Distance. New York for Gallup. (*Pause*)
New York Operator. New York.
Long Distance. Gallup, New Mexico, calling Beechwood 2-0828.

(*Fade*)

Adams. I had read somewhere that love could banish demons. It was the middle of the morning. I knew Mother would be home. I pictured her,

---

12. **Beechwood 2-0828:** phone number. At the time of this story, phone numbers in the United States began with two letters (called an exchange), followed by five numbers. Names (called exchange names) like Beechwood were used to tell callers which two letters to dial—usually the first two letters of the name (e.g., *BE* for *Beechwood*).

N **Literary Focus** **Plot** Why do you think the man appears unless Adams drives at 85 miles per hour? What is the author setting up?

O **Read and Discuss** How has the play circled back to the beginning here?

tall, white-haired, in her crisp housedress, going about her tasks. It would be enough, I thought, merely to hear the even calmness of her voice. . . . **℗**

Long Distance. Will you please deposit three dollars and eighty-five cents for the first three minutes? When you have deposited a dollar and a half, will you wait until I have collected the money?

[Sound: *Clunk of six coins.*]

Long Distance. All right, deposit another dollar and a half.

[Sound: *Clunk of four coins.*]

Long Distance. Ready with Brooklyn—go ahead, please.

℗ **Literary Focus** **Character** Why does Adams try to call his mother? What does his desire to speak to her reveal about his reaction to his situation?

Adams. Hello.

Mrs. Whitney. Mrs. Adams's residence.

Adams. Hello. Hello—Mother?

Mrs. Whitney (*very flat and rather proper*). This is Mrs. Adams's residence. Who is it you wished to speak to, please?

Adams. Why—who's this?

Mrs. Whitney. This is Mrs. Whitney.

Adams. Mrs. Whitney? I don't know any Mrs. Whitney. Is this Beechwood 2-0828?

Mrs. Whitney. Yes.

Adams. Where's my mother? Where's Mrs. Adams?

Mrs. Whitney. Mrs. Adams is not at home. She is still in the hospital.

Adams. The hospital!

Mrs. Whitney. Yes. Who is this calling, please? Is it a member of the family?

Adams. What's she in the hospital for?

Mrs. Whitney. She's been prostrated[13] for five days. Nervous breakdown. But who is this calling?

Adams. Nervous breakdown? But—my mother was never nervous.

Mrs. Whitney. It's all taken place since the death of her oldest son, Ronald.

Adams. Death of her oldest son, Ronald . . . ? Hey—what is this? What number is this?

Mrs. Whitney. This is Beechwood 2-0828. It's all been very sudden. He was killed just six days ago in an automobile accident on the Brooklyn Bridge.

---

13. **prostrated** (PRAHS tray tihd): overcome by exhaustion or grief; weak.

Operator (*breaking in*). Your three minutes are up, sir. (*Pause*) Your three minutes are up, sir. (*Pause*) Your three minutes are up, sir. (*Fade*) Sir, your three minutes are up. Your three minutes are up, sir.

Adams (*in a strange voice*). And so, I am sitting here in this deserted auto camp in Gallup, New Mexico. I am trying to think. I am trying to get hold of myself. Otherwise, I shall go mad. . . . Outside it is night—the vast, soulless night of New Mexico. A million stars are in the sky. Ahead of me stretch a thousand miles of empty mesa, mountains, prairies—desert. Somewhere among them, he is waiting for me. Somewhere I shall know who he is, and who . . . I . . . am. . . . **Ⓠ**

[Music: *Up.*]

Ⓠ **Reading Focus** **Analyzing Cause and Effect** What really happened at the beginning of the story on the Brooklyn Bridge? Read that section again, if necessary.

Applying Your Skills

Reading Standard 3.2 Analyze the effect of the qualities of the character (e.g., courage or cowardice, ambition or laziness) on the plot and the resolution of the conflict.

The Hitchhiker
Literary Response and Analysis

Reading Skills Focus
Quick Check

1. When does Adams first see the hitchhiker?
2. How does Adams's <u>attitude</u> toward the hitchhiker change as the play goes on?

Read with a Purpose

3. What does Adams eventually discover about himself on his cross-country drive? What finally triggers his discovery?

Reading Skills: Analyzing Cause and Effect

4. Review the flowchart you created as you read. Does knowing what really happened on the Brooklyn Bridge change your view of the cause-and-effect relationships? Revise your chart as necessary. Then, add a box labeled "Main Cause and Effect" to the end of your chart. Record the cause and effect that you think forms the basis of the plot.

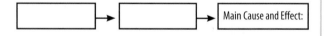

Main Cause and Effect:

Vocabulary Check

Tell whether each statement is true or false.

5. A **coincidence** is always planned in advance.
6. **Sinister** people are friendly and kind.

Literary Skills Focus
Literary Analysis

7. **Infer** Whom or what do you think the hitchhiker represents?
8. **Extend** In a way, this play doesn't end at all—Adams and the reader are kept in suspense. What do you think Adams will do after the end of the play? Use details from the play to support your answer.

Literary Skills: Plot and Character

9. **Analyze** How does the fact that Adams is describing his own experiences in the play help you identify his character traits?
10. **Analyze** How does Adams's behavior affect the **plot**? When he encounters the hitchhiker in Texas, he says, "Perhaps I should have spoken to him then, fought it out then and there." How would the plot be different if Adams had taken action?
11. **Analyze** How does the playwright increase your curiosity about what will happen next throughout the play? Give three examples of **foreshadowing** and other elements of suspense.

Writing Skills Focus
Think as a Reader/Writer

Use It in Your Writing Write a scene for a play in which a conflict causes a character to make a crucial telephone call. Use **foreshadowing** to create suspense in your scene.

Reading Standard 3.2 Analyze the effect of the qualities of the character (e.g., courage or cowardice, ambition or laziness) on the plot and the resolution of the conflict.

In the Fog / The Hitchhiker

Writing Skills Focus
Write a Comparison-Contrast Essay

In an essay, compare and contrast the characters and plots in the two plays. Be sure to analyze the effects of the doctor's and Adams's qualities, or character traits, on the plots and the playwrights' use of suspense. There are two ways you can organize your essay:

- Use the **block method** to organize your essay, and discuss one play at a time. Write all about one play in one paragraph and all about the other play in another paragraph. For each play, explain the qualities of the main character and their effect on the plot and conflict. Then, explain how the playwright creates suspense.

- Use the **point-by-point method** to organize your essay. In one paragraph, compare and contrast the qualities of the doctor and Adams and their effects on the plot and conflict. In another paragraph, compare and contrast the playwrights' use of suspense in the two plays.

At the end of the essay, explain which play you prefer. Which play was more suspenseful?

Use the workshop on writing a Comparison-Contrast Essay, pages 450–458, for help with this assignment.

What Do You Think Now? How have these plays affected your view of the ways in which people react to an unknown threat?

CHOICES

As you respond to the Choices, use these **Academic Vocabulary** words as appropriate: <u>attitude</u>, <u>communicate</u>, <u>conveyed</u>, <u>illustrate</u>.

REVIEW
Write a Review

Write a short review of an imaginary production of either play. Describe the main character and his conflict. Explain the effect of his qualities on the plot. (Don't give away the ending!) Rate the effectiveness of the playwright's use of suspense, and critique the acting and the staging. Convince your reader that the play is—or is not—worth attending.

CONNECT
Write Text Messages

TechFocus Choose one of the plays. Imagine that it takes place today and the main character has a cell phone. Write the text messages that the main character and a friend send back and forth.

EXTEND
Prepare an Oral Report

Oral Report Research an aspect of the Battle of Gettysburg for an oral report. You can focus on the fighting, the men who led the battle, the effect on the people living nearby, or President Lincoln's address commemorating the battle. Write an outline, and make notes for your report.

Learn It Online
Give your report in a whole new way. Try digital storytelling—we'll show you how on:
go.hrw.com | H6-311 | Go

INFORMATIONAL TEXT FOCUS
Following Instructions

CONTENTS

Animals often seem to be part of the family. What can people do to give animals comfortable homes?

 QuickWrite

Think about the responsibilities of caring for an animal. What qualities and attitudes do you think are important in a pet owner? Write a paragraph detailing these qualities.

APPLICATION
Preparing to Read

 Reading Standard 2.5 Follow multiple-step instructions for preparing applications (e.g., for a public library card, bank savings account, sports club, league membership).

Pet Adoption Application

Informational Text Focus

Following Instructions: Preparing an Application In the years ahead, you'll be asked to fill out applications for all kinds of things. Right now, if you want to get a library card or adopt a pet from a shelter, you will be asked to fill out an application.

Into Action These are the steps you need to follow when you fill out an application.

1. **Read the application all the way through** before you do anything. You can often learn a great deal about whatever you're applying for by reading through the application.
2. If there is a question that requires more than a quick answer, **write down or type your response before you write it on the application** itself. Review and, if necessary, revise what you've written. Then, copy your response onto the application.
3. **Answer questions truthfully.**
4. **Print or type** the information carefully, with no cross-outs.
5. **Fill in** all the blanks. Write *n/a* (for "not applicable") in response to questions that don't apply to you.
6. Check your **spelling.**
7. After you fill out the application, read it through carefully to **make sure you didn't miss anything.**
8. **Sign and date** your application.

   Some applications require references. A **reference** is someone (possibly a teacher or family friend) who can provide information about your abilities and qualities. You should list only adults as references. Always ask permission first so that your references will have a chance to prepare useful information about you—and so they won't be surprised if they receive a phone call.

Writing Skills Focus

Preparing for **Timed └Writing** Note the main headings, boldface terms, and other features that help guide you through the application.

 **Reader/Writer Notebook**
Use your **RWN** to complete the activities for these selections.

Vocabulary

contribution (kahn truh BYOO shuhn) *n.*: payment given for a specific purpose. *I gave the shelter at which I found my cat a contribution to help other lost animals.*

occupation (ahk yoo PAY shuhn) *n.*: work a person does regularly. *I had to list my occupation when applying for a pet.*

supervisor (SOO puhr vy zuhr) *n.*: person in charge. *Did someone call my supervisor to ask if I was dependable?*

Language Coach

Latin Origins and Root Words
Many words commonly used in business, like the three Vocabulary words above, are Latinate words, words from ancient Latin roots. Latin was the language of the ancient Romans, who had a rich vocabulary for dealing in business, law, and government. Latinate words are often rather long because they are built from two or more word parts consisting of a root and one or more affixes.

In a dictionary, look up the words above. What are their Latin roots?

Learn It Online
Use the interactive Reading Workshop for an example of how to prepare an application:

| go.hrw.com | H6-313 | Go |

Read with a Purpose

Read to discover the kinds of information requested on applications.

INSTRUCTIONS: Adopter, print carefully in UNSHADED AREAS ONLY— do not write in shaded areas.

☐ Puppy ☐ Kitten ☐ Dog ☐ Cat

Ⓐ

					1		Program	H	T	**Adoption Number**
Date / /		Single Adoption	Double Adoption	Age				D	O	1
								L	R	
Day	Time	Breed		Color			MTA MID	G	circle one	2

		Sex	☐ Mr. ☐ Mrs. ☐ Ms. ☐ Miss

☐ Adopter's Last Name   First Name

Voluntary Contribution | Size: S_____ M_____ L_____ | Spay/Neuter

Cash	$	☐ Pure	☐ Mix	Vaccine Type	Street Address	Apt. #
Check	$	Pet's Name		Vaccine Date		
D V M A circle one	$	ASC. Int.	No.	Rabies Tag		
Credit A/R	$			Rabies Date	City	State Zip Code
Total Voluntary Contribution	$			Wormed		

X_____ | Med. Given | Home Phone ( ) – | Business Phone ( ) –

Name of Reference	Address	City	State	Telephone	**ID Source**
				( ) –	☐ Yes ☐ No
				( ) –	

1. WHOM IS THE PET FOR? ☐ Self ☐ Gift For whom?_____ Adopter's age: _____

2. IF YOU ARE SINGLE: Do you live alone? ☐ Yes ☐ No Do you live with family? ☐ Yes ☐ No
Do you work? ☐ Yes ☐ No What are your hours? _____

IF YOU ARE MARRIED: Do you both work? ☐ Yes ☐ No Husband's hours: _____ Wife's hours: _____
How many children do you have at home? _____ Ages: _____, _____, _____, _____, _____, _____
Who will be responsible for the pet? ☐ Husband ☐ Wife ☐ Children ☐ Other

3. DO YOU: ☐ Own ☐ Rent (CHECK ONE) ☐ House ☐ Apt. Floor # _____ Elevator in building? ☐ Yes ☐ No (CHECK ONE)
If renting, does your lease allow pets? ☐ Yes ☐ No Are you moving? ☐ Yes ☐ No When? _____
Do you have use of a private yard? ☐ Yes ☐ No Is it fenced? ☐ Yes ☐ No Fence height: _____
Where will your pet be kept? _____ / _____ Any allergy to pets? ☐ Yes ☐ No
                              DAYTIME   NIGHTTIME

4. DO YOU HAVE OTHER PETS? ☐ Yes ☐ No Breed: _____
Where did you get the pet? _____ How long have you had it? _____

5. YOUR OCCUPATION: _____ Business Phone: ( ) _____
Company: _____ Supervisor's Name: _____

Ⓑ

Vet's Name	City, State	Zip Code

Adopter's Signature

Ⓐ **Informational Focus** **Following Instructions**
What information is required in the upper-right-hand area?

Ⓑ **Read and Discuss** What did you learn about pet adoption?

Vocabulary **contribution** (kahn truh BYOO shuhn) *n.*: payment given for a specific purpose.
occupation (ahk yoo PAY shuhn) *n.*: work a person does regularly.
supervisor (SOO puhr vy zuhr) *n.*: person in charge.

Applying Your Skills

Reading Standard 2.5 Follow multiple-step instructions for preparing applications (e.g., for a public library card, bank savings account, sports club, league membership).

Pet Adoption Application

Standards Review

Informational Text and Vocabulary

1. Which of the following people would *not* be a suitable reference on a pet adoption form?

 A a teacher

 B a former employer

 C a fellow Boy Scout

 D a minister

2. The *main* thing the shelter wants to know about an applicant is

 A whether the applicant will feed the animal the right food.

 B whether the applicant plans to let the animal run free through the neighborhood.

 C whether the applicant will take good care of the pet.

 D what kind of dog or cat the applicant wants.

3. The abbreviation *n/a* stands for "not applicable." What does the term *not applicable* mean?

 A none of your business

 B does not apply to me

 C not again

 D no answer

4. Why would the agency care if the pets were to be given as gifts?

 A The agency might charge an extra fee.

 B The agency would want to send a card.

 C The agency wants to know that the actual owner is responsible.

 D The agency disapproves of giving pets as gifts.

5. A person is most likely to give a *contribution* to

 A an employer.

 B a new pet.

 C a good cause.

 D a neighbor.

6. Another word for *occupation* is

 A application.

 B pet.

 C volunteer.

 D job.

7. *Supervisor* means

 A boss.

 B veterinarian.

 C reference.

 D clergyman.

Writing Skills Focus

Timed └Writing Write a paragraph explaining the most important things a person should do when filling out an application.

 What Do You Think Now

What information is the shelter *really* looking for when it asks what pets you have and whether you rent or own your home?

INSTRUCTIONS
Preparing to Read

Reading Standard 2.5 Follow multiple-step instructions for preparing applications (e.g., for a public library card, bank savings account, sports club, league membership).

Going Batty! How to Build a Bat House

Informational Text Focus

Following Instructions: Analyzing Directions **Directions** are step-by-step instructions that explain how to complete a task, put something together, or repair something. You've probably followed directions when working on projects in art class or setting up a new computer. Good directions <u>communicate</u> a great deal of information in very few words.

Into Action To make the best use of directions, follow these strategies in order. Summarize these strategies on a card or piece of paper that you can keep as a handy reference.

- Preview the task by reading all the **directions** carefully so you know the scope, or extent, of the project, including how long it will take. If there are any safety precautions or hazardous-materials warnings, ask for permission and work with adult supervision.
- Study any **diagrams** that <u>illustrate</u> the materials you'll need, recommended methods of working, or examples of the finished product.
- Set up your work space by gathering all the tools and **materials** you'll need. Have them all in one place so that you won't have to stop to go to the store or to search your garage or workshop.
- Start following the directions in sequence, from the beginning until the end. **Sequence** is the order in which actions are meant to be done. Here, it means the order of the steps in the directions.
- *Always* work with **safety** in mind: Carefully follow any safety precautions or warnings about hazardous materials.

Writing Skills Focus

Preparing for **Timed Writing** As you read the directions that follow on the next few pages, notice the way they are organized in a sequence.

Vocabulary

literally (LIHT uh uh lee) *adv.:* actually; in truth. *Bats literally hang from the ceilings of their homes.*

structure (STRUHK chuhr) *n.:* something built or constructed. *This wooden structure would make a good home for a bat colony.*

exterior (ehk STIHR ee uhr) *adj.:* outdoor. *Exterior-grade wood is specially treated so it can withstand harsh weather.*

Language Coach

Usage The word *literally* means "true to the exact meaning of the words." Many people use *literally* incorrectly, though. For example, someone might say, "My headache was so bad, my head was literally splitting." Unless the speaker was actually rushed to the hospital because his or her head had split open, the use of the word *literally* here can't be taken—well—literally!

Reader/Writer
Notebook
Use your **RWN** to complete the activities for this selection.

Learn It Online
Become vocabulary savvy with Word Watch at:

| go.hrw.com | H6-316 | Go |

GOING BATTY!
How to Build a Bat House

by THE WORLD ALMANAC®

Read with a Purpose
Read this article and its instructions to learn a lesson in sequencing.

Bats have gotten a bad name from horror stories and movies. That's too bad, because bats can be great little guys to have around. Give a bat a place to live, and it will help you cut down on mosquitoes and other insect nuisances.

These tiny creatures, the world's only flying mammals, don't ask for much. They want a warm, enclosed space where they can hang out—literally! Bats climb the walls when home, and yes, they do sleep upside down. So they need a surface to grip with their tiny claws. They also like a place that stays dark at night and is near water. (Eating bugs makes a bat thirsty!)

This easy-to-build structure will welcome a small colony of helpful bats. (Caution: Never touch a bat in case the bat is sick.) **Ⓐ**

Ⓐ Read and Discuss What point about bats is the author making?

Vocabulary **literally** (LIHT uhr uh lee) *adv.*: actually; in truth.
structure (STRUHK chuhr) *n.*: something built or constructed.

Materials

- 1 sheet ½" exterior-grade untreated plywood, at least 2' x 4'
- 1 piece 1" x 2" x 8' untreated pine (for sides)
- 1" x 4" x 28" untreated board (for roof)
- Window screen or mesh (optional), 5 sq. ft.
- 20 to 30 exterior-grade 1-inch screws
- Small box 1-inch nails
- Dark-colored, water-based paint or stain
- Heavy-duty hanging hooks and wire (optional)

Tools (Caution: Always wear safety goggles when using tools, and get an adult to help!)

- Table saw or handsaw
- Hammer
- Screwdriver
- Drill and drill bits
- Staple gun
- Paintbrush
- Caulk gun

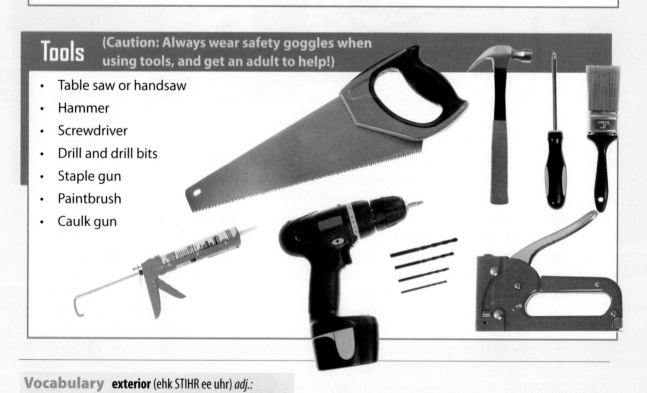

Vocabulary **exterior** (ehk STIHR ee uhr) *adj.:* outdoor.

Let's Get Started: Steps to Building a Bat House

1 Cut the plywood into three pieces as follows if you live in a warm climate. (See step 7 for measurements if you live in a cold climate.)

   a) 26½" x 24" (1 back)

   b) 26" x 24" (1 top front)

   c) 5" x 24" (1 bottom front)

2 Cut the pine into three pieces as follows:

   a) 24" (1 ceiling)

   b) 20½" (2 side walls)

3 Paint or stain the wood. The dark color absorbs sunlight and keeps the bat house warm.

4 Using the staple gun, cover one side of the back panel with the screen so that bats can grab on to it. (If you don't want to use a screen, you can rough up the surface of the board with a file.)

5 Line up the side walls with the longer sides of the back panel. Screw into place. There will be ½ inch of extra back panel at the bottom for bats to land on.

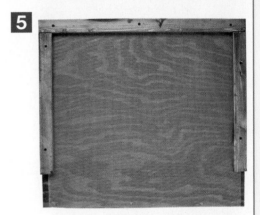

6 Place the ceiling at the top of the back panel, between the side walls. Screw into place.

7 Place the top front panel on the house. Line it up with the ceiling, and screw into place. Place the bottom front panel on the house, leaving a ½-inch vent space between the top and bottom front panels. If you live in a cold climate, you can eliminate this vent. Simply cut a single front piece that's 23 inches long.

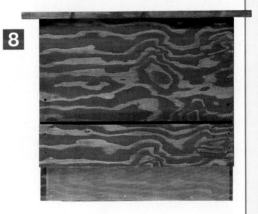

8 Carefully nail the roof over the top.

9 For best results, apply caulk to the joints. **Ⓑ**

Ⓑ **Informational Focus** **Following Instructions** The first strategy on page 316 says to preview the directions by reading all the steps first. What would you do if you got to step 9 and realized you did not know what the word *joints* or *caulk* meant? How might not understanding a word affect your completing the project?

The Comforts of Home

- Look for a wall facing south or east with a water source nearby.
- Hang your bat house at least 12 feet off the ground to help keep other critters out.
- Choose an area away from lighting, such as porch lights.
- Bats like to live in neighbor-hoods, so consider building more than one bat house. You could create a bat city! **C**

Analyzing Visuals   **Connecting to the Text** What information in the text does this photograph illustrate? Point out details.

C **Informational Focus** **Following Instructions** This last bulleted list has four more instructions, but they do not follow as strong a sequence as the building instructions do. Are these items in the best sequence? How would you order the information?

Applying Your Skills

Reading Standard 2.5 **Follow multiple-step instructions** for preparing applications (e.g., for a public library card, bank savings account, sports club, league membership).

Going Batty! How to Build a Bat House

Standards Review

Informational Text and Vocabulary

1. Which of the following is *not* required for building a bat house?

A plywood

B hanging hooks

C exterior-grade screws

D hammer

2. What should you do if you find a bat near your house?

A Feed it mosquitoes.

B Find the rest of its colony.

C Put it in a wooden box.

D Do not touch it.

3. Why should the roof be installed over the ceiling?

A so bats can land more easily

B because it uses less plywood

C so rain won't get inside the house

D so the caulking will fill the joints

4. Why should you create an air vent in the house if you live in a warm climate?

A so the bats can drink water

B so the house can get some light

C so there is something for bats to hold on to

D so air can flow through the house

5. Another term for *literally* is

A in truth.

B greedily.

C with excitement.

D spookily.

6. A *structure* is

A a plywood sheet.

B an enclosed space.

C a bat colony.

D a building.

7. The opposite of *exterior* is

A damp.

B inside.

C unquestionable.

D untreated.

8. What challenges might you encounter when building this bat house?

A avoiding injury from tools

B following all the details in the instructions

C getting all the required materials

D all of the above

Writing Skills Focus

Timed ⏱ Writing Write a set of **directions** explaining how to make or do something: crochet a scarf, make a grilled cheese sandwich, shoot a basket, take a good digital photograph. Make a list of all the **materials** and tools required for the project. Then, organize the directions into a **sequence** of steps.

What Do **You Think Now**

How might you and your family benefit from having bats living near your home?

Writing Workshop

Problem-Solution Explanation

Write with a Purpose

Write an essay that describes a problem and provides a successful solution to the problem. Your **audience** includes your teacher and classmates. Your **purpose** is to convince them that your solution is reasonable and practical.

A Good Problem-Solution Essay

- clearly defines the problem, considering its causes and effects
- clearly states a proposed solution
- supports the problem and the solution with relevant evidence
- anticipates and addresses possible objections
- is organized by order of importance with the most important solutions presented first
- summarizes the problem and solution and may end with a convincing call to action

See page 330 for complete rubric.

Reader/Writer Notebook

Use your **RWN** to complete the activities for this workshop.

Think as a Reader/Writer

In life you will often want to address problems and find solutions for these problems. One way to do this is to write a problem-solution explanation. A problem-solution explanation discusses an important problem, proposes a solution, and convinces readers why the proposed solution is the best one. Take a few minutes to read this excerpt from an essay titled "The U.S. Has a Garbage Crisis," by William Dudley.

> We are running out of places to put all the garbage we produce. About 80 percent of it is now buried in landfills. There are 6,000 landfills currently operating, but many of them are becoming full. The Environmental Protection Agency estimates that one-half of remaining landfills will run out of space and close within the next five to ten years. . . .
>
> The only real solution to the garbage crisis is for Americans to reduce the amount of trash they throw away. There are two methods of doing this. One is recycling—reusing garbage. . . . Environmentalist Barry Commoner estimates that we can reduce 70 percent of our garbage by recycling.
>
> We must also reduce the amount of garbage we produce in the first place. . . . Consumers should buy foods and goods that use less packaging. We also should buy reusable products rather than things that are used once and thrown away.

← The first paragraph states the **problem** and provides relevant **evidence** of the problem.

← The proposed **solution** is clearly stated at the beginning of the second paragraph.

← Note **suggestions** on how to reach the solution, plus a **call for action**.

Think About the Professional Model

With a partner, discuss the following questions about the model:

1. How does the writer get your attention with the problem statement?
2. Is the problem statement effective? Why or why not?
3. Is the proposed solution realistic? What information is used to persuade the reader that this is a realistic solution?
4. Is the explanation organized in a coherent manner?

Writing Standard 1.2 Create multiple-paragraph expository compositions: a. Engage the interest of the reader and state a clear purpose. b. Develop the topic with supporting details and precise verbs, nouns, and adjectives to paint a visual image in the mind of the reader. c. Conclude with a detailed summary linked to the purpose of the composition. 1.3 Use a variety of effective and coherent organizational patterns, including comparison and contrast; organization by categories; and arrangement by spatial order, order of importance, or climactic order. 2.2 Write expository compositions (e.g., description, explanation, comparison and contrast, problem and solution): a. State the thesis or purpose. b. Explain the situation. c. Follow an organizational pattern appropriate to the type of composition. d. Offer persuasive evidence to validate arguments and conclusions as needed.

Prewriting

Choose a Problem

The first step in writing a problem-solution explanation is choosing a problem that is important to you and your audience. Work in a small group to brainstorm a list of problems. The Idea Starters at right may help you generate ideas. Then, choose two or three problems that are most important to you. Thinking about the **causes** and **effects** of those problems, consider some realistic solutions. Then, choose a problem that has a valid and promising solution.

Develop a Thesis

Once you've identified a particular problem, write a **thesis statement,** or opinion statement, that clearly states the problem. (The solution will come later in your essay.) Here is an example of a student's thesis statement: *Sibling rivalry, or competition between brothers and sisters, can seriously harm families.*

Find a Solution

The solution is the heart of the matter, your reason for writing. There's no one "correct" way to go about finding a solution. One person might begin by brainstorming different possibilities, while another might write freely about the problem just to put words on paper. If you take the second approach, you might want to imagine that you're writing a letter to a friend about the problem.

   Whatever approach you take, be sure you clearly explain your solution to your readers. You might stress how practical your solution is, how easy it is to accomplish, or the consequences of taking no action at all. Fill in a chart like the one below to keep track of some possible solutions to the problem you've chosen. This chart is partially completed for the model on page 322.

Problem	Possible Solution
Landfills are filling up, and there's no place to put garbage.	Reduce garbage by recycling.
	Reduce garbage produced in the first place.

Idea Starters

Think about problems involving

- you and your classmates
- your school or community
- the global community
- a situation you noticed recently

Your Turn _____

Get Started Record in your **RWN** the **problem** and **solution** you have selected. Then, spend some time thinking about both. Is the problem one your audience will care about? Are there any flaws in your solution to the problem? Can you think of a better solution? Use this information as you plan your draft.

Learn It Online
See how one writer develops a problem-solution essay at:

go.hrw.com   H6-323   Go

Peer Review

Getting together with a classmate who can serve as your "practice audience" is a good way to help you think through the objections you might face to your proposed solution. Sit down with a partner and ask him or her to "punch holes" in your argument. Your partner may see weaknesses in your solution that you are unable to see or haven't considered.

Gather Evidence

In order to persuade others that you've identified a real problem and that you've found a good solution, you must support your position with organized and relevant **evidence.** Here are some types of evidence you might use:

• facts (including statistics)

• expert opinions

• analysis of whether the solution is practical (in terms of cost, time, and difficulty)

• comparisons of solutions (mention other solutions that might be—or have been—tried in order to show they are not as good as yours)

You may want to include anecdotes and other examples from personal experience to make your essay more engaging, but those stories and examples are not considered evidence.

Consider Your Purpose and Audience

Remember that your **purpose** is not only to persuade your **audience** that your problem is valid but also to convince them that your solution is the very best one. However, that doesn't mean you should present your solution as the only possible solution. In fact, a powerful technique is to discuss other reasonable solutions, as well as possible objections to the solution you are offering.

Always take time to consider the point of view, or perspective, of your audience. It's easy to persuade readers who are likely to agree with your ideas from the beginning. People who are already recycling don't need to be convinced to recycle plastic. (This is sometimes called "preaching to the choir.") The real challenge in presenting a solution is to change the minds of people who may not agree with you at first. Anticipate the concerns and counterarguments of those readers. Imagine yourself in the shoes of readers who are unlike you—who perhaps see things differently. What parts of your solution might seem weak to them? Openly acknowledge the pros and cons of each solution. Anticipate your audience's objections, and plan a response to each objection. This approach lets your readers know that you've given full consideration to the problem. A flowchart like this one can help you think through the process.

Your Turn _____

Plan Your Essay Use research and your knowledge of the problem and its solution to plan your essay. Use a flowchart like the one on this page to plan and organize your information.

Problem → Solution → Readers' arguments → My answers

Drafting

Follow the Writer's Framework
The Writer's Framework at right outlines how to plan your draft to create an effective problem-solution explanation.

Discuss the Pros and Cons
As you write your draft, analyze your proposed solution and evidence as your readers would. Ask yourself questions like these:

- Is my solution adequate and practical?
- Have I considered the problem's causes and effects?
- Is my evidence persuasive and accurate?
- What are other possible solutions, and what are their pros and cons?
- What are some possible concerns about or objections to my solution?
- What evidence shows that my solution is best?

Write a Strong Conclusion
Your conclusion should restate the problem and your solution, repeating why your solution is best. If you want your readers to do something to help solve the problem, include a call to action—a request urging them to take a specific action. If you end with a call to action, make it reasonable and specific. Tell your readers what you want them to do, and remind them why they should do it.

A Problem-Solution Framework

Introduction
- State the problem and why it is important.
- Include evidence that it is a serious problem.

Body
- Present and describe your proposed solution.
- Provide details about the solution.
- Provide evidence, in order of importance, that explains the benefits of the solution.
- Answer possible objections to the solution.

Conclusion
- Restate the problem.
- Summarize your proposed solution.
- End with a strong call to action.

● Writing Tip
Try one of the following techniques to draft a strong introduction:

- Tell an anecdote that puts the problem on a personal level.
- Present a startling fact or statistic about the problem.
- Include a quotation by an authority on the topic.

● Writing Tip
A call to action is a specific suggestion about something your readers can do about the problem. It is a powerful way to end your essay.

Your Turn
Write Your Draft Following your plan, write a draft of your essay. Be sure to think about the following questions:

- What other possible solutions will you discuss?
- What possible objections will you answer?
- What, if any, call to action will you present?

Grammar Link Using Numbers Correctly
You may need to use numbers to state your problem or its solution or to write a strong conclusion. Use the following guidelines and examples if you do.

Use numerals for indicating numbers over ten.	Use a hyphen with compound numbers from twenty-one to ninety-nine.	Spell out the numbers *ten* and below.
"There are 6,000 landfills…." "…reduce 70 percent of our garbage…"	"…over seventy-five wells had to be closed…."	"…within the next five to ten years…"

Peer Review

Get together with a classmate to review your draft. Ask your classmate to answer the questions in the chart at the right as he or she reviews your essay. Be sure to write down your partner's suggestions so you can use them when you revise your draft.

Evaluating and Revising

Your draft is merely the starting point of the writing process. Now it's time to evaluate your essay to look for any weak areas and to improve your essay by revising those weak areas.

Problem-Solution Explanation: Guidelines for Content and Organization

Evaluation Question	Tip	Revision Technique
1. Does your introduction get the reader's attention and clearly state the problem?	**Underline** the attention-getting opening. **Highlight** the thesis, or statement of the problem.	**Add** a strong statement, statistic, or example of the problem. **Clarify** your statement of the problem.
2. Do you provide details that describe the problem and relevant causes and effects?	**Put stars** next to details that describe the problem.	**Add** evidence that reveals the seriousness of the problem.
3. Do you propose a solution to the problem? Do you examine the pros and cons of the solution?	**Circle** statements that suggest a solution. **Bracket** the pros and cons discussed.	**Write** a clear statement of the solution, if needed. **Add** pros and cons of the solution.
4. Have you provided strong reasons and persuasive evidence to support your proposed solution?	**Put a check mark** next to each reason or piece of evidence.	**Add** facts, statistics, anecdotes, examples, or expert opinions, as needed.
5. Have you organized your solutions by order of importance?	**Number** the solutions to your problem, giving a number 1 to the most important solution, a number 2 to the next most important solution, and so on.	**Rearrange** your solutions so they are organized in order of importance.
6. Does the conclusion include a convincing argument, a summary, or a call to action?	**Draw a box** around the argument, summary, or call to action.	**Add** a call to action, or **revise** your conclusion to make it more persuasive.

Read this student's draft and the comments about it as a model for revising your own problem-solution explanation.

Household Hazardous Wastes

by Michelle Burrows, Paradise Canyon Elementary

In daily life, for work or pleasure, people use products that later become hazardous wastes. Household items such as beauty products, car-care products, cleaning supplies, and gardening products are a few examples. When no longer usable or wanted, these products are thrown in the trash and become hazardous wastes. If they are disposed of improperly, they pose a threat to the health of our environment and the organisms living in it.

Improperly stored and disposed of household products can cause serious problems. Accidental poisonings can occur. Hazardous products may ignite or explode, threatening the environment and workers. If hazardous products make it to the landfill, waste liquids can go into our surface water or groundwater, our drinking water. When these wastes go down the drain, they can kill the organisms that make the system work.

← Michelle clearly states the **problem** in the first sentence.

← Michelle provides further **details** about the problem.

← Consequences of ignoring the **problem** are presented through cause-effect reasoning.

MINI-LESSON ▶ How to Use Cause and Effect to Support Evidence

In her second paragraph, Michelle explained the effects of hazardous wastes. After working with a partner, she realized that some of the cause-effect relationships are unclear. She revised her explanation to make the causes clearer and to specify how and why the hazards exist. The revisions strengthen her essay.

Michelle's Revision of Paragraph Two

Improperly stored and disposed of household products can cause serious problems. ~~Accidental poisonings can occur. Hazardous products may ignite or explode, threatening the environment and workers.~~

Hazardous wastes, such as bleach and cleaning supplies, that are left within children's reach can cause accidental poisoning. When you place combustible items such as paint and paint thinner in the trash, the garbage can may ignite or explode, injuring workers and threatening the environment.

If hazardous products make it to the landfill, waste liquids can go into our surface water or groundwater, *poisoning* our drinking water. When these wastes go down the drain, they can kill the organisms that make the system work.

Student Draft *continues*

Michelle's **solution** includes several specific suggestions.

This problem may seem hopeless, but it is not. Remember this handy mnemonic device the three *R*'s, which stands for *Reduce, Reuse,* and *Recycle.* The first *R* is to *reduce*--avoid purchasing household products with labels containing words such as *caustic, corrosive, danger, explosive, flammable, poison, toxic, volatile,* or *warning.* You can find books that suggest safer alternatives in a library or bookstore. When you must use a certain product, buy only the amount you need. Remember the second *R* and *reuse* whatever products you can. Finally, consider the third *R* and contact your local solid waste officials for *recycling* locations in your area. When the three *R*'s cannot be used, there is another option: *Relocation.* Keep the product in its original container, label it clearly, and take it to a hazardous waste collection site.

A less-desirable but realistic **solution** is presented as an alternative.

The final paragraph provides a brief **summary** of the problem and proposed solution.

Household hazardous waste management is a problem, but not one without solutions. Use the three *R*'s or *Relocation* to protect our health and our environment.

MINI-LESSON **How to Write a Call to Action**

Michelle proposes realistic solutions to the problem. She concludes with a broad suggestion for action, but she decides to write a more direct call to action by asking her readers to do something specific. The revision gives her conclusion the persuasive power it needs.

Michelle's Draft of the Final Paragraph

Household hazardous waste management is a problem, but not one without solutions. Use the three *R*'s or *Relocation* to protect our health and our environment.

Your Turn

Write a Call to Action As you revise your draft, consider the following questions about your conclusion:

- What action have you asked your readers to take?
- Is the action likely to be effective?
- Can you be more specific about what you want your readers to do?

Michelle's Revision of the Final Paragraph

Household hazardous waste management is a problem, but not one without solutions. ~~Use the three *R*'s or *Relocation*~~

If every person takes one small action, we will add far less hazardous waste to the environment. Choose just one thing to do. For example, make your own natural cleaner, buy smaller amounts of gardening products, or recycle one reusable item in your garage. Taking action now will help

for the future

to protect our health and our environment.

Proofreading and Publishing

Proofreading

You have evaluated and revised your problem-solution explanation to improve its content and organization. Now it's time to put the final touches on it and prepare it for publication. You do this by reading it with the critical eyes of a proofreader. Edit your writing for misspellings, punctuation errors, grammar errors, and problems in sentence structure.

Grammar Link Punctuating Appositives

An **appositive** is a noun or pronoun that identifies or describes more specifically another noun or pronoun beside it. An appositive phrase is an appositive with modifiers. Use commas to separate an appositive from the rest of the sentence.

As she was proofreading, Michelle found an appositive that needed to be set off by a comma.

> Remember this handy mnemonic device, the three R's, which stands for
>
> *Reduce, Reuse*, and *Recycle*.

Publishing

Now it is time to publish your problem-solution explanation to reach a wider audience. Here are some ways to share your explanation:

- Present your explanation to your school newspaper as an editorial.
- Publish your explanation in your community's newspaper.
- Post your explanation on a community Internet site to see how readers respond to your ideas.
- Read your explanation on a local or school television broadcast that addresses problems in your school or community.

Reflect on the Process   In your **RWN,** write a short response to each of the following questions:

1. What was the most difficult part of writing a problem-solution essay? Why do you think it was difficult?
2. What did you learn about your audience and their possible objections to your solution?
3. What did you learn here that will be useful in other types of writing?

● Proofreading Tip

Get help from at least two of your classmates during the proofreading process. Ask each person to focus on only one area, such as spelling, punctuation, or sentence structure.

Your Turn _____

Proofread and Publish As you proofread your writing, look closely for appositives that lack punctuation. Corrrect them and any other errors in punctuation, usage, or spelling before you publish your explanation.

Scoring Rubric

You can use the rubric below to evaluate your problem-solution explanation.

	Expository Writing	Organization and Focus	Sentence Structure	Conventions
4	• *Clearly* defines the problem and *convincingly* states a proposed solution. • *Strongly* supports the problem and solution with *relevant* evidence. • *Convincingly* anticipates and addresses the reader's concerns and expectations.	• *Clearly* addresses all parts of the writing task. • Demonstrates a *clear* understanding of purpose and audience. • Maintains a *consistent* focus and organizational structure, ending with a *clear* and *concise* summary.	• Includes sentence *variety* (e.g., simple, complex, compound-complex).	• Contains *few, if any,* errors in the conventions of the English language (grammar, punctuation, capitalization, spelling). These errors do **not** interfere with the reader's understanding of the writing.
3	• *Generally* defines the problem and states a proposed solution. • Supports the problem and solution with *relevant* evidence. • Anticipates and addresses the reader's concerns and expectations.	• Addresses *most* of the writing task. • Demonstrates a *general* understanding of purpose and audience. • Maintains a *mostly consistent* focus and organizational structure, ending with a *relatively* clear and concise summary.	• Includes *some* sentence variety (e.g., simple, complex, compound-complex).	• Contains *some errors* in the conventions of the English language (grammar, punctuation, capitalization, spelling). These errors do **not** interfere with the reader's understanding of the writing.
2	• *Vaguely* defines the problem and states a proposed solution. • *Partially* supports the problem and solution with *somewhat relevant* evidence. • *May* anticipate and address the reader's concerns and expectations.	• Addresses *some* of the writing task. • Demonstrates *little* understanding of purpose and audience. • Maintains an *inconsistent* focus and/or organizational structure, ending with an *unclear* summary.	• Includes *little* sentence variety.	• Contains *several errors* in the conventions of the English language (grammar, punctuation, capitalization, spelling). These errors **may** interfere with the reader's understanding of the writing.
1	• *Fails* to define a problem or a solution. • Provides *little* or *no* evidence. • *Fails* to anticipate and address the reader's concerns and expectations.	• Addresses *only one* or *no* part of the writing task. • Demonstrates *no* understanding of purpose and audience. • *Lacks* a focus and organizational structure, and includes either *no* summary or a *rambling* one.	• Includes *no* sentence variety.	• Contains *serious errors* in the conventions of the English language (grammar, punctuation, capitalization, spelling). These errors interfere with the reader's understanding of the writing.

Problem-Solution Explanation

> **Writing Standard 2.2** Write expository compositions (e.g., description, explanation, comparison and contrast, **problem and solution**): a. State the thesis or purpose. **b. Explain the situation.** c. Follow an organizational pattern appropriate to the type of composition. **d. Offer persuasive evidence to validate arguments and conclusions as needed.**

When responding to an on-demand problem-solution prompt, use the models you have read, what you've learned from writing your own problem-solution essay, the rubric on page 330, and the steps below.

Writing Prompt

School officials have decided that students should not be allowed to eat lunch on the football field because they leave too much litter. Write a problem-solution explanation in which you propose a solution to the problem. Write your explanation in the form of a letter to your principal, and provide evidence to persuade him or her to agree with you.

Study the Prompt

Begin by reading the prompt carefully. Note what is required in your explanation: a proposed **solution** to a litter problem at your school. You know that your **audience** is your school principal, and your **purpose** is to persuade your principal to agree with your proposed solution.

Tip: Spend about five minutes studying the prompt.

Plan Your Response

Since you already know your topic,

- write down some background information on the problem
- think about all sides of the problem
- write down the solution you will propose
- write down several reasons why your audience should agree with your solution
- consider any objections your audience might have to your solution, and think about how you'll answer those objections.

Tip: Spend about ten minutes planning your response.

Respond to the Prompt

Using the notes you've just made, draft your explanation. Follow these guidelines:

- In the introduction, state the **problem** and tell why it is important.
- In the body, describe and give details about your **solution**, provide reasons or **evidence** that explains why your solution is best, and address possible **objections** to your solution.
- In the conclusion, wrap up your explanation with a **summary** of the problem and solution or a **call to action.**

As you are writing, remember to use persuasive language. You may need to change the way your audience thinks about the problem. Also try to write as neatly as you can.

Tip: Spend about twenty minutes writing your draft.

Improve Your Response

Revising Go back over the key aspects of the explanation. Did you state your solution clearly? Did you provide reasons for all your points?

Proofreading Proofread your explanation to correct errors in grammar, spelling, punctuation, and capitalization. Make sure all your edits are neat, and erase any stray marks.

Checking Your Final Copy Before you turn in your explanation, read it one more time to catch any errors you may have missed.

Tip: Save five to ten minutes to improve your paper.

Giving a Problem-Solution Presentation

Speak with a Purpose

Present your problem-solution essay as a speech. Practice the speech, and then present it to your class.

● Listening Tip

One important way of learning how to deliver a problem-solution presentation is to pay close attention to your classmates' speeches. As you watch and listen to your classmates' presentations, notice both **content**—what the speaker says—and **delivery**—how the speaker says it.

Think as a Reader/Writer You've already written a persuasive problem-solution essay. Now you will try your hand at delivering it as an oral presentation. When delivering a problem-solution presentation, you may need to pay more attention to your audience (the listeners) than you did in your essay.

Adapt Your Essay

Make It Clear

Your presentation will address the same problem and propose the same solution as your essay. You have only one opportunity, however, to persuade your audience when you give a problem-solution presentation. Listeners cannot go back and re-read your words. It is essential to capture your audience's attention and help them recognize the problem you are discussing as well as the solution you propose. Make sure to emphasize all salient, or main, points in your presentation.

Problem Solved

These guidelines will ensure that your presentation will persuade listeners to agree with you.

- Clearly define the **problem** you wish to address.
- **Theorize,** or speculate, on the possible causes and effects of the problem. To identify causes and effects, consult your research on the problem. Note one or two noticeable causes as well as one or two apparent effects.
- Establish connections between the **problem** you have defined and the proposed **solution**. The connection might be the way your solution limits the causes or reduces the effects of the problem. Transitional expressions such as *therefore, as a result,* and *for this reason* can clarify cause-and-effect relationships.
- Include persuasive **evidence**, such as facts, statistics, descriptions and quotations from experts. The evidence should **validate,** or prove, that you defined the problem correctly and that your proposed solution is reasonable and viable.

Listening and Speaking Standard
1.1 Relate the speaker's verbal communication (e.g., word choice, pitch, feeling, tone) to the nonverbal message (e.g., posture, gesture). **1.5** Emphasize salient points to assist the listener in following the main ideas and concepts. **2.5** Deliver presentations on problems and solutions: a. Theorize on the causes and effects of each problem and establish connections between the defined problem and at least one solution. b. Offer persuasive evidence to validate the definition of the problem and proposed solution.

Deliver Your Oral Response

Even the most persuasive ideas can fall flat if they aren't delivered well. For example, if you get affected by distractions, mumble, or speak in a dull monotone, your listeners are not going to be engaged. Practice your speech to make sure you don't fall into any of these bad speaking habits. As you practice, concentrate on using **verbal elements** (what your voice does as you speak) and **nonverbal elements** (what your face and body do as you speak).

Verbal Elements

When you give a problem-solution presentation, it is important to speak at a slow **rate** so your audience can comprehend your ideas. You should also speak at a loud enough **volume** so the people in the back of the room can hear you. Varying your **vocal modulation,** or **pitch**—the rise and fall of your speaking voice—can help keep your audience interested. Adjusting the **tone,** or attitude, of your voice to match your message helps the audience understand your feelings about the issue. When giving a persuasive speech, your tone should be enthusiastic and believable so that your audience will be more likely to agree with your position.

Nonverbal Elements

Your **posture, eye contact** with the audience, **gestures,** and **facial expressions** are examples of nonverbal elements. Standing tall while looking directly at your audience shows that you are confident, and using appropriate gestures and facial expressions can help **emphasize** important ideas.

Dealing with Distractions

Try not to let noises or unexpected events distract you. For example, if your presentation is interrupted by continuous or recurring background noise, ignore it and speak louder. If you are interrupted by a more noticeable but temporary noise, pause until the noise stops, and then continue. Similarly, if you realize you accidentally skipped a minor point in your speech, go on as if nothing happened. If you skip an important point, explain the point to your listeners and then resume your presentation.

A Good Problem-Solution Presentation

- includes a clear statement of the problem
- theorizes on the causes and effects of the problem
- provides a variety of evidence that supports the definition of the problem, emphasizing salient points
- proposes a clearly stated solution to the problem
- makes effective use of verbal and nonverbal techniques

 Speaking Tip

A good speaker provides a strong message and uses his or her voice and body language together to effectively present that message. For example, when stating a key point in a presentation, a speaker may point or nod.

 Learn It Online
An interactive graphic organizer can help you organize your ideas. Try one at:

go.hrw.com | H6-333 | **Go**

Literary Skills Review

Theme **Directions:** Read this story and respond to the questions that follow.

As a boy growing up in the New York City neighborhood of Harlem, the author Claude Brown ran with a tough crowd and often got into trouble, some of it very serious. He was first sent away to reform school when he was eleven. While there, a teacher who was encouraging Claude to stay out of trouble told him this story.

A vat is a very large container. Milk vats are often filled with milk that has just come from the cow, so the milk contains a lot of fat. When milk is churned, the fat turns to butter.

Two Frogs and the Milk Vat

by **Claude Brown**

There were two frogs sitting on a milk vat one time. The frogs fell into the milk vat. It was very deep. They kept swimming and swimming around, and they couldn't get out. They couldn't climb out because they were too far down. One frog said, "Oh, I can't make it, and I'm going to give up."

And the other frog kept swimming and swimming. His arms became more and more tired, and it was harder and harder and harder for him to swim. Then he couldn't do another stroke. He couldn't throw one more arm into the milk. He kept trying and trying; it seemed as if the milk was getting hard and heavy. He kept trying; he knows that he's going to die, but as long as he's got this little bit of life in him, he's going to keep on swimming. On his last stroke, it seemed as though he had to pull a whole ocean back, but he did it and found himself sitting on top of a vat of butter.

Reading Standard 3.6 Identify and analyze features of themes conveyed through characters, actions, and images.

1. The second frog could *best* represent a person who
   A always looks for an easy way.
   B makes life harder than it has to be.
   C has hope, even when all else looks bad.
   D lives as if today is the best day of his life.

2. The first frog decides to stop swimming because
   A he is a very weak swimmer.
   B he thinks there is no chance of escape.
   C he does not want to get into trouble.
   D he knows that it will help the other frog.

3. The writer uses the image of a huge vat of milk to
   A make the frogs look hopeless and out of place.
   B give the story a sense of humor.
   C allow the milk fat to turn into butter.
   D keep the frogs from getting out easily.

4. The action of swimming could *best* represent
   A an excuse for trouble.
   B escape on a summer day.
   C freedom for city kids.
   D the struggle to live.

5. Which one of the following sentences is a theme of this story?
   A Hope can save those who give up.
   B One frog gives up, but the other gets out.
   C If you give up, you lose.
   D Don't worry; no one ever drowns in milk.

Timed Writing

6. Look back at the note that introduces the story, and consider this message: *We learn about ourselves when we tell stories about animals.* Explain how this message, or theme, might be appropriate for this fable. Does the message still apply today?

Informational Skills Review

Following Instructions   **Directions:** Read the following application form. Then, read and respond to the questions that follow.

Natural History Museum Volunteer Application

1. Name: _____

   Address: _____   City, State, Zip code: _____

   Home telephone: _____   E-mail: _____

   Social Security number: _____   Age: ☐ Under 18   ☐ Over 18

2. Education   School most recently attended: _____

3. Employment   If a résumé is available, please submit it along with your application.
   (Please check *Past* or *Present*.)
   ☐ Past   ☐ Present   Volunteer work: _____

   Special skills or training: _____

   Computer skills: _____

   Fluency in other languages (please specify): _____

4. Is there a specific department or program at the museum in which you
   would like to work if a volunteer job is available? _____

5. Availability   Please check the times you are available to volunteer.

	Mon.	Tues.	Wed.	Thurs.	Fri.	Sat.	Sun.
9:00 A.M.–1:00 P.M.							
1:00 P.M.–5:00 P.M.							
5:00 P.M.–8:30 P.M.	■	■	■	■			■

   When can you start? _____

   A minimum commitment of one year is required. Can you meet this requirement? ☐ Yes   ☐ No

   **I HAVE READ AND AM IN POSSESSION OF A COPY OF THE
   "VOLUNTEER REGULATIONS AND PROCEDURES."**

   Signature: _____   Date: _____

1. In what section should you indicate that you speak more than one language?

   A 1

   B 2

   C 3

   D 4

2. The purpose of section 5 is to find out

   A what hours you're available to work.

   B what work experience you have.

   C where you live.

   D what your educational background is.

3. For what department is the museum accepting volunteers?

   A tours

   B research

   C sales

   D The application doesn't say.

4. Which applicant below *best* meets the qualifications to be a volunteer at the Natural History Museum?

   A Joaquin, who works every afternoon except Sundays

   B Bailey, whose family is moving away in ten months

   C Tong, who speaks English and Mandarin and knows computer programs

   D R. J., who would rather have a paying job and is filling out only section 1

5. Which of the following statements belongs in section 4?

   A I can design Web sites.

   B I've always been interested in dinosaurs.

   C I can start work immediately.

   D I am a skilled scuba diver.

6. For how long must you agree to work if you are accepted as a volunteer?

   A six months

   B one year

   C two years

   D three months

Timed Writing

7. What is the purpose of section 3? Explain the purpose of the section in one or two sentences.

Vocabulary Skills Review

Reading Standard 1.2 Identify and **interpret** figurative language and **words with multiple meanings.**

Multiple-Meaning Words   **Directions:** The sentences in quotation marks are from the story "Ta-Na-E-Ka." Read each sentence. Then, choose the answer in which the italicized word is used in the same way.

1. "As my birthday *drew* closer, I had awful nightmares about it."
   A My grandfather *drew* the blinds to stop the afternoon sun from beating in through the window.
   B The year *drew* to a close with the usual shouts and hugs at midnight.
   C In art class we *drew* self-portraits using only pen and ink.
   D I reached into the can and *drew* the name of the raffle winner.

2. "I was reaching the *age* at which all Kaw Indians had to participate in Ta-Na-E-Ka."
   A A person's *age* does not have to be filled in on the entry form.
   B Sometimes my mom says that we *age* her every time we do something risky.
   C Would you say that the modern era is the *age* of the computer?
   D My uncle taught me to *age* avocados more quickly by putting them in a brown paper sack.

3. "Many of the younger families on the *reservation* were beginning to give up the old customs."
   A I accept your offer to help with my chores without *reservation*.
   B We made a *reservation* at the restaurant so we would be sure to get a table.
   C He grew up on a Hopi *reservation* in Arizona.
   D My aunt is a *reservation* agent for a major airline.

4. "I even complained to my teacher, Mrs. Richardson, feeling that, as a white woman, she would *side* with me."
   A He had bruises on his *side* even though he wore pads during football practice.
   B They needed a freezer to store the *side* of beef they won from the meat market.
   C When I watch sports, I always seem to cheer for the losing *side*.
   D Unfortunately, my brother did not *side* with me in the argument I had with her.

5. "I was up early enough to watch the sun rise . . . , and I went to bed after it *set*."
   A After the moon *set*, the night grew dark.
   B After just one *set* of tennis, I was tired.
   C One of my chores on Thanksgiving is to *set* the tables—all four of them!
   D I *set* a match to the papers in the fireplace to get the logs burning.

Academic Vocabulary

Directions: Choose the answer in which the word in italics is used in the same way as it is used in sentence 6.

6. Please *illustrate* your point so I can understand it.
   A Please *illustrate* the poem with a sketch.
   B He wants to *illustrate* books for a living.
   C You might want to use some examples to *illustrate* your idea.
   D The story would be more appealing if it had drawings to *illustrate* it.

Writing Skills Review

Problem and Solution Explanation

Directions: Read the following paragraph from a problem-solution essay. Then, answer each question that follows.

Writing Standard 2.2 Write expository compositions (e.g., description, explanation, comparison and contrast, problem and solution): a. State the thesis or purpose. b. Explain the situation. c. Follow an organizational pattern appropriate to the type of composition. d. Offer persuasive evidence to validate arguments and conclusions as needed.

(1) Our nation is facing a growing problem with the number of overweight young people. (2) Studies show that an increasing number of children are carrying around an excessive amount of weight. (3) Being overweight creates medical problems, and it can even lead to serious diseases. (4) Most people care about the way they look. (5) The major causes of the problem have been identified. (6) Many children eat lots of food high in calories and they don't get enough exercise. (7) To attack this problem we need widespread public education about good eating habits. (8) What everyone can do immediately is to pay close attention to the foods they eat and adopt a sensible program of physical exercise.

1. This paragraph would be strengthened
   A by a discussion of hereditary diseases.
   B by comparison of various methods of dieting.
   C by a definition for the term *obesity*.
   D by a reference to the number of overweight adults.

2. Which sentence is beside the point and could be deleted?
   A. sentence 2
   B sentence 3
   C sentence 4
   D sentence 6

3. The problem the essay will address is identified in
   A sentence 1.
   B sentence 4.
   C sentence 5.
   D sentence 6.

4. Sentence 2 could be improved by
   A. adding statistics showing the number of overweight children.
   B naming the specific scientific studies.
   C identifying precisely the age groups of affected youth.
   D all of the above.

5. Which sentence could be improved by adding specific illnesses, such as diabetes and heart disease?
   A sentence 2
   B sentence 3
   C sentence 5
   D sentence 6

6. The audience for this essay would most likely be
   A children and teenagers.
   B healthcare workers.
   C parents.
   D all of the above.

Read On

Fiction

The Heart of a Chief

The award-winning author Joseph Bruchac mixes dialogue and first-person narration to present the compelling story of an eleven-year-old Pennacock boy, Chris Nicola, in *The Heart of a Chief*. You'll come to understand his harsh life on a reservation and the trials he experiences at his school and in his community. Despite the conditions Chris must deal with, his inner qualities and family traditions help him to recognize his potential.

Bat 6

A fifty-year-old tradition of softball rivalry between sixth-graders from two nearby towns is threatened with disaster. It is 1949, and the shadow of World War II still looms over people in the towns. The conflict between two girls from different backgrounds explodes in Virginia Euwer Wolff's *Bat 6* as the novel takes a brave look at prejudice, responsibility, and growing up.

The Pigman

In Paul Zindel's novel *The Pigman*, John and Lorraine befriend Mr. Pignati, a lonely widower with a weakness for bad jokes and miniature pigs. He also has a passion for life. This unlikely hero becomes a model of joy, freedom, and courage for John and Lorraine. Read about these three characters and find yourself learning from their situations.

A Dog's Life: Autobiography of a Stray

Have you ever wondered what a dog is thinking? This diary by a dog named Squirrel lets you in on her puppyhood, from life with her mother and brother in a warm and secure shed to her later life without her family or home. She tells you of her brutal life as a stray, with its constant and dangerous hunt for food and shelter. "Translated" by the well-loved author Ann Martin, *A Dog's Life: Autobiography of a Stray* may change how you think and feel about lost and abandoned dogs.

Nonfiction

Heroic Stories

Anthony Masters looks at the lives of twenty-four exceptional people in *Heroic Stories*. Some are people you've heard of, like Martin Luther King, Jr., and Anne Frank. Others, though, are lesser known people, like Christy Brown, who succeeded despite a devastating lifelong disability, and Pauline Cutting, who worked tirelessly under the conditions of war in Beirut's hospitals. Read *Heroic Stories* to learn more about these people and twenty others who have lived heroic lives.

Endangered Bats

The bat is a misunderstood little mammal. Around the world, humans disturb bat colonies when they enter caves or other places where bats roost. People make up terrifying stories about bats, and some even attempt to exterminate them. *Endangered Bats* gives you a close-up view of these magnificent animals and teaches you about how they live so you will understand why bats should be protected. Perhaps you'll be inspired to build a bat house to protect the bats, the world's only flying mammals.

Under the Greenwood Tree: Shakespeare for Young People

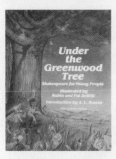

Every page of this lavishly illustrated book offers a song, a sonnet, or a story from a play by William Shakespeare. Lively portrayals will draw you into the world of Shakespeare's characters. In *Under the Greenwood Tree*, editor Barbara Holdridge and illustrator Robin Dewitt provide an attractive introduction to Shakespeare's world-famous poems and plays.

Orphan Train Rider

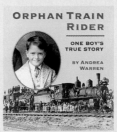

Many children were sent west to new families during the late 1800s and early 1900s. Lee Nailling was one such child. Author Andrea Warren recounts Nailling's experiences and eventual happiness in *Orphan Train Rider*. She also presents the history of those train rides and describes the difficulties the children often faced with their new families.

Learn It Online
Find tips for choosing, reading, and studying works with *NovelWise* at:

go.hrw.com   H6-341   Go

CHAPTER 4

Forms of Fiction

INFORMATIONAL TEXT FOCUS
Structural Features of Popular Media

California Standards

Here are the Grade 6 standards you will work toward mastering in Chapter 4.

Word Analysis, Fluency, and Systematic Vocabulary Development
1.2 Identify and interpret figurative language and words with multiple meanings.

Reading Comprehension (Focus on Informational Materials)
2.1 Identify the structural features of popular media (e.g., newspapers, magazines, online information) and use the features to obtain information.

Literary Response and Analysis
3.1 Identify the forms of fiction and describe the major characteristics of each form.

3.6 Identify and analyze features of themes conveyed through characters, actions, and images.

Writing Applications (Genres and Their Characteristics)
2.2 Write expository compositions (e.g., description, explanation, comparison and contrast, problem and solution):
  a. State the thesis or purpose.
  b. Explain the situation.
  c. Follow an organizational pattern appropriate to the type of composition.
  d. Offer persuasive evidence to validate arguments and conclusions as needed.

"We need to travel that road of danger and laughter, of mystery and understanding, which has always been the road of stories."

—Joseph Bruchac

What Do You Think   In what ways are stories an important part of your life?

Erosion (2000) by Jacek Yerka.

Learn It Online
Learn more about fiction online at *NovelWise:*

go.hrw.com   H6-343   Go

Literary Skills Focus

by **Linda Rief**

What Are the Forms of Fiction?

Have you ever played the telephone game? The sentence that the players begin with is usually not what the last person hears. Fiction writers play a kind of telephone game. They start out with a "whisper in the ear"—an idea, image, feeling, or character. Then they ask the question "What if?"—and begin to play.

The Oldest Forms of Fiction

Why do people love **fiction**—made-up stories that are purely products of the imagination? Perhaps people value how fiction depicts, or shows, them meaningful parts of life. Fiction may not be factual, but what it reveals can be *true*.

The oldest forms of fiction were created by forgotten or unknown storytellers who worked in the **oral tradition.** This body of cultural knowledge and wisdom has been passed down by word of mouth from generation to generation.

Myths and Epics Ancient peoples created stories called **myths** to provide explanations about their world by answering questions such as these:

- Why is there day, and why is there night?
- What causes the seasons to change?
- Why does death exist?

Characters in myths often appear in long stories called **epics**—tales about the deeds of heroes who possess qualities valued by their cultures.

> *"People of Uruk!"* cried Gilgamesh. "I go to the Forest of Cedar Trees. . . . There I shall do battle with Huwawa, the Evil One."
> from "Gilgamesh the Hero" by Geraldine McCaughrean

Fables A **fable** is a very brief "teaching tale" that presents a lesson regarding life, usually warning us about the effects of human weaknesses. Many fables end with a **moral,** a statement of the lesson they teach.

> If you let flattery go to your head, you'll pay the price.
> from "The Fox and the Crow" by Aesop

Folk Tales, Fairy Tales, Legends, and Tall Tales A **folk tale** is a fictional tale created by an unknown, or anonymous (uh NAHN uh muhs), writer that has been passed down orally for generations. A special form of folk tale is the **fairy tale,** which often begins with the words "Once upon a time" and involves fantasy, a conflict between good and evil, and a happy ending. A **legend** is a folk tale or epic with some basis in historical fact, such as the tales of King Arthur. Most tales from the oral tradition exist in many versions. There are hundreds of "Cinderella" stories all over the world!

> "Better had let me tell you somethin," Bruh Rabbit said, "for I've seen Man, and I know him the real king of the forest."
> from "He Lion, Bruh Bear, and Bruh Rabbit" by Virginia Hamilton

Fiction Today

When people talk about fiction today, they are usually referring to short stories and novels. You can also experience fictional worlds in movies, TV shows, comic books, manga, video games, and other storytelling media. Readers often place fiction into specific categories, or **genres** (ZHAHN ruhz): mystery, romance, science fiction, historical fiction, adventure, fantasy, and so on.

Short Stories A **short story** is just what it sounds like: a brief story that is generally five to twenty pages long. Short stories usually focus on one or two major characters, one main setting, and one central theme.

> Why did he raise his hand and volunteer?
> Why couldn't he have just sat there like
> the rest of the kids and not said anything?
> from "La Bamba" by Gary Soto

Novels A **novel** is a long fictional story, more than one hundred pages, that tends to have more characters, settings, and themes than a short story. Due to a novel's length, its plot can be more complex, the characters and settings can be more detailed, and there can be more than one theme.

Novellas Shorter than a novel but longer than a short story, a **novella** is often published with a collection of short stories or as a small book by itself.

> So my father slept. But that bothered me.
> I needed him awake. I was afraid of the
> dark and of the woods and of whatever
> lurked there.
> from *The Gold Cadillac*
> by Mildred D. Taylor

Other Forms of Fiction Fiction appears in many other forms, too, and you'll find some of those forms in this book. **Plays** (or **dramas**), radio and television **scripts, narrative poems** (poems that tell a story), **graphic stories** and novels (illustrated stories told in comic-book style), and **comic strips** are all forms of fiction that writers use to entertain us—as well as give us new insights into our lives.

"Yo, novella!"

©The New Yorker Collection 2004. Danny Shanahan from cartoonbank.com. All Rights Reserved.

Your Turn Identify Forms of Fiction

1. Identify one myth, one folk tale, one short story, and one novel you know.

2. Pair up with a classmate, and identify at least one example of each of the following forms of fiction: adventure, fantasy, romance, historical fiction, science fiction, mystery, and horror. From your experiences as a reader, describe the major characteristics of each form to the class.

Learn It Online
Explore forms of fiction with *PowerNotes* at:

go.hrw.com   H6-345   Go

Reading Skills Focus

by **Kylene Beers**

What Skills and Strategies Can Help You Read Forms of Fiction?

Reading fiction is often enjoyable, but that doesn't mean stories don't pose challenges—even for good readers. If you get stuck or lost while reading a story, setting a purpose for your reading and making and adjusting predictions can help you find your way.

Monitoring Comprehension

Have you ever finished reading a work of fiction, only to realize you haven't grasped its basic meaning? You read the words, but you couldn't understand what the author was trying to say. The way to figure out the meaning of all those words is to monitor your comprehension.

Comprehension means "understanding." When you **monitor your comprehension,** you check to make sure you *really* understand what you're reading. The steps in the flowchart below show you how to stay focused and uncover the text's meaning:

1. Read a passage of the text, such as a paragraph or section, and then pause.

2. Ask yourself, "What just happened?" or "What did the writer just explain?" Answer in your own words.

3. If you are able to give a clear answer in your own words, continue reading. (Go back to Step 1.) If you are unable to answer, go to Step 4.

4. Use the "fix-it" strategies on the right to aid your comprehension.

Comprehension "Fix-It" Strategies These "fix-it" strategies offer more techniques to help you monitor your comprehension.

What Happened?	How Do I Fix It?
First, try to figure out why you didn't understand the meaning of the text. Ask yourself the following questions:	When you've figured out the source of your difficulty, use these strategies to get back on track:
Did you **read too fast**?	**Re-read the passage** more slowly and carefully.
Are there **unfamiliar words** in the passage?	Try to **figure out the meaning** of unfamiliar words. Use a dictionary if necessary.
Have **new ideas** been introduced?	Consult a **reference source,** such as an encyclopedia or a trustworthy Web site, if there are ideas you don't understand.
Did you **forget key information** from earlier in the text?	**Re-read earlier passages** to refresh your memory about major details.

Setting a Purpose for Reading Fiction

When you read the latest book in your favorite fantasy series, you probably won't read it the same way you read your science textbook. Your main **purpose,** or reason, for reading the fantasy is to be entertained, so you will probably read it much more quickly than the textbook. The table below shows some general purposes for reading a few different forms of fiction.

Text	Purposes for Reading Fiction
Comic book	to be entertained
Historical novel	to be entertained; to learn more about a historical period
Fable	to be entertained; to gain insight into human nature

When you **set a purpose** for reading, you define your specific reading goals and decide what you, as a reader, need to do to meet those goals. Having a clear purpose in mind can help you choose texts to read and get the most out of them. Often, you will have multiple purposes for reading, and they may even change as you read.

Making and Adjusting Predictions

Have you ever figured out the conclusion to a mystery novel before the truth was revealed? If so, you made a correct prediction. **Predictions** are educated guesses about what will happen next in a story. You make predictions based on a combination of prior knowledge (what you already know) and information in the text. When you get new information as you read, you may need to **adjust** the predictions you made earlier. Don't worry if your predictions aren't always correct—part of the fun of reading is being surprised, and a good writer will often surprise you.

A Model for Predicting Read the excerpt below from Gary Soto's story "La Bamba." Notice how a reader might make and later have to adjust a prediction. You'll have to read the selection yourself to see if this reader was correct.

Manuel thought they had a great talent show. The entire school would be amazed. His mother and father would be proud, and his brothers and sisters would be jealous and pout. It would be a night to remember.

← **Prediction:** Manuel just seems too confident here. He thinks everything will go perfectly in the talent show, but I think he may be in for a big surprise.

Your Turn Apply Reading Skills

1. You finish reading a paragraph and realize that there were several important words you didn't understand. What can you do?

2. What purpose might you set if you are going to read a myth?

3. In a story about a lovable soccer team that keeps losing, the team gets a new coach who teaches them to believe in themselves. What do you predict might happen in the story?

Now go to the Skills in Action: Reading Model

Learn It Online
For tips on applying reading strategies to longer works, visit *NovelWise* at:

go.hrw.com | H6-347 | Go

Build Background

"The Storytelling Stone" comes from the **oral tradition** of the Seneca people. The Seneca originally lived in the woodlands of what is now New York State. They were one of the five nations of the Iroquois League, which also included the Cayuga, Onondaga, Oneida, and Mohawk.

Read with a Purpose Read the following folk tale to discover the Seneca people's explanation of the origin, or beginning, of stories.

The Storytelling Stone

retold by **John Cech**

Literary Focus

Forms of Fiction: Folk Tale
One characteristic of tales from the oral tradition is that they often begin with phrases like "In another time before this one," which indicates the story takes place a long time ago.

Reading Focus

Monitoring Comprehension
Pause here to make sure you understand what just happened. (The boy discovers that the stone is speaking to him.) If you begin monitoring your comprehension early in your reading, you will remain focused and figure out the story's meaning.

In another time before this one, there was a boy who hunted every day in the forest. Once, late in the afternoon, he stopped beside a large rock and sat down near it to fix his bow and make new points on his arrows.

A man's voice spoke to him. "I will tell you a story," it said.

The boy was startled and a little afraid, but he searched all around the stone to find the source of the voice. It could only be the rock, he thought. It must have *orenda,* the magic power the old men talk about. So he spoke to it.

"What did you say you wanted to tell me?"

"They are called stories; they are traditions. But first you must give me a present for telling it to you."

"Will this partridge do?" asked the boy, placing one of the birds he had hunted that day on the stone.

"Come back in the evening," the stone said, "and you will hear a legend about the world that was."

In the evening the boy sat on the stone again. The voice told him of the people who lived in the sky above, the "first people," the ones with great magic. Among them lived an old woman who dreamed that the large tree with the white blossoms that stood in the center of her village should be dug up by its roots. When she told her people about this, they followed the dream's instructions, uprooting the tree. They were frightened and angry over the hole it left and threw the old woman into it. She fell to earth, and the earth, which was completely under water then, had to be brought up from the depths by the animals and put upon the turtle's back and patted by the beavers' tails and allowed to grow before it could receive her who had fallen from the sky.

When he finished the tale, he noticed the boy had dozed off and so he said, "You must tell me if you become sleepy, and we can rest. If you sleep you will not hear. It is better that you come back tomorrow evening, and I will tell you more. Remember to bring my present."

Next day the boy hunted and in the evening returned to the rock with a string of birds. This time he did not miss a word. He came the next evening and the one after that.

"Where do you disappear to at night?" his friend asked him one day when they were out hunting together.

"I go to hear stories," he replied.

"What are they?"

"I don't know how to tell you about them, but come with me tonight and you will hear for yourself."

Reading Focus

Monitoring Comprehension
Re-read and break down long sentences like this one. Identify who fell and how the animals prepared for the fall.

Reading Focus

Making and Adjusting Predictions Predictions are often based on prior knowledge. You know that folk tales are passed down by storytellers and that the boy loves hearing stories. You might predict that the boy will become a storyteller himself.

So he brought his friend to the stone, and its voice filled their ears with the tales of Genonsgwa and the stone coats, the Flying Heads, and the Porcupine people until the boys were sleepy and the stone sent them home to their beds.

Soon the whole village was buzzing with the news of the stone and the tales. The boys led the tribe to the place where the stone stood. The people carried fresh game with them which they left for the stone. They marveled over the things called tales that fell from its mouth. No one had ever heard about "The Master of Life" and "He Who Is Our Grandfather," or his enemy "He Who Is Clad in Ice." They did not know about such things as the songs of the corn or the prayer for harvest, and the wisest among them knew then that they had known nothing until the stone had begun to speak. It took four years for the stone to tell all the tales, but the nights passed quickly.

The rock called the boy one evening after the others had left and said to him, "One day you will become old and be unable to hunt. These tales will help you in your old age. Tell the legends to others, but make sure that they give you something in return for them." And after it had told the boy the last story, the stone was silent and never spoke again.

The boy grew up and grew old. He did not forget the legends, and he told them to anyone who came to his lodge to listen. Many traveled from faraway tribes to hear the stories from the old man who had learned them from the stone when

Reading Focus

Making and Adjusting Predictions As you get more information, you may have to adjust your predictions. At this point, though, the earlier prediction about the boy becoming a storyteller still seems likely.

Analyzing Visuals

Connecting to the Text
How would hearing stories from this storyteller differ from hearing the storytelling stone recite them?

he was a boy. They gladly gave him tobacco, meat, and pelts, for he knew the stories of their beginnings, too, and could tell them as well as the ones about his own tribe. There were few nights when his lodge did not have a crowd of listeners, enthralled[1] and intent, catching the tales to take home with them to their own hearths.

That is the way stories came to be and why there are many stories in the world where none had been before. The people from the other world before ours, the ones who had the strong and wonderful magic that the stone told about, are the ones we cannot stop telling stories about, even today.

1. **enthralled** (ehn THRAWLD): fascinated; held captive by interest.

Read with a Purpose According to this folk tale, how did stories come to be?

Literary Focus

Forms of Fiction: Folk Tale Characters in folk tales are often simple "types" rather than complicated individuals. The boy, whose name we never learn, is now an old man who passes down the stories he heard. The fact that people pay him for his storytelling suggests that stories are an essential part of the Seneca culture.

Reading Focus

Setting a Purpose for Reading By setting a purpose at the beginning, you were able to think about possible answers to this question as you read.

John Cech
(1944–   )

A Born Storyteller

It's no wonder that John Cech is interested in the origin of stories—he's been telling them his whole life. When he was a child, he made up tales about the famous fictional detective Sherlock Holmes to entertain his friends. According to a teacher's note on his third-grade report card, however, he spent too much time telling stories and not enough working on class assignments! That teacher would probably be proud of Cech today. He successfully balances his classroom duties as an English professor with his ongoing love of storytelling.

Literature for Kids

In fact, stories—including Cech's recollections of his own childhood—have served him well in his profession. An award-winning writer and scholar, Cech serves as director of the University of Florida's Center for Children's Literature and Culture. The center is devoted to the study of literature and other media, both classic and modern, produced for young audiences. Cech himself has written several children's books, as well as books, articles, and reviews for adults.

Time for *Recess!*

One way that Cech shares his insights into childhood with interested adults is through *Recess!*—the daily three-minute radio show that he produces and hosts. The program airs on public radio stations across the country and explores topics in children's culture. It features book and movie reviews, historical notes, and original stories and essays.

"In the events and the literature of childhood lie the seeds . . . of the imagination."

Think About the Writer Cech often writes for young people. What characteristics of a story would capture the attention of a reader your age?

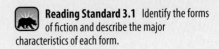

Reading Standard 3.1 Identify the forms of fiction and describe the major characteristics of each form.

Into Action: Monitoring Comprehension

You should have stopped regularly to monitor your comprehension as you read "The Storytelling Stone." Using the question-and-answer chart below, make sure that you understood the main events of the story. If you can't answer a particular question, go back and re-read the passage.

What happened? Q and A	
Q: What does the stone want to tell the boy? What does it expect from him?	A:
Q: How do the villagers react to the stories they hear?	A:
Q: When the boy is an old man, to whom does he tell stories?	A:

Talk About . . .

1. "The Storytelling Stone" illustrates the power and importance of stories. Choose a partner, and discuss why you think people enjoy reading and listening to stories, in various forms. Try to use each Academic Vocabulary word listed on the right at least once in your discussion.

Write About . . .

Answer the following questions about "The Storytelling Stone." Definitions of the underlined Academic Vocabulary words are in the column on the right.

2. Identify some of the special <u>characteristics</u> of folk tales that are evident in this story.

3. Explain the <u>concept</u> of an oral tradition. How are you able to read "The Storytelling Stone" today even though it wasn't written down for generations and its original author is unknown?

Writing Skills Focus
Think as a Reader/Writer

In Chapter 4, you'll read different forms of fiction. The Writing Skills Focus activities on the Preparing to Read pages show you how each writer makes his or her writing unique and interesting. On the Applying Your Skills pages, you'll practice using these aspects of a writer's craft in your own writing.

Academic Vocabulary for Chapter 4

Talking and Writing About Forms of Fiction

Academic Vocabulary is the language you use to write and talk about literature. Use these words to discuss the fiction you read in this chapter. They are underlined throughout the chapter.

characteristics (kar ihk tuh RIHS tihks) *n.*: important, typical parts or features. *The different forms of fiction each have defining characteristics.*

concept (KAHN sehpt) *n.*: idea of how something is or could be. *The concept of storytelling exists in all cultures.*

indicate (IHN duh kayt) *v.*: show; express; suggest. *What characteristics of "The Storytelling Stone" indicate that the story is a folk tale?*

interpret (ihn TUR priht) *v.*: decide on the meaning of something. *When we interpret stories, we can learn lessons about life.*

Your Turn

Copy the words from the Academic Vocabulary list into your *Reader/Writer Notebook*. Then, use each word in different sentences about your favorite story. Practice using these Academic Vocabulary words as you discuss and write about the selections in this chapter.

La Bamba

by **Gary Soto**

What Do You Think?

How can reading stories about events in the life of a young person like yourself give you insights into your own life?

 QuickWrite

Most lists of "Top Ten Things People Fear Most" include "public speaking" and "performing in front of an audience." When have you had to perform in front of an audience? What was it like? Record a few notes about the experience.

Reader/Writer Notebook

Use your **RWN** to complete the activities for this selection.

Reading Standard 3.1 Identify the forms of fiction and describe the major characteristics of each form.

Literary Skills Focus

Forms of Fiction: Identifying the Characteristics of the Short Story Some forms of fiction have existed for centuries, but the short story is a newcomer. It became popular in the United States during the nineteenth century. At that time, magazines were beginning to be published, and new stories appeared in each issue.

A **short story** is a brief fictional narrative that is usually five to twenty pages long. Short stories can cover any subject.

Reading Skills Focus

Story and Structure Short stories are built in the same way as other forms of fiction: They have a character or characters dealing with a **conflict** (problem), main events that lead to a **climax,** and a **resolution** of the conflict. You can use a chart like the one on the right to map the structure of most stories. These building blocks are also found in novels and novellas, but the short story is defined by its shorter length. The typical short story has just one or two main characters and one conflict. Good short stories deliver an emotional punch, and they deliver it quickly.

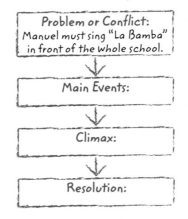

Problem or Conflict: Manuel must sing "La Bamba" in front of the whole school.

↓

Main Events:

↓

Climax:

↓

Resolution:

Into Action Complete a chart like the one above as you read "La Bamba."

Writing Skills Focus

Think as a Reader/Writer

Find It in Your Reading As you read this short story, identify at least five details that help make the main character, Manuel, and his experiences come alive for you. Record these details in your *Reader/Writer Notebook*.

Vocabulary

jammed (jamd) *v.:* got stuck and became unworkable. *When the lever jammed, Mr. Roybal frowned.*

maneuvered (muh NOO vuhrd) *v.:* moved, as a group, into position. *The students maneuvered back onto the stage.*

groove (groov) *n.:* state of being comfortable. *Manuel got into the groove once he felt more relaxed on the stage.*

cast (kast) *n.:* group of performers in a play or event. *The audience appreciated the cast's efforts.*

Language Coach

Oral Fluency Two of the words above have the same vowel sound, but that vowel sound is spelled in a different way in each word. Identify the two words that have the same vowel sound but very different spellings.

Learn It Online
For a preview of this story, see the video introduction on:

go.hrw.com   H6-355   **Go**

Learn It Online
Read more about Soto online at:
go.hrw.com H6-356 Go

Gary Soto
(1952–)

"My Friends . . . Jump Up and Down on the Page"

Gary Soto grew up in a Mexican American family in California's San Joaquin (SAN waw KEEN) Valley. He remembers himself as an active kid who liked the playground better than the classroom and loved to compete against others in games. He was not a very good student, he claims, until he went to college and discovered poetry—and an urge to become a writer himself. He won recognition by recapturing the world of his childhood in words.

> "When I first started writing recollections and short stories . . . I needed full-fledged stories and the patience of a monk. I needed to recall the narrative, characters, small moments, dates, places, etc. I was responsible for my writing, and, thus, it was tremendous work to keep it all in order. When I was writing *Living Up the Street* . . . I wrote, rewrote, and rewrote the rewrite, so that my friends would jump up and down on the page."

Think About the Writer How does a writer many years older than you are, like Soto, convey what it's like to be your age?

Build Background

The first digitally recorded music came on the market in the early 1980s in the form of audio CDs. The birth of the CD signaled the end of the long era of the vinyl record, which had been the primary audio format of the twentieth century.

Records are vinyl disks that contain cut grooves. These grooves correspond to sound waves. Putting a stylus, or needle, into the grooves and rotating the record on a turntable, or record player, made the stylus vibrate, which reproduced the recorded sounds.

Records got scratched easily by being dropped or mishandled—or even from a slip of the stylus that read the grooves. A scratch could ruin a record by making the needle get stuck, playing the same section of music over and over.

Preview the Selection

Manuel is the story's main character, an average kid attending a typical school. As the story begins, he is regretting his decision to participate in his school's talent show.

La Bamba

by **Gary Soto**

Manuel was the fourth of seven children and looked like a lot of kids in his neighborhood: black hair, brown face, and skinny legs scuffed from summer play. But summer was giving way to fall: The trees were turning red, the lawns brown, and the pomegranate trees were heavy with fruit. Manuel walked to school in the frosty morning, kicking leaves and thinking of tomorrow's talent show. He was still amazed that he had volunteered. He was going to pretend to sing Ritchie Valens's[1] "La Bamba" before the entire school.

Why did I raise my hand? he asked himself, but in his heart he knew the answer. He yearned for the limelight. He wanted applause as loud as a thunderstorm and to hear his friends say, "Man, that was bad!" And he wanted to impress the girls, especially Petra Lopez, the second-prettiest girl in his class. The prettiest was already taken by his friend Ernie. Manuel knew he should be reasonable since he himself was not great-looking, just average. **Ⓐ**

Manuel kicked through the fresh-fallen leaves. When he got to school, he realized he had forgotten his math workbook. If the teacher found out, he would have to stay after school and miss practice for the talent show. But fortunately for him, they did drills that morning.

During lunch Manuel hung around with Benny, who was also in the talent show. Benny was going to play the trumpet in spite of the fat lip he had gotten playing football.

"How do I look?" Manuel asked. He cleared his throat and started moving his lips in pantomime. No words came out, just a hiss that sounded like a snake. Manuel tried to look emotional, flailing his arms on the high notes and opening his eyes and mouth as wide as he could when he came to "Para bailar la baaaaammmba."[2]

After Manuel finished, Benny said it looked all right but suggested Manuel dance while he sang. Manuel thought for a moment and decided it was a good idea.

"Yeah, just think you're like Michael

---

1. **Ritchie Valens** (1941–1959), the professional singer mentioned in the story, was the first Mexican American rock star. In 1959, when he was only seventeen, Valens was killed in a plane crash.

2. **para bailar la bamba** (PAH rah BY lahr lah BAHM bah): Spanish for "to dance the bamba."

Ⓐ **Read and Discuss** What is the author letting you know about Manuel?

Jackson or someone like that," Benny suggested. "But don't get carried away."

During rehearsal, Mr. Roybal, nervous about his debut as the school's talent co-ordinator, cursed under his breath when the lever that controlled the speed on the record player jammed.

"Darn," he growled, trying to force the lever. "What's wrong with you?"

"Is it broken?" Manuel asked, bending over for a closer look. It looked all right to him.

Mr. Roybal assured Manuel that he would have a good record player at the talent show, even if it meant bringing his own stereo from home. **B**

Manuel sat in a folding chair, twirling his record on his thumb. He watched a skit about personal hygiene, a mother-and-daughter violin duo, five first-grade girls jumping rope, a karate kid breaking boards, three girls singing "Like a Virgin," and a skit about the pilgrims. If the record player hadn't been broken, he would have gone after the karate kid, an easy act to follow, he told himself.

As he twirled his forty-five record, Manuel thought they had a great talent show. The entire school would be amazed. His mother and father would be proud, and his brothers and sisters would be jealous and pout. It would be a night to remember. **C**

Benny walked onto the stage, raised his trumpet to his mouth, and waited for his cue. Mr. Roybal raised his hand like a symphony conductor and let it fall dramatically. Benny inhaled and blew so loud that Manuel dropped his record, which rolled across the cafeteria floor until it hit a wall. Manuel raced after it, picked it up, and wiped it clean.

"Boy, I'm glad it didn't break," he said with a sigh.

That night Manuel had to do the dishes and a lot of homework, so he could only practice in the shower. In bed he prayed that he wouldn't mess up. He prayed that it wouldn't be like when he was a first-grader. For Science Week he had wired together a C battery and a bulb and told everyone he had discovered how a flashlight worked. He was so pleased with himself that he practiced for hours pressing the wire to the battery, making the bulb wink a dim, orangish light. He showed it to so many kids in his neighborhood that when it was time to show his class how a flashlight worked, the battery was dead. He pressed the wire to the battery, but the bulb didn't respond. He pressed until his thumb hurt and some kids in the back started snickering.

But Manuel fell asleep confident that nothing would go wrong this time.

The next morning his father and mother beamed at him. They were proud that he was going to be in the talent show.

"I wish you would tell us what you're doing," his mother said. His father, a

---

B **Reading Focus** **Story and Structure** Based on this conversation between Manuel and Mr. Roybal, what do you predict will be the story's main conflict?

C **Read and Discuss** What do Manuel's thoughts about his family indicate about him?

Vocabulary **jammed** (jamd) *v.*: got stuck and became unworkable.

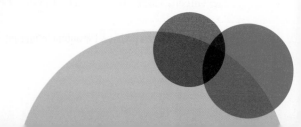

pharmacist who wore a blue smock with his name on a plastic rectangle, looked up from the newspaper and sided with his wife. "Yes, what are you doing in the talent show?"

"You'll see," Manuel said, with his mouth full of Cheerios.

The day whizzed by, and so did his afternoon chores and dinner. Suddenly he was dressed in his best clothes and standing next to Benny backstage, listening to the commotion as the cafeteria filled with school kids and parents. The lights dimmed, and Mr. Roybal, sweaty in a tight suit and a necktie with a large knot, wet his lips and parted the stage curtains. **Ⓓ**

"Good evening, everyone," the kids behind the curtain heard him say. "Good evening to you," some of the smart-alecky kids said back to him.

"Tonight we bring you the best John Burroughs Elementary has to offer, and I'm sure that you'll be both pleased and amazed that our little school houses so much talent. And now, without further ado, let's get on with the show." He turned and, with a swish of his hand, commanded, "Part the curtain." The curtains parted in jerks. A girl dressed as a toothbrush and a boy dressed as a dirty gray tooth walked onto the stage and sang:

Brush, brush, brush
Floss, floss, floss
Gargle the germs away—hey! hey! hey!

After they finished singing, they turned to Mr. Roybal, who dropped his hand. The toothbrush dashed around the stage after

Why do you think Manuel chooses to pantomime a song by the 1950s Latino rock star Ritchie Valens, shown here?

the dirty tooth, which was laughing and having a great time until it slipped and nearly rolled off the stage.

Mr. Roybal jumped out and caught it just in time. "Are you OK?"

The dirty tooth answered, "Ask my dentist," which drew laughter and applause from the audience.

The violin duo played next, and except for one time when the girl got lost, they sounded fine. People applauded, and

Ⓓ **Literary Focus** **Short Story** What are the main events of the story so far? Who is the main character, and what does he want? What might stand in his way?

some even stood up. Then the first-grade girls maneuvered onto the stage while jumping rope. They were all smiles and bouncing ponytails as a hundred cameras flashed at once. Mothers "awed" and fathers sat up proudly.

The karate kid was next. He did a few kicks, yells, and chops, and finally, when his father held up a board, punched it in two. The audience clapped and looked at each other, wide-eyed with respect. The boy bowed to the audience, and father and son ran off the stage.

Manuel remained behind the stage, shivering with fear. He mouthed the words to "La Bamba" and swayed left to right. Why did he raise his hand and volunteer? Why couldn't he have just sat there like the rest of the kids and not said anything? While the karate kid was onstage, Mr. Roybal, more sweaty than before, took Manuel's forty-five record and placed it on a new record player. **(E)**

"You ready?" Mr. Roybal asked.
"Yeah . . ."

Mr. Roybal walked back on stage and announced that Manuel Gomez, a fifth-grader in Mrs. Knight's class, was going to pantomime Ritchie Valens's classic hit "La Bamba."

The cafeteria roared with applause. Manuel was nervous but loved the noisy crowd. He pictured his mother and father applauding loudly and his brothers and sisters also clapping, though not as energetically.

Manuel walked on stage and the song started immediately. Glassy-eyed from the shock of being in front of so many people, Manuel moved his lips and swayed in a made-up dance step. He couldn't see his parents, but he could see his brother Mario, who was a year younger, thumb-wrestling with a friend. Mario was wearing Manuel's favorite shirt; he would deal with Mario later. He saw some other kids get up and head for the drinking fountain, and a baby sitting in the middle of an aisle sucking her thumb and watching him intently.

What am I doing here? thought

(E) Read and Discuss How would you interpret Manuel's behavior now?

Vocabulary   maneuvered (muh NOO vuhrd) *v.*: moved, as a group, into position.

Manuel. This is no fun at all. Everyone was just sitting there. Some people were moving to the beat, but most were just watching him, like they would a monkey at the zoo. **F**

But when Manuel did a fancy dance step, there was a burst of applause and some girls screamed. Manuel tried another dance step. He heard more applause and screams and started getting into the groove as he shivered and snaked like Michael Jackson around the stage. But the record got stuck, and he had to sing

Para bailar la bamba
Para bailar la bamba
Para bailar la bamba
Para bailar la bamba
again and again. **G**

Manuel couldn't believe his bad luck. The audience began to laugh and stand up in their chairs. Manuel remembered how the forty-five record had dropped from his hand and rolled across the cafeteria floor. It probably got scratched, he thought, and now it was stuck, and he was stuck dancing and moving his lips to the same words over and over. He had never been so embarrassed. He would have to ask his parents to move the family out of town.

After Mr. Roybal ripped the needle across the record, Manuel slowed his dance steps to a halt. He didn't know what to do except bow to the audience, which applauded wildly, and scoot off the stage, on the verge of tears. This was worse than the homemade flashlight. At least no one laughed then; they just snickered.

Manuel stood alone, trying hard to hold back the tears as Benny, center stage, played his trumpet. Manuel was jealous because he sounded great, then mad as he recalled that it was Benny's loud trumpet playing that made the forty-five record fly out of his hands. But when the entire cast lined up for a curtain call, Manuel received a burst of applause that was so loud it shook the walls of the cafeteria. Later, as he mingled with the kids and parents, everyone patted him on the shoulder and told him, "Way to go. You were really funny." **H**

Funny? Manuel thought. Did he do something funny?

Funny. Crazy. Hilarious. These were the words people said to him. He was confused but beyond caring. All he knew was that people were paying attention to him, and his brothers and sisters looked at him with a mixture of jealousy and awe. He was going to pull Mario aside and punch him in the arm for wearing his shirt, but he cooled it. He was enjoying the limelight. A teacher brought him cookies and punch, and the popular kids who had never before given him the time of day now clustered around him. Ricardo, the editor of the school bulletin, asked him how he made the needle stick.

"It just happened," Manuel said, crunching on a star-shaped cookie.

At home that night his father, eager

F [Read and Discuss] What does Manuel mean when he says that people "were watching him, like they would a monkey at the zoo"? What is he feeling at this point in the story?

G [Reading Focus] **Story and Structure** What is the cause of Manuel's conflict?

H [Read and Discuss] What is the reaction to Manuel's performance? Explain whether this matches his <u>concept</u> of what happened.

Vocabulary **groove** (groov) *n.*: state of being comfortable.
cast (kast) *n.*: group of performers in a play or event.

Analyzing Visuals

Connecting to the Text
Is this audience reacting the way you imagined Manuel's audience reacted? Why or why not?

to undo the buttons on his shirt and ease into his La-Z-Boy recliner, asked Manuel the same thing, how he managed to make the song stick on the words "Para bailar la bamba."

Manuel thought quickly and reached for scientific jargon he had read in magazines. "Easy, Dad. I used laser tracking with high optics and low functional decibels per channel." His proud but confused father told him to be quiet and go to bed. **❶**

"Ah, que niños tan truchas,"[3] he said as

---

3. **que niños tan truchas** (kay NEEN yohs tahn TROO chahs): Spanish for "what smart kids."

he walked to the kitchen for a glass of milk. "I don't know how you kids nowadays get so smart."

Manuel, feeling happy, went to his bedroom, undressed, and slipped into his pajamas. He looked in the mirror and began to pantomime "La Bamba," but stopped because he was tired of the song. He crawled into bed. The sheets were as cold as the moon that stood over the peach tree in their backyard.

He was relieved that the day was over. Next year, when they asked for volunteers for the talent show, he wouldn't raise his hand. Probably. **❿**

---

❶ **Literary Focus** Short Story *Interpret* Manuel's answer to his father's question. Why does he give his father a different answer than he gave Ricardo?

❿ **Read and Discuss** What do you learn about Manuel when he decides that he *probably* won't volunteer for the talent show next year?

Applying Your Skills

Reading Standard 3.1 Identify the forms of fiction and describe the major characteristics of each form.

La Bamba
Literary Response and Analysis

Reading Skills Focus
Quick Check

1. What did Manuel volunteer to do at the talent show? *Why* did he volunteer?

2. What almost breaks during a rehearsal? What effect does this incident have on the story?

Read with a Purpose

3. How does Manuel feel about the talent show before, during, and after his performance?

Reading Skills: Story and Structure

4. Review the structure chart you filled in as you read the story. Now, add a final box in which you state the story's main emotional impact. Was it humorous? nostalgic? rousing? Explain your answer.

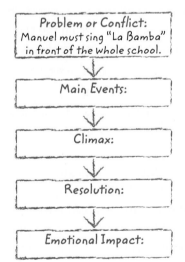

Problem or Conflict:
Manuel must sing "La Bamba"
in front of the whole school.

↓

Main Events:

↓

Climax:

↓

Resolution:

↓

Emotional Impact:

Literary Skills Focus
Literary Analysis

5. **Compare** Compare Manuel's <u>concept</u> of what being in the talent show would be like with his actual experience onstage. Why didn't the audience view Manuel's performance as a disaster?

6. **Describe** What words or phrases in the story best <u>indicate</u> the type of person Manuel is?

7. **Interpret** A **simile** is a comparison between two very different things using a word such as *like* or *as*. Identify the simile used to describe the audience as Manuel takes the stage. What does this comparison <u>indicate</u> about Manuel?

Literary Skills: Short Story

8. **Analyze** What is the major **conflict,** or problem, that Manuel must overcome in this story? How is the conflict finally resolved?

9. **Extend** How do you imagine a novel about Manuel's experiences would differ from this short story? Compare and contrast the <u>characteristics</u> of each form.

Literary Skills Review: Character

10. **Evaluate** Manuel remembers his attempt to show how a flashlight works. What does this memory tell you about Manuel's **character**?

Writing Skills Focus
Think as a Reader/Writer
Use It in Your Writing Write a short narrative about another talent show participant. Use descriptive details to bring the character to life.

What Do
You
Think
Now

How would you react to an embarrassing situation such as Manuel's talent show experience?

Applying Your Skills

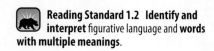

La Bamba

Vocabulary Development

Words with Multiple Meanings

Multiple-meaning words have more than one meaning. Often, the different meanings are completely unrelated to one another. When you look up a multiple-meaning word in a dictionary, you'll find a numbered list of definitions, as in this example:

shower (SHOW uhr) *n.* **1.** a brief rainfall **2.** a party at which someone is honored and given gifts **3.** a bath in which water pours down on the body —*v.* **1.** to spray **2.** to pour forth like a shower **3.** to take a shower

If you see a multiple-meaning word and you're not sure which definition is intended, look at the word's **context,** or the words that surround it. If the word *shower* appears with words like *weather*, *rain*, *soaked*, or *umbrella*, you know that *shower* must refer to rainfall. If you're still confused, look at the definitions listed in a dictionary and choose the one that makes the most sense in the sentence.

Here is a sentence from "La Bamba." Which definition of *shower* fits in this context?

> "That night Manuel had to do the dishes and a lot of homework, so he could only practice in the shower."

The sentence below is not from the story. Which definition of *shower* fits in this context?

> Manuel's family threw his older sister a shower before her wedding.

Your Turn

Choose two of the Vocabulary words at the right. For each one, write *two* sentences that demonstrate *two* distinct meanings of the word. Use a dictionary for help.

jammed
maneuvered
groove
cast

Language Coach

Oral Fluency Many words in English have the same vowel sound but different spellings. The two examples listed here have the same /oo/ sound, but each is spelled in a different way. A Vocabulary word above, *maneuvered,* shows you a third way to spell this /oo/ sound. Think of three words that contain the same vowel sound spelled in different ways.

new
boot

Academic Vocabulary

Talk About . . .
Describe Manuel's <u>concept</u> of his family. What do his views <u>indicate</u> about his relationship with them? <u>Interpret</u> Manuel's ideas about his family, and write your ideas in your *Reader/Writer Notebook*.

 **Learn It Online**
For vocabulary tutorials, visit *WordSharp* on:
go.hrw.com H6-364 **Go**

Grammar Link
Choosing the Correct Forms of Pronouns

The **case** of a pronoun shows how it is used in a sentence. A pronoun that is the subject of a verb is in the **nominative case:**

He was in the talent contest.

A pronoun that is a direct object, indirect object, or object of a preposition is in the **objective case:**

The record player confused *them*. (direct object)
Manuel watched *her* jump rope. (indirect object)
The audience laughed loudly at *him*. (object of a preposition)

If you know whether a pronoun is acting as the subject or the object of the verb, you can choose the correct form of the pronoun. Most personal pronouns have different forms for the nominative and objective cases, as shown below.

SINGULAR PERSONAL PRONOUNS

Nominative Case	Objective Case
I	me
you	you
he, she, it	him, her, it

PLURAL PERSONAL PRONOUNS

Nominative Case	Objective Case
we	us
you	you
they	them

Your Turn

Identify the correct pronoun in the parentheses.
1. He gave (he, him) the record.
2. (They, Them) jumped rope in the talent show.
3. Mr. Roybal introduced (she, her) to the audience.

CHOICES

As your respond to the Choices, use these **Academic Vocabulary** words as appropriate: characteristics, concept, indicate, interpret.

REVIEW
Analyze the Story

Timed ⏱Writing In a brief essay, identify the characteristics of "La Bamba" that make it a short story. Then, using your structure chart from page 363, describe the story's **conflict, climax,** and **resolution.** Indicate whether you think the resolution is believable. Support your conclusion with details from the story.

CONNECT
Create a Brochure

Group Work With a small group, develop a concept for a brochure called "How to Deal with Stage Fright." Find articles and books on the topic and interview people who often perform or speak in public, such as musicians and business consultants. Write up the information you've collected in the form of a brochure.

EXTEND
Research Two Technologies

TechFocus Find information in a library or on the Internet that explains the way sound is recorded and played back on vinyl records and compact discs. Draw diagrams to help explain the process of recording sounds. Add captions that point out which features are similar and which are different for the two formats.

Learn It Online
Learn more with the Internet links at:
go.hrw.com | H6-365 | Go

Preparing to Read

The Gold Cadillac

by **Mildred D. Taylor**

What Do **You** Think? | How can a fictional story give us different insights into historical events than a nonfiction account can?

QuickWrite

At one time in the United States, African Americans were not allowed to eat in certain restaurants, which were for whites only. Write down your thoughts about this.

Reader/Writer
Notebook
Use your **RWN** to complete the
activities for this selection.

Reading Standard 3.1 Identify the forms
of fiction and describe the major characteristics of each form.

Literary Skills Focus

**Forms of Fiction: Identifying the Characteristics of the
Novella** The novel, novella, and short story are all members of the
family of fiction. They each have a plot, characters, a setting, and a
theme—elements you've learned about in Chapters 1 through 3. A
novella is short enough to be published with other stories yet long
enough to be published by itself. *The Gold Cadillac* is a novella; it was
first published as a short book.

Literary Perspectives Apply the literary perspective described on
page 369 as you read this novella.

Reading Skills Focus

Making and Adjusting Predictions When you read, you use clues
from the text and your own experiences to **make predictions** about
what will happen next in the plot or will be revealed about a character
next. As you continue reading, new information may cause you to <u>interpret</u> what is going on in a new way and to **adjust your predictions.**

Into Action When you are prompted to make a prediction—or when
one occurs to you—stop and use a chart like the one below to <u>indicate</u>
what's happening in the story. Then, record your prediction and give a
reason for it. Adjust your predictions as necessary.

In the story	I predict	Because
the narrator and her sister see the Cadillac	that the father bought it	the father drives up in it and is grinning

Writing Skills Focus

Think as a Reader/Writer

Find It in Your Reading As you read this novella, use your *Reader/
Writer Notebook* to record details from the story that relate to such
<u>concepts</u> as beauty, richness, pride, and luxury. Identify where these
details appear, and explain what they add to the story.

Learn It Online
Check out the *PowerNotes* introduction to this story
online at:

go.hrw.com   H6-367   **Go**

Learn It Online
Read more about Taylor online at:
go.hrw.com H6-368 Go

Mildred D. Taylor
(1943–   )

Weaving Memories into Fiction

Mildred D. Taylor was born in Mississippi, but her family moved to the North when she was only a few months old, escaping segregation, the enforced separation of white people and African Americans. Taylor has always drawn upon her memories of both the North and South in her work.

Road Trips

Even though Taylor's family relocated, they maintained their ties to Mississippi and the South. They made a yearly trek back to Mississippi to visit the relatives who remained. In fact, car trips became an important part of family life.

> "Because my father, my uncles, and my older male cousins all loved cars, we often rode in caravan out to the park, where the men would park their cars in a long, impressive row and shine them in the shade of the trees. . . . And sometimes we took even longer trips, down country highways into the land called the South."

Nancy N. Jacobs

Think About the Writer

If you were a writer, which of your own experiences would you draw on for *your* stories?

Build Background

This story takes place around 1950—a period between the end of the Civil War (1861–1865), when African Americans were freed from slavery, and the civil rights era (1955–1968), in which they were finally granted full and equal rights in American society. During this time, black Americans were segregated, or kept apart, from white Americans in many ways. For example, African Americans often had to use separate bathrooms, sit in the backs of buses, or see movies in their own theaters. Segregation was especially widespread and severe in the South.

By 1950, the U.S. Army had already been desegregated. Therefore, black soldiers could serve and fight alongside white soldiers. Some of the characters in this story served in the military. Although black soldiers served their country honorably abroad, at home they faced discrimination.

Preview the Selection

The narrator of this story goes by a somewhat unusual nickname—**'lois.** (The apostrophe means it's short for her full first name.) The other members of 'lois's immediate family are her older sister, **Wilma,** her mother, **Dee,** and her father, **Wilbert.**

The Gold Cadillac

by **Mildred D. Taylor**

My sister and I were playing out on the front lawn when the gold Cadillac rolled up and my father stepped from behind the wheel. We ran to him, our eyes filled with wonder. "Daddy, whose Cadillac?" I asked.

And Wilma demanded, "Where's our Mercury?"

My father grinned. "Go get your mother and I'll tell you all about it."

"Is it ours?" I cried. "Daddy, is it ours?"

"Get your mother!" he laughed. "And tell her to hurry!"

Wilma and I ran off to obey, as Mr. Pondexter next door came from his house to see what this new Cadillac was all about. We threw open the front door, ran through the downstairs front parlor and straight through the house to the kitchen, where my mother was cooking and one of my aunts was helping her. "Come on, Mother-Dear!" we cried together. "Daddy say come on out and see this new car!"

"What?" said my mother, her face showing her surprise. "What're you talking about?" Ⓐ

"A Cadillac!" I cried.

"He said hurry up!" relayed Wilma.

And then we took off again, up the back stairs to the second floor of the duplex. Running down the hall, we banged on all the apartment doors. My uncles and their wives stepped to the doors. It was good it was a Saturday morning. Everybody was home.

Literary Perspectives

The following perspective will help you think about the characters and events in *The Gold Cadillac*.

Analyzing Credibility in Literature All fiction asks us to suspend disbelief—to let ourselves be pulled into the world of a story even though we know it is not real. In myths, fables, and folk tales, we expect magical occurrences and other unrealistic characteristics. In realistic fiction, however, we expect the characters and plot to be more believable, or credible. For example, if a character doesn't talk and act the way a real person might, we find ourselves questioning the credibility of that character. Credibility is particularly important in historical fiction—fiction based on things that really happened. Consider the credibility of this novella, an example of historical fiction. As you read, pay attention to the questions in the text, which will guide you in using this perspective.

Ⓐ **Reading Focus Making Predictions** How do you predict 'lois's mother will react when she sees the new car?

"We got us a Cadillac! We got us a Cadillac!" Wilma and I proclaimed in unison.[1] **B**

We had decided that the Cadillac had to be ours if our father was driving it and holding on to the keys. "Come on see!" Then we raced on, through the upstairs sunroom, down the front steps, through the downstairs sunroom, and out to the Cadillac. Mr. Pondexter was still there. Mr. LeRoy and Mr. Courtland from down the street were there too, and all were admiring the Cadillac as my father stood proudly by, pointing out the various features.

"Brand-new 1950 Coupe deVille!" I heard one of the men saying.

"Just off the showroom floor!" my father said. "I just couldn't resist it."

My sister and I eased up to the car and peeked in. It was all gold inside. Gold leather seats. Gold carpeting. Gold dashboard. It was like no car we had owned before. It looked like a car for rich folks.

"Daddy, are we rich?" I asked. My father laughed.

"Daddy, it's ours, isn't it?" asked Wilma, who was older and more practical than I. She didn't intend to give her heart too quickly to something that wasn't hers.

"You like it?"

"Oh, Daddy, yes!"

He looked at me. "What 'bout you, 'lois?" **C**

---

1. **in unison** (ihn YOO nuh suhn): in chorus; in the same words, spoken at the same time.

"Yes, sir!"

My father laughed again. "Then I expect I can't much disappoint my girls, can I? It's ours, all right!"

Wilma and I hugged our father with our joy. My uncles came from the house, and my aunts, carrying their babies, came out too. Everybody surrounded the car and owwed and ahhed. Nobody could believe it. **D**

Then my mother came out.

Everybody stood back grinning as she approached the car. There was no smile on her face. We all waited for her to speak. She stared at the car, then looked at my father, standing there as proud as he could be. Finally she said, "You didn't buy this car, did you, Wilbert?"

"Gotta admit I did. Couldn't resist it."

"But . . . but what about our Mercury? It was perfectly good!"

"Don't you like the Cadillac, Dee?"

"That Mercury wasn't even a year old!"

My father nodded. "And I'm sure whoever buys it is going to get themselves a good car. But we've got ourselves a better one. Now stop frowning, honey, and let's take ourselves a ride in our brand-new Cadillac!"

My mother shook her head. "I've got food on the stove," she said and, turning away, walked back to the house.

There was an awkward silence, and then my father said, "You know Dee never did much like surprises. Guess this here Cadillac was a bit too much for her. I best go smooth things out with her."

B | Read and Discuss | What has the author set up for you so far?

C | Literary Focus | Novella Who is the main character in this novella? How can you tell?

D | Read and Discuss | What does this scene reveal about the relationship between the sisters and their father?

Elm and Cumberland View #3 by Connie Hayes.

Everybody watched as he went after my mother. But when he came back, he was alone.

"Well, what she say?" asked one of my uncles.

My father shrugged and smiled. "Told me I bought this Cadillac alone, I could just ride in it alone."

Another uncle laughed. "Uh-oh! Guess she told you!"

"Oh, she'll come around," said one of my aunts. "Any woman would be proud to ride in this car." **E**

"That's what I'm banking on," said my father as he went around to the street side of the car and opened the door. "All right! Who's for a ride?" **F**

"We are!" Wilma and I cried.

All three of my uncles and one of my aunts, still holding her baby, and Mr. Pondexter climbed in with us, and we took off for the first ride in the gold Cadillac. It was a glorious ride, and we drove all through the city of Toledo. We rode past the church and past the school. We rode through Ottawa

---

E [Read and Discuss] How has Dee acted in this scene? How do you interpret her behavior?

F **Literary Perspectives** Analyzing Credibility in Literature Does the dialogue (the characters' spoken words) here make these characters seem more credible or less credible? Explain.

Hills, where the rich folks lived, and on into Walbridge Park and past the zoo, then along the Maumee River. But none of us had had enough of the car, so my father put the car on the road and we drove all the way to Detroit. We had plenty of family there, and everybody was just as pleased as could be about the Cadillac. My father told our Detroit relatives that he was in the doghouse with my mother about buying the Cadillac. My uncles told them she wouldn't ride in the car. All the Detroit family thought that was funny, and everybody, including my father, laughed about it and said my mother would come around. **G**

It was early evening by the time we got back home, and I could see from my mother's face she had not come around. She was angry now not only about the car, but that we had been gone so long. I didn't understand that, since my father had called her as soon as we reached Detroit to let her know where we were. I had heard him myself. I didn't understand either why she did not like that fine Cadillac and thought she was being terribly disagreeable with my father. That night, as she tucked Wilma and me in bed, I told her that too.

"Is this your business?" she asked.

"Well, I just think you ought to be nice to Daddy. I think you ought to ride in that car with him! It'd sure make him happy."

"I think you ought to go to sleep," she said and turned out the light.

Later I heard her arguing with my father. "We're supposed to be saving for a house!" she said.

"We've already got a house!" said my father.

"But you said you wanted a house in a better neighborhood. I thought that's what we both said!"

"I haven't changed my mind."

"Well, you have a mighty funny way of saving for it, then. Your brothers are saving for houses of their own, and you don't see them out buying new cars every year!"

"We'll still get the house, Dee. That's a promise!"

"Not with new Cadillacs we won't!" said my mother, and then she said a very loud good night, and all was quiet.

The next day was Sunday, and everybody figured that my mother would be sure to give in and ride in the Cadillac. After all, the family always went to church together on Sunday. But she didn't give in. What was worse, she wouldn't let Wilma and me ride in the Cadillac either. She took us each by the hand, walked past the Cadillac where my father stood waiting, and headed on toward the church three blocks away. I was really mad at her now. I had been looking forward to driving up to the church in that gold Cadillac and having everybody see. **H**

On most Sunday afternoons during the summertime, my mother, my father, Wilma, and I would go for a ride. Sometimes we just rode around the city and visited friends and family. Sometimes we made short trips over to Chicago or Peoria or Detroit to see relatives there or to Cleveland, where we had relatives too, but we could also see the Cleveland Indians play. Sometimes we

---

G **Literary Focus** Novella So far, where have the events of this novella taken place?

H **Read and Discuss** What does this section indicate about Dee's anger regarding the Cadillac purchase?

joined our aunts and uncles and drove in a caravan[2] out to the park or to the beach. At the park or the beach, Wilma and I would run and play. My mother and my aunts would spread a picnic, and my father and my uncles would shine their cars.

But on this Sunday afternoon, my mother refused to ride anywhere. She told Wilma and me that we could go. So we left her alone in the big, empty house, and the family cars, led by the gold Cadillac, headed for the park. For a while I played and had a good time, but then I stopped playing and went to sit with my father. Despite his laughter he seemed sad to me. I think he was missing my mother as much as I was. **①**

That evening, my father took my mother to dinner down at the corner cafe. They walked. Wilma and I stayed at the house, chasing fireflies in the backyard. My aunts and uncles sat in the yard and on the porch, talking and laughing about the day and watching us. It was a soft summer's evening, the kind that came every day and was expected. The smell of charcoal and of barbecue drifting from up the block, the sound of laughter and music

and talk drifting from yard to yard were all a part of it. Soon one of my uncles joined Wilma and me in our chase of fireflies, and when my mother and father came home, we were at it still. My mother and father watched us for a while, while everybody else watched them to see if my father would take out the Cadillac and if my mother would slide in beside him to take a ride. But it soon became evident that the dinner had not changed my mother's mind. She still refused to ride in the Cadillac. I just couldn't understand her objection to it. **①**

Though my mother didn't like the Cadillac, everybody else in the neighborhood certainly did. That meant quite a few folks too, since we lived on a very busy block. On one corner was a grocery store, a cleaner's, and a gas station. Across the street was a beauty shop and a fish market, and down the street was a bar, another grocery store, the Dixie Theater, the cafe, and a drugstore. There were always people strolling to or from one of these places, and because our house was right in the middle of the block, just about everybody had to pass our house and the gold Cadillac. Sometimes people took in the Cadillac as they walked, their heads turning for a longer look as they passed. Then

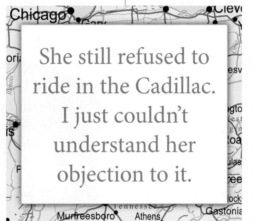

She still refused to ride in the Cadillac. I just couldn't understand her objection to it.

---

2. **caravan** (KAR uh van): group of cars traveling together.

---

① **Literary Perspectives** **Analyzing Credibility in Literature** Nobody seems to agree with Dee's objection to the Cadillac purchase. Explain whether you think her reaction is believable or not.

① **Read and Discuss** How have these scenes added to what you know about 'lois's father and mother?

Vocabulary **evident** (EHV uh duhnt) *adj.*: easily seen or understood; obvious.

there were people who just outright stopped and took a good look before continuing on their way. I was proud to say that car belonged to my family. I felt mighty important as people called to me as I ran down the street. "'Ey, 'lois! How's that Cadillac, girl? Riding fine?" I told my mother how much everybody liked that car. She was not impressed and made no comment. **(K)**

Since just about everybody on the block knew everybody else, most folks knew that my mother wouldn't ride in the Cadillac. Because of that, my father took a lot of good-natured kidding from the men. My mother got kidded too, as the women said if she didn't ride in that car, maybe some other woman would. And everybody laughed about it and began to bet on who would give in first, my mother or my father. But then my father said he was going to drive the car south into Mississippi to visit my grandparents, and everybody stopped laughing.

My uncles stopped.

So did my aunts.

Everybody.

"Look here, Wilbert," said one of my uncles, "it's too dangerous. It's like putting a loaded gun to your head."

"I paid good money for that car," said my father. "That gives me a right to drive it where I please. Even down to Mississippi."

My uncles argued with him and tried to talk him out of driving the car south. So did my aunts, and so did the neighbors, Mr. LeRoy, Mr. Courtland, and Mr. Pondexter. They said it was a dangerous thing, a mighty dangerous thing, for a black man to drive an expensive car into the rural South.

Analyzing Visuals **Connecting to the Text** What character traits do you infer that the girl in this portrait has in common with 'lois?

Harlem Girl 1 (1925) by Fritz Winold Reiss.

Museum of Art and Archaeology, University of Missouri-Columbia. Gift of Mr. W. Tjark Reiss.

(K) Read and Discuss | What does this part of the novella show you about 'lois?

Vocabulary **rural** (RUR uhl) *adj.*: having to do with country life.

"Not much those folks hate more'n to see a northern Negro coming down there in a fine car," said Mr. Pondexter. "They see those Ohio license plates, they'll figure you coming down uppity, trying to lord your fine car over them!"

I listened, but I didn't understand. I didn't understand why they didn't want my father to drive that car south. It was his.

"Listen to Pondexter, Wilbert!" cried another uncle. "We might've fought a war to free people overseas, but we're not free here! Man, those white folks down south'll lynch[3] you soon's look at you. You know that!" **L**

Wilma and I looked at each other. Neither one of us knew what *lynch* meant, but the word sent a shiver through us. We held each other's hand.

My father was silent, then he said: "All my life I've had to be heedful of what white folks thought. Well, I'm tired of that. I worked hard for everything I got. Got it honest, too. Now I got that Cadillac because I liked it and because it meant something to me that somebody like me from Mississippi could go and buy it. It's my car, I paid for it, and I'm driving it south." **M**

My mother, who had said nothing through all this, now stood. "Then the girls and I'll be going too," she said.

---

3. **lynch** (lihnch): kill a person without legal authority, usually by hanging. Lynchings are committed by violent mobs that have taken the law into their own hands.

"No!" said my father.

My mother only looked at him and went off to the kitchen.

My father shook his head. It seemed he didn't want us to go. My uncles looked at each other, then at my father. "You set on doing this, we'll all go," they said. "That way we can watch out for each other." My father took a moment and nodded. Then my aunts got up and went off to their kitchens too.

All the next day, my aunts and my mother cooked and the house was filled with delicious smells. They fried chicken and baked hams and cakes and sweet potato pies and mixed potato salad. They filled jugs with water and punch and coffee. Then they packed everything in huge picnic baskets, along with bread and boiled eggs, oranges and apples, plates and napkins, spoons and forks and cups. They placed all that food on the back seats of the cars. It was like a grand, grand picnic we were going on, and Wilma and I were mighty excited. We could hardly wait to start.

My father, my mother, Wilma, and I got into the Cadillac. My uncles, my aunts, my cousins got into the Ford, the Buick, and the Chevrolet, and we rolled off in our caravan headed south. Though my mother was finally riding in the Cadillac, she had no praise for it. In fact, she said nothing about it at all. She still seemed upset, and since she still seemed to feel the same about the car, I wondered why she had insisted upon making this trip with my father. **N**

L **Reading Focus** **Making Predictions** From Mr. Pondexter's and the uncles' warnings, what do you think will happen on the trip?

M **Literary Focus** **Novella** What is the main conflict, or problem, in this novella?

N **Read and Discuss** What is 'lois thinking about during the trip? What does this tell you about her?

We left the city of Toledo behind, drove through Bowling Green and down through the Ohio countryside of farms and small towns, through Dayton and Cincinnati, and across the Ohio River into Kentucky. On the other side of the river, my father stopped the car and looked back at Wilma and me and said, "Now from here on, whenever we stop and there're white people around, I don't want either one of you to say a word. *Not one word!* Your mother and I'll do the talking. That understood?"

"Yes, sir," Wilma and I both said, though we didn't truly understand why.

My father nodded, looked at my mother, and started the car again. We rolled on, down Highway 25 and through the bluegrass hills of Kentucky. Soon we began to see signs. Signs that read: "White Only, Colored Not Allowed." Hours later, we left the Bluegrass State and crossed into Tennessee. Now we saw even more of the signs saying: "White Only, Colored Not Allowed." We saw the signs above water fountains and in restaurant windows. We saw them in ice cream parlors and at hamburger stands. We saw them in front of hotels and motels, and on the restroom doors of filling stations. I didn't like the signs. I felt as if I were in a foreign land.

I couldn't understand why the signs were there, and I asked my father what the signs meant. He said they meant we couldn't drink from the water fountains. He said they meant we couldn't stop to sleep in the motels. He said they meant we couldn't stop to eat in the restaurants. I looked at the grand picnic basket I had been enjoying so much. Now I

understood why my mother had packed it. Suddenly the picnic did not seem so grand. **O**

Finally we reached Memphis. We got there at a bad time. Traffic was heavy and we got separated from the rest of the family. We tried to find them but it was no use. We had to go on alone. We reached the Mississippi state line, and soon after, we heard a police siren. A police car came up behind us. My father slowed the Cadillac, then stopped. Two white policemen got out of their car. They eyeballed the Cadillac and told my father to get out. **P**

"Whose car is this, boy?" they asked.

I saw anger in my father's eyes. "It's mine," he said.

"You're a liar," said one of the policemen. "You stole this car."

"Turn around, put your hands on top of that car, and spread-eagle," said the other policeman.

My father did as he was told. They searched him and I didn't understand why.

I didn't understand either why they had called my father a liar and didn't believe that the Cadillac was his. I wanted to ask, but I remembered my father's warning not to say a word, and I obeyed that warning.

The policemen told my father to get in the back of the police car. My father did. One policeman got back into the police car. The other policeman slid behind the wheel of our Cadillac. The police car started off. The Cadillac followed. Wilma and I looked at each other and at our mother. We didn't know what to think. We were scared.

The Cadillac followed the police car into a small town and stopped in front of

---

O Read and Discuss What is 'lois thinking about the grand picnic now?

P Reading Focus Making Predictions What do you predict the police will do to 'lois's father? Why?

Greetings from MISSISSIPPI

© CURT TEICH & CO., INC.

9A-H16

Analyzing Visuals **Connecting to the Text** Compare and contrast the tone of this postcard to the kind of greeting that 'lois and her family have received in Mississippi so far.

the police station. The policeman stepped out of our Cadillac and took the keys. The other policeman took my father into the police station.

"Mother-Dear!" Wilma and I cried. "What're they going to do to our daddy? They going to hurt him?"

"He'll be all right," said my mother. "He'll be all right." But she didn't sound so sure of that. She seemed worried. **Q**

We waited. More than three hours we waited. Finally my father came out of the police station. We had lots of questions to ask him. He said the police had given him a ticket for speeding and locked him up. But then the judge had come. My father had paid the ticket and they had let him go.

He started the Cadillac and drove slowly out of the town, below the speed limit. The police car followed us. People standing on steps and sitting on porches and in front of stores stared at us as we passed. Finally we were out of the town. The police car still followed. Dusk was falling. The night

Q [Read and Discuss] How does 'lois handle the unfolding events with the police?

Vocabulary **dusk** (duhsk) *n.*: period of time when the sky darkens as the sun goes down.

The Gold Cadillac **377**

Black Mountain, U.S. 70 (1957) by Joseph Garlock. Gouache on board (29" × 37").

grew black, and finally the police car turned around and left us.

We drove and drove. But my father was tired now and my grandparents' farm was still far away. My father said he had to get some sleep, and since my mother didn't drive, he pulled into a grove of trees at the side of the road and stopped.

"I'll keep watch," said my mother.

"Wake me if you see anybody," said my father.

"Just rest," said my mother.

So my father slept. But that bothered me. I needed him awake. I was afraid of the dark and of the woods and of whatever lurked there. My father was the one who kept us safe, he and my uncles. But already the police had taken my father away from us once today, and my uncles were lost.

"Go to sleep, baby," said my mother. "Go to sleep." **R**

But I was afraid to sleep until my father woke. I had to help my mother keep watch. I figured I had to help protect us too, in case the police came back and tried to take my father away again. There was a long, sharp knife in the picnic basket, and I took hold of it, clutching it tightly in my hand. Ready to strike, I sat there in the back of the car, eyes wide, searching the blackness outside the Cadillac. Wilma, for a while, searched the night too, then she fell asleep. I didn't want to sleep, but soon I found I couldn't help myself as an unwelcome drowsiness came over me. I had an uneasy sleep, and when I woke, it was dawn and my father was gently shaking me. I woke with a start and my hand went up, but the knife wasn't there. My mother had it.

R **Read and Discuss** How do you think Dee is feeling at this point?

My father took my hand. "Why were you holding the knife, 'lois?" he asked.

I looked at him and at my mother. "I—I was scared," I said.

My father was thoughtful. "No need to be scared now, sugar," he said. "Daddy's here and so is Mother-Dear." **S**

Then after a glance at my mother, he got out of the car, walked to the road, looked down it one way, then the other. When he came back and started the motor, he turned the Cadillac north, not south.

"What're you doing?" asked my mother.

"Heading back to Memphis," said my father. "Cousin Halton's there. We'll leave the Cadillac and get his car. Driving this car any farther south with you and the girls in the car, it's just not worth the risk."

And so that's what we did. Instead of driving through Mississippi in golden splendor, we traveled its streets and roads and highways in Cousin Halton's solid, yet not so splendid, four-year-old Chevy. When we reached my grandparents' farm, my uncles and aunts were already there. Everybody was glad to see us. They had been worried. They asked about the Cadillac. My father told them what had happened, and they nodded and said he had done the best thing.

We stayed one week in Mississippi. During that week I often saw my father, looking deep in thought, walk off alone across the family land. I saw my mother watching him. One day I ran after my father, took his hand, and walked the land with him. I asked him all the questions that were on my mind. I asked him why the policemen had treated him the way they had and why people didn't want us to eat in the restaurants or drink from the water fountains or sleep in the hotels. I told him I just didn't understand all that.

My father looked at me and said that it all was a difficult thing to understand and he didn't really understand it himself. He said it all had to do with the fact that black people had once been forced to be slaves. He said it had to do with our skins being colored. He said it had to do with stupidity and ignorance. He said it had to do with the law, the law that said we could be treated like this here in the South. And for that matter, he added, any other place in these United States where folks thought the same as so many folks did here in the South. But he also said, "I'm hoping one day though we can drive that long road down here and there won't be any signs. I'm hoping one day the police won't stop us just because of the color of our skins and we're riding in a gold Cadillac with northern plates." **T**

When the week ended, we said a sad goodbye to my grandparents and all the Mississippi family and headed in a caravan back toward Memphis. In Memphis, we returned Cousin Halton's car and got our Cadillac. Once we were home, my father put the Cadillac in the garage and didn't drive it. I didn't hear my mother say any more about the Cadillac. I didn't hear my father speak of it either. **U**

S **Reading Focus** Making Predictions Will the family keep going south, or will they go back? What makes you think so?

T **Read and Discuss** What effect do you think 'lois's questions have on her father?

U **Reading Focus** Making Predictions What do you predict the family will do with the Cadillac?

Vocabulary ignorance (IHG nuhr uhns) n.: lack of knowledge.

Some days passed, and then on a bright Saturday afternoon while Wilma and I were playing in the backyard, I saw my father go into the garage. He opened the garage doors wide so the sunshine streamed in and began to shine the Cadillac. I saw my mother at the kitchen window staring out across the yard at my father. For a long time, she stood there watching my father shine his car. Then she came out and crossed the yard to the garage, and I heard her say, "Wilbert, you keep the car."

He looked at her as if he had not heard.

"You keep it," she repeated and turned and walked back to the house.

My father watched her until the back door had shut behind her. Then he went on shining the car and soon began to sing. About an hour later he got into the car and drove away. That evening when he came back, he was walking. The Cadillac was nowhere in sight.

"Daddy, where's our new Cadillac?" I demanded to know. So did Wilma.

He smiled and put his hand on my head. "Sold it," he said as my mother came into the room.

"But how come?" I asked. "We poor now?"

"No, sugar. We've got more money towards our new house now, and we're all together. I figure that makes us about the richest folks in the world." He smiled at my mother, and she smiled too and came into his arms. **(V)**

After that, we drove around in an old 1930s Model A Ford my father had. He said he'd factory-ordered us another Mercury, this time with my mother's approval. Despite that, most folks on the block figured we had fallen on hard times after such a splashy showing of good times, and some folks even laughed at us as the Ford rattled around the city. I must admit that at first I was pretty much embarrassed to be riding around in that old Ford after the splendor of the Cadillac. But my father said to hold my head high. We and the family knew the truth. As fine as the Cadillac had been, he said, it had pulled us apart for a while. Now, as ragged and noisy as that old Ford was, we all rode in it together, and we were a family again. So I held my head high.

Still, though, I thought often of that Cadillac. We had had the Cadillac only a little more than a month, but I wouldn't soon forget its splendor or how I'd felt riding around inside it. I wouldn't soon forget either the ride we had taken south in it. I wouldn't soon forget the signs, the policemen, or my fear. I would remember that ride and the gold Cadillac all my life. **(W)**

> I would remember that ride and the gold Cadillac all my life.

(V) Literary Perspectives Analyzing Credibility in Literature How credible is this turn of events? Explain why it seems either believable or unbelievable to you.

(W) Literary Focus Novella What is the theme, or main message, of this novella?

Applying Your Skills

The Gold Cadillac
Literary Response and Analysis

Reading Skills Focus
Quick Check

1. Why doesn't 'lois's mother like the new Cadillac? How does the rest of the family feel about the car?

2. What do the police think 'lois's father did wrong?

Read with a Purpose

3. What does 'lois learn from her trip to the South? What does her father learn?

Reading Skills: Making and Adjusting Predictions

4. Add a fourth column to the predictions chart you filled out, and note whether your predictions were correct. Use a check mark (✓) for "yes" and an *X* for "no." What new information caused you to adjust the incorrect predictions?

In the story	I predict	Because	
the narrator and her sister see the Cadillac	that the father bought it	the father drives up in it and is grinning	✓
the girls go get their mother			

Literary Skills Focus
Literary Analysis

5. **Analyze** What do you think the gold Cadillac represents for Wilbert and his neighbors? What details <u>indicate</u> this?

6. **Infer** How can you tell that 'lois's parents love each other even though they disagree about the car?

7. **Literary Perspectives** How is the credibility of *The Gold Cadillac*'s **plot** (the events that make up the story) dependent on the **setting** (where and when the story takes place)?

Literary Skills: Novella

8. **Extend** If you were Mildred Taylor and had to edit *The Gold Cadillac* to half its length, what would you choose to change? Which <u>characteristics</u> of the story would have to remain for the <u>concept</u> to stay the same?

Literary Skills Review: Theme

9. **Analyze** In one or two words, state what you think the **subject** of this story is. Then, in a complete sentence, state what you see as the story's **theme.** Find at least one passage in the story that supports the theme.

Writing Skills Focus
Think as a Reader/Writer

Use It in Your Writing Look at your list of details about beauty, richness, pride, and luxury. Think about something meaningful to you, such as a possession, a place, or an activity. Write a descriptive paragraph about it, using details that show its importance to you and what it adds to your life.

What Do You Think Now

What has this story shown you about the power of historical fiction?

The Gold Cadillac

Vocabulary Development

Synonyms and Antonyms

Words have relationships with other words. For example, words can be **synonyms** (have the same or similar meanings) or **antonyms** (have opposite or nearly opposite meanings). A **semantic map,** like the one below, is a good way of showing certain word relationships.

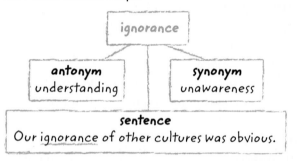

ignorance

antonym
understanding

synonym
unawareness

sentence
Our ignorance of other cultures was obvious.

Your Turn

Using the semantic map above as a model, map the three other Vocabulary words: *evident, rural,* and *dusk.*

evident
rural
dusk

Multiple-Meaning Words

A multiple-meaning word is like a fork in the road: Each road, and each definition, will take you in a different direction. To make things even more complicated, many multiple-meaning words can function as different parts of speech.

Dad came _back_ to the car. [Here, *back* **is an adverb meaning "toward an earlier position."]**

Mother decided to back Dad's plan. [Here, *back* **is a verb meaning "support."]**

To decide on the correct meaning of a multiple-meaning word, decide what part of speech it is and look at its context.

Your Turn

Define the underlined word in each set of sentences, and tell what part of speech it is.

1. Tired of arguing, he decided to <u>smooth</u> things out with his wife.
   I kept slipping on the <u>smooth</u> floor.
2. I finally asked the question that had been on my <u>mind</u>.
   <u>Mind</u> your little sister while I go to the store.
   Would you <u>mind</u> closing that door?

Language Coach

Word Forms You can often change one word to another, related word by adding to or changing the end of the word. For example, to change the noun *importance* to the adjective *important,* you change the ending, or suffix, like this:

importance (*n.*) + *–ant* = important (*adj.*)

Try changing each Vocabulary word into a different part of speech by adding a suffix. Use a dictionary if you need help.

Academic Vocabulary

Write About . . .
Which details in *The Gold Cadillac* <u>indicate</u> that it is set in the past? In a paragraph, describe the events of the novella that clearly distinguish it from life today. What <u>concept</u> of the past does this story present?

Grammar Link
Direct and Indirect Objects

A **direct object** is a noun or pronoun that receives the action of the verb or that shows the result of the action. A direct object tells *what* or *whom* after a transitive (action) verb.

Every sentence has a subject and verb. The subject tells you *who* did something, and the verb tells you *about* the action—*what* he, she, or it did. The direct object tells *who* or *what* receives the action of the verb. The example tells *what* Wilbert bought.

S   V   DO

EXAMPLE Wilbert bought a *Cadillac.*

An **indirect object** is a noun or pronoun that comes between the verb and the direct object. An indirect object tells *to whom* or *to what* or *for whom* or *for what* the action of the verb is done.

S   V   IO   DO

EXAMPLE Wilbert bought his *family* a Cadillac.

The example tells *for whom* Wilbert bought a Cadillac—his family.

Your Turn

Identify the direct objects and the indirect objects in the following sentences. Write DO above the direct objects and IO above the indirect objects. Remember that a sentence can have more than one direct object and indirect object.

1. Wilbert drove the Cadillac.
2. Dee did not like the Cadillac.
3. Wilbert's siblings gave him a warning.
4. Dee packed her family a grand picnic lunch.
5. Wilbert sold the Cadillac to earn money for the family's new house.

CHOICES

As you respond to the Choices, use these **Academic Vocabulary** words as appropriate: <u>characteristics</u>, <u>concept</u>, <u>indicate</u>, <u>interpret</u>.

REVIEW
Reflect on Forms of Fiction

Timed ⌐Writing Mildred Taylor based this novella on some of her own memories. Why didn't she write an autobiographical account of one of those memories instead of creating fictional characters and events? In a paragraph, discuss how this story would be different if it were written as nonfiction instead of fiction.

CONNECT
Draw a Map

Group Activity Using pencils or a computer drawing tool, create a map of the route that 'lois's family drives in their gold Cadillac. Use color and other methods to show features such as the states that had segregation laws. Be sure to <u>indicate</u> where major events in the story occur.

EXTEND
Research the Facts

Oral Report Before the Civil Rights Act of 1964, the South was a very different place than it is today. List some of the things 'lois sees that puzzle or disturb her. Then, in a library or on the Internet, research articles and find photographs about the pre–civil rights South. Has the author accurately depicted what the South was like around 1950? Share your findings with the class.

Learn It Online
Take a deeper look at this story using the Internet links at:

go.hrw.com   H6-383   **Go**

He Lion, Bruh Bear, and Bruh Rabbit

African American folk tale
retold by **Virginia Hamilton**

The Fox and the Crow *and*
The Wolf and the House Dog

by **Aesop**

What Do
You?
Think

Why do we like stories
about clever animals who
outsmart their enemies?

QuickWrite

Write about the things trickster animals say and do
in stories. Start with tricksters you may know from
cartoons, such as Bugs Bunny and the Road Runner.

Little Red Riding Hood (1992)
by William Wegman.

Reader/Writer Notebook

Use your **RWN** to complete the activities for these selections.

Literary Skills Focus

Forms of Fiction: Identifying the Characteristics of Folk Tales and Fables **Folk tales** and **fables** have been around for thousands of years—much longer than novels, novellas, and short stories. Traditional folk tales and fables were shared aloud long before they were written down. The folk tale that follows originally comes from Africa. On the surface, stories like this one seem to be entertaining tales about big, mean animals and small, crafty ones. If you read between the lines, however, you often find that the point the storyteller is making has to do with people, not animals.

The Trickster A major <u>characteristic</u> of many folk tales is the **trickster**—a character who outsmarts bigger, more powerful enemies. Most tricksters are underdogs—weak characters who seem unlikely to win. Tricksters triumph because they're clever, even if they seem silly or even ignorant. Their tricks often teach important lessons. Brer Rabbit, who is called Bruh (Brother) Rabbit in this story, is one of the trickiest.

Reading Skills Focus

Monitoring Comprehension To check your understanding of the stories, pause regularly and ask yourself questions about the texts.

Into Action Asking questions about what you've read is key to **monitoring your comprehension.** Stop at least twice—once in the middle and once at the end—as you read each of the tales.

The Big Questions	... and Answers
What just happened?	
Why did it happen?	
What characters were involved?	

Writing Skills Focus

Think as a Reader/Writer

Find It in Your Reading As you read these folk tales and fables, keep lists of the strong characters and the weak characters in each story. Explain what makes each character weak or strong.

Language Coach

Homophones Homophones (HAHM uh fohnz) are words that sound the same but are spelled differently and mean different things. The word *bear*, for example, sounds like the word *bare*. You have to remember what each word means.

1. If you were referring to an animal, which word would you use? (*bear/bare*)

2. If you were referring to a tree with no leaves, which word would you use? (*bear/bare*)

Learn It Online
Read more on Hamilton's life at:
go.hrw.com H6-386 Go

Virginia Hamilton
(1936–2002)

For most of her life, Virginia Hamilton lived where she was born and raised: Yellow Springs, Ohio. Her grandfather settled there after escaping from slavery in pre–Civil War days. Hamilton recalls her family fondly:

"My mother's 'people' were warm-hearted, tight with money, generous to the sick and landless, close-mouthed, and fond of telling tales and gossip about one another and even their ancestors. They were a part of me from the time I understood that I belonged to all of them."

Aesop
(sixth century B.C.)

Not much is known about Aesop. According to an ancient historian, he came from Africa and was held in slavery in Greece. The fables he is said to have written may have originally come from ancient India. Aesop eventually won his freedom, but he met a violent death, perhaps because his fables made dangerous political points about such concepts as liberty.

Think About the Writers

Why do you think people throughout time have used fictional tales to teach important lessons?

Build Background

Folk tales and fables like the following ones usually present an idea or lesson that we humans need to learn.

Preview the Selections

In the folk tale, **he Lion** thunders through the forest, scaring the small animals, who go to **Bruh Bear** and **Bruh Rabbit** for help.

In the fables, **Fox** tries to get **Crow** to give up a chunk of cheese, and **House Dog** tries to persuade **Wolf** to try living in the village.

Read with a Purpose Read this fable, and decide if he Lion gets what he deserves.

He Lion, Bruh Bear, and Bruh Rabbit

African American folk tale retold by **Virginia Hamilton**

Say that he Lion would get up each and every mornin. Stretch and walk around. He'd roar, "ME AND MYSELF. ME AND MYSELF," like that. Scare all the little animals so they were afraid to come outside in the sunshine. Afraid to go huntin or fishin or whatever the little animals wanted to do.

"What we gone do about it?" they asked one another. Squirrel leapin from branch to branch, just scared. Possum playin dead, couldn't hardly move him.

He Lion just went on, stickin out his chest and roarin, "ME AND MYSELF. ME AND MYSELF."

The little animals held a sit-down talk, and one by one and two by two and all by all, they decide to go see Bruh Bear and Bruh Rabbit. For they know that Bruh Bear been around. And Bruh Rabbit say he has, too.

So they went to Bruh Bear and Bruh Rabbit. Said, "We have some trouble. Old he Lion, him scarin everybody, roarin every mornin and all day, 'ME AND MYSELF. ME

AND MYSELF', like that." **Ⓐ**

"Why he Lion want to do that?" Bruh Bear said.

"Is that all he Lion have to say?" Bruh Rabbit asked.

"We don't know why, but that's all he Lion can tell us and we didn't ask him to tell us that," said the little animals. "And him scarin the children with it. And we wish him to stop it."

"Well, I'll go see him, talk to him. I've known he Lion a long kind of time," Bruh Bear said.

"I'll go with you," said Bruh Rabbit. "I've known he Lion most long as you." **Ⓑ**

That bear and that rabbit went off through the forest. They kept hearin somethin. Mumble, mumble. Couldn't make it out. They got farther in the forest. They heard it plain now. "ME AND MYSELF. ME AND MYSELF."

"Well, well, well," said Bruh Bear. He wasn't scared. He'd been around the whole forest, seen a lot.

"My, my, my," said Bruh Rabbit. He'd

Ⓐ Reading Focus Monitoring Comprehension
Who are the characters so far, and what is their problem?

Ⓑ Read and Discuss What have you learned so far?

He Lion, Bruh Bear, and Bruh Rabbit **387**

found him. Kept their distance. He watchin them and they watchin him. Everybody actin cordial.[1]

"Hear tell you are scarin everybody, all the little animals, with your roarin all the time," Bruh Rabbit said.

"I roars when I pleases," he Lion said.

"Well, might could you leave off the noise first thing in the mornin, so the little animals can get what they want to eat and drink?" asked Bruh Bear.

"Listen," said he Lion, and then he roared: "ME AND MYSELF. ME AND MYSELF. Nobody tell me what not to do," he said. "I'm the king of the forest, *me and myself.*"

"Better had let me tell you somethin," Bruh Rabbit said, "for I've seen Man, and I know him the real king of the forest." **C**

He Lion was quiet awhile. He looked straight through that scrawny lil Rabbit like he was nothin at all. He looked at Bruh Bear and figured he'd talk to him.

"You, Bear, you been around," he Lion said.

"That's true," said old Bruh Bear. "I been about everywhere. I've been around the whole forest."

"Then you must know somethin," he Lion said.

"I know lots," said Bruh Bear, slow and quiet-like.

"Tell me what you know about Man," he Lion said. "He think him the king of the forest?"

"Well, now, I'll tell you," said Bruh Bear,

seen enough to know not to be afraid of an old he lion. Now old he lions could be dangerous, but you had to know how to handle them.

The bear and the rabbit climbed up and up the cliff where he Lion had his lair. They

---

1. **cordial** (KAWR juhl): warm and friendly.

C **Reading Focus** Monitoring Comprehension Why does Bruh Rabbit say this to he Lion?

Vocabulary **lair** (lair) *n.*: home of a wild animal; den.

"I been around, but I haven't ever come across Man that I know of. Couldn't tell you nothin about him."

So he Lion had to turn back to Bruh Rabbit. He didn't want to but he had to. "So what?" he said to that lil scrawny hare.

"Well, you got to come down from there if you want to see Man," Bruh Rabbit said. "Come down from there and I'll show you him." **D**

He Lion thought a minute, an hour, and a whole day. Then, the next day, he came on down.

He roared just once, "ME AND MYSELF. ME AND MYSELF. Now," he said, "come show me Man."

So they set out. He Lion, Bruh Bear, and Bruh Rabbit. They go along and they go along, rangin the forest. Pretty soon, they come to a clearin. And playin in it is a little fellow about nine years old.

"Is that there Man?" asked he Lion.

"Why no, that one is called Will Be, but it sure is not Man," said Bruh Rabbit.

So they went along and they went along. Pretty soon, they come upon a shade tree. And sleepin under it is an old, olden fellow, about ninety years olden.

"There must lie Man," spoke he Lion. "I knew him wasn't gone be much."

"That's not Man," said Bruh Rabbit. "That fellow is Was Once. You'll know it when you see Man." **E**

So they went on along. He Lion is gettin tired of strollin. So he roars, "ME AND

MYSELF. ME AND MYSELF." Upsets Bear so that Bear doubles over and runs and climbs a tree.

"Come down from there," Bruh Rabbit tellin him. So after a while Bear comes down. He keepin his distance from he Lion, anyhow. And they set out some more. Goin along quiet and slow.

In a little while they come to a road. And comin on way down the road, Bruh Rabbit sees Man comin. Man about twenty-one years old. Big and strong, with a big gun over his shoulder.

"There!" Bruh Rabbit says. "See there, he Lion? There's Man. You better go meet him."

"I will," says he Lion. And he sticks out his chest and he roars, "ME AND MYSELF. ME AND MYSELF." All the way to Man he's roarin proud, "ME AND MYSELF, ME AND MYSELF!"

D [Literary Focus] **Folk Tale** In this folk tale, who's most likely the trickster, Bruh Bear or Bruh Rabbit? Why do you think so?

E [Read and Discuss] What is Bruh Rabbit talking about when he refers to *Man*, *Will Be*, and *Was Once?*

389

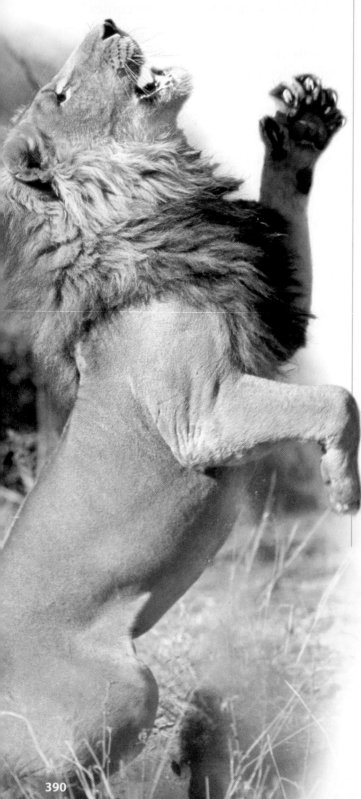

"Come on, Bruh Bear, let's go!" Bruh Rabbit says.

"What for?" Bruh Bear wants to know.

"You better come on!" And Bruh Rabbit takes ahold of Bruh Bear and half drags him to a thicket. And there he makin the Bear hide with him.

For here comes Man. He sees old he Lion real good now. He drops to one knee and he takes aim with his big gun.

Old he Lion is roarin his head off: "ME AND MYSELF! ME AND MYSELF!"

The big gun goes off: PA-LOOOM!

He Lion falls back hard on his tail.

The gun goes off again. PA-LOOOM!

He Lion is flyin through the air. He lands in the thicket.

"Well, did you see Man?" asked Bruh Bear.   **F**

"I seen him," said he Lion. "Man spoken to me unkind, and got a great long stick him keepin on his shoulder. Then Man taken that stick down and him speakin real mean. Thunderin at me and lightnin comin from that stick, awful bad. Made me sick. I had to turn around. And Man pointin that stick again and thunderin at me some more. So I come in here, cause it seem like him throwed some stickers at me each time it thunder, too."   **G**

F **Literary Focus** **Folk Tale** Humor is part of many folk tales. What is humorous about this scene?

G **Reading Focus** **Monitoring Comprehension** What happens when he Lion meets Man?

"So you've met Man, and you know zactly what that kind of him is," says Bruh Rabbit.

"I surely do know that," he Lion said back.

A while after he Lion met Man, things were some better in the forest. Bruh Bear knew what Man looked like so he could keep out of his way. That rabbit always did know to keep out of Man's way. The little animals could go out in the mornin because he Lion was more peaceable. He didn't walk around roarin at the top of his voice all the time. And when he Lion did lift that voice of his, it was like, "Me and Myself and Man. Me and Myself and Man." Like that.

Wasn't too loud at all.

H **Read and Discuss** What is the story's resolution?

I **Literary Focus** **Folk Tale** What <u>concept</u> of bullies and bullying does this folk tale present? What lesson does it teach?

Analyzing Visuals **Connecting to the Text** How do the bear and rabbit in this picture reflect the outcome of the story?

The Fox and the Crow. Ⓐ

by **Aesop**

Greek fable, dramatized by **Mara Rockliff**

Narrator. One fine morning a Fox was wandering through the woods, enjoying the lovely spring weather.

Fox. Lovely spring weather is all very well, but a fox can't live on sunshine and fresh air. I could use some breakfast right about now.

Narrator. Suddenly he noticed a Crow sitting on the branch of a tree above him. The Fox didn't think much of crows as a rule, but this particular Crow had something very interesting in her beak.

Fox. Cheese. Mmm. A nice big yellow chunk of cheese. I would love that cheese. I deserve that cheese. But how can I get that cheese? Ⓑ

Narrator. The Fox thought awhile, and then he called up to the Crow.

Fox. Good morning, you fabulous bird.

Narrator. The Crow looked at him suspiciously. But she kept her beak closed tightly on the cheese and said nothing.

Fox. What beautiful beady eyes you have! And you certainly look great in black feathers. I've seen a lot of birds in my time, but you outbird them all. A bird with your good looks must have a voice to match. Oh, if only I could hear you sing just one song. Then I would know you were truly the Greatest Bird on Earth. Ⓒ

Narrator. Listening to all this flattery, the Crow forgot her suspicion of the Fox. She forgot her cheese, too. All she could think of was impressing the Fox with a song. So she opened her beak wide and let out a loud "Caw!" Down fell the cheese, right into the Fox's open mouth.

Fox. Thanks! That tasted every bit as good as it looked. Well, now I know you have a voice—and I hope I never have to hear it again. But where are your brains?

All Together. If you let flattery go to your head, you'll pay the price.

Ⓐ **Literary Focus** Fable What behaviors do you associate with foxes and with crows?

Ⓑ **Read and Discuss** What problem does Fox have?

Ⓒ **Literary Focus** Fable Who is the trickster in this fable, and how do you know?

Vocabulary **suspicion** (suh SPIHSH uhn) *n.*: feeling that someone is guilty of something.

impressing (ihm PREHS ihng) *v.*: making someone feel admiration.

flattery (FLAT uhr ee) *n.*: praise that is false or pretended.

The Wolf and the House Dog

by **Aesop**

Greek fable, dramatized by **Mara Rockliff**

Narrator. Once there was a Wolf who never got enough to eat. Her mouth watered when she looked at the fat geese and chickens kept by the people of the village. But every time she tried to steal one, the watchful village dogs would bark and warn their owners.

Wolf. Really, I'm nothing but skin and bones. It makes me sad just thinking about it.

Narrator. One night the Wolf met up with a House Dog who had wandered a little too far from home. The Wolf would gladly have eaten him right then and there.

A **Reading Focus** Monitoring Comprehension Why is the Wolf so hungry?

Wolf. Dog stew . . . cold dog pie . . . or maybe just dog on a bun, with plenty of mustard and ketchup . . .

Narrator. But the House Dog looked too big and strong for the Wolf, who was weak from hunger. So the Wolf spoke to him very humbly and politely.

Wolf. How handsome you are! You look so healthy and well fed and delicious—I mean, uh, terrific. You look terrific. Really.

House Dog. Well, you look terrible. I don't know why you live out here in these miserable woods, where you have to fight so hard for every crummy little scrap of food. You should come live in the village like me. You could eat like a king there.

Wolf. What do I have to do?

House Dog. Hardly anything. Chase kids on bicycles. Bark at the mailman every now and then. Lie around the house letting people pet you. Just for that they'll feed you till you burst—enormous steak bones with fat hanging off them, pizza crusts, bits of chicken, leftovers like you wouldn't believe. **Ⓑ**

> How handsome you are! You look so healthy and well fed and delicious— I mean, uh, terrific. You look terrific.

Narrator. The Wolf nearly cried with happiness as she imagined how wonderful her new life was going to be. But then she noticed a strange ring around the Dog's neck where the hair had been rubbed off.

Wolf. What happened to your neck?

House Dog. Oh . . . ah . . . nothing. It's nothing, really. **Ⓒ**

Wolf. I've never seen anything like it. Is it a disease?

House Dog. Don't be silly. It's just the mark of the collar that they fasten my chain to.

Wolf. A chain! You mean you can't go wherever you like?

House Dog. Well, not always. But what's the difference?

Wolf. What's the difference? Are you kidding? I wouldn't give up my freedom for the biggest, juiciest steak in the world. Never mind a few lousy bones.

Narrator. The Wolf ran away, back to the woods. She never went near the village again, no matter how hungry she got.

All Together. Nothing is worth more than freedom. **Ⓓ**

Ⓑ **Read and Discuss** What does the conversation between the Wolf and the House Dog reveal?

Ⓒ **Reading Focus** **Monitoring Comprehension** How does House Dog feel when he says these words? How do you know?

Ⓓ **Literary Focus** Fable The moral, or lesson, is a major characteristic of a fable. State this tale's moral in your own words.

Applying Your Skills

**Reading Standard 3.1** Identify the forms of fiction and describe the major characteristics of each form.

He Lion, Bruh Bear, and Bruh Rabbit / The Fox and the Crow / The Wolf and the House Dog

Literary Response and Analysis

Reading Skills Focus
Quick Check

1. Retell the events of each tale by writing sentences that start with these words:

   First, _____
   As a result, _____
   However, _____
   Then, _____
   Finally, _____

Read with a Purpose

2. In "He Lion, Bruh Bear, and Bruh Rabbit," do you think the punishment handed out by Bruh Bear and Bruh Rabbit was appropriate for he Lion's actions? Explain.

3. In "The Fox and the Crow," why do you think the Crow wants to impress the Fox? Explain.

4. In "The Wolf and the House Dog," why does the Wolf value freedom so much? What is she willing to give up for freedom?

Reading Skills: Monitoring Comprehension

5. Did your comprehension break down at any point as you read these selections? If so, how did pausing regularly and asking and answering questions about the text help you?

Literary Skills Focus
Literary Analysis

6. **Interpret** What does he Lion mean when he roars, "ME AND MYSELF. ME AND MYSELF"?

7. **Infer** At the end of "He Lion . . . ," he Lion roars less loudly and less often. What does this change in his behavior <u>indicate</u>?

8. **Extend** What kind of people are like he Lion and the Crow? What do these tales tell you about such people?

Literary Skills: Folk Tales and Fables

9. **Analyze** Folk tales and fables present **morals,** or lessons about how to get along in the world. What lessons are taught in these stories? What do you think about each lesson?

Literary Skills Review: Character

10. **Analyze** What qualities associated with real rabbits and foxes make people think they would be good tricksters? Would a lion or bear be a likely trickster? Why or why not?

11. **Analyze** In these three selections, the characters are animals who talk and act like people. What do these animal characters show you about human nature?

Writing Skills Focus
Think as a Reader/Writer

Use It in Your Writing Review your list of weak and powerful characters, and think about the lessons in these tales. Then, write two paragraphs in response to these questions: How can a character who seems powerful be outsmarted by a weaker character? Is it better to be clever or strong?

 What Do You Think Now

Why are stories about small and weak characters cleverly outsmarting large and powerful characters still popular today?

He Lion, Bruh Bear, and Bruh Rabbit

Vocabulary Development
Words with Multiple Meanings

Multiple-meaning words can be confusing. A multiple-meaning word is always spelled the same way, but it means different things in different **contexts.** To find the correct meaning of a word, look at its context—the words around it. Then, try out each meaning in the context of the sentence.

Your Turn

Choose the correct meaning of each italicized word.

1. Does a fox know the difference between *right* and wrong?
   a. opposite of left
   b. what is just and proper
2. He broke every *rule* in the forest.
   a. law
   b. line
3. He Lion went flying through the *air*.
   a. appearance
   b. sky
4. "I surely do know that," he Lion answered *back*.
   a. in return
   b. part of a chair

Language Coach

Homophones *To, too,* and *two* are **homophones**—words that sound alike but are spelled differently and have different meanings. (The word *homophone* comes from the Greek words *homos,* meaning "same," and *phōnē,* meaning "sound.") The best way to keep from confusing homophones is to just memorize them.

to: toward; in the direction of (*to* is also part of the infinitive form of a verb)
too: also; more than enough
two: a number—one plus one

Choose the correct word in the underlined pair in each sentence.
The little animals go <u>to/two</u> see Bruh Bear and Bruh Rabbit because he Lion is making <u>too/to</u> much noise. He Lion doesn't like talking <u>too/to</u> Bruh Rabbit.

Academic Vocabulary

Talk About . . .
With a partner, take a close look at one of the stories you just read. Take turns sharing how each of you <u>interprets</u> the story. Then, discuss what the story says about a <u>concept</u> such as freedom. Use the underlined Academic Vocabulary words in your discussion.

Learn It Online
Sharpen your word skills with *WordSharp* at:

go.hrw.com | H6-396 | GO

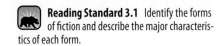
Grammar Link

Predicate Nominatives

A **predicate nominative** is a word or word group that is in the predicate of a sentence and that identifies or refers to the subject. It may be a noun, a pronoun, or a word group functioning as a noun. Here are some examples:

Bruh Bear was a fearless *animal*.

[*Animal* is the predicate nominative completing the meaning of the linking verb *was*.]

The rulers of the forest were *human*.

[*Human* is the predicate nominative completing the meaning of the linking verb *were*.]

It is important to remember that a predicate nominative always completes the meaning of a *be* linking verb.

He Lion became a better *neighbor*.

[*Neighbor* completes the meaning of the linking verb *became*.]

If two words are connected by an action verb, that complement is usually a direct object, not a predicate nominative.

Your Turn

Identify the predicate nominative in each of the sentences below.

1. Bruh Rabbit is a smart fellow.
2. Bruh Bear and Bruh Rabbit were friends.
3. Will Become was still a boy.
4. Sometimes, he Lion was a fool.

CHOICES

As you respond to the Choices, use these **Academic Vocabulary** words as appropriate: characteristics, concept, indicate, interpret.

REVIEW
Respond to a Moral

Timed ⏱ **Writing** Write a personal response to one of the morals in the two Aesop's fables you have read. Explain whether you agree or disagree with the moral, a defining characteristic of this fictional form, by using examples from your personal experience and your own knowledge.

CONNECT
Create a Graphic Fable

TechFocus Use software tools or other media to create an original fable in graphic story form that could teach one of these lessons: "Kindness is never wasted" or "The grass is always greener on the other side of the fence." Keep these characteristics of graphic stories in mind: They are told in panels, and the words characters speak are put in word balloons.

EXTEND
Perform a Story

Group Activity Form a group, and present "He Lion, Bruh Bear, and Bruh Rabbit" or another folk tale of your choice in an oral reading. Break the story into scenes, and decide whether you need a narrator. Then, write out each character's lines, and indicate how they should be spoken.

Learn It Online
Expand your understanding of these stories at:

go.hrw.com   H6-397   **Go**

Do or Die *from* Gilgamesh the Hero

retold by **Geraldine McCaughrean**

What Do
You
Think?

In what ways might a hero in a
story from five thousand years ago
be similar to and different from a
hero in a story written today?

Reader/Writer
Notebook

Use your **RWN** to complete the activities for this selection.

Literary Skills Focus

Forms of Fiction: Identifying the Characteristics of Myths and Epics **Myths** are probably the world's oldest stories. They deal with such basic human issues as love, war, and death. There are two main kinds of myth. The **origin myth** explains how something in the world began or was created. The **hero myth** describes the adventures of a superhuman hero who goes on a quest, or journey, to perform great deeds.

The story of Gilgamesh is a type of hero myth called an **epic**—a long story about the quest of a hero who is a leader in his culture.

Reading Skills Focus

Setting a Purpose When you **set a purpose** for reading, you decide on your reading goals. Are you reading to be entertained, or are you looking for information? Reading with a purpose means that you will probably stop often, ask and answer questions, and re-read passages as you go along.

Into Action Use a chart like the one below to set a purpose for reading. List any new purposes, and check off completed purposes.

What's Your Purpose?

Purpose 1	to read an exciting story about a hero with superhuman powers	☐
Purpose 2		☐

Writing Skills Focus

Think as a Reader/Writer

Find It in Your Reading List examples of the most vivid descriptions, details, and images in "Do or Die." How do these features of the writing bring the characters and events to life?

TechFocus Many video games are quests. As you read, decide whether the story of Gilgamesh and Enkidu would be the basis for a good video game.

Vocabulary

clenched (klehnchd) *v.*: closed tightly. *Gilgamesh clenched his fists angrily.*

splendor (SPLEHN duhr) *n.*: brightness; glory. *Gilgamesh praised Shamash's splendor.*

rash (rash) *adj.*: reckless; impatient. *Gilgamesh made a rash decision.*

invincible (ihn VIHN suh buhl) *adj.*: unable to be defeated. *The counselors warned that Huwawa was invincible.*

erupt (ih RUHPT) *v.*: burst forth. *Gilgamesh saw a volcano erupt in his dream.*

- **clenched** his fist
- seemed impatient and **rash**
- fought an **invincible** foe
- The hero Gilgamesh
- saw a volcano **erupt** in his dream
- praised the **splendor** of Shamash

Language Coach

Multiple-Meaning Words If you saw the word *bat* by itself, you would not know if it meant a winged mammal, a piece of baseball equipment, or the action of hitting a ball. If you saw *bat* in a sentence, however, you would be able to tell which meaning was intended. Which Vocabulary word above has two very different meanings?

Geraldine McCaughrean
(1951–)

Her Dream Job

A resident of Berkshire, England, Geraldine McCaughrean (ma KAWRK ruhn) has won some of the United Kingdom's highest honors for children's writers. Early in her career, though, she was happy just to consider herself a professional writer. Today, with more than 130 books to her credit, she continues to feel lucky: "It still seems almost wicked to do something so enjoyable for a living."

Old Stories Made New

One thing McCaughrean enjoys as much as writing new stories is "rewriting" old ones—that is, making up new versions of classic stories for today's readers. Many of her books are based on myths and legends first told countless years ago. Among these classics are some of the world's oldest stories—like Gilgamesh.

"I discovered a passion for myth. Perhaps it is because myths were never told 'for children' or 'for adults,' but to whole communities who understood the importance and magic of storytelling."

Think About the Writer

Geraldine McCaughrean loves working as a writer. What would be *your* ideal job?

Build Background

One of the oldest written stories is the *Epic of Gilgamesh,* from the part of the Middle East that today includes Iraq. Almost five thousand years old, the epic tells the story of a proud king with superhuman powers who battles monsters and goes on a quest to find the secret of eternal life. This episode from a retelling of the epic by a contemporary writer focuses on Gilgamesh's determination to make a name for himself by killing the greatest monster of all.

Preview the Selection

Use this list to help you identify the cast of characters.

Gilgamesh (GIHL guh mehsh)—part god and part man, possessing special powers; he is the king of the city of Uruk.

Enkidu (EHN kee doo)—also called the Wild Man, he lived among wild animals before becoming Gilgamesh's best friend.

Ishtar (IHSH tahr)—goddess of love and war.

Huwawa (hoo WAH wah)—an enormous and powerful monster, also called Guardian or Protector of the Cedar Forests.

Shamash (SHAW mush)—the Sun God.

Ninsun (NIHN suhn)—Gilgamesh's mother, a goddess.

Read with a Purpose Read this myth to discover the qualities of an
ancient hero named Gilgamesh and what he truly values.

Do or Die
from Gilgamesh the Hero
retold by Geraldine McCaughrean

Like the axe in his dream, Gilgamesh
wore Enkidu at his side and swore
never to be parted from him. "I must
have been mad to contemplate marriage," he
told Enkidu, "especially to Ishtar!"

Gilgamesh schooled Enkidu in the ways
of civilization, and then Enkidu taught him
the way of the wild places: how the honey-
ant gathers its winter food, how mistletoe
grows without a root, how water can be
mined out of the driest desert.

They wrestled and raced and hunted and
talked, and the people of Uruk breathed a
sigh of relief and gave thanks to the gods.

Enkidu had roamed far afield, into the
wildest places. He had seen things which
Gilgamesh had never seen. He had swum
in both the Tigris and the Euphrates, had
stood on the summit of Mount Nisir where
the ark ran aground after the Great Flood;
had seen the monstrous Huwawa, Protector
of the Cedar Forests, and the Scorpionmen
who guard the roadway to the Garden of
the Gods. One day, as Gilgamesh showed
Enkidu the sights of the city, he pointed

out the carved stone friezes[1] recording the
deeds of Uruk's great men. **Ⓐ**

"Where are the deeds of Gilgamesh?"
asked Enkidu.

"Here!" cried Gilgamesh, spread-eagling
himself against the wall. "This blank. So far
I've done nothing worth carving in stone.
But soon! Soon, Enkidu! You and I are
going on such an adventure that no wall will
be large enough to record it!" **Ⓑ**

"We are?" Enkidu too flattened himself against the wall, striking a grand pose.
"Where? When? Now?" The very ends of his
long hair crackled with energy.

"It was you who gave me the idea. Who's
the most frightening foe in the whole world?"

Enkidu racked his brains. "Gilgamesh is.
Ask his enemies."

Gilgamesh laughed. "Someone far more
dangerous! We are going to fight Huwawa,
Guardian of the Cedar Forests, and kill him
and bring home cedarwood to build new
gates for Uruk!"

---

1. **friezes** (FREEZ ehz): ornamental bands of decora-
tion around a building.

Ⓐ Literary Focus Myth What details in this paragraph
indicate that this is a myth and not some other kind of story?

Ⓑ Read and Discuss What is Gilgamesh planning? Why?

Enkidu stepped away from the wall. "Ah, now, listen. You're forgetting, I've *seen* Huwawa. He's a monster among monsters! The trees are small alongside him. His strength is the stuff of legends. He never sleeps. When a fox stamps its paw sixty leagues[2] away, Huwawa hears it. He lives for battle! He was made for no other purpose than to guard the forest. No one goes there, for fear of him . . . Besides, a kind of magic surrounds Him. You can't go close without your strength ebbing away. If you had seen Huwawa . . ."

"I would have killed him already!" declared Gilgamesh. "We have to make our mark! Don't we? What are you afraid of?"

"Of getting killed," said Enkidu candidly.

Gilgamesh spread his arms high above his head as if reaching up to clutch the hems of the gods. "Then we'll have died gloriously, won't we? And our names will be written in clouds of glory on the noonday sky! . . . Fame is everything, Enkidu, isn't it? Why live if not to make a mark on the world? To blaze a trail through it! To do deeds worthy of remembrance! Do or die!" Both his fists were clenched, his feet set square on to life, like a prize-fighter. **C**

A surge of love and pride thrilled through Enkidu. "Do or die!" he cried, and closed his own hand around the King's upraised fist. "Just do me one favor. The Cedar Forest

belongs to Shamash the Sun. Don't fly in the face of the gods. Tell Shamash what you want to do. Ask his blessing." **D**

That is how Gilgamesh came to be standing, at high noon, in the full glare of the sun, a white kid[3] at his feet, and in his right hand a silver scepter[4] which caught the sunbeams as he spoke. "O Sun! O lord and master, who sees all! Only help me do this thing, and I shall build you a temple all of cedar wood—wood from your own forests. O Sun, you who are robed in fiery splendor, surely you understand a man's need to cloak himself in glory?"

Swaying as he prayed, Gilgamesh felt the tears on his cheeks dry to streaks of white salt. Then it was as if a red hot hand rested on the crown of his head. Shamash had given his blessing.

Crowds of curious onlookers had gathered, round-eyed, fearful, wondering. *"People of Uruk!"* cried Gilgamesh. "I go to the Forest of Cedar Trees, to cut cedar for new city gates and a temple to the god Shamash! There I shall do battle with Huwawa, the Evil One. Pray for me, and make offerings to the Sun. I shall bring back such glory to Uruk that the name of Uruk will live forever in the annals of the world!" **E**

The crowd gave a nervous laugh and burst out singing. A clumsy, shuffling dance carried them home to their houses.

---

2. **leagues** (leegz): units of distance, from about 2.4 to 4.6 miles.

3. **kid:** young goat.

4. **scepter** (SEHP tuhr): staff or baton carried by a ruler on ceremonial occasions. Often decorated and made of special materials, it is a symbol of authority.

C **Reading Focus** Setting a Purpose What details would you pay attention to here if your purpose in reading this story were to answer the question "What kind of hero is Gilgamesh?"

D **Read and Discuss** What is Gilgamesh's plan?

E **Literary Focus** Myth and Epic The hero of an epic usually tries to gain resources or glory for his people. What details in these last three paragraphs indicate that Gilgamesh is an epic hero?

Vocabulary **clenched** (klehnchd) *v.:* closed tightly.
splendor (SPLEHN duhr) *n.:* brightness; glory.

Gilgamesh and Enkidu went to the forges and gave orders for two axes and two swords. Armorers and craftsmen went out into the ancient groves and cut willow and box wood for axe handles and spear shafts. But they sent to Anshan in Persia for wood fine enough to make the King's bow. The axe of Gilgamesh was called "Might of Heroes," his bow "Anshan." Every stage of the craftsmanship was watched over by Gilgamesh and Enkidu, for they knew that their lives would depend on these weapons. **F**

As the golden sparks flew up from the anvil, the elderly counselors of Uruk gathered in the doorway of the forge. Their old heads were white with the snow of wisdom. "You are young, Gilgamesh. Youth is rash. We beg you to reconsider. This Huwawa is a thing of spirit and magic—invincible!"

But Gilgamesh only laughed. "What do you want me to do, gentlemen? Sit at home for three score years? Wrap up warm in winter and keep cool in the summer, and stay safe here in Uruk?" The blacksmith passed a finished sword into his outstretched hands. It weighed as much as a grown man, but he handled it as delicately as a newborn baby.

The counselors shook their wise old heads. There is no telling young people anything they do not want to hear. They comforted themselves on the way home, saying, "If anyone can do this thing, it is Gilgamesh and his friend, the Wild Man." **G**

Analyzing Visuals   Connecting to the Text
What scene from the story does this illustration depict?

F | Read and Discuss | What are Gilgamesh and Enkidu doing?

G | Read and Discuss | What do you learn from the conversation between Gilgamesh and the counselors?

Vocabulary   **rash** (rash) *adj.*: reckless; impatient.
invincible (ihn VIHN suh buhl) *adj.*: unable to be defeated.

Ninsun, the King's mother, sent for Enkidu. "Remember to dig a well every evening, Enkidu, and offer up pure water to the Sun God every day . . . Oh, look after him, Enkidu! You are not my son: I did not give birth to you. But bring Gilgamesh safe home and I shall adopt you as my own. I'm relying on you, Enkidu!"

The Wild Man bowed his head. For the first time, he realized that there was someone else in the word who loved Gilgamesh as much as he did.

What a way it was to the land of the cedar forests! Even though the friends walked fifty leagues a day, and accomplished in three days what it would take others six weeks to do, they still had seven mountains to cross before they stood at the forest gate.

Carved in a dozen languages were warnings and prohibitions:[5]

"DO NOT ENTER"

"CUT NO TREES, ON PAIN OF DEATH"

"THIS FOREST IS PROTECTED BY HUWAWA, TERROR OF THE EARTH" **H**

And yet the woodlands beyond the gate were as greenly peaceful as the bottom of a lake. Birdsong rippled outwards from it in tinkling wavelets. Enkidu shoved open the gate.

His knees sagged. His head spun, his hands prickled as though stabbed by a thousand splinters. He jumped awkwardly backwards. "Gilgamesh! Don't go in there! The magic is too strong! The moment I touched the gate, my strength failed me!"

But Gilgamesh was already whistling his way along the broad green pathways of the wood. **I**

In the center of the forest stood a green mountain—a perfect cone rising up so high that its peak was hidden by cloud. Its peaceful slopes seemed a perfect place to sleep. Without even troubling to dig a well and refill their water skins, the friends stretched out on the ground. Still, they slept hand-in-hand, so as to wake one another at the first sign of danger.

At midnight, Enkidu woke to the feeling of his knuckles being crushed together. Gilgamesh was sitting bolt upright, his eyes glistening in the dark. "I had a dream!" he said. "I dreamt the top of the mountain melted, and the earth spewed out its blood—fire and molten rock, and so much smoke and ash that the sun turned black. What does it mean?"

Enkidu laughed and extricated his hand. "It means we've come to the land of volcanoes, friend," he said, "In this part of the world the mountains erupt like spots on a young man's cheek. What else did you dream?"

"I dreamt that the earth trembled under me, and clouds of dust flew up so that I couldn't breathe, couldn't see, and everything around me caught fire like kindling!

---

5. **prohibitions** (proh uh BIHSH uhnz): orders forbidding something.

H **Reading Focus** Setting a Purpose Explain whether your purpose in reading this story has changed at all. If so, why has it changed?

Vocabulary **erupt** (ih RUHPT) *v.*: burst forth.

I **Literary Focus** Myth and Epic One characteristic of epics is that the heroes often travel with companions who are different from them. How is Enkidu similar to and different from Gilgamesh?

Cuneiform and Sumerian Writing

Gilgamesh's story was written thousands of years ago on clay tablets that seem to be covered with scratch marks. These marks are cuneiform (kyoo NEE uh fawrm), the world's oldest writing. Cuneiform was pressed into the surfaces of soft clay tablets with a pointed stick, or stylus. The tablets were then left in the sun to dry and harden.

The Sumerians, skilled traders who lived in Mesopotamia (part of modern-day Iraq) more than five thousand years ago, developed cuneiform to keep track of what they traded. Very few of the ancient tablets that have been discovered are literary works. Most of them are bookkeeping, inventory, and tax records!

Ask Yourself
Would you expect most cultures to use writing more for recording stories or for informational purposes like business? Why?

What kind of portent[6] is that for the gods to send me? What does it mean?"

Again Enkidu laughed. "It means we are in the land of earthquakes! Do you know nothing? The world's skin is like the skin of a lizard—now and then the scales twitch, and the earth shakes. What else did you dream?"

"I dreamt a bull," said Gilgamesh, his teeth chattering at the memory of it. "Not just a bull, I mean: a giant of a bull—bigger than twenty bulls. It was head-down and charging right at you, and there was nothing I could do! Nothing! Nothing!"

Enkidu scratched his head. "Huwawa is nothing like a bull," he said, puzzled. "His face is like a lion and he has fangs like a

---

6. **portent** (PAWR tehnt): omen; sign or warning of something, usually evil.

J [Read and Discuss] What has Gilgamesh been telling Enkidu? How has Enkidu responded?

dragon. I don't know why you should dream a . . . Gilgamesh?" **J**

But Gilgamesh had fallen asleep, his head on Enkidu's shoulder. When daylight came, he was still sound asleep. Enkidu touched him. Enkidu shook him. Enkidu took hold of him by the ears and banged his head on the ground, but he would not wake up. He was under the influence of Huwawa's magic. **K**

The whole day came and went, and still Gilgamesh slept. Enkidu was panic-stricken. *"Wake up!"* he bellowed in his friend's ear. *"Wake up!* Must I tell your mother that I let you die in your sleep? Do you want Huwawa to find you like this?"

He slapped Gilgamesh. He rolled him down the hill. He held their empty water skins over his friend—oh, why had he not

---

K [Literary Focus] Myth What <u>characteristics</u> and details here tell you that you are reading a myth and not, for example, a typical adventure story?

heeded Ninsun's advice? Enkidu dug and dug, but found no water. He ran and ran, until pebbles flew from under his feet as sparks had from the blacksmith's hammer. At last he heard the soft tinkle of trickling water. Splashing into the stream, he scooped the water skin through the cool, delicious water. Then back he ran and, upending the bag, emptied it in the King's face.

At last, the dark brown eyes opened. Stretching himself, Gilgamesh picked up his breast plate and put it on. He was perfectly calm. "Let us go and meet our enemy."

Enkidu kicked aside his bow in disgust. "You go if you like, but I'm going back to the city. You have no idea . . . You don't know what you are up against! Me, I'll go back and tell your mother how brave you are, how heroic, how glorious . . . how dead."

Gilgamesh calmly strung his bow. "Don't launch the funeral barge yet. What can go wrong with the two of us side by side?"

"Do you really want me to tell you?" said Enkidu. **L**

Inside his cedarwood house, the giant Huwawa cocked his giant head on one side and listened. A smile came to his lips which curled like the bark from a silver birch. He reached out and took down his first cloak of splendor. Six more hung alongside it, woven out of magic and the fibers of the forest. He opened his door, stuck out his head and bellowed.

"WHO HAS COME INTO THE FOREST? LET HIM DIE!"

All the acorns fell from the trees—all

L Read and Discuss What is happening in this dialogue between Enkidu and Gilgamesh?

Analyzing Visuals   **Connecting to the Text**
In this illustration, which features of Huwawa's face express his personality and reputation?

the nests of the previous spring. He looked, and as he looked, the beam of his looking scythed[7] down trees. He nodded his head, and malign[8] magic rolled through the forest, bluer and deeper than drifts of bluebells. Then he stepped out of doors. The green forest was like grass around his feet. He blotted out the sun.

Gilgamesh, caught in the coal-black shadow, looked up. "Oh, Enkidu," he said. He had never thought anything could be so big.

Then Shamash the Sun looked down and saw Gilgamesh and his friend like two tiny ants in the path of an elephant's stampede.

The Sun breathed in, fetching the warm winds. He reached out to sea and grasped the north wind and the waterspouts, lightning and phosphorescent[9] fire. He turned about and about, and the elements were twisted into a single whiplash, its thongs sharp with hail and sleet.

But the Guardian only ran back into his house and grabbed his second cloak. He had been formed to protect the forests, and even the master of those forests could not call him to heel.

Gilgamesh was wielding his axe now, hacking at the outermost wall of the lodge to bring it down. Seven walls, one inside another, and inside the seventh the Guardian, bellowing flame and destruction. Huwawa put on the third of his seven cloaks.

---

7. **scythed** (sythd): cut with a tool that has a long, curved handle and a single-edged, curved blade.
8. **malign** (muh LYN): evil; showing strong ill will.
9. **phosphorescent** (fahs fuh REHS uhnt): glowing; giving off low light after exposure to a light source.

But with every passing moment, more of the winds of Heaven piled up around the cedarwood lodge. They turned back Huwawa's powers like a mirror turns back light. The Guardian put on the fourth of his seven cloaks, and the wall of his lodge bowed outwards, so great was the magic within. Huwawa put on the fifth and sixth of his seven cloaks and for twenty thousand leagues, the cedar forests trembled. **Ⓜ**

At last the seventh cedar wall fell, and Gilgamesh and Enkidu, axes in hand, came face to face with Huwawa. Seven cloaks billowed round him like the rays of a rainbow; magic shone from his open mouth, from the heels of his hands, from the fabric of his skin. Huwawa might be terrible, but he was also magnificent. **Ⓝ**

Suddenly, a cyclone of twisted wind and heat bound him round: he was powerless to strike the heroes dead. "Let me go, Gilgamesh!" he said. "Spare me and I shall be your slave, and cut down the trees myself to build you a fitting palace."

Gilgamesh hesitated. He glanced sideways at Enkidu.

"Don't listen to him!" urged Enkidu. "It's a trick. Kill him!"

Gilgamesh swung back his axe over one shoulder. "But, Enkidu . . . if we kill him, all that glory will be lost to the world forever!"

"Don't let him fool you, Gilgamesh!" (He was not at all sure how long those ropes of wind binding Huwawa's arms would hold him, how long before the giant would squirm free.)

Ⓜ Literary Focus Myth Gods and goddesses often appear in myths to help—or hinder—the hero. How is Shamash, the Sun, playing a role in Gilgamesh's quest?

Ⓝ Read and Discuss Describe Huwawa. In what specific instances could a foe be both "terrible" and "magnificent"?

It took three blows to dispatch the Guardian of the Forests. He sprawled on his face, the trees falling flat for acres around. The phosphorescent glory which had hung about Huwawa went out like a blown candle. He was a mound of vegetable matter, a hummock in the landscape.

Dead. **O**

Gilgamesh, walking the length of the Guardian's dead body, felt the spark of life flare up inside his own. He had survived! He was alive—even more alive than before. All the colors of the forest were more bright, the birdsong sweeter, the smells more delectable. The touch of his friend's hand on his arm made him dizzy with joy.

They found the tallest cedar tree in the entire forest and hacked it down. It fell with a deafening hiss of leaves. From this the carpenters of Uruk would fashion a mighty gate to the city. **P**

Then, in reverence to the Sun, Gilgamesh washed himself in the river, put on clean robes and made an offering of cold water to Shamash, holding up the silver bowl while the noonday heat drank it up in steamy white sips.

And looking down, Ishtar, goddess of Love, saw the finest sight the world had to offer—a young man, covered in glory, triumphant, silhouetted against the sinking sun, a silver bowl upraised, face shining with pent-up happiness—King Gilgamesh. **Q**

Analyzing Visuals **Connecting to the Text** How does this image relate to the description of Gilgamesh in the final paragraph?

O **Reading Focus** **Setting a Purpose** If your purpose in reading this story were to look out for details familiar to you from other stories in books or media, what would you notice here?

P **Literary Focus** **Myth and Epic** In what ways is Gilgamesh fulfilling the role of an epic hero?

Q **Read and Discuss** How has the story ended for Gilgamesh? for Huwawa? Where do you suppose Enkidu is now?

Do or Die
Literary Response and Analysis

Reading Skills Focus
Quick Check

1. Why does Gilgamesh show Enkidu a blank wall? What does Gilgamesh say he wants to put there?

2. How does Enkidu react to Gilgamesh's plan to go to the Cedar Forest? Why?

3. How does Huwawa's magic affect Gilgamesh?

4. Who helps Gilgamesh and Enkidu against the monster Huwawa? How is Huwawa defeated?

5. What will Gilgamesh bring back to Uruk from the forest?

Read with a Purpose

6. What are Gilgamesh's heroic qualities? What do his actions indicate about what he values?

Reading Skills: Setting a Purpose

7. Review the chart you made to track your purposes for reading. How many times did your purpose change, and why?

What's Your Purpose?

Purpose 1:	to read an exciting story about a hero with superhuman powers	☐
Purpose 2:		☐

Literary Skills Focus
Literary Analysis

8. **Interpret** What qualities do Gilgamesh and Enkidu share? How are the two friends different? Explain how their differences work for them—or against them.

9. **Infer** When Gilgamesh is so close to victory, why does he hesitate to kill Huwawa? What does this tell you about Gilgamesh?

Literary Skills: Myth and Epic

10. **Analyze** One of the major characteristics of an epic is that the hero usually undertakes adventures for the good of his people. In what ways is Gilgamesh acting for the good of his people? What else might be motivating him?

11. **Evaluate** This story is almost five thousand years old. What is it about the story's concept that makes it enjoyable for audiences today? What modern stories might be loved and remembered hundreds of years from now?

Literary Skills Review: Setting

12. **Evaluate** **Setting** is the location and time period of a work of fiction. Setting can be so important that a story could not happen in any other time or place. Could this story be set in a different time and place? Explain.

Writing Skills Focus
Think as a Reader/Writer

Use It in Your Writing Choose one character from this story, and write your own description of him or her. Build on the author's descriptions you noted in your *Reader/Writer Notebook*.

What Do **You Think Now** What new thoughts do you have about heroes and people's need for them after reading about Gilgamesh?

Do or Die

Reading Standard 1.2 Identify and interpret figurative language and **words with multiple meanings** **1.5** Understand and explain "shades of meaning" in related words (e.g., softly and quietly).

Vocabulary Development

Connotations

The feelings and ideas connected with words are called **connotations.** For example, if a friend told you that you were *self-confident,* you'd probably be flattered. How would you feel, though, if your friend said you were *bossy, conceited,* or *pushy*? Your experience with words tells you that it is better to be called *self-confident* than *conceited. Self-confident* has a positive connotation; *conceited* has the negative connotation of "thinking too much of oneself."

Consider the word in italics in this sentence:

"The counselors shook their *wise* old heads."

Smart, intelligent, and *knowledgeable* are all words related to *wise,* but *wise* has the most positive connotation, of mature knowledge and experience.

Think about the connotations of words as you read. Be especially aware of words that have strong positive or negative associations.

Your Turn

Use a Vocabulary word from the list on the right to replace the word or words in italics in each sentence below. Then, next to each sentence, write *negative, neutral,* or *positive* to identify each Vocabulary word's connotation.

clenched
splendor
rash
invincible
erupt

1. The elders worried that Gilgamesh was simply an *impatient* young man.
2. Gilgamesh *tightened* his fists and stood firm.
3. The monster Huwawa seemed *unbeatable.*
4. Did the mountains *burst up* from the earth?
5. The Sun God Shamash shone with *brightness.*

Language Coach

Multiple-Meaning Words Words that are spelled the same and sound the same can have completely different meanings. *Rash* can mean "reckless" or "hasty," but it can also refer to red spots on your skin! For each of the words to the right, write two sentences, each using different meanings of the same word. You may use a dictionary if needed.

deed
stamps
mark
blaze
score

Academic Vocabulary

Talk About . . .

With a small group, <u>interpret</u> this statement by Gilgamesh: "Fame is everything, Enkidu, isn't it?" What do you think is Gilgamesh's <u>concept</u> of fame? Include specific examples from the text that <u>indicate</u> what fame means to Gilgamesh and how it motivates his actions. Use the underlined Academic Vocabulary words in your discussion.

Learn It Online
Explore shades of meaning with *WordSharp:*

go.hrw.com   H6-410   **Go**

Grammar Link

Add Interest with Predicate Adjectives

A story without adjectives would be colorless and dull, like a black-and-white picture of a rainbow. Adjectives can be used in the subject or the predicate of a sentence. When an adjective in the predicate modifies the subject of a sentence or clause, it is called a **predicate adjective.**

EXAMPLE Enkidu's pose was grand.

Enkidu's pose = subject; *was* = verb; *grand* = predicate adjective

The adjective *grand* completes the verb *was* and modifies, or describes, the subject *Enkidu's pose.*

A predicate adjective is one kind of **subject complement.** It *completes* the meaning of a verb and identifies or modifies the *subject.* A predicate adjective may be compound, which means it contains more than one adjective.

EXAMPLE Huwawa was tall and powerful.

Huwawa = subject; *was* = verb; *tall and powerful* = compound predicate adjective

A predicate adjective may even come *before* the subject and verb.

EXAMPLE How curious the onlookers were!

curious = predicate adjective; *the onlookers* = subject; *were* = verb

Your Turn

Identify the predicate adjective in each sentence.

1. The crowd was nervous.
2. Gilgamesh was young and rash.
3. He was asleep.
4. How frightening was that story!

CHOICES

As you respond to the Choices, use these **Academic Vocabulary** words as appropriate: characteristics, concept, indicate, interpret.

REVIEW

Write a Letter to the Editor

Timed ⏱ Writing As one of Gilgamesh's subjects, write a letter to the editor of the *Daily Tablet.* Explain why he is an epic hero, and express how you interpret Gilgamesh's actions. Was Gilgamesh being brave or irresponsible? Do you think he acted to benefit his people, or was he motivated by selfish needs? Cite details from the story to support your views.

CONNECT

Design the Characters

TechFocus Review the author's descriptions of Gilgamesh, Enkidu, and Huwawa. Imagine how they might be designed as characters in a video game. Draw, paint, sculpt, adapt an action figure, or make a collage of your concept of these characters. Display your work in class.

EXTEND

Discuss a Modern Gilgamesh

Partner Talk With another student, describe a concept for a modern-day Gilgamesh. What kind of person would today's Gilgamesh be—a king, a politician, an athlete? What would his goals be, and how would he achieve them? What values would he fight for? Who would be his Enkidu, and who (or what) would be the Huwawa they fight against? Share your ideas with the class.

Learn It Online
There's more to this story than meets the eye. Expand your view at:

go.hrw.com   H6-411   Go

Author Study: Walter Dean Myers

CONTENTS

What Do You Think? What truths about our own lives can a writer's messages teach us?

🕐 **QuickWrite**

Pretend you have an eager audience, ready to hear a message you would like to share about life. What is your message? What have you read or seen on television or in the movies that is similar to your message? Write your ideas.

Preparing to Read

An Interview with Walter Dean Myers / The Game / The Golden Serpent / Love That Boy

Literary Skills Focus

A Writer's Themes, or Messages Walter Dean Myers has written a huge number of works. Many of them are about the problems and adventures of teenagers from urban backgrounds like his own.

Most narratives contain a message, or **theme**—the big idea or truth that goes beyond the specific events of the narrative. One theme you'll find throughout Myers's works is that people must accept responsibility for their own lives and try to understand the lives of others—especially those very different from themselves.

Reading Skills Focus

Drawing Conclusions When you **draw conclusions,** you put together different pieces of information in order to see what they all have in common. You may find similar details and ideas in works by the same writer. These recurring <u>concepts</u> may be part of the messages that are most important to that writer.

Into Action For each selection, use a chart like the one below to gather evidence about what's important to Walter Dean Myers.

"Interview"	"The Game"
Some important <u>concepts</u> in the interview with Myers are . . .	Some important <u>concepts</u> in "The Game" are . . .

My conclusion about Walter Dean Myers's work is . . .

Writing Skills Focus
Think as a Reader/Writer

Find It in Your Reading Write down at least two details or ideas from each work that you connect to—anything that makes you think, "I like the way he said that" or "That's how I feel, too."

Reader/Writer
Notebook
Use your **RWN** to complete the activities for these selections.

Language Coach
Related Words The words *defend* and *defensive* are related to the word *defense.* Write a short paragraph in which you use each of these three words in its proper context.

 Learn It Online
Increase your understanding of words at:

go.hrw.com	H6-413	Go

Walter Dean Myers
(1937–   )

Michael
L. Printz
AWARD

"Writing, being a writer, is wonderful," says Walter Dean Myers. "I love it more than anything else in the world" Myers grew up in New York City's Harlem. He began to write when he was nine or ten.

"It was one of the few things I did get encouragement for. I wasn't a very good kid. I talked incessantly, and I fought a lot. I had a speech impediment, and that started lots of fights. Schools were much stricter then, but I guess there was room for one bad Walter. By the time I got to high school, I was more sullen and withdrawn, but I kept writing the whole time. It was something I enjoyed doing. The other kids seemed interested in me because of my writing. It was the one thing I was praised for."

"It changed my life because I had no real education, and I needed something to validate myself. I needed to find value, and publishing gave me that value."

Key Elements of Myers's Writing

Different styles of language reflect the variety of genres (types of works) he explores in his writing and the different subjects he writes about. Most often, his characters speak in **everyday language** that sounds the way people really speak.

Characters are often young African American men trying to achieve something in urban **settings,** such as Harlem.

Interesting, suspenseful plots entertain readers, making them want to keep reading to find out what's going to happen.

Messages focus on exploring his characters' relationships to the world and their responsibilities to one another.

Think About the Writer

What qualities do you think help make Myers a successful writer?

A Myers Time Line

1940s	1950s	1970	1980	1990	2000
1940 Adopted by Dean family	**1954** Drops out of high school to join army	**1970** Takes job as editor	**1980** Wins Coretta Scott King Award for *The Young Landlords*	**1989** *Scorpions* named Newbery Honor Book	**2000** First winner of Michael L. Printz Award for *Monster*
1937 Born on August 12 in West Virginia	**1969** Wins contest and publishes first book		**1975** Publishes first novel, *Fast Sam, Cool Clyde, and Stuff* **1977** Starts writing full time	**2004** Publishes 80th book **2007** With son Christopher, publishes *Blues Journey and Jazz*	

1940   1950   1960   1970   1980   1990   2000

Read with a Purpose

Read this interview to learn more about Myers's life and how he became a writer.

Build Background

Barbara Hoffman interviewed Walter Dean Myers in October 2004, just after his eightieth book, *Here in Harlem*, was published. She asked him questions that eighth-graders from Demarest School in New Jersey had put together, and Myers answered them. The interview first appeared in the newspaper the *New York Post*.

If you're anywhere near middle-school age, chances are you've read *Hoops*. Or *Monster* or *Scorpions*. Or any of the many other books by Walter Dean Myers.

His newest—and 80th—book came out this month. It's called *Here in Harlem,* and, unlike the gritty young-adult fiction he's famed for, it's a book of poems about his hometown, and the people—students, teachers, jazzmen—who made it tick.

"I have no memory of my mother at all," Myers told the *Post*. Born 67 years ago, in tiny Martinsburg, West Virginia, he was a year and a half old when she died. His father had seven children and was too poor to care for them, so the Dean family of Harlem adopted Walter when he was 3. (He later took their name by way of thanks.)

It was years before he saw his brothers and sisters and father again.

Still, said Myers, a father of three who lives in Jersey City, if he hadn't moved, he probably wouldn't have become writer:

"I had such a good experience with reading and books in the New York City school system," he says.

"I loved Yeats, Shakespeare, what have you. When I first began to write, I wrote odes[1] to everything," he says with laugh.

"Then I got older and discovered the fiction of James Baldwin. That gave me permission, so to speak, to write about African-American life, Harlem and the experiences of the poor." Ⓐ

---

1. **odes:** formal, somewhat long poems, usually written in praise of someone or something.

Ⓐ **Read and Discuss** What does Myers want to write about?

Walter Dean Myers and his brother George in front of Church of the Master at 122nd Street, Harlem, 1947.

He's been writing ever since. Recently, several dozen fans—Kathie Nolan's eighth-graders at the Demarest (N.J.) Middle School—had a bunch of questions for him. Here's how he answered them:

Barbara Hoffman: Are most of your books about your own life? Which ones?

Walter Dean Myers: Most of them are based on my own life or my own world view. *Somewhere in the Darkness* is about a boy who meets his father for the first time when he's a teenager. I met my father when he moved to my neighborhood. **B**

Hoffman: Who were your role models growing up?

Myers: I wanted to be an athlete—that's what I saw growing up. Sugar Ray Robinson[2] would come around our block and box with the kids; Willie Mays[3] would play stickball. I wanted to be a basketball player, but I left school at 17 to join the Army. When I got out, I just struggled to make a living. I worked at the post office, I worked tearing down buildings, I worked as a messenger—I was a twister in an electrical-cable factory. A big cable came out of the machine and I had to grab the cable and twist it.

Hoffman: What inspired your first book?

Myers: I saw a contest for children's books writers. I entered the picture book category, not knowing exactly what a picture book was. I did the text—about a father who takes a group of children to Central Park, and one child asked, "Where does the day go, at night?" And each child came up with an answer. The name of the book was *Where Does the Day Go?* It came out in 1969.

Hoffman: Did you take writing classes—and did they help?

Myers: I took a class with Lajos Egri, a Hungarian writer, in New York. He liked me very much and was very encouraging. I couldn't afford to take any more classes, and he let me stay for free. Years later, I took

---

2. **Sugar Ray Robinson:** an African American boxer in the 1940s and 1950s who is recognized as one of the greatest boxers of all time.
3. **Willie Mays:** an African American baseball player who played for the New York Giants in the 1950s and 1960s.

B Literary Focus A Writer's Themes, or Messages When Myers says his books are based on his "own world view," what do you think he means?

a writing class at the New School[4] and was kicked out. The guy said I just didn't have the ability. He was very apologetic and said, "Some people have it and some don't." But I kept writing. **C**

Hoffman: How many revisions do you go through before you're finished?

Myers: Usually four or five. Before I begin a book, if it's a novel, I'll go through hip-hop magazines and pick out pictures of my characters; then my wife will put them on a large piece of oaktag and make a montage. Sometimes, she'll even create a scene I'll tell her about. That montage goes on my wall behind the computer. So whenever I sit down to work, I look up and there are all my characters, looking up at me.

---

4. **New School:** a well-known institution in New York City that offers courses for adults taught by scholars, artists, and professionals.

Hoffman: If you had one chance to change something about the world, what would you do?

Myers: Oy vey! [He laughs.] You know, I would give all children philosophy courses, because so many children don't understand that you have to make decisions early in life. We sort of let kids drift. When I go to places like Rikers Island[5] and see so many kids who've drifted into lives of crime, I wish someone had told them that education is a necessity—that how you conduct your life at 15 or 16 is going to affect you for as long as you live. There's no do-over. That's why, in my books, I write about the moral decisions kids have to make. Some people think I'm preachy—and I agree! **D**

---

5. **Rikers Island:** a jail complex run by the New York City Department of Correction.

C Reading Focus **Drawing Conclusions** What would make you keep writing after someone whose opinion you should respect said you didn't have the ability?

D Read and Discuss How does Myers approach the writing process? How does he choose the topics he writes about?

Vocabulary montage (mahn TAHZH) *n.:* combination of pictures.

Analyzing Visuals

Connecting to the Text
What sort of story could you write based on the pictures in this montage?

Handbook for Boys Mural by Constance Myers.

Applying Your Skills

Reading Standard 3.6 Identify and analyze features of themes conveyed through characters, actions, and images.

An Interview with Walter Dean Myers
Literary Response and Analysis

Reading Skills Focus
Quick Check

1. What does Walter Dean Myers write about in most of his books?

2. What was Myers's first published book? Why did he write it?

3. What would Myers change about the world?

Read with a Purpose

4. How did Myers become a writer?

Reading Skills: Drawing Conclusions

5. Review the evidence you gathered about the author's ideas as you read the interview with Walter Dean Myers. What conclusions can you draw about him from this interview?

Evidence from the Text

> Some important <u>concepts</u> in the interview with Walter Dean Myers are . . .

↓

> The conclusions about Walter Dean Myers that I drew from the interview are . . .

✓ Vocabulary Check

Answer the following question.
6. What does Myers's wife use to create a **montage**?

Literary Skills Focus
Literary Analysis

7. **Draw Conclusions** Myers talks about his good experience with reading in the New York City school system. Why is reading a major part of becoming a writer?

8. **Interpret** Why does Myers cut pictures out of magazines? Why does he keep these pictures in front of him as he works?

Literary Skills: A Writer's Themes, or Messages

9. **Evaluate** Why does Walter Dean Myers think children should study philosophy? What does a person achieve by studying philosophy? What view of life does this idea express?

10. **Infer** Walter Dean Myers says, "How you conduct your life at 15 or 16 is going to affect you for as long as you live. There's no do-over." What <u>concept</u> is Myers delivering here? What view of life does it express?

11. Describe a situation in which characters, action, and images could convey the view of life you identified in question 10.

Writing Skills Focus
Think as a Reader/Writer

Use It in Your Writing What did you like about Myers's responses? Did he say anything in this interview with which you especially agreed? Read through the details that you collected as you read. Choose one detail, and write a short paragraph to explain how his words connect to your own life.

THE GAME

by Walter Dean Myers

Read with a Purpose

Read this story to find out whether the narrator's team wins the championship.

Preparing to Read for this selection is on page 413.

Build Background

Although the word *basketball* doesn't appear until more than halfway through the story, "the game" refers to a basketball game—a championship basketball game. Walter Dean Myers writes about basketball often because basketball was a big part of his life as he grew up in Harlem. This story comes from Myers's first novel for young adults, *Fast Sam, Cool Clyde, and Stuff.*

We had practiced and practiced until it ran out of our ears. Every guy on the team knew every play. We were ready. It meant the championship. Everybody was there. I never saw so many people at the center at one time. We had never seen the other team play but Sam said that he knew some of the players and that they were good. Mr. Reese told us to go out and play as hard as we could every moment we were on the floor. We all shook hands in the locker room and then went out. Mostly we tried to ignore them warming up at the other end of the court but we couldn't help but look a few times. They were doing exactly what we were doing, just shooting a few lay-ups[1] and waiting for the game to begin. Ⓐ

They got the first tap and started passing the ball around. I mean they really started passing the ball around faster than anything I had ever seen. Zip! Zip! Zip! Two points! I didn't even know how they could *see* the ball, let alone get it inside to their big man.[2] We brought the ball down and one of their players stole the ball from Sam. We got back on defense but they weren't in a hurry. The same old thing. Zip! Zip! Zip! Two points! They could pass the ball better than anybody I ever saw. Then we brought the ball down again and Chalky missed a jump shot. He missed the backboard, the rim, everything. One of their players caught the ball and then brought it down and a few seconds later the score was 6–0. We couldn't even get

---

1. **lay-ups:** shots taken close to the basket, usually banked off the backboard.

2. **their big man:** the center; this player is usually tall and plays close to the basket.

Ⓐ **Reading Focus** Drawing Conclusions What is the setting of this story? What kind of center is this? Who are the teams competing for the championship?

Vocabulary **defense** (dih FEHNS) *n.*: team acting to keep the opposing team from scoring points.

close enough to foul[3] them. Chalky brought the ball down again, passed to Sam cutting across the lane,[4] and Sam walked. They brought the ball down and it was 8–0. **Ⓑ**

They were really enjoying the game. You could see. Every time they scored they'd slap hands and carry on. Also, they had some cheerleaders. They had about five girls with little pink skirts on and white sweaters cheering for them. **Ⓒ**

Clyde brought the ball down this time, passed into our center, a guy named Leon, and Leon turned and missed a hook. They got the rebound and came down, and Chalky missed a steal and fouled his man. That's when Mr. Reese called time out.

"Okay, now, just trade basket for basket. They make a basket, you take your time and you make a basket—don't rush it." Mr. Reese looked at his starting five. "Okay, now, every once in a while take a look over at me and I'll let you know when I want you to make your move. If I put my hands palm down, just keep on playing cool. If I stand up and put my hands up like this"—he put both hands up near his face—"that means to make your move. You understand that?" **Ⓓ**

Everyone said that they understood. When the ball was back in play Chalky and

Sam and Leon started setting picks[5] from the outside and then passed to Clyde for our first two points. They got the ball and started passing around again. Zip! Zip! Zip! But this time we were just waiting for that pass underneath and they knew it. Finally they tried a shot from outside and Chalky slapped it away to Sam on the break. We came down real quick and scored. On the way back Mr. Reese showed everybody that his palms were down. To keep playing cool.

They missed their next shot and fouled Chalky. They called time out and, much to my surprise, Mr. Reese put me in. My heart was beating so fast I thought I was going to have a heart attack. Chalky missed the foul shot but Leon slapped the ball out to Clyde, who passed it to me. I dribbled about two steps and threw it back to Leon in the bucket. Then I didn't know what to do so I did what Mr. Reese always told us. If you don't know what to do then, just move around. I started moving toward the corner and then I ran quickly toward the basket. I saw Sam coming at me from the other direction and it was a play. Two guards cutting past and one of the defensive men gets picked off. I ran as close as I could to Sam, and his man got picked off. Chalky threw the ball into him for an easy lay-up. They came down and missed again but one of

---

3. **foul:** make an illegal move on the court, such as grabbing a player.

4. **lane:** section of the basketball court that players can't enter during a free throw.

5. **setting picks:** blocking defensive players to free up a teammate to make a shot.

Ⓑ [Read and Discuss] How do occasional short sentences and phrases like "Zip! Zip! Zip!" help you visualize what is happening in this segment?

Ⓒ [Reading Focus] **Drawing Conclusions** Who is the narrator of this story? How do you know?

Ⓓ [Read and Discuss] What does Mr. Reese's advice show you about him and how he views his players?

their men got the rebound in. We brought the ball down and Sam went along the base line for a jump shot, but their center knocked the ball away. I caught it just before it went out at the corner and shot the ball. I remembered what Mr. Reese had said about following your shot in, and I started in after the ball but it went right in. It didn't touch the rim or anything. Swish! **E**

One of their players said to watch out for 17—that was me. I played about two minutes more, then Mr. Reese took me out. But I had scored another basket on a lay-up. We were coming back. Chalky and Sam were knocking away just about anything their guards were throwing up, and Leon, Chalky, and Sam controlled the defensive backboard. Mr. Reese brought in Cap, and Cap got fouled two times in two plays. At the end of the half, when I thought we were doing pretty well, I found out the score was 36–29. They were beating us by seven points. Mr. Reese didn't seem worried, though.

"Okay, everybody, stay cool. No sweat. Just keep it nice and easy." **F**

We came out in the second half and played it pretty cool. Once we came within one point, but then they ran it up to five again. We kept looking over to Mr. Reese to see what he wanted us to do and he would just put his palms down and nod his head for us to play cool. There were six minutes to go when Mr. Reese put me and another guy named Turk in. Now I didn't really understand why he did this because I know

I'm not the best basketball player in the world, although I'm not bad, and I know Turk is worse than me. Also, he took out both Sam and Chalky, our two best players. We were still losing by five points, too. And they weren't doing anything wrong. There was a jump ball between Leon and their center when all of a sudden this big

---

E **Reading Focus** Drawing Conclusions The narrator says that he threw the ball to Leon "in the bucket." What does that mean? Where is Leon? What evidence did you use to figure that out?

F **Read and Discuss** How is Mr. Reese's coaching paying off?

cheer goes up and everybody looks over to the sidelines. Well, there was Gloria, BB, Maria, Sharon, Kitty, and about four other girls, all dressed in white blouses and black skirts and with big T's on their blouses and they were our cheerleaders. One of their players said something stupid about them but I liked them. They looked real good to me. We controlled the jump and Turk drove right down the lane and made a lay-up. Turk actually made the lay-up. Turk once missed seven lay-ups in a row in practice and no one was even guarding him. But this one he made. Then one of their men double-dribbled and we got the ball and I passed it to Leon, who threw up a shot and got fouled. The shot went in and when he made the foul shot it added up to a three-point play. They started down court and Mr. Reese started yelling for us to give a foul. **G**

"Foul him! Foul him!" he yelled from the sidelines.

Now this was something we had worked on in practice and that Mr. Reese had told us would only work once in a game. Anybody who plays basketball knows that if you're fouled while shooting the ball you get two foul shots and if you're fouled while not shooting the ball you only get one. So when a guy knows you're going to foul him he'll try to get off a quick shot. At least that's what we hoped. When their guard came across the mid-court line, I ran at him as if I was going to foul him. Then, just as I was going to touch him, I stopped short and moved around him without touching him. Sure enough, he threw the ball wildly toward the basket. It went over the base line and it was our ball. Mr. Reese took me out and Turk and put Sam and Chalky back in. And the game was just about over. **H**

We hadn't realized it but in the two minutes that me and Turk played the score had been tied. When Sam and Chalky came back in they outscored the other team by four points in the last four minutes. We were the champs. We got the first-place trophies and we were so happy we were all jumping around and slapping each other on the back. Gloria and the other girls were just as happy as we were, and when we found that we had an extra trophy we gave it to them. Then Mr. Reese took us all in the locker room and shook each guy's hand and then went out and invited the parents and the girls in. He made a little speech about how he was proud of us and all, and not just because we won tonight but because we had worked so hard to win. When he finished everybody started clapping for us and, as usual, I started boo-hooing. But it wasn't so bad this time because Leon started boo-hooing worse than me.

You know what high is? We felt so good the next couple of days that it was ridiculous. We'd see someone in the street and we'd just walk up and be happy. Really. **I**

G [Read and Discuss] What do Mr. Reese's decisions to put the narrator and Turk into the game add to what you already know about the coach?

H [Read and Discuss] What's all this about fouling players?

I [Literary Focus] A Writer's Themes, or Messages How would you express the theme of this story? How do the characters' feelings and actions help convey the theme?

Applying Your Skills

Reading Standard 3.6 Identify and analyze features of themes conveyed through characters, actions, and images.

The Game
Literary Response and Analysis

Reading Skills Focus
Quick Check

1. Review "The Game," and fill in a story map like the one below.

   Title and Author: _____

   Setting: _____

   Characters: _____

   Events: _____

Read with a Purpose

2. How does the narrator's team win the championship?

Reading Skills: Drawing Conclusions

3. What important concepts does Myers present in this story? Review the evidence of his ideas and messages you gathered as you read "The Game." What conclusions can you draw about Myers and his work from this evidence?

   Some important ideas in "The Game" are...

   ↓

   My conclusion about Myers's work is...

✓ Vocabulary Check

4. What is an antonym for the **defense** on a team?

   a. defenseless   c. defenders
   b. offense   d. offenders

Literary Skills Focus
Literary Analysis

5. **Interpret** By the time Mr. Reese calls the first timeout, what conclusion has the narrator already drawn about the other team? On what evidence does he base this conclusion?

6. **Evaluate** The story is told from the first-person point of view of one of the players. How does this point of view affect the way Myers tells the story and the way you interpret events?

7. **Interpret** The narrator asks at the end: "You know what high is?" How does he define *high*? What does this tell you about the effect winning had on him?

Literary Skills: A Writer's Themes, or Messages

8. **Analyze** In the interview, Walter Dean Myers talked about decisions youths need to make early in life. What decisions have the boys in this story made? How do their decisions relate to the theme of the story?

9. **Interpret** How do the words and actions of Mr. Reese help the boys work together to achieve their goal?

Writing Skills Focus
Think as a Reader/Writer

Use It in Your Writing Look at the sentences and lines of dialogue that you liked and wrote down in your *Reader/Writer Notebook*. Think of one of your experiences that you could write about. Write it as if you were talking to a friend.

The Golden Serpent

retold by **Walter Dean Myers**

Read with a Purpose
Read this fable to learn how the wise man Pundabi solves the mystery of the Golden Serpent.

Preparing to Read for this selection is on page 413.

Build Background
"The Golden Serpent" was first published as a book. Although many of Myers's books are connected to his own background and to the life experience of African Americans, "The Golden Serpent" has characters, a plot, and a setting completely different from those of most of his other works. The story is based on an ancient fable from India.

There was once a very wise man. He lived on a high mountain and was called Pundabi. With him lived a young boy. The boy's name was Ali.

Each morning Ali would come down the mountain. He would sit in the shade of a fig tree. Many people would come to him. They brought him loaves of bread. In the bread were pieces of fine linen. There would be questions on the linen for the wise Pundabi to answer. They would be questions of life and death, or about the search for happiness.

Each evening Ali would climb the mountain and give the loaves of bread to Pundabi. Pundabi would answer all the questions. Then they would eat the bread.

Ali would take the answers down the mountain. He would give them to the waiting people. Pundabi and Ali lived well this way, and the people loved them dearly. ⓐ

One day a tall shadow fell across Ali. It was the shadow of the king himself.

"Are you Ali?" the king asked.

"I am he," Ali answered.

"And you live with the wise man Pundabi?"

"That is so," Ali replied.

ⓐ **Read and Discuss** What has the author told you so far about Pundabi and Ali?

Vocabulary **linen** (LIHN uhn) *n.*: fine-quality writing paper, once made from linen rags.

"And it is true that he is very wise?"

"Yes, it is true," said Ali.

"Then you must bring him to me," the king said.

So Ali went up the mountain. He told Pundabi of the king's request. Pundabi and Ali came down the mountain. They set out for the palace. They went past the river and through the marketplace. They went through the village. Finally they reached another high mountain. **B**

On top of this mountain was the palace.

"I want you to solve a mystery for me." The king spoke from his high throne. "But first we must have lunch." He clapped his hands twice.

Five men brought in five trays of food. There was a tray for Pundabi. There was a tray for Ali. And three trays for the king.

"I am very rich," the king said. "I have much gold and many rubies. And you, Pundabi, are very wise. I can pay you very well."

"What is the mystery?" asked Pundabi.

"I do not know," said the king. "That is for you to discover!"

"But how can Pundabi solve a mystery"—Ali wrung his hands—"if there is none to solve?"

"If you are truly wise, Pundabi, it will be done. If you do not solve it, then you are a fraud. I will put you in jail where you belong."

Ali was very afraid. He began to shake.

But Pundabi said, "Let us take a walk. Perhaps our eyes will speak to us." **C**

B Reading Focus **Drawing Conclusions** Why does Pundabi, without question or hesitation, come down the mountain and make his way to the palace?

C Read and Discuss Now what is happening to Pundabi?

Vocabulary **fraud** (frawd) *n.*: someone who pretends to be what he or she is not.

The Golden Serpent **425**

So they began to walk. They walked by the river.

They walked through the village. They stopped by the home of an old woman. They walked around the marketplace. Pundabi's eyes spoke to him.

Then Pundabi began to walk up the mountain toward the palace.

"We will surely go to jail," Ali said. "We cannot solve the mystery. We do not know what it is."

"But we do know what the mystery is." Pundabi spoke, a smile upon his face. "And perhaps we can solve it. Let us go and see the king."

"Have you solved the mystery yet?" the king asked.

"No," said Pundabi. "But we know what the mystery is! It is the mystery of the Golden Serpent."

"The Golden Serpent?" said the king.

"Yes," Pundabi said. "Where is your Golden Serpent?"

"I didn't know I had one," the king said.

"The thief must be very clever," Pundabi said.

"You must find it for me," said the king.

"Let us see," Pundabi said. "Someone must have taken it to sell. Let us go to the market."

So the king called his guards. And off they went to the market. **Ⓓ**

In the market they came upon a young boy. The boy was turning wood.[1]

---

1. **turning wood:** shaping wood with a tool called a lathe. The lathe the boy is using is operated by a pedal, which accounts for the boy's bent leg.

"Perhaps he has stolen the Golden Serpent." The king seized the boy by the arm.

"I have no Golden Serpent," the boy said. "I could not run away with it. My leg is bent from turning."

But the guards searched him well. They searched his blouse and the hay upon which he slept. They even looked at his bent leg.

"It is true," the guards said. "He has nothing. He can hardly walk."

Next they went to the village. They stopped at the house of a widow.

"We are searching for the Golden Serpent," said Pundabi, "which was stolen from the king."

"I do not have it," said the widow. "I have only this small cup of grain."

But the king did not trust her. So the guards searched her hut. They looked in the corners. They looked in the cupboard.

"It is true," said the guards. "She has nothing but this cup of grain."

"Let us go from this dismal place," the king said.

Outside they heard a strange cry. Three men walked together. They sang a sad song. The first had a stick. He swung it before him as he walked. The second walked behind the first. The third walked behind the second. Each had a hand on the other's shoulder.

"Perhaps," said Pundabi, "these are your thieves."

"These?" said the king. "Why, they cannot see!"

Ⓓ **Read and Discuss** How are things looking for Pundabi? What does the king think of Pundabi's discovery?

Vocabulary **dismal** (DIHZ muhl) *adj.*: cheerless; depressing.

"How clever of them," said Pundabi. **E**

So they stopped the three blind men and asked of the king's Golden Serpent.

"No," said the first. "I have only this stick for comfort."

"No," said the second. "I have only the few coins I am given."

"No," said the third. "I have but these two friends."

But the king did not trust them. So the guards searched the three blind men.

"They have nothing," said the guards, "except a worm-eaten stick and a few coins. Nothing more." **F**

"Let us return to the palace," the king said.

"But we have not found the Golden Serpent," Pundabi said.

"I no longer want it," the king said bitterly. "I will pay you and you can leave." **G**

At the palace, the king had his counters pay Pundabi in gold coins.

"And what about your people?" Pundabi asked.

"My people?" asked the king.

"Yes. The crippled boy, the poor widow, and the blind beggars," said Ali.

"What about them, indeed!" said the king. "They did not find my Golden Serpent."

E Reading Focus **Drawing Conclusions** What does Pundabi mean by this comment? Why does he say this to the king?

F Reading Focus **Drawing Conclusions** Why does Pundabi take the king to see all these unfortunate people and suggest to him that they have taken his Golden Serpent?

G Read and Discuss What are the king and Pundabi up to now? How is their search going?

"Ah," said Pundabi, "I see. But I have solved your mystery. I know where the Golden Serpent is."

"You do?" said the king. "How splendid!"

"You must close your eyes and count slowly until you reach a hundred. But make sure you are alone so that no one can steal the Golden Serpent again. Then open your eyes. The Golden Serpent will be in your room."

The king closed his eyes and began to count slowly as Pundabi picked up his bag of gold and left the palace.

He went down the steep hill.

He gave some of the gold to the crippled boy.

He gave some to the widow. He gave some to the blind beggars.

"Pundabi," said Ali. "You are both wise and generous. But there is still one problem."

"And what is that?" asked Pundabi.

"When the king opens his eyes," said Ali, "he will still not find the Golden Serpent." **H**

"No," said Pundabi. "Some people never do. But that is another mystery." **I**

H **Reading Focus** Drawing Conclusions   Do you know more now about the Golden Serpent? What do you think the Golden Serpent is?

I **Literary Focus** A Writer's Themes, or Messages
What is the theme of this fable? Why do some people never find the Golden Serpent? Why is that a "mystery"?

Love That Boy

by **Walter Dean Myers**

Read with a Purpose
Read this poem to see how the speaker cherishes his young son.

Preparing to Read for this selection is on page 413.

Build Background
Walter Dean Myers started writing poems when he was in fifth grade. Almost fifty years later, he wrote "Love That Boy" for his book *Brown Angels*. The book is an album of turn-of-the-century photographs of African American children. Myers collected the photos from antique shops, flea markets, and auctions.

Love that boy,
like a rabbit loves to run
I said I love that boy
like a rabbit loves to run
5 Love to call him in the morning
love to call him
"Hey there, son!"

He walk like his grandpa
grins like his uncle Ben
10 I said he walk like his grandpa
and grins like his uncle Ben
Grins when he happy
when he sad he grins again **Ⓐ**

His mama like to hold him
15 like to feed him cherry pie
I said his mama like to hold him
feed him that cherry pie
She can have him now
I'll get him by and by **Ⓑ**

20 He got long roads to walk down
before the setting sun
I said he got a long, long road
to walk down,
before the setting sun
25 He'll be a long stride walker
and a good man before he done **Ⓒ**

Ⓐ Reading Focus Drawing Conclusions What is the speaker saying about his son?

Ⓑ Read and Discuss What does the speaker mean when he says, "I'll get him by and by"?

Ⓒ Literary Focus A Writer's Themes, or Messages What is the author's theme, or message, in this poem?

Applying Your Skills

Reading Standard 3.6 Identify and analyze features of themes conveyed through characters, actions, and images.

The Golden Serpent / Love That Boy
Literary Response and Analysis

Reading Skills Focus
Quick Check

1. How does being wise enable Pundabi to support himself and Ali?

2. Why does the king summon Pundabi?

3. Who is the speaker in "Love That Boy"?

Read with a Purpose

4. In "The Golden Serpent," how does Pundabi solve the mystery? In "Love That Boy," how does the speaker show his love for his son?

Reading Skills: Drawing Conclusions

5. Review the evidence of Myers's ideas and messages you gathered as you read "The Golden Serpent" and "Love That Boy." What conclusions can you draw about Walter Dean Myers and his work from this evidence?

> Evidence from the Text
>
> Some important ideas in "The Golden Serpent" are . . .   Some important ideas in "Love That Boy" are . . .
>
> ↓
>
> My conclusion about Walter Dean Myers's work is . . .

✔ Vocabulary Check

6. What would you be writing on if you wrote something on **linen**?

7. Why would Pundabi be a **fraud** if he could not solve the mystery?

8. Which is more likely to be a **dismal** place: a palace or a jail? Why?

Literary Skills Focus
Literary Analysis

9. **Interpret** Who or what *is* the Golden Serpent? Support your answer with evidence from the fable.

10. **Analyze** Myers uses **repetition** throughout "Love That Boy"; that is, he repeats words and sentences. Why do you think he uses repetition? What does it add to the poem?

11. **Evaluate** In the interview, Walter Dean Myers says he has no memory of his mother and didn't see his father again until long after his adoption. How does knowing this affect your appreciation of "Love That Boy"?

Literary Skills: A Writer's Themes, or Messages

12. **Analyze** Walter Dean Myers has said that one of the messages he believes and carries through all of his work is that we fulfill our lives when we try to understand the lives of others. How does this theme come across in "The Golden Serpent" and "Love That Boy"?

Writing Skills Focus
Think as a Reader/Writer

Use It in Your Writing What did you most like—or dislike—about the way Myers wrote "The Golden Serpent" and "Love That Boy"? How did Myers help you connect to these works? Were you able to connect more to one than the other? Using the details that you collected in your *Reader/Writer Notebook,* respond to these questions in one or two paragraphs.

Reading Standard 3.6 Identify and analyze features of themes conveyed through characters, actions, and images.

Author Study: Walter Dean Myers

Writing Skills Focus
Think as a Reader/Writer

Making Connections to a Writer's Works Look back at the examples of Myers's writing that you recorded in your *Reader/Writer Notebook*. Which characteristics of his writing did you find most effective? Evaluate his straightforward descriptions, the way his characters talk, the way his characters act and interact, and the rhythm of his words. What sentences, descriptions, lines of dialogue, and even entire passages most help you connect with Myers's different fictional "worlds"?

Use It in Your Writing Myers once said, "Ultimately, what I want to do with my writing is to make connections—to touch the lives of my characters and, through them, those of my readers." In a two-paragraph essay, explain whether you felt connections to Myers's characters and their situations. If you felt more connected to some works, themes, or characters than others, explain why. Use examples from your *Reader/Writer Notebook* to support your opinions.

What Do You Think Now?

What truths about life does Myers share in these works? How do these truths connect to your own life?

CHOICES

As you respond to the Choices, use these **Academic Vocabulary** words as appropriate: characteristics, concept, indicate, interpret.

REVIEW
Write about Theme

Timed ⏱ **Writing** In two or three paragraphs, interpret the theme of one of the texts by Myers presented in this Author Study. Explain how the characters, actions, and images of the text support Myers's theme.

CONNECT
Write Your Own Tribute Poem

Myers's poem "Love That Boy" was the inspiration for Sharon Creech's book *Love That Dog,* which tells the story of a boy who discovers the power of words and poetry. Following the model of "Love That Boy," write your own tribute poem to someone or something you love.

EXTEND
Write a Screenplay

TechFocus With several others, choose "The Game" excerpt or "The Golden Serpent," and write all or part of it as a screenplay. Write dialogue and camera directions. To create a storyboard showing the sequence of events, see the template on the *Digital Storytelling* site.

Learn It Online
"The Game" is a novel excerpt. For more on novels, see:

| go.hrw.com | H6-431 | Go |

Structural Features of Popular Media

Tales (1988) by Jonathan Green. Oil on masonite (24" x 36"). From the collection of Kuuna Riihimaki.

CONTENTS

What Do You Think

What can we learn from stories of times past?

 QuickTalk

Name some popular stories from you and most of your classmates these stories so memorable?

Preparing to Read

Reading Standard 2.1 Identify the structural features of popular media (e.g., newspapers, **magazines**, online information) and use the features to obtain information.

Making It Up as We Go

Informational Text Focus

Structural Features of Popular Media: Magazines The word *media* means "ways of communicating or expressing ideas." When people use television, radio, magazines, newspapers, and the Internet to provide news and information to audiences of millions around the world, that "way of communicating" is called *mass media*.

Magazines have special structural features that give you an overview of what is inside—the contents.

- **The cover** The cover's art and main headline usually announce the lead article and other feature articles.
- **The contents page** The contents at the front of the magazine lists the articles and tells you what pages they are on.

Before you read your next **magazine article,** take a minute to notice the way it is structured.

- **The title** Most magazine articles have titles that are written to catch the reader's interest.
- **The subtitle** An article may have a **subtitle,** a secondary title that tells you more about the article's subject. Beneath the subtitle, the **name of the writer** of the article may be listed.
- **Headings** Headings are words or phrases used to break up the text of an article into sections. They are often printed in a size or color intended to stand out. You can sometimes **outline** the main points of an article by listing the headings.
- **Illustrations** Many articles are illustrated with drawings, photographs, maps, and such to help you picture something described and to provide more information. They may be accompanied by brief printed explanations, called **captions.**

Writing Skills Focus

Preparing for **Timed** ○ **Writing** Record the main points of "Making It Up As We Go." You'll use them to answer a question later.

Reader/Writer
Notebook
Use your **RWN** to complete the activities for this selection.

Vocabulary

prehistoric (pree hihs TAWR ihk) *adj.:* relating to the time before written history. *The prehistoric cave art was skillfully done.*

permanent (PUR muh nuhnt) *adj.:* lasting; unchanging. *The art might have provided a permanent record of a story.*

intriguing (ihn TREE gihng) *adj.:* causing great interest. *Scientists have intriguing ideas about the purpose of the cave art.*

Language Coach

Word Origin The word *intriguing* comes from the Latin word *intricare*, which means "to tangle up." Explain how you think the meaning of the Latin term is related to the meaning of *intriguing*.

Learn It Online
Explore an interactive magazine article with the Reading Workshop online:

go.hrw.com   H6-433   **Go**

Making It Up as We Go

The **title** is often a catchy phrase intended to grab your interest.

THE HISTORY OF STORYTELLING

The **subtitle** tells you more about the article.

by Jennifer Kroll

THE WORLD ALMANAC

Read with a Purpose

Read the following magazine article, paying attention to what you can learn from its structural features.

On an autumn day in 1879, eight-year-old Maria Sanz de Sautuola explored a cave on her family's land in Altamira, Spain. As her candle lit up a large chamber, Maria was startled and called to her father. "Look, Papa! Oxen!" she cried. The chamber was filled with animal paintings. From where she stood, oxen seemed to be running across the ceiling.

Similar paintings have since been found in more than 200 caves in Spain and France. The artwork shows such animals as mammoths, reindeer, and horses. Sometimes, symbols have been drawn on or near the creatures. At a cave called Font-du-Gaume, these symbols include upside-down *T*s and side-by-side circles with arches above them.

What did these pictures and symbols mean to the people who made them? We cannot know. But it is reasonable to wonder whether the images were used as a way of preserving stories—or as an aid in telling them.

Headings break up the text into sections.

STONE-AGE STORYTELLERS

Maria and her father, Marcelino, found stone tools, pieces of pottery, oyster shells, and animal bones nearby before uncovering the art. Marcelino figured the items, and therefore the artwork, were created by prehistoric people called Cro-Magnons. Cro-Magnons were

Marcelino Sanz de Sautuola and his daughter Maria discover the cave paintings at Altamira. Ⓐ

hunters and gatherers who lived from about 40,000 to 10,000 years ago. They did not have written language as we do. But surely they had stories.

Imagine a Cro-Magnon storyteller standing in the Altamira cave, lighting up pictures to show parts of a story. Perhaps he stood where Maria stood. Maybe the flicker of fire from his torch made the oxen seem to run. Ⓑ

PASS IT ON, PASS IT DOWN

Writing is a recent invention, only about 5,000 to 6,000 years old. Among the first people to develop a writing system were the Sumerians. They lived in the region that is now Iraq. Their writing system, called

---

Ⓐ **Informational Focus** Structural Features Point out the text that the illustration at the right describes. What is the information that the drawing helps you understand?

Ⓑ **Read and Discuss** How does this new information add to what you have already learned?

Vocabulary prehistoric (pree hihs TAWR ihk) *adj.*: relating to the time before written history.

FROM DRAWING TO WRITING

The Sumerians first wrote by using pictures to represent things and ideas. Gradually, the pictures became more like abstract symbols and less like illustrations of what they represented. These examples show how Sumerian writing changed over time.

	3300 B.C.	2800 B.C.	2400 B.C.	1800 B.C.
Heaven				
Grain				
Fish				
Bird				
Water				

Illustrations help you picture things described in the article.

THE RARE AND WONDERFUL WRITTEN WORD

JUST HOW NEW AND NOVEL IS WRITING? CONSIDER THESE FACTS:

- Modern humans (*Homo sapiens*) have existed for between 100,000 and 150,000 years. The earliest written language, though, dates from only 5,000 to 6,000 years ago.

- Perhaps tens of thousands of different languages have existed in human history. Stories have been told orally in most of these languages.

- **Written** stories exist in only a small percentage of all languages—about 106!

- About 6,000 languages are spoken in the world today. Only about 78 of them have a written form that is used for recording and saving stories.

- Even today, hundreds of languages with no written form are being used all over the world. **C**

C [Read and Discuss] The author has given you a number of facts here. What is the point of this information?

cuneiform, dates back to before 3000 B.C. The Sumerians wrote by pressing marks into moist clay tablets with a sharp reed. The tablets would be baked, hardening the clay so that it would last. The Sumerians kept detailed business and government records. They also wrote down stories. The *Epic of Gilgamesh* is a Sumerian story that's still told today. It was written on clay tablets that have lasted for thousands of years.

Before developing writing, the Sumerians kept stories alive in the way most groups have throughout time. They passed on tales by word of mouth. Many of these ancient stories were written into the *Epic of Gilgamesh*. But the tales were passed from person to person for years before being pressed into clay.

A culture that passes on stories by word of mouth is said to have an *oral tradition*. The stories of such a culture differ from those of a *chirographic* (ky ruh GRAF ihk), or writing, culture in some ways. For one thing, written stories remain the same with each reading. But unwritten stories change with every telling. Each storyteller cannot help but give each story his or her own twist.

PREHISTORIC BLOGGERS? Ⓓ

The idea that a story may never be told the same twice might seem to go against the belief that a story is a permanent creation. Then again, maybe not. After all, we're used to seeing stories change as they shift forms—when a novel is made into a film, for example, or a film into a comic book.

The **caption** explains what is shown in an illustration.

American tall tales, like those about Paul Bunyan and Babe the Blue Ox (the subjects of this California sculpture), are examples of stories spread by word of mouth.

We still pass on stories by word of mouth, just as our ancestors did. Think of campers telling scary stories around a fire or fishers swapping "biggest catch" stories. Most people like to give a story their own "spin." Think of news passed around the school cafeteria or by Internet bloggers. Most Web writers don't just tell you what happened; they tell you what they *think* about what happened. The journalists Gregory Curtis and Daniel Burnstein have (separately) suggested that the Cro-Magnons might have done something similar when they drew symbols around cave paintings. Could the symbols be comments added to a story by later viewers or tellers? It is an intriguing idea. What do you think? Ⓔ

Read with a Purpose

Which structural feature most contributed to your understanding of this article?

Ⓓ **Informational Focus** Structural Features How do headings like this one help you while you read the article?

Ⓔ **Read and Discuss** How does early storytelling relate to some of today's forms of storytelling?

Vocabulary **permanent** (PUR muh nuhnt) *adj.:* lasting; unchanging.
intriguing (ihn TREE gihng) *adj.:* causing great interest.

MAGAZINE ARTICLE
Applying Your Skills

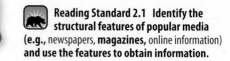

Reading Standard 2.1 **Identify the structural features of popular media (e.g.,** newspapers, **magazines,** online information) **and use the features to obtain information.**

Making It Up as We Go
Standards Review

Informational Text and Vocabulary

1. The article's title, "Making It Up as We Go," is written to grab interest, whereas the subtitle, "The History of Storytelling," is written to

   A inform.

   B entertain.

   C increase interest.

   D catch the reader's eye.

2. "Pass It On, Pass It Down" is

   A the magazine title.

   B a caption.

   C a heading.

   D an illustration.

3. The illustrations in this article

   A depict the animals painted in Altamira cave.

   B tell a story in the chirographic tradition.

   C show the marks made next to cave paintings.

   D support points made in the article.

4. This article was written *mainly* to

   A teach readers about prehistoric paintings in the Altamira cave.

   B explain that Cro-Magnons lived in caves.

   C show how Sumerian writing changed gradually over time.

   D suggest that the long tradition of story-telling may go back to prehistoric times.

5. The term *prehistoric* most closely means

   A before humans.

   B recorded in writing.

   C before speech.

   D before recorded history.

6. *Permanent* does *not* mean

   A indelible.

   B brief.

   C constant.

   D lasting.

7. An *intriguing* person is

   A interesting.

   B toughened.

   C confusing.

   D confused.

Writing Skills Focus

Timed ⌊Writing** Use the notes you took while reading this article to describe the <u>characteristics</u> of storytelling from the oral tradition.

What Do
You
Think
Now

What might the most ancient storytellers have in common with storytellers today?

Preparing to Read

Reading Standard 2.1 Identify the structural features of popular media (e.g., **newspapers**, magazines, online information) and use the features to obtain information.

Iraqi Treasures Hunted

Informational Text Focus

Structural Features of Popular Media: Newspapers Like other forms of informational materials, **newspapers** have special structural features that help you find and understand the information you are looking for. Follow these tips when you are reading a newspaper:

- Learn about your newspaper's **sections.** A newspaper may be divided into sections for world and national news, local news, sports, weather, comics, entertainment, and other subjects. Decide which section is most likely to have the information you want.
- Scan the **headlines.** Headlines usually appear in large, heavy type and are not complete sentences. Headlines <u>indicate</u> what an article is about and usually grab your attention.
- Beneath a headline, you will sometimes find a **byline,** the name of the writer. The article itself may begin with a **dateline,** which includes the name of the place where the news event happened and often the date when it happened.
- For the most important information, check the **lead,** the beginning of the article. News articles usually answer most or all of the *5W-How?* questions—*who? what? where? when? why?* and *how?*—in the lead. The less important information usually comes at the end of the article. Having the most important information up front makes skimming and scanning a newspaper much easier for readers.
- Some newspaper articles have pictures or graphics with **captions,** or short explanations. Newspapers may also have special side features called **sidebars**—additional information that is related to the article but placed in a separate box.

Writing Skills Focus

Preparing for **Timed Writing** As you read, observe how structural features of a newspaper help you find information. You'll answer a timed-writing question about structural features later.

Vocabulary

recovered (rih KUHV uhrd) *v.:* got back something lost. *Many of the stolen items have been recovered by the museum.*

civilizations (sihv uh luh ZAY shuhnz) *n.:* advanced cultures that are characteristic of particular times and places. *Mesopotamia was home to some of the earliest civilizations.*

authorities (uh THAWR uh teez) *n.:* people with the official responsibility for something. *Many artifacts were returned to the authorities.*

Language Coach

Base Words A base word can stand alone. It is a complete word all by itself, although other word parts may be added to it to make new words. If you know a certain base word, you can often discover another word's meaning if it shares the same base. For instance, you have learned the meaning of *civilizations*. What do you think the words *civilized*, *civility*, and *civilian* might mean? What is the base word of all these words?

Reader/Writer
Notebook
Use your **RWN** to complete the activities for this selection.

Learn It Online
Learn about the features of a newspaper through *PowerNotes* online:

| go.hrw.com | H6-439 | Go |

©AFP/Getty Images.

The **headline** tells you what the news story is about.

Iraqi workers repair a damaged statue.

IRAQI TREASURES
HUNTED

Long after the looting of the National Museum, Iraq's treasures remain at risk.

The **byline** tells you who wrote the article.

by Barbara Bakowski

THE WORLD ALMANAC

Read with a Purpose
Read the following article to find out the fate of Iraq's archaeological treasures.

Build Background
In the days following the invasion of Iraq in 2003, U.S.–led military forces struggled to maintain order. As the city of Baghdad fell, it was easy for thieves, or looters, to take advantage of the confusion and disorder. Looters were even able to steal some of the nation's greatest treasures: ancient, priceless artifacts from Iraq's National Museum.

STONY BROOK, N.Y., January 14 — Nearly four years have passed since looters removed thousands of items from Iraq's National Museum. Many of the missing pieces have been recovered. Historians and art experts, however, say Iraq's historical artifacts are still in danger.

After the robberies, museum director Donny George walled off much of the collection to protect the remains. George left Iraq in 2006 and is serving as a visiting professor at New York's Stony Brook University. Now looters are stealing items from throughout Iraq, says his Stony Brook colleague Dr. Elizabeth Stone, an expert in the archaeology of the Middle East. Dig sites are the new targets. Some of the objects being taken date back to the world's earliest civilizations.

"Mesopotamia had the world's first cities, first writing," Stone says. "All our ideas of how we live in cities came from there." Ⓐ

Birthplace of Civilization

Present-day Iraq occupies the land once called Mesopotamia. The name comes from a Greek word meaning "the land between rivers." In the plains between the Tigris and Euphrates rivers, some of the world's earliest settlements were founded: Sumer, Babylonia, and Assyria. "It was the cradle of civilization" more than 5,000 years ago, Stone says.

Early Mesopotamians were ahead of their time in many ways. They improved farming methods, created irrigation systems, learned how to measure time, wrote a set of laws, and invented the wheeled chariot. The Sumerians also invented cuneiform, one of the first writing systems in the world, before 3000 B.C. *The Epic of Gilgamesh,* a famous work of Sumerian literature, was recorded on clay tablets that still survive. It was written down in about 2000 B.C.

Ancient Objects Stolen

Iraq's National Museum, founded in 1923, held the physical record of Mesopotamia's long history. The museum housed at least 500,000 valuable items. Then, in April 2003, U.S.-led troops moved into Baghdad. Looters used the resulting confusion as an opportunity to steal statues, coins, and more. In the final count, about 14,000 items from the museum were stolen, including the 5,000-year-old Warka mask and a copper sculpture known as the Bassetki statue.

Iraqi authorities, the United Nations, the U.S. government, and international law-enforcement officials began a search. Researchers at the Oriental Institute at the University of Chicago listed photographs and descriptions of the stolen objects on a Web site to aid in their recovery.

Relics Returned

Officials adopted a "no-questions-asked" policy to encourage the safe return of the missing

— *Continued on Page 443* —

Ⓐ **Informational Focus** **Structural Features** What do the structural features and the information on pages 440 and 441 indicate about the article? Use details to explain.

Vocabulary **recovered** (rih KUHV uhrd) *v.:* got back something lost.
civilizations (sihv uh luh ZAY shuhnz) *n.:* advanced cultures that are characteristic of particular times and places.
authorities (uh THAWR uh teez) *n.:* people with the official responsibility for something.

The full-page *sidebar* goes into greater detail about a point in the article.

Riches from the Ruins

B

Status: Found

Warka Mask—5,000-year-old marble mask from the Sumerian city of Uruk; one of the world's oldest realistic carvings and one of the world's oldest masks

Warka Vase—Stone (alabaster) vase from about 3,000 B.C.; badly damaged during theft

Bassetki Statue—Copper sculpture from about 2,300 B.C.

Nimrud Gold—Gold jewelry and precious stones dating from the eighth and ninth centuries B.C.

Golden Harp of Ur—Gold and ivory harp from about 2,600 B.C.; also badly damaged during looting

Clay Pot from Tall Hassuna—Clay pot dating to the sixth millennium B.C., at least 1,500 years before the invention of the wheel

Status: Still Missing

Nimrud Lioness—Carved ivory and gold plaque dating to 800 B.C.

Hatra Goddess of Victory—Life-size head, made of copper, from the third century B.C.

Ninhursag Bull—One of two copper bulls from a temple built by the King of Ur around 2,475 B.C.; the other has been recovered

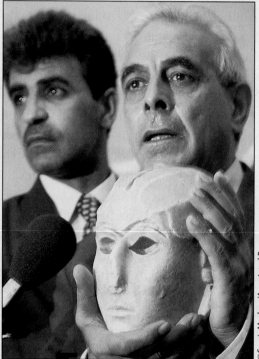

©Samir Mezban/Associated Press.

The 5,000-year-old Warka mask, one of the most important artifacts stolen from Iraq's National Museum, is held up by Iraqi Minister of Culture, Mufeed Muhammad Jawad Al Jazairee, after it was found and returned.

Lagash Statue—Headless inscribed limestone statue from about 2,450 B.C.

Hatra Heads—Five statue heads from a city that thrived in the first century A.D.

Cuneiform Bricks—Nine bricks bearing royal inscriptions from the ancient Akkadian, Babylonian, and Sumerian empires

B **Informational Focus** **Structural Features** Why do you think the writer chose to put this information in a sidebar?

— Continued from Page 441 —

treasures. A few months after the looting, the Warka mask was returned to the museum. A police raid later in the year turned up the Bassetki statue. It had been hidden in a sewer in Iraq. A headless stone statue of a Sumerian king was recovered by American agents after it had been smuggled through Syria into the United States. Other treasures were found in the Netherlands, Britain, and Italy and were returned to Baghdad.

More than 5,000 of the stolen artifacts have been recovered. Experts say it may take decades to locate the rest. Some may never be found. Meanwhile, the National Museum remains closed to the public.

Looting Goes On

C

Experts in the United States and other countries say dig sites in Iraq are still being raided. "One of the many unfortunate consequences [of instability in Iraq is] widespread looting of archaeological sites," says Susan B. Downey. She is an art historian at the University of California, Los Angeles.

Iraqi law makes it illegal to remove artifacts from dig sites without government permission.

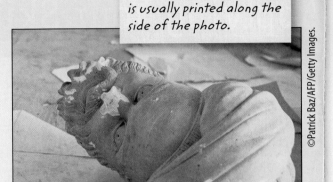

*The photographer's **credit** is usually printed along the side of the photo.*

©Patrick Baz/AFP/Getty Images.

*The **caption** explains what is shown in a picture.*

The head of a broken sculpture lies in a pile of rubble after looters plundered Iraq's National Museum for its treasures.

But thieves digging at any of thousands of sites may be able to smuggle priceless goods out of the country. Those objects have not yet been recorded or photographed, and therefore will be easier for smugglers to sell. **D**

Read with a Purpose

Go back to the lead of the article (the first three paragraphs) and decide if any important information should be included, or unimportant information removed.

Analyzing Visuals

Connecting to the Text
What do you think happened in the museum before this photograph was taken?

©Patrick Robert/CORBIS.

C **Informational Focus** Structural Features
Outline the main points of the article by listing the headings and giving a one-sentence description of each section.

D **Read and Discuss** How do archaeological digs figure into the problem of stolen objects?

Applying Your Skills

Reading Standard 2.1 Identify the structural features of popular media (e.g., **newspapers**, magazines, online information) and use the features to obtain information.

Iraqi Treasures Hunted
Standards Review

Informational Text and Vocabulary

1. In which section of the newspaper would you *most* likely find this article?

  A health

  B national news

  C entertainment

  D world news

2. The **byline** tells you

  A what information is most important.

  B who wrote the article.

  C who is in charge of the museum.

  D what the article is about.

3. Where in the article is the most detailed list of lost-and-found artifacts?

  A the lead

  B the sidebar

  C the headline page

  D the section "Ancient Objects Stolen"

4. Which statement *best* sums up the point of the news story?

  A Thousands of artifacts were stolen from the Iraqi National Museum.

  B Many stolen artifacts have been returned to the Iraqi museum.

  C The Iraqi National Museum remains closed.

  D Ancient Iraqi artifacts are still at risk of being stolen.

5. Another term for *authorities* is

  A politicians.

  B researchers.

  C officials.

  D journalists.

6. The closest meaning of *civilization* is

  A society.

  B ancient city.

  C country.

  D artifact.

7. *Recovered* does *not* mean

  A regained.

  B reclaimed.

  C reworked.

  D retrieved.

Writing Skills Focus

Timed ⌐Writing How did the structural features of this article help you find information? Use details from the article to support your answer.

What Do You Think Now

In what sense can ancient artifacts be seen as stories from the past? What can these "stories" tell us?

Reading Standard 2.1 Identify the structural features of popular media (**e.g.,** newspapers, magazines, **online information**) and use the features to obtain information.

CAVE Online

Informational Text Focus

Structural Features of Popular Media: Web Site In the past, if a writer wanted to research a topic, he or she would probably look in a reference book or in a library. Today, we have another important source of information—the Internet.

There are several ways to find information on the Internet. You can go directly to a **Web site** if you know the URL (uniform resource locator), or address of the site. Sometimes you will want to use a **search engine** when you do research. A search will produce a list of Web sites relating to your topic. You can just click on the site name to go directly to the site. If you get too many results, you can refine your search by choosing more specific search terms. (Always keep in mind that not all Web sites contain reliable information. If you are doing research, you need to be sure that the Web site you are using has been created and is monitored by a trustworthy source.)

Getting Information Most Web sites share some basic structural features. Knowing them can help you find information online.

- Most of the features a site offers are shown on the site's **home page.** Start out by finding and reading basic information about the site, usually at the top or center of the home page.
- Look for a **table of contents,** a list of the site's other pages. This often appears on the side of the home page. You can generally reach the other pages of a site by clicking on the items listed in the table of contents.
- Look for **links,** Web sites related to the one you're exploring. You can often reach a link by clicking on its name. You can usually find a link in the table of contents or on the home page.

Vocabulary

techniques (tehk NEEKS) *n.:* ways of doing complex activities. *The new techniques will capture better images of the cave art.*

projection (pruh JEHKT shuhn) *n.:* display of an image made by shining light through a small version of the image. *The projection of the cave paintings made me feel as if I were in the actual cave.*

vivid (VIHV ihd) *adj.:* producing strong, clear images. *The vivid images of the cave drawings look like the real thing.*

Language Coach

Pronunciation and Fluency When you are learning how to pronounce unfamiliar words, it's important to pay attention to which syllable is stressed. In the word list above, look inside the parentheses for the syllable written in capital letters. That syllable is stressed. Practice pronouncing these words with a partner.

Writing Skills Focus

Preparing for **Timed Writing** See how the structural features of a Web site can help you find information. You'll answer a timed-writing question about structural features later.

Reader/Writer
Notebook
Use your **RWN** to complete the activities for this selection.

Learn It Online
To learn more about analyzing Web sites, visit *MediaScope* on:

go.hrw.com | H6-445 | **Go**

File Edit View Favorites Tools Help

Back Forward Stop Refresh Home | Search Favorites History | Mail Print

Address http://www.cavewonders.org/lascaux/ | Go

Read with a Purpose
Read this Web article to learn about structural features on Web sites.

INTRODUCTION

IN THIS ISSUE

Fungus Among Us:
A Dangerous Lascaux Intruder

News Board

Education

Ask the Digger

NEWS BOARD

PAST ISSUES

By Date

Contents: The list above tells you what other topics the site covers.

 CAVE — in cooperation with the Natural History Society

HOME | ABOUT | EXPLORER'S BLOG | SITE MAP | CONTACT **Ⓐ**

FINDING YOUR WAY AROUND
EARTH'S UNDERGROUND WONDERS

SEARCH   print   e-mail   fax

 by THE WORLD ALMANAC®

Home Page: These features at the top of the page outline the structure of the Web site.

NEWS BOARD

Copy That
Picture this: A team of artists is at work, creating a copy of prehistoric art from Lascaux (la SKOH) cave in France. The tools being used are laser techniques and photographic projection. Therefore, the fake promises to be vivid and realistic. Team leader Renaud Sanson tells a Canadian newspaper that "advances in technology allow us to reproduce the tiniest detail." **Ⓑ**

The replica will tour several cities around the world, carrying images of the famous

Detail of a painting showing a bull and horse in Lascaux cave. <u>Click to enlarge.</u>

Ⓐ **Informational Focus** Structural Features Where would you click to get more information about CAVE?

Ⓑ **Read and Discuss** What role does technology play in the world of prehistoric art?

Vocabulary **techniques** (tehk NEEKS) *n.*: ways of doing complex activities.
projection (pruh JEHKT shuhn) *n.*: display of an image made by shining light through a small version of the image.
vivid (VIHV ihd) *adj.*: producing strong, clear images.

Artists work to create a replica of the Lascaux cave art.

17,000-year-old cave art to a wide audience. If all goes as planned, the exhibit will be ready for showing in 2008. It will begin its tour near the Eiffel Tower in Paris.

Lascaux cave in southwestern France was an accidental discovery made by teens in 1940. It has astounded the art world and the public ever since. Rock paintings show bison, horses, stags, and other animals. The different stages of a hunt are clearly visible, as are the talents of those who did the artwork.

The site has been closed to the public since 1963 to protect the paintings. It attracted so many people—over a thousand a day—that the paintings were being damaged by the carbon dioxide from visitors' breath! That's why a professor of fine arts, Benjamin Britton, decided to design software in 1990 that would allow people to go on "virtual visits" of Lascaux. Britton, who had to work from photographs, became a finalist for a 1995 Discover Award. Sanson has been able to go one better than Britton: He has been given special permission to enter the cave to complete this latest high-tech project.

Not the First Replica

In 1983, long before Renaud Sanson began his painstaking reproduction of the Lascaux cave paintings, a replica of Lascaux opened not far from

Ⓒ **Informational Focus** Structural Features What do the headings of the Web article on this site tell you about its topic?

A visitor to Lascaux II. This replica of two of the finest cave rooms opened in 1983. Click to enlarge. Ⓓ

RELATED LINKS

Official Lascaux Cave Web Site

Discover Awards

Virtual Lascaux Software

Links: Clicking on an item in this list takes you to another Web site and more information.

the original site. This replica, called Lascaux II, is an accurate copy of two of the most famous sections of the cave: the Great Hall of the Bulls and the Painted Gallery. (The real Lascaux is a system of caves. Other sections of the system have been given colorful names based on the type of art found in them: the Shaft of the Dead Man, the Chamber of Felines, and the Chamber of Engravings.) Visitors can go inside Lascaux II's re-creation of the Great Hall of the Bulls, where paintings covering a huge area of the cave walls show horses, bulls, stags, and a creature with twisted horns that is sometimes called "the unicorn." They can also see what is probably the largest single cave-art image in the world—a 17-foot-long bull. True to the original cave paintings, these animals are colorfully drawn in red, black, and a dark yellow-gold color called ocher (OH kuhr). Visitors to Lascaux II can also see the Painted Gallery, which features what many art historians see as the finest paintings. Wild oxen, horses, bison, ibexes, cows, and a stag cover nearly 100 feet of wall space—including the ceiling.

And the replicas don't end there. Tourists can go to the town of Le Thot, France, to see more reproductions of Lascaux cave paintings at the Center of Prehistoric Art.

Read with a Purpose
Which structural features of this Web site can help you continue to explore the topic of the Lascaux cave paintings?

Ⓓ **Informational Focus** Structural Features How does this feature add to your understanding of what you're reading?

🌐 Internet

Applying Your Skills

Reading Standard 2.1 Identify the structural features of popular media (e.g., newspapers, magazines, online information) and use the features to obtain information.

CAVE Online

Standards Review

Informational Text and Vocabulary

1. The **main purpose** of the article on this **Web site** is to
   A criticize the work of Benjamin Britton.
   B describe the paintings inside Lascaux cave.
   C explain the importance of cave paintings.
   D let people know about the exhibit of cave paintings.

2. What part of this **Web site** tells you that there are other topics discussed on it?
   A search field
   B table of contents
   C links section
   D photo captions

3. What is the **URL** for this Web article?
   A www.worldalmanac.org
   B http://www.cavewonders.org/lascaux/
   C http://www.cavewonders.org
   D www.naturalhistorysociety.org/cave/lascaux/

4. Which of the following statements *best* sums up the **main idea** of this **Web site**?
   A The Natural History Society helps publish *CAVE* magazine.
   B Lascaux cave is closed to tourists because their presence damages the artwork.
   C Benjamin Britton was a finalist for a 1995 Discover Award.
   D Scientists are recording the images in Lascaux so they can re-create them for a traveling exhibit.

5. Another term for *projection* is
   A drawing.
   B laser technique.
   C map.
   D display.

6. *Techniques* are
   A the reproduction of tiny details.
   B software programs that contain photographs.
   C methods for doing things.
   D ways to record cave art.

7. A *vivid* image is
   A bright.
   B blurry.
   C photographed.
   D enlarged.

Writing Skills Focus

Timed └**Writing** There are many kinds of Web sites. Explain one purpose they all share.

What Do You Think Now

What stories do you think the prehistoric artists might have told using the paintings in the Lascaux cave?

Writing Workshop

Comparison-Contrast Essay

Write with a Purpose

Write a comparison-contrast essay that explores the similarities and differences between two literary works or two literary elements, such as characters, plot, or setting. The **purpose** of your essay is to inform your **audience**—in this case, your teacher or classmates.

A Good Comparison-Contrast Essay

- identifies the subjects being compared and states the main idea, or thesis, in the introduction
- includes at least two similarities and two differences
- uses consistent and coherent organization, such as the block method or point-by-point method
- supports statements with specific details and examples
- restates the main idea in the conclusion

See page 458 for complete rubric.

 Reader/Writer Notebook

Use your **RWN** to complete the activities for this workshop.

Think as a Reader/Writer

You probably made comparisons as you read different forms of fiction in this chapter. Before you write a comparison-contrast essay, read this excerpt from World Almanac's *Olympic Glory: Victories in History,* from page 197 of this book.

The ancient Games were summertime events. In the modern world, however, there are Winter Games as well. Like the ancient Games, the modern Summer and Winter Olympics are each held every four years, with the two alternating on even-numbered years.

← This specific **detail** illustrates a **similarity.**

When the Olympics began in 776 B.C., they consisted of one footrace—covering a distance of 600 feet. In contrast, twenty-eight summer sports were set for the year 2008, and seven sports were scheduled for the 2010 Winter Games. "The range of sports has expanded enormously," says [David] Potter [professor of Greek and Latin at the University of Michigan]. "The Olympians established a very small canon of sports initially. Now it appears to be an Olympian sport in itself to see what can be added each time."

← **Point-by-point organization** is used to **contrast** the number of sports included in the games.

Ancient Olympians battled the Mediterranean heat, so to toughen up, they practiced in the sun. At the events, according to historians, they wore little or no clothing. Such a dress code would be shocking to modern sensibilities and a blow to manufacturers of sportswear and accessories—who, like shoemakers, make certain to place their products in the public eye during the Olympic Games.

← Statements are supported with **examples,** including vivid images.

Think About the Professional Model

With a partner, discuss the following questions about the model.

1. What kind of evidence does the author use to support this comparison-contrast?
2. What details illustrate the contrast between ancient and modern Olympic Games?

Writing Standard 1.3 Use a variety of effective and coherent organizational patterns, including **comparison and contrast; organization by categories;** and arrangement by spatial order, order of importance, or climactic order. **1.6** Revise writing to improve the organization and consistency of ideas within and between paragraphs **2.2** **Write expository compositions** (**e.g.** description, explanation, **comparison and contrast,** problem and solution): a. **State the thesis or purpose.** b. Explain the situation. c. **Follow an organizational pattern appropriate to the type of composition.** d. **Offer** persuasive **evidence to validate** arguments and **conclusions as needed.**

Prewriting

Choose Your Subjects

Select any two literary works that share at least one interesting point of comparison, such as similar characters, settings, subjects, or themes. You can begin by looking back through the selections in this collection and thinking about the Idea Starters at right.

Think About Your Subject, Purpose, and Audience

As you think about possible subjects for your essay, consider your purpose (why you are writing) and audience (your readers).

- Your main **purpose** is to give readers information about how two subjects are similar and how they are different.

- Your **audience** is a reader or readers who may—or may not—be familiar with the works you are comparing. If they are not familiar with the works, you must decide what kind of (and how much) background information you need to provide for them so that they can follow your ideas.

Find Similarities and Differences

Which features will you compare and contrast? If you choose to compare and contrast two short stories, discuss the same aspects of both works: plot elements, characters, or themes, for example. If you choose two characters, focus on each character's physical traits, actions, thoughts, and feelings. Describe the characters' main conflicts and how they resolve these conflicts.

A **Venn diagram** can help you brainstorm ideas about how your subjects are alike and different. Here's a Venn diagram based on the professional model on the previous page. The similarities are written where the circles overlap, and the differences are written where they don't overlap.

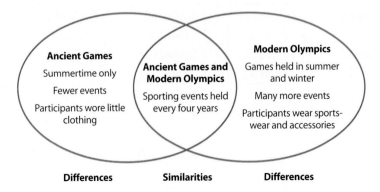

Ancient Games
Summertime only
Fewer events
Participants wore little clothing

Ancient Games and Modern Olympics
Sporting events held every four years

Modern Olympics
Games held in summer and winter
Many more events
Participants wear sportswear and accessories

Differences   **Similarities**   **Differences**

Idea Starters

- two characters with similar conflicts
- similar themes in two stories
- the role of setting in two works
- two myths, fables, or folk tales from different cultures

Peer Review

Survey your classmates to see how many of them are familiar with the works you plan to compare. You won't need to provide as much background for familiar works as you will for works that few others have read.

Your Turn _____

Get Started List some subjects for **comparison** in your **RWN.** Narrow your choices until you have decided on the two that would make the most interesting comparison. Then, create a Venn diagram to list the **similarities** and **differences** you'll discuss in your essay.

Learn It Online
Try the interactive Venn diagram online at:

go.hrw.com   H6-451   Go

Comparison-Contrast Essay

Gather Supporting Details

You may have a clear understanding of your subjects, but your audience will need more information. Look at the points of comparison you have listed in your Venn diagram. What specific examples would help your reader get the picture? If you say the settings of two stories are similar, support your statement with examples of *how* they're similar. For example, the two stories may both take place in a large city, or they may both take place in the same historical period.

Organize Your Ideas

The details in a comparison-contrast essay usually are organized in a particular pattern, using either the block method or the point-by-point method. Use a chart like one of those below to help you plan.

- **Block method:** In the block method, all points of comparison for a subject are presented at one time. For example, if you were comparing and contrasting two settings, you would present all the features of one setting in the first paragraph or section—where the setting is located, what time of day it is, what it looks like, and so on. Then, in the next paragraph or section, you would present all the same information about the features of the other setting.

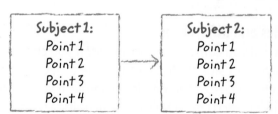

- **Point-by-point method:** In the point-by-point method, you present each point of comparison for both subjects before moving on to the next point of comparison. For example, you would compare both settings' geographical locations, then what time of year (or day) it is in each setting, then what the settings look like, and so on.

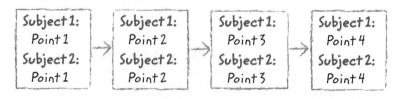

Your Turn _____

Choose Your Method of Organization Look at your subjects, your points of comparison, and the details you want to include. Which method of **organization** would be most appropriate for your comparison? Create a chart in your **RWN** like one of those shown on this page to help you map out your key points.

Drafting

Follow the Writer's Framework

Use the **Writer's Framework** at right to help you write your first draft. Once you have written your draft, compare it with the framework to make sure you haven't forgotten anything.

Use Transitional Words and Phrases

Using words and phrases that signal **transitions,** or changes from one idea to another, can clarify your essay's organization, help paragraphs flow easily from one to the next, and enable your readers to follow your ideas. These words and phrases show similarities: *also, another, as well as, both, in addition, just as, like, neither, similarly, too.* These words and phrases show differences: *although, but, however, in contrast, instead, in spite of, nevertheless, on the other hand, unlike.* Use transitional words and phrases to shift from one point of comparison to the next or to introduce supporting examples.

> ### A Writer's Framework
>
> **Introduction**
> - Capture your reader's attention with a strong beginning.
> - Identify your subject at the beginning of the essay.
>
> **Body**
> - Use the block method or point-by-point method.
> - Explore at least two similarities and two differences between your subjects.
> - Support your points of comparison with details and examples.
>
> **Conclusion**
> - Sum up the main points about your subjects.
> - Restate your main idea.

● Writing Tip

Re-read your draft before you write your conclusion. A good conclusion should be more than just a summary. Elaborate on the main idea, or thesis, that you presented in your introduction. You might also extend the conclusion to cover related works or topics.

Grammar Link Use Introductory Adverbial Phrases

Another useful kind of transition is the **adverbial phrase**—a prepositional phrase used as an adverb. Adverbial phrases answer the questions *when? where? how? why? how often? how long? to what extent?* An adverbial phrase may come before or after the word it modifies, but as a transition it is best used at the beginning of a sentence. Study these examples from the professional model on page 450:

> **"In the modern world,** however, there are Winter Games as well."

> **"At the events,** according to historians, they wore little or no clothing."

Your Turn _____

Write Your Draft Follow your plan and framework to write a draft of your essay. Be sure to consider the following:
- How can you capture your reader's interest?
- What **introductory adverbial phrases** can you use?

Peer Review

Working with a classmate, review each other's drafts and trade revision suggestions. Answer each question in the chart to identify where and how your drafts can be improved. As you discuss your papers, be sure to write down your classmate's suggestions. You can refer to your notes as you revise your draft.

Evaluating and Revising

After your draft is completed, it's time to go back through and smooth out the rough spots. You can improve your draft by using the evaluation questions and revision techniques shown below.

Comparison-Contrast Essay: Guidelines for Content and Organization

Evaluation Question	Tip	Revision Technique
1. Does your introduction state your thesis, or main idea?	**Underline** the thesis statement.	**Add** a thesis statement if one is missing.
2. Do you discuss two or more similarities and two or more differences?	**Put a star** next to each example of comparison or contrast.	If necessary, **add** examples of comparison and contrast. **Delete** any statements that don't belong.
3. Is the body of your essay organized by either the block method or the point-by-point method?	**Label** the method of organization in the margin. **Write** *A* above each point about the first subject and *B* above each point about the second subject.	If necessary, **rearrange** statements into either block order or point-by-point order.
4. Do details and examples support points of comparison?	**Put a check mark** next to supporting details and examples.	**Add support** with details and examples, if necessary.
5. Do you use introductory phrases to transition from one point to the next?	**Highlight** introductory phrases used as transitions.	**Add** introductory adverbial phrases if transitions are needed.
6. Does your conclusion restate and expand on the main idea?	**Bracket** the thesis statement. **Underline** statements that expand your thesis.	**Summarize** the thesis. **Elaborate** on statements that may need to be expanded.

Read this student's draft along with the comments on its structure, its strengths, and how it could be made even better.

Student Draft

Oh No! The Earth Is Exploding!

by Erica Graham, Owasso Sixth-Grade Center

"Earth" by Oliver Herford and "Earth" by John Hall Wheelock are two poems about the destruction of Earth as viewed by a creature on another planet. Although the subjects are identical, the poems differ greatly in description and point of view.

In Herford's poem, the explosion of Earth is a beautiful sight to an innocent child who simply sees lights and color. Herford describes in great detail how the child from a planet far away witnesses the explosion as a beautiful shooting star rushing through the sky. Lines 6–12 paint a picture of what happens to the planet's creatures as Earth falls through space.

In Wheelock's poem, on the other hand, a Martian astronomer watches the destruction of Earth and states that it was bound to happen. His adult point of view is that the catastrophe means nothing to the Martians. The Martian astronomer dryly says the explosion proves that highly intelligent beings had been living there. He thinks that they are responsible for destroying their own planet.

← In the first sentence, Erica introduces the **subjects** she is going to compare and contrast. In the second sentence, her **main idea** statement includes both similarities and differences.

← Erica uses the **block** method, discussing each poem in a separate paragraph.

← Erica uses a **transitional phrase**, *on the other hand*, to link the paragraphs. She discusses the point of view of the Martian astronomer in Wheelock's poem.

MINI-LESSON ▸ **How to Use the Block Method of Organization**

Since Erica has chosen the block method of organization, she must demonstrate a consistency of ideas by addressing **both** points established in her thesis statement: description and point of view. Her third paragraph addresses only point of view, so Erica revises her draft to add a reference to the description—or lack of it—in the second poem.

Erica's Draft (end of third paragraph)

He thinks that they are responsible for destroying their own planet.

Erica's Revision (end of third paragraph)

He thinks that they are responsible for destroying their own planet. ∧ *Even though the astronomer is watching the event, he does not describe it at all. The lack of description emphasizes how unimportant this event is to the Martian astronomer.*

Your Turn _____

Use an Organizational Method
Read your draft and ask yourself:
- Is my organizational method effective and coherent?
- Do I need to add support for any points of comparison?

Make any revisions that will strengthen the organization of your essay.

Comparison-Contrast Essay

The **conclusion** restates the **thesis** from the introduction and makes a **connection to the reader.**

→ Both Oliver Herford's "Earth" and John Hall Wheelock's "Earth" are poems that view the Earth's destruction through the eyes of a creature on another planet. The child in Herford's poem may be easier to relate to than Wheelock's Martian astronomer, but their responses to Earth's destruction are equally surprising.

MINI-LESSON ▸ **How to Expand the Main Idea in the Conclusion**

In concluding your comparison-contrast essay, remember to restate your main points about the two subjects you are comparing. You may want to take your conclusion one step further and expand on your main points to give your reader something to consider. Can you make a connection to something beyond your topic that will make your comparison even more meaningful?

Erica revised her conclusion, summarizing her main points and making a connection to a deeper meaning. She shows how the two poems may deliver an important message about the planet Earth.

Erica's Revision

Both Oliver Herford's "Earth" and John Hall Wheelock's "Earth" are

poems that view the Earth's destruction through the eyes of a creature on

another planet. ∧Herford's poem provides a vivid description of the event, while Wheelock's is curiously lacking in description or emotion.

The child in Herford's poem may be easier to relate to than Wheelock's

Martian astronomer, but their responses to Earth's destruction are equally

surprising. ∧Readers may be shocked that neither the child nor the astronomer views the Earth's destruction as such a bad thing. However, both poems force readers to consider that the Earth is fragile. These poems send the strong message that the Earth must be protected and cared for if it is to survive.

Your Turn _____

Expand Your Conclusion

Review your conclusion. Have you summarized your main points? Is there anything you can add to show why these points are important?

Proofreading and Publishing

Proofreading

After you have revised your comparison-contrast essay, it's time to go back through it one more time to correct any errors in grammar, usage, or mechanics. It's easy to overlook your own errors, so you may want to have a classmate proofread, or edit, your essay as well.

> #### Grammar Link Using Comparatives Correctly
>
> A **comparative** is an adjective or adverb used to compare two things: *easier, better.* A **superlative** is an adjective or adverb used to compare three or more things: *easiest, best.* Erica looked closely at her work so that she could edit for two common mistakes people make when using comparatives:
>
> - Use the comparative form, not the superlative, when you are comparing only two things.
>
>   "The child in Herford's poem may be ~~easiest~~ *easier* to relate to than Wheelock's Martian astronomer. . . ."
>
> - Don't use *more* with *–er* to form a comparative.
>
>   "The child in Herford's poem may be ~~more~~ easier to relate to than Wheelock's Martian astronomer. . . ."

Publishing

Now it is time to publish your comparison-contrast essay, sharing it with a wider audience. Here are some ways to share your essay:

- Add photos or illustrations to your essay, and print the results in book form.
- Share your comparison-contrast essay orally. Practice reading it aloud, and then present it to your classmates.

Reflect on the Process
In your *Reader/Writer Notebook,* write a short response to the following questions as you think about how you wrote your comparison-contrast essay.

1. How did you decide on your subjects for comparison? Were they easy to compare and contrast? Why or why not?
2. What strategies helped you select points of comparison?
3. Which organizational pattern did you choose and why?
4. Was the revision process helpful in improving your essay? What revision suggestions did you find most useful?

● Proofreading Tip

Getting a "second pair of eyes"—having someone else edit your work—is a time-honored method of proofreading. Ask a classmate to proofread your essay, looking for misspellings, punctuation errors, and problems in sentence structure.

Your Turn _____
Proofread and Publish

Proofread your essay, paying special attention to your use of comparatives. Correct any errors you find, including errors in grammar, usage, and punctuation. Then, publish your essay for an audience.

Scoring Rubric

You can use the rubric below to evaluate your comparison-contrast essay.

	Comparison-Contrast Writing	Organization and Focus	Sentence Structure	Conventions
4	• *Clearly* states the two elements being compared with a *coherent* introduction and a *comprehensive* conclusion. • Offers *thoughtful, creative* comparisons and ideas.	• *Clearly* addresses all parts of the writing task. • Demonstrates a *clear* understanding of purpose and audience. • Focuses *consistently* on a *logical* comparison of two elements. • Shows *effective* and *coherent* block method or point-by-point organization. • Develops comparisons thoroughly using *relevant* facts, details, and/or explanations as evidence.	• Includes sentence *variety* (e.g., simple, complex, compound-complex).	• Contains *few, if any,* errors in the conventions of the English language (grammar, punctuation, capitalization, spelling). These errors do **not** interfere with the reader's understanding of the writing.
3	• States the two elements being compared with a *relatively clear* introduction and conclusion. • Offers *generally thoughtful* comparisons and ideas.	• Addresses *most* of the writing task. • Demonstrates a *general* understanding of purpose and audience. • Focuses *mainly* on a comparison of two elements. • Shows *relatively effective* block method or point-by point organization. • Develops comparisons using *mostly relevant* facts, details, and/or explanations as evidence.	• Includes some sentence *variety* (e.g., simple, complex, compound-complex).	• Contains *some errors* in the conventions of the English language (grammar, punctuation, capitalization, spelling). These errors do **not** interfere with the reader's understanding of the writing.
2	• *Vaguely* states the two elements being compared with a *somewhat clear* introduction and conclusion. • Offers *some* comparisons and ideas.	• Addresses *some* of the writing task. • Demonstrates *little* understanding of purpose and audience. • Maintains an *inconsistent* focus and/or organizational structure. • *Ineffectively* develops comparisons using *limited* facts, details, and/or explanations as evidence.	• Includes *little* sentence variety.	• Contains *several errors* in the conventions of the English language (grammar, punctuation, capitalization, spelling). These errors **may** interfere with the reader's understanding of the writing.
1	• *Fails* to state the two elements being compared and offers no introduction and/or conclusion. • *Fails* to offer comparisons or ideas.	• Addresses *only one or no* part of the writing task. • Demonstrates *no* understanding of purpose and audience. • *Lacks* a focus and organizational structure. • *Lacks* a comparison but may contain *marginally related* facts, details and/or explanations as evidence.	• Includes *no* sentence variety.	• Contains *serious errors* in the conventions of the English language (grammar, punctuation, capitalization, spelling). These errors interfere with the reader's understanding of the writing.

Comparison-Contrast Essay

Writing Standard 2.2 Write expository compositions (e.g., description, explanation, **comparison and contrast,** problem and solution): **a. State the thesis or purpose.** b. Explain the situation. **c. Follow an organizational pattern appropriate to the type of composition. d. Offer** persuasive **evidence to validate** arguments and **conclusions.**

When responding to an on-demand writing task with a comparison-contrast prompt, use what you've learned from the models you've read, from writing your own comparison-contrast essay, and from the rubric on page 458. Use the steps below to develop a comparison-contrast essay.

Writing Prompt

Think of two literary characters who are similar in some important way although they may be from two separate literary selections. Write a comparison-contrast essay about how the characters are similar and different. Be sure to use specific examples and details to develop your essay.

Study the Prompt

Begin by reading the prompt carefully. Note what is required in the prompt: selecting two literary characters that have something in common, stating **similarities** and **differences,** and providing **support** for your statements.

Tip: Spend about five minutes studying the prompt.

Plan Your Response

Ask yourself questions about the prompt. Think about questions that will help you identify subjects, points of comparison, and support.

- What two characters do you know well? What do they have in common?
- How are the characters similar? How are they different?
- What evidence from the literary selections can you use to support the similarities and differences?
- What organizational method should you use: block method or point-by-point method?
  Tip: Spend about ten minutes studying the prompt.

Respond to the Prompt

Now it's time to start writing your response. Don't worry too much about your introduction for now. You can always come back and revise it later. As you write, remember the following:

- In the introduction, state your **topic,** identify the titles and authors of the works being compared, and state the **thesis,** or main idea, about how your subjects are alike and different.
- In the body, present two or three of the most important similarities and differences, along with **examples** and **details** to support your statements.
- In the conclusion, **restate your thesis** and **summarize** the points you made in the body of your paper.
  Tip: Spend about twenty minutes writing your draft.

Improve Your Response

Revising Go back over the key aspects of the prompt. Did you use the block or point-by-point method of organization? Did you include supporting evidence for your points of comparison?

Proofreading Take a few minutes to proofread your essay to correct errors in grammar, spelling, punctuation, and capitalization. Make sure all your edits are neat and your paper is easy to read.

Checking Your Final Copy Before you turn in your paper, read it one more time to catch any errors you may have missed.

Tip: Save five to ten minutes to improve your paper.

Using Electronic Texts to Locate Information

Write with a Purpose

Choose a topic that you would like to know more about. Search the various electronic text sources mentioned here for your topic. Then present the types, names, and location of the sources that have information on your topic to your class.

● Techno Tip

You can use **e-mail** to reach institutions, businesses, and individuals. When you e-mail places like museums, you may be able to ask **experts** about a topic you're researching. An e-mail address is made up of a **user name,** the **domain name,** and a suffix that indicates what **top-level domain** it belongs to (see the Techno Tip on the next page for a description of top-level domains). Electronic **bulletin boards** are online systems where you can share, request, or discuss information on just about any topic. Because they are open to the public, follow the same criteria to evaluate a bulletin board as you would a Web site.

Think as a Reader/Writer

Explore the electronic options besides the Internet at your library—the online catalog, databases, encyclopedias on CD-ROM, even e-mail. To use electronic text effectively, you need to understand the features of each type of text and the methods for using each type.

Search Electronic Texts

Visit a Library

Many libraries have computers for research available to the public. To find a book, audiotape, film, or video in a library, start by looking in its catalog. Ask a librarian for help with locating other electronic texts.

- **online catalog:** An online catalog will tell you whether a book is available for checkout and where in the library it is located. You can either search by **title, author,** or **subject** in some catalogs; with others simply enter **keywords** for the subject you need.
- **periodical database:** A database such as the *Readers' Guide to Periodical Literature* has magazine articles that will fit your search.
- **CD-ROM:** A "compact disc-read only memory" is played on a computer. A disc often contains sources such as an encyclopedia. You can find information by typing keywords into its search box.
- **Web sites:** You can find text, graphics, photographs, and video clips on a Web site. Not all sites are accurate; stick to ones sponsored by trustworthy organizations.
- **e-mail:** You can use e-mail to ask experts directly for information.

Identify Your Keyword

When you use most electronic texts to search for information, you need to think of a keyword. A **keyword,** or search term, is a word or phrase that identifies your specific topic. You may need to experiment with keywords in order to find the information you need. If you get too few choices when you enter your keyword, use a more general one. If you get too many choices, use a more specific word.

Use the Internet

Features of the Internet

The **Internet** (the Net) is a huge network of computers. Libraries, news services, government agencies, schools, and organizations communicate and share information on the Net. It lets you chat online with students around the world by **e-mail, bulletin boards,** and **newsgroups.**

World Wide Web The easiest way to do research on the Internet is on the World Wide Web, where information is stored in easy-to-access files called **Web pages.** The most common way to search on the Net is by using a software tool called a **search engine.** Just go to a search engine's form and enter a keyword. A list of Web pages containing your search term, and the first few lines of each page, will appear.

Search Operators A search term such as *Frost* may produce thousands of results, or **hits,** including weather data on frost. If you are searching for the poet Robert Frost, most of those thousands of hits will be of no use. To find useful material, you have to narrow your search. To focus your research, use **search operators,** like the words AND or NOT, to create a string of keywords. If you are looking for material on Robert Frost and his life in Vermont, for example, you might enter the following keywords:

Frost AND Vermont NOT weather

The more focused search term yields pages that contain both *Frost* and *Vermont* and nothing about weather. The chart below explains how several search operators work.

Common Search Operators and What They Do			
AND	Demands that both terms appear on the page; narrows search	**–**	Excludes a word from consideration; narrows search
+	Demands that both terms appear on the page; narrows search.	**NEAR**	Demands that two words be close together; narrows search
OR	Yields pages that contain either term; widens search	**ADJ**	Demands that two words be close together; narrows search
NOT	Excludes a word from consideration; narrows search	**" "**	Demands an exact phrase; narrows search

Good Criteria to Evaluate Web Sources

- Who is the author? Trust respected sources, such as the Smithsonian Institution, not a person's newsletter or home page.
- How trustworthy, or accurate, is the information? Check information from one site against information from at least two other sites.
- What is the author's perspective? Find out whether the information is objective or has a bias or hidden purpose.
- Is the information up-to-date?

Techno Tip

To evaluate a Web source, look at the top-level domain (the suffix after the dot, or period) in the URL. Here is a sample URL: http://www.loc.gov The top-level domain is *gov*, which represents a government agency. Schools' URLs end in *edu*; commercial sites' addresses end in *com*; and organizations' URLs end in *org*. Try to stick with sites sponsored by trustworthy groups, often those with the endings *edu, gov,* or *org*.

Literary Skills Review

Forms of Fiction   **Directions:** Read the following folk tale. Then, answer each question that follows.

Little Mangy One

Lebanese folk tale, retold by **Inea Bushnaq**

Once upon a time three little goats were grazing on the side of a stony hill. Their names were Siksik, Mikmik, and Jureybon, the Little Mangy One. Soon a hyena scented them and loped up. "Siksik!" called the hyena. "Yes sir!" answered the goat. "What are those points sticking out of your head?" "Those are my little horns, sir," said the goat. "What is that patch on your back?" continued the hyena. "That is my hair, sir," replied the goat. "Why are you shivering?" roared the hyena. "Because I am afraid of you, sir," said the goat. At this the hyena sprang and gobbled him right up. Next the hyena turned to Mikmik, who answered like his brother, and he too was quickly devoured.

Then the hyena approached Jureybon, the Little Mangy One. Before the hyena came within earshot, Jureybon began to snort. As the hyena drew nearer, Jureybon bellowed, "May a plague lay low your back, O cursed one! What have you come for?" "I wish to know what the two points on your head are," said the hyena. "Those?

Why, those are my trusty sabers!" said the goat. "And the patch on your back, what is that?" said the hyena. "My sturdy shield, of course!" sneered the goat. "Then why are you shivering?" asked the hyena. "Shivering? I'm trembling with rage! I'm shaking with impatience, for I cannot wait to throttle you and squeeze your very soul till it starts out of your eye sockets!" snarled the goat, and began to advance on the hyena.

The hyena's heart stopped beating for an instant; then he turned and ran for his life. But Jureybon sprang after him over the rocks and gored him with his sharp little horns, slitting open his belly and freeing his two little brothers inside.

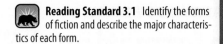

1. Which characteristics of a folk tale does "Little Mangy One" have?
   A It is about gods and heroes.
   B It ends with a stated moral.
   C It is based on a historical event.
   D It has talking animals.

2. What important lesson about life does this folk tale give you?
   A Scaring others is never a good idea.
   B Cleverness can beat strength.
   C Always run away from dangerous people and situations.
   D Brothers should take separate paths in life.

3. You can tell that this is a folk tale because it features each of the following *except*
   A a trickster hero.
   B a lesson to be learned.
   C a large, strong villain.
   D a short rhyming poem.

4. Folk tales, like the ones that inspired "Little Mangy One,"
   A are connected with some major religions.
   B have famous hero characters.
   C have several well-known authors.
   D change from year to year, teller to teller.

Timed Writing
5. Folk tales were passed along orally long before they were written down. What makes "Little Mangy One" a popular story to tell aloud? List at least three reasons.

Informational Skills Review

Structural Features of Popular Media—Web Page

Directions: Read the Web page. Then, read and answer each question that follows.

File   Edit   View   Favorites   Tools   Help

Back   Forward   Stop   Refresh   Home   Search   Favorites   History   Mail   Print

Address   http://www.starlinkuniverse.org   Go

StarLink Universe

Contact Us | Search

HOME   NEWS   MISSIONS   PLANETS   PEOPLE   TECHNOLOGY

TABLE OF CONTENTS

RELATED LINKS

NASA Site Network
Kids Astronomy
Stars at Night
Star Child
Windows to the Universe

All pages and content copyrighted by StarLink Universe ©2008

This site last modified August 20, 2008, 2:15 P.M.

The Solar System

What is the solar system? It consists of the Earth's Sun and everything that travels around it as a result of gravity. The solar system consists of eight planets and their 162 (currently known) moons; three dwarf planets, including Pluto, and their four (currently known) moons; and billions of comets, asteroids, meteoroids, other space objects, and interplanetary dust.

The Sun is the largest object in the solar system, and because it is so large, its powerful gravity pulls all of the objects in the solar system toward it. At the same time, these objects, since they are moving so fast, are trying to fly into outer space. As a result of the two opposing, physical forces, the objects remain in orbit.

The solar system is elliptical, or egg-shaped, with the Sun in the middle. The planets orbit continuously around the Sun, with Mercury being the closest. Next closest is Venus, followed by Earth, Mars, Jupiter, Saturn, Uranus, and Neptune. Six of these planets, including Earth, are orbited by moons.

1. The main purpose of this Web page is to
   A analyze scientific studies of Pluto.
   B give information about the planets of the solar system.
   C describe NASA's current missions.
   D encourage space exploration.

2. The source of this Web page is
   A the National Aeronautics and Space Administration (NASA).
   B StarLink Universe.
   C the astronauts of the International Astronomical Union (IAU).
   D a famous university's science department.

3. If you want to find information about NASA, you would go to
   A Windows to the Universe.
   B Contact Us.
   C NASA Site Network.
   D Technology.

4. This page was last updated on
   A August 20, 2008.
   B March 15, 2008.
   C December 3, 2007.
   D date not given.

5. If you want to find out about the second closest planet to the Sun, which of these could you click on?
   A "Mercury" in the table of contents
   B "Neptune" at the bottom of the page
   C "Venus" in the table of contents
   D "Mars" at the bottom of the page

6. What in the table of contents might help you find out about faraway stars?
   A The Sun
   B Earth's Moon
   C The Farthest Regions
   D Mars's Moons

7. If you want to send a letter or e-mail to StarLink Universe, you would click on
   A Contact Us.
   B Missions.
   C Search.
   D Windows to the Universe.

Timed Writing

8. Compare and contrast the information available in the table of contents with what's pictured in the main illustration.

Vocabulary Skills Review

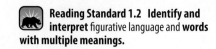

Reading Standard 1.2 Identify and interpret figurative language and **words with multiple meanings.**

Multiple-Meaning Words **Directions:** Each of the sentences below is from a story in this collection. Read the sentence, and then choose the answer in which the italicized word is used in the same way.

1. "During rehearsal, Mr. Roybal, nervous about his debut as the school's talent co-ordinator, cursed under his breath when the lever that controlled the speed on the record player *jammed*."

   A The musicians met in Mike's garage and *jammed* for hours.

   B I *jammed* my hand into the cookie jar, only to find it empty.

   C We had to run the lawn mower at full speed after the throttle *jammed*.

   D Sarah *jammed* her thumb badly while playing basketball.

2. "He heard more applause and screams and started getting into the *groove* as he shivered and snaked like Michael Jackson around the stage."

   A My writing desk has a *groove* to hold pencils.

   B The school drill team got into a *groove* with the music, and their dance routine was flawless.

   C The old ax was so well used that it had a hand *groove* worn in its wooden handle.

   D My grandparents are stuck in a *groove* of eating the same breakfast at the cafe every Saturday.

3. "But when the entire *cast* lined up for a curtain call, Manuel received a burst of applause that was so loud it shook the walls of the cafeteria."

   A The *cast* was very strong except for the boy who played the jester; his acting was way too stiff.

   B After dinner on the beach, we walked to the water's edge and *cast* rocks into the surf.

   C Kelly's broken arm still hurt a little, but she allowed us to draw elaborate pictures all over her *cast*.

   D Fly fishing is very rewarding once you learn how to *cast* correctly.

4. "Youth is *rash*."

   A Juan gets a horrible *rash* from ant bites.

   B Dad complained that my brother's decision about college was *rash*.

   C Mary's skateboard continued down the sidewalk as she scrambled to her feet and examined her new *rash*.

   D The city received a *rash* of complaints when the swimming pool closed.

Academic Vocabulary

Directions: Choose the *best* synonym for the Academic Vocabulary word in italics.

5. The word *concept* most closely means

   A structure.

   B vision.

   C feature.

   D idea.

Writing Skills Review

Comparison-Contrast Essay   Directions: Read the following paragraph from a comparison-contrast essay. Then, answer each question that follows.

Reading Standard 2.2 Write expository compositions (e.g., description, explanation, comparison and contrast, problem and solution): a. State the thesis or purpose. b. Explain the situation. c. Follow an organizational pattern appropriate to the type of composition. d. Offer persuasive evidence to validate arguments and conclusions as needed.

(1) In Greek mythology the gods and goddesses live on Mount Olympus; in Norse mythology the deities live in Asgard. (2) Olympus and Asgard are very much alike. (3) On Olympus the family of gods enter and leave through a gate of clouds. (4) The palace of Zeus is a great hall where the gods and goddesses feast each day on ambrosia and nectar. (5) As they eat, Apollo plays his lyre. (6) When the sun sets, the gods return to their own homes to sleep. (7) Asgard is entered by crossing a rainbow bridge. (8) The great mansion of Odin is called Valhalla. (9) In Valhalla, Odin entertains the war heroes who have fallen in battle. (10) The Norse gods drink mead. (11) The flesh of the boar Schrimnir is cooked every day and then becomes whole again. (12) When not feasting, the warriors practice battle moves.

1. Which of the following statements would follow sentence 2 the *best*?
   A The gods and goddesses work very hard.
   B Warriors are important in Norse mythology.
   C However, they are different: Rules of Olympus ban mortals, whereas the Norse gods' laws welcome human heroes.
   D All gods and goddesses live in splendid palaces.

2. All of the following points of comparison are noted *except*
   A the entrances to the homes of the gods and goddesses.
   B the names of the homes.
   C the food that is eaten.
   D the appearance of the palaces.

3. What would be the *best* way to combine sentences 8 and 9?
   A The great mansion of Odin is called Valhalla, and in Valhalla, Odin entertains the war heroes who have fallen in battle.
   B The great mansion of Odin, Valhalla, is where Odin entertains the war heroes who have fallen in battle.
   C In his great mansion of Valhalla, Odin entertains the war heroes who have fallen in battle.
   D Valhalla is the great mansion of Odin, where the war heroes who have fallen in battle are entertained.

4. This passage could be improved by
   A identifying Zeus, Apollo, and Odin.
   B explaining what ambrosia and nectar are.
   C defining *mead*.
   D all of the above.

Read On

For Independent Reading

Fiction

Sounder

In his novel *Sounder*, William H. Armstrong tells the story of an African American sharecropper who is arrested for stealing food for his starving family. His son spends years searching for him; then one day the young man and Sounder, the family's hunting dog, hear footsteps approaching the house. This beloved story, winner of a Newbery Award in 1970, was made into a classic film in 1972.

Love That Dog

Do only girls write poetry? That's what the boy in *Love That Dog* thinks. As you follow the story of a boy and his dog, you'll see how encouragement, a pencil and some paper, and a great dog can help a guy find his voice. Sharon Creech's *Love That Dog* has won or been nominated for more than thirty awards.

World Myths and Folk Tales

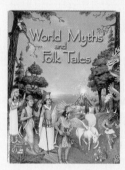

For thousands of years people have been telling stories to better understand themselves, their communities, and their world. The enduring stories of many cultures appear together in *World Myths and Folk Tales*. From creation myths to Aesop's fables, these stories sometimes explain cultural beliefs, sometimes teach moral lessons, and almost always entertain. It's no wonder they have been told and retold for generations.

The Ch'i-Lin Purse

Linda Fang has collected her favorite ancient Chinese stories in *The Ch'i-Lin Purse*. Some of the stories come from ancient Chinese novels and operas, while others are inspired by actual historical events. All include twists and turns that will keep you on your toes. The stories are accompanied by lively illustrations.

Nonfiction

The Mexican American Family Album

In *The Mexican American Family Album*, Dorothy and Thomas Hoobler detail some of the historical events that have shaped the lives of Mexican Americans. The book contains photographs and firsthand accounts of generations of Mexicans who immigrated to the United States.

Ashanti to Zulu: African Traditions

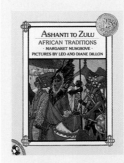

Margaret Musgrove introduces you to the cultures of twenty-six different African peoples in *Ashanti to Zulu: African Traditions*. Accompanying the text are Leo and Diane Dillon's highly detailed illustrations depicting life among these peoples. *Ashanti to Zulu* won the 1977 Caldecott Award for best illustrated book.

Ancient Mesopotamia: The Sumerians, Babylonians, and Assyrians

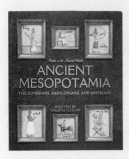

Three ancient civilizations thrived in the land of Mesopotamia. This colorful and inviting text by Virginia Schomp gives you background on Gilgamesh's people, the Sumerians, who built the first cities. It also discusses the lawmaker Babylonians and the warrior Assyrians. The way people lived, from the king to the peasants, is described for each culture. You'll find a helpful time line and a biographical dictionary, which describes important historical figures.

But That's Another Story: Favorite Authors Introduce Popular Genres

Edited by Sandy Asher, *But That's Another Story: Famous Authors Introduce Popular Genres* explores different genres of fiction—suspense, humor, adventure, science fiction, and more. Each genre is represented by an original story from a well-known writer. The stories are sure to tempt you to dive deeper into your favorite genre.

 Learn It Online
Explore other novels—and find tips for choosing, reading, and studying novels—at:

go.hrw.com H6-469 **Go**

CHAPTER 5

Elements of
Poetry

California Standards

Here are the Grade 6 standards you will work toward mastering in Chapter 5.

Word Analysis, Fluency, and Systematic Vocabulary Development
1.2 Identify and interpret figurative language and words with multiple meanings.

Literary Response and Analysis
3.4 Define how tone or meaning is conveyed in poetry through word choice, figurative language, sentence structure, line length, punctuation, rhythm, repetition, and rhyme.

Writing Applications (Genres and Their Characteristics)
2.2 Write expository compositions (e.g., description, explanation, comparison and contrast, problem and solution):
a. State the thesis or purpose.
b. Explain the situation.
c. Follow an organizational pattern appropriate to the type of composition.
d. Offer persuasive evidence to validate arguments and conclusions as needed.

"The best and most beautiful things in the world cannot be seen or even touched—they must be felt with the heart."

—Helen Keller

What Do
You **?**
Think

How can poetry help us experience "the best and most beautiful things in the world"?

Learn It Online
Listen to the poetry in this collection come alive online at:

| go.hrw.com | H6-471 | Go |

LITERARY RESPONSE AND ANALYSIS

Literary Skills Focus

by **Linda Rief**

How Do the Sounds of Poetry Convey Tone and Meaning?

Do you have trouble getting a favorite song out of your head? That's probably because the sounds and the words work together to create a powerful feeling. Poets, like songwriters, convey the meaning and tone of their work through rhythm, rhyme, and repetition.

Tone: It's an Attitude

If you respond to a joke by saying, "That's funny," what do you really mean? A light, cheerful tone of voice would show that you think the joke is funny. An angry, sarcastic tone of voice, however, would show that you were offended by the joke. **Tone** is the speaker's attitude toward his or her subject or audience. Tone is created by many verbal elements, including sounds and word choice. One thing is sure: unless you catch a poem's tone, you won't catch its meaning.

Rhythm

The musical quality produced by repeated sound patterns is called **rhythm.** To help convey the tone and meaning of a sad poem, a poet might use a slow, heavy rhythm that would communicate the speaker's feelings of sorrow. A poet who wanted to convey the tone and meaning of a happy poem might use, instead, a lively, bouncy rhythm.

Meter The most obvious kind of rhythm is **meter,** a regular pattern of stressed and unstressed syllables.

Scanning To find a poem's meter, read the poem aloud. Mark each stressed syllable you hear with the symbol / and each unstressed syllable with the symbol ◡. Marking this pattern is called **scanning.** The following lines are scanned. Read them aloud, and notice how the beat creates a bouncy, light tone.

◡ ◡ / ◡◡ / ◡
Now, the Star-Belly Sneetches
◡ / ◡ ◡ /
Had bellies with stars.
◡ / ◡◡ / ◡
The Plain-Belly Sneetches
◡ / ◡◡ /
Had none upon thars.

from "The Sneetches" by Dr. Seuss

Rhyme

Words **rhyme** when they end with the same vowel or vowel-consonant sound, as in the words *clown* and *noun* (both have an -ow- sound followed by an -n- sound). Rhyme, like rhythm, can be used to create different effects. It can emphasize the seriousness or the silliness of a poem, for example, and thus can help convey the poem's tone and meaning. Most rhymes are **end rhymes:**

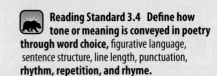
Reading Standard 3.4 Define how tone or meaning is conveyed in poetry through **word choice,** figurative language, sentence structure, line length, punctuation, **rhythm, repetition, and rhyme.**

The last word in one line is paired with the last word in the next line. In Dr. Seuss's "The Sneetches," *stars* and *thars* are end rhymes. Dr. Seuss has made up the word *thars* to rhyme with *stars,* creating humor. Sometimes rhymes occur within lines. This is called **internal rhyme.** Listen for internal rhymes in these lines:

> The rumbling, tumbling stones,
> And "Bones, bones, bones!"
> from "The Sea" by James Reeves

Rhyme Scheme The pattern of rhyming sounds at the ends of lines in a poem is the **rhyme scheme.** In addition to marking the meter in a poem, you can also mark the rhyme scheme. To mark the rhyme scheme, identify words that rhyme by labeling them with the same letter. The rhyme scheme in these lines is *a-b-a-b.* Listen:

> I'll tell you the story of Jimmy Jet—   *a*
> And you know what I tell you is true.   *b*
> He loved to watch his TV set   *a*
> Almost as much as you.   *b*
> from "Jimmy Jet and His TV Set"
> by Shel Silverstein

Free Verse Many poets today write in **free verse,** which means they do not worry about regular meter or rhyme schemes. Poetry written in free verse sounds like regular conversation. Here's the beginning of a poem written in free verse:

> Fifty cents apiece
> To eat our lunch
> We'd run
> Straight from school
> Instead of home
> from "Good Hot Dogs"
> by Sandra Cisneros

Other Sound Effects

Repetition and Refrain Rhythm and rhyme are forms of **repetition.** A poet may also repeat a word, phrase, line, or group of lines to make a **refrain.** Poets, like songwriters, use refrain to emphasize key ideas and to create rhythm.

Alliteration The repetition of consonant sounds in words that are close together is called **alliteration.** Alliteration, which often occurs at the beginnings of words, can contribute to the poem's music and its tone. Listen to the repetition of the -l- and -wh- sounds in these lines:

> It laughs a lovely whiteness,
> And whitely whirs away,
> from "Cynthia in the Snow"
> by Gwendolyn Brooks

Your Turn Analyze Sounds, Tone, and Meaning

Tone may be humorous, sarcastic, sad, joyful, playful, and so on. Choose a favorite song. First, explain what the song means—what is its message? Next, identify the way the songwriter uses sound effects. Finally, describe the tone of the song. How do the sounds of the song reinforce its tone and meaning?

Learn It Online
Try the *PowerNotes* version of this lesson at:
go.hrw.com   H6-473   **Go**

Literary Skills Focus

by **Linda Rief**

How Do Word Choice, Figurative Language, and Structure Convey Tone and Meaning?

Think of a popular song, such as "America the Beautiful." How can a song create such powerful feelings using only two elements: words and sounds?

Tone and Meaning

All of the choices a poet makes about how to use language affect not only the poem's meaning but also its **tone.** Tone is the speaker's attitude toward a subject. Tone can be playful or serious, joyous or sad, mournful or humorous, and so on.

Figurative Language

Poets have a special talent for making imaginative comparisons—for describing one thing in terms of something else, something very different. These comparisons are called **figures of speech.** Using figurative language, instead of expressing their thoughts directly, enables poets to convey meaning in rich ways. Compare these two sentences:

> *His friendship was valuable.*
> *His friendship was like a gift.*

By using figurative language to compare friendship to a gift in the second sentence above, the poet not only conveys that the friendship was valuable but also that it was given freely—without any expectation of receiving something in return. The comparison also suggests that the friendship might have been unexpected or surprising and that it was gratefully received. Whereas the first sentence above lacks tone, the

figurative language in the second sentence creates a strong tone of appreciation.

Three of the most common figures of speech are metaphor, simile, and personification.

Metaphor A **metaphor** directly compares two unlike things. If you said, "My brother is a rat," you'd be using a metaphor that suggests some hostility toward your brother, since few people like rats. Poets use unexpected and original comparisons to create metaphors such as this one:

> The sea is a hungry dog,
> Giant and gray.
> from "The Sea" by James Reeves

A single comparison that is explored in great depth and detail, sometimes through the entire length of a poem, is called an **extended metaphor.**

Simile If you had a change of heart and exclaimed, "My brother's as good as gold!" you would be using a simile. A **simile** is a comparison between unlike things that uses specific words of comparison, such as *like* or *as*. Here's a poem that begins with a simile:

He's white
As spilled milk,
My cat who sleeps
With his belly
Turned toward
The summer sky.

from "Ode to Mi Gato" by Gary Soto

Personification A common type of figurative language is **personification**—speaking of something that is not human as if it had human abilities, emotions, and reactions: "The sky wept bitterly all day." The personification in this sentence not only conveys that it rained hard all day but also creates a gloomy tone by comparing the rain to tears.

Word Choice

Every word counts in a poem. Choosing the right word—the one that is most vivid and precise—is essential for conveying a poem's meaning and tone. You can understand the importance of word choice by examining the imagery in a poem—the use of language that appeals to the senses of sight, hearing, touch, taste, or smell.

What precise images do the words in this poem help you see? How would the sense of the poem differ if the word *upset* were used instead of the words *bad-tempered*?

Bad-tempered, I got back:
Then, in the garden,
The willow tree.

by Ōshima Ryōta

Sentence Structure

Meaning and tone in a poem depend on many things, including the structure of the poem's sentences. Short, punchy sentences can create emphasis or drama or nervousness. Long sentences can create a rolling rhythm. Read the following lines aloud. Notice how dramatic the short line is. The poem is about snow.

It laughs a lovely whiteness,
And whitely whirs away,
To be
Some otherwhere,

from "Cynthia in the Snow"
by Gwendolyn Brooks

Your Turn Analyze Figurative Language and Tone

Write two descriptions of fire or water, using a metaphor, simile, and personification in each description. In one description, use words to create a tone of terror or horror. In the other description, use words to create a tone of wonder or awe.

Learn It Online
See this lesson in a new way with *PowerNotes*:
go.hrw.com   H6-475   Go

Reading Skills Focus

by **Kylene Beers**

What Strategies Help You Identify How Tone and Meaning Are Conveyed in Poetry?

It's not hard to identify how tone and meaning are conveyed in a poem once you know some basic strategies: Read the poem aloud. Focus on each word—because every word counts! Re-read as many times as you need to, and use the questioning strategy to uncover meaning and tone.

Reading a Poem

Reading a poem is not like reading a novel or a note from a friend. You need to take a different approach to reading a poem.

Steps for Reading a Poem Following these steps will help you identify how tone and meaning are conveyed in poetry.

1. Pay attention to the **title.** Think about the images it creates and the associations it evokes. What images and associations come to mind when you read the title of the poem "Cynthia in the Snow" in this chapter?

2. Read the poem silently. Note where sentences begin and end. Pay attention to **punctuation.** Pause briefly at commas and semicolons, and pause longer after periods. If you see a dash, expect a sudden shift in thought. If there's no punctuation at the end of a line, don't pause.

3. Read the poem aloud. *Hear* how it sounds. Feel the poem's **rhythm** as you read. Listen for **rhyme** and the **repetition** of words, phrases, lines, or sounds.

4. Pay attention to **word choice.** Use context clues to figure out the meanings of unfamiliar words. Think about shades of meaning in the words the poet has chosen. Each word was chosen for a reason.

Peanuts reprinted by permission of United Feature Syndicate, Inc.

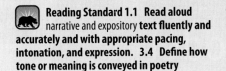

Reading Standard 1.1   Read aloud narrative and expository **text fluently and accurately and with appropriate pacing, intonation, and expression.   3.4   Define how tone or meaning is conveyed in poetry** through word choice, figurative language, sentence structure, line length, **punctuation, rhythm, repetition, and rhyme.**

5. Visualize the poem's **images** as you read. Think about the emotions conveyed by the images.

6. Identify **figurative language.** Look for **metaphors** and **similes,** which are imaginative comparisons, and **personification,** or instances in which human or living qualities are given to something that is not human. What feelings are created by these figures of speech?

7. Finally, think about how all these elements work together to create the poem's tone and meaning. How does the speaker feel about the subject? What message or meaning does the poem convey to you?

Re-reading a Poem

As you re-read, focus on figurative language and imagery. Be sure you understand each figure of speech and that you visualize each image. Then, focus on the sounds of the poem. How do all of these elements contribute to the poem's meaning?

Reading Fluency and Reading Rate   It's especially helpful to re-read a poem aloud to improve your reading fluency and reading rate. **Reading fluency** (how well you read) and **reading rate** (how fast you read) are related. If you want to improve your fluency, record yourself as you read the poem aloud (so that you can listen to yourself later) or read it to a friend or family member. Fluent reading has these characteristics:

- You read with expression.
- You know when to pause and when to come to a full stop.
- You correctly read by phrases or thought groups instead of word by word.

- You know how to adjust your rate, reading certain passages more quickly and other passages more slowly, depending on the content of what you are reading.

Questioning

Think of the **questioning** strategy as a way of having a conversation with the poet. As you read, ask questions and note your observations about the poem—things you like, things you find interesting, things with which you agree or disagree. As you re-read the poem, you can answer your questions, make new observations, and even ask more questions. Use a chart like this one for "The Sneetches" to record your thoughts:

Observations	Questions	Answers
There are 2 kinds of Sneetches.	What is a Sneetch?	

Your Turn   Apply Reading Skills

1. Read the lyrics of a song you like, following the steps listed for reading for a poem on page 476. What is the meaning or message of the song? What tone do you hear in the song—that is, how does the singer feel about his or her subject?

2. Explain why re-reading is an important strategy for defining how tone and meaning are conveyed in a poem.

Now go to the Skills in Action: Reading Model

Learn It Online
Use online graphic organizers as you read:

go.hrw.com   H6-477   **Go**

Reading Skills Focus   **477**

Read with a Purpose Read to discover one poet's unique way of describing the sea.

The Sea

by **James Reeves**

Literary Focus

Figurative Language A **metaphor** is a type of figurative language that makes a direct comparison between two unlike things. In this poem the metaphor is extended throughout every stanza of the poem. A stanza in a poem is like a paragraph in prose. It often expresses one idea or unit of thought.

Reading Focus

Reading a Poem Pay attention to punctuation as you read the poem aloud. Don't stop at the ends of lines that have no punctuation. Here, the poet wants you to keep reading without pause until you reach the comma after *stones*.

The sea is a hungry dog,
Giant and gray.
He rolls on the beach all day.
With his clashing teeth and shaggy jaws
Hour upon hour he gnaws
The rumbling, tumbling stones,
And "Bones, bones, bones!"
The giant sea dog moans,
Licking his greasy paws.

And when the night wind roars
And the moon rocks in the stormy cloud,
He bounds to his feet and snuffs and sniffs,
Shaking his wet sides over the cliffs,
And howls and hollos long and loud.

But on quiet days in May or June,
When even the grasses on the dune
Play no more their reedy tune,
With his head between his paws
He lies on the sandy shores,
So quiet, so quiet, he scarcely snores.

Read with a Purpose What characteristics of the sea does Reeves describe?

Literary Focus

Rhyme and Repetition
Notice that the rhyme scheme for this stanza is *a-b-c-c-b*. The poet uses **alliteration** (the repetition of consonant sounds in words that are close together) to connect words and create sound effects. The repetition of the *w* sound in *when* and *wind* is one example of alliteration in this stanza. Listen for others.

Reading Focus

Re-reading and Questioning
When you finish the poem, re-read it. Write down your observations and questions about words or images that you don't completely understand. Finally, re-read the poem a third time—or more—to answer your questions and to define how tone and meaning are conveyed in the poem.

James Reeves
(1909–1978)

A Reader and a Writer

James Reeves was born in a suburb of London, but he grew up in the small county of Buckinghamshire, England. As a child, Reeves loved reading, and he started writing poetry when he was only eleven years old.

Reeves attended Cambridge University and then taught for many years before becoming a writer and an editor. Reeves wrote poetry and edited books for a series called the Poetry Bookshelf. Even though Reeves is known primarily for his poetry, he also had a particular interest in folk tales and myths. As a result, he wrote various adaptations of traditional tales and classics.

"A Continuing Craving for Poetry"

When he was forty-one years old and already established as a respected author of books for adults, Reeves turned his attention to writing for children. He edited various prose and poetry anthologies for children that proved popular. Critics praised his original poems for children, which had widespread appeal. Reeves once declared:

"We must always provide poetry in such a way that it creates and nourishes a continuing craving for poetry and does not kill it by making poetry seem something childish."

Think About the Writer Why might Reeves have started writing poetry for children after he had already been writing it for adults?

The Giant (1923) by N. C. Wyeth (1882–1945).
Collection of Westtown School, Westtown, PA.
Photography courtesy of Brandywine River Museum.

Reading Standard 3.4 Define how tone or meaning is conveyed in poetry through word choice, figurative language, sentence structure, line length, punctuation, rhythm, repetition, and rhyme.

Into Action: Re-reading and Questioning

Fill in a chart like this one with your observations and questions about "The Sea." Re-read the poem, and think about what's clearer to you on the second reading. Continue re-reading until you can answer all your questions, or as many as possible.

Questions	Observations	Answers
How are the sea and a dog similar?	The sea is compared to a large, hungry gray dog.	Both the sea and a dog roll on the beach.

Talk About . . .

1. Discuss with a partner how you could extend the metaphor in "The Sea" even further. For example, what might happen when the napping dog wakes up? Try to use each Academic Vocabulary word listed on the right at least once in your discussion.

Write About . . .

Answer the following questions about "The Sea." For definitions of the underlined Academic Vocabulary words, see the column on the right.

2. Which <u>visual</u> images helped you <u>appreciate</u> the poem's meaning the most? Why?

3. What tone do you <u>detect</u> in the poem: amusement, disgust, fear, or anger? What details create that tone?

4. The <u>device</u> of the extended metaphor forms the heart of the poem. How would the poem's tone and meaning change if the poet had compared the sea to a different type of dog, such as a well-fed one?

Writing Skills Focus
Think as a Reader/Writer

The Writing Skills Focus activities in Chapter 5 will draw your attention to each poet's style. You'll then be given the chance to write about and use the same elements of poetry used by these poets.

Academic Vocabulary for Chapter 5

Talking and Writing About Poetry

Academic Vocabulary is the language you use to write and talk about literature. Use these words to discuss the poetry you read in this chapter. The words are underlined throughout the chapter.

appreciate (uh PREE shee ayt) *v.*: understand and enjoy the good qualities or value of something. *Careful reading can help you appreciate poetry.*

detect (dih TEHKT) *v.*: notice or discover, especially something that is not easy to see, hear, and so on. *Read a poem aloud to detect how the rhyme scheme changes.*

device (dih VYS) *n.*: way of achieving a particular purpose. *Figurative language is a device for conveying tone and meaning.*

visual (VIHZH oo uhl) *adj.*: related to seeing or to sight. *Color words are visual and help you imagine an object more clearly.*

Your Turn

Copy the Academic Vocabulary words into your *Reader/Writer Notebook*. Use each word in a sentence about your personal thoughts on poetry.

The Sounds of Poetry

CONTENTS

 What Do **You** **Think**

What is a "beautiful sound"? How can sounds affect our emotions?

 QuickWrite

Why do some word combinations sound "just right"? What is it like to read, listen to, or recite words that sound good to your ears?

Reading Standard 3.4 Define how tone or meaning is conveyed in poetry through **word choice,** figurative language, sentence structure, line length, punctuation, **rhythm,** repetition, and **rhyme.**

The Sneetches

Reader/Writer
Notebook
Use your **RWN** to complete the activities for this selection.

Literary Skills Focus

Rhythm and Rhyme You know what rhythm and rhyme are from the nursery rhymes and silly songs you heard as a young child. **Rhythm** is the musical quality created by repeated sound patterns. **Meter** is a regular pattern of stressed and unstressed syllables. Words that **rhyme** end with the same vowel or vowel-consonant sounds. Dr. Seuss uses the <u>devices</u> of rhythm and rhyme to keep this poem galloping along, but don't be deceived by the poem's sound. As you read, think about the serious **tone,** or attitude, and meaning that lie beneath the poem's surface.

Reading Skills Focus

Reading a Poem This poem begs to be read aloud. Reading a poem aloud helps you identify sound patterns. To identify the **rhyme scheme** (the pattern of **end rhymes**—rhymes created by the last words in lines), mark the first line and the lines that rhyme with it *a*; mark the second line and the lines that rhyme with it *b*; and so on. To **scan** a poem, or identify its meter, mark each stressed syllable with the symbol ´ and each unstressed syllable with the symbol ˘.

Into Action As you read the poem aloud, record your observations in a chart like the one below.

Rhythm/Meter	Rhyme
1.	

Writing Skills Focus
Think as a Reader/Writer

Find It in Your Reading In your *Reader/Writer Notebook*, list your favorite rhymes in this poem—especially real words that rhyme with made-up words.

Language Coach

Vowel Sounds In the Vocabulary word *keen*, the long -e- sound is spelled *ee*. There are several other ways the sound can be spelled: *ea* as in *mean*; *ie* as in *chief*; *ei* as in *receive*. (Remember how to determine whether to write *ie* or *ei* for the long -e- sound: After *c*, write *ei*. Otherwise, usually write *ie*.) The long -e- sound is also created by the letter *e* followed by a consonant and a silent *e*, as in *these*. For each spelling of the long -e- sound, list two other words that can serve as examples.

Learn It Online
Practice your vocabulary with Word Watch online:

go.hrw.com   H6-483   **Go**

Learn It Online
Get more on the author's life at:
go.hrw.com H6-484 Go

Theodor Seuss Geisel
(1904–1991)

Pulitzer Prize WINNER

Wacky Wisdom in Rhythm and Rhyme

Dr. Seuss (soos) is the pen name of Theodor Seuss Geisel, who began drawing fantastic animal cartoons while he was still a child. An art teacher told him that he would never learn to draw, and twenty-seven publishers rejected his first children's book, *And to Think That I Saw It on Mulberry Street* (1937). Even so, Dr. Seuss went on to write and illustrate more than forty children's classics, full of rhymes and wacky creatures. Dr. Seuss often used his zany characters to look at serious issues as if "through the wrong end of a telescope."

Dr. Seuss explained how he decided on his pen name:

"The 'Dr. Seuss' name is a combination of my middle name and the fact that I had been studying for my doctorate when I decided to quit and become a cartoonist. My father had always wanted to see a Dr. in front of my name, so I attached it. I figured by doing that, I saved him about ten thousand dollars."

Think About the Writer What kind of person do you think Geisel was? What makes you think so?

Build Background

Once, when he was asked, "What is rhyme?" Dr. Seuss replied, "A rhyme is something without which I would probably be in the dry-cleaning business." To keep his poems galloping along with catchy rhymes, Dr. Seuss often invented words. In "The Sneetches" he rhymes the real word *stars* with the made-up word *thars*—and *Sneetches* with *beaches*. Seuss's playful way with words has delighted generations of children who have grown up with his simple-seeming but masterful rhymes and his wacky characters, like the Cat in the Hat and the Grinch.

"The Sneetches" is a **narrative poem**— a long poem that tells a story.

Preview the Selection

In "The Sneetches" we enter a world inhabited by **Star-Belly Sneetches** and **Plain-Belly Sneetches.** See what happens when a "Fix-it-Up Chappie" named **Sylvester McMonkey McBean** comes along. (A "chappie" is a *chap*—a British term for "fellow" or "guy.")

THEODOR SEUSS GEISEL
USA 37
2004

Read with a Purpose Underneath the clever wordplay and lively rhythms of Dr. Seuss's works, there is usually a serious message, or moral. Read to discover what point Dr. Seuss is making about people and the way they treat one another.

The SNEETCHES

by **Dr. Seuss
(Theodor Geisel)**

Now, the Star-Belly Sneetches
Had bellies with stars.
The Plain-Belly Sneetches
Had none upon thars.

5   Those stars weren't so big. They were really so small
You might think such a thing wouldn't matter at all.

But, because they had stars, all the Star-Belly Sneetches
Would brag, "We're the best kind of Sneetch on the beaches."
With their snoots in the air, they would sniff and they'd snort
10 "We'll have nothing to do with the Plain-Belly sort!"
And whenever they met some, when they were out walking,
They'd hike right on past them without even talking. **Ⓐ**

When the Star-Belly children went out to play ball,
Could a Plain-Belly get in the game . . . ? Not at all.
15 You only could play if your bellies had stars
And the Plain-Belly children had none upon thars.

Ⓐ **Literary Focus** **Rhyme** Which words rhyme in this
stanza? What does the rhyme add the tone of the poem so far?

When the Star-Belly Sneetches had frankfurter roasts
Or picnics or parties or marshmallow toasts,
They never invited the Plain-Belly Sneetches.
20   They left them out cold, in the dark of the beaches.
They kept them away. Never let them come near.
And that's how they treated them year after year. **B**

Then ONE day, it seems . . . while the Plain-Belly Sneetches
Were moping and doping alone on the beaches,
25   Just sitting there wishing their bellies had stars . . .
A stranger zipped up in the strangest of cars! **C**

"My friends," he announced in a voice clear and keen,
"My name is Sylvester McMonkey McBean.
And I've heard of your troubles. I've heard you're unhappy.

B Read and Discuss What has Dr. Seuss set up here?

C Reading Focus **Reading a Poem** Read this stanza
aloud. What is its rhyme scheme?

Vocabulary **keen** (keen) *adj.*: eager; enthusiastic.

486

Photo courtesy of the Springfield Museum.

The Grinch and his dog, Max.

Seussmania!

How influential is Dr. Seuss? Consider these facts:

- Educators have praised his Beginner Books series for teaching generations of children to become successful readers.
- His books have sold more than 200 million copies, stayed in print for decades, and been translated into more than fifteen languages.
- His works have inspired eleven television specials, several feature films, and a Broadway musical called *Seussical*.
- He earned dozens of awards and medals, including a Pulitzer Prize in 1984 for his contributions to children's literature.
- His hometown (Springfield, Massachusetts) honored him with the Dr. Seuss National Memorial in 2002—a sculpture garden with bronze statues of his characters.

Ask Yourself
Why do you think Dr. Seuss's creations have become a part of our culture?

30   But I can fix that. I'm the Fix-it-Up Chappie.
And I've come here to help you. I have what you need.
And my prices are low. And I work at great speed.
And my work is one hundred per cent guaranteed!"

Then, quickly, Sylvester McMonkey McBean
35   Put together a very peculiar machine.
And he said, "You want stars like a Star-Belly Sneetch . . . ?
My friends, you can have them for three dollars each!"

"Just pay me your money and hop right aboard!"
So they clambered inside. Then the big machine roared
40   And it klonked. And it bonked. And it jerked. And it berked    **D**
And it bopped them about. But the thing really worked!
When the Plain-Belly Sneetches popped out, they had stars!
They actually did. They had stars upon thars!

D **Literary Focus** Rhythm What words are stressed in line 40? How does the sound of the line imitate the actions of the machine?

Vocabulary **guaranteed** (gair uhn TEED) *v.* used as *adj.*: being subject to a promise that something will be paid for or replaced if it is not satisfactory.
peculiar (pih KYOOL yuhr) *adj.*: strange.

Then they yelled at the ones who had stars at the start.
45 "We're exactly like you! You can't tell us apart.
We're all just the same, now, you snooty old smarties!
And now we can go to your frankfurter parties."

"Good grief!" groaned the ones who had stars at the first.
We're *still* the best Sneetches and they are the worst.
50 But, now, how in the world will we know," they all frowned,
"If which kind is what, or the other way round?" **E**

Then up came McBean with a very sly wink
And he said, "Things are not quite as bad as you think.
So you don't know who's who. That is perfectly true.
55 But come with me, friends. Do you know what I'll do?
I'll make you again, the best Sneetches on beaches
And all it will cost you is ten dollars eaches."

"Belly stars are no longer in style," said McBean.
What you need is a trip through my Star-*Off* Machine.
60 This wondrous contraption will take *off* your stars
So you won't look like Sneetches who have them on thars."
And that handy machine
Working very precisely
Removed all the stars from their tummies quite nicely.

65 Then, with snoots in the air, they paraded about
And they opened their beaks and they let out a shout,
"We know who is who! Now there isn't a doubt.
The best kind of Sneetches are Sneetches without."

E Read and Discuss How are the original Star-Belly Sneetches reacting to the news?

488

Then, of course, those with stars all got frightfully mad.
70 To be wearing a star now was frightfully bad.
Then, of course, old Sylvester McMonkey McBean
Invited *them* into his Star-Off Machine.

Then, of course from THEN on, as you probably guess,
Things really got into a horrible mess.

75 All the rest of the day, on those wild screaming beaches,
The Fix-it-Up Chappie kept fixing up Sneetches.
Off again! On again!
In again! Out again!
Through the machines they raced round and about again,
80 Changing their stars every minute or two.
They kept paying money. They kept running through
Until neither the Plain nor the Star-Bellies knew
Whether this one was that one . . . or that one was this one
Or which one was what one . . . or what one was who. **F**

85 Then, when their last cent
Of their money was spent,
The Fix-it-Up Chappie packed up
And he went.

And he laughed as he drove
90 In his car up the beach,
"They never will learn.
No. You can't teach a Sneetch!"

But McBean was quite wrong. I'm quite happy to say
That the Sneetches got really quite smart on that day,
95 The day they decided that Sneetches are Sneetches
And no kind of Sneetch is the best at the beaches.
That day, all the Sneetches forgot about stars
And whether they had one, or not, upon thars. **G**

F Reading Focus **Reading a Poem** Read this stanza
aloud. Where did you pause or stop, and why?

G Read and Discuss How does McBean influence the behavior
of the Sneetches?

Reading Standard 3.4 Define how **tone or meaning is conveyed in poetry through word choice,** figurative language, sentence structure, line length, punctuation, **rhythm,** repetition, and **rhyme.**

The Sneetches

Literary Response and Analysis

Reading Skills Focus

Quick Check

1. Why does one group of Sneetches think it is better than the other group?

2. How does McBean offer to help both groups?

Read with a Purpose

3. What point does Dr. Seuss make in this poem about the way people treat one another?

Reading Skills: Reading a Poem

4. Review your chart, and look back at the poem. Which stanzas have a different rhyme scheme? Do the differences "make a difference"?

5. Copy two stanzas onto a piece of paper. Mark the stressed and unstressed syllables in each line. Is the meter identical in every line?

6. How do the variations in rhyme scheme and rhythm, or meter, affect the poem as a whole? Add a row, labeled "Conclusions," to the bottom of your chart, and write down your ideas.

Rhythm/Meter	Rhyme
1. Meter for 1st two lines: ∪∪′∪∪′∪∪′ ∪∪′	1. Rhyme scheme for 1st stanza: a-b-a-b

Conclusions:

✓ Vocabulary Check

7. Use each Vocabulary word in a sentence about "The Sneetches": **keen, guaranteed, peculiar.**

Literary Skills Focus

Literary Analysis

8. **Connect** Where and when might people like McBean show up in everyday life?

9. **Analyze** Why do the Sneetches finally change their behavior?

Literary Skills: Rhythm and Rhyme

10. **Analyze** What **tone** do you <u>detect</u> underneath the funny nonsense rhymes and bouncy rhythms? Do you think the rhyme and rhythm make this seem like a children's poem, or is it meant for adults as well? Explain.

Literary Skills Review: Character

11. **Analyze** "The Sneetches" is a narrative poem containing a plot and characters. How do McBean's qualities affect the plot? What quality of the Sneetches affects the resolution?

Writing Skills Focus

Think as a Reader/Writer

Use It in Your Writing Write a few rhyming lines that include both real and made-up words.

What Do **You Think Now** Why might nonsense verse with a strong rhythm be effective in making a serious point about human behavior?

Reading Standard 3.4 Define how tone or meaning is conveyed in poetry through **word choice, figurative language,** sentence structure, line length, punctuation, rhythm, **repetition,** and rhyme.

John Henry

Literary Skills Focus

Repetition and Refrain In poetry and songs, certain words, phrases, lines, stanzas, and even sounds may be repeated again and again. This poetic <u>device</u> is called **repetition.** Poets use repetition to emphasize important ideas and to convey **tone,** or the speaker's attitude toward a subject or the audience. One of the simplest kinds of repetition is **refrain**—a word, phrase, line, or group of lines that is repeated regularly throughout a work at intervals. (The wording of a refrain may change slightly from time to time.) As you read "John Henry," listen for the refrains, and think about how they help convey the tone of the song.

Reading Skills Focus

Questioning Asking questions as you read will make you a more active reader. Questioning can help you find the meaning in a poem and experience it in a way that is meaningful to you.

Into Action Use a chart like this one to record your questions and observations as you read. Some examples are included.

Observations	Questions
A three-day-old boy holding a hammer and singing is pretty unrealistic and exaggerated.	Are we supposed to think that John Henry is superhuman?
The captain says he's going to bring in a steam drill.	Why does John Henry want to die with a hammer in his hand?

Language Coach

Hyperbole When a friend says, "I just ate a mountain of food," you know that she didn't literally eat a mountain-size portion of food; she simply means that she ate a *lot* of food. She is using a kind of **figurative language** called **hyperbole** (hy PUHR buh lee). Hyperbole exaggerates or overstates a situation to produce a comical effect or to make a strong point. "John Henry" relies on hyperbole, starting with the lines "John Henry was about three days old / Sittin' on his papa's knee." We're not supposed to believe that John Henry was literally three days old and already working with a hammer; the writer is just trying to tell us that John Henry seemed born to be a "steel-driving man" from the beginning. What other examples of hyperbole can you find in this ballad? How do they fit its subject, theme, and tone?

Writing Skills Focus
Think as a Reader/Writer

Find It in Your Reading Almost all of the refrains in this song rely on **imagery,** or language that appeals to the senses. In your *Reader/Writer Notebook*, write down the refrains that you think contain the most vivid images, and note the senses to which these images appeal.

Reader/Writer
Notebook

Use your **RWN** to complete the activities for this selection.

Learn It Online
Hear a professional actor read this ballad. Visit the selection online at:

go.hrw.com   H6-491   **Go**

The Story of John Henry

Working on the Railroad

In the years following the Civil War, laborers toiled long and hard to build America's railroads. African Americans and recent immigrants from China did much of the work. In those days no unions protected the railroad construction crews. The men sweated long hours, cutting down trees, digging tunnels, and laying track. "Steel drivers" used a ten-pound hammer and a drill to crack the rock so that they could carve out a tunnel. Many of these laborers lost their jobs to the newly invented steam drill, which could do their work faster and more cheaply.

Mystery Song, Mystery Man

Nobody knows who wrote this popular song about John Henry. In fact, no one even knows whether John Henry was a real person. According to legend, he was an African American laborer in the crew constructing the Big Bend Tunnel of the Chesapeake and Ohio Railroad. Someone set up a contest between John Henry and a steam drill. This contest between man and machine became the subject of various **tall tales**—exaggerated folk tales about larger-than-life men and women. John Henry joined the ranks of America's tall-tale figures, such as Pecos Bill and Paul Bunyan, and became the subject of stories, poems, and songs in the 1870s. The "steel-driving man" is an enduring part of America's cultural legacy.

32 USA

JOHN HENRY

Think About the Writer What point do you think the people who sang this song wanted to make?

Build Background

"John Henry" is a **ballad,** a song or songlike poem that tells a story. Ballads are often about a hero or an important event. They usually have refrains and a regular rhythm and rhyme scheme. Try to find one of the many recordings of "John Henry" sung by rock, blues, or folk musicians.

Preview the Selection

John Henry is a "steel-driving man" practically born holding a hammer. He's strong and determined to hold his own against a machine that threatens to take his job.

Read with a Purpose

Read to learn why John Henry feels he has to compete with a machine.

John Henry on the Right, Steam Drill on the Left (1944–1947)
by Palmer C. Hayden.

The Museum of African American Art, Los Angeles, California, Palmer C. Hayden Collection, gift of Miriam A. Hayden.

JOHN HENRY

Anonymous African American

John Henry was about three days old
Sittin' on his papa's knee.
He picked up a hammer and a little piece of steel
Said, "Hammer's gonna be the death of me, Lord, Lord!
5   Hammer's gonna be the death of me."   Ⓐ

Ⓐ **Literary Focus** Repetition What feeling is conveyed through the repeated sentences?

John Henry **493**

The captain said to John Henry,
"Gonna bring that steam drill 'round
Gonna bring that steam drill out on the job
Gonna whop that steel on down, Lord, Lord!
10   Whop that steel on down."

John Henry told his captain,
"A man ain't nothin' but a man
But before I let your steam drill beat me down
I'd die with a hammer in my hand, Lord, Lord!
15   I'd die with a hammer in my hand."   **B**

John Henry said to his shaker,°
"Shaker, why don't you sing?
I'm throwing thirty pounds from my hips on down
Just listen to that cold steel ring, Lord, Lord!
20   Listen to that cold steel ring."

John Henry said to his shaker,
"Shaker, you'd better pray
'Cause if I miss that little piece of steel
Tomorrow be your buryin' day, Lord, Lord!
25   Tomorrow be your buryin' day."

The shaker said to John Henry,
"I think this mountain's cavin' in!"
John Henry said to his shaker, "Man,
That ain't nothin' but my hammer suckin' wind,
          Lord, Lord!
30   Nothin' but my hammer suckin' wind."   **C**

The man that invented the steam drill
Thought he was mighty fine
But John Henry made fifteen feet
The steam drill only made nine, Lord, Lord!
35   The steam drill only made nine.   **D**

16. shaker (SHAY kuhr): the worker who holds the drill.

B Read and Discuss   What have you learned about John Henry so far?

C Reading Focus   Questioning   What questions do you have about the shaker and about what is happening here? Record your questions and reactions.

D Read and Discuss   What has happened?

The Museum of African American Art, Los Angeles, California, Palmer C. Hayden Collection, gift of Miriam A. Hayden.

He Laid Down His Hammer and Cried (1944–1947) by Palmer C. Hayden.

John Henry hammered in the mountain
His hammer was striking fire
But he worked so hard, he broke his poor heart
He laid down his hammer and he died, Lord, Lord!
40   He laid down his hammer and he died.

John Henry had a little woman
Her name was Polly Ann
John Henry took sick and went to his bed
Polly Ann drove steel like a man, Lord, Lord!
45   Polly Ann drove steel like a man.   **E**

John Henry had a little baby
You could hold him in the palm of your hand
The last words I heard that poor boy say,
"My daddy was a steel-driving man, Lord, Lord!
50   My daddy was a steel-driving man."

They took John Henry to the graveyard
And they buried him in the sand
And every locomotive comes a-roaring by
Says, "There lies a steel-driving man, Lord, Lord!
55   There lies a steel-driving man."   **F**

Well, every Monday morning
When the bluebirds begin to sing
You can hear John Henry a mile or more
You can hear John Henry's hammer ring, Lord, Lord!
60   You can hear John Henry's hammer ring.   **G**

E **Reading Focus** **Questioning** What questions do you have
about Polly Ann? Record your questions and reactions.

F **Read and Discuss** How do things turn out for John Henry?

G **Literary Focus** **Refrain** What point is conveyed through the final refrain
in the ballad?

Reading Standard 3.4 Define how tone or meaning is conveyed in poetry **through word choice**, figurative language, sentence structure, line length, punctuation, rhythm, **repetition,** and rhyme.

John Henry
Literary Response and Analysis

Reading Skills Focus
Quick Check

1. What does John Henry predict as a child?
2. What happens to John Henry in the end?

Read with a Purpose

3. Was John Henry heroic or foolish for wanting to compete with a machine? Explain, citing lines from the ballad.

Reading Skills: Questioning

4. Add a column to your chart. As you think about the ballad and re-read it, record the answers you find to your questions. Discuss any unanswered questions with a partner.

Observations	Questions	Answers
A three-day-old boy holding a hammer and singing is pretty unrealistic and exaggerated.	Are we supposed to think that John Henry is superhuman?	I think John Henry is like a tall tale hero.
The captain says he's going to bring in a steam drill.	Why does John Henry want to die with a hammer in his hand?	

Literary Skills Focus
Literary Analysis

5. **Interpret** John Henry says, "A man ain't nothin' but a man." What does the ballad prove about this statement? Who or what ends up winning the contest, and why?

6. **Connect** What other stories about people challenging machines do you know? What is usually the point of such stories? Explain whether we can still <u>appreciate</u> and find meaning in such stories today.

Literary Skills: Repetition and Refrain

7. **Analyze** Identify the **refrains** in this ballad. How could the refrains be sung or spoken differently to suggest different feelings?

8. **Analyze** What is the **tone** of this ballad—humorous, proud, sad, angry, or something else? How is this tone conveyed through the **refrains**? Use examples from the ballad to explain your answer.

Literary Skills Review: Character

9. **Analyze** What heroic qualities does John Henry demonstrate in this ballad? What details suggest that John Henry lives on?

Writing Skills Focus
Think as a Reader/Writer
Use It in Your Writing Write an idea for a ballad about someone today who challenges a machine. Write the refrain(s) for your ballad, using imagery to convey meaning and tone.

What Do **You Think Now** How does the refrain of this ballad affect your feelings about John Henry?

POEMS
Preparing to Read

Cynthia in the Snow / Full Fathom Five / A Nash Menagerie

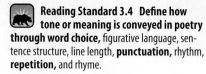

Reading Standard 3.4 Define how tone or meaning is conveyed in poetry through **word choice,** figurative language, sentence structure, line length, **punctuation,** rhythm, **repetition,** and rhyme.

Reader/Writer Notebook
Use your **RWN** to complete the activities for these selections.

Literary Skills Focus

Repetition and Alliteration One common form of repetition used in poetry is **alliteration** (uh liht uh RAY shuhn), the repetition of the same or similar consonant sounds in words that are close together. Alliteration usually occurs at the beginnings of words, as in "the **d**eep, **d**ark forest." Poets use alliteration to imitate sounds, to create a feeling, or to emphasize certain words in order to help convey the tone and meaning of their poems. As you read, think about the purpose and effect of the alliteration in these poems.

Reading Skills Focus

Reading a Poem Punctuation is used to break up or to connect ideas. When you read, it's important to pay attention to punctuation in order to understand a poem's full meaning. Make a full stop at periods, question marks, and exclamation points. Pause briefly at commas, and pause longer at colons, semicolons, and dashes. If there is no punctuation at the end of a line, don't stop. Go on to the next line or lines, which will contain the rest of the poet's idea.

Into Action For each poem, fill in a chart like the one below for "Cynthia in the Snow." Record notes about how to use punctuation to guide you in reading the poem.

"Cynthia in the Snow"

Line(s)	Comments
2–3	These lines contain one thought.

Writing Skills Focus
Think as a Reader/Writer
Find It in Your Reading As you read, record in your *Reader/Writer Notebook* the most effective or striking examples of alliteration that you find in the poems.

Vocabulary

A Nash Menagerie

marvel (MAHR vuhl) *v.:* wonder at. *The speaker can only marvel at the octopus and its many limbs.*

behold (bih HOHLD) *v.:* look at; see. *In his poetry, Nash invites the reader to behold many kinds of animals.*

extinct (ehk STIHNGKT) *adj.:* no longer existing. *The speaker cautions that humans might become extinct if we are not careful.*

Language Coach
Word Roots The adjective *extinct,* like the verb *extinguish,* comes from the Latin verb *exstinguere.* How are the meanings of *extinct* and *extinguish* similar? What are some other related words? Use a dictionary to help you answer these questions if necessary.

Learn It Online
Use Word Watch to improve your vocabulary at:
go.hrw.com | H6-498 | GO

The Granger Collection, New York.

Gwendolyn Brooks (1917–2000)

Gwendolyn Brooks spent much of her childhood reading and writing. She published her first poem at the age of fourteen. After finishing junior college, Brooks worked several different jobs before she went on to write more than twenty books and to win a Pulitzer Prize for poetry.

Pulitzer Prize WINNER

The Granger Collection, New York.

William Shakespeare (1564–1616)

William Shakespeare was born in Stratford-upon-Avon, England, during the Renaissance. At eighteen, Shakespeare left Stratford for a life in the theater in London. He began to act and to write such famous plays as *Romeo and Juliet*. He also wrote some of the best poetry of his day. Today he is considered the greatest English playwright.

Ogden Nash (1902–1971)

Generations of readers have appreciated Ogden Nash for his comical poetry and clever rhymes. He taught and worked in advertising and publishing before turning to writing "silly" verse. A master of the English language, Nash admitted having intentionally ignored or mangled every known rule of grammar and spelling.

Think About the Writers
What kinds of poems would you expect each of these writers to write?

Build Background

"Full Fathom Five" is an excerpt from *The Tempest*, one of Shakespeare's most widely read plays and one of the last ones he wrote. The English language has changed a lot since Shakespeare's time, so you'll notice words we no longer use, such as *thy* ("your") and *doth* ("does").

In the Nash Menagerie you'll also notice some odd words, such as *thou* ("you") and the made-up *anther* ("answer")—not because Nash wrote long ago but because he enjoyed playing with language.

Preview the Selections

In "Cynthia in the Snow" the speaker is reflecting on the beauty of snowfall.

In "Full Fathom Five" the sprite, or spirit, **Ariel** is singing to **Ferdinand,** who believes that his father has drowned in a shipwreck.

The Nash Menagerie introduces us to some interesting creatures—and a poet's unique sense of humor. A *menagerie* (muh NAJ uhr ee) is a collection or assortment of animals, usually in a zoo.

Read with a Purpose Read this poem to learn how the speaker feels about snow.

Cynthia
in the
Snow

by **Gwendolyn Brooks**

It SHUSHES.
It hushes
The loudness in the road.
It flitter-twitters,
5   And laughs away from me.
It laughs a lovely whiteness,
And whitely whirs away,   **A**
To be   **B**
Some otherwhere,
10   Still white as milk or shirts.
So beautiful it hurts.   **C**

A **Literary Focus** **Alliteration** Identify the alliteration in lines 6–7. What do the sounds make you "hear"?

B **Reading Focus** **Reading a Poem** Since there is no punctuation at the end of this line, how should you read it?

C **Read and Discuss** What visual images does this poem create for you?

Read with a Purpose   Read this poem to learn how Ferdinand's father has been changed by the sea.

Full Fathom Five

from *The Tempest*
by **William Shakespeare**

Full Fathom Five by Edmund Dulac. Illustration from an edition of William Shakespeare's *The Tempest*.

Full fathom° five thy father lies:
Of his bones are coral made;   **Ⓐ**
Those are pearls that were his eyes:
   Nothing of him that doth fade
But doth suffer a sea-change   **Ⓑ**
Into something rich and strange.
Sea-nymphs° hourly ring his knell:°
   Ding-dong.
Hark! now I hear them—ding-dong, bell.   **Ⓒ**

1. fathom (FATH uhm): unit of measurement equal to about six feet, used to measure the depth of water.

7. sea-nymphs (see nihmfs): goddesses once thought to inhabit the sea. **knell** (nehl): sound of a bell rung after someone has died.

Ⓐ **Reading Focus** **Reading a Poem**   Notice the semicolon at the end of this line. How should you read the line?

Ⓑ **Read and Discuss**   What does "But doth suffer a sea-change" mean?

Ⓒ **Literary Focus** **Alliteration**   What examples of alliteration can you find in this poem? Which consonants do you hear most?

Read with a Purpose Read these poems to discover what Nash thinks of the octopus, the panther, the camel, the duck, an extinct bird—and people.

A Nash Menagerie
by Ogden Nash

The Octopus

Tell me, O Octopus, I begs,
Is those things arms, or is they legs? **Ⓐ**
I marvel at thee, Octopus;
If I were thou, I'd call me Us.

The Panther

The panther is like a leopard,
Except it hasn't been peppered. **Ⓑ**
Should you behold a panther crouch,
Prepare to say Ouch.
Better yet, if called by a panther,
Don't anther.

Ⓐ **Literary Focus** **Alliteration** Notice the alliteration here. What sounds are repeated in this line?

Ⓑ **Read and Discuss** What does this line mean?

Vocabulary **marvel** (MAHR vuhl) v.: wonder at.
behold (bih HOHLD) v.: look at; see.

The Duck

Behold the duck
It does not cluck.
A cluck it lacks.
It quacks.
It is especially fond
Of a puddle or pond.
When it dines or sups,
It bottoms ups. **C**

The Camel

The camel has a single hump;
The dromedary, two;
Or else the other way around.
I'm never sure. Are you? **D**

C Read and Discuss What aspect of duck behavior is this line describing?

D Reading Focus Reading a Poem Read the last line of this poem aloud.
How do the two punctuation marks in this line affect the way you read it?

A Caution to Everybody

Consider the auk;°
Becoming extinct because he forgot
　how to fly, and could only walk.
Consider man, who may well
　become extinct
Because he forgot how to walk and
　learned how to fly before he
　thinked.

---

1. **auk** (awk): the great auk, a large, flightless bird once common in
　North Atlantic regions but now extinct.

Analyzing Visuals

Connecting to the Text
How does this photograph
relate to the meaning of the
poem on this page?

Vocabulary **extinct** (ehk STIHNGKT) *adj.:* no longer existing.

Applying Your Skills

Reading Standard 3.4 Define how tone or meaning is conveyed in poetry through word choice, figurative language, sentence structure, line length, **punctuation**, rhythm, repetition, and rhyme.

Cynthia in the Snow / Full Fathom Five /
A Nash Menagerie

Literary Response and Analysis

Reading Skills Focus

Quick Check

1. What are the qualities of the snow described in "Cynthia in the Snow"?
2. In "Full Fathom Five," what are two of the changes that the drowned body undergoes?

Read with a Purpose

3. In "Cynthia in the Snow," how would you describe the speaker's feelings about snow?
4. In "Full Fathom Five," what makes the drowned man's fate seem magical?
5. What do Ogden Nash's observations in the five poems have in common?

Reading Skills: Reading a Poem

6. Use your charts to guide you in re-reading the poems. Then, in a new row, record your thoughts about each poem's meaning.

"Cynthia in the Snow"

Line(s)	Comments
2–3	These lines contain one thought.

Poem's meaning:

✔ Vocabulary Check

Match each Vocabulary word in the left-hand column with its definition in the right-hand column.

7. marvel   **a.** see
8. behold   **b.** no longer existing
9. extinct   **c.** wonder at

Literary Skills Focus

Literary Analysis

10. **Interpret** How would you explain the meaning of the last lines of "A Caution to Everybody"?
11. **Analyze Onomatopoeia** (ahn uh maht uh PEE uh) is the use of a word whose sound imitates or suggests its meaning, such as *boom* and *bang*. Find three examples of onomatopoeia in these poems, and explain their effects.

Literary Skills: Repetition and Alliteration

12. **Analyze** Review the examples of **alliteration** you recorded in your *Reader/Writer Notebook*. Then, explain how the alliteration in two poems helps convey their **tone**.

Literary Skills Review: Metamorphosis

13. **Analyze** A **metamorphosis** is a change from one form to another. What metamorphoses are imagined in "Full Fathom Five"?

Writing Skills Focus

Think as a Reader/Writer

Use It in Your Writing Write a funny or serious poem. Use alliteration to convey tone and meaning.

 What Do You Think Now

How can the sounds of a poet's words convey the feeling—and the meaning—of a poem?

Language and Structure in Poetry

CONTENTS

What Do **You** **Think**? How can the simple details of everyday life make good subjects for poems?

 **QuickWrite**

Write down three things you saw or did on the way to school today—no matter how simple or unimportant they may seem to you. Choose one of the three, and describe it using two or more images.

Preparing to Read

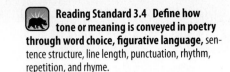

Reading Standard 3.4 Define how tone or meaning is conveyed in poetry through word choice, figurative language, sentence structure, line length, punctuation, rhythm, repetition, and rhyme.

Reader/Writer
Notebook
Use your **RWN** to complete the activities for these selections.

Ode to Mi Gato / In a Neighborhood in Los Angeles / Hard on the Gas

Literary Skills Focus

Figurative Language There are three main types of **figurative language,** or language that describes one thing in terms of something else. A **metaphor** is a direct comparison between two unlike things. When poets use an **extended metaphor,** they develop a comparison through many lines or even through an entire poem. A **simile** is a comparison between unlike things using a word such as *like* or *as*. When poets use **personification,** they talk about a nonhuman thing as if it were human. As you'll see when you read these poems, poets use figurative language to convey meaning in rich ways that appeal to our imagination and senses. They also use it to convey **tone,** a speaker's attitude toward, or feelings about, a subject.

Literary Perspectives Apply the literary perspective described on page 509 as you read "Ode to Mi Gato."

Reading Skills Focus

Re-reading Read each poem straight through to get a sense of it. Then, re-read the poem to clarify your understanding.

Into Action Set up a chart like the one below. As you read each poem, record words, lines, or sections you want to pay particular attention to when you re-read.

Ode to Mi Gato	In a Neighborhood in Los Angeles	Hard on the Gas
Line 13	Fish canneries?	"bar above your right shoulder"?
Line 27, "Porque"	lines 28–30	

Writing Skills Focus

Find It in Your Reading As you read, record in your *Reader/Writer Notebook* your responses to the figurative language used in these poems. Which types of figurative language vividly convey meaning or feelings? Which ones create clear pictures in your mind?

Vocabulary

Ode to Mi Gato

dribble (DRIHB uhl) *n.:* irregular drops that flow slowly. *The cat loved to lick the dribble of milk that came out of old milk cartons.*

dangled (DANG guhld) *v.:* held something or swung it loosely. *The speaker dangled food in front of his cat.*

abandoned (uh BAN duhnd) *adj.:* not used or taken care of any longer. *The speaker found the cat on an abandoned car.*

Hard on the Gas

clutch (kluhch) *v.:* hold something tightly. *When she clutched the rail in fear, her grandfather knew she needed encouragement.*

Language Coach

Multiple-Meaning Words Two of the words above can be used as both a verb and a noun. Can you identify them? Use a dictionary if necessary.

Learn It Online
For a preview of "Ode to Mi Gato," see the introductory video at:

| go.hrw.com | H6-507 | Go |

Learn It Online
Get more on Soto's life at:
go.hrw.com H6-508 Go

Gary Soto
(1952–   )

Gary Soto grew up in a Mexican American family in California's San Joaquin Valley. He dreamed of being a hobo, a geographer, a priest, and a paleontologist. He was not a very good student until he discovered poetry in college. Soon afterward, he yearned to become a writer—to recapture the world of his childhood in words. Soto has won awards and widespread recognition for his poems, short stories, and novels.

Francisco X. Alarcón
(1954–   )

Francisco X. Alarcón, who grew up in the United States and in Mexico, says that his family has belonged to two countries for four generations. Alarcón's roots are important to him. He regularly visits the Mexican village where his ancestors lived. Alarcón was brought up mainly in Los Angeles by his grandmother, the woman he celebrates in his poem "In a Neighborhood in Los Angeles."

Janet S. Wong
(1962–   )

Janet S. Wong bases many of her poems on her experiences growing up as an Asian American. Wong decided to become a poet after working as a lawyer for several years. For Wong, "Poetry is, in a way, like shouting. Since you can't yell at the top of your lungs for a long time, you have to decide what you really need to say, and say it quickly."

Think About the Writers

Why do you think poets use childhood experiences as subject matter?

Build Background

Gary Soto's poem "Ode to Mi Gato" is a special form of poetry called an **ode**—a poem written to honor or celebrate someone or something. The word *ode* is often applied to a poem that is written in a grand, dignified style and is dedicated to an important subject, such as a famous person. Soto, though, takes a playful approach with his ode, using ordinary language and the rhythms of everyday speech to celebrate an ordinary but much-loved *gato,* or cat.

Preview the Selections

The speaker of "Ode to Mi Gato" describes his relationship with his cat over time.

The speaker of "In a Neighborhood in Los Angeles" fondly recalls the Mexican grandmother who raised him.

"Hard on the Gas" describes a young girl's reaction to her grandfather's driving and the lesson it taught her about life.

Read with a Purpose Read this poem to
discover why a white cat is special to the speaker.

Ode to Mi Gato

by **Gary Soto**

He's white
As spilled milk,
My cat who sleeps
With his belly
5   Turned toward
The summer sky.
He loves the sun,
Its warmth like a hand.
He loves tuna cans
10   And milk cartons
With their dribble
Of milk. He loves
Mom when she rattles
The bag of cat food,
15   The brown nuggets
Raining into his bowl.   **A**
And my cat loves
Me, because I saved
Him from a dog,
20   Because I dressed him
In a hat and a cape
For Halloween,   **B**

Literary Perspectives

Analyzing Responses to Literature The way a poet uses
literary elements such as word choice contributes to your reaction to a poem. As you read "Ode to Mi Gato," think about the
way the literary elements shape your response to the work. As
you read, pay attention to the questions in the text, which will
guide you in using this perspective.

A Read and Discuss What is the speaker telling you?
B Literary Perspectives Analyzing Responses to
Literature What words help clarify the way the speaker feels
about his cat?

Vocabulary **dribble** (DRIHB uhl) *n.*: irregular drops that
flow slowly.

Analyzing Visuals

Connecting to the Text
How is the cat in this painting similar to or different from the cat described in the poem?

Cat Lying on Yellow Cushion
by Franz Marc.

Because I dangled
A sock of chicken skin
25 As he stood on his
Hind legs. I love mi gato,
Porque I found
Him on the fender
Of an abandoned car.
30 He was a kitten,
With a meow
Like the rusty latch
On a gate. I carried
Him home in the loop
35 Of my arms.
I poured milk
Into him, let him
Lick chunks of
Cheese from my palms,
40 And cooked huevo
After huevo

Until his purring
Engine kicked in
And he cuddled
45 Up to my father's slippers. **C**
That was last year.
This spring,
He's excellent at sleeping
And no good
50 At hunting. At night
All the other cats
In the neighborhood
Can see him slink
Around the corner,
55 Or jump from the tree
Like a splash of
Milk. We lap up
His love and
He laps up his welcome. **D**

C | Read and Discuss | So far, what have you learned about the speaker and his cat?

D | Literary Focus | **Figurative Language** How has the comparison between the white cat and milk been developed?

Vocabulary dangled (DANG guhld) *v.:* held something or swung it loosely.
abandoned (uh BAN duhnd) *adj.:* not used or taken care of any longer.

In a Neighborhood in Los Angeles

by **Francisco X. Alarcón**

I learned
Spanish
from my grandma

mijito°
5 don't cry
she'd tell me

on the mornings
my parents
would leave

10 to work
at the fish
canneries

---

4. *mijito* (mee HEE toh): contraction of *mi hijito,* Spanish for "my little child."

my grandma
would chat
15 with chairs

sing them
old
songs

dance
20 waltzes with them
in the kitchen Ⓐ

when she'd say
niño barrigón°
she'd laugh

---

23. ***niño barrigón*** (NEEN yo bah
ree GOHN): Spanish for
"potbellied boy."

25 with my grandma
I learned
to count clouds

to point out
in flowerpots
30 mint leaves

my grandma
wore moons
on her dress

Mexico's mountains
35 deserts
ocean

in her eyes
I'd see them
in her braids

40 I'd touch them
in her voice
smell them

one day
I was told:
45 she went far away

but still
I feel her
with me Ⓑ

whispering
50 in my ear
mijito Ⓒ

Ⓐ **Reading Focus** **Re-reading** Re-read lines 13–21. Why do you think the grandmother sings to chairs and chats and dances with them?

Ⓑ **Read and Discuss** What is the speaker letting you know?

Ⓒ **Literary Focus** **Tone** What is the tone of the poem's ending?

Downtown Los Angeles, California.

Analyzing Visuals **Connecting to the Text**
How do these images add to the poem's meaning and what you learn about the grandmother's personality?

Mexico.

Read with a Purpose Read this poem to discover what the speaker learns from her grandfather's driving.

HARD ON THE GAS

by **Janet S. Wong**

My grandfather taught himself
    to drive   **Ⓐ**
rough, the way he learned to live,

push the pedal, hard on the gas,
rush up to 50,
coast a bit,

rush, rest, rush, rest—   **Ⓑ**

When you clutch the bar above your
    right shoulder
he shoots you a look that asks,
Who said the ride would
    be smooth?   **Ⓒ**

Ⓐ Reading Focus Re-reading Why do you think the poet broke the first line after "drive"? What is the effect of beginning the second line with "rough"?

Ⓑ Literary Focus Figurative Language What two things is the speaker comparing in the poem?

Ⓒ Read and Discuss Now what has happened? What does the speaker's grandfather think of the speaker's actions?

Vocabulary   clutch (kluhch) *v.:* hold something tightly.

Applying Your Skills

Reading Standard 3.4 Define how tone or meaning is conveyed in poetry through word choice, figurative language, sentence structure, line length, punctuation, rhythm, repetition, and rhyme.

Ode to Mi Gato / In a Neighborhood in Los Angeles / Hard on the Gas

Literary Response and Analysis

Reading Skills Focus

Quick Check

1. What does the speaker's grandmother teach him in "In a Neighborhood in Los Angeles"?

2. Which word in "Hard on the Gas" best describes the grandfather's driving?

Read with a Purpose

3. What do you learn about each poem's speaker from the way he or she describes the subject of the poem?

Reading Skills: Re-reading

4. Review the notes you took while reading the poems. Now, make notes about what you learned after re-reading the poems.

Ode to Mi Gato	In a Neighborhood in Los Angeles	Hard on the Gas
Line 13: The speaker might be a child, since he talks about Mom.	Fish canneries? A place where fish are processed and canned	"bar above your right shoulder?" bar to grasp for safety

✔ Vocabulary Check

Match each of the numbered Vocabulary words on the left with its definition on the right:

5. **dribble**   a. hold tightly
6. **dangled**   b. not taken care of
7. **abandoned**   c. irregular drops
8. **clutch**   d. swung

Literary Skills Focus

Literary Analysis

9. **Literary Perspectives** Soto uses Spanish words in his poem. What do you think of this technique? What effect does the use of Spanish words have on the poem?

Literary Skills: Figurative Language

10. **Analyze** How do Soto's **similes** and the **metaphor** describing the family cat convey his poem's **tone** and meaning?

11. **Analyze** What does the **personification** in Alarcón's poem help you understand about the grandmother's qualities and the poem's meaning?

12. **Analyze** Explain the **extended metaphor** in Wong's poem. What point does it relate about the grandfather's life?

Literary Skills Review: Repetition

13. **Analyze** How does the repetition of the word *love* in Soto's poem help to express the poem's **tone** and meaning?

Writing Skills Focus

Think as a Reader/Writer

Use It in Your Writing Write a poem using figurative language to convey a speaker's feelings.

 What Do You Think Now

What important things do poets celebrate by describing everyday events?

Preparing to Read

Reading Standard 1.1 **Read aloud** narrative and expository **text fluently and accurately and with appropriate pacing, intonation, and expression.** **3.4** **Define how tone or meaning is conveyed in poetry through word choice, figurative language, sentence structure, line length, punctuation,** rhythm, repetition, and rhyme.

Poem / Motto

Literary Skills Focus

Structure Poets, of course, rely on words to express their ideas, but line length, sentence structure, and punctuation all play a role in helping them communicate their thoughts and feelings. Note, for example, how the punctuation and italics suggest different meanings and **tones**—attitudes or feelings—in these two sentences: "I *won!*" (suggests joy); "*I won?*" (suggests surprise or doubt). As you read these two poems by Langston Hughes, note how the structure of his ideas and his use of punctuation help convey the poems' meanings and create two very different tones.

Reading Skills Focus

Reading Fluency and Reading Rate **Reading fluency** is how easily and well you read. Being a fluent reader means that you are able to read with expression, pausing and stopping appropriately. It means that you know how to adjust your **reading rate**—how quickly or slowly you read something.

Into Action As you read each poem, fill in a chart like the one below for "Poem." Record notes to help you read the poem fluently.

"Poem"

Line(s)	Comments
1	Full sentence. Read slowly and stop.

Writing Skills Focus

Find It in Your Reading As you read, take notes in your *Reader/ Writer Notebook* about the choices Hughes made concerning line length, sentence structure, and punctuation. Why do you think he made these choices? How would different choices have affected the poems?

Vocabulary

motto (MAHT oh) *n.*: short statement that expresses the aims or beliefs of a person or institution. *The boy had a catchy motto to describe his view of life.*

Language Coach

Slang Slang is informal, nonstandard language, usually spoken by members of a group who share some common bond. Slang usually changes frequently; a term popular in one time period may seem dated or may even be forgotten in a few years. In "Motto," Langston Hughes uses slang words popular with jazz musicians of his time, including *cool, dig,* and *jive.* Which of these slang words survive today? What slang words used today do you think will still be around years from now?

Reader/Writer Notebook

Use your **RWN** to complete the activities for these selections.

Learn It Online
Listen for the tone in these poems through the audio versions online:

go.hrw.com   H6-515   **Go**

Get more on the author's life and work at:

go.hrw.com | H6-516 | Go

Langston Hughes

(1902–1967)

Langston Hughes was a lonely child until he found a home in the world of books. Hughes wrote his first poem in elementary school—but only *after* his classmates had elected him class poet:

> "[My class] had elected all the class officers, but there was no one in our class who looked like a poet, or had ever written a poem. . . . The day I was elected, I went home and wondered what I should write. Since we had eight teachers in our school, I thought there should be one verse for each teacher, with an especially good one for my favorite teacher. I felt the class should have eight, too. So my first poem was about the longest poem I ever wrote—sixteen verses, which were later cut down. In the first half of the poem, I said that our school had the finest teachers there ever were. And in the latter half, I said our class was the greatest class ever graduated. So at graduation, when I read the poem, naturally everybody applauded loudly. That was the way I began to write poetry."

Hughes grew up in the Midwest, but he eventually moved to New York City, where he became a leading figure in the cultural movement known as the Harlem Renaissance. His poems often echo the rhythms of blues and jazz.

Think About the Writer What surprises you about the way Hughes became a poet?

The Granger Collection, New York.

Read with a Purpose Read this poem to learn how the speaker feels about a friend who is no longer around.

Poem

by **Langston Hughes**

I loved my friend.
He went away from me.
There's nothing more to say.
The poem ends,
Soft as it began— **Ⓐ**
I loved my friend. **Ⓑ**

Ⓐ Literary Focus Punctuation Why might Hughes have chosen to use a dash here?

Ⓑ Read and Discuss Sometimes you learn things not from what is said, but from what is *not* said. How does the speaker convey his or her feelings more powerfully by *not* telling you everything?

Analyzing Visuals

Connecting to the Text
Explain whether this image conveys the same tone, or feeling, as Hughes's poem.

MOTTO

by **Langston Hughes**

I play it cool
And dig all jive.
That's the reason
I stay alive. **Ⓐ**

My motto,
As I live and learn,
is:
Dig And Be Dug
In Return. **Ⓑ**

Ⓐ **Literary Focus** Tone How would you describe the speaker's attitude here?

Ⓑ **Reading Focus** **Reading Fluency and Reading Rate** How would you recite the last two lines?

Vocabulary **motto** (MAHT oh) *n.:* short statement that expresses the aims or beliefs of a person or institution.

Analyzing Visuals

Connecting to the Text
How does this painting match the tone of the poem?

Cool Hand by Gil Mayers.

Applying Your Skills

Reading Standard 3.4 Define how tone or meaning is conveyed in poetry through word choice, figurative language, sentence structure, line length, punctuation, rhythm, repetition, and rhyme.

Poem / Motto

Literary Response and Analysis

Reading Skills Focus
Quick Check

1. In "Poem," what has happened?
2. In "Motto," how does the speaker describe the way he lives his life?

Read with a Purpose

3. In "Poem," how does the speaker feel about the friend? Explain the speaker's motto, or the idea he lives by, in "Motto."

Reading Focus: Reading Fluency and Reading Rate

4. Review each chart. Then, read each poem aloud to a partner, and record his or her feedback in your chart. Re-read the poem to improve your fluency and reading rate.

"Poem"

Line(s)	Comments
1	Full sentence. Read slowly and stop.

Feedback:

✓ Vocabulary Check

5. Write a **motto** for someone who excels at sports.

Literary Skills Focus
Literary Analysis

6. **Interpret** What do you think is the untold story behind "Poem"? What does "He went away from me" mean?
7. **Connect** In "Motto," what does "playing it cool" allow the speaker to do? What are the costs and benefits of such an attitude?

Literary Skills: Structure

8. **Analyze** Describe the **tone** of "Poem." How do the line length, sentence structure, and punctuation help convey this tone? How does the repetition of the first line affect the tone?
9. **Analyze** What is the **tone** of "Motto"? Look carefully at the second stanza. How do the line length, sentence structure, and punctuation convey this tone and emphasize the stanza's meaning?

Literary Skills Review: Character

10. **Analyze** Think about the "I" in "Motto." What qualities do you think this speaker has?

Writing Skills Focus
Think as a Reader/Writer

Use It in Your Writing Write a short poem about a friend or a motto. Use line length, sentence structure, and punctuation to help convey tone and meaning.

What Do You Think Now?

How do these short poems convey strong feelings with few words?

Preparing to Read

Reading Standard 3.4 Define how tone or meaning is conveyed in poetry through word choice, figurative language, sentence structure, line length, punctuation, rhythm, repetition, and rhyme.

Reader/Writer Notebook

Use your **RWN** to complete the activities for these selections.

Haiku

Literary Skills Focus

Word Choice **Haiku** (HY koo) is a Japanese poetry form with a strict structure. Each haiku consists of three lines and seventeen syllables: five syllables each in lines 1 and 3 and seven syllables in line 2. (The number of syllables may vary in English translations.) In haiku, poets must pack meaning into just a few phrases, so choosing just the right word is essential. As you'll see when you read these poems, haiku poets rely on language that appeals to the senses, or **imagery,** to convey tone and meaning.

Reading Skills Focus

Questioning Asking questions as you read haiku will help you analyze the way imagery creates meaning.

Into Action For each haiku, make a chart like the one below. The questions refer to the traditional content that haiku poets generally include in their poems. (See Build Background, p. 521.)

Title: "An old silent pond"

What specific things does the haiku describe?	pond; frog
What images are used?	Sight—pond; frog jumps Sound—silence; splash; silence
What are the contrasting images?	
What season is being described?	
What discovery about life is made?	

Writing Skills Focus

Find It in Your Reading In your *Reader/Writer Notebook*, record your responses to the images in these haiku. What feelings and associations do you connect with these images?

Vocabulary

balmy (BAH mee) *adj.*: warm and pleasant. *The balmy wind felt good as the man sat outdoors, thinking.*

recall (rih KAWL) *v.*: remember; bring to mind. *The speaker cannot recall the memory stirred up by the wind.*

Language Coach

Shades of Meaning **Synonyms** are words with the same or nearly the same meaning. For example, *stone* and *rock* are synonyms. Synonyms are not always interchangeable, though; there are usually shades of meaning that make them a bit different from each other. For example, the Vocabulary word *balmy* above refers to warm and pleasant weather, often involving a mild breeze. The words *calm* and *mild* have similar meanings with respect to weather. Of the three words, however, only *balmy* suggests a pleasant breeze. Be aware of such shades of meaning when you choose which word to use in your writing.

Learn It Online
Build vocabulary skills and increase learning comprehension at:

go.hrw.com | H6-520 | **Go**

Matsuo Bashō and Nozawa Bonchō
(1644–1694)   (16??–1714)

Matsuo Bashō is one of Japan's most famous poets. He took his pen name from a banana tree (*bashō* in Japanese) that he planted in his yard. Bashō was born into a wealthy family and grew up in a village in western Japan. He began writing verse when he was nine. By the time Bashō was thirty, he was traveling around Japan as a professional poetry teacher.

Nozawa Bonchō was one of Bashō's students. Many of the haiku written by Bashō and his students were inspired by the natural world. Bashō encouraged students like Bonchō to look for the "true nature of things." He insisted that haiku should be written in simple language and deal with everyday life.

Ōshima Ryōta
(1707–1787)

Ōshima Ryōta wrote haiku and created paintings inspired by Zen, a form of Buddhism that emphasizes meditation and oneness with nature.

Richard Wright
(1908–1960)

Modern poets in many countries have written haiku, finding beauty and discipline in the form. **Richard Wright,** an African American writer famous for his autobiography *Black Boy*, composed more than four thousand haiku in the two years before his death.

Think About the Writers
Why do you think these writers wanted to write haiku? What is special about the form?

Build Background

Haiku writing follows strict rules, not just in form but also in content. Here are some rules that haiku poets generally follow when crafting their poems:

1. A haiku is about a simple moment in daily life.
2. A haiku describes particular things, often two contrasting things.
3. A haiku records a moment of enlightenment—a sudden discovery of a truth about life.
4. A haiku is usually about a particular season of the year. Often a haiku contains a *kigo*, or "season word," like *frog* for summer or *willow* for spring.

Preview the Selections

"An old silent pond," "Winter rain," and "Bad-tempered, I got back" all examine the poets' relationship with nature.

Read with a Purpose   Read these haiku to see how skilled poets can create powerful images in just three lines.

Haiku

Night Rain at Oyama by Utagawa Toyokuni.

An old silent pond . . .
A frog jumps into the pond,
splash! Silence again.   **Ⓐ**
          —Matsuo Bashō

Winter rain:
A farmhouse piled with firewood,
A light in the window.   **Ⓑ**
              —Nozawa Bonchō

Bad-tempered, I got back:
Then, in the garden,
The willow tree.   **Ⓒ**
              —Ōshima Ryōta

Ⓐ **Read and Discuss** What do the images in the poem help you see and hear?

Ⓑ **Literary Focus** **Word Choice** Think about the poet's use of three separate images. How do these images combine to create one picture in your mind?

Ⓒ **Reading Focus** **Questioning** What questions do you have after reading this poem?

Analyzing Visuals   **Connecting to the Text**   Which haiku uses sensory language to capture the moment in time shown in this picture?

A balmy spring wind
Reminding me of something
I cannot recall **D**
      —Richard Wright

D **Literary Focus** **Word Choice**   The poet uses the words *reminding* and *recall.* What state of mind do these words suggest?

Vocabulary   **balmy** (BAH mee) *adj.:* warm and pleasant.
recall (rih KAWL) *v.:* remember; bring to mind.

Applying Your Skills

Haiku
Literary Response and Analysis

Reading Skills Focus
Quick Check

1. Which season do you think each haiku describes? (Remember that a frog is often used to suggest summer and a willow tree to suggest spring.)

Read with a Purpose

2. What images formed in your mind as you read these haiku?

Reading Skills: Questioning

3. Try to answer any unanswered questions in your charts. Then, compare each chart with a friend's, and discuss your ideas.

Title: "An old silent pond"

What specific things does the haiku describe?	pond; frog
What images are used?	Sight—pond; frog jumps Sound—silence; splash; silence
What are the contrasting images?	splash and silence
What season is being described?	Probably summer. "Frog" is a season word for summer.
What discovery about life is made?	

✔ Vocabulary Check

4. Write a sentence using each Vocabulary word: **balmy, recall.**

Literary Skills Focus
Literary Analysis

5. **Analyze** Review your questioning charts. Which haiku contain contrasting images? What are the effects of these contrasts?

Literary Skills: Word Choice

6. **Analyze** Describe the **tone** of each haiku. Which words in the haiku convey this tone?

7. **Analyze** Review your questioning chart for each haiku. How would you express the poem's **theme,** or message? How is this meaning conveyed through sensory language?

Literary Skills Review: Punctuation

8. **Analyze** What purposes does the punctuation serve in Bashō's haiku? What is the effect of the lack of punctuation in Wright's haiku?

Writing Skills Focus
Think as a Reader/Writer

Use It in Your Writing Write a three-line poem about nature. Use imagery to evoke feelings and associations and to convey tone and meaning.

What Do You Think Now What did these haiku teach you about what makes a good subject for poetry?

Vocabulary Development
Figurative Language

Figurative language is based on comparisons; it is not meant to be understood literally. These are three of the most common types of figurative language: **similes,** or comparisons between two unlike things using a word such as *like*; **metaphors,** or direct comparisons between unlike things; and **personification,** the giving of human traits to nonhuman things.

Your Turn

For each quotation, identify the two things being compared, explain how they're alike, and identify the kinds of figurative language being used: simile, metaphor, or personification.

1. "O my Love is like a red, red rose . . ." —Robert Burns
2. "I wandered lonely as a cloud / That floats on high o'er vales and hills . . ." —William Wordsworth
3. "The Lightning is a yellow Fork / From Tables in the sky . . ." —Emily Dickinson
4. "I hear America singing, the varied carols I hear . . ." —Walt Whitman

Academic Vocabulary

Write About . . .
Which poem in this section did you most appreciate? Was there a particular literary device or visual image that made the poem stand out for you? Write down your thoughts.

CHOICES

As you respond to the Choices, use these **Academic Vocabulary** words as appropriate: appreciate, detect, device, visual.

REVIEW
Create a Poetry Presentation

TechFocus Choose one poem in this section, and define how tone and meaning are conveyed through its literary devices. Then, choose a piece of music that you think suits the poem's tone and meaning. Record yourself reading the poem to the music. Be sure to read the poem expressively, paying attention to punctuation as well as rhythm and other sound devices. Play your recording for your classmates.

CONNECT
Write About Poetry

Timed LWriting Write a paragraph or two in response to this statement: "Good poetry can be about anything, from old socks to an ordinary person. Poetry can make even the most common things seem beautiful and important." Cite examples from the poems you have read.

EXTEND
Organize a Poetry Collection

Group Work Start a class poetry collection. Ask each person to bring to class at least one poem and to write a brief introduction explaining why he or she appreciates it. Decide how to organize the collection into a booklet. Make a special section for original poems written by students.

Learn It Online
There's more to these poems than meets the eye. Expand your view at:

go.hrw.com   H6-525   Go

Comparing Tone

Baile en 1958 by Carmen Lomas Garza.
Alkyds and oils, 24 x 32 inches.

CONTENTS

What Do **You Think**

How can poetry express the power of love?

QuickWrite

Imagine a photo taken of you with an important person in your life. What would the photo show? What would it tell about your relationship? Write down your thoughts.

Preparing to Read

Reading Standard 3.4 Define how tone or meaning is conveyed in poetry through word choice, figurative language, sentence structure, line length, punctuation, rhythm, **repetition,** and rhyme.

Yes, It Was My Grandmother / In the Blood / That Day / About "That Day"

Literary Skills Focus

Tone The poems you are about to read all focus on family, but each poem has a distinct tone. **Tone** refers to the speaker's attitude—the way the speaker feels about the subject of the poem. When you talk to people face to face, you can usually tell how they feel from their expressions and voices. When you read a poem, however, you have to depend on words and the way in which the poet uses language to learn how the speaker feels. As you read these poems, think about how the poets convey tone through **word choice,** especially **imagery,** and the <u>devices</u> of **figurative language** and **repetition.**

Reading Skills Focus

Questioning Asking questions and making observations as you read will help you focus your attention on key details that a poet uses to convey tone and meaning. You'll probably discover that by the time you finish reading a poem, you'll be able to answer many of your questions. Re-reading will strengthen your understanding of the poem and help you answer the rest of your questions.

Into Action As you read each poem, write down your observations and questions in a chart like the one below.

"Yes, It Was My Grandmother"

Observations	Questions
Grandmother is respected for training horses.	How did Grandmother free the speaker from cooking?

Writing Skills Focus

Find It in Your Reading As you read each poem, record the words and phrases that seem most important. How do these words and phrases provide clues to the poem's meaning or tone?

Vocabulary

Yes, It Was My Grandmother

tangles (TANG guhlz) *v.:* becomes twisted into knots. *Her hair tangles in the wind and is difficult to comb.*

That Day

gesture (JEHS chuhr) *n.:* act performed to show feelings. *The poet thought his father's playing ball with him was a beautiful gesture.*

previously (PREE vee uhs lee) *adv.:* before now. *After his father played ball with him, the son realized that he had previously not appreciated his father's love.*

Language Coach

Antonyms Words that are opposite in meaning are called **antonyms.** Can you think of a word that means the opposite of one of the Vocabulary words above?

Reader/Writer Notebook

Use your **RWN** to complete the activities for these selections.

Learn It Online
Focus on words with Word Watch:

| go.hrw.com | H6-527 | **Go** |

Luci Tapahonso
(1953–)

Luci Tapahonso, a member of the Navajo nation, was born and raised in Shiprock, New Mexico. Ever since she was young, Tapahonso and her family have shared stories and songs. This storytelling tradition has been a rich source of material for her.

Pat Mora (1942–)

Pat Mora is a Mexican American who grew up in Texas. Much of her poetry is about the ways Hispanic culture has blended into American society. In addition to poetry, she has written children's books based on her own experiences.

David Kherdian
(1931–)

The award-winning author David Kherdian was born in Racine, Wisconsin, to parents from Armenia. Kherdian has written more than sixty books, including novels, memoirs, biographies, and poetry collections.

Think About the Writers

What might inspire writers such as these to write poety?

Build Background

The hard-riding, horse-training grandmother in Luci Tapahonso's poem is not an oddity in Navajo culture. Navajo women have always been respected as leaders and have traditionally been the ones who have passed down cultural identity as well as a family's possessions—even land and livestock.

Pat Mora writes because she believes Hispanics need to take their rightful place in American literature. "In the Blood" appears in both English and Spanish. If you know Spanish, compare the two poems as you read. If you don't, look for words in the Spanish version that remind you of English words.

In "That Day," David Kherdian remembers a time when his Armenian-born father attempted to participate in one of his son's American activities—and how that gesture taught Kherdian about the power of love.

Preview the Selections

In "Yes, It Was My Grandmother" the speaker talks about her grandmother, a horse trainer.

In "In the Blood" the speaker describes a family relationship.

In "That Day," David Kherdian presents a memorable childhood experience.

In "About 'That Day,'" David Kheridan recalls the feelings that inspired his poem.

Yes, It Was My Grandmother

by **Luci Tapahonso**

Yes, it was my grandmother
who trained wild horses for pleasure
    and pay.
People knew of her, saying:
    She knows how to handle them.
5   Horses obey that woman.

She worked,
skirts flying, hair tied securely in the
    wind and dust.
She rode those animals hard and was
    thrown,
time and time again.
10 She worked until they were meek
and wanting to please.
    She came home at dusk,
    tired and dusty,
    smelling of sweat and horses.

15 She couldn't cook,
my father said smiling,
your grandmother hated to cook. **A**

Oh, Grandmother,
who freed me from cooking. **B**
20 Grandmother, you must have made
    sure
I met a man who would not share the
    kitchen. **C**

I am small like you and
do not protect my careless hair
from wind or rain—it tangles often,
25 Grandma, and it is wild and untrained.

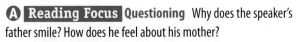

Analyzing Visuals

Connecting to the Text
What qualities does the woman shown in this photograph share with the grandmother described in the poem?

A **Reading Focus** **Questioning** Why does the speaker's father smile? How does he feel about his mother?

B **Literary Focus** **Tone** What word would you use to describe the tone of lines 18–19?

C **Read and Discuss** What is the speaker saying here?

Vocabulary **tangles** (TANG guhlz) *v.*: becomes twisted into knots.

Read with a Purpose

Read this poem to learn about the relationship between a child and her grandfather.

Preparing to Read for this selection is on page 527.

In the Blood

by **Pat Mora**

The brown-eyed child
and the white-haired grandfather
dance in the silent afternoon.
They snap their fingers
to a rhythm only those
who love can hear.   **B**

En la Sangre

La niña con ojos cafés
y el abuelito con pelo blanco
bailan en la tarde silenciosa.
Castañetean los dedos
a un ritmo oído solamente
por los que aman.

Baile en 1958 (detail) by Carmen Lomas Garza.
Alkyds and oils, 24 x 32 inches.

A **Reading Focus** **Questioning** How does the poem's title relate to the rest of the poem?

B **Reading Focus** **Questioning** What do the last three lines mean?

Applying Your Skills

Reading Standard 3.4 Define how tone or meaning is conveyed in poetry through word choice, figurative language, sentence structure, line length, punctuation, rhythm, repetition, and rhyme.

Yes, It Was My Grandmother / In the Blood

Literary Response and Analysis

Reading Skills Focus

Quick Check

1. In "Yes, It Was My Grandmother," how does the grandmother approach her job of training horses?

2. What scene is described in "In the Blood"?

Read with a Purpose

3. In Tapahonso's poem, how has the granddaughter's life been affected by her grandmother?

4. What do you think the relationship between the child and the grandfather is like in Mora's poem?

Reading Skills: Questioning

5. Add a column, labeled "Answers," to your charts. Which questions can you answer now that you've read all of each of the poems? Re-read the poems, and then try to answer any remaining questions.

"Yes, It Was My Grandmother"

Observations	Questions	Answers
Grandmother is respected for training horses.	How did Grandmother free the speaker from cooking?	

✔ Vocabulary Check

6. Name three things that can be used to complete this sentence: _____ **tangles** easily.

Literary Skills Focus

Literary Analysis

7. **Infer** In Tapahonso's poem, why do you think the speaker's father points out that her grandmother couldn't cook? How might the grandmother have been different from many women of her time?

8. **Analyze** In Tapahonso's poem, what does the speaker's "wild and untrained" hair tell you about her?

9. **Evaluate** Why is "In the Blood" a good title for Mora's poem? What does this title mean?

Literary Skills: Tone

10. **Analyze** What words would you use to describe the speaker's **tone,** or feelings toward her grandmother, in Tapahonso's poem? Note that the speaker directly addresses her absent grandmother three times. How does this **repetition** help convey the poem's tone?

11. **Analyze** What **images,** or sensory impressions, do you find in Mora's poem? Describe the **tone** of Mora's poem. How do you think the speaker feels about family relationships?

Writing Skills Focus
Think as a Reader/Writer
Use It in Your Writing Write a poem about a family relationship. Choose your words carefully to convey a particular tone.

Read with a Purpose

Read to learn why the speaker is surprised when his father joins in a softball game.

Preparing to Read for this selection is on page 527.

THAT DAY

by **David Kherdian**

Just once
my father stopped on the way
into the house from work
and joined in the softball game
5   we were having in the street,
and attempted to play in *our*
game that *his* country had never
known. Ⓐ

Just once
10 and the day stands out forever
in my memory
as a father's living gesture
to his son,
that in playing even the fool
15 or clown, he would reveal
that the lines of their lives
were sewn from a tougher fabric
than the son had previously known. Ⓑ

Ⓐ **Read and Discuss** What event is being described?

Ⓑ **Reading Focus** **Questioning** What is the "tougher fabric" to which the speaker is referring?

Vocabulary **gesture** (JEHS chuhr) *n.*: act performed to show feelings.
previously (PREE vee uhs lee) *adv.*: before now.

Preparing to Read for this selection is on page 527.

About "THAT DAY"

by **David Kherdian**

David as a boy.

In many ways my father and I were strangers to each other. At home I was his Armenian son, but in the streets I was an American stranger. I'm putting this a little bluntly. I'm exaggerating. So far as I knew, children did not play games in the Old Country. Therefore I did not believe that he understood any of the games I was involved in. And then, one day, while walking home from work, along the street where we were playing a pick-up game of softball, he stopped and either pitched the ball, or picked up the bat and tried to give the ball a hit. He was *intentionally* participating, he was joining in, and by doing so he was sharing with me something that was of value in my life that I did not believe had any importance in his life. I was deeply touched by this, though why I was touched, or where I was touched, or even how I was touched, was beyond my understanding at the time. Which brings me to poetry and why I write: But that's another story, and has to do with why I wrote *all* of my poems, not just the one you are looking at today. Ⓐ

Ⓐ ⎡Read and Discuss⎤ David Kherdian did not completely understand his own reaction to his father's gesture. What does that suggest about the reason he writes?

Applying Your Skills

Reading Standard 3.4 Define how tone or meaning is conveyed in poetry through word choice, figurative language, sentence structure, line length, punctuation, rhythm, repetition, and rhyme.

That Day / About "That Day"

Literary Response and Analysis

Reading Skills Focus
Quick Check

1. What did the poet's father do to please his son in "That Day"?

2. According to Kherdian, why were he and his father strangers?

Read with a Purpose

3. In "That Day," why was the poet surprised that his father joined in the softball game?

Reading Skills: Questioning

4. Now that you've read both the poem and the essay, try answering your questions about the poem, and record your answers in a new column in your chart. (You may want to re-read both works.) Does the essay help you understand the poem better?

"That Day"

Observations	Questions	Answers
Father is from a different country.	Why does the father join in the game?	

✔ Vocabulary Check

5. Use each Vocabulary word in a sentence: **gesture, previously.**

Literary Skills Focus
Literary Analysis

6. **Analyze** The poet says, "The day stands out forever / in my memory." Why does this day stand out?

7. **Interpret** What is the father's "living gesture" in the poem? What kinds of living gestures might we encounter in life?

8. **Analyze** What feeling did the father show for his son? Use details from the poem to explain your answer.

Literary Skills: Tone

9. **Analyze** What words would you use to describe the **tone** of "That Day"? What is the speaker's attitude toward his father?

10. **Analyze** Find the **metaphor** at the end of the poem that compares the life of the family to fabric. Explain this metaphor in your own words. How does this metaphor help convey the poem's **tone**?

11. **Analyze** How does the **repetition** of the phrase "Just once" affect the poem's **tone**?

Writing Skills Focus
Think as a Reader/Writer

Use It in Your Writing Write your own poem titled "That Day" in which you repeat the phrase "Just once." Pay careful attention to your word choice: What tone do you want your words to convey?

Reading Standard 3.4 Define how tone or meaning is conveyed in poetry through word choice, **figurative language,** sentence structure, line length, punctuation, rhythm, **repetition,** and rhyme.

Yes, It Was My Grandmother / In the Blood / That Day / About "That Day"

Writing Skills Focus
Write a Comparison-Contrast Essay

Write an essay in which you compare and contrast the tone of the three poems you have just read. Compare and contrast as well the <u>devices</u> each poet uses to convey the poem's tone, such as imagery, figurative language, and repetition. You can organize your essay according to these guidelines:

1. Name the poems; identify each one's tone.
2. Discuss the first poem by defining its tone and explaining how the poet conveys it. Use details from the poem in your discussion.
3. Do the same for the second and third poems.
4. In a concluding paragraph, summarize the similarities and differences in the tones of the three poems and in the <u>devices</u> used to express those tones.

Use the workshop on writing a comparison-contrast essay, pages 450–458, for help with this assignment.

What Do
You
Think
Now

What do these poems tell you about the relationships that are important in our lives?

CHOICES

As you respond to the Choices, use these **Academic Vocabulary** words as appropriate: <u>appreciate</u>, <u>detect</u>, <u>device</u>, <u>visual</u>.

REVIEW
Evaluate a Poem

Timed ⌚ **Writing** Imagine that a poetry contest is being held, and you have been asked to vote for one of the three poems you have just read. Which poet conveys the tone and meaning of his or her poem most effectively? Why? Write one or two paragraphs explaining your opinion. Use details from the poem in your evaluation.

CONNECT
Conduct an Interview

TechFocus Who is special to you? Who has influenced you over the years? Arrange to interview this person, and ask permission to record the interview. Before the interview, write at least three questions you want to ask. Make a recording of the interview, and give a copy to this important person as a thank-you gift.

EXTEND
Create a Collage

Group Work With a group of classmates, make a collage about the people and events in one of the poems you have just read. A collage can be made up of pictures, objects, and words. It should have <u>visual</u> appeal, but it can also appeal to our sense of touch. What makes a collage interesting is how all the different items are put together. How does your collage compare with your classmates' collages about the same poem?

Writing Workshop

Descriptive Essay

Write with a Purpose

Choose a subject that you would enjoy observing and describing: a place, a person, an object, an animal, or an event. Write a descriptive essay about this subject for an **audience** of students your age. Your **purpose** is to bring the subject to life through detailed description.

A Good Descriptive Essay

- clearly identifies the subject being described
- uses sensory details and figures of speech to help the reader hear, see, smell, taste, or feel the subject
- organizes details in a clear way
- reveals the writer's thoughts and feelings about the subject
- states why the subject is important to the writer

See page 544 for complete rubric.

Reader/Writer Notebook

Use your **RWN** to complete the activities for this workshop.

Think as a Reader/Writer

In this chapter you've seen how poets bring images to life. In addition, you've learned how figures of speech, such as similes and metaphors, can be used to create vivid and memorable descriptions. These same techniques are used in descriptive writing. In a descriptive essay, you use words to paint a precise picture of an object, place, animal, person, or event. You choose nouns, verbs, and adjectives that will help your readers to see, hear, smell, taste, and feel the qualities of the subject you're describing. As part of your descriptive essay, you may also choose to include your thoughts, memories, and feelings about your subject, sharing your views and perspective with your readers.

Before you begin your own descriptive essay, read this excerpt from *Two in the Far North,* by Margaret E. Murie. This book is about life in the Alaskan backcountry during the early 1920s. The paragraph excerpted here describes the arctic plain after nightfall.

> The sky is midnight blue and fully spangled with stars, and the moon is rising brighter and brighter behind the pointed trees. In the north a flicker of green and yellow; then an unfurled bolt of rainbow ribbon shivering and shimmering across the stars—the Aurora. The dogs begin to speed up; we must be nearing a cabin; yes, there it is, a little black blotch on the creek bank. The air is cold and tingling, fingers are numb. A great dark form flops slowly across the trail—a great horned owl, the speaking spirit of the wilderness.

← The writer creates a vivid image by describing specific colors and objects in the night sky.

← **Sensory details** that appeal to sight and touch draw the reader into the scene.

Think About the Professional Model

With a partner, discuss the following questions about the model:

1. Which sentence engages you most strongly? Why does that sentence affect you more powerfully than the others?
2. How does the writer seem to feel about the subject?
3. No sounds or smells are included in this description. How might the writer have described the sounds and smells of this scene?

Writing Standard 1.3 Use a variety of effective and coherent organizational patterns, including comparison and contrast; organization by categories; and **arrangement by spatial order, order of importance, or climactic** order. **2.2** Write expository compositions (e.g., **description**, explanation, comparison and contrast, problem and solution): **a. State the thesis or purpose. b.** Explain the situation. **c. Follow an organizational pattern appropriate to the** type of composition. **d.** Offer persuasive evidence to validate arguments and conclusions as needed.

Prewriting

Choose a Subject

A good subject for a descriptive essay must meet these criteria:

- You can observe it directly or picture it clearly in your mind.
- You can describe it with a variety of sensory details.
- You can fully decribe it in a short essay; its "scope" is manageable.
- You have a strong reaction to it because it is important or meaningful to you.
- It will actively engage your reader.

As you think of an idea for a subject, try freewriting about it for a few minutes. Then, using what you've written, try to fill in all the bubbles of an idea web like the one below. List the sensory details that apply to each bubble heading. The Idea Starters in the margin might help you think of some subject ideas.

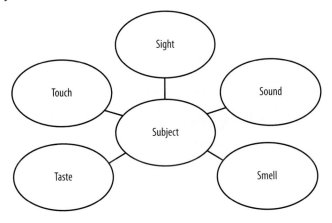

Gather Details

Gather details about your subject by observing it directly or by using your memory. Try to include both **sensory details** and **factual details** (details that can be proved true). Ask yourself:

- What does the subject look like? (What color, size, and shape is it?)
- What does the subject sound like? (What sounds can you hear?)
- What does the subject smell like? (Is there a particular scent?)
- What does the subject taste like? (Is it sweet, sour, salty?)
- What does the subject feel like? (Is it silky, rough, gritty, moist?)
- How do I feel about the subject? Why is it meaningful to me?

Idea Starters

- an interesting person
- an animal
- a fascinating, beautiful, or weird place
- a strange or useful object
- a spectacular event
- something you see every day that has unexpected and interesting qualities

Writing Tip

Sensory details tell what something looks, sounds, smells, tastes, or feels like. **Factual details** tell what something *is,* rather than what it looks, sounds, smells, tastes, or feels like.

Your Turn _____

Get Started Record your subject in your **RWN,** and write down why you have chosen the subject. Record details about your subject that appeal to each of the five senses. Also list factual details, such as measurements, numbers, and names.

 Learn It Online

Plan and organize your essay with an interactive graphic organizer. Try one at:

go.hrw.com | H6-537 |

Focus on Your Dominant Impression

As you think about the sensory details you'll use to describe your subject, you should also consider your **thoughts** and **feelings** about the subject. Together, these form the **dominant impression** about the subject that you'll leave with your readers.

Thinking about the impression you want to leave with readers will help you decide which details to keep and which to leave out. For example, if you want your reader to experience the peace and beauty of a mountain lake, you might decide to leave out details about a crowded lodge on its shores.

Organize Ideas

There are three common ways to organize descriptive essays. Choose the organizational pattern that is most effective for your topic.

- **Spatial Order:** Tell where details are located, moving from right to left, top to bottom, or near to far, for example.
- **Chronological Order:** Put details in the order that they occur.
- **Order of Importance:** Present details from most to least important or least to most important.

Once you decide on your organization, you can create a simple chart to list your details in correct order. This chart shows the combination of spatial and chronological order used in the student draft on pages 541–542.

> ### Order of Details for "The Smoky Mountains"
> 1. I follow the mountain path.
> 2. The path snakes upward in the distance.
> 3. The brook runs downhill, mirroring the trail's ascent.
> 4. I make my way to a rock by the bank.
> 5. I step back to the mossy ground.
> 6. I return to the path.

Think About Purpose and Audience

Your **purpose** is to inform and entertain your audience with a description of a place, person, object, animal, or event. As you choose your subject and consider the details you'll include, think about what will appeal to your **audience.** Select details to which your audience can easily relate, but point out unexpected details as well.

⬤ Writing Tip

Use transition words to keep your organization clear. Here are some transition words that match each organizational method.

- **Spatial:** *across from, near, far, by, around, inside, outside, between, down, next to, beside, up, under*
- **Chronological:** *first, next, last, after, now, before, eventually, finally, then, later*
- **Order of Importance:** *to begin with, mainly, then*

Your Turn _____

Plan Your Description To help you plan your descriptive essay, use your **RWN** to record your **dominant impression** and a list of **details** you'll use. Then, decide how you'll **organize** your details, and make a chart that shows the **order** in which you'll present them. Share your plan with a classmate, and revise your plan as needed. Keep in mind your **purpose** and **audience.**

Drafting

Use Precise Language

Precise language makes details come alive and engages the reader. Use specific nouns, verbs, adjectives, and adverbs rather than general words. The description "the lake was *cold* and *beautiful*" is vague and weak; it doesn't help the reader form a mental image. Compare that with a precise description: "The *icy* waters *shimmered* in the morning sun, as if the *sleepy* mountain lake was slowly *awakening* and still *shivering* from the *clear* and *frigid* night."

> **A Writer's Framework**
>
> **Introduction**
> - identifies the subject, time, and place and provides background
>
> **Body**
> - presents details in clear order
> - includes sensory and factual details as well as figures of speech
>
> **Conclusion**
> - includes a dominant impression
> - expresses thoughts and feelings
> - tells why the subject is important

Use Figurative Language

Figurative language—descriptive language that compares one thing to another—adds color to your writing. In the description above, for example, a mountain lake is described as having human characteristics (*sleepy*, *awakening*, *shivering*). There are three types of figurative language:

- **Similes** compare two unlike things using *like* or *as.*
  My *cat is like a race car,* slender and built for speed.
- **Metaphors** compare two unlike things by saying one *is* the other.
  My cat's *claws are sharpened daggers*.
- **Personification** uses human characteristics to describe something nonhuman.
  My *cat scowls* at me when I accidentally step on his tail.

Grammar Link Using Present Participles

An effective way to draw the reader into your description is to use present participles to add movement and action to your descriptions. Present participles are made from verbs but are used as adjectives. Murie uses participles as a part of her description of Alaska.

> "... rainbow ribbon, **shivering** and **shimmering** across the stars ..."

When used at the end of a sentence, the participial phrase is separated from the main clause by a comma.

> "... a great horned owl, the **speaking** spirit of the wilderness."

When used as a simple adjective, the participle is not separated by a comma.

⬤ Writing Tip
Vivid Verbs

Vivid verbs increase the action, movement, and interest in your description. Instead of weak, over-used verbs like *appear, take, move, give, hold, seem, look, has, had, was, going,* and *went,* try to use precise, action-oriented verbs that paint a picture. For example, use *grabbed* instead of *took*; *swayed* instead of *moved*; *shuffled away* instead of *went away*.

Your Turn _____

Write Your Draft Following your plan, write a draft of your essay. Remember to think about the following:

- What precise words can you use?
- What kind of figurative language can you use?

Peer Review

Working with a peer, review your draft. Answer each question in this chart to decide where and how your drafts can be improved. As you discuss your essays, be sure to take notes about each other's suggestions.

Evaluating and Revising

Read the questions in the left column of the chart, and then use the tips in the middle column to help you make revisions to your essay. The right column suggests techniques you can use to revise your draft.

Descriptive Essay: Guidelines for Content and Organization

Evaluation Question	Tip	Revision Technique
1. Does your introduction catch the reader's attention? Does it identify the subject?	**Bracket** interesting or surprising statements. **Circle** the subject of the essay.	**Add** an attention-getting statement or a quotation. **Add** a sentence that identifies the subject.
2. Does your description include a variety of precise and vivid details and figures of speech?	**Highlight** sensory details and imaginative comparisons. **Put an S** above sensory details. **Put an F** above sentences that employ figures of speech.	**Add** sensory details and figures of speech. **Delete** irrelevant details.
3. Are the details arranged in a clear effective, and coherent order?	In the margin, **write** the method of organization used—spatial, chronological, or order of importance.	**Rearrange** details if necessary. **Add** transitions for greater coherence.
4. Does your description include your thoughts and feelings?	**Put a check mark** next to any statement of your thoughts or feelings.	**Add** specific details about your thoughts and feelings.
5. Does your conclusion state why the subject is important to you? Does it convey a clear impression of the subject?	**Underline** the statement that tells why the experience is important. **Put parentheses** around statements that hint at the main impression.	**Add** a statement explaining why the experience is important. **Add** a statement that conveys the main impression of the subject.

Read this student's draft and the comments about it as a model for revising your own descriptive essay.

The Smoky Mountains
by Melissa Jones, Murchison Middle School

The summer sun tickles my face as a calming breeze swirls my hair. The rolling foothills envelop me with their blue, smoky mist as I follow the dirt mountain path. In the distance, the path snakes up the mountain, mirroring the brook's journey downward.

I draw the warm air into my lungs and admire the natural beauty around me. I stare into a sky so blue that the clouds floating in it appear to be puffs of cotton. I carefully make my way over to a large rock by the bank of the brook. The running water made a gurgling, babbling noise that calms me. All around me, majestic pines shaded me from the sun, except for random sunbeams filtering like spider webs through the lush greenery.

← Melissa uses **spatial organization** to describe her walk up a mountain path.

← Notice Melissa's use of **vivid action verbs.**

← **Sensory details** describe how the scene feels, looks, and sounds.

MINI-LESSON ▶ How to Include Thoughts and Feelings

In addition to including factual details, Melissa could share her thoughts and feelings to help draw readers into the setting. This will also give the readers a dominant impression of the place she is describing and its effect on her.

Melissa's Draft of the First Paragraph

The summer sun tickles my face, as a calming breeze swirls my hair. The rolling foothills envelop me with their blue, smoky mist as I follow the dirt mountain path. In the distance, the path snakes up the mountain, mirroring the brook's journey downward.

Melissa's Revision of the First Paragraph

Breathing deeply, I smile with anticipation. Nothing makes me feel quite as free and complete as spending time in the mountains.

The summer sun tickles my face, as a calming breeze swirls my hair. The rolling foothills envelop me with their blue, smoky mist as I follow the dirt mountain path. In the distance, the path snakes up the mountain, mirroring the brook's journey downward.

Your Turn _____

Include Your Thoughts and Feelings Read your draft and ask yourself the following:

- Are my thoughts and feelings coming through?
- What dominant impression about the subject am I leaving with the reader?

Student Draft *continues*

Melissa provides specific details that appeal to the senses of **hearing, sight,** and **touch.**

> As birds chirp in the distance, I absorb the beauty of the brook. There's a fog that's hovering over the water. It hugs the surface like a winter blanket. As the water dips over a tiny waterfall, it swirls in foamy rapids at the base. The sun seems to cast a spell on the water, making it sparkle in the light. I dip my fingers into the bone-chilling, crystal-clear water. Its chill runs up my arm and down my spine. The breeze whirls through the trees and makes me shiver. The beauty and mystery of the mountains make me feel so alive.

A combination of **spatial** and **chronological organization** guides the reader along the trail, and Melissa ends by stating how the experience makes her feel.

> I step back onto the mossy ground and return to the sunny dirt path. I faintly smell jasmine as I make my way through the trees up the mountain. Today is the perfect day for hiking in the Smokies.

MINI-LESSON ▸ How to Add Figurative Language

In her draft, Melissa uses a variety of precise and vivid sensory details. Her description is clear, but Melissa can make it even more appealing by adding figurative language. When she evaluates her essay, she looks for descriptions that can be revised to include a simile, a metaphor, or personification.

Melissa's Draft of Paragraph Three

> . . . The sun seems to cast a spell on the water, making it sparkle in the light. I dip my fingers into the bone-chilling, crystal-clear water. Its chill runs up my arm and down my spine. The breeze whirls through the trees and makes me shiver. The beauty and mystery of the mountains make me feel so alive.

In her revision, Melissa focuses on "cast a spell" as the basis for a simile.

Melissa's Revision of Paragraph Three

> *Like a wizard waving a golden wand,*   *transforming it into a pool*
> The sun seems to cast a spell on the water, ~~making it sparkle in the light~~
>
> *of sparkling gemstones.*
>
> I dip my fingers into the bone-chilling, crystal-clear water. Its chill runs
>
> up my arm and down my spine. The breeze whirls through the trees and
>
> makes me shiver. The beauty and mystery of the mountains make me
>   *It is magic.*
> feel so alive.

Your Turn _____

Add Figurative Language With a partner, look for descriptions in your essay that can be revised to include figurative language. Remember that figurative language is used to compare two unlike things. Share your revisions with your partner.

Proofreading and Publishing

Proofreading

Now that you have revised your descriptive essay, it is time to edit it and eliminate any errors that might confuse or distract your readers. Proofread your essay carefully, looking for misspellings, punctuation errors, or problems with sentence structure.

Proofreading Tip

There are three main areas to focus on when editing, so it makes sense to involve three people in proofreading. Ask two classmates to help you. Have each person focus on just one area: spelling, punctuation, or sentence structure.

Grammar Link Using Consistent Verb Tense

Be careful to use a consistent verb tense throughout your essay. You can use past tense to describe something as if it has already happened, or you can use present tense to make the reader feel more a part of the description. When she first proofread her description, Melissa noticed that she had used present tense in all but two sentences. She revised those sentences, changing them from past tense to present tense for consistency.

> The running water ~~made~~ *makes* a gurgling, babbling noise that calms me.
>
> All around me majestic pines ~~shaded~~ *shade* me from the sun, except for random sunbeams filtering like spider webs through the lush greenery.

Publishing

Now it is time to publish your descriptive essay for a wider audience. Here are some ways to share your essay:

- Add illustrations or photos, and publish your essay as a small booklet.
- Create a multimedia presentation to enhance the sensory details you have included in your essay.

Reflect on the Process In your **RWN**, write a short response to each of the following questions:

1. How did you organize your ideas during the brainstorming part of the assignment?
2. How did you think of figurative language to include in your essay?
3. What did you learn from writing a descriptive essay that you can use in other types of writing?

Your Turn _____

Proofread and Publish

Proofread to make sure you have used a consistent verb tense throughout your essay. Then, publish your description.

Scoring Rubric

You can use the rubric below to evaluate your descriptive essay.

	Descriptive Writing	Organization and Focus	Sentence Structure	Conventions
4	• *Thoroughly* engages the interest of the reader. • Focuses *consistently* on describing a single subject. • Offers *thoughtful, creative* descriptions. • Develops the descriptions *throughout,* using factual details as well as *precise* and *vivid* sensory details.	• *Clearly* addresses all parts of the writing task. • Demonstrates a *clear* understanding of purpose and audience. • Shows *effective* and *coherent* organization throughout, with smooth transitions. • Describes subject matter *completely* and *seamlessly* within a manageable scope.	• Includes sentence *variety* (e.g., simple, complex, compound-complex).	• Contains *few, if any,* errors in the conventions of the English language (grammar, punctuation, capitalization, spelling). These errors do **not** interfere with the reader's understanding of the writing.
3	• Engages the interest of the reader. • Focuses on describing a single subject, with *minor* digressions. • Offers *mostly thoughtful* descriptions. • Develops the descriptions *adequately,* with *some* factual and sensory details.	• Addresses *most* of the writing task. • Demonstrates a *general* understanding of purpose and audience. • Shows *effective* organization, with *minor* lapses. • Describes subject matter within a *manageable* scope.	• Includes some sentence *variety* (e.g., simple, complex, compound-complex).	• Contains *some errors* in the conventions of the English language (grammar, punctuation, capitalization, spelling). These errors do **not** interfere with the reader's understanding of the writing.
2	• *Attempts* to engage the interest of the reader. • Includes some *loosely related* material that distracts from the writer's descriptive focus. • Offers *routine, predictable* descriptions. • Develops the descriptions with *uneven* use of factual and sensory details.	• Addresses *some* of the writing task. • Demonstrates *little* understanding of purpose and audience. • Shows *some* organization, with *noticeable* flaws. • *Has difficulty* describing subject matter within a manageable scope.	• Includes *little* sentence variety.	• Contains *several errors* in the conventions of the English language (grammar, punctuation, capitalization, spelling). These errors **may** interfere with the reader's understanding of the writing.
1	• *Doesn't attempt* to engage the interest of the reader. • Shows *little awareness* of the topic and the descriptive purpose. • Offers *unclear and confusing* descriptions. • Uses factual and sensory details in a *minimal* way, if at all.	• Addresses *only one or no* part of the writing task. • Demonstrates *no* understanding of purpose and audience. • *Lacks* organization. • Subject matter *rambles* and does *not* fit within a manageable scope.	• Includes *no* sentence variety.	• Contains *serious errors* in the conventions of the English language (grammar, punctuation, capitalization, spelling). These errors interfere with the reader's understanding of the writing.

Descriptive Essay

When responding to an on-demand prompt for a descriptive essay, use the models you have read, what you've learned from writing your own descriptive essay, the rubric on page 544, and the steps below.

Writing Standard 2.2 Write expository compositions (e.g., description, explanation, comparison and contrast, problem and solution). a. State the thesis or purpose. b. Explain the situation. c. Follow an organizational pattern appropriate to the type of composition. d. Offer persuasive evidence to validate arguments and conclusions as needed.

Writing Prompt

Your pen pal in another country wants to know what a school cafeteria in the United States is like. Write a descriptive essay illustrating what a school cafeteria looks, sounds, smells, tastes, and feels like. Make your writing precise with sensory details and figures of speech, and choose the best method of organizing your description.

Study the Prompt

Read the prompt carefully. The prompt tells you that your **audience** is a pen pal in another country. Your **purpose** and **subject,** describing a school cafeteria, are also provided for you. The prompt reminds you how to write a lively description using **sensory details** and **figures of speech,** and it asks you to choose a pattern of **organization. Tip:** Spend about five minutes studying the prompt.

Plan Your Response

Plan your response by considering the following:

- What **background** information will my audience need to know about the subject?
- What are the main **sensory details** I should include to describe the subject?
- What **figures of speech** could I use to relate the subject to something my audience knows?
- How can I **organize** my essay: by chronological or spatial organization? by order of importance?
- What **dominant impression** do I want to create? What thoughts and feelings do I want to convey?
  Tip: Spend about ten minutes planning your response.

Respond to the Prompt

Using the notes you've just made, draft your essay. Follow these guidelines:

- In the introduction, identify the subject, identify the time and place, and give background information.
- In the body, present sensory details and figures of speech in a clear order.
- In the conclusion, sum up the main, or dominant, impression you want to leave your reader with, or explain why the subject is important.

   As you are writing, remember to use exact verbs. **Precise language** makes descriptions more vivid and lively. Write as neatly as you can. If your essay can't be read easily, it won't be scored. **Tip:** Spend about twenty minutes writing your draft.

Improve Your Response

Revising Go back over the key aspects of the essay. Did you provide vivid language for your reader? Did you organize your details in the most effective way to create a dominant impression?

Proofreading Proofread your essay to correct errors in grammar, spelling, punctuation, and capitalization. Make sure all your edits are neat, and erase any stray marks.

Checking Your Final Copy Before you turn in your essay, read it one more time to catch any errors you may have missed. You'll be glad you took the extra time for one final review. **Tip:** Save five or ten minutes to read and improve your paper.

Analyzing Propaganda on TV

View with a Purpose

In this workshop you will identify and analyze propaganda techniques on television. You will also learn how to

- distinguish between persuasive techniques and propaganda techniques
- identify false and misleading information on TV

🔘 Listening Tip

A persuasive message that includes propaganda techniques may be logical and sound—as long as it is based on accurate supporting evidence. The term *propaganda* describes a message that relies too heavily on propaganda techniques. Propaganda may also contain false or misleading information.

Reader/Writer Notebook

Use your **RWN** to record your ideas about this workshop.

Think as a Reader/Writer Persuasive messages are everywhere—newspaper editorials, magazine articles, Web pages, politicians' speeches. You also find them in television, radio, and movies. The persuasive messages you listen to and view usually contain *persuasive techniques* or *propaganda techniques*. The information presented here will help you identify persuasive techniques from propaganda ones. These skills will help you make well-informed decisions when watching TV.

Identify Persuasive Techniques

Consider the Message

To be persuasive, a message must make sense. Signs of persuasive techniques include

- a **clearly stated opinion**, or claim
- **logical reasons** for the opinion supported by relevant **evidence**
- an **appeal** to the interests and backgrounds of an **audience**

Watch for these signs as you view, but don't automatically accept a message that includes them. First, check for propaganda techniques.

Recognize Propaganda Techniques

Think—Do Not Just Feel

Like persuasive techniques, propaganda techniques are used to persuade you to believe, feel, or act a certain way. Their messages appeal more to your emotions than to your common sense or logic. The major difference between the two techniques is that propaganda does not hold up under a critical and thoughtful review. Below are some types of propaganda techniques (see page 714 for a more detailed explanation).

- **bandwagon appeal** a statement that encourages you to do something because everyone else is doing it
- **testimonial** a famous person's promotion of a product
- **stereotype** a fixed idea about all the members of a group; one that doesn't allow for individual differences
- **name-calling** the use of labels to stir up negative feelings about someone
- **snob appeal** persuasion that appeals to one's desire to be special

Find False and Misleading Information

A **propagandist,** one who uses propaganda techniques, counts on your being led by your emotions and not your intelligence. In fact, even if you wanted to look critically at a propaganda message, you would have very little substance to compare because propaganda is strongly biased. That means it favors one point of view and ignores (or lies about) information that supports another point of view. Watch for these signals that a message might contain misleading information:

- **Presenting Opinions as Facts Opinions** are beliefs or claims that cannot be tested and proved true (as a fact can). For example, a news report may quote an expert who says, "Space exploration is necessary for the future of human survival." It may sound sensible at first, but how could such a statement be proved true?

- **Missing Information** A persuasive message may downplay or leave out negative information. Consider a car commercial: Often a car commercial will downplay or avoid the auto's high cost, and instead feature only its design, comfort, speed, or gas mileage. To avoid believing false information, consider the source of the facts. Is the source possibly biased?

The following steps will help you identify and analyze examples of false and misleading information on television.

Analyzing False and Misleading Information

Step 1	**Focus on a specific program or advertisement. Briefly describe the message and how it makes you feel.**	You might pick an interview on a talk show, a segment of a newscast, a sports broadcast, or a commercial.
Step 2	**Identify the main message, or claim, of the program or ad.**	State it in one simple sentence.
Step 3	**Ask yourself, "Is the claim a fact, which can be proved true, or is it someone's opinion?"**	Remember that scientific-sounding words do not necessarily point to factual information.
Step 4	**Ask yourself, "What is missing from the message?"**	Is there any information you still don't know after watching the program/ad?
Step 5	**Using your answers from the previous questions, decide whether you think the TV program or ad is misleading or not.**	Explain your answer.

A Good Critical TV Viewer

- listens and observes carefully
- identifies the purpose, or goal, of the program
- determines if it is attempting to entertain, inform, or persuade
- analyzes the values and ideas that the program represents
- is able to understand the difference between opinions and facts
- makes one's own judgment

● Viewing Tip

Entertainment programs may also show bias. Think of programs that address controversial topics. Do these programs present equal, nonjudgmental information on both sides of a topic? Or do they show one side as correct or at least preferable to another?

Learn It Online

Learn more about persuasion in modern media through MediaScope online at:

 go.hrw.com H6-547   Go

Literary Skills Review

Poetry   **Directions:** Read the following poem. Then, read and respond to the questions that follow.

This poem describes a moment in the 1998 National Basketball Association Finals game between the Chicago Bulls and the Utah Jazz. Bulls superstar Michael Jordan scored the winning shot with just 5.2 seconds left in the game. This victory brought the team their sixth NBA title. The game, which took place on June 14, 1998, in Salt Lake City, Utah, was Jordan's last with the Chicago Bulls.

Forty-one Seconds on a Sunday in June, in Salt Lake City, Utah

for Michael Jordan by **Quincy Troupe**

rising up in time, michael jordan hangs like an icon,° suspended in space,
cocks his right arm, fires a jump shot for two, the title game on the line,
his eyes two radar screens screwed like nails into the mask of his face

bore in on the basket, gaze focused, a thing of beauty, no shadow, or trace,
5   no hint of fear, in this, his showplace, his ultimate place to shine,
rising up in time michael jordan hangs like an icon, suspended in space,

after he has moved from baseline to baseline, sideline to sideline, his coal-face
shining, wagging his tongue, he dribbles through chaos, snaking serpentine,°
his eyes two radar screens screwed like nails into the mask of his face,

10   he bolts a flash up the court, takes off, floats in for two more in this race
for glory, it is his time, what he was put on earth for, he can see the headline,
rising up in time, michael jordan hangs like an icon, suspended in space,

inside his imagination, he feels the moment he will embrace, knows his place
is written here, inside this quickening pace of nerves, he will define,
15   his eyes two radar screens screwed like nails into the mask of his face,

---

1. icon (Ȳ kahn): image; also, person or thing regarded with great respect and admiration.
8. serpentine (SUR puhn teen): in a snakelike way.

inside this moment he will rule on his own terms, quick as a cat he interfaces°
time, victory & glory, as he crosses over his dribble he is king of this shrine,°
rising up in time, michael jordan hangs like an icon, suspended in space,
his eyes two radar screens screwed like nails into the mask of his face

---

16. **interfaces** (IHN tuhr fays ihz): brings together; joins.
17. **shrine** (shryn): place held in high honor because of its association with an event, a person, or a holy figure.

---

1. Which groups of words from the poem help to create its tone?

   A beauty; floats; glory; king

   B time; space; trace; face

   C jump shot; basket; court; dribble

   D rising; knows; hangs; nails

2. The poet compares Jordan's eyes to radar screens because

   A Jordan worked with radar in the navy.

   B fellow players can read his next idea.

   C Jordan sees as well as a radar screen.

   D his head moves like a radar screen.

3. Which of the following phrases from the poem is *not* an example of figurative language?

   A "hangs like an icon"

   B "quick as a cat"

   C "eyes two radar screens"

   D "it is his time"

4. Which of the following statements describes the poem's structure?

   A The first and third lines of each stanza rhyme.

   B Each stanza begins with the same line.

   C Each line has the same number of words.

   D The first and second lines of each stanza rhyme.

5. How does the poet create his tone?

   A He sets the poem at Jordan's last game during the NBA finals.

   B He describes Jordan's playing with surprising figurative language.

   C He uses only lowercase letters and only commas for punctuation.

   D He keeps the length of each of the lines about the same.

Timed Writing

6. Write two or three sentences explaining how the poet uses figurative language to help convey the meaning of the poem. Use examples from the poem in your description.

Vocabulary Skills Review

Reading Standard 1.2 Identify and interpret figurative language and words with multiple meanings.

Synonyms

Directions: Identify the word or group of words that is closest in meaning to the italicized Vocabulary word in each item.

1. If a person is *keen* about doing something, he or she is

  A nervous.

  B bored.

  C eager.

  D proud.

2. If you *marvel* at something you have seen, you

  A show off.

  B admire it.

  C find it unsatisfactory.

  D act it out.

3. *Previously* means

  A before.

  B sadly.

  C later.

  D greatly.

4. When something *tangles*, it

  A falls.

  B stops.

  C dances.

  D twists.

5. To *behold* something is to

  A pick it up.

  B look at it.

  C buy it.

  D become it.

6. Something that has been *abandoned* has been

  A left.

  B turned.

  C angered.

  D fixed.

7. *Recall* means the same as

  A receive.

  B respect.

  C remember.

  D retell.

Academic Vocabulary

Directions: Use context clues to identify the synonyms of the italicized Academic Vocabulary words below.

8. If you examine the painting very closely, you can *detect* the artist's signature.

  A disapprove

  B discover

  C describe

  D delete

9. The *device* the detective used to catch the thief was simple—fingerprinting.

  A detail

  B trap

  C confession

  D technique

Writing Skills Review

Writing Standard 2.2 Write expository compositions (e.g., **description**, explanation, comparison and contrast, problem and solution). a. State the thesis or purpose. b. Explain the situation. c. Follow an organizational pattern appropriate to the type of composition. d. Offer persuasive evidence to validate arguments and conclusions as needed.

Descriptive Writing   **Directions:** Read the following paragraph from a descriptive essay. Then, answer the questions that follow.

(1) My favorite time to be on the beach is at the end of the day in late summer, after the crowds have packed up and gone home. (2) I love walking along the edge of the beach, looking for seashells. (3) I collect various sea-shells that I put in glass vases. (4) I use them to decorate my room. (5) The sky is streaked with rays of color from the setting sun—purple, orange, and gold. (6) Sunrise at the beach is also beautiful. (7) My toes sink into the soothing sand. (8) I enjoy wading in the water, which has absorbed the sun's rays all summer and is now warm. (9) The scent of spicy, grilled food from someone's backyard barbecue comes on a light breeze. (10) In the distance I hear the gentle music of wind chimes tinkling when blown by the wind.

1. Which answer choice correctly matches a sensory detail with the sentence in which it appears?

    A   sentence 5: smell

    B   sentence 7: touch

    C   sentence 9: sound

    D   sentence 10: sight

2. What is the *best* way to combine sentences 2, 3, and 4?

    A   I love walking along the edge of the beach, and I decorate my room and put the seashells I collect in glass vases.

    B   I love walking along the edge of the beach, collecting various seashells to put in glass vases to decorate my room.

    C   I love collecting various seashells along the edge of the beach that I use to deco-rate my room in glass vases.

    D   To collect various seashells to use in dec-orating my room, I love walking along the edge of the beach.

3. Which of the following is the *best* way to revise sentence 9?

    A   A light breeze brings the scent of spicy, grilled food from someone's backyard barbecue.

    B   Someone is cooking spicy, grilled food, and a light breeze brings the scent in a backyard barbecue.

    C   There is the scent of spicy, grilled food on a light breeze from someone's back-yard barbecue.

    D   On a light breeze from someone's back-yard barbecue is brought the scent of spicy, grilled food.

4. Which sentence is out of place and should be deleted?

    A   sentence 5

    B   sentence 6

    C   sentence 9

    D   sentence 10

Read On

For Independent Reading

Poetry

Rimshots: Basketball Pix, Rolls, and Rhythms

Charles R. Smith, Jr., combines his love for basketball, photography, and reading into *Rimshots,* a Parents' Choice Silver Award–winning title. His poems are like basketball: quick and energetic, with sounds of scuffling feet and swishing baskets. Also included in *Rimshots* are short prose selections written with the same passion for the game.

The Tree Is Older Than You Are: A Bilingual Gathering of Poems and Stories from Mexico

The author and poet Naomi Shihab Nye has collected poems and folk tales from all over Mexico, including some by well-known writers such as Octavio Paz and Rosario Castellanos. Most of the poems are written in Spanish, but some are in Mayan languages. In *The Tree Is Older Than You Are,* you'll find an English translation next to each selection as well as artwork by various Mexican artists.

Rainbows Are Made

The winner of two of the most acclaimed book awards in the United States—the Pulitzer Prize and the National Book Award—Carl Sandburg left his mark on poetry in the twentieth century. Chosen with young people in mind, the selections in *Rainbows Are Made* include seventy poems, both humorous and serious, dealing with people, wordplay, nature, and other aspects of life. The quality of the writing is matched by strong, dramatic wood engravings.

Langston Hughes: Young Black Poet

The famous poet Langston Hughes was one of the first African American writers to win worldwide favor. This biography focuses on Hughes's early life, when he developed a love of storytelling and an appreciation for hard work from his grandmother. Read Montrew Dunham's *Langston Hughes: Young Black Poet* to imagine yourself experiencing Hughes's childhood. Then, see what poetry might come from you.

Poetry

Whisked Away: Poems for More Than One Voice

This collection of new poems was written to be read aloud, preferably by more than one voice. When read aloud, the poems in *Whisked Away* become conversations, chants, demands, and spoken thoughts. Notes at the back of the book give practical guidance on volume, pace, actions, and sound effects to ensure that you get the most out of every poem—and that every poem gets the most out of you.

Poetry Matters: Writing a Poem from the Inside Out

Have you ever been asked to write a poem? Have you ever struggled to start or even to come up with ideas? Ralph Fletcher's *Poetry Matters* gives you a nuts-and-bolts approach to creating poetry. The text includes chapters on generating ideas, dealing with images, and creating music within your poem. You'll also find interviews with published poets, such as Janet S. Wong, discussing how they write. The interviews are followed by examples of poems that prove the techniques work.

Home: A Journey Through America

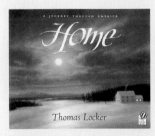

In this collection by Thomas Locker, famous American writers (including Willa Cather, Henry David Thoreau, and Eloise Greenfield) from different regions of the United States give voice to the region that each calls home. Lavish oil paintings that accompany each passage take you from the crashing waves of the Pacific Coast to the vast expanse of the Great Plains to the bluebonnet prairie of Texas. Come along on a spectacular literary journey through America.

The Yearling

Have you ever dreamed of finding a wild baby animal that you could raise? That dream comes true for Jody Baxter in *The Yearling*. Imagery, rural dialogue, and the rhythms of nature are interwoven into this adventure story. Marjorie Kinnan Rawlings was awarded the 1939 Pulitzer Prize for this novel, which is set near her home in the wilds of central Florida.

Learn It Online
Use *NovelWise* to go further in your exploration of novels at:

go.hrw.com   H6-553   **Go**

CHAPTER 6

Biography and Autobiography

INFORMATIONAL TEXT FOCUS

Connecting and Clarifying Main Ideas

California Standards

Here are the Grade 6 standards you will work toward mastering in Chapter 6.

Word Analysis, Fluency, and Systematic Vocabulary Development
1.4 Monitor expository text for unknown words or words with novel meanings by using word, sentence, and paragraph clues to determine meaning.

Reading Comprehension (Focus on Informational Materials)
2.3 Connect and clarify main ideas by identifying their relationships to other sources and related topics.

Literary Response and Analysis
3.5 Identify the speaker and recognize the difference between first- and third-person narration (e.g., autobiography compared with biography).

3.7 Explain the effects of common literary devices (e.g., symbolism, imagery, metaphor) in a variety of fictional and nonfictional texts.

Writing Applications (Genres and Their Characteristics)
2.3 Write research reports:
   a. Pose relevant questions with a scope narrow enough to be thoroughly covered.
   b. Support the main idea or ideas with facts, details, examples, and explanations from multiple authoritative sources (e.g., speakers, periodicals, online information searches).
   c. Include a bibliography.

"The biggest adventure you can ever take is to live the life of your dreams."

—**Oprah Winfrey**

What Do
You
Think

In what ways is life an adventure? How can you make your dreams in life come true?

 Learn It Online
Find graphic organizers online to help you take notes as you read:

| go.hrw.com | H6-555 | Go |

Walking to the Sky
by Jonathan Borofsky.

Literary Skills Focus

by **Linda Rief**

What Is the Difference Between First- and Third-Person Narration?

Who is speaking? When you're reading, that is one of the first questions you should ask. Nonfiction writers often tell their own life stories, but they also frequently describe the lives of others. It's important to identify the **speaker,** or narrator, and to recognize different types of narration in order to analyze how a writer shapes a story.

Autobiography and First-Person Point of View

The most personal kind of nonfiction writing is **autobiography**—a writer's account of his or her own life. The word *autobiography* is made up of three parts that explain its meaning. The prefix *auto–* means "self," the root word *–bio–* means "life," and the suffix *–graphy* means "writing."

First-Person Narration Since the narrator is telling his or her own story, an autobiography is written from the first-person point of view. That means the writer uses first-person pronouns—*I, me, we, us, our, my, mine.* You learn the writer's thoughts and feelings because the writer can directly tell you what is going on inside his or her own head and heart. Here is an example of the first-person point of view in an autobiography:

> Bailey was the greatest person in my world. And the fact that he was my brother, my only brother, and I had no sisters to share him with, was such good fortune that it made me want to live a Christian life just to show God that I was grateful.
>
> from "Brother" by Maya Angelou

Biography and Third-Person Point of View

A **biography** is a person's life story written by another person. Biographers spend a lot of time—sometimes many years—learning as much as they can about their subject. They read firsthand accounts, such as interviews, letters, and diaries, as well as secondhand accounts, such as newspaper and magazine articles. If a biographer is writing about a person who lived long ago, he or she reads historical accounts of the time in order to understand the world in which the subject lived.

Third-Person Narration Biographers do not write as "I" because they are not the subject of the life story. Instead, they write about their subject from the **third-person point of view,** using third-person pronouns such as *his, her, their, he, she, they,* and *them.* On the next page is an example from a biography of Harriet Tubman that you will read. Compare it with the excerpt you just read by Maya Angelou to recognize the difference between first- and third-person narration.

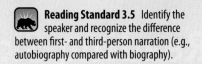

Reading Standard 3.5 Identify the speaker and recognize the difference between first- and third-person narration (e.g., autobiography compared with biography).

> When Harriet heard of the sale of her sisters, she knew that the time had finally come when she must leave the plantation.
>
> from "A Glory over Everything"
> by Ann Petry

What a writer chooses to leave out of a biography is as important as what he or she puts in it. No book is large enough to tell everything about a person's life. The biographer chooses events that reveal something important about the person. When you read a biography, think about the specific details that are included and what they tell you about the subject.

Shifting Points of View

In both autobiographies and biographies, writers may sometimes change the point of view from which they record events. Here, the writer of the autobiography *The Land I Lost* describes his own life, using the **first-person point of view:**

> I was born on the central highlands of Vietnam in a small hamlet on a riverbank that had a deep jungle on one side and a chain of high mountains on the other.
>
> from *The Land I Lost*
> by Huynh Quang Nhuong

In the same autobiography the author decides to tell a story he heard about a young couple, so he switches to the **third-person point of view:**

> Trung was happiest when Lan was helping his mother. They did not talk to each other but they could look at each other when his mother was busy with her work.
>
> from *The Land I Lost*
> by Huynh Quang Nhuong

Your Turn Analyze Narration

1. Explain the difference between an autobiography and a biography.

2. Choose an event from your life, and write about it using first-person narration.

3. Write about the same event using third-person narration.

4. How are your two accounts different? How are they the same?

Learn It Online
For more on this lesson, see *PowerNotes:*
go.hrw.com H6-557 **Go**

Literary Skills Focus **557**

Reading Skills Focus

by **Kylene Beers**

What Skills Help You Analyze Different Types of Narration?

Imagine that you're standing in a hallway of your school and you overhear some classmates talking about you. You might want to know *what* they're saying about you—the main idea of the conversation. You might wonder if what they're saying is true or just their opinion. You might also want to know *why* they're telling the story—their purpose. It's important to make similar determinations when you read autobiographies and biographies.

Main Idea

The topic and the main idea of a nonfiction text are not the same. The **topic** is what the text is all about: movies, for example. The **main idea** is the most important point the writer is making about that topic: *This year's top-grossing movies were all low-budget comedies.*

Finding the Main Idea In most texts the main idea is not stated directly. You have to infer it, or figure it out from clues. This chart shows you the key steps to follow when you want to find the main idea:

1. Identify the topic.

Tip: The topic can usually be stated in one or two words. Sometimes it's in the title.

2. Look for important details.

Tip: Keep the topic in mind. What are the most important details the writer gives you about the topic?

3. Write a statement that expresses the main idea.

Tip: Ask yourself, "What is the writer saying about the topic?" Try to write the answer in one sentence.

More Than One Main Idea There will often be more than one main idea in a nonfiction text. It takes practice to uncover all the main ideas. As you read, use a chart to organize your thinking about possible main ideas. Here is a chart you might develop for a nonfiction selection about a person's relationship with an animal:

Possible Main Ideas	
Main Idea 1 Humans and animals have a special bond.	**Main Idea 2** There are many things about animals that humans can't explain.
Main Idea 3 Animals may understand humans better than humans understand animals.	**Main Idea 4** Humans can learn from their animal friends.

Comparing Selections for Main Ideas When you read two or more selections about the same topic, you can compare the main ideas to see how they're connected and how they are different. Collecting main ideas for each selection in a chart like the one above can help you with your comparisons.

Facts and Opinions

Nonfiction is based on **facts**—information that can be proved true. However, even fact-filled nonfiction may contain a writer's **opinions,** or personal beliefs, feelings, and attitudes. When you read nonfiction, it is important to be able to tell facts from opinions. Compare these statements about Maya Angelou's brother, Bailey, from her autobiography *I Know Why the Caged Bird Sings.*

Term	Definition	Example
Fact	Information that can be proved true	*Bailey is the author's only brother.*
Opinion	A personal belief or attitude	*Bailey is the greatest brother in the world.*

As a reader, you need to watch for opinions stated as facts. Always ask yourself, "Can this statement be proved true?" Look for words that signal opinions, such as these: *believe, seem, may, think, probably, possibly.* Also look for strongly emotional language, like *greatest, best, finest,* and *worst.*

Supported and Unsupported Opinions In nonfiction writing some opinions are supported by facts, while others are not. When you identify opinions in a nonfiction text, ask yourself whether the facts in the text support them. Determining whether opinions are supported is especially important when you are deciding whether to agree or disagree with a writer's position on something. You want to identify examples of **bias**—personal ideas and values the writer holds that may lead to conclusions the text does not support. Always suspect bias when you see that only one side of an issue is being addressed.

Author's Purpose

There are many different reasons, or **purposes,** that an author might write a biography or an autobiography. The following are common examples of an **author's purpose:**

- to inform
- to persuade
- to express feelings
- to entertain

The author's purpose affects not only *what* he or she says but also *how* he or she says it. For example, to entertain the reader, an author might use first-person narration to tell stories of her childhood in the 1960s. To inform the reader, she might use third-person narration to tell about important political figures in the 1960s. Keep in mind that an author may have several purposes for writing, but one usually stands out as most important.

Your Turn   Apply Reading Skills

1. What would you expect an author's main purpose to be in writing an autobiography? a biography? Explain.

2. Write one fact and one opinion about a subject related to your life.

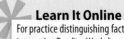

Now go to the Skills in Action: Reading Model

Learn It Online

For practice distinguishing fact from opinion, visit the interactive Reading Workshops at:

go.hrw.com	H6-559	Go

Read with a Purpose Read this true story to learn how a famous writer feels about the ugly jacket he wore in grade school.

THE JACKET

by **Gary Soto**

My clothes have failed me. I remember the green coat that I wore in fifth and sixth grades, when you either danced like a champ or pressed yourself against a greasy wall, bitter as a penny toward the happy couples.

When I needed a new jacket and my mother asked what kind I wanted, I described something like bikers wear: black leather and silver studs with enough belts to hold down a small town. We were in the kitchen, steam on the windows from her cooking. She listened so long while stirring dinner that I thought she understood for sure the kind I wanted. The next day when I got home from school, I discovered draped on my bedpost a jacket the color of day-old guacamole.[1] I threw my books on the bed and approached the jacket slowly, as if it were a stranger whose hand I had to shake. I touched the vinyl sleeve, the collar, and peeked at the mustard-colored lining.

From the kitchen Mother yelled that my jacket was in the closet. I closed the door to her voice and pulled at the rack of clothes in the closet, hoping the jacket on the bedpost wasn't for me but my mean brother. No luck. I gave up. From my bed, I stared at the jacket. I wanted to cry because it was so ugly and so big that I knew I'd have to wear it a long time. I was a small kid,

---

1. **guacamole** (gwah kuh MOH lay): a thick green spread made from avocados.

thin as a young tree, and it would be years before I'd have a new one. I stared at the jacket, like an enemy, thinking bad things before I took off my old jacket whose sleeves climbed halfway to my elbow.

I put the big jacket on. I zipped it up and down several times, and rolled the cuffs up so they didn't cover my hands. I put my hands in the pockets and flapped the jacket like a bird's wings. I stood in front of the mirror, full face, then profile, and then looked over my shoulder as if someone had called me. I sat on the bed, stood against the bed, and combed my hair to see what I would look like doing something natural. I looked ugly. I threw it on my brother's bed and looked at it for a long time before I slipped it on and went out to the backyard, smiling a "thank you" to my mom as I passed her in the kitchen. With my hands in my pockets I kicked a ball against the fence, and then climbed it to sit looking into the alley. I hurled orange peels at the mouth of an open garbage can, and when the peels were gone, I watched the white puffs of my breath thin to nothing.

I jumped down, hands in my pockets, and in the backyard on my knees I teased my dog, Brownie, by swooping my arms while making bird calls. He jumped at me and missed. He jumped again and again, until a tooth sunk deep, ripping an L-shaped tear on my left sleeve. I pushed Brownie away to study the tear as I would a cut on my arm. There was no blood, only a few loose pieces of fuzz. Darn dog, I thought, and pushed him away hard when he tried to bite again. I got up from my knees and went to my bedroom to sit with my jacket on my lap, with the lights out.

That was the first afternoon with my new jacket. The next day I wore it to fifth grade and got a *D* on a math quiz. During the morning recess, Frankie T., the playground terrorist, pushed me to the

Reading Focus

Main Idea The topic of this autobiography is the narrator's jacket. To find the main idea, look for important details about what the narrator once thought about the jacket—and about himself.

ground and told me to stay there until recess was over. My best friend, Steve Negrete, ate an apple while looking at me, and the girls turned away to whisper on the monkey bars. The teachers were no help: they looked my way and talked about how foolish I looked in my new jacket. I saw their heads bob with laughter, their hands half covering their mouths.

Even though it was cold, I took off the jacket during lunch and played kickball in a thin shirt, my arms feeling like Braille from goose bumps. But when I returned to class, I slipped the jacket on and shivered until I was warm. I sat on my hands, heating them up, while my teeth chattered like a cup of crooked dice. Finally warm, I slid out of the jacket but a few minutes later put it back on when the fire bell rang. We paraded out into the yard where we, the fifth-graders, walked past all the other grades to stand against the back fence. Everybody saw me. Although they didn't say out loud, "Man, that's ugly," I heard the buzz-buzz of gossip and even laughter that I knew was meant for me.

And so I went, in my guacamole jacket. So embarrassed, so hurt, I couldn't even do my homework. I received C's on quizzes, and forgot the state capitals and the rivers of South America, our friendly neighbor. Even the girls who had been friendly blew away like loose flowers to follow the boys in neat jackets.

I wore that thing for three years until the sleeves grew short and my forearms stuck out like the necks of turtles. All during that time no love came to me—no little dark girl in a Sunday dress she wore on Monday. At lunchtime I stayed with the ugly boys who leaned against the chain-link fence and looked around with propellers of grass spinning in our mouths. We saw girls walk by alone, saw couples, hand in hand, their heads like bookends pressing air together. We saw them and spun our propellers so fast our faces were blurs.

I blame that jacket for those bad years. I blame my mother for her bad taste and her cheap ways. It was a sad time for the heart. With a friend I spent my sixth-grade year in a tree in the alley, waiting for something good to happen to me in that jacket, which had become the ugly brother who tagged along wherever I went. And it was about that time that I began to grow. My

Reading Focus

Fact and Opinion Be aware that some information presented as fact may be opinion. The narrator says that the teachers were laughing at his jacket, but that is his interpretation. It is unlikely that they were actually doing so.

Reading Focus

Author's Purpose In this autobiography, Soto's main purpose is to express feelings he had as a child. As you continue reading, keep in mind other purposes he may have.

Reading Focus

Fact and Opinion "The Jacket" contains many opinions, beginning with what the narrator thinks about his new jacket. Here, he states his opinions about this time in his life and his mother's taste.

chest puffed up with muscle and, strangely, a few more ribs. Even my hands, those fleshy hammers, showed bravely through the cuffs, the fingers already hardening for the coming fights. But that L-shaped rip on the left sleeve got bigger; bits of stuffing coughed out from its wound after a hard day of play. I finally Scotch-taped it closed, but in rain or cold weather the tape peeled off like a scab and more stuffing fell out until that sleeve shriveled into a palsied arm.[2] That winter the elbows began to crack and whole chunks of green began to fall off. I showed the cracks to my mother, who always seemed to be at the stove

Analyzing Visuals Connecting to the Text Whose point of view in "The Jacket" might this image reflect? Explain.

with steamed-up glasses, and she said that there were children in Mexico who would love that jacket. I told her that this was America and yelled that Debbie, my sister, didn't have a jacket like mine. I ran outside, ready to cry, and climbed the tree by the alley to think bad thoughts and watch my breath puff white and disappear.

But whole pieces still casually flew off my jacket when I played hard, read quietly, or took vicious spelling tests at school. When it became so spotted that my brother began to call me "camouflage," I flung it over the fence into the alley. Later, however, I swiped the jacket off the ground and went inside to drape it across my lap and mope.

I was called to dinner: Steam silvered my mother's glasses as she said grace; my brother and sister, with their heads bowed,

Literary Focus

Autobiography Throughout "The Jacket," Soto shares the thoughts and emotions of his childhood. The use of first-person narration enables writers to express personal thoughts.

---

2. **palsied** (PAWL zeed) **arm:** Palsy is a condition that leaves muscles weak. A palsied arm would look limp and thinner than a healthy arm.

Reading Model

made ugly faces at their glasses of powdered milk. I gagged too, but eagerly ate big rips of buttered tortilla that held scooped up beans. Finished, I went outside with my jacket across my arm. It was a cold sky. The faces of clouds were piled up, hurting. I climbed the fence, jumping down with a grunt. I started up the alley and soon slipped into my jacket, that green ugly brother who breathed over my shoulder that day and ever since.

Reading Focus

Main Idea Pay special attention to the last paragraph for clues to the main idea. From this ending, you can infer that the main idea relates not only to the jacket but also to the narrator himself and how he remembers his childhood.

Read with a Purpose How did the jacket affect Soto in his youth? How might these years have been the same or different if he'd had a different jacket?

MEET THE WRITER

Gary Soto
(1952–   )

A Working Life

Gary Soto was born in Fresno, California. His father worked at a raisin factory and his mother at a potato-processing plant. Soto has written autobiographical works—like "The Jacket"—that describe his experiences growing up in a working-class Mexican American family, but he is perhaps best known as a fiction writer and poet. Whether writing poetry, fiction, or nonfiction, Soto continues to celebrate "commonplace, everyday things," the joys and sorrows of average people who take walks, play games, experience love, and muddle through life with its joys and sorrows. His writing focuses on "the small moments which add up to a large moment—life itself."

"In short, not all my work is autobiographical, but it could be."

Think About the Writer What might Soto mean in saying that all of his work "could be" autobiographical?

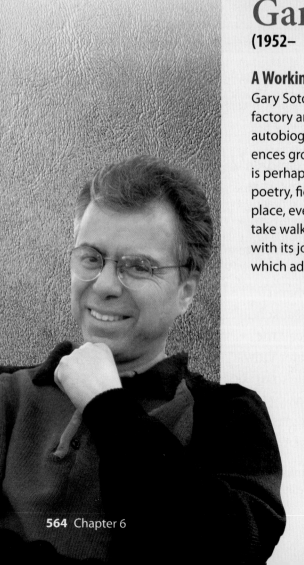

SKILLS IN ACTION
Wrap Up

Reading Standard 3.5 Identify the speaker and recognize the difference between first- and third-person narration (e.g., autobiography compared with biography).

Into Action: Distinguishing Between Fact and Opinion

Complete a chart like the one below to identify the main idea of "The Jacket."

Step 1 Identify the topic of "The Jacket"	Topic: The narrator's jacket
Step 2 Look for important details. List details and make inferences about the topic to help you identify the most important message.	
Step 3 Write a one-sentence statement that answers "What about the topic?" and expresses the main idea.	

Talk About . . .

1. With a partner, discuss the author's purpose for writing "The Jacket." How does the use of first-person narration help him achieve this purpose? Try to use each of the Academic Vocabulary words listed on the right at least once in your discussion.

Write About . . .

Answer the following questions about "The Jacket." For definitions of the underlined Academic Vocabulary words, see the column on the right.

2. How would the story be different if it were written from the <u>perspective</u> of the mother using third-person narration?

3. How is this autobiography <u>distinct</u> from a fictional story?

4. How does this autobiography <u>contribute</u> to your understanding of Gary Soto?

Writing Skills Focus
Think as a Reader/Writer

In Chapter 6, you'll read more autobiographies and biographies. You'll learn more about how writers use first- and third-person narration, and you'll write about and practice these methods yourself.

Academic Vocabulary for Chapter 6

Talking and Writing About Biography and Autobiography

Academic Vocabulary is the language you use to write and talk about literature. Use these words to discuss the biographies and autobiographies you read in this chapter. The words are underlined throughout the chapter.

contribute (kuhn TRIHB yoot) *v.*: give or add something, such as resources or ideas. *Writers contribute important ideas through their books.*

distinct (dihs TIHNGKT) *adj.*: distinguishable; clearly different or of a different type. *Autobiographies are distinct from biographies.*

perspective (puhr SPEHK tihv) *n.*: mental view or outlook; way of thinking. *Biographies and autobiographies can change your perspective on people.*

uniform (YOO nuh fawrm) *adj.*: having the same shape, size, quality, or other characteristics. *Biographies have certain uniform characteristics, such as the use of third-person narration.*

Your Turn

Copy the Academic Vocabulary words into your *Reader/Writer Notebook*. Write an easy-to-remember synonym next to each Academic Vocabulary word.

Brother

from *I Know Why the Caged Bird Sings*
by **Maya Angelou**

What Do You Think?

How can the people closest to you inspire you to live life to the fullest?

QuickWrite

Which family member, or other person close to you, do you admire, and why? How does this person bring out the best in you?

Fruit Vendor II (1996) by Hyacinth Manning.

Reader/Writer
Notebook
Use your **RWN** to complete the activities
for this selection.

**Reading Standard 3.5 Identify the
speaker and recognize** the difference
between **first-** and third-**person narration (e.g.,
autobiography** compared with biography).

Literary Skills Focus

First-Person Narration An **autobiography** is the true story of a
person's life written by that person. Autobiographies are written in the
first-person point of view. That means the writer speaks in the first
person, using pronouns such as *I, we, me, us, mine,* and *ours.* Reading an
autobiography lets you see the world through another person's eyes
and gain a different <u>perspective</u>.

Reading Skills Focus

Distinguishing Between Fact and Opinion A **fact** is information
that can be proved true with evidence: *My brother is older than I am* . An
opinion is a personal belief: *My brother is the bravest boy in the neighborhood.* In "Brother," Maya Angelou presents a portrait of her brother,
Bailey. Because she knew her brother personally, she is able to present
many facts about him. Someone else who knew Bailey could confirm
these facts. Angelou's account is also filled with her opinions. Others
who knew Bailey might not share her opinions of him.

Into Action As you read, identify facts and opinions in "Brother."
Record them in a chart like this one.

Fact	Opinion
Bailey was her only brother.	"Bailey was the greatest person in my world."
Bailey was small.	Bailey was "graceful" and "smooth."

Writing Skills Focus
Think as a Reader/Writer

Find It in Your Reading Angelou uses specific details about her
brother's actions to share her <u>perspective</u> of him. As you read, record in
your *Reader/Writer Notebook* examples of these details. What do these
details tell you about her view of her brother?

Vocabulary

outrageous (owt RAY juhs) *adj.:*
extreme; shocking. *Somehow, Bailey
always got away with his outrageous
actions.*

acquaintance (uh KWAYN tuhns) *n.:*
friend; someone known casually.
*Bailey described the way an acquain-
tance moved.*

precision (prih SIHZH uhn) *n.:* exactness; accuracy. *Bailey moved with
precision.*

apt (apt) *adj.:* skilled; capable. *Bailey
was apt at stealing pickles, a skill his
sister admired.*

sift (sihft) *v.:* strain or filter through
something. *Bailey and his sister used
a strainer to sift the flour.*

Language Coach

Word Families *Outrageous* is an
adjective formed from *outrage,* a
word that can be either a noun or
a verb. (The noun *outrage* refers to
extreme anger. The verb *outrage*
means "to offend, insult, or anger.")
Think of three other words that
end in *–ous.* How many of them
are adjectives? Use each word in a
sentence.

Learn It Online
Delve into vocabulary using Word Watch at:

| go.hrw.com | H6-567 | Go |

Learn It Online
Get more on the author's life at:
go.hrw.com H6-568 Go

Maya Angelou
(1928–   )

"All Things Are Possible"

The remarkable career of Maya Angelou (AN juh loo) has taken her far from the days when she was Bailey's lonely, awkward sister. Angelou has held many jobs in her long life: streetcar conductor, waitress, singer, dancer, actress, civil rights worker, professor, TV producer, and, above all, writer. In an interview, Angelou talked about how she has triumphed, both as a person and a writer, over life's obstacles. She said, "I believe all things are possible for a human being, and I don't think there's anything in the world I can't do. Of course, I can't be five feet four because I'm six feet tall. I can't be a man because I'm a woman. The physical gifts are given to me, just like having two arms is a gift. In my creative source, wherever that is, I don't see why I can't sculpt. Why shouldn't I? Human beings sculpt. I'm a human being." Her strength and determination have made her one of America's most admired writers.

> "All my work is meant to say, 'You may encounter many defeats, but you must not be defeated.'"

Think About the Writer Do you agree that "all things are possible"? How would you describe Angelou's view of life?

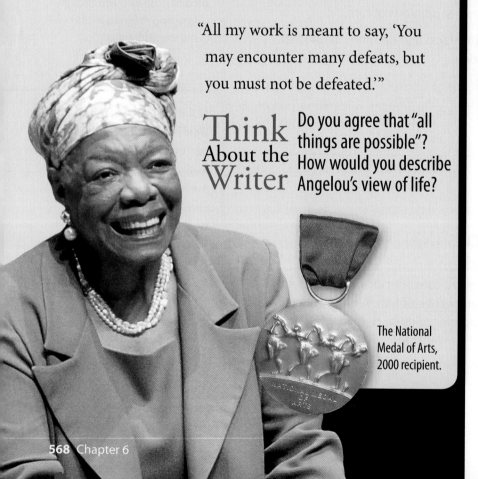

The National Medal of Arts, 2000 recipient.

Build Background

In the following selection, which takes place in the 1930s, Angelou's brother figures out a way to sneak some pickles out of the barrel in his family's store. Pickle barrels were a common sight in stores in both the North and South until recent times. The barrels, as tall as a young child, would sit in the aisle of the corner store or deli, and customers or the store owner would use slotted spoons or tongs to pick out the pickles to purchase. Biting into a big, juicy pickle fresh from the barrel was seen as a treat by most kids.

Preview the Selection

"Brother" is an excerpt from the autobiography of writer **Maya Angelou.** She describes herself and her only brother, **Bailey,** as children and tells why their relationship was so important to her.

Read with a Purpose Read to understand how Maya Angelou feels about her brother, and why.

Brother

from I Know Why the Caged Bird Sings by **Maya Angelou**

Bailey was the greatest person in my world. And the fact that he was my brother, my only brother, and I had no sisters to share him with, was such good fortune that it made me want to live a Christian life just to show God that I was grateful. Where I was big, elbowy, and grating,[1] he was small, graceful, and smooth. . . . He was lauded[2] for his velvet-black skin. His hair fell down in black curls, and my head was covered with black steel wool. And yet he loved me. **(A)**

When our elders said unkind things about my features (my family was handsome to a point of pain for me), Bailey would wink at me from across the room, and I knew that it was a matter of time before he would take revenge. He would allow the old ladies to finish wondering how on earth I came about, then he would ask, in a voice like cooling bacon grease, "Oh Mizeriz[3] Coleman, how is your son? I saw him the other day, and he looked sick enough to die." **(B)**

Aghast,[4] the ladies would ask, "Die? From what? He ain't sick."

And in a voice oilier than the one before, he'd answer with a straight face, "From the Uglies." **(C)**

I would hold my laugh, bite my tongue, grit my teeth, and very seriously erase even the touch of a smile from my face. Later, behind the house by the black-walnut tree, we'd laugh and laugh and howl.

---

1. **grating** (GRAY tihng): irritating; annoying.
2. **lauded** (LAWD ihd): praised highly.
3. **Mizeriz:** dialect term for "Mrs."
4. **aghast** (uh GAST) : shocked; horrified.

(A) Reading Focus Fact and Opinion State the facts you learn about Bailey in this opening paragraph. What opinions does Angelou express? How can you tell the difference between fact and opinion here?

(B) Literary Focus First-Person Narration Which pronouns signal that Angelou is using first-person narration? Who is the speaker? Who is speaking the words in quotation marks?

(C) Read and Discuss So far, what has Angelou told you about her brother? What do these details contribute to her portrait of him?

Bailey could count on very few punishments for his consistently outrageous behavior, for he was the pride of the Henderson/Johnson family.

His movements, as he was later to describe those of an acquaintance, were activated with oiled precision. He was also able to find more hours in the day than I thought existed. He finished chores, homework, read more books than I, and played the group games on the side of the hill with the best of them. He could even pray out loud in church and was apt at stealing pickles from the barrel that sat under the fruit counter and Uncle Willie's nose.

Once when the Store was full of lunchtime customers, he dipped the strainer, which we also used to sift weevils[5] from meal and flour, into the barrel and fished for two fat pickles. He caught them and hooked the strainer onto the side of the barrel, where they dripped until he was ready for them. When the last school bell rang, he picked the nearly dry pickles out of the strainer, jammed them into his pockets, and threw the strainer behind the oranges. We ran out of the Store. It was

---

5. **weevils:** small beetles that feed on grains, cotton, and other crops.

summer and his pants were short, so the pickle juice made clean streams down his ashy legs, and he jumped with his pockets full of loot and his eyes laughing a "How about that?" He smelled like a vinegar barrel or a sour angel. **D**

After our early chores were done, while Uncle Willie or Momma minded the Store, we were free to play the children's games as long as we stayed within yelling distance. Playing hide-and-seek, his voice was easily identified, singing, "Last night, night before, twenty-four robbers at my door. Who all is hid? Ask me to let them in, hit 'em in the head with a rolling pin. Who all is hid?" In follow the leader, naturally he was the one who created the most daring and interesting things to do. And when he was on the tail of the pop the whip, he would twirl off the end like a top, spinning, falling, laughing, finally stopping just before my heart beat its last, and then he was back in the game, still laughing.

Of all the needs (there are none imaginary) a lonely child has, the one that must be satisfied, if there is going to be hope and a hope of wholeness, is the unshaking need for an unshakable God. My pretty black brother was my Kingdom Come. **E**

D [Read and Discuss] How does this information about Bailey connect with what you already know?

E [Reading Focus] Fact and Opinion What does the author mean when she says, "My pretty black brother was my Kingdom Come"? Is this statement a fact or an opinion?

Applying Your Skills

Reading Standard 3.5 Identify the speaker and recognize the difference between **first-** and third-**person narration** (e.g., **autobiography** compared with biography).

Brother

Literary Response and Analysis

Reading Skills Focus
Quick Check

1. How is the writer's appearance <u>distinct</u> from that of other family members?

2. According to Angelou, what does a lonely child need most?

Read with a Purpose

3. Why was Bailey so important to Angelou?

Reading Skills: Distinguishing Between Fact and Opinion

4. Compare your Fact/Opinion chart with a partner's. Where was it hard to separate facts from opinions? Did this selection consist of mostly facts or mostly opinions? Explain.

Fact	Opinion	Difficult to Separate?
Bailey was her only brother.	"Bailey was the greatest person in my world."	
Bailey was small.	Bailey was "graceful" and "smooth."	

Literary Skills Focus
Literary Analysis

5. **Analyze** How would you describe Bailey's personality? What do you think of him?

6. **Infer** What qualities in a person did Angelou value when she was a child? What kind of person do you think she wanted to be?

Literary Skills: First-Person Narration

7. **Infer** Although the subject of this selection is Bailey, you also learn a great deal about Angelou through her **first-person narration.** How do you think Angelou felt about herself when she was young? Why do you think so?

8. **Evaluate** From which point of view is this description of Bailey told—first person or third person? How do you know?

Literary Skills Review: Characterization

9. **Analyze** Writers reveal characters' qualities through their appearance, words, actions, thoughts, and other characters' reactions. They also directly state characters' qualities. Which methods of **characterization** does Angelou use to reveal Bailey's character? Which does she *not* use? Why?

Writing Skills Focus
Think as a Reader/Writer

Use It in Your Writing Use first-person narration to describe a person. Use specific details to show why this person is important to you.

What Do You Think Now

How has this selection affected your ideas about how the people close to you can inspire you?

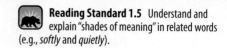

Brother

Vocabulary Development

Shades of Meaning

Synonyms are words that have the same or nearly the same meaning. The synonyms' **shades of meaning** are what make them <u>distinct</u>. Writers pay careful attention to words' shades of meaning in order to make their writing rich and precise.

Think, for example, about why Maya Angelou says that Bailey "was *lauded*"—and not *praised* or *acclaimed*—for his appearance. *Lauded* implies great praise. It's a much stronger word than *praised* and conveys people's admiration for Bailey. *Acclaimed* suggests that people clapped or cheered to show their approval. Angelou probably didn't want to suggest that people applauded Bailey for his appearance!

You can use a thesaurus to find synonyms for words. Be sure, though, to check the definition of each synonym in a dictionary to make sure you understand its shades of meaning. Sometimes a dictionary will include a list of synonyms at the end of an entry for a word, along with an explanation of each synonym's shades of meaning.

Your Turn

Look up each Vocabulary word in a thesaurus. List two or three synonyms you find for each word. Then, go back to the text and substitute the synonyms for each Vocabulary word. Write a few sentences explaining which synonyms work best, considering their different shades of meaning.

> outrageous
> acquaintance
> precision
> apt
> sift

Language Coach

Word Families Some adjectives are made from words that can be both verbs and nouns, like the Vocabulary word *outrageous*.

> grating
> oiled
> daring
> interesting

Work with a partner to identify the verb forms of each of the adjectives from "Brother" in the box above. First, write the meanings of all four adjectives. Then, write a sentence that uses the verb form of each of these words. For example, *His tone of voice really grated on my nerves.*

Academic Vocabulary

Write About . . .

People seldom share a <u>uniform</u> view of things. You may see someone in a way that's different from the way others see that person. Bailey's family let him get away with things because, from their <u>perspective</u>, he was wonderful and could do no wrong. Do you think others saw him this way? Explain.

Learn It Online
For more on synonyms and antonyms see *WordSharp*:
go.hrw.com   H6-572   Go

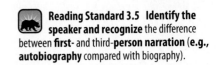

Reading Standard 3.5 Identify the speaker and recognize the difference between **first-** and third-**person narration (e.g., autobiography** compared with biography).

Grammar Link
Subject-Verb Agreement

It's easy for a sentence to go astray when its subject and verb don't agree: *The pickles is nearly dry now*. A verb should agree in number with its subject: *The pickles are nearly dry now*. Singular subjects need singular verbs, and plural subjects need plural verbs.

EXAMPLES

> **Bailey was** the greatest person in my world. [The singular subject **Bailey** agrees with the singular verb **was**.]

> The **pickles drip** until he is ready for them. [The plural subject **pickles** agrees with the plural verb **drip**.]

When a sentence contains a verb phrase like *has been given,* make sure the first helping verb in the phrase agrees with the subject.

EXAMPLES

> **Bailey has** been stealing pickles.
> **We have** been stealing pickles.

Your Turn

Writing Applications Rewrite each sentence, changing the subject and verb from singular to plural or from plural to singular.

EXAMPLE

> The **elders talk** unkindly about my features.
> The **elder talks** unkindly about my features.

1. The pickle juice runs in streams down his legs.
2. Bailey was seldom punished for his pranks.
3. He has fun playing hide-and-seek and follow-the-leader.

CHOICES

As you respond to the Choices, use these **Academic Vocabulary** words as appropriate: contribute, distinct, perspective, uniform.

REVIEW
Write a New Version
Narrative Writing Rewrite the paragraph in which Angelou describes how Bailey steals the pickles. Describe the incident from Bailey's point of view, using first-person narration. Replace any details that convey Angelou's perspective with ones that show what Bailey thinks and feels.

CONNECT
Write a Character Sketch
Timed Writing Who is the "greatest person" in *your* world? Your choice may be someone you know or a public figure you admire. Write a character sketch describing why this person is the greatest. What does he or she contribute to your world? Use first-person narration, and be sure to make your perspective clear by presenting facts about the person and your opinions.

EXTEND
Create a Movie About "Brother"
TechFocus Imagine you were making a short movie based on "Brother." Whom would you cast as Maya and as Bailey? What scenes from the selection would you include in the movie, and how would you expand these scenes to make an interesting film? Write a summary of the movie in a paragraph.

Learn It Online
To make a digital story, go to:
go.hrw.com | H6-573 | Go

Preparing to Read

from
The
Land I Lost

by **Huynh Quang Nhuong**

What Do
You
Think?
What kinds of inspi-
ration can you get
from true stories?

QuickWrite

What lessons have you learned from reading
or listening to other people's true stories?
Write about a true story that inspired you.

Reader/Writer
Notebook

Use your **RWN** to complete the activities for this selection.

Literary Skills Focus

Narrators: First Person and Third Person This excerpt from an **autobiography** starts with **first-person narration.** The writer, Huynh Quang Nhuong (hoon kwang nyoon), uses the pronoun *I* to tell about his boyhood in Vietnam. This autobiography is the story of more than one person, though. As the narrative progresses, Nhuong switches to the **third person.** You'll notice that when he tells the story of Lan and Trung, "So Close," Nhuong describes the thoughts and feelings of many of the characters. He tells his story from the point of view of someone outside it.

Reading Skills Focus

Analyzing Author's Purpose Authors write with a **purpose,** such as to inform, to persuade, to express feelings, or to entertain. They may write with more than one purpose in mind—to persuade and to entertain, for example—or their purpose may shift in the course of a work. To determine an author's purpose(s), ask yourself, "*Why* is the author telling me this? *Why* is the author telling me this *in this way*?"

Into Action As you read, record the writer's purpose in different parts of the autobiography in a chart like this.

Inform	Persuade	Express Feelings	Entertain
He tells what Vietnam was like before the war.			He tells a story about his neighbors.

TechFocus Think about a story from your own past that you enjoy telling people. How would it look as a movie?

Writing Skills Focus

Find It in Your Reading The speaker describes Lan's and Trung's actions to reveal what they are like. As you read, record in your *Reader/Writer Notebook* at least three ways their actions help you understand them.

Language Coach

Synonyms Synonyms are words that are similar in meaning. You can find synonyms in a thesaurus or at the end of the dictionary entry for some words. With a partner, brainstorm synonyms for each of the Vocabulary words above. You can use a thesaurus or dictionary for extra help, if necessary.

Learn It Online
For a preview of this autobiography, see the video introduction on:

go.hrw.com | H6-575 | Go

Huynh Quang Nhuong

(1946–   )

To Make People Happy

Huynh Quang Nhuong (hoong KWAHN nyoong) was born in a small village in Vietnam between a deep jungle and a chain of high mountains. At age six, Huynh learned to tend his family's herd of water buffaloes. Tank, his favorite water buffalo, takes part in many of the adventures described in *The Land I Lost*.

Nhuong left his village to study chemistry at the University of Saigon. When war broke out, he recalls, "the land I love was lost to me forever." Nhuong was drafted into the army of South Vietnam. On the battlefield he was shot and paralyzed.

In 1969, Nhuong left Vietnam to receive special medical treatment in the United States. He stayed, earned degrees in literature and French, and settled in Columbia, Missouri. His writing helps form a link between his two countries. He says:

"I hope that my books will make people from different countries happy, regardless of their political adherences, creeds, and ages."

Think About the Writer Nhuong wants his books to make people happy. What does that tell you about what he values?

Build Background

One place where you're likely to meet up with a crocodile is Vietnam, a tropical country in Southeast Asia with many warm, muddy rivers and swamps. Vietnam is about the size of New Mexico, and as the period map shows, it extends south from China in a long, narrow S-curve.

Most Americans probably still associate Vietnam with war. In this excerpt from his autobiography, Huynh Quang Nhuong recalls a peaceful time in his beautiful country. His story helps you picture the people of Vietnam and gives you a perspective on their relationship with the land and with the animals that live in it.

Preview the Selection

Huynh Quang Nhuong, the author, describes his life as a child in a South Vietnamese village. Then, he tells the story of two neighbors. **Lan** is a young woman who becomes engaged to **Trung,** a fisherman.

Read with a Purpose   Read to find out what happens when a crocodile shows up on a happy couple's wedding night.

from
The Land I Lost

by **Huynh Quang Nhuong**

I was born on the central highlands of Vietnam in a small hamlet on a riverbank that had a deep jungle on one side and a chain of high mountains on the other. Across the river, rice fields stretched to the slopes of another chain of mountains. **Ⓐ**

There were fifty houses in our hamlet, scattered along the river or propped against the mountainsides. The houses were made of bamboo and covered with coconut leaves, and each was surrounded by a deep trench to protect it from wild animals or thieves. The only way to enter a house was to walk across a "monkey bridge"—a single bamboo stick that spanned the trench. At night we pulled the bridges into our houses and were safe.

There were no shops or marketplaces in our hamlet. If we needed supplies—medicine, cloth, soaps, or candles—we had to cross over the mountains and travel to a town nearby. We used the river mainly for traveling to distant hamlets, but it also provided us with plenty of fish. **Ⓑ**

During the six-month rainy season, nearly all of us helped plant and cultivate fields of rice, sweet potatoes, Indian mustard, eggplant, tomatoes, hot peppers, and corn. But during the dry season, we became hunters and turned to the jungle.

Wild animals played a very large part in our lives. There were four animals we feared the most: the tiger, the lone wild hog, the crocodile, and the horse snake. Tigers were

---

Ⓐ Literary Focus **First- and Third-Person Narration**
What does the opening paragraph tell you about the speaker's identity?

Ⓑ **Read and Discuss** Can you imagine living in this village? How do you think you would deal with living there?

always trying to steal cattle. Sometimes, however, when a tiger became old and slow it became a man-eater. But a lone wild hog was even more dangerous than a tiger. It attacked every creature in sight, even when it had no need for food. Or it did crazy things, such as charging into the hamlet in broad daylight, ready to kill or to be killed.

The river had different dangers: crocodiles. But of all the animals, the most hated and feared was the huge horse snake. It was sneaky and attacked people and cattle just for the joy of killing. It would either crush its victim to death or poison it with a bite.

Like all farmers' children in the hamlet, I started working at the age of six. My seven sisters helped by working in the kitchen, weeding the garden, gathering eggs, or taking water to the cattle. I looked after the family herd of water buffaloes. Someone always had to be with the herd because no matter how carefully a water buffalo was trained, it always was ready to nibble young rice plants when no one was looking. Sometimes, too, I fished for the family while I guarded the herd, for there were plenty of fish in the flooded rice fields during the rainy season. **C**

> A lone wild hog was even more dangerous than a tiger. It attacked every creature in sight, even when it had no need for food.

I was twelve years old when I made my first trip to the jungle with my father. I learned how to track game, how to recognize useful roots, how to distinguish edible mushrooms from poisonous ones. I learned that if birds, raccoons, squirrels, or monkeys had eaten the fruits of certain trees, then those fruits were not poisonous. Often they were not delicious, but they could calm a man's hunger and thirst.

My father, like most of the villagers, was a farmer and a hunter, depending upon the season. But he also had a college education, so in the evenings he helped to teach other children in our hamlet, for it was too small to afford a professional schoolteacher.

My mother managed the house, but during the harvest season she could be found in the fields, helping my father get the crops home; and as the wife of a hunter, she knew how to dress and nurse a wound and took good care of her husband and his hunting dogs.

I went to the lowlands to study for a while because I wanted to follow my father as a teacher when I grew up. I always planned to return to my hamlet to live the rest of my life there. But war disrupted my dreams. The land I love was lost to me forever. **D**

These stories are my memories. . . .

C **Literary Focus** First- and Third-Person Narration
What have you learned about the speaker and his life so far?

D **Literary Focus** First- and Third-Person Narration
What were the speaker's dreams? What happened to them?

So Close

My grandmother was very fond of cookies made of banana, egg, and coconut, so my mother and I always stopped at Mrs. Hong's house to buy these cookies for her on our way back from the marketplace. My mother also liked to see Mrs. Hong because they had been very good friends since grade-school days. While my mother talked with her friend, I talked with Mrs. Hong's daughter, Lan. Most of the time Lan asked me about my older sister, who was married to a teacher and lived in a nearby town. Lan, too, was going to get married—to a young man living next door, Trung. **E**

Trung and Lan had been inseparable playmates until the day tradition did not allow them to be alone together anymore. Besides, I think they felt a little shy with each other after realizing that they were man and woman. **F**

Lan was a lively, pretty girl, who attracted the attention of all the young men of our hamlet. Trung was a skillful fisherman who successfully plied[1] his trade on the river in front of their houses. Whenever Lan's mother found a big fish on the kitchen windowsill, she would smile to herself. Finally, she decided that Trung was a fine

---

1. **plied:** worked at.

E **Read and Discuss** How are we first introduced to Lan and Trung?

F **Literary Focus** **First- and Third-Person Narration** What is the point of view now? Why has it shifted?

young man and would make a good husband for her daughter. **G**

Trung's mother did not like the idea of her son giving good fish away, but she liked the cookies Lan brought her from time to time. Besides, the girl was very helpful; whenever she was not busy at her house, Lan would come over in the evening and help Trung's mother repair her son's fishing net.

Trung was happiest when Lan was helping his mother. They did not talk to each other, but they could look at each other when his mother was busy with her work. Each time Lan went home, Trung looked at the chair Lan had just left and secretly wished that nobody would move it.

One day when Trung's mother heard her son call Lan's name in his sleep, she decided it was time to speak to the girl's mother about marriage. Lan's mother agreed they should be married and even waived[2] the custom whereby the bridegroom had to give the bride's family a fat hog, six chickens, six ducks, three bottles of wine, and thirty kilos[3] of fine rice, for the two families had known each other for a long time and were good neighbors.

> Each time Lan went home, Trung looked at the chair Lan had just left and secretly wished that nobody would move it.

The two widowed mothers quickly set the dates for the engagement announcement and for the wedding ceremony. Since their decision was immediately made known to relatives and friends, Trung and Lan could now see each other often. . . . **H**

At last it was the day of their wedding. Friends and relatives arrived early in the morning to help them celebrate. They brought gifts of ducks, chickens, baskets filled with fruits, rice wine, and colorful fabrics. Even though the two houses were next to each other, the two mothers observed all the proper wedding day traditions.

First, Trung and his friends and relatives came to Lan's house. Lan and he prayed at her ancestors' altars and asked for their blessing. Then they joined everyone for a luncheon. **I**

After lunch there was a farewell ceremony for the bride. Lan stepped out of her house and joined the greeting party that was to accompany her to Trung's home. Tradition called for her to cry and to express her sorrow at leaving her parents behind and forever becoming the daughter of her husband's family. In some villages the bride was even supposed to cling so tightly to her mother that it would take several friends to pull her away from her

---

2. **waived:** gave up voluntarily.
3. **kilos:** kilograms, about 2.2 pounds each.

G **Read and Discuss** Why is Trung leaving the fish?

H **Read and Discuss** What are the two mothers thinking and planning?

I **Reading Focus** Author's Purpose The author is telling a story here. What might his purpose be?

home. But instead of crying, Lan smiled. She asked herself, why should she cry? The two houses were separated by only a garden; she could run home and see her mother anytime she wanted to. So Lan willingly followed Trung and prayed at his ancestors' altars before joining everyone in the big welcome dinner at Trung's house that ended the day's celebrations. **J**

Later in the evening of the wedding night, Lan went to the river to take a bath. Because crocodiles infested the river, people of our hamlet who lived along the riverbank chopped down trees and put them in the river to form barriers and protect places where they washed their clothes, did their dishes, or took a bath. This evening, a wily crocodile had avoided the barrier by crawling up the riverbank and sneaked up behind Lan. The crocodile grabbed her and went back to the river by the same route that it had come. **K**

Trung became worried when Lan did not return. He went to the place where she was supposed to bathe, only to find that her clothes were there, but she had disappeared. Panic-stricken, he yelled for his relatives. They all rushed to the riverbank with lighted torches. In the flickering light they found traces of water and crocodile claw-prints on the wet soil. Now they knew that a

---

J Read and Discuss Why are the houses so important in the wedding traditions?

K Read and Discuss What just happened at the river?

Vocabulary infested (ihn FEHST ihd) *v.:* inhabited in large numbers (said of something harmful).
wily (WY lee) *adj.:* sly; clever in a sneaky way.

The Vietnam War

The Vietnamese had struggled against domination by China for centuries, but by the early 1880s, it was France that ruled Vietnam. Starting in 1941, a large group of Vietnamese, led by Ho Chi Minh, worked toward a communist revolution they believed could free Vietnam from French rule. The United States, concerned that a communist victory would contribute to the spread of communism in Southeast Asia, supported France with military aid.

When the French left in the early 1950s, Vietnam was divided into North Vietnam, which had a communist government, and South Vietnam, which had a Western-style government. Yet many Vietnamese longed to reunite the country under communism, and the American anti-communist military effort grew into all-out war: the Vietnam War, which lasted from 1959 to 1975.

Ask Yourself

How can living through war change a person's perspective on life?

crocodile had grabbed the young bride and dragged her into the river.

Since no one could do anything for the girl, all of Trung's relatives returned to the house, urging the bridegroom to do the same. But the young man refused to leave the place; he just stood there, crying and staring at the clothes of his bride.

Suddenly the wind brought him the sound of Lan calling his name. He was very frightened, for according to an old belief, a crocodile's victim must lure a new victim to his master; if not, the first victim's soul must stay with the beast forever. **Ⓛ**

Trung rushed back to the house and woke all his relatives. Nobody doubted he thought he had heard her call, but they all believed that he was the victim of a hallucination. Everyone pleaded with him and tried to convince him that nobody could survive when snapped up by a crocodile and dragged into the river to be drowned and eaten by the animal.

The young man brushed aside all their arguments and rushed back to the river. Once again, he heard the voice of his bride in the wind, calling his name. Again he rushed back and woke his relatives. Again they tried to persuade him that it was a hallucination, although some of the old folks suggested that maybe the ghost of the young girl was having to dance and sing to placate[4] the angry crocodile because she failed to bring it a new victim.

---

4. **placate:** calm or soothe (someone who is angry).

Ⓛ [Read and Discuss] What is going on with Trung here?

Vocabulary **hallucination** (huh loo suh NAY shuhn) *n.*: sight or sound of something that isn't really there.

No one could persuade Trung to stay inside. His friends wanted to go back to the river with him, but he said no. He resented them for not believing him that there were desperate cries in the wind.

Trung stood in front of the deep river alone in the darkness. He listened to the sound of the wind and clutched the clothes Lan had left behind. The wind became stronger and stronger and often changed direction as the night progressed, but he did not hear any more calls. Still he had no doubt that the voice he had heard earlier was absolutely real. Then at dawn, when the wind died down, he again heard, very clearly, Lan call him for help. **Ⓜ**

Her voice came from an island about six hundred meters away. Trung wept and prayed: "You were a good girl when you were still alive, now be a good soul. Please protect me so that I can find a way to kill the beast in order to free you from its spell and avenge your tragic death." Suddenly, while wiping away his tears, he saw a little tree moving on the island. The tree was jumping up and down. He squinted to see better. The tree had two hands that were waving at him. And it was calling his name. **Ⓝ**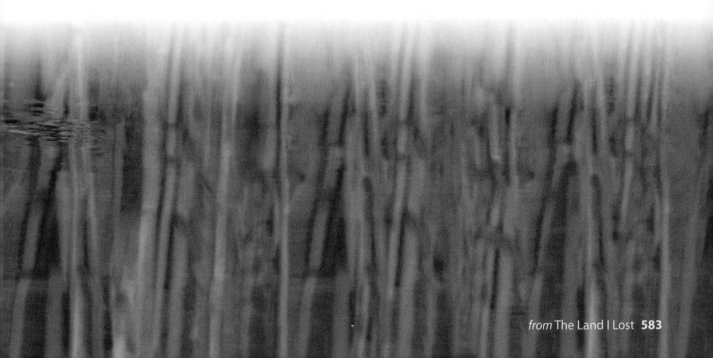

Trung became hysterical and yelled for help. He woke all his relatives and they all rushed to his side again. At first they thought that Trung had become stark mad. They tried to lead him back to his house, but he fiercely resisted their attempt. He talked to them incoherently[5] and pointed his finger at the strange tree on the island. Finally his relatives saw the waving tree. They quickly put a small boat into the river,

---

5. **incoherently:** not clearly.

Ⓜ **Reading Focus** **Author's Purpose** What is the author's purpose in describing these scenes of Trung listening for Lan? What other stories does *The Land I Lost* remind you of so far?

Ⓝ **Read and Discuss** What is the narrator describing here?

Vocabulary **desperate** (DEHS puhr iht) *adj.:* having a great and urgent need.
avenge (uh VEHNJ) *v.:* get even for; get revenge for.

and Trung got into the boat along with two other men. They paddled to the island and discovered that the moving tree was, in fact, Lan. She had covered herself with leaves because she had no clothes on.

At first nobody knew what had really happened because Lan clung to Trung and cried and cried. Finally, when Lan could talk, they pieced together her story.

Lan had fainted when the crocodile snapped her up. Had she not fainted, the crocodile surely would have drowned her before carrying her off to the island. Lan did not know how many times the crocodile had tossed her in the air and smashed her against the ground, but at one point, while being tossed in the air and falling back onto the crocodile's jaw, she regained consciousness. The crocodile smashed her against the ground a few more times, but Lan played dead. Luckily the crocodile became thirsty and returned to the river to drink. At that moment Lan got up and ran to a nearby tree and climbed up it. The tree was very small.

Lan stayed very still for fear that the snorting, angry crocodile, roaming around trying to catch her again, would find her

> Lan stayed very still for fear that the snorting, angry crocodile, roaming around trying to catch her again, would find her and shake her out of the tree.

and shake her out of the tree. Lan stayed in this frozen position for a long time until the crocodile gave up searching for her and went back to the river. Then she started calling Trung to come rescue her. **❶**

Lan's body was covered with bruises, for crocodiles soften up big prey before swallowing it. They will smash it against the ground or against a tree, or keep tossing it into the air. But fortunately Lan had no broken bones or serious cuts. It was possible that this crocodile was very old and had lost most of its teeth. Nevertheless, the older the crocodile, the more intelligent it usually was. That was how it knew to avoid the log barrier in the river and to snap up the girl from behind.

Trung carried his exhausted bride into the boat and paddled home. Lan slept for hours and hours. At times she would sit up with a start and cry out for help, but within three days she was almost completely recovered.

Lan's mother and Trung's mother decided to celebrate their children's wedding a second time because Lan had come back from the dead. **❶**

---

❶ ▢ Read and Discuss ▢ What is Lan explaining about her plan to get home?

❶ ▢ Read and Discuss ▢ How does the story conclude? How does the near tragedy <u>contribute</u> to the joy at the end?

Applying Your Skills

from The Land I Lost
Literary Response and Analysis

Reading Skills Focus
Quick Check

1. How is the river important in the lives of the people in the village?
2. What four animals do the villagers fear the most? Why?

Read with a Purpose

3. What is surprising about Lan and Trung's story? Why?

Reading Skills: Analyzing Author's Purpose

4. Review your chart. What do you think is the author's main purpose? Why?

Inform	Persuade	Express Feelings	Entertain
He tells what Vietnam was like before the war.			He tells a story about his neighbors.

Main purpose: _____

Literary Skills Focus
Literary Analysis

5. **Analyze** How did the author lose the land he loved? How does the story of Lan and Trung fit with this idea of the loss of a homeland?
6. **Connect** What values and feelings do you share with Nhuong's people?
7. **Extend** Does the story about Trung, Lan, and the crocodile seem like a tall tale? How could this story be proved true?

Literary Skills: First- and Third-Person Narration

8. **Analyze** What do you learn about the **speaker's** qualities and his goals and dreams in the first section of the autobiography? Use examples to explain your answer.
9. **Analyze/Connect** Why does the author shift his point of view from the first person to the third person? What <u>distinct</u> qualities of each point of view most help to reveal the <u>perspectives</u> of the people he is writing about?

Literary Skills Review: Characterization

10. **Interpret** A writer reveals character through **characterization.** Think of what you learned about Lan before the crocodile attack. How did the author prepare you for the story's outcome through his characterization of Lan?

Writing Skills Focus
Think as a Reader/Writer

Use It in Your Writing Look at your notes on how the author uses characters' actions to reveal their traits. Write a paragraph about a real or imagined person, using the character's actions to help your reader "see" and understand the character.

What Do You Think Now

What lessons did you learn from Nhuong's story? What can we learn from other people's stories in general?

Applying Your Skills

Reading Standard 1.4 Monitor expository text for unknown words or words with novel meanings by using word, sentence, and paragraph clues to determine meaning.

from **The Land I Lost**

Vocabulary Development

Context Clues

When you read, use **context clues**—or word, sentence, and paragraph clues—to determine the meanings of unknown words. These clues can appear before or after the unknown word.

Your Turn

infested
wily
hallucination
desperate
avenge

Paragraph Clues Locate the paragraph in the story where each Vocabulary word in the box is used. Find clues in the paragraph that help explain the word's meaning. Put the context clues for the Vocabulary words in cluster diagrams like this one, which contains clues for the word *infested*.

> Crocodiles infested the river—the word must refer to something dangerous.
>
> **infested**
>
> People had to put up barriers to keep them out.

Monitoring Text Answer these questions about other words and context clues in the selection.

1. Find the word *hamlet* in the first paragraph. Which words in the first three paragraphs provide clues to the meaning of *hamlet*? How would you define the word?

2. Find the term *monkey bridge* in the second paragraph. Where does the writer provide a definition of this term?

Language Coach

Synonyms Synonyms are words with the same or nearly the same meaning. For example, *stone* and *rock* are synonyms. Synonyms are not always interchangeable, though. Fill out a chart like the one below for the following Vocabulary words: *wily, hallucination, desperate,* and *average.*

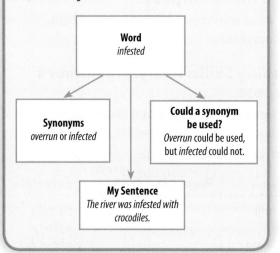

Word
infested

Synonyms
overrun or *infected*

Could a synonym be used?
Overrun could be used, but *infected* could not.

My Sentence
The river was infested with crocodiles.

Academic Vocabulary

Talk About . . .
Huynh Quang Nhuong writes from the unique <u>perspective</u> of a Vietnamese villager. How does his viewpoint influence your opinion of whether the story of Lan and Trung is true or fictional? What else does his <u>perspective</u> <u>contribute</u>?

Learn It Online
Learn about context clues with *WordSharp* on:

go.hrw.com | H6-586 | Go

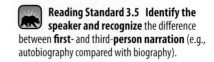

Reading Standard 3.5 Identify the speaker and recognize the difference between **first-** and third-**person narration** (e.g., autobiography compared with biography).

Grammar Link
Run-on Sentences and Fragments

It is very easy to mistakenly write run-on sentences and fragments, but a few simple rules will help you avoid those mistakes. A **run-on sentence** is two complete sentences run together or combined with just a comma. To revise a run-on, either make two separate sentences or use a comma and a conjunction such as *and, but,* or *or.*

RUN-ON SENTENCE
> Lan bakes cookies, Trung fishes.

REVISED
> Lan bakes cookies**.** Trung fishes.
> Lan bakes cookies **and** Trung fishes.

A **fragment** is missing a part of the sentence, but it is capitalized and punctuated as if it were a complete sentence. (Remember that a complete sentence must have a subject and a predicate and must make sense on its own.)

FRAGMENT
> Frightened the villagers.

REVISED
> **The snake** frightened the villagers.

Your Turn _____

Revise each of the following items to eliminate run-on sentences and fragments.

1. Allowed to go into the jungle alone.
2. Trung and Lan are having a luncheon after the wedding everyone will come.
3. The animals frighten us all the time, we must be very careful.
4. Mrs. Hong's house to take those cookies to her.

CHOICES

As you respond to the Choices, use these **Academic Vocabulary** words as appropriate: contribute, distinct, perspective, uniform.

REVIEW
Describe a Place

In the first section of his autobiography, Nhuong describes life in his village. Write a description of everyday life in your own city, town, or village. Write as if you were going to publish your description in a different country, where little is known about the United States—where people live, what they eat, how they make a living. Open your description with the words *I was born in* or *I live in.* End your description with a statement telling how you feel about your hometown.

CONNECT
Write a Memoir

Timed ⌐Writing Imagine that you have to leave home today and can never return. Write a short essay from your own perspective, using the first-person point of view, that describes what you would and would not miss.

EXTEND
Go Digital: Screen Your Story

TechFocus Write a brief autobiographical narrative of one or two paragraphs, choosing details that make your story interesting. Then, use the *Digital Storytelling* instructions on Learn It Online to create a short movie of your story.

Learn It Online
Tell your story in a whole new way. Try digital storytelling. We'll show you how at:

go.hrw.com   H6-587   **Go**

A GLORY OVER
Everything

by **Ann Petry**

QuickWrite

Is following a dream for a better future ever worth risking everything—even your life? Would you risk your life to gain something as essential as your freedom?

Harriet Tubman by Stephen Alcorn.

Reader/Writer
Notebook
Use your **RWN** to complete the activities
for this selection.

Reading Standard 3.5 Identify the
speaker and **recognize** the difference
between first- and **third-person narration** (e.g.,
autobiography compared with **biography**).

Literary Skills Focus

Third-Person Narration This selection is from a **biography,** the
true story of a person's life written by another person. Using **third-
person narration**—signaled by the use of pronouns such as *he, she,*
and *they*—the author writes from the <u>perspective</u> of someone *outside*
the narrative. As you read, note how the author presents what she
imagines her real-life subjects must have thought and felt.

Literary Perspectives Use the Analyzing Responses to Literature
perspective on page 591 as you read this biography.

Reading Skills Focus

Finding the Main Idea The **main idea** is the most important point
made in a nonfiction text. Although first and last paragraphs often
give clues to the main idea, you must infer, or make an educated guess
about, the main idea from details the writer provides throughout the
text.

Into Action To figure out the main idea in "A Glory over Everything,"
use a chart like the one below to take notes as you read the selection.
List key details and important passages.

Notes for Finding the Main Idea in "A Glory over Everything"

Details in the First Paragraph	A white woman askes about Harriet's scar.
Important Passages/Other Key Details	Dr. Thompson starts selling slaves.
Details in the Last Paragraph	

Language Coach
Words That Describe Two of the four
Vocabulary words are adjectives, words
used to modify, or describe, a noun or
pronoun by telling what kind, which one,
how many, or how much. Match each
adjective from the Vocabulary list with one
of the following nouns it can describe:

rebels   concerns

Writing Skills Focus
Think as a Reader/Writer
Find It in Your Reading As you read this biography, use your
Reader/Writer Notebook to record dialogue that <u>contributes</u> to
your understanding of Harriet Tubman.

Learn It Online
Use Word Watch to explore the meaning of terms at:

go.hrw.com   H6-589   **Go**

Ann Petry

(1908–1997)

A Writer at Work

Ann Petry worked as a certified pharmacist in her family's drug-store in Old Saybrook, Connecticut. Later, while living in New York City, she was a journalist and teacher, as well as an actor in the American Negro Theatre.

Petry is best known for presenting the tragedy of slavery in two biographies for young readers: one about Harriet Tubman and the other about Tituba, a young woman from Barbados who was held in slavery by a family in Salem, Massachusetts, and accused of witchcraft in 1692.

Making History Speak

Speaking about her two celebrated subjects, Harriet Tubman and Tituba, Petry said the following:

"These women were slaves. I hoped that I had made them into real people. I tried to make history speak across the centuries in the voices of people—young, old, good, evil, beautiful, ugly."

Think About the Writer Why do you think Petry chose to write about two women who were enslaved?

Build Background

The Underground Railroad wasn't a railroad, and it didn't run underground. It was made up of people from both the North and the South who offered food, shelter, and protection to African Americans escaping from slavery to freedom in the North. To keep the route secret, the organization used railroad terms, such as *stations* for the houses along the way and *conductors* for the people who offered help.

Harriet Tubman, who escaped from slavery, became one of the most famous "conductors" on the railroad. She helped more than three hundred men, women, and children along the road to freedom.

Preview the Selection

In this part of Petry's biography of **Harriet Tubman,** you will meet Tubman in 1849, when she was working as a field hand on the Brodas plantation in Maryland. Tubman knew that as a slave she could be sold at any time, so she had to plan her escape quickly.

A GLORY OVER Everything

by **Ann Petry**

One day in 1849, when Harriet was working in the fields near the edge of the road, a white woman wearing a faded sunbonnet went past, driving a wagon. She stopped the wagon and watched Harriet for a few minutes. Then she spoke to her, asked her what her name was, and how she had acquired the deep scar on her forehead. **Ⓐ**

Harriet told her the story of the blow she had received when she was a girl. After that, whenever the woman saw her in the fields, she stopped to talk to her. She told Harriet that she lived on a farm near Bucktown. Then one day she said, not looking at Harriet but looking instead at the overseer far off at the edge of the fields, "If you ever need any help, Harriet, ever need any help, why, you let me know."

That same year the young heir to the Brodas estate[1] died. Harriet mentioned the fact of his death to the white woman in the

faded sunbonnet the next time she saw her. She told her of the panic-stricken talk in the quarter, told her that the slaves were afraid

Literary Perspectives

Analyzing Responses to Literature When you analyze your responses to a work of literature, you consider how the distinct literary elements—plot, setting, character, theme, literary devices—contributed to your responses. Perhaps you think the characters in the story are people you'd want to know. You might analyze how their qualities affected the plot. Did their bravery, kindness, helpfulness, humor, or sense of adventure lead to a happy ending?

If you felt inspired to be a better person by reading a text, you'd surely want to think about its theme. What message inspired you? Did the author convey that message through the characters and their actions, through images, or through a direct statement?

As you read this biography, answer the Literary Perspective questions at the bottom of the page.

---

1. **Brodas estate:** Edward Brodas, the previous owner of the plantation, died in 1849 and left his property to his heir, who was not yet old enough to manage it. In the meantime the plantation was placed in the hands of the boy's guardian, Dr. Thompson.

Ⓐ Literary Focus Third-Person Narration How can you recognize that the author is using third-person narration?

that the master, Dr. Thompson, would start selling them. She said that Doc Thompson no longer permitted any of them to hire their time.[2] The woman nodded her head, clucked to the horse, and drove off, murmuring, "If you ever need any help—"

The slaves were right about Dr. Thompson's intention. He began selling slaves almost immediately. Among the first ones sold were two of Harriet Tubman's sisters. They went south with the chain gang on a Saturday.

When Harriet heard of the sale of her sisters, she knew that the time had finally come when she must leave the plantation. She was reluctant to attempt the long trip north alone, not because of John Tubman's threat to betray her[3] but because she was afraid she might fall asleep somewhere along the way and so would be caught immediately.

She persuaded three of her brothers to go with her. Having made certain that John was asleep, she left the cabin quietly and met her brothers at the edge of the plantation. They agreed that she was to lead the way, for she was more familiar with the woods than the others. **(B)**

---

2. **hire their time:** Some slaveholders allowed the people they held in slavery to hire themselves out for pay to other plantation owners who needed extra help. In such cases, the workers were permitted to keep their earnings.

3. **threat to betray her:** Harriet's husband, John Tubman, was a free man who was content with his life. He violently disapproved of his wife's plan to escape and threatened to tell the master if she carried it out.

The three men followed her, crashing through the underbrush, frightening themselves, stopping constantly to say, "What was that?" or "Someone's coming."

She thought of Ben[4] and how he had said, "Any old body can go through a woods crashing and mashing things down like a cow." She said sharply, "Can't you boys go quieter? Watch where you're going!" **(C)**

One of them grumbled, "Can't see in the dark. Ain't got cat's eyes like you."

"You don't need cat's eyes," she retorted. "On a night like this, with all the stars out, it's not black dark. Use your own eyes."

She supposed they were doing the best they could, but they moved very slowly. She kept getting so far ahead of them that she had to stop and wait for them to catch up with her, lest they lose their way. Their progress was slow, uncertain. Their feet got tangled in every vine. They tripped over fallen logs, and once one of them fell flat on his face. They jumped, startled, at the most ordinary sounds: the murmur of the wind in the branches of the trees, the twittering of a bird. They kept turning around, looking back.

They had not gone more than a mile when she became aware that they had stopped. She turned and went back to them. She could hear them whispering. One of them called out, "Hat!"

"What's the matter? We haven't got time to keep stopping like this."

---

4. **Ben:** Harriet Tubman's father. Her mother is called Old Rit.

(B) Literary Perspectives **Responses to Literature** What do you think of Tubman so far? What literary elements contributed to your response?

(C) Read and Discuss What does Harriet's behavior during their escape tell you about her?

Analyzing Visuals

Connecting to the Text
How does this image illustrate Harriet Tubman's desire for freedom, as Petry conveys it, in this biography?

Under the Midnight Blues (2003) by Colin Bootman.

"We're going back."

"No," she said firmly. "We've got a good start. If we move fast and move quiet—"

Then all three spoke at once. They said the same thing, over and over, in frantic hurried whispers, all talking at once:

They told her that they had changed their minds. Running away was too dangerous. Someone would surely see them and recognize them. By morning the master would know they had "took off." Then the handbills advertising them would be posted all over Dorchester County. The patterollers[5] would search for them. Even

if they were lucky enough to elude the patrol, they could not possibly hide from the bloodhounds. The hounds would be baying after them, snuffing through the swamps and the underbrush, zigzagging through the deepest woods. The bloodhounds would surely find them. And everyone knew what happened to a runaway who was caught and brought back alive.

She argued with them. Didn't they know that if they went back they would be sold, if not tomorrow, then the next day, or the next? Sold south. They had seen the chain gangs. Was that what they wanted? Were they going to be slaves for the rest of their lives? Didn't freedom mean anything to them? **Ⓓ**

---

5. **patterollers:** patrollers.

Ⓓ Reading Focus Main Idea How do Harriet's words here relate to finding the main idea of the story?

Vocabulary **elude** (ih LOOD) *v.*: escape the notice of; avoid detection by.

"You're afraid," she said, trying to shame them into action. "Go on back. I'm going north alone."

Instead of being ashamed, they became angry. They shouted at her, telling her that she was a fool and they would make her go back to the plantation with them. Suddenly they surrounded her, three men, her own brothers, jostling her, pushing her along, pinioning[6] her arms behind her. She fought against them, wasting her strength, exhausting herself in a furious struggle.

She was no match for three strong men. She said, panting, "All right. We'll go back. I'll go with you."

She led the way, moving slowly. Her thoughts were bitter. Not one of them was willing to take a small risk in order to be free. It had all seemed so perfect, so simple, to have her brothers go with her, sharing the dangers of the trip together, just as a family should. Now if she ever went north, she would have to go alone. **E**

Two days later, a slave working beside Harriet in the fields motioned to her. She bent toward him, listening. He said the water boy had just brought news to the field hands,

> They shouted at her, telling her that she was a fool and they would make her go back to the plantation with them.

and it had been passed from one to the other until it reached him. The news was that Harriet and her brothers had been sold to the Georgia trader and that they were to be sent south with the chain gang that very night. **F**

Harriet went on working but she knew a moment of panic. She would have to go north alone. She would have to start as soon as it was dark. She could not go with the chain gang. She might die on the way because of those inexplicable sleeping seizures. But then she—how could she run away? She might fall asleep in plain view along the road. **G**

But even if she fell asleep, she thought, the Lord would take care of her. She murmured a prayer, "Lord, I'm going to hold steady on to You, and You've got to see me through."

Afterward, she explained her decision to run the risk of going north alone in these words: "I had reasoned this out in my mind; there was one of two things I had a *right* to, liberty or death; if I could not have one, I would have the other; for no man should take me alive; I should fight for my liberty as long as my strength lasted, and when the time came for me to go, the Lord would let them take me." **H**

---

6. **pinioning** (PIHN yuhn ihng): pinning.

E **Literary Perspectives** Responses to Literature Do you agree with Harriet or her brothers? What elements in the text contribute to your reaction?

F Read and Discuss What has Harriet just learned?

G **Literary Focus** Third-Person Narration In this paragraph, Petry shows Harriet's thoughts and fears almost as if they are her own. Why do you think she writes this way?

H Read and Discuss How does Harriet's decision fit in with what you already know about her?

At dusk, when the work in the fields was over, she started toward the Big House.[7] She had to let someone know that she was going north, someone she could trust. She no longer trusted John Tubman and it gave her a lost, lonesome feeling. Her sister Mary worked in the Big House, and she planned to tell Mary that she was going to run away, so someone would know.

As she went toward the house, she saw the master, Doc Thompson, riding up the drive on his horse. She turned aside and went toward the quarter. A field hand had no legitimate reason for entering the kitchen of the Big House—and yet—there must be some way she could leave word so that afterward someone would think about it and know that she had left a message.

As she went toward the quarter, she began to sing. Dr. Thompson reined in his horse, turned around, and looked at her. It was not the beauty of her voice that made him turn and watch her, frowning; it was the words of the song that she was singing and something defiant in her manner that disturbed and puzzled him.

> When that old chariot comes,
>   I'm going to leave you,
> I'm bound for the promised land,
>   Friends, I'm going to leave you.
> I'm sorry, friends, to leave you,
>   Farewell! Oh, farewell!

> But I'll meet you in the morning,
>   Farewell! Oh, farewell!
> I'll meet you in the morning,
>   When I reach the promised land;
> On the other side of Jordan,
>   For I'm bound for the promised land. ❶

That night when John Tubman was asleep and the fire had died down in the cabin, she took the ash cake that had been baked for their breakfast and a good-sized piece of salt herring and tied them together in an old bandanna. By hoarding this small stock of food, she could make it last a long time, and with the berries and edible roots she could find in the woods, she wouldn't starve.

She decided that she would take the quilt[8] with her, too. Her hands lingered over it. It felt soft and warm to her touch. Even in the dark, she thought she could tell one color from another because she knew its pattern and design so well.

Then John stirred in his sleep, and she left the cabin quickly, carrying the quilt carefully folded under her arm.

Once she was off the plantation, she took to the woods, not following the North Star, not even looking for it, going instead toward Bucktown. She needed help. She was going to ask the white woman who had stopped to talk to her so often if she would help her. Perhaps she wouldn't. But she would soon find out.

---

7. **Big House:** plantation owner's house.

8. **the quilt:** Tubman had painstakingly stitched together a quilt before her wedding.

❶ **Read and Discuss** What is the point of Harriet's singing?

Vocabulary **legitimate** (luh JIHT uh miht) *adj.:* reasonable; justified.
defiant (dih FY uhnt) *adj.:* disobedient; boldly resistant.

When she came to the farmhouse where the woman lived, she approached it cautiously, circling around it. It was so quiet. There was no sound at all, not even a dog barking or the sound of voices. Nothing.

She tapped on the door, gently. A voice said, "Who's there?" She answered, "Harriet, from Dr. Thompson's place."

When the woman opened the door, she did not seem at all surprised to see her. She glanced at the little bundle that Harriet was carrying, at the quilt, and invited her in. Then she sat down at the kitchen table and wrote two names on a slip of paper and handed the paper to Harriet.

She said that those were the next places where it was safe for Harriet to stop. The first place was a farm where there was a gate with big white posts and round knobs on top of them. The people there would feed her, and when they thought it was safe for her to go on, they would tell her how to get to the next house or take her there.

For these were the first two stops on the Underground Railroad—going north, from the eastern shore of Maryland.

Thus Harriet learned that the Underground Railroad that ran straight to the North was not a railroad at all. Neither did it run underground. It was composed of a loosely organized group of people who offered food and shelter, or a place of concealment, to fugitives who had set out on the long road to the North and freedom. **J**

Harriet wanted to pay this woman who had befriended her. But she had no money. She gave her the patchwork quilt, the only beautiful object she had ever owned.

That night she made her way through the woods, crouching in the underbrush whenever she heard the sound of horses' hoofs, staying there until the riders passed. Each time, she wondered if they were already hunting for her. It would be so easy to describe her, the deep scar on her forehead like a dent, the old scars on the back of her neck, the husky speaking voice, the lack of height, scarcely five feet tall. The master would say she was wearing rough clothes when she ran away, that she had a bandanna on her head, that she was muscular and strong. **K**

She knew how accurately he would describe her. One of the slaves who could read used to tell the others what it said on those handbills that were nailed up on the trees along the edge of the roads. It was easy to recognize the handbills that advertised runaways because there was always a picture in one corner, a picture of a black man, a little running figure with a stick over his shoulder and a bundle tied on the end of the stick.

Whenever she thought of the handbills, she walked faster. Sometimes she stumbled over old grapevines, gnarled and twisted, thick as a man's wrist, or became entangled in the tough sinewy vine of the honeysuckle. But she kept going.

In the morning she came to the house where her friend had said she was to stop.

J Read and Discuss How are things turning out for Harriet so far? What is the Underground Railroad?

K Literary Focus Third-Person Narration What does the author reveal here? How might the author know this?

Vocabulary **befriended** (bih FREHND ihd) *v.*: helped out; acted as a friend.

She showed the slip of paper that she carried to the woman who answered her knock at the back door of the farmhouse. The woman fed her and then handed her a broom and told her to sweep the yard.

Harriet hesitated, suddenly suspicious. Then she decided that with a broom in her hand, working in the yard, she would look as though she belonged on the place; certainly no one would suspect that she was a runaway.

That night the woman's husband, a farmer, loaded a wagon with produce. Harriet climbed in. He threw some blankets over her, and the wagon started.

It was dark under the blankets and not exactly comfortable. But Harriet decided that riding was better than walking. She was surprised at her own lack of fear, wondered how it was that she so readily trusted these strangers who might betray her. For all she knew, the man driving the wagon might be taking her straight back to the master.

She thought of those other rides in wagons, when she was a child, the same clop-clop of the horses' feet, creak of

Analyzing Visuals **Connecting to the Text** What do you learn about Harriet Tubman from her room and her physical appearance? What qualities of Tubman are conveyed in both this image and the biography?

597

the wagon, and the feeling of being lost because she did not know where she was going. She did not know her destination this time either, but she was not alarmed. She thought of John Tubman. By this time he must have told the master that she was gone. Then she thought of the plantation and how the land rolled gently down toward the river, thought of Ben and Old Rit, and that Old Rit would be inconsolable because her favorite daughter was missing. "Lord," she prayed, "I'm going to hold steady onto You. You've got to see me through." Then she went to sleep.

The next morning, when the stars were still visible in the sky, the farmer stopped the wagon. Harriet was instantly awake.

He told her to follow the river, to keep following it to reach the next place where people would take her in and feed her. He said that she must travel only at night and she must stay off the roads because the patrol would be hunting for her. Harriet climbed out of the wagon. "Thank you," she said simply, thinking how amazing it was that there should be white people who were willing to go to such lengths to help a slave get to the North.

> "Thank you," she said simply, thinking how amazing it was that there should be white people who were willing to go to such lengths to help a slave get to the North.

When she finally arrived in Pennsylvania, she had traveled roughly ninety miles from Dorchester County. She had slept on the ground outdoors at night. She had been rowed for miles up the Choptank River by a man she had never seen before. She had been concealed in a haycock[9] and had, at one point, spent a week hidden in a potato hole in a cabin which belonged to a family of free Negroes. She had been hidden in the attic of the home of a Quaker. She had been befriended by stout German farmers, whose guttural[10] speech surprised her and whose well-kept farms astonished her. She had never before seen barns and fences, farmhouses and outbuildings, so carefully painted. The cattle and horses were so clean they looked as though they had been scrubbed. **L**

When she crossed the line into the free state of Pennsylvania, the sun was coming up. She said, "I looked at my hands to see if I was the same person now I was free. There was such a glory over everything, the sun came like gold through the trees and over the fields, and I felt like I was in heaven." **M**

---

9. **haycock:** pile of hay in a field.
10. **guttural:** harsh; rasping.

L **Read and Discuss** The author has presented a lot of detail about Harriet's journey. What point is the author trying to make?

M **Reading Focus** Main Idea What thoughts do you have now about the main idea of this selection? What clues does this final paragraph hold?

Applying Your Skills

Reading Standard 3.5 Identify the speaker and **recognize the difference between first- and third-person narration** (e.g., autobiography compared with biography).

A Glory over Everything
Literary Response and Analysis

Reading Skills Focus
Quick Check

1. What happened at the plantation that had the enslaved workers worried?
2. Why do Harriet's brothers change their minds about escaping with her?

Read with a Purpose

3. How did Harriet Tubman escape from slavery?

Reading Skills: Main Idea

4. Review your notes from "A Glory over Everything." Use the details you recorded to make inferences about the main idea. State the main idea in your own words.

Notes for Finding the Main Idea in "A Glory over Everything"

Details in the First Paragraph	A white woman askes about Harriet's scar.
Important Passages/ Other Key Details	Dr. Thompson starts selling slaves.
Details in the Last Paragraph	

Literary Skills Focus
Literary Analysis

5. **Interpret** In the last paragraph, why does Tubman say, "There was such a glory over everything"? (Here, *glory* means "great beauty.") What is she feeling at that moment? Why?

6. **Extend** In the Bible, the Israelites escaping slavery in Egypt eventually cross the Jordan River and enter the land they believe was promised to them by God. What is Tubman's Jordan? What is her Promised Land?

Literary Skills: Third-Person Narration

7. **Analyze** Re-read the paragraph on page 595 that begins, "As she went toward the quarter . . ." Explain why this passage could appear in a biography, which uses **third-person narration,** but probably not in an autobiography, which uses **first-person narration.**

8. **Evaluate** Petry never knew Tubman personally, yet she describes Tubman's thoughts and feelings. Do you think it's right for a biographer to include such details? Explain.

Literary Skills Review: Character

9. **Analyze** What are Harriet Tubman's main qualities? How do they enable her to gain her freedom?

Writing Skills Focus
Think as a Reader/Writer

Use It in Your Writing Write a one-page biography of a friend or family member. Use dialogue to help reveal the person's qualities.

What Do You Think Now?

How did this text affect your thoughts about the value of freedom? Would you be willing to do what Tubman did?

Applying Your Skills

Reading Standard 1.4 Monitor expository text for unknown words or words with novel meanings by using word, sentence, and paragraph clues to determine meaning.

A Glory over Everything

Vocabulary Development
Context Clues

Identifying word, sentence, and paragraph clues—or **context clues**—when you read will help you determine the meanings of unknown words. There are several types of context clues. For instance, the clues can be synonyms (words with similar meanings), antonyms (words with opposite meanings), or examples that show the meanings of the unknown words.

Your Turn

Answer the following questions to practice using context clues to determine the meanings of unknown words.

> elude
> legitimate
> defiant
> befriended

1. In the paragraph on page 593 containing *elude*, several context clues help you determine the word's meaning by expressing an opposite meaning. What are these clues?

2. What context clues can you identify in the paragraph on page 595 containing *legitimate*?

3. How do Dr. Thompson's reactions provide clues to the meaning of *defiant* in the paragraph containing the word on page 595?

4. Find the paragraph containing *befriended* on page 596. How do the woman's actions in the previous paragraphs show what it means to *befriend* someone?

Language Coach

Words That Describe In the box to the right are descriptive words from the selection you just read. Use a dictionary to learn the meaning of each word. Then, write a descriptive paragraph about Harriet Tubman, using at least three of the words.

> faded
> murmuring
> tangled
> zigzagging
> jostling

Academic Vocabulary

Talk About . . .

With a partner, discuss the meaning of *freedom* from Tubman's <u>perspective</u>. How did the selling of Tubman's sisters <u>contribute</u> to Tubman's decision to seek freedom? What would her future have been like if she had not risked her life to gain her freedom? Use the underlined Academic Vocabulary words in your discussion.

Learn It Online
For action-packed vocabulary lessons, visit:

go.hrw.com   H6-600   Go

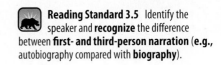

Reading Standard 3.5 Identify the speaker and **recognize** the difference between **first- and third-person narration** (e.g., autobiography compared with **biography**).

Grammar Link

Troublesome Verbs

The **past tense** and **past participle** of most verbs are formed by adding –*d* or –*ed,* but **irregular verbs** change in unexpected ways. You just have to memorize their forms. The past participle is the form you use with the helping verbs *has, have,* and *had.*

Here are some irregular verbs from "A Glory over Everything."

Base Form	Past Tense	Past Participle
sell	sold	(have) sold
wear	wore	(have) worn
see	saw	(have) seen
run	ran	(have) run

Your Turn

Fill in the chart of irregular verbs below.

Base Form	Past Tense	Past Participle
take		
think		
awake		
begin		

Writing Applications Write a brief summary of "A Glory over Everything." In your summary, include past tense and past participle forms of these irregular verbs: *tell, sell, wear, see, run, think, begin.*

CHOICES

As you respond to the Choices, use these **Academic Vocabulary** words as appropriate: contribute, distinct, perspective, uniform.

REVIEW
Write a Biography

Think of a person from history or someone living today who has struggled for freedom or equal rights. Write one or two paragraphs about that person's struggle. Use third-person narration, and try to convey the perspectives—the opinions or beliefs—of that person.

CONNECT
Be a Character in the Story

Timed └Writing Imagine that you are one of the people mentioned in "A Glory over Everything," such as one of Harriet's brothers, someone in the Underground Railroad, or Harriet herself. Tell the story from your own perspective, using first-person narration. What are your feelings and motivations?

EXTEND
Write an Obituary

Research Read part of a biography or an encyclopedia article to find out how Harriet Tubman lived the rest of her life after she gained her freedom. What did she contribute to society? Then, write an obituary for Tubman that summarizes the highlights of her life.

Learn It Online
There's more to this story than meets the eye. Expand your view at:

go.hrw.com   H6-601   **Go**

Comparing Literary Devices in Fiction and Nonfiction

CONTENTS

Utopie (1999)
by Bob Lescaux.

What lessons do you have
to learn before you can
achieve your dreams?

🕐 **QuickWrite**

Think about a life lesson you've learned that helped you
accomplish something or solve a problem. In a few sentences, describe the lesson and the way you learned it.

Literary Skills Focus

Reading Standard 3.7 Explain the effects of common literary devices (e.g., symbolism, imagery, metaphor) in a variety of fictional and nonfictional texts.

How Do Writers Use Literary Devices in Fiction and Nonfiction?

Literary Devices

You probably associate **literary devices,** such as imagery and metaphors, with poetry, but writers of fiction and nonfiction also use such devices. Writers use literary devices as tools to reach our emotions, appeal to our imaginations, and convey meaning. Literary devices give life to a work. Their effect is to make a work interesting, meaningful, moving, or exciting. Without them, a work would seem like just words on a page. Here are three of the most common types of literary devices:

Imagery Language that appeals to our senses is called **imagery.** Imagery creates pictures in our minds. It can also help us hear, smell, or taste something and feel its textures and temperature. Note how Gary Paulsen uses imagery in this passage to describe his dog Storm:

> Then he raised his lips, bared his teeth, and growled at the stove.
>
> from "Storm"
> by Gary Paulsen

Paulsen *shows* us that Storm is angry by using imagery to help us see and hear Storm.

Figurative Language There are many kinds of **figurative language,** or language that makes an imaginative comparison and is not meant to be taken literally. In a **simile** a writer compares two unlike things using words such as *like, as, than,* and *resembles.* In a **metaphor** a writer directly compares two unlike things without using a comparison word. Note how Avi uses a simile to help us picture a homeless man and to convey that people don't see his true identity:

> His matted, streaky gray hair hung like a ragged curtain over a dirty face.
>
> from "What Do Fish Have to Do with Anything?" by Avi

When writers use **personification,** they describe something nonhuman as if it were human, as you will see in Paulsen's descriptions of his dog Storm.

Symbolism A **symbol** is a person, place, thing, or event that stands for itself and for something beyond itself as well. We all agree on the meanings of public symbols; for example, a red rose symbolizes love, and a white dove symbolizes peace. Writers often create their own symbols. The effect is to add layers of meaning to their works.

MEET THE WRITERS

Learn It Online
Get more on the authors' lives at:
go.hrw.com H6-604 Go

Gary Paulsen
(1939–   )

Newbery Medal WINNER

A Passion for Writing
As an army officer's son, Gary Paulsen lived over-seas and all over this country when he was a boy. Because he was always moving, he had trouble making friends. He developed a passion for reading, which led to a passion for writing. Paulsen says of his craft, "I have not done anything else in life that gives me the personal satisfaction that writing does."

Russell Freedman
(1929–   )

Newbery Medal WINNER

Studying Mr. Lincoln
Russell Freedman has written more than three dozen books on historical topics. He says of Abraham Lincoln, "The Lincoln I grew up with was a cardboard figure, too good to believe. . . . When I had some inkling he was a complicated person in his own right, I decided I wanted to know more about him."

Avi
(1937–   )

Newbery Medal WINNER

Writing out of Sheer Stubbornness
Determined to prove he could become a writer, Avi says he succeeded out of "sheer stubbornness." He discovered his true audience when he became a father and started writing for children and young adults. "Writing for kids has been at the center of my life ever since."

Think About the Writers
What motivates each of these writers?

Preview the Selections

In "Storm," you'll meet **Storm,** a dog with a sense of humor, and his owner, **Gary Paulsen.**

In "The Mysterious Mr. Lincoln," you'll discover the complex personality of **Abraham Lincoln,** one of our nation's greatest presidents.

In "What Do Fish Have to Do with Anything?" you'll meet a thoughtful boy named **Willie;** his mother, **Mrs. Markham;** and a **homeless man** whom they see from a very different perspectives.

Preparing to Read

Storm

Reading Standard 3.7 Explain the effects of common literary devices (e.g., symbolism, **imagery**, metaphor) **in** a variety of fictional and **nonfictional texts.**

Literary Skills Focus

Imagery Language that appeals to our senses is called **imagery.** Writers of nonfiction use imagery to help us see a ship in the distance, hear the whistling wind, smell and taste fresh bread, and imagine what a snake feels like. Nonfiction writers use imagery to re-create real-life experiences and to convey their perspectives on these experiences; the effect of imagery is to make things real for us. As you read "Storm," an excerpt from Gary Paulsen's autobiography, think about how Paulsen uses imagery to bring his dog Storm to life.

Reading Skills Focus

Analyzing Author's Purpose A writer's purpose for writing a piece of nonfiction may be to **inform,** to **persuade,** to **express feelings,** or simply to **entertain.** A writer may have more than one purpose, but usually one is more important than the others. To determine a writer's purpose, think about *why* he or she is telling you something. Do the ideas prove a point? Do they show you how the writer feels? Think, too, about the effects of literary devices. Does an image provide information? Does it make you laugh?

Into Action Make a pie chart, and divide it into four sections, one for each purpose. As you read, record images and other details that support each purpose.

Writing Skills Focus
Think as a Reader/Writer

Find It in Your Reading Record in your *Reader/Writer Notebook* the images that have the greatest effect in making Storm's and Paulsen's experiences seem real to you. Identify the sense or senses to which these images appeal.

Vocabulary

resembled (rih ZEHM buhld) *v.:* was similar to. *The dog resembled a bear.*

Language Coach

Prefixes A prefix is a word part added to the beginning of a word. Knowing the meanings of common prefixes will help you determine the definitions of unfamiliar words. The Vocabulary word *resembled* comes from the Latin prefix *re–,* meaning "again," and the Latin root word *simulare,* meaning "to feign or imitate." *Rearrange* and *rebuild* also contain the prefix *re–.* What other words can you name that contain this prefix? How does knowing the meaning of *re–* help you understand these words?

Reader/Writer
Notebook

Use your **RWN** to complete the activities for this selection.

Learn It Online
For previews of these stories, see the video introductions on:

go.hrw.com   H6-605   Go

Storm

from Woodsong by **Gary Paulsen**

Siberian Husky
by Scott Kennedy.

Read with a Purpose

Read to learn what qualities make a dog named Storm very special to Gary Paulsen.

Build Background

"Storm" is taken from *Woodsong*, Gary Paulsen's account of his adventures in northern Minnesota. There he ran a team of sled dogs. Paulsen later ran the Iditarod (y DIHT uh rahd), the famous—and dangerous—dog sled race between Anchorage and Nome, Alaska.

It is always possible to learn from dogs, and in fact the longer I'm with them, the more I understand how little I know. But there was one dog who taught me the most. Just one dog. Storm. First dog. . . .

Joy, loyalty, toughness, peacefulness—all of these were part of Storm. Lessons about life and, finally, lessons about death came from him. **A**

He had a bear's ears. He was brindle colored[1] and built like a truck, and his ears were rounded when we got him, so that

---

1. **brindle colored:** gray or brown and streaked or spotted with a dark color.

A **Read and Discuss** What has Paulsen told you so far?

they looked like bear cub ears. They gave him a comical look when he was young that somehow hung on to him even when he grew old. He had a sense of humor to match his ears, and when he grew truly old, he somehow resembled George Burns.[2]

At peak, he was a mighty dog. He pulled like a machine. Until we retired him and used him only for training puppies, until we let him loose to enjoy his age, he pulled, his back over in the power curve, so that nothing could stop the sled. **B**

In his fourth or fifth year as a puller, he started doing tricks. First he would play jokes on the dog pulling next to him. On long runs he would become bored, and when we least expected it, he would reach across the gang line and snort wind into the ear of the dog next to him. I ran him with many different dogs and he did it to all of them—chuckling when the dog jumped and shook his or her head—but I never saw a single dog get mad at him for it. Oh, there was once a dog named Fonzie who nearly took his head off, but Fonzie wasn't really mad at him so much as surprised. Fonzie once nailed me through the wrist for waking him up too suddenly when he was sleeping. I'd reached down and touched him before whispering his name. **C**

Small jokes. Gentle jokes, Storm played. He took to hiding things from me. At first I couldn't understand where things were going. I would put a bootie down while working on a dog, and it would disappear. I lost a small ladle[3] I used for watering each dog, a cloth glove liner I took off while working on a dog's feet, a roll of tape, and finally, a hat.

He was so clever.

When I lost the hat, it was a hot day and I had taken the hat off while I worked on a dog's harness. The dog was just ahead of Storm, and when I knelt to work on the harness—he'd chewed almost through the side of it while running—I put the hat down on the snow near Storm.

Or thought I had. When I had changed the dog's harness, I turned and the hat was gone. I looked around, moved the dogs, looked under them, then shrugged. At first I was sure I'd put the hat down; then, when I couldn't find it, I became less sure, and at last I thought perhaps I had left it at home or dropped it somewhere on the run.

Storm sat quietly, looking ahead down the trail, not showing anything at all. **D**

I went back to the sled, reached down to disengage the hook, and when I did, the dogs exploded forward. I was not quite on the sled when they took off, so I was knocked slightly off balance. I leaned over to the right to regain myself, and when I did, I accidentally dragged the hook through the snow.

And pulled up my hat.

It had been buried off to the side of the trail in the snow, buried neatly with the snow smoothed over the top, so that it was

---

2. **George Burns** (1896–1996): American comedian and actor with large ears.

3. **ladle:** cup-shaped spoon with a long handle for dipping out liquids.

B Literary Focus **Imagery** Which images in the last two paragraphs best help you picture Storm?

C Read and Discuss What have you learned about Storm?

D Read and Discuss What new information about Storm has Paulsen given you?

Vocabulary **resembled** (rih ZEHM buhld) *v.*: was similar to.

Eager to Run by Scott Kennedy.

completely hidden. Had the snow hook not scraped down four or five inches, I never would have found it.

I stopped the sled and set the hook once more. While knocking the snow out of the hat and putting it back on my head, I studied where it had happened.

Right next to Storm.

He had taken the hat, quickly dug a hole, buried the hat and smoothed the snow over it, then gone back to sitting, staring ahead, looking completely innocent.

When I stopped the sled and picked up the hat, he looked back, saw me put the hat on my head, and—I swear—smiled. Then he shook his head once and went back to work pulling. **E**

Along with the jokes, Storm had scale eyes. He watched as the sled was loaded, carefully calculated the weight of each item, and let his disapproval be known if it went too far.

One winter a friend gave us a parlor stove with nickel trim. It was not an enormous stove, but it had some weight to it and some bulk. This friend lived twelve miles away—twelve miles over two fair hills followed by about eight miles on an old, abandoned railroad grade.[4] We needed the stove badly (our old barrel stove had started to burn through), so I took off with the team to pick it up. I left early in the morning because I wanted to get back that same day. It had snowed four or five inches, so the dogs would have to break trail. By the time we had done the hills and the railroad grade, pushing in new snow all the time, they were ready for a rest. I ran them the last two miles to where the stove was and unhooked their tugs so they could rest while I had coffee.

We stopped for an hour at least, the dogs

---

4. **railroad grade:** rise or elevation in a railroad track.

E **Reading Focus** Author's Purpose What does this image tell you about the author's purpose?

sleeping quietly. When it was time to go, my friend and I carried the stove outside and put it in the sled. The dogs didn't move.

Except for Storm.

He raised his head, opened one eye, did a perfect double take—both eyes opening wide—and sat up. He had been facing the front. Now he turned around to face the sled—so he was facing away from the direction we had to travel when we left—and watched us load the sled. **F**

It took some time, as the stove barely fit on the sled and had to be jiggled and shuffled around to get it down between the side rails.

Through it all, Storm sat and watched us, his face a study in interest. He did not get up but sat on his back end, and when I was done and ready to go, I hooked all the dogs back in harness—which involved hooking the tugs to the rear ties on their harnesses. The dogs knew this meant we were going to head home, so they got up and started slamming against the tugs, trying to get the sled to move.

All of them, that is, but Storm. **G**

Storm sat backward, the tug hooked up but hanging down. The other dogs were screaming to run, but Storm sat and stared at the stove.

Not at me, not at the sled, but at the stove itself. Then he raised his lips, bared his teeth, and growled at the stove.

When he was finished growling, he snorted twice, stood, turned away from the stove, and started to pull. But each time we stopped at the tops of the hills to let the dogs catch their breath after pulling the sled and stove up the steep incline, Storm turned and growled at the stove.

The enemy.

The weight on the sled. **H**

F Read and Discuss How is Storm's reaction different from the uniform reactions of the other dogs?

G Reading Focus **Analyzing Author's Purpose** How is Paulsen letting you know that he's about to present another amusing example of Storm's personality?

H Literary Focus **Imagery** Describe the scene here. How do Paulsen's images make you see the stove as Storm sees it?

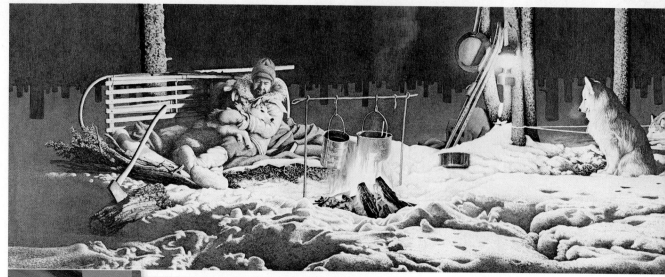

Connecting to the Text Explain whether the images in this painting accurately show the relationship between Paulsen, Storm, and the other dogs.

Never Alone by Scott Kennedy.

* * *

I do not know how many miles Storm and I ran together. Eight, ten, perhaps twelve thousand miles. He was one of the first dogs and taught me the most, and as we worked together, he came to know me better than perhaps even my own family. He could look once at my shoulders and tell how I was feeling, tell how far we were to run, how fast we had to run—knew it all. ❶

When I started to run long, moved from running a work team, a trap line team, to training for the Iditarod, Storm took it in stride, changed the pace down to the long trot, matched what was needed, and settled in for the long haul.

He did get bored, however, and one day while we were running a long run, he started doing a thing that would stay with him— with us—until the end. We had gone forty or fifty miles on a calm, even day with no bad wind. The temperature was a perfect ten below zero. The sun was bright, everything was moving well, and the dogs had settled into the rhythm that could take them a hundred or a thousand miles.

And Storm got bored.

At a curve in the trail, a small branch came out over the path we were running, and as Storm passed beneath the limb, he jumped up and grabbed it, broke a short piece off—about a foot long—and kept it in his mouth.

All day.

And into the night. He ran, carrying the stick like a toy, and when we stopped to feed or rest, he would put the stick down, eat, then pick it up again. He would put the stick down carefully in front of him, or across his paws, and sleep, and when he awakened, he would

---

❶ **Read and Discuss** What point about Storm is the author trying to make?

pick up the stick, and it soon became a thing between us, the stick.

He would show it to me, making a contact, a connection between us, each time we stopped. I would pet him on top of the head and take the stick from him—he would emit a low, gentle growl when I took the stick. I'd "examine" it closely, nod and seem to approve of it, and hand it back to him.

Each day we ran, he would pick a different stick. And each time I would have to approve of it, and after a time, after weeks and months, I realized that he was using the sticks as a way to communicate with me, to tell me that everything was all right, that I was doing the right thing. **J**

Once, when I pushed them too hard during a pre-Iditarod race—when I thought it was important to compete and win (a feeling that didn't last long)—I walked up to Storm, and as I came close to him, he pointedly dropped the stick. I picked it up and held it out, but he wouldn't take it. He turned his face away. I put the stick against his lips and tried to make him take it, but he let it fall to the ground. When I realized what he was doing, I stopped and fed and rested the team, sat on the sled, and thought about what I was doing wrong. After four hours or so of sitting—watching other teams pass me—I fed them another snack, got ready to go, and was gratified to see Storm pick up the stick. From that time forward I looked for the stick always, knew when I saw it out to the sides of his head that I was doing the right thing. And it was always there. **K**

Through storms and cold weather, on the long runs, the long, long runs where there isn't an end to it, where only the sled and the winter around the sled and the wind are there, Storm had the stick to tell me it was right, all things were right.

J **Literary Focus** **Imagery** What images show that Storm uses the sticks to communicate?

K **Read and Discuss** What does this information contribute to what you have learned about Storm and the sticks?

Applying Your Skills

Reading Standard 3.7 Explain the effects of common literary devices (e.g., symbolism, **imagery**, metaphor) in a variety of fictional and **nonfictional texts.**

Storm

Literary Response and Analysis

Reading Skills Focus
Quick Check

1. From whose <u>perspective</u> is "Storm" told?
2. What two stories does the narrator tell to illustrate Storm's sense of humor?
3. Why does Storm carry sticks?

Read with a Purpose

4. What qualities make Storm special?

Reading Skills: Analyzing Author's Purpose

5. Writers often have more than one purpose for writing their autobiographies. Use your pie chart to analyze Paulsen's purposes in writing "Storm." Beneath the chart, complete this sentence: *The author's main purpose is to . . .* Then, provide reasons for your answer in one or two sentences.

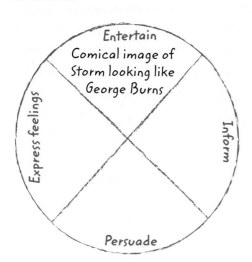

✓ Vocabulary Check

6. What animal might you think a dog **resembled** if it were covered in snow?

Literary Skills Focus
Literary Analysis

7. **Analyze** Explain why Paulsen values Storm as "the dog who taught [him] the most."
8. **Analyze** Paulsen's descriptions of Storm give clues to Paulsen's own character. What qualities do you think Paulsen possesses? Why?
9. **Evaluate** Do you think Paulsen exaggerates in his description of Storm? Should autobiographers try to be completely truthful, or is it permissible to stretch the truth to make their accounts more interesting? Explain.

Literary Skills: Imagery

10. **Analyze** To which senses do most of Paulsen's **images** appeal? What is the effect of using this particular type of imagery?
11. **Evaluate** Think about the effects of Paulsen's use of **imagery.** Does his imagery make Storm and his own experiences seem real to you? Why or why not?

Writing Skills Focus
Think as a Reader/Writer

Use It in Your Writing Write a description of an animal interacting with a person. Use imagery to make this interaction real for your reader.

Preparing to Read

The Mysterious Mr. Lincoln

Literary Skills Focus

Figurative Language **Figurative language** refers to imaginative comparisons made between seemingly unlike things. A **metaphor** makes a comparison by saying something *is* something else: *You're a fish out of water.* A **simile** makes a comparison using *like* or *as: The moon is like a silver platter.* **Personification** gives human qualities to something that is not human: *The wind slapped us.*

Through figurative language, writers can create pictures in our minds, call up associations, and help us see ordinary things in fresh ways. The overall effect of figurative language is to make a writer's points richer. As you read this biography, think about how figurative language can be used to make a point as well as—if not better than—hundreds of words can.

Reading Skills Focus

Distinguishing Between Fact and Opinion It is important to distinguish between fact and opinion when evaluating a work of nonfiction. Facts can be proved true with evidence, while opinions are personal beliefs and attitudes.

Into Action As you read the biography, record important facts and opinions about President Lincoln in a chart like the one below.

Facts	Opinions
Lincoln was 6 feet 4 inches tall.	Sitting, "he seemed no taller than" others.

Writing Skills Focus

Think as a Reader/Writer

Find It in Your Reading As you read, record examples of figurative language. How do these examples affect your view of Lincoln?

Reader/Writer
Notebook

Use your **RWN** to complete the activities for this selection.

Vocabulary

defy (dih FY) *v.*: resist. *Lincoln's beliefs defy easy explanations.*

ambitious (am BIHSH uhs) *adj.*: very much wanting success. *Lincoln was ambitious and wanted to achieve great things.*

cautious (KAW shuhs) *adj.*: careful. *Lincoln's approach to the war was cautious.*

Language Coach

Multiple-Meaning Words Many words in the English language have multiple meanings. It's important to learn a word's different definitions so that you can fully understand a writer's point and use the word appropriately yourself. Use a dictionary to identify the multiple meanings of the Vocabulary words *defy* and *ambitious.* Then, for each word, write two sentences that illustrate two different meanings of the word.

Learn It Online
There's more to words than just definitions. Get the whole story on:

go.hrw.com | H6-613 | Go

The Mysterious

Mr. Lincoln

by **Russell Freedman**

Read with a Purpose

Read this selection to learn why Russell Freedman considers Abraham Lincoln "mysterious."

Build Background

This selection comes from Russell Freedman's book *Lincoln: A Photobiography*. Freedman's biography of Lincoln won the Newbery Medal for the most distinguished contribution to children's literature in 1988.

Abraham Lincoln wasn't the sort of man who could lose himself in a crowd. After all, he stood six feet four inches tall, and to top it off, he wore a high silk hat.

His height was mostly in his long, bony legs. When he sat in a chair, he seemed no taller than anyone else. It was only when he stood up that he towered above other men.

At first glance most people thought he was homely. Lincoln thought so too, referring once to his "poor, lean, lank face." As a young man he was sensitive about his gawky[1] looks, but in time, he learned to laugh at himself. When a rival called him "two-faced" during a political debate, Lincoln replied: "I leave it to my audience. If I had another face, do you think I'd wear this one?" **Ⓐ**

According to those who knew him, Lincoln was a man of many faces. In repose[2] he often seemed sad and

The Granger Collection, New York.

---

1. **gawky** (GAW kee): clumsy; awkward.
2. **repose** (rih POHZ): state of rest or inactivity.

Ⓐ | **Read and Discuss** | What is the author telling you about Lincoln?

Abraham Lincoln (1860) by George Peter Alexander Healy.

gloomy. But when he began to speak, his expression changed. "The dull, listless[3] features dropped like a mask," said a Chicago newspaperman. "The eyes began to sparkle, the mouth to smile; the whole countenance[4] was wreathed in animation, so that a stranger would have said, 'Why, this man, so angular and solemn a moment ago, is really handsome!'" **B**

Lincoln was the most photographed man of his time, but his friends insisted that no photo ever did him justice. It's no

wonder. Back then, cameras required long exposures. The person being photographed had to "freeze" as the seconds ticked by. If he blinked an eye, the picture would be blurred. That's why Lincoln looks so stiff and formal in his photos. We never see him laughing or joking.

Artists and writers tried to capture the "real" Lincoln that the camera missed, but something about the man always escaped them. His changeable features, his tones, gestures, and expressions, seemed to defy description.

Today it's hard to imagine Lincoln as he really was. And he never cared to reveal

---

3. **listless** (LIHST lihs): lifeless; lacking in interest or energy.
4. **countenance** (KOWN tuh nuhns): face.

B **Literary Focus** **Figurative Language** Identify the simile in this paragraph. What is its purpose and effect?

Vocabulary **defy** (dih FY) *v.*: resist.

much about himself. In company he was witty and talkative, but he rarely betrayed his inner feelings. According to William Herndon, his law partner, he was "the most secretive—reticent[5]—shut-mouthed man that ever lived." **C**

In his own time, Lincoln was never fully understood even by his closest friends. Since then, his life story has been told and retold so many times he has become as much a legend as a flesh-and-blood human being. While the legend is based on truth, it is only partly true. And it hides the man behind it like a disguise.

The legendary Lincoln is known as Honest Abe, a humble man of the people who rose from a log cabin to the White House. There's no doubt that Lincoln was a poor boy who made good. And it's true that he carried his folksy manners and homespun speech to the White House with him. He said "howdy" to visitors and invited them to "stay a spell." He greeted diplomats while wearing carpet slippers, called his wife "mother" at receptions, and told bawdy[6] jokes at cabinet meetings.

Lincoln may have seemed like a common man, but he wasn't. His friends agreed that he was one of the most ambitious people they had ever known. Lincoln struggled hard to rise above his log-cabin origins, and he was proud of his achievements. By the time he ran for president he was a wealthy man, earning a large income from his law practice and his many investments. As for the nickname Abe, he hated it. No one who knew him well ever called him Abe to his face. They addressed him as Lincoln or Mr. Lincoln.

Lincoln is often described as a sloppy dresser, careless about his appearance. In fact, he patronized the best tailor in Springfield, Illinois, buying two suits a year. That was at a time when many men lived, died, and were buried in the same suit.

It's true that Lincoln had little formal "eddication," as he would have pronounced it. Almost everything he "larned" he taught himself. All his life he said "thar" for *there*, "git" for *get*, "kin" for *can*. Even so, he became an eloquent public speaker who could hold a vast audience spellbound and a great writer whose finest phrases still ring in our ears. He was known to sit up late into the night, discussing Shakespeare's plays with White House visitors.

He was certainly a humorous man, famous for his rollicking stories. But he was also moody and melancholy,[7] tormented by long and frequent bouts of depression. Humor was his therapy. He relied on his yarns,[8] a friend observed, to "whistle down sadness."

> As for the nickname Abe, he hated it.

---

5. **reticent** (REHT uh suhnt): reserved; tending to speak little.
6. **bawdy:** not considered decent; crude.

7. **melancholy** (MEHL uhn kahl ee): sad; gloomy.
8. **yarns:** entertaining stories filled with exaggeration. Storytellers like Lincoln could be said to "spin" yarns.

C Read and Discuss From what you've read so far, what is your sense of Lincoln now?

Vocabulary **ambitious** (am BIHSH uhs) *adj.:* very much wanting success.

Analyzing Visuals

Connecting to the Text
What qualities in this photograph can be explained by what you learned about early photography on page 615?

Abraham Lincoln and his son Tad (1865).

He had a cool, logical mind, trained in the courtroom, and a practical, common-sense approach to problems. Yet he was deeply superstitious, a believer in dreams, omens, and visions. **D**

We admire Lincoln today as an American folk hero. During the Civil War, however, he was the most unpopular president the nation had ever known. His critics called him a tyrant, a hick, a stupid baboon who was unfit for his office. As commander in chief of the armed forces, he was denounced as a bungling amateur who meddled in military affairs he knew nothing about. But he also had his supporters.

They praised him as a farsighted statesman, a military mastermind who engineered the Union victory.

Lincoln is best known as the Great Emancipator, the man who freed the slaves. Yet he did not enter the war with that idea in mind. "My paramount[9] object in this struggle *is* to save the Union," he said in 1862, "and is *not* either to save or destroy slavery." As the war continued, Lincoln's attitude changed. Eventually he came to regard the conflict as a moral crusade[10] to wipe out the sin of slavery. **E**

9. **paramount:** main; most important.
10. **crusade:** struggle for a cause or belief.

D Read and Discuss What does the contrast in this paragraph tell you about Lincoln?

E Reading Focus Fact and Opinion What facts does this paragraph contain?

Connecting to the Text Explain whether this sculpture captures the qualities of Lincoln described in this biography.

No black leader was more critical of Lincoln than the fiery abolitionist[11] writer and editor Frederick Douglass. Douglass had grown up as a slave. He had won his freedom by escaping to the North. Early in the war, impatient with Lincoln's cautious leadership, Douglass called him "preeminently the white man's president, entirely devoted to the welfare of white men." Later, Douglass changed his mind and came to admire Lincoln. Several years after the war, he said this about the sixteenth president: "His greatest mission was to accomplish two things: first, to save his country from dismemberment[12] and ruin; and second, to free his country from the great crime of slavery. . . . Taking him for all in all, measuring the tremendous magnitude of the work before him, considering the necessary means to ends, and surveying the end from the beginning, infinite wisdom has seldom sent any man into the world better fitted for his mission than Abraham Lincoln." **F**

11. **abolitionist:** person who supported abolishing, or ending, slavery in the United States.

12. **dismemberment:** separation into parts; division.

Vocabulary **cautious** (KAW shuhs) *adj.:* careful.

F [Read and Discuss] How do Douglass's opinions of Lincoln mentioned in this part connect to the text as a whole?

Applying Your Skills

Reading Standard 3.7 Explain the effects of common literary devices (e.g., symbolism, imagery, **metaphor**) in a variety of fictional and **nonfictional texts**.

The Mysterious Mr. Lincoln

Literary Response and Analysis

Reading Skills Focus
Quick Check

1. What did Lincoln think of his own looks?
2. How did Lincoln's goals change during the course of the Civil War?

Read with a Purpose

3. How accurate is the word *mysterious* in describing Lincoln? Explain.

Reading Skills: Distinguishing Between Fact and Opinion

4. Review the chart you filled in as you read. Given the facts and opinions Freedman chose to include in this selection, what do you think is his perspective on Lincoln and his overall opinion of the man? Add a row, labeled "Conclusion," to the bottom of your chart, and record your response.

Facts	Opinions
Lincoln was 6 feet 4 inches tall.	Sitting, "he seemed no taller than" others.

Conclusion:

Literary Skills Focus
Literary Analysis

5. **Analyze** Choose three of Lincoln's contrasting qualities, and explain what these contrasts tell you about his character.
6. **Extend** How successful would Lincoln be if he ran for president today? Explain.

Literary Skills: Figurative Language

7. **Analyze** Explain the **simile** Freedman uses when he says that the legend of Lincoln "hides the man behind it like a disguise." How does this simile help Freedman convey his point?
8. **Interpret** We usually associate **metaphors** with poetry, but metaphors are used in all kinds of writing and speaking. Freedman uses metaphor when he says that Lincoln "towered above other men" and that he was "a man of many faces." Explain these comparisons— what do they tell you about Lincoln?
9. **Identify** Using another metaphor, a rival called Lincoln "two-faced." What does this commonly used metaphor mean?
10. **Analyze** Explain the **personification** Frederick Douglass uses when he says that Lincoln's great mission was "to save his country from dismemberment." (In addition to meaning "division," *dismemberment* means "the cutting or tearing off of limbs.") How does this personification add to the point Douglass is making?

Writing Skills Focus
Think as a Reader/Writer

Use It in Your Writing Think about the picture you formed of Lincoln as you read this selection. Then, write a description of Lincoln. Use at least two of your own examples of figurative language to create a distinct portrait.

Applying Your Skills

The Mysterious Mr. Lincoln

Reading Standard 1.1 Read aloud narrative and expository text fluently and accurately and with appropriate pacing, intonation, and expression. **1.2 Identify** and interpret figurative language and **words with multiple meanings.**

Vocabulary Development

Developing Fluency

Follow these steps to read narrative and expository texts fluently (or easily and well) and accurately:

- Make sure that you know the meanings and pronunciations of unfamiliar words.
- Determine appropriate pacing by deciding when to speed up, slow down, pause, or stop as you read. Remember to read by phrases or thought groups instead of word by word.
- Read with expression to convey the meaning of a text.
- Vary your intonation, or the tone or sound of your voice, to suit the text's meaning. Avoid a uniform tone.

Your Turn

Fluency in Word Usage To develop fluency, answer these questions about the Vocabulary words in the box at the right.

| defy |
| ambitious |
| cautious |

1. Why might a person's behavior *defy* explanation?
2. Name three goals that an *ambitious* person might want to achieve.
3. What is the difference between *cautious* and bold actions?

Reading Fluently Choose a passage in "The Mysterious Mr. Lincoln" that is 150–200 words long. Read it silently a few times. Then, read it aloud to a partner, using the steps listed above to help you read fluently. Ask your partner for feedback, and then read the passage aloud again to improve your fluency.

Language Coach

Multiple-Meaning Words
In the box at the right are multiple-meaning words from the selection you just read. List the multiple meanings of each word. Then, for each word, write two sentences that illustrate two different meanings of the word. Use a dictionary if necessary to help you complete this activity.

| face |
| dull |
| common |
| cool |
| regard |

Academic Vocabulary

Talk About . . .
With a partner, discuss what Lincoln contributed to this country in his role as president. What were his distinct achievements, according to the information and perspectives presented in "The Mysterious Mr. Lincoln"?

Preparing to Read

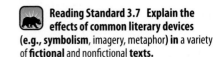
What Do Fish Have to Do with Anything?

Literary Skills Focus

Symbolism A **symbol** is a person, place, thing, or action that has meaning in itself and that stands for something else as well. Many symbols are traditional. They're easily understood because people have agreed on their meaning. A skull and crossbones, for example, symbolizes danger. Peter Pan is a symbol of everlasting childhood. Uncle Sam is a symbol of the United States.

Symbolism, the use of symbols, adds another layer of meaning to texts, from poetry to fiction and nonfiction. In this story the writer uses things, like cave-dwelling fish and a poundcake, to mean what they are—and much more.

Reading Skills Focus

Sequencing Often the events in a story are placed in **chronological order,** or time order. Writers use words such as *before* and *after* to indicate the **sequence,** or order, of events and the amount of time that has passed. Identifying the sequence of events will help you understand the plot and track how a writer builds a symbol's meaning in a story.

Into Action As you read, fill in a flowchart like the one below to identify the sequence of events. Add as many boxes as you need.

> Willie and his mother see a homeless man.

↓

>

Writing Skills Focus
Think as a Reader/Writer
Find It in Your Reading As you read, record instances where fish and poundcake are mentioned. Why does the writer mention them?

Reader/Writer
Notebook
Use your **RWN** to complete the activities for this selection.

Vocabulary

urgency (UR juhn see) *n.:* pressure; insistence. *Hearing the urgency in her voice, Willie quickly turned around.*

ashamed (uh SHAYMD) *adj.:* embarrassed. *She was ashamed of being alone.*

Language Coach

Word Families When you learn a new word, you can quickly expand your vocabulary by learning other words in its family. A word family contains related words. For example, the word family for the Vocabulary word *ashamed* includes *shame* and *shameful.* Create a word family for the Vocabulary word *urgency.* Write down the definition and part of speech of each word in the family. You might want to use a dictionary to help you complete this activity.

Learn It Online
Check out the *PowerNotes* introduction to this story on:

| go.hrw.com | H6-621 | Go |

What Do FISH Have to Do with Anything?

by **Avi**

Read with a Purpose
Read this story to learn what the unusual title means.

Build Background
The fish in the title are a strange kind of creature called cave fish. In the United States these fish are found mostly in eastern and southern states, but they are also found all over the world. In fact, dozens of different species have been identified so far. The <u>uniform</u> traits they all share are a whitish or colorless appearance (some of the fish seem nearly transparent) and a lack of eyes!

Every day Mrs. Markham waited for her son, Willie, to come out of school when it was over. They walked home together. If asked why, Mrs. Markham would say, "Parents need to protect their children."

One Monday afternoon as they approached their apartment building, she suddenly tugged at Willie. "Don't look that way," she said.

"Where?"

"At that man over there."

As they walked, Willie stole a look back over his shoulder. A man Willie had never seen before was sitting on a red plastic milk crate near the curb. His matted, streaky gray hair hung like a ragged curtain over a dirty face. His shoes were torn. Rough hands lay upon his knees. One hand was palm up.

"What's the matter with him?" Willie asked.

Keeping her eyes straight ahead, Mrs. Markham said, "He's sick." She pulled Willie around. "Don't stare. It's rude." **Ⓐ**

"What kind of sick?"

Mrs. Markham searched for an answer. "He's unhappy," she said.

"What's he doing?"

"Come on, Willie; you know. He's begging."

"Did anyone give him anything?"

"I don't know. Now come on, don't look."

"Why don't you give him anything?"

Ⓐ **Read and Discuss** What have you learned so far about Mrs. Markham?

"We have nothing to spare."

When they got home, Mrs. Markham removed a white cardboard box from the refrigerator. It contained poundcake. Using her thumb as a measure, she carefully cut a half-inch-thick piece of cake and gave it to Willie on a clean plate. The plate lay on a plastic mat decorated by images of roses with diamondlike dewdrops. She also gave him a glass of milk and a folded napkin. **B**

Willie said, "Can I have a bigger piece of cake?"

Mrs. Markham picked up the cake box and ran a manicured pink fingernail along the nutrition information panel. "A half-inch piece is a portion, and a portion contains the following nutrients. Do you want to hear them?"

"No."

"It's on the box, so you can accept what it says. Scientists study people and then write these things. If you're smart enough, you could become a scientist. Like this." Mrs. Markham tapped the box. "It pays well."

Willie ate his cake and drank the milk. When he was done, he took care to wipe the crumbs off his face as well as to blot the milk moustache with the napkin.

His mother said, "Now go on and do your homework. You're in fifth grade. It's important." **C**

Willie gathered up his books that lay on the empty third chair. At the kitchen entrance he paused. "What *kind* of unhappiness does he have?"

"Who's that?"

"That man."

Mrs. Markham looked puzzled.

"The begging man. The one on the street."

"Could be anything," his mother said, vaguely. "A person can be unhappy for many reasons."

"Like what?"

"Willie . . ."

"Is it a doctor kind of sickness? A sickness you can cure?"

"I wish you wouldn't ask such questions."

"Why?"

"Questions that have no answers shouldn't be asked."

"Can I go out?"

"Homework first."

Willie turned to go.

"Money," Mrs. Markham suddenly said. "Money will cure a lot of unhappiness. That's why that man was begging. A salesperson once said to me, 'Maybe you can't buy happiness, but you can rent a lot of it.' You should remember that."

B **Literary Focus** **Symbolism** This is the first reference to the poundcake. What details seem important?

C **Read and Discuss** What is the author letting you know about Mrs. Markham and Willie?

A cave fish

623

The apartment had three rooms. The walls were painted mint green. Willie walked down the hallway to his room, which was at the front of the building. By climbing up on the windowsill and pressing against the glass, he could see the sidewalk five stories below. The man was still there.

It was almost five when he went to tell his mother he had finished his school assignments. She was not there. He found her in her bedroom, sleeping. Since she had begun working the night shift at a convenience store—two weeks now—she took naps in the late afternoon.

For a while Willie stood on the threshold,[1] hoping his mother would wake up. When she didn't, he went to the front room and looked down on the street again. The begging man had not moved.

Willie returned to his mother's room.

"I'm going out," he announced softly.

Willie waited a decent interval[2] for his mother to waken. When she did not, Willie made sure his keys were in his pocket. Then he left the apartment.

Standing just outside his door, he could keep his eyes on the man. It appeared as if he had still not moved. Willie wondered how anyone could go on without moving for so long in the chilly October air. Was staying in one place part of the man's sickness?

During the twenty minutes that Willie watched, no one who passed looked in the beggar's direction. Willie wondered if they even saw the man. Certainly no one put any money into his open hand.

A lady leading a dog by a leash went by. The dog strained in the direction of the man sitting on the crate. The dog's tail wagged. The lady pulled the dog away. "Heel!" she commanded.

The dog—tail between its legs—scampered to the lady's side. Even so, the dog twisted around to look back at the beggar.

Willie grinned. The dog had done exactly what he had done when his mother told him not to stare.

Pressing deep into his pocket, Willie found a nickel. It was warm and slippery. He wondered how much happiness you could rent for a nickel. **Ⓓ**

Squeezing the nickel between his fingers, Willie walked slowly toward the man. When he came before him, he stopped, suddenly nervous. The man, who appeared to be looking at the ground, did not move his eyes. He smelled bad.

"Here." Willie stretched forward and dropped the coin into the man's open right hand.

"Bless you," the man said hoarsely, as he folded his fingers over the coin. His eyes, like high beams on a car, flashed up at Willie, then dropped.

Willie waited for a moment, then went back up to his room. From his front room he looked down on the street. He thought he saw the coin in the man's hand but was not sure.

After supper Mrs. Markham got ready to go to work. She kissed Willie good night. Then, as she did every night, she said,

---

1. **threshold** (THRESH hohld): doorway; entrance.
2. **interval:** period of time between events.

Ⓓ [Read and Discuss] What is Willie about to do?

Analyzing Visuals Connecting to the Text
What scene and symbol in the story does this photograph show?

"If you have regular problems, call Mrs. Murphy downstairs. What's her number?"

"274–8676," Willie said.

"Extra bad problems, call Grandma."

"369–6754."

"Super-special problems, you can call me."

"962–6743."

"Emergency, the police."

"911."

"Don't let anyone in the door."

"I won't."

"No television past nine."

"I know."

"But you can read late."

"You're the one who's going to be late," Willie said.

"I'm leaving," Mrs. Markham said.

After she went, Willie stood for a long while in the hallway. The empty apartment felt like a cave that lay deep below the earth. That day in school Willie's teacher had told them about a kind of fish that lived in caves. These fish could not see. They had no eyes. The teacher had said it was living in the dark cave that made them like that. **E**

Before he went to bed, Willie took another look out the window. In the pool of light cast by the street lamp, Willie saw the man.

On Tuesday morning when Willie went to school, the man was gone. But when he came home from school with his mother, he was there again.

"*Please* don't look at him," his mother whispered with some urgency.

During his snack Willie said, "Why shouldn't I look?"

"What are you talking about?"

"That man. On the street. Begging." **F**

E **Literary Focus** Symbolism Think about the fish introduced by the author. In what ways is Willie's situation similar to that of an eyeless fish in a dark cave? Who else in the story might be compared to a fish that cannot see?

F Read and Discuss What does it say about Willie that he keeps thinking about the homeless man?

Vocabulary urgency (UR juhn see) *n*.: pressure; insistence.

"I told you. He's sick. It's better to act as if you never saw them. When people are that way, they don't wish to be looked at."

"Why not?"

Mrs. Markham thought for a while. "People are ashamed of being unhappy."

"Are you sure he's unhappy?"

"You don't have to ask if people are unhappy. They tell you all the time."

"Is that part of the sickness?"

"Oh, Willie, I don't know. It's just the way they are."

Willie contemplated the half-inch slice of cake his mother had just given him. He said, "Ever since Dad left, you've been unhappy. Are you ashamed?"

Mrs. Markham closed her eyes. "I wish you wouldn't ask that."

Willie said, "Are you?"

"Willie . . ."

"Think he might come back?"

"It's more than likely," Mrs. Markham said, but Willie wondered if that was what she really thought. He did not think so. "Do you think Dad is unhappy?"

"Where do you get such questions?"

"They're in my mind."

"There's much in the mind that need not be paid attention to."

"Fish that live in caves have no eyes."

"What are you talking about?"

"My teacher said it's all that darkness. The fish forget to see. So they lose their eyes."

"I doubt she said that."

"She did."

"Willie, you have too much imagination."

After his mother went to work, Willie gazed down onto the street. The man was there. Willie thought of going down, but he knew he was not supposed to leave the building when his mother worked at night. He decided to speak to the man tomorrow.

Next afternoon—Wednesday—Willie said to the man, "I don't have any money. Can I still talk to you?" **G**

The man's eyes focused on Willie. They were gray eyes with folds of dirty skin beneath them. He needed a shave.

"My mother said you were unhappy. Is that true?"

"Could be," the man said.

"What are you unhappy about?"

The man's eyes narrowed as he studied Willie intently. He said, "How come you want to know?"

Willie shrugged.

"I think you should go home, kid."

"I am home." Willie gestured toward the apartment. "I live right here. Fifth floor. Where do you live?"

"Around."

"*Are* you unhappy?" Willie persisted.

The man ran a tongue over his lips. His Adam's apple bobbed.

Willie said, "I'm trying to learn about unhappiness."

"Why?"

"I don't think I want to say."

"A man has the right to remain silent," the man said and closed his eyes.

Willie remained standing on the pavement for a while before walking back to his apartment. Once inside his own room, he

---

Vocabulary   **ashamed** (uh SHAYMD) *adj.*: embarrassed.

G **Reading Focus** Sequencing Explain the sequence of events that prompts Willie to talk to the man.

looked down from the window. The man was still there. At one moment Willie was certain he was looking at the apartment building and the floor on which Willie lived.

The next day—Thursday—after dropping a nickel in the man's palm, Willie said, "I've decided to tell you why I want to learn about unhappiness."

The man gave a grunt.

"See, I've never seen anyone look so unhappy as you do. So I figure you must know a lot about it."

The man took a deep breath. "Well, yeah, maybe."

Willie said, "And I need to find a cure for it."

"A *what*?"

"A cure for unhappiness."

The man pursed his lips and blew a silent whistle. Then he said, "Why?"

"My mother is unhappy."

"Why's that?"

"My dad left."

"How come?"

"I don't know. But she's unhappy all the time. So if I found a cure for unhappiness, it would be a good thing, wouldn't it?"

"I suppose."

Willie said, "Would you like some cake?"

"What kind?"

"I don't know. Cake."

"Depends on the cake."

On Friday Willie said to the man, "I found out what kind of cake it is." **H**

"Yeah?"

"Poundcake. But I don't know why it's

> "I've decided to tell you why I want to learn about unhappiness."

called that."

"Probably doesn't matter."

For a moment neither said anything. Then Willie said, "In school my teacher said there are fish that live in caves and the caves are dark, so the fish don't have eyes. What do you think? Do you believe that?"

"Sure."

"You do? How come?"

"Because you said so."

"You mean, just because someone *said* it you believe it?"

"Not someone. You."

Willie said, "But, well, maybe it *isn't* true."

The man grunted. "Hey, do you believe it?"

Willie nodded.

"Well, you're not just anyone. You got eyes. You see. You ain't no fish." **I**

"Oh."

"What's your name?"

"Willie."

"That's a boy's name. What's your grownup name?"

Willie thought for a moment. "William, I guess."

"And that means another thing."

"What?"

"I'll take some of that cake."

Willie smiled. "You will?"

"Just said it, didn't I?"

"I'll get it."

Willie ran to the apartment. He took the box from the refrigerator as well as a knife, then hurried back down to the street. "I'll

---

H [Read and Discuss] What is going on between Willie and the homeless man?

I [Literary Focus] Symbolism What does the homeless man mean here? In what ways is Willie "not a fish"?

What Do Fish Have to Do with Anything? **627**

cut you a piece," he said.

As the man looked on, Willie opened the box, then held his thumb against the cake to make sure the portion was the right size. With a poke of the knife he made a small mark for the proper width.

Just as he was about to cut, the man said, "Hold it!"

Willie looked up. "What?"

"What were you doing with your thumb there?"

"I was measuring the right size. The right portion. One portion is what a person is supposed to get."

"Where'd you learn that?"

"It says so on the box. You can see for yourself." He held out the box.

The man studied the box, then handed it back to Willie. "That's just lies," he said.

"How do you know?"

"William, how can a box say how much a person needs?"

"But it does. The scientists say so. They measured, so they know. Then they put it there."

"Lies," the man repeated.

Willie studied the man. His eyes seemed bleary.[3] "Then how much should I cut?" he asked.

The man said, "You have to look at me, then at the cake, and then you're going to have to decide for yourself." **J**

"Oh." Willie looked at the cake. The piece was about three inches wide. Willie looked up at the man. After a moment he cut the cake into two pieces, each an inch and a half wide. He gave one piece to the man and kept the other.

"Bless you," the man said, as he took the piece and laid it in his left hand. He began to break off pieces with his right hand and one by one put them into his mouth. Each piece was chewed thoughtfully. Willie watched him piece by piece. **K**

When the man was done, he dusted his hands of crumbs.

"Now I'll give you something," the man said.

"What?" Willie said, surprised.

---

3. **bleary** (BLIHR ee): blurred; misty; dim.

J **Literary Focus** **Symbolism** How does the author use the symbol of the cake to communicate a message? What is the message?

K **Read and Discuss** What does the interaction between Willie and the man tell you about them?

Analyzing Visuals

Connecting to the Text What might the gesture pictured here symbolize?

"The cure for unhappiness."

"You know it?" Willie asked, eyes wide.

The man nodded.

"What is it?"

"It's this: What a person needs is always more than they say."

Willie thought for a while. "Who's *they*?" he asked.

The man pointed to the cake box. "The people on the box," he said.

Willie thought for a moment; then he gave the man the other piece of cake.

The man took it, saying, "Good man," and then ate it. **Ⓛ**

The next day was Saturday. Willie did not go to school. All morning he kept looking down from his window for the man, but it was raining and he did not appear. Willie wondered where he was but could not imagine it.

Willie's mother woke about noon. Willie sat with her while she ate the breakfast he had made. "I found the cure for unhappiness," he announced.

"Did you?" his mother said. She was reading a memo from the convenience store's owner.

"It's, 'What a person needs is always more than they say.'"

His mother put her papers down. "That's nonsense. Where did you hear that?"

"That man."

"What man?"

"On the street. The one who was begging. You said he was unhappy. So I asked him."

"Willie, I told you I didn't want you to even look at that man."

"He's a nice man . . ."

"How do you know?"

"I've talked to him."

"When? How much?"

Willie shrank down. "I did, that's all."

"Willie, I forbid you to talk to him. Do you understand me? Do you? Answer me!"

"Yes," Willie said, but in his mind he decided he would talk to the man one more time. He needed to explain why he could not talk to him anymore.

On Sunday, however, the man was not there. Nor was he there on Monday.

"That man is gone," Willie said to his mother as they walked home from school.

"I saw. I'm not blind."

"Where do you think he went?"

"I couldn't care less. And you might as well know, I arranged for him to be gone."

Willie stopped short. "What do you mean?"

"I called the police. We don't need a nuisance like that around here. Pestering kids."

"He wasn't pestering me."

"Of course he was."

"How do you know?"

"Willie, I have eyes. I can see."

Willie stared at his mother. "No, you can't. You're a fish. You live in a cave."

"Willie, don't talk nonsense."

"My name isn't Willie. It's William." Turning, he walked back to the school playground. **Ⓜ**

Mrs. Markham watched him go. "Fish," she wondered to herself; "what do fish have to do with anything?" **Ⓝ**

Ⓛ [Read and Discuss] What did you learn here?

Ⓜ [Read and Discuss] What are Willie and his mother trying to say to each other?

Ⓝ [Literary Focus] **Symbolism** Who is the blind cave fish in the story? Explain.

Applying Your Skills

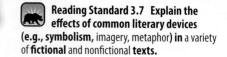
Reading Standard 3.7 Explain the effects of common literary devices (e.g., symbolism, imagery, metaphor) in a variety of fictional and nonfictional texts.

What Do Fish Have to Do with Anything?
Literary Response and Analysis

Reading Skills Focus
Quick Check

1. Why does Mrs. Markham refuse to give the homeless man money?
2. What happens to the man at the end?

Read with a Purpose

3. What does the story's title mean? Can you answer the question the title asks?

Reading Skills: Sequencing

4. Review your flowchart. What is your opinion of the story's ending? Were you surprised by it? Do you think it is a logical outcome of the sequence of events in the story? Below your flowchart, write a few sentences explaining your opinion.

> Willie and his mother see a homeless man.
>
> ↓
>
> [ ]
>
> My Opinion: _____

✔ Vocabulary Check

Answer the following questions:
5. What are you feeling when you speak with **urgency**?
6. If someone was **ashamed** of something, would he or she talk about it a lot? Why or why not?

Literary Skills Focus
Literary Analysis

7. **Analyze** Why do you think Willie wants to be called "William" at the end? What does this show about how his character has grown?
8. **Make Judgments** Mrs. Markham expresses several ideas about life in this story. Choose one statement below, and explain why you agree or disagree with it.
   - "Questions that have no answers shouldn't be asked."
   - "Money will cure a lot of unhappiness."
   - "People are ashamed of being unhappy."

Literary Skills: Symbolism

9. **Interpret** Why does Willie end up giving the man both pieces of cake? What might the cake stand for, or **symbolize**? Explain how the use of this symbol affects your understanding of the story.
10. **Interpret** Avi mentions the fish four times in the story. What might the fish **symbolize**? Imagine that Avi had not mentioned the fish at all. How would the story be different? What is the effect of the symbolism on the story?

Writing Skills Focus
Think as a Reader/Writer

Use It in Your Writing Write a plot outline for a story of your own. Include notes about where and how you will make references to a symbol in order to build the symbol's meaning.

COMPARING TEXTS
Wrap Up

Storm / The Mysterious Mr. Lincoln / What Do Fish Have to Do with Anything?

Writing Skills Focus
Write a Comparison-Contrast Essay

Choose *two* of the selections you've just read, and write an essay in which you compare how each writer uses literary devices—imagery, figurative language, symbolism—to support his message. You can organize your essay in one of these ways:

1. **Organize by selection.** In the first paragraph, describe one writer's use of literary devices. Also discuss how the literary devices support the author's purpose or message. In the second paragraph, do the same for the second selection.

2. **Organize by literary device and effect.** In the first paragraph, compare the two writers' use of literary devices. In the second paragraph, discuss how both writers use literary devices to strengthen and convey their messages.

In your conclusion, explain which writer you think uses literary devices more effectively.

Use the workshop on writing a Comparison-Contrast Essay, pages 450–458, for help with this assignment.

What Do You Think Now? What lessons did you learn from these three selections? How could these lessons help you achieve your dreams?

CHOICES

As you respond to the Choices, use these **Academic Vocabulary** words as appropriate: <u>contribute</u>, <u>distinct</u>, <u>perspective</u>, <u>uniform</u>.

REVIEW
Describe a Character

Use three <u>distinct</u> literary devices to bring a favorite fictional character or a real person to life. Use imagery and figurative language to describe the figure and a symbol to stand for something important about him or her.

CONNECT
Record a Learning Experience

TechFocus Some radio programs use a combination of interviews, narration, and music to tell real-life stories. With a partner, record a five- to ten-minute radio show about an interesting "learning experience" from your own or someone else's life. Play the recording for the class.

EXTEND
Write a Letter to the Author

Timed Writing Avi advises young writers: "Don't be satisfied with answers others give you. Don't assume that because everyone believes a thing, it is right *or* wrong. Reason things out for yourself." Write a letter to Avi explaining what you think of this <u>perspective</u>. Use examples from "What Do Fish Have to Do with Anything?" to support your opinion.

Learn It Online
There's more to these stories than meets the eye. Expand your view at:

go.hrw.com   H6-631   **Go**

Connecting and Clarifying Main Ideas

CONTENTS

Wanted: Douglass, Tubman, Truth (1997), American Collection #10, by Faith Ringgold.
Acrylic on canvas with fabric borders (77" × 82¼").

What Do **You** Think? How can individual people make a positive difference in the lives of others?

QuickWrite
Think about someone you believe is a hero—someone who has made a difference. Explain what this person did and how it changed others' lives.

Reading Standard 2.3 Connect and clarify main ideas by identifying their relationships to other sources and related topics.

All Aboard with Thomas Garrett / *from* Harriet Tubman: The Moses of Her People / *from* The Life of Harriet Tubman

Informational Text Focus

Identifying the Main idea The **topic** of a nonfiction text can usually be stated in just a word or two: *slavery, Underground Railroad*. The **main idea** is the most important point the writer makes *about* the topic: *Conductors on the Underground Railroad took great risks to help slaves gain their freedom.* To identify a text's main idea, look for important details and think about what these details tell you about the topic. Identify key passages, and look for a major idea that the writer repeats. Keep in mind that a text may contain more than one main idea.

Connecting and Clarifying Main Ideas When you read several sources about the same or similar topics, think about the relationships between the texts' main ideas. How are the main ideas similar? How are they different? Making connections between main ideas will help clarify the ideas. Think, too, about how a source and its main ideas are connected to related topics. Recognizing connections will expand your understanding of ideas and broaden your knowledge of the world.

Into Action If you read "A Glory over Everything," you already know about Harriet Tubman. You are about to read three more sources related to Tubman. Copy the chart of main ideas, on the next page. As you read, fill in the chart by adding evidence from the three sources. Look for more main ideas to include in the chart, adding as many boxes as you need. You don't have to fill in every box for each selection; some main ideas will apply to only one source.

Writing Skills Focus

Preparing for **Timed Writing** The following selections all deal with the same topic, but not in the same way. Pay attention to how the writers and the artist present the same facts. Consider their <u>perspectives</u> on the topic and their audience. Are their messages <u>uniform</u>, or does each work convey a <u>distinct</u> message?

Reader/Writer
Notebook
Use your **RWN** to complete the activities for these selections.

Vocabulary

prudent (PROO duhnt) *adj.:* wise; sensible. *The runaways stayed with Garrett until it was prudent for them to leave.*

hazardous (HAZ uhr duhs) *adj.:* dangerous; risky. *The runaways made the hazardous journey north.*

diligence (DIHL uh juhns) *n.:* steady effort. *Garrett's diligence helped people escape from slavery.*

jubilant (JOO buh luhnt) *adj.:* joyful. *Crowds of jubilant people celebrated the passage of the amendment.*

Language Coach

Related Words Each of the Vocabulary words above is part of a "family tree" of related words. *Jubilant*, for example, comes from the Latin root word *jubilare*, "to shout for joy." In a dictionary you can find the related words *jubilee, jubilation,* and *jubilance*. Make a dictionary search on the remaining Vocabulary words, and make a family tree for each word.

Learn It Online
Increase you word comprehension with Word Watch:

go.hrw.com   H6-633   **Go**

Connecting Main Ideas Across Sources

Main Ideas	Evidence and Support from Sources		
	"All Aboard with Thomas Garrett"	from Harriet Tubman: The Moses of Her People	from The Life of Harriet Tubman
Idea 1: It was important for free people to help those who were enslaved.	1. No runaway "was ever turned away from his door." 2.	1. "I was free, and they should be free. . . ." 2.	1. "Here, she and the fugitives were fed and clothed and sent on their way." 2.
Idea 2: People fleeing slavery were in constant danger.	1. "Slave catchers" searched the streets of Wilmington for runaways. 2.	1.	1. Runaways had to travel at night and hide during the day. 2.
Idea 3: Freeing people from slavery required hard work and sacrifice.			
Idea 4:			

Related topics: *The Frederick Douglass Series* by Jacob Lawrence; work of Quakers in antislavery movement; Virginia Hamilton's novel *House of Dies Drear* (about Underground Railroad).

Harriet Tubman.

Thomas Garrett.

All Aboard *with* Thomas Garrett

by Alice P. Miller

Read with a Purpose

Read this account to learn how one heroic man stood by his antislavery principles.

The elderly couple walked sedately down the stairs of the red brick house, every detail of their costumes proclaiming their respectability. The small lady was wearing an ankle-length gray gown, a snowy-white lawn kerchief, and a pleated gray silk bonnet, draped with a veil. The tall white-haired gentleman wore the wide-brimmed beaver hat and the long black waistcoat that was customary among Quakers.

When they reached the sidewalk, he assisted her into the four-wheeled barouche[1] that stood at the curb. Then he climbed into the barouche himself. The driver drove the horses away at a leisurely pace. Not until they were beyond the city limits did he allow the horses to prance along at a brisk pace across the few miles that separated Wilmington, Delaware, from the free state of Pennsylvania.

That tall white-haired gentleman was Thomas Garrett, a white man who had for many years been breaking the law by sheltering runaway slaves. And the little lady at his side was runaway slave Harriet Tubman,

---

1. **barouche** (buh ROOSH): type of horse-drawn carriage.

---

clad in clothes donated by his wife. On the preceding night Harriet had slept in a small room secreted behind one wall of Garrett's shoe store, a room that never remained unoccupied for very long. It was Harriet's first visit to Garrett, but she would be returning many times in the future. **A**

Runaway slaves remained with Garrett for one night or two or three until such time as Garrett considered it prudent to send them along to the next station on the Underground Railroad. He provided them with clothing and outfitted them with new shoes from his shoe store. He fed them hearty meals and dressed their wounds. He also forged passes for them so that any slave stopped by a slave catcher would have evidence that he or she was on a legitimate errand.

Some of the money he needed to cover the cost of his hospitality came out of his own pocket, but he was not a rich man. He could not have taken care of so many fugitives were it not for donations made by fellow abolitionists in the North as well as from supporters in foreign countries. There was never quite enough money, but no fugitive was ever turned

---

A **Read and Discuss** What is the author showing you by describing Harriet Tubman's and Thomas Garrett's actions?

Vocabulary **prudent** (PROO duhnt) *adj.*: wise; sensible.

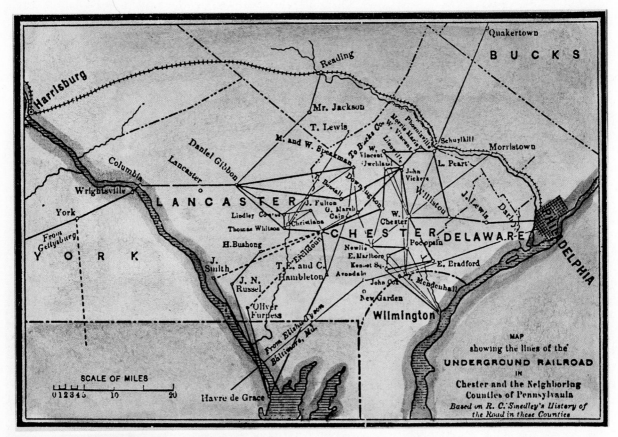

Map of the Underground Railroad. The Granger Collection, New York.

away from his door. He would have gone without food himself before he would have refused food to a hungry slave.

Garrett, who was born in Upper Darby, Pennsylvania, in 1789, had been helping runaway slaves ever since 1822, when he rescued a young black woman who was trying to escape from her master. At that time he vowed to devote the rest of his life to helping fugitives, and he remained faithful to that vow. **B**

Of all the stations on the Underground Railroad his was probably the most efficiently run and the one most frequently used. The fact that Wilmington was so close to Pennsylvania made it the most hazardous stop on the route. Slave catchers prowled the streets of Wilmington, on the alert for any indication that a black person might be a runaway. They kept a sharp eye on all roads leading north from Wilmington. **C**

For many years Garrett managed to get away with his illegal activities

B **Informational Focus** Connecting and Clarifying Main Ideas Recall that Tubman first escaped to freedom in 1849. What can you conclude from the fact that Garrett first began helping runaways in 1822?

C Read and Discuss What does Thomas Garrett's life's work tell us about him?

Vocabulary **hazardous** (HAZ uhr duhs) *adj.*: dangerous; risky.

Connecting to the Text What connections can you make between this image of enslaved people escaping through the Underground Railroad and the source you are reading?

On to Liberty (1867) by Theodor Kaufmann. Oil on canvas (91.4 cm × 142.2 cm).

because he was a clever man and knew ways to avoid detection by the slave catchers. Sometimes he disguised a slave, as he had done with Harriet. Sometimes he dressed a man in a woman's clothing or a woman in a man's clothing or showed a young person how to appear like one bent over with age. Another reason for his success was that he had many friends who admired what he was doing and who could be trusted to help him. They might, for example, conceal slaves under a wagonload of vegetables or in a secret compartment in a wagon.

The slave catchers were aware of what he was doing, but they had a hard time finding the kind of evidence that would stand up in court. At last, in 1848, he was sued by two Maryland slave owners who hoped to bring a stop to his activities by ruining him financially. **D**

The suit was brought into the federal circuit court of New Castle under a 1793 federal law that allowed slave owners to recover penalties from any person who harbored a runaway slave. The case was heard by Willard Hall, United States District Judge, and by Roger B. Taney, Chief Justice of the United States Supreme Court. Bringing in a verdict in favor of the slave owners, the jurors decided that the slave owners were entitled to $5,400 in fines.

Garrett didn't have anywhere near that much money, but he stood up and addressed the court and the spectators in these words:

"I have assisted fourteen hundred slaves in the past twenty-five years on their way to the North. I now consider this penalty imposed upon me as a license for the remainder of my life. I am now past sixty and have not a dollar to my name, but be that as it may, if anyone knows of a poor slave who needs shelter and a breakfast, send him to me, as I now publicly pledge myself to double my diligence and never neglect an opportunity to assist a slave to obtain freedom, so help me God!"

As he continued to speak for more than an hour, some of the spectators hissed while others cheered. When he finished, one juror leaped across the benches and pumped Garrett's hand. With tears in his eyes, he said, "I beg your forgiveness, Mr. Garrett." **E**

After the trial Garrett's furniture was auctioned off to help pay the heavy fine. But he managed to borrow money from friends and eventually repaid those loans, rebuilt his business, and became prosperous. Meanwhile he went on sheltering slaves for many more years. By the time President Lincoln issued the Emancipation Proclamation[2] in 1863, Garrett's records showed that he had sheltered more than 2,700 runaways. **F**

During those years he had many encounters with Harriet Tubman, as she kept returning to the South and coming back north with bands of slaves. Much of what we know about Harriet today is based on letters that he sent to her or wrote about her. A portion of one of those letters reads thus:

"I may begin by saying, living as I have in a slave State, and the laws being

---

2. **Emancipation Proclamation:** presidential order freeing slaves in states still at war with the Union.

D **Informational Focus** Connecting and Clarifying Main Ideas Considering the slaveholders' actions here and those described in "A Glory over Everything," what can you conclude about their determination to keep slaves from escaping?

E **Read and Discuss** How do things turn out in court for Garrett?

F **Informational Focus** Identifying the Main Idea What personal sacrifice does Garrett make because of his convictions?

Vocabulary **diligence** (DIHL uh juhns) *n.*: steady effort.

Analyzing Visuals

Connecting to the Text
How does this image of sheltering runaway slaves connect to this article?

than she did in the State of New York or Canada, for she said she ventured only where God sent her, and her faith in the Supreme Power truly was great." **G**

In April, 1870, the black people of Wilmington held a huge celebration upon the passage of the fifteenth amendment to the Constitution of the United States. That amendment provided that the right of citizens to vote should not be denied or abridged by the United States or by any state on account of race, color, or previous condition of servitude.[3]

Jubilant blacks drew Garrett through the streets in an open carriage on one side of which were inscribed the words "Our Moses." **H**

Read with a Purpose How did Thomas Garrett stand by his principles?

very severe where any proof could be made of anyone aiding slaves on their way to freedom, I have not felt at liberty to keep any written word of Harriet's labors as I otherwise could, and now would be glad to do; for in truth I never met with any person, of any color, who had more confidence in the voice of God, as spoken direct to her soul. . . . She felt no more fear of being arrested by her former master, or any other person, when in his immediate neighborhood,

---

3. **servitude** (SUR vuh tood): condition of being under another person's control.

G **Informational Focus** Connecting and Clarifying **Main Ideas** How is this description of Tubman consistent with the one in "A Glory over Everything"?

H **Read and Discuss** What does this celebration show you?

Vocabulary **jubilant** (JOO buh luhnt) *adj.*: joyful.

Applying Your Skills

Reading Standard 2.3 Connect and clarify main ideas by identifying their relationships to other sources and related topics.

All Aboard with Thomas Garrett
Standards Review

Informational Text and Vocabulary

1. Thomas Garrett helped people fleeing slavery in all of the following ways *except*

   A by giving them shoes to wear.

   B by hiding them in his store.

   C by feeding them meals.

   D by taking them to Canada.

2. Tubman and Garrett were both fearless conductors on the Underground Railroad. Which of the following **main ideas** can be used to identify them?

   A Moses is a name given to people who led enslaved people to freedom.

   B People of African descent led one another to safety.

   C Only people who had been held in slavery would dare to work on the Underground Railroad.

   D The courts in the North put Underground Railroad conductors in jail.

3. Which of the following statements does Garrett's court speech *best* support?

   A After his conviction, Garrett retired from the Underground Railroad.

   B Garrett admitted that he had been wrong to assist slaves.

   C The guilty verdict made Garrett even more determined to shelter runaways.

   D Garrett's powerful speech changed the verdict to "not guilty."

4. A *prudent* person is

   A sensible.

   B warlike.

   C modest.

   D generous.

5. A *hazardous* task is

   A easy.

   B complicated.

   C risky.

   D impossible.

6. *Diligence* is

   A severe penalty.

   B voting rights.

   C moral behavior.

   D steady effort.

Writing Skills Focus

Timed └Writing Connect the methods Tubman used to avoid capture as described in this article and in "A Glory over Everything." What main idea about the difficulty in escaping from slavery do both sources present? Identify a related topic, such as the life of a freed slave, and write a few sentences explaining its relationship to this main idea.

What Do **You Think Now?** How did Thomas Garrett's vow to help fugitives affect the lives of those who sought his help?

from *Harriet Tubman: The Moses of Her People*

by Sarah Bradford

Read with a Purpose
Read this account to learn why Harriet Tubman decided to guide other slaves to freedom.

Preparing to Read for this selection is on pages 633 and 634.

Build Background
During the Civil War, Harriet Tubman worked for the Union Army as a spy, scout, and nurse. She refused payment for her services because she wanted to set an example of self-sufficiency and independence. When she returned to her home in New York after the war, she found that she was about to lose her house because she couldn't pay for it. To help Tubman, the abolitionist Sarah Bradford wrote a biography of her in 1869; she revised it in 1886. Bradford turned over to Tubman the earnings from both editions. This part of Bradford's biography starts where Petry's "A Glory over Everything" ends.

After many long and weary days of travel, she[1] found that she had passed the magic line, which then divided the land of bondage from the land of freedom. But where were the lovely white ladies whom in her visions she had seen, who, with arms outstretched, welcomed her to their hearts and homes. All these visions proved deceitful: She was more alone than ever; but she had crossed the line; no one could take her now, and she would never call her man "Master" more.

"I looked at my hands;" she said, "to see if I was the same person now I was free. There was such a glory over everything, the sun came like gold through the trees and over the fields, and I felt like I was in heaven." **Ⓐ**

But then came the bitter drop in the cup of joy. She was alone, and her kindred were in slavery, and not one of them had the courage to dare what she had dared. Unless she made the effort to liberate them, she would never see them more, or even know their fate. **Ⓑ**

"I knew of a man;" she said, "who was sent to the State Prison for twenty-five years. All these years he was always thinking of his home, and counting by years, months, and days, the time till he should be free, and

---

1. **she:** Harriet Tubman.

Ⓐ **Informational Focus** Connecting and Clarifying **Main Ideas** This quotation was also used in "A Glory over Everything." What main idea does it suggest?

Ⓑ **Read and Discuss** How does Harriet view her new freedom? What realization then changes her mood? Why?

(above) 1911 photograph of Tubman. (left) *Step on Board* by Fern Cunningham. Boston, Massachusetts.

Analyzing Visuals   **Connecting to the Text** How does this statue of Tubman connect to a main idea in this source?

see his family and friends once more. The years roll on, the time of imprisonment is over, the man is free. He leaves the prison gates, he makes his way to his old home, but his old home is not there. The house in which he had dwelt in his childhood had been torn down, and a new one had been put up in its place; his family were gone, their very name was forgotten, there was no one to take him by the hand to welcome him back to life."

"So it was with me;" said Harriet; "I had crossed the line of which I had so long been dreaming. I was free; but there was no one there to welcome me to the land of freedom,

I was a stranger in a strange land, and my home after all was down in the old cabin quarter, with the old folks and my brothers and sisters. But to this solemn resolution I came: I was free, and they should be free also; I would make a home for them in the North, and, the Lord helping me, I would bring them all there. Oh, how I prayed then, lying all alone on the cold, damp ground. "Oh, dear Lord," I said, "I haven't got a friend but you. Come to my help, Lord, for I'm in trouble!"   **C**

Read with a Purpose
Why did Harriet Tubman decide to help other enslaved people escape?

C [Read and Discuss] How does Harriet's story of the jailed man connect to her decision to help free her relatives? What does this thought process show you about Harriet?

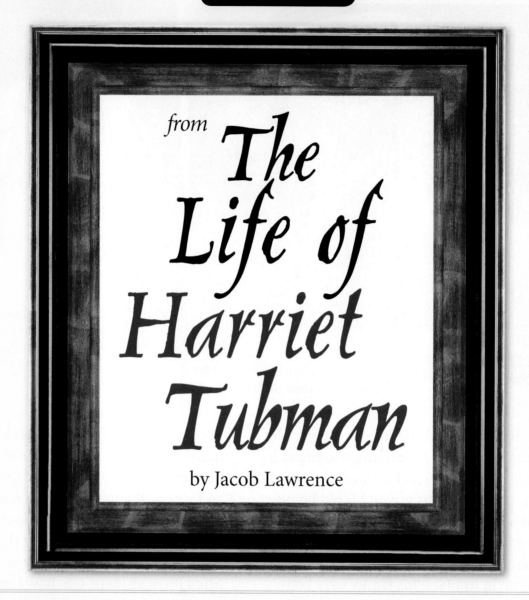

from
The Life of Harriet Tubman

by Jacob Lawrence

Read with a Purpose

As you look at these paintings and read the captions, notice how the text and the images work together to tell Harriet Tubman's story.

Preparing to Read for this selection is on pages 633 and 634.

Build Background

Jacob Lawrence (1917–2000) created *The Life of Harriet Tubman,* a series of thirty-one paintings, between 1939 and 1940. The series is a visual biography that depicts Tubman's work with the Underground Railroad and her service in the Civil War. The series is one of Lawrence's most famous works.

Lawrence wrote long captions to go with the paintings because at the time he created the series, most people knew little about Tubman's life. Much of the information in the captions comes from Sarah Bradford's biographies of Tubman.

Analyzing Visuals **Connecting to the Text** Who are the small figures? What effect does the artist achieve by making the people so small against an enormous sky? Which idea in the caption below is reflected in this painting?

The Life of Harriet Tubman (1939–1940), No. 15, by Jacob Lawrence.

In the North, Harriet Tubman worked hard. All her wages she laid away for the one purpose of liberating her people, and as soon as a sufficient amount was secured, she disappeared from her Northern home, and as mysteriously appeared one dark night at the door of one of the cabins on the plantation, where a group of trembling fugitives was waiting. Then she piloted them North, traveling by night, hiding by day, scaling the mountains, wading the rivers, threading the forests—she, carrying the babies, drugged with paregoric. So she went, nineteen times liberating over three hundred pieces of living, breathing "property." 🅐

🅐 **Read and Discuss** What do Tubman's actions show you about the Underground Railroad and her own character?

Analyzing Visuals

Connecting to the Text
Who are the figures in the painting? What is each group doing?

The Life of Harriet Tubman (1939–1940), No. 19, by Jacob Lawrence.

Such a terror did she become to the slaveholders that a reward of forty thousand dollars was offered for her head, she was so bold, daring, and elusive. **B**

B **Informational Focus** **Connecting and Clarifying Main Ideas** What main idea does this painting and its caption share with "All Aboard with Thomas Garrett"?

The Life of Harriet Tubman (1939–1940), No. 22, by Jacob Lawrence.

Harriet Tubman, after a very trying trip North in which she had hidden her cargo by day and had traveled by boat, wagon, and foot at night, reached Wilmington, where she met Thomas Garrett, a Quaker who operated an Underground Railroad station. Here, she and the fugitives were fed and clothed and sent on their way. **C**

C **Informational Focus** **Connecting and Clarifying Main Ideas** How does the painting below and its caption connect to ideas in "All Aboard with Thomas Garrett"?

Analyzing Visuals **Connecting to the Text** Notice the body language and expressions of Tubman and her fellow fugitives. How does the journey seem to have affected them?

© 2007 The Jacob and Gwendolyn Lawrence Foundation, Seattle/Artists Rights Society (ARS), New York.

The Life of Harriet Tubman (1939–1940), No. 20, by Jacob Lawrence.

In 1850, the Fugitive Slave Law was passed, which bound the people north of the Mason and Dixon Line to return to bondage any fugitives found in their territories—forcing Harriet Tubman to lead her escaped slaves into Canada. **D**

Read with a Purpose

How do the paintings and their captions tell the story of Harriet Tubman in a way that's different from the other sources?

Analyzing Visuals

Connecting to the Text
What feeling, which also describes Tubman's life in the North, do you get from this painting?

© 2007 The Jacob and Gwendolyn Lawrence Foundation, Seattle/ Artists Rights Society (ARS), New York.

D Read and Discuss How were Tubman's journeys north affected by laws concerning escaped slaves?

Applying Your Skills

All Aboard with Thomas Garrett / *from* Harriet Tubman: The Moses of Her People / *from* The Life of Harriet Tubman

Standards Review

Informational Text

1. Which **main idea** is presented in all three sources about Tubman?

   A Tubman dedicated herself to helping people escape from slavery.

   B Thomas Garrett spent most of his money sheltering runaways.

   C African Americans celebrated the passage of the Fifteenth Amendment.

   D A large reward was offered for Harriet Tubman's capture.

2. Which of the following statements is a **main idea** about Harriet Tubman in both "All Aboard with Thomas Garrett" and the excerpt from *Harriet Tubman: The Moses of Her People*?

   A Tubman was overcome by loneliness once she was free.

   B Thomas Garrett played an important role in helping Tubman gain her freedom.

   C Tubman believed that God would help her lead slaves to freedom.

   D Tubman feared being returned to a slave-holder.

3. Which of the following **main ideas** does the statement "I was free, and they should be free also" connect to?

   A Garrett gave runaways great sums of money.

   B Runaways often faced harsh conditions when they headed north.

   C Tubman would not rest until she had helped many more people escape from slavery.

   D Tubman feared being returned to a slave-holder.

4. The writers of the three sources would *most likely* agree that

   A runaways felt no obligation toward the people they left behind.

   B African Americans enjoyed a comfortable life as soon as they reached the North.

   C freeing people from slavery required great coordination between many people.

   D everyone Tubman met was eager to help her.

5. From the three sources, you can infer that all of the writers

   A were friendly with Harriet Tubman.

   B knew Thomas Garrett.

   C sympathized with the slaves seeking freedom.

   D grew up under harsh conditions.

Writing Skills Focus

Timed ⌐Writing Review the main-idea chart you made while reading these three sources. Use the chart to write a paragraph connecting the main ideas about Harriet Tubman and the Underground Railroad in these texts. Conclude by identifying two or three related topics and explaining their relationship to these main ideas.

What Do **You Think Now**

Based on Tubman's and Garrett's actions, what can you conclude about the value of an individual's efforts in fighting injustice?

Writing Workshop

Research Report

Write with a Purpose

Write a research report about a topic that interests you, and that supports your thesis with evidence from several sources. The **audience** for your report will include your classmates and your teacher. Your **purpose** is to share information about a subject you care about and that might interest your readers.

A Good Research Report

- narrowly focuses on a thesis, or main idea, supported by relevant details, facts, and explanations
- includes accurately documented information from several sources
- uses clear organization to present information
- ends with a detailed summary or by drawing an overall conclusion
- includes a bibliography

See page 658 for complete rubric.

Reader/Writer Notebook

Use your **RWN** to complete the activities for this workshop.

Think as a Reader/Writer

In this collection, you have learned about the techniques writers use in nonfiction. Some of the nonfiction texts were based on the authors' personal experiences. Others, such as the biographies, required research. Now it's time for you to research a topic and write a report that draws on information from several sources. Before you begin, take a few minutes to read this excerpt from an article on the California gold rush, written by Kathy Wilmore and published in *Junior Scholastic* magazine:

Thousands of Forty-Niners made the trek to California with the idea of striking it rich, then returning home to spend their wealth. But for every Forty-Niner whose labor paid off handsomely, countless others had to find other ways of making a living.

← The report opens with **background information,** followed immediately by the **thesis statement.**

Among those were thousands of Chinese. Word of "Gold Mountain"—the Chinese name for California—lit new hope among poverty-stricken peasants in China. In 1849, only 54 Chinese lived in California; by 1852, the number had risen to 14,000.

← **Facts** are used as **evidence** to develop and support the thesis.

Chinese miners faced the resentment of many white Forty-Niners who saw them as unfair competition…. Looking for less risky ways of earning a living, many Chinese turned to service work: cooking meals, toting heavy loads, and washing clothes. Miners happily plunked down money for such service.

← **Details** further support the thesis.

Think About the Professional Model

With a partner, discuss the following questions about the model:

1. Why might the author have placed the thesis at the very end of the first paragraph?
2. How does the organization of this excerpt affect its clarity?
3. Which piece of evidence most directly supports the thesis? Why?

Writing Skills 1.2 **Create multiple-paragraph expository compositions:** **a. Engage the interest of the reader and state a clear purpose. b. Develop the topic with supporting details** and precise verbs, nouns, and adjectives to paint a visual image in the eye of the reader. c. **Conclude with a detailed summary linked to the purpose of the composition. 2.3** Write research reports: **a.** Pose relevant questions with a scope narrow enough to be thoroughly covered. **b.** Support the main idea or ideas with facts, details, examples, and explanations from multiple authoritative sources (e.g. speakers, periodicals, online information searches). **c.** Include a bibliography.

Prewriting

Choose and Narrow a Topic

Begin by brainstorming broad subjects that interest you, such as sports, nature, animals, or art. The Idea Starters in the margin may help you brainstorm subjects. Then, narrow your focus to a manageable topic for your report by using an inverted triangle like those shown below.

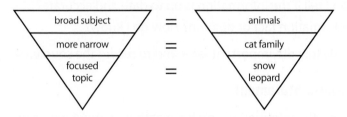

This process involves repeatedly narrowing the subject until you have a focused topic. A focused topic will enable you to write a strong **thesis statement,** or main idea statement, and to cover your topic in a single paper.

Once you have selected your subject, answer the following questions:

- What about your subject do you find especially interesting?
- What do you already know about the subject?
- Where can you find reliable information about the subject?
- Will your audience be interested in the subject? How can you interest them? What will they want to know?

Ask Questions

Make a list of things you already know about your topic. Put a question mark next to information that you will want to verify, or double-check, when doing your research. Then, make a list of questions you would like to answer about your topic. As you research your topic, carefully record the answers to your questions, along with information about the source. Always record the source information, and keep all of your information together where you can find it and use in your bibliography. For help in recording source information, see the Handbook section in the Resource Center.

Your Turn _____

Get Started Following the procedure above, do some brainstorming to choose a few subjects that interest you. Select one for your report, and begin listing questions about your topic.

Learn It Online
See an online example of a full research report at:

go.hrw.com   H6-651   **Go**

Peer Review

Learning to schedule your time on a research project is an important skill. Get together with a partner to work out realistic deadlines for each of these tasks:

- find information
- take notes from sources
- organize notes
- write first draft

To fill in dates, work backward from the final due date your teacher gives you to a good starting date for each task. Check in with your partner regularly to see if you're both keeping to your schedules.

Gather Facts and Evaluate Sources

Plan to use at least three **sources** of information for your report, such as books, magazines, encyclopedias, newspapers, and the Internet. Evaluate the reliability, or truthfulness and accuracy, of each source. Look for nonfiction sources created by people and organizations that are experts in that field. Make sure a Web site has been created by an authoritative source, not just someone interested in the subject. Ask yourself the following:

- Is the creator of the source an expert? How do I know?
- How can I tell if the information is up to date and accurate?
- Is the information fact or opinion? How do I know?

Use note cards to write important facts and to record the source.

Write Your Thesis Statement

Thinking about the information you have gathered about your topic, write a **thesis statement**. The thesis states your topic and your main idea about it. Here's an example from the Student Draft on page 655.

> topic: the microbe
>
> main idea: helpful in unlocking doors to science
>
> thesis: A bug known as a microbe has been the key to unlocking many doors to science.

Make a Plan

To make an informal plan, sort your notes into categories, and divide each category into subtopics. The informal plan below was completed for the Student Draft on pages 655–656.

Informal Plan for "Nature's Recyclers"

Category 1: Facts about microbes	Category 2: Effects of microbes	Category 3: Uses of Microbes
Subtopics: microscopic organisms, bacteria	Subtopics:	Subtopics: create fertilizer, clean oil spills

Your Turn _____

Gather Information and Write a Thesis Statement Using your questions as a guide, gather information about your topic. Write a **thesis statement** that expresses your **main idea** about the topic. Make an informal plan to organize the information. As you plan, keep your **audience** and **purpose** in mind and consider feedback as you revise your plan.

Think About Purpose and Audience

You have two **purposes** for writing a research report: to discover information for yourself and to share it with your **audience.** Consider what your audience will *need* to know as well as what they'll *want* to know.

Drafting

Paraphrase Information

Use the **Writer's Framework** at right to help write your draft. Most of your source information can be **paraphrased,** or rewritten in your own words, keeping the essential meaning the same. A paraphrase should be a straightforward summary of the original writer's information, usually shorter than the original text. It should not use any of the original author's style or exact wording. If you need to use exact words from a source, put them in quotation marks, and identify the source.

A Writer's Framework
Introduction:
• A hook to interest readers
• A clear thesis statement
Body:
• Paragraph 1—subtopic and supporting evidence
• Paragraph 2—subtopic and supporting evidence
(Add as many paragraphs/subtopics as needed to support your thesis—no fewer than three.)
Conclusion:
• Summary of main points
• Reflection on the topic

Cite Your Sources

At the end of your paper, provide a **Works Cited** list or **bibliography** that credits all the sources used in your research report. Include the following for each book you cite: author (last name first), title (underlined or in italics), place of publication, publisher, and date published.

Here is an example of how to cite a book in a Works Cited list:

Farrell, Jeanette. Invisible Allies: Microbes That Shape Our Lives.

New York: Farrar, Straus and Giroux, 2005.

Grammar Link Using Italics and Quotation Marks in Titles

When you write your Works Cited list, be sure to follow the rules for using italics and quotation marks with titles.

• **Use italics for the titles of major works.** Major works include books, encyclopedias, magazines, newspapers, databases, Web sites, movies, and television series.
  Example: *Encyclopaedia Britannica*
• **Use quotation marks for the titles of short works.** Short works include chapters of books; articles from encyclopedias, magazines, and newspapers; individual pages from Web sites; and individual television episodes.
  Example: "The California Gold Rush," *Junior Scholastic*

● Writing Tip

Copying exact words from a source and presenting them as your own is called **plagiarism.** Plagiarizing is the same as stealing another writer's work.

Your Turn _____

Write Your Draft Following the plan you've developed, write a draft of your research report. Remember to think about the following:

• What information is important enough to be quoted word for word? What should you paraphrase?
• What source information will you include in your Works Cited list?

Peer Review

Work with a partner to review your draft. Answer each question in the chart at the right to find out how your draft can be improved. Take notes on what you and your partner discuss so that you can refer to them when you revise your draft.

Evaluating and Revising

You may think your work is over once you've written your draft, but you've really just begun the writing process. Now it's time to review your draft carefully, looking for areas that can be improved. This chart will help you evaluate and revise your draft.

Research Report: Guidelines for Content and Organization

Evaluation Question	Tip	Revision Technique
1. Does your introduction contain a clear thesis statement?	**Underline** your thesis statement.	**Add** a thesis statement, including your topic and main point, if necessary.
2. Does each paragraph in the body of your paper develop one subtopic?	In the margin, **label** each paragraph with the subtopic it develops.	Where necessary, **rearrange** information into separate paragraphs that each discuss one subtopic. **Delete** unrelated ideas.
3. Does each body paragraph contain supporting evidence?	**Highlight** the facts, examples, and quotations that support each subtopic.	**Add** facts and examples from your notes, if necessary.
4. Does your conclusion summarize your findings?	**Put a check mark** next to your final statement or summary.	**Summarize** your research. **Revise** your final statement to clarify your point, if necessary.
5. Have you included at least three sources in your bibliography or Works Cited list?	**Number** the sources listed.	**Add** information from other sources, if needed. **Add** those sources to your list.
6. Does the Works Cited list use the correct format?	**Check** the format and punctuation by referring to page 653.	**Add** correct format and punctuation as needed.

Read this student's draft and the comments about it as a model for revising your own research report.

Nature's Recyclers
by Allison Hamilton, Hillsboro Middle School

A bug known as a microbe has been the key to unlocking many doors to science.

Microbe is the name for any of millions of microscopic organisms. Microbes are tiny cells. They are so small you can't see them without a microscope. Some of the most common are the ones called bacteria. Bacteria are some of the oldest life forms, and some of the simplest, not having the cell nucleus found in most other microbes.

Most bacteria are harmless to plants and animals. Only a small fraction cause disease. Some attack living things after they're dead. If it weren't for bacteria, animal wastes and dead organisms would build up. Bacteria also make the soil rich. . . .

← Allison clearly states her **thesis** in the first sentence.

← Allison **defines** an important term and provides background information.

← Allison narrows her **focus.**

MINI-LESSON ▶ **How to Create an Interesting Introduction**

Allison's draft begins with a clear thesis statement, but she could use a "hook" to make her introduction more interesting. Just as a fishhook dangling in the water catches a fish, an interesting hook catches the attention of a reader. A fact, an unusual image, a striking quote, an unexpected comparison, or a question addressed to the reader may be used as a hook. Allison might use a combination of techniques. She could begin with a question and lead to a memorable image.

Allison's Draft of Paragraph One

A bug known as a microbe has been the key to unlocking many doors to science.

Allison's Revision of Paragraph One

If there was an oil spill off the coast of Alaska, how would you clean it up? You may think this is a machine's job, but scientists have proven that a tiny bug, usually invisible to the naked eye, could take on the work of a one-hundred-ton piece of steel. A bug known as a microbe has been the key to unlocking many doors to science.

● Writing Tip

Organize ideas around comparisons to make facts interesting and vivid to your readers. Imagine starting out with a fact like this: "If you think public restrooms are the favorite gathering places for germs, think again: The typical desk of an office worker holds an astounding population of ten million germs." To clarify, you add a comparison: "That's about four hundred times more germs than a toilet in a public restroom!"

Your Turn _____

Create a Hook Try one of these ways of "hooking" your audience:
- State a surprising fact.
- Open with a question.
- Begin with a memorable quote.
- Create an image for the reader.

. . . They take nitrogen gas from the air and convert it to a form that green plants use for growth. Bacteria create fertilizer, too. They break down compost made of soil and dead plants.

Scientists have discovered how to use microbes to clean up oil spills. The scientists found a type of bacteria that feeds on oil and breaks it down into hydrogen, carbon, and oxygen. Microbial decomposition of petroleum by hydrocarbon-oxidizing bacteria and fungi is of considerable ecological importance.

The microbe is very important to us. I guess you could look at it as nature's recycler. Life as we know it would not exist without these powerful bugs. Scientists have explored only a fraction of these amazing creatures' potential. Discovering the benefits and uses of microbes is an important step into the future.

Allison's report is **organized** effectively and clearly. Each paragraph discusses a new subtopic and provides supporting **evidence.**

The conclusion includes a **summary** of Allison's findings.

MINI-LESSON ▸ How to Avoid Plagiarism

Allison has used the exact words from a source and has forgotten to use quotation marks. She can either add quotation marks and keep the exact words, or she can paraphrase the information in her own words and leave out quotation marks.

Allison's Draft of Paragraph Four, Sentence Three

Microbial decomposition of petroleum by hydrocarbon-oxidizing bacteria and fungi is of considerable ecological importance.

Allison decided the language of the original was too technical for her audience, so she paraphrased the information to make it easier to understand and ended with a shorter direct quotation from her authoritative source.

Allison's Revision of Paragraph Four, Sentence Three

~~Microbial decomposition of petroleum by hydrocarbon-oxidizing bacte~~

According to the Encyclopaedia Britannica, using microbes to decompose oil

~~ria and fungi~~ "is of considerable ecological importance."

Your Turn _____

Check for Plagiarism Review your draft to make sure you haven't presented a source's ideas or exact words as your own. Look for sentences that don't sound like your writing. Then, insert quotation marks around exact quotes. Giving proper credit to your sources helps you avoid plagiarism, and it also lends credibility to your report.

Proofreading and Publishing

Proofreading

Now that you have evaluated and revised your research report, it is time to give it one last cleanup and prepare it for publication. Edit your report carefully, correcting any errors in spelling, punctuation, or sentence structure.

> ### Grammar Link Varying Sentence Structure
>
> Varying your sentence structure will make your report easier and more interesting to read. Analyze the sentences in your draft. Have you used mostly simple sentences?
>
> When she proofread her paper, Allison combined two simple sentences into a compound sentence by adding a comma and the coordinating conjunction *and*.
>
> Most bacteria are harmless to plants and animals. Ønly a small fraction
> ,and
> cause disease.
>
> Allison created a complex sentence by using a subordinating conjunction to more clearly show the relationship between two ideas.
>
> Bacteria create fertilizer, too. *Because* They break down compost made of
> soil and dead plants.

Publishing

It is time to share your report with a wider audience. Here are some suggestions for sharing your report:

- If you have written about a historical event, e-mail a copy of your report to a friend or relative who is a history buff.
- Have a "discovery day" in class. You and your classmates can form into small groups and share your research.

Reflect on the Process
In your **RWN**, write a short response to each of the following questions to reflect on your writing process:

1. Where did you find the best information about your topic? Are there some types of sources that you will avoid in the future? Why?
2. What part of your report do you think is the strongest? What makes it strong?
3. What is the most surprising fact you learned?

● Proofreading Tip
If you have used terms in your report that are not part of your everyday vocabulary, be sure to double-check the spelling in a dictionary. Ask a peer to read your draft and circle any terms that might need to be defined for your audience.

● Proofreading Tip
Review the overall look of your document. Make sure to use appropriate formatting for margins, tabs, spacing, and so on. Use word processing skills to create a document that is easy to read and pleasing to the eye.

Your Turn
Proofread and Publish
Proofread your report, paying particular attention to sentence structure. If your report contains mostly short, simple sentences, try to vary the sentence structure by combining some of the sentences. Publish your report to share your research findings.

Scoring Rubric

You can use the rubric below to evaluate your research report.

	Research Report	Organization and Focus	Sentence Structure	Conventions
4	• Provides a *thoroughly developed* thesis that is appropriately narrow in focus. • Has a clearly stated main idea, *fully supported* with facts, details, and examples from authoritative sources. • Demonstrates *advanced ability* to locate and use information in print and electronic texts.	• *Clearly* addresses all of the writing tasks. • Demonstrates a *clear* understanding of purpose and audience. • Maintains a *consistent* point of view and *smooth* transitions. • Includes a complete and *well-formatted* bibliography. • Uses *consistently appropriate* formatting (margins, tabs, spacing, etc.).	• Includes sentence *variety*.	• Contains *few, if any,* errors in the conventions of the English language (grammar, punctuation, capitalization, spelling). These errors do **not** interfere with the reader's understanding of the writing.
3	• Provides an *adequately developed* thesis that is *appropriately* narrow in focus. • Has a *relatively clear* main idea, *mostly supported* with facts, details, and examples from authoritative sources. • Demonstrates *good ability* to locate and use information in print and electronic texts.	• Addresses *most* of the writing task. • Demonstrates a *general* understanding of purpose and audience. • Maintains a *mostly consistent* point of view and *usually smooth* transitions. • Includes a *mostly complete* and *adequately formatted bibliography*. • Uses mostly *appropriate* formatting (margins, tabs, spacing, etc.).	• Includes *some* sentence *variety*.	• Contains *some errors* in the conventions of the English language (grammar, punctuation, capitalization, spelling). These errors do **not** interfere with the reader's understanding of the writing.
2	• Provides a *minimally developed* thesis that is *not sufficiently* narrow in focus. • Has an unclear main idea, *minimally supported* with facts, details, and examples from authoritative sources. • Shows *minimal* success in attempting to locate and use information in print and electronic texts.	• Addresses *some* of the writing task. • Demonstrates *little* understanding of purpose and audience. • Maintains an *inconsistent* point of view and *awkward* transitions. • Includes an *incomplete* and *inconsistently formatted* bibliography. • Uses *inconsistent* formatting.	• Includes *little* sentence variety.	• Contains *several errors* in the conventions of the English language (grammar, punctuation, capitalization, spelling). These errors **may** interfere with the reader's understanding of the writing.
1	• *Lacks* a thesis and focus. • Has *no* main idea and *doesn't* provide facts, details, and examples from authoritative sources. • Makes *no* attempt to locate or use information in print and electronic texts.	• Addresses *only one* part of the writing task. • Demonstrates *no* understanding of purpose and audience. • *Lacks* a point of view and transitions. • *Lacks* a bibliography. • Uses *no* formatting.	• Includes *no* sentence variety.	• Contains *serious errors* in the conventions of the English language (grammar, punctuation, capitalization, spelling). These errors interfere with the reader's understanding of the writing.

Preparing for Timed ⏲ Writing

Expository Writing: Informative Essay

Writing Standard 2.2 **Write expository compositions** (e.g., description, explanation, comparison and contrast, problem and solution): **a. State the thesis or purpose. b. Explain the situation. c. Follow an organizational pattern appropriate to the type of composition. d. Offer persuasive evidence to validate arguments and conclusions as needed.**

When responding to a prompt for an on-demand informative essay, use the models you have read, what you've learned from writing your research report, the rubric on page 658, and the steps below.

Writing Prompt

Think of an important historical figure that you have studied. Write an informative essay for your school paper in which you provide factual information about this person. Be sure to organize your ideas clearly and present the information without revealing your own opinion.

Study the Prompt

Read the prompt carefully, and identify all parts of your task. Your **thesis** will be about a historical figure you've studied at school or on your own. Make sure you choose a subject whom you know enough about and can explain with facts and details. Remember that your **purpose** is to **inform** your readers about your subject.

Tip: Spend about five minutes studying the prompt.

Plan Your Response

Thesis Focus your thesis by repeatedly narrowing it from a broad subject to a more specific subject. **Ask:** *What historical figure have I studied recently, and what factual information do I know about the person?* Your answers will help focus your thesis.

Support After focusing your thesis, quickly write down as many details, facts, and examples as you can think of to support the thesis.

Organization Decide how to organize your information so it is clear to your readers.

Tip: Spend about ten minutes planning your response.

Respond to the Prompt

You have your thesis and support, so go ahead and start writing. Look for your most fascinating **detail, fact,** or **example,** and try to work it into your introduction, if possible. Don't worry about getting your introduction perfect the first time. If necessary, you can come back to it later to make it more focused and interesting.

Tip: Spend about twenty minutes writing your response.

Improve Your Response

Revising Re-read the prompt, and make sure your written response addresses the key aspects. Have you provided factual information about a historical figure? Have you organized your ideas clearly? Is your response free of personal opinion and bias? Have you supported your conclusions with evidence that is factual and persuasive?

Proofreading Take a few minutes to proofread your response and correct any errors in grammar, spelling, punctuation, and capitalization. Make sure your edits are neat and that your paper is legible.

Checking Your Final Copy Before you turn in your essay, read it one more time to catch any errors you may have missed and to make any finishing touches. A final read is worthwhile to make sure you're presenting your best writing.

Tip: Save five or ten minutes to read and improve your draft.

Listening & Speaking Workshop

Giving an Informative Presentation

Speak with a Purpose

Adapt your research report as an oral presentation. Practice your presentation, and then share it with your class.

Think as a Reader/Writer Researchers sometimes present their findings in a formal presentation or speech, in addition to sharing the information in a written report. As in your written report, you'll want to present a clear thesis and support the thesis by sharing the salient, or most important, points of your research. Here is your chance to share your research findings through an informative presentation.

Adapt Your Report

Even the most interesting information can sound dull if a speaker reads it word for word. To turn your research report into an oral presentation, carefully plan your **content.**

Choose Carefully

You may not want to present exactly the same points in your oral presentation that you used in your written report. Time considerations may limit the number of ideas and explanations you can present. To choose the content for your presentation, follow these suggestions.

- **Narrow your focus.** Limiting the scope of your topic to the most relevant points will ensure that the issues raised can be thoroughly answered. Keep your audience in mind as you narrow down your questions—what aspects of the topic will they find most interesting or surprising?
- **Remember your purpose.** Your **purpose** is to inform your listeners about your topic. Your **point of view** should be objective; that is, you should not appear to favor one side of an issue. If your research revealed varied opinions about your subject, share them with your audience.
- **Plan your support.** Look at the plan you created for your report. Identify the information you will use to answer the research questions you have chosen. This information should provide detailed evidence that includes facts, details, examples, and explanations from several sources.

Make Note Cards

Create a separate note card for each research question that you'll address in your presentation. On each note card, write words or phrases from your research notes, or written report that will help you remember the main ideas you want to share with your audience.

🔵 Speaking Tip

If you choose to use visual displays or technology, practice this part of your speech as well. Use appropriate technology, and be sure you can hold and point to displays easily. Have everything ready to go so that you will not fumble around during your presentation trying to get a piece of equipment to work.

Reader/Writer Notebook

Use your **RWN** to complete the activities for this workshop.

Speaking Standard 1.1 Relate the speaker's verbal communication (e.g., word choice, pitch, feeling, tone) to the nonverbal message (e.g. posture, gesture). **1.5** Emphasize salient points to assist the listener in following the main ideas and concepts. **1.6** Support opinions with detailed evidence and with visual or media displays that use appropriate technology. **2.2** Deliver informative presentations: a. Pose relevant questions sufficiently limited in scope to be completely and thoroughly answered. b. Develop the topic with facts, details, examples, and explanations from multiple authoritative sources, (e.g., speakers, periodicals, online information).

Deliver Your Research Presentation

Once you know *what* you will say, you need to practice *how* you will say it. Follow these suggestions.

Use Effective Verbal Strategies

Practice your speech out loud. Because the occasion for giving your speech is fairly formal, use **formal English.** Avoid using slang or clichés. Consider your **volume** and **rate,** speaking loudly and slowly. Everyone in your audience—including people at the back of the room—should be able to hear and understand you.

Practice using your voice to add meaning to your ideas. Slow down your rate of speech or change the **modulation** (pitch) of your voice to emphasize an important point. Make sure your **tone** of voice reflects a neutral **point of view.**

Use Effective Nonverbal Elements

Match your gestures and facial expressions to what you say. Raising your voice while pointing a finger, for example, can cue your audience that you are making an important point.

Practice making eye contact. As you rehearse your speech, make eye contact with a practice audience of friends, or glance from one object in the room to another if you practice alone.

Consider Using a Visual or Media Display

Maps, charts, graphs, slide shows, and video segments can be very effective in helping emphasize important ideas in your speech. The design of any display should be clear and direct. Use the display to support the ideas you explain in your speech. Do not overuse visual displays; include only items that clearly support the important points, the main idea, or the purpose of the speech. Add cues to your note cards to remind you when to use supporting visuals or displays during your speech.

A Good Oral Presentation of Research

- includes a clear thesis statement
- organizes, presents, and emphasizes salient points to assist the audience in following the main ideas and concepts.
- adequately supports every main idea with a variety of evidence from different sources
- shows that the speaker fully understands the topic
- effectively communicates ideas both verbally and nonverbally

Listening Tip

It is natural to focus on verbal messages and forget the importance of nonverbal communication when listening to an informative presentation. After all, you're there to pick up information, not to notice the speaker. Actually, it is quite important to pay attention to the speaker's nonverbal cues as well. The speaker may pause, raise the tone of his or her voice, use varied facial expressions, or gesture to emphasize major points.

 Learn It Online
A media display can bring your report to life.
Take a look at *MediaScope* on:

| go.hrw.com | H6-661 | Go |

Listening and Speaking Workshop **661**

Literary Skills Review

Biography and Autobiography   **Directions:** Read the following two selections. Then, answer each question that follows.

John Brown (1800–1859) was an abolitionist, someone working to end slavery. In this selection from a biography of John Brown, Gwen Everett writes from the point of view of Brown's daughter Annie. Annie recalls her father's fateful raid on a federal arsenal in Harpers Ferry, Virginia, in 1859. He was searching for weapons.

from John Brown: One Man Against Slavery by **Gwen Everett**

We listened carefully to Father's reasons for wanting to end slavery.

None of us questioned his sincerity, for we knew he believed God created everyone equal, regardless of skin color. He taught us as his father had taught him: To own another person as property—like furniture or cattle—is a sin. When Father was twelve years old, he witnessed the cruel treatment of black men, women, and children held in bondage and he vowed, then and there, that one day he would put an end to the inhumanity.

"I once considered starting a school where free blacks could learn to read and write, since laws in the South forbid their education," he told us. "And, when we moved to North Elba, New York, we proved that black and white people could live together in peace and brotherhood."

"One person—one family—can make a difference," he said firmly. "Slavery won't end by itself. It is up to us to fight it."

Father called us by name: Mary, John, Jason, Owen, and Annie (me). He asked us to say a prayer and swear an oath that we, too, would work to end slavery forever. Then he told us his plan.

He would lead a small group of experienced fighting men into a state that allowed slavery. They would hide in the mountains and valleys during daylight. And, under the cover of night, members of his "liberation army" would sneak onto nearby plantations and help the slaves escape.

Freed slaves who wished to join Father's army would learn how to use rifles and pikes—spear-shaped weapons. Then, plantation by plantation, Father's liberation army would move deeper south—growing larger and stronger—eventually freeing all the slaves.

Father's idea sounded so simple. Yet my brothers and I knew this was a dangerous idea. It was illegal for black people to handle firearms and for whites to show them how. It was also against the law to steal someone else's property; and, in effect, Father was doing this by encouraging slaves to leave their masters.

The fateful night of Sunday, October 16, 1859, Father and eighteen of his men marched into Harpers Ferry. They succeeded in seizing the arsenal and several buildings without firing a single shot. By morning the townspeople discovered the raiders and began to fight back. Then a company of marines led by Lieutenant Colonel Robert E. Lee arrived to reinforce the local troops.

The fighting lasted almost two days. When it was over, Father was wounded and four townspeople and ten of Father's men were dead. Newspapers across the country reported every detail of the trial, which was held during the last two weeks of October in Charles Town, Virginia. On October 31, the jury took only forty-five minutes to reach its decision. They found Father guilty of treason against the Commonwealth of Virginia, conspiring with slaves to rebel, and murder.

On December 1, my mother visited him in jail, where they talked and prayed together for several hours. I wished I could have been there to tell Father how courageous I thought he was.

He was executed the next morning.

Father's raid did not end slavery. But historians said that it was one of the most important events leading to the Civil War, which began in April 1861. The war destroyed slavery forever in our country, but it also took 619,000 lives and ruined millions of dollars' worth of property. My father must have known this would come to pass, for the day he was hanged, he wrote: "I, John Brown, am now quite certain that the crimes of this guilty land will never be purged away but with Blood."

Years after Father's death, I still had sleepless nights. Sometimes I recalled our conversations. Other times I found comfort in the verse of a song that Union soldiers sang about Father when they marched into battle.

> His sacrifice we share! Our sword
>   will victory crown!
> For freedom and the right remember
>   old John Brown!
> His soul is marching on.

Yes indeed, I think to myself, one man against slavery did make a difference.

In 1850, Congress passed the Fugitive Slave Law. This law required federal officials to arrest people fleeing slavery and return them to their "owners." Here, Harriet Tubman comes to the aid of a captured runaway who is in danger of being returned to slavery.

from Harriet Tubman: Conductor on the Underground Railroad
by **Ann Petry**

On April 27, 1860, [Harriet Tubman] was in Troy, New York. She had spent the night there and was going on to Boston to attend an antislavery meeting. That morning she was on her way to the railroad station. She walked along the street slowly. She never bothered to find out when a train was due; she simply sat in the station and waited until a train came which was going in the direction she desired.

It was cold in Troy even though it was the spring of the year. A northeast wind kept blowing the ruffle on her bonnet away from her face. She thought of Maryland and how green the trees would be. Here they were only lightly touched with green, not yet in full leaf. Suddenly she longed for a sight of the Eastern Shore with its coves and creeks, thought of the years that had elapsed since she first ran away from there.

She stopped walking to watch a crowd of people in front of the courthouse, a pushing, shoving, shouting crowd. She wondered what had happened. A fight? An accident? She went nearer, listened to the loud excited voices. "He got away." "He didn't." "They've got him handcuffed." Then there was an eruptive movement, people pushing forward, other people pushing back.

Harriet started working her way through the crowd, elbowing a man, nudging a woman. Now and then she asked a question. She learned that a runaway slave named Charles Nalle had been arrested and was being taken inside the courthouse to be tried.

When she finally got close enough to see the runaway's face, a handsome frightened face, his guards had forced him up the courthouse steps. They were trying to get through the door but people blocked the way.

She knew a kind of fury against the system, against the men who would force this man back into slavery when they themselves were free. The Lord did not intend that people should be slaves, she thought. Then without even thinking, she went up the steps, forced her way through the crowd, until she stood next to Nalle.

There was a small boy standing near her, mouth open, eyes wide with curiosity. She grabbed him by the collar and whispered to him fiercely, "You go out in the street and holler 'Fire, fire' as loud as you can."

The crowd kept increasing and she gave a nod of satisfaction. That little boy must have got out there in the street and must still be hollering that there's a fire. She bent over, making her shoulders droop, bending her back in the posture of an old woman. She pulled her sunbonnet way down, so that it shadowed her face. Just in time, too. One of the policemen said, "Old woman, you'll have to get out of here. You're liable to get knocked down when we take him through the door."

Harriet moved away from Nalle, mumbling to herself. She heard church bells ringing somewhere in the distance, and more and more people came running. The entire street was blocked. She edged back toward Nalle. Suddenly she shouted, "Don't let them take him! Don't let them take him!"

She attacked the nearest policeman so suddenly that she knocked him down. She wanted to laugh at the look of surprise on his face when he realized that the mumbling old woman who had stood so close to him had suddenly turned into a creature of vigor and violence. Grabbing Nalle by the arm, she pulled him along with her, forcing her way down the steps, ignoring the blows she received, not really feeling them, taking pleasure in the fact that in all these months of inactivity she had lost none of her strength.

When they reached the street, they were both knocked down. Harriet snatched off her bonnet and tied it on Nalle's head. When they stood up, it was impossible to pick him out of the crowd. People in the street cleared a path for them, helped hold back the police. As they turned off the main street, they met a man driving a horse and wagon. He reined in the horse. "What goes on here?" he asked.

Harriet, out of breath, hastily explained the situation. The man got out of the wagon. "Here," he said, "use my horse and wagon. I don't care if I ever get it back just so that man gets to safety."

Nalle was rapidly driven to Schenectady and from there he went on to the West—and safety.

Literary Skills Review

Reading Standard 3.5 Identify the speaker and recognize the difference between first- and third-person narration (e.g., autobiography compared with biography).

1. The account called *John Brown: One Man Against Slavery* was written

   A in the third person.

   B in the first person.

   C by Harriet Tubman.

   D by John Brown himself.

2. With which of the following statements would both John Brown and Harriet Tubman be *most* likely to agree?

   A One person fighting against slavery can make a difference.

   B The Fugitive Slave Law was fair and just.

   C Slavery could be ended without violence.

   D People should not involve family members in attempts to end slavery.

3. Which of the following sentences is an example of first-person narration?

   A "Harriet started working her way through the crowd…."

   B "Years after Father's death, I still had sleepless nights."

   C "She knew a kind of fury against the system…."

   D "People in the street cleared a path for them…."

4. *Harriet Tubman: Conductor on the Underground Railroad* is

   A a biography.

   B an autobiography.

   C an essay.

   D a short story.

5. Which of these titles seems *most* likely to be the title of an autobiography?

   A *The Civil War: 1861–1865*

   B *How I Gained My Freedom*

   C *Work Songs and Field Hollers*

   D *The History of the Underground Railroad*

Timed Writing

6. In one or two sentences, explain the difference between the speakers and the types of narration used in Ann Petry's account and Gwen Everett's account.

Informational Skills Review

Connecting and Clarifying Main Ideas **Directions:** Read the following passages. Then, answer each question that follows.

Pet Heroes

We got Max from a group that traps wild kittens and tames them. When Max came to us, he was scrawny and little. Now he's a broad-shouldered, sun-yellow cat, the biggest cat in the 'hood. Max is my hero because he's a gentle giant with a soft meow. Yet he's kept some of his wild ways. He runs from everybody except me and my parents. He insists on his freedom to roam outside, especially on moon-lit nights. He won't eat cat food unless he's really, really hungry. He prefers the mice and rats he catches on his own. Max knows we don't want him to catch birds, so he just watches them. He's kind to other cats—as long as they show him respect. He hates being pounced on. He loves curling up next to the sweet-smell-ing lavender plants in our yard, jumping from high places, cuddling at night, and getting stroked and scratched while giv-ing me a cat massage with his big paws. I used to worry when he took off for a few days, but he always comes back. Max is my golden boy. He has a little voice but a big heart.

—Lynn

Rita is a small, shaggy, sandy-brown fluff ball. She's what some people call a mix—some poodle, some terrier, and a bit of something else. Rita is my hero because she's my hearing-ear dog. A woman from a place that trains dogs for deaf people found Rita in an animal shelter. Rita had been there for weeks, and nobody had claimed her. She went through five months of training. Then I got lucky. I was chosen to be the one who got to take her home.

I get along well by using American Sign Language, but having Rita tell me when she hears sounds like the ringing of an alarm clock or a telephone makes me feel even more independent. I love Rita. She is my special friend.

—Alex and Rita

Before I got Mopsy, I didn't know a bunny could be so much fun. Mopsy likes to play jokes on our cat. She creeps up behind him and nibbles his tail. She follows me around like a hop-ping shadow. Sometimes, to get attention, she jumps straight up in the air. Then, when she gets tired, she flops down and

Informational Skills Review

Reading Standard 2.3 Connect and clarify main ideas by identifying their relationships to other sources and related topics.

takes a power nap. Mopsy loves to play, and she's never mean. My mom says that Mopsy must have learned her playful ways from her mother, who was a classroom rabbit.

Once a week we take Mopsy to visit my great-grandfather at his nursing home. He and his friends love to see her. Mopsy gets to sit on their laps and on their beds. She is quiet and never bites. That's why she's my hero.

—Michael

1. Which title fits all three sources?
   A "Giving Humans a Helping Hand"
   B "My Pet Is My Hero"
   C "Courageous Critters"
   D "Keeping Animals Safe"

2. Which of the following main ideas is found in all three sources?
   A To be considered a hero, an animal must show great courage.
   B Animals make better use of their time than humans do.
   C Owning a pet can be very rewarding.
   D People should spend more time with their pets.

3. All of the following titles describe articles that *most likely* deal with topics related to these sources *except*
   A "Tips on Caring for Your Dog."
   B "Can Pets Make People Happy?"
   C "My Iguana Is a Good Friend."
   D "When Rover Made My Day."

4. Which of the following statements about pets is *not* a fact?
   A Cats make better pets than dogs.
   B Dogs can be trained to help deaf people.
   C Some cats like to hunt for their own food.
   D Mopsy visits a nursing home every week.

Timed Writing

5. What main idea about pets serving as friends is expressed in all three sources? Explain the idea in a few sentences. Then, identify one or two related topics, and write a sentence or two explaining their relationship to these sources and this main idea.

Vocabulary Skills Review

Reading Standard 1.4 Monitor expository text for unknown words or words with novel meanings by using word, sentence, and paragraph clues to determine meaning.

Context Clues **Directions:** Use **context clues** to help you determine what the italicized words mean. Then, choose the best answer.

1. In "Brother," Maya Angelou describes her brother Bailey's behavior as *outrageous* when he insults the child of an elder.

    In this passage, *outrageous* means

    A inspiring.

    B respected.

    C shocking.

    D predictable.

2. Bailey was so *apt* at playing group games that he could compete with the best players.

    In this passage, *apt* means

    A skilled.

    B selfish.

    C emotional.

    D interested.

3. In *The Land I Lost,* the villagers believe a very old, very *wily* crocodile grabbed Lan from behind.

    In this passage, *wily* means

    A stubborn.

    B crazy.

    C ugly.

    D clever.

4. Lan is *desperate* for Trung to notice her in the tree, so she waves her arms frantically.

    In this passage, *desperate* means

    A not wanting.

    B urgently needing.

    C calmly waiting.

    D silently hoping.

5. Trung wants to kill the crocodile in order to *avenge* what he believes to be Lan's death.

    In this passage, *avenge* means

    A properly mourn.

    B show his fear of.

    C get even for.

    D cover up.

6. In "A Glory over Everything," Harriet's brothers become nervous about their ability to *elude* those who will be hunting for them.

    In this passage, *elude* means

    A confront.

    B betray.

    C escape the notice of.

    D change the minds of.

7. At first Harriet is *defiant* when her brothers want to turn around, but she returns with them because they won't let her go on alone.

    In this passage, *defiant* means

    A happy.

    B relieved.

    C agreeable.

    D resistant.

8. When Harriet finally escapes, she moves *cautiously* to avoid capture.

    In this passage, *cautiously* means

    A fearlessly.

    B bravely.

    C carefully.

    D slowly.

9. Harriet Tubman found plenty of ways to disguise herself and other runaway slaves in order to look as if they had *legitimate* reasons for being in places far from the plantations they had fled.

    In this passage, *legitimate* means

    A foolish.

    B justified.

    C practical.

    D unusual.

Academic Vocabulary

Directions: Use context clues to help you determine what the Academic Vocabulary words in italics mean. Then, choose the *best* answer.

10. A white woman *contributed* to Harriet's escape by hiding her and helping her along the Underground Railroad.

    In this passage, *contributed* means

    A added.

    B stopped.

    C began.

    D simplified.

11. The people who ran stations along the Underground Railroad had a *uniform* opinion of slavery.

    In this passage, *uniform* means

    A same.

    B formal.

    C immoral.

    D enthusiastic.

Directions: Choose the *best* synonym for each italicized Academic Vocabulary word.

12. The *perspective* of the speaker of an autobiography is his or her

    A language.

    B outlook.

    C background.

    D talent.

13. When you *contribute* to a class discussion, you

    A distract from it.

    B criticize it.

    C add to it.

    D improve it.

Writing Skills Review

Writing Standard 2.3 Write research reports: **a.** Pose relevant questions with a scope narrow enough to be thoroughly covered; **b.** Support the main idea or ideas with facts, details, examples, and explanations from multiple authoritative sources (e.g., speakers, periodicals, online information searches); **c.** Include a bibliography.

Research Report **Directions:** Read the following paragraph from a research report. Then, answer each question that follows.

(1) One of the North American Indian groups who built mounds was the Adena. (2) They built the mounds as burial places in what is now southern Ohio. (3) Mounds made by other groups are found in Indiana, Michigan, Illinois, Wisconsin, Iowa, Missouri, and Canada. (4) The Adena buried most of their dead in simple graves within the mounds, covering the bodies with dirt and stone. (5) Leaders and other important people from the village were buried in log tombs before being covered with dirt and stones. (6) Gifts were often placed in the tombs. (7) A pipe made of clay or stone was a usual gift placed in the tombs. (8) Grave Creek Mound is one of the largest mounds built by the Adena. (9) At about seventy feet high, it is a mysteriously beautiful monument.

1. Which of the following research questions does the information in this paragraph best answer?
   A Why did the Adena build mounds?
   B How were the Adena leaders chosen?
   C When did the Adena build mounds?
   D Who are the other mound builders?

2. If the writer wanted to add a fact to develop this paragraph, which of the following sentences would be most appropriate for a research report?
   A I would like to go to Hillsboro, Ohio, to see burial mounds.
   B The mounds should be protected.
   C The Adena began to build mounds around 700 B.C.
   D It is amazing to think how the mounds were built.

3. If you were revising this paragraph to improve its focus, which sentence might you delete?
   A sentence 1
   B sentence 3
   C sentence 5
   D sentence 8

4. Which transitional word could be added to the beginning of sentence 5 to show how it relates to sentence 4?
   A Therefore,
   B Finally,
   C Next,
   D However,

5. If you were to use the information above in an oral presentation, which visual display would best support sentence 9?
   A a drawing of a clay or stone pipe
   B maps of the United States and Canada
   C a time line showing when mounds were built
   D a photograph of Grave Creek Mound

Nonfiction

Year of Impossible Goodbyes

After World War II ended, Korea was divided into two sections: the north, controlled by the communist Soviet Union, and the south, controlled by the United States. Many Koreans in the north feared living under communism. *Year of Impossible Goodbyes* is an autobiographical story based on author Sook Nyul Choi's escape to South Korea. Because of a betrayal, ten-year-old Sookan and her brother are separated from their mother and have to continue the dangerous journey on their own.

Shipwreck at the Bottom of the World: The Extraordinary True Story of Shackleton and the Endurance

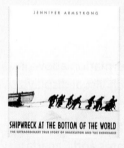

Imagine that your ship and crew of twenty-seven are trapped by a crushing sea of ice in the coldest place on Earth—Antarctica. Your ship breaks up and the only hope for survival is for some of you to trek eight hundred miles for help. You never know what life-or-death challenge is coming next when you read Jennifer Armstrong's *Shipwreck at the Bottom of the World,* the true story of Ernest Shackleton's Antarctic expedition.

My Life in Dog Years

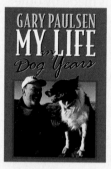

In the story "Storm," Gary Paulsen tells us about one of his favorite dogs. In his autobiography *My Life in Dog Years,* he remembers many of the dogs that have influenced his life, such as Snowball, his first dog, who saved him from a poisonous snake; Dirk, who chased bullies away from a school-age Paulsen; and his beloved husky Cookie, who risked her life to save him from drowning after he fell through ice. Paulsen's appreciation of these and other animal companions comes through in these humorous and touching stories.

Blizzard

In 1888, weather forecasting was more luck than science. When snow began to fall on the East Coast one day in March of that year, no one expected the storm that would later become known as the Great White Hurricane. Three days of fierce winds and heavy snowfall brought down telegraph lines, stopped all trains, and made getting food and coal almost impossible. Historian Jim Murphy researched newspaper articles and personal stories from 1888 and gathered photographs and drawings in order to retell the harrowing story of this historic blizzard.

America's Story from America's Library

The Web site www.americaslibrary.gov is brought to you by the Library of Congress, our nation's library and the largest one in the world. (It has almost 530 miles of books—that's enough to make a line of books from New Orleans to Oklahoma City!) Designed with you in mind, this students' site is entertaining, interactive, and instructive. Take a look at this site to find out what happened on your birth date; listen to be-bop, a type of music invented long before hip-hop; watch Thomas Edison's favorite movie; and enjoy many more features.

Faces Magazine

This magazine is designed to get you interested in travel, with just the turn of a page. In it, you can discover what people are like on the other side of the world or find out what kids in Australia do for fun. *Faces* takes you to different continents and introduces you to people and cultures that are very different from yours, yet very similar too. Stories about daily life and traditions, biographies, activities, and more fill each issue. Every story is accompanied by beautiful color photographs and drawings that show you faces from all over our planet.

Science News for Kids

Check out www.sciencenewsforkids.org, a Web site that explores different and surprising zones of science. One zone has games to challenge your logic and memory; another gives exercises for writing science fiction stories. There's an interactive laboratory zone that gives hands-on activities as well as ideas for science projects. *Science News for Kids* will inspire you to let your imagination take off in all directions scientific.

Time for Kids

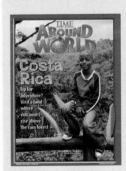

When a news story breaks, the magazine *Time for Kids* is there to report it. For the latest on current events, sports, and culture, pick up the magazine or look at its Web site, www.timeforkids.com. Make your own thoughts count in *Time for Kids* by participating in its polls and writing letters in response to its features and opinions.

Learn It Online
Use *NovelWise* to break down the elements needed to understand and analyze texts:

go.hrw.com   H6-673   **Go**

CHAPTER 7

Expository Critique: Persuasive Texts and Media

INFORMATIONAL TEXT FOCUS

Persuasion and Propaganda

California Standards

Here are the Grade 6 standards you will work toward mastering in Chapter 7.

Reading Comprehension (Focus on Informational Materials)

2.6 Determine the adequacy and appropriateness of the evidence for an author's conclusions.

2.7 Make reasonable assertions about a text through accurate, supporting citations.

2.8 Note instances of unsupported inferences, fallacious reasoning, persuasion, and propaganda in text.

Writing Applications (Genres and Their Characteristics)

2.5 Write persuasive compositions:
  a. State a clear position on a proposition or proposal.
  b. Support the position with organized and relevant evidence.
  c. Anticipate and address reader concerns and counterarguments.

"How wonderful it is that nobody need wait a single moment before starting to improve the world."

—**Anne Frank**

What Do
You
Think

What actions can individuals take to improve the world?

Learn It Online
Explore modern methods of persuasion on MediaScope:

| go.hrw.com | H6-675 | Go |

Informational Text Focus

by **Linda Rief**

How Do Writers Persuade You?

You and your parents disagree about whether you should upgrade your computer. You state your case clearly, presenting reasons to support your cause, and your parents do the same. Then you respectfully critique their argument by making a claim supported by evidence. If you present a strong critique, you might actually persuade your parents to agree with you!

Persuasion

When a writer's purpose is to influence readers to believe something or do something, the writer is using **persuasion.** The writer of a persuasive text presents a **claim** or an **opinion**—a belief—about a subject. He or she makes an argument to try to convince, or **persuade,** readers that this opinion is one that should be believed and accepted.

A writer builds a case by using **logic,** or correct reasoning. You're using logic when you put information together and conclude that "if this is true, then that must be true." A logical persuasive argument is built on an opinion that is supported by reasons and evidence. **Reasons** tell *why* writers hold particular opinions. **Evidence** is support or proof that backs up the reasons. This pyramid diagram shows how evidence is the foundation of persuasive writing.

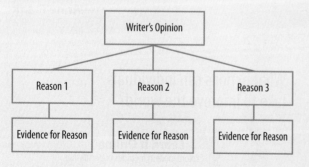

Types of Evidence

Here are some common types of evidence that authors use in persuasive writing.

- **Facts** are statements that can be proved true. You can use information from reliable sources to confirm facts.

> Today there are dozens of peace parks on five continents.
>
> from "Peace Parks Help Environment and Communities" by Sarah Ives

- **Quotations** are the documented record of people's comments about a topic. **Direct quotations**—people's exact words—are always enclosed in quotation marks. A statement made by an expert, such as a professor, on a topic is called an **expert opinion.**

> "[The parks] will let animals wander over larger parts of southern Africa, much as they did centuries ago," said Jack Shepherd, a professor of Environmental Studies at Dartmouth College. . . .
>
> from "Peace Parks Help Environment and Communities" by Sarah Ives

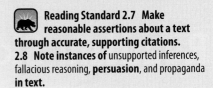

Reading Standard 2.7 Make reasonable assertions about a text through accurate, supporting citations. 2.8 Note instances of unsupported inferences, fallacious reasoning, **persuasion**, and propaganda **in text.**

- **Statistics** are information expressed as numbers. Statistics may be presented in the text, as in this example, or in charts or graphs.

> It turned out that life expectancy at age 35 was extended by as much as one and a half years simply by going to school for one extra year.
>
> from "A Surprising Secret to a Long Life: Stay in School" by Gina Kolata

- **Examples** are specific instances or illustrations of a general idea. Specific examples are sometimes called **case studies,** especially when they are based on scientific research.

> In one large federal study of middle-aged people, Smith reports, those with less education were less able to think ahead.
>
> from "A Surprising Secret to a Long Life: Stay in School" by Gina Kolata

- **Anecdotes** are brief personal stories that illustrate a point.

Logical and Emotional Appeals

When writers use facts and statistics to support an argument, they are using **logical appeals** aimed at your thinking abilities. When writers use evidence that appeals to emotions, such as fear and love, they are using **emotional appeals.** Since you are most likely to be persuaded by arguments that appeal to your mind *and* your heart, writers usually use both types of appeals. Still, don't be swayed by emotional appeals alone. Make sure the writer's position is also supported by facts.

Expository Critique

It's important to **critique,** or evaluate, all forms of persuasion carefully to judge if the opinion is valid. You can express your evaluation by making and supporting assertions about the opinion and the argument. An **assertion** is a statement or claim. A **citation** is evidence that supports an assertion. Follow these steps to make an assertion about a text:

- Identify the author's opinion.
- Identify the author's evidence, and determine whether the author has presented a convincing argument.
- Make your own assertion, or claim, about the author's argument, and support your assertion with citations from the author's text.
- Evaluate your assertion by making sure that it is reasonable—that it is sensible and shows solid judgment. Be sure that your assertion is supported by accurate evidence from the text.

See pages 678 and 679 for strategies to help you critique persuasive texts and media.

Your Turn   Analyze Persuasion

1. Give an example of a statistic you've heard or read. What opinion might it support?
2. Describe a television commercial you've seen that included an emotional appeal. To which emotion did it appeal? What assertion can you make about the commercial?

Learn It Online
Try the *PowerNotes* version of this lesson on:

| go.hrw.com | H6-677 | Go |

Reading Skills Focus

by **Kylene Beers**

What Skills Help You Critique Persuasive Texts and Media?

"How do you know?" you ask your friend, who has just told you some gossip. "I just know" is all your friend can say. That's not good enough. Your friend isn't using evidence to support his or her opinion or claim. It's important to determine someone's purpose and to evaluate his or her evidence and conclusions. Then, you'll know if you should (or should not) be persuaded to accept the person's claim as true.

Evaluating Evidence

Read persuasive texts carefully to determine if the evidence is strong enough to support the claims.

Adequate Evidence Determine if there is **adequate,** or enough, evidence to support the writer's points. Sometimes, a direct quotation from a respected expert in the field may be enough evidence all by itself. At other times, the writer may need to provide several facts and statistics.

Appropriate Evidence Make sure the writer uses **appropriate** evidence that relates directly to his or her ideas and supports the writer's claim. When something in the text makes you ask, "What does this have to do with anything?" you're dealing with **inappropriate evidence**—unrelated information that doesn't support the ideas.

Accurate Evidence Make sure the writer's evidence is **accurate,** or correct, and comes from a source you trust. Don't assume everything you see in print is accurate! If information doesn't sound right, check the source.

Evaluating Conclusions

Evaluating the writer's evidence leads directly to evaluating the writer's **conclusions,** judgments or opinions based on evidence. When you read persuasive texts, you expect the writer's evidence to add up to a conclusion that makes sense. Don't be fooled—writers are not perfect. The fact that a text looks nice and neat on a printed page doesn't mean that the ideas are well thought out.

Summarizing Evidence One way to determine if a writer's evidence supports his or her conclusion is to summarize the evidence, and then review your summary. Does all the evidence clearly add up to and support the conclusion?

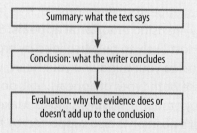

Summary: what the text says

↓

Conclusion: what the writer concludes

↓

Evaluation: why the evidence does or doesn't add up to the conclusion

Distinguishing Between Facts and Opinions

In persuasive writing, if the writer's position is well supported, you'll find many facts in the text. A writer may also present opinions, such as those of experts, to support his or her position. As a critical reader, you need to distinguish between facts and opinions. Remember these differences:

- **Facts** are information that can be proved true.
- **Opinions** are personal beliefs or attitudes.
- Some opinions are supported by facts, while others are not.

Distinguishing between facts and opinions will help you evaluate the adequacy and appropriateness of a writer's evidence.

CORNERED © 2001 Mike Baldwin. Reprinted with permission of UNIVERSAL PRESS SYNDICATE. All rights reserved.

Analyzing an Author's Purpose

In persuasive texts and media, an author's **purpose**—or reason for writing—is, of course, to persuade. There are many different ways, however, that an author can try to persuade you to accept his or her opinion or claim. To evaluate the evidence for an author's conclusions, it's important to analyze the purpose of each type of evidence or persuasive technique. Ask yourself, for example, if the author is presenting evidence or using a persuasive technique to appeal to your

- sense of logic
- emotions
- sense of what's right or wrong
- desire to fit in with other people
- desire to be special or important

Your Turn   Apply Reading Skills

1. Explain how to determine whether evidence is adequate, appropriate, and accurate in supporting a writer's conclusions.

2. How can you tell the difference between facts and opinions in persuasive writing?

3. Choose a magazine or newspaper advertisement. What is the purpose of each statement in the ad? What is the purpose of the art or graphics?

> **Now go to the Skills in Action: Reading Model**

Learn It Online
Get organized! Find interactive graphic organizers at:

| go.hrw.com | H6-679 | Go |

Read with a Purpose Read to learn what a "global classroom" is and how much it is like—or is not like—your own classroom.

The Global Classroom

by  **THE WORLD ALMANAC**

In Jeanne Agnello's sixth-grade classroom in Cold Spring Harbor, N.Y., a globe sits on a cart full of laptop computers. In the time it takes the social studies teacher to spin the globe, her students can connect with classrooms on the other side of the country—or the other side of the world.

The Internet has shrunk the planet. People can now send ideas and images across the world in seconds. The Web connects more than a billion users worldwide, providing instant access to a vast amount of information. The walls of the classroom have virtually disappeared—and that's good news for the future of education.

Clearing Language Barriers

Many schools recognize that students must be prepared to live as citizens of a global community. The U.S. government does as well. In 2006, President George W. Bush proposed a plan to increase the number of Americans who speak and teach foreign languages. Stress was placed on "critical-need languages." Those are languages spoken in important or rapidly developing areas of the world. They include Arabic, Chinese, Korean, Japanese, Russian, and Farsi (or Persian, the language of Iran).

Analyzing Visuals **Connecting to the Text** What statement from the article does this photograph support?

"To prepare young Americans to understand the peoples who will help define the 21st century, nothing is more important than our ability to converse in their native languages," said U.S. Secretary of State Condoleezza Rice.

East Meets West

With help from the government and nonprofit groups, many more public schools are teaching Chinese and Arabic. China is becoming an economic powerhouse, so Mandarin Chinese is growing in popularity in U.S. schools.

At Glenwood Elementary School in Chapel Hill, N.C., some classes are taught in both English and Mandarin. Students at McCormick Elementary School are among 3,000 students in Chicago schools who are learning Chinese. At Brookwood School in Manchester-by-the-Sea, which is a town on Cape Ann, Mass., even preschoolers learn to count and sing in Mandarin. The classes also help students understand the values and traditions of people in other lands, say teachers.

Informational Text Focus

Types of Evidence Writers use different types of evidence to support statements and conclusions. One is a **direct quotation**—a person's exact words set within quotation marks. Quotations from experts, such as this one, can be especially persuasive.

Reading Focus

Evaluating Evidence To support this statement, the writer lists specific schools that have begun teaching Mandarin Chinese. The evidence seems adequate and appropriate to support the claim. Specific evidence like this can be verified, or checked, so it's possible to prove (or disprove) its accuracy.

Distinguishing Between Fact and Opinion The first highlighted sentence is a **fact**—a statement that can be proved true. The second is an **opinion**—a belief or judgment. This opinion is supported by facts (examples of schools teaching Arabic). Facts and supported opinions can provide strong evidence.

The official language in many Middle Eastern nations is Arabic—a language that, until recently, was rarely taught in American classrooms. In the 21st century, however, Arabic is increasingly being seen as a language that's helpful to know in a changing world. At several high schools in Seattle, students are learning to read, write, and speak Arabic in after-school programs. Students at Annandale High School in Virginia are already in their third and fourth years of the language program.

New York City planned to open, in fall 2007, its first public school teaching Arabic language and culture. Students at Khalil Gibran International Academy will eventually have half of their lessons in Arabic. "We are . . . looking to attract as many diverse students as possible," said Debbie Almontaser, the school's principal. "We really want to give them the opportunity to expand their horizons and be global citizens."

World of Knowledge

Language classes are just part of a shift to a global outlook in education. The International Baccalaureate Organization (IBO), based in Geneva, Switzerland, has a special program in more than 100 U.S. elementary schools. The program encourages

students, beginning with preschoolers, to become multilingual. It aims to help them understand and value other cultures. Every subject takes a world view, from math and science to literature and social studies.

Many schools use e-mail and online exchanges that link students throughout the world. The International Education and Resource Network (iLEARN) is a network of schools teaching students ages 5 to 19 in more than 115 countries. Students and teachers interact in more than 30 languages to carry out online projects with peers worldwide.

One iLEARN project is a newsmagazine, *Backtalk Journal,* in which students from many countries contribute interviews. The stories highlight people "who play some kind of leadership role in service to sustainable development" in their communities. Another ongoing iLEARN project concerns endangered great apes in Africa and Asia. The project includes online activities, research projects, and art exchanges.

Another worldwide network is Global Learning and Observations to Benefit the Environment (GLOBE). This is an elementary and a secondary school science program. It connects students, teachers, and scientists in more than 19,000 schools in 109 countries.

The National Aeronautics and Space Administration and the National Science Foundation help GLOBE students carry out studies. Students take air, water, and soil measurements. They use the measurements to create maps and graphs. Teams in Bahrain, Honduras, Sri Lanka, and other nations work together. They share their findings through the GLOBE Web site. In doing so, students "develop awareness, respect, and appreciation for one another's cultures and environmental habitats," according to the American Forum for Global Education.

Going Places

The push to produce graduates who understand the world is increasing opportunities to study abroad. Numerous districts have programs helping U.S. students get schooled in other

Informational Text Focus

Types of Evidence Notice the information that the writer gives here and elsewhere in the form of numbers. **Statistics,** or number facts, are another form of evidence that writers use to support their claims.

countries. These experiences prepare students to take part in "an increasingly interconnected international community that demands cross-cultural skills and knowledge." That's according to the Strategic Task Force on Education Abroad.

The U.S. Senate even designated 2006 the official Year of Study Abroad. In that year, more than 2,600 American high school students spent a semester or full year studying abroad, according to the Council on Standards for International Education Travel. Nearly 28,000 international students studied in the United States.

By "globalizing" education, schools seek to improve students' knowledge. Educators want students to better understand geography, culture, language, and international viewpoints. Business leaders and government officials agree: A global education helps students understand their role as world citizens. It helps them make connections between local and international communities.

"There's no turning back," says Agnello of her connected classroom. As students look forward to their future in a changing world, they can be pleased that global education is here to stay, helping them to become active, engaged citizens in an exciting new era.

Read with a Purpose What is a "global classroom"? Explain whether or not your classroom is one.

Reading Focus

Evaluating the Writer's Conclusions Think critically about the conclusions a writer makes. Has the writer convinced you? One way to check a writer's conclusions is to summarize the evidence in your own words and then determine what conclusions you can draw.

Informational Text Focus

Emotional Appeals The writer ends this article with an **emotional appeal**—a statement that will appeal to most people's feelings. This persuasive statement appeals to positive emotions such as hope and excitement.

Reading Standard 2.6 Determine the adequacy and appropriateness of the evidence for an author's conclusions. **2.7** Make reasonable assertions about a text through accurate, supporting citations.

Into Action: Evaluating Evidence

Complete a chart like the one below. Identify two of the author's conclusions and the evidence used to support them. Is the evidence adequate and appropriate? Explain.

Conclusion	Evidence
"Educators want students to better understand geography . . . and international viewpoints."	

Talk About . . .

1. With a partner, critique the author's argument. Express your opinion by making an assertion and supporting it with evidence from the text.

Write About . . .

Answer the following questions. For definitions of the underlined Academic Vocabulary words, see the column on the right.

2. What evidence in the article shows that it is crucial for students to have access to the Internet?

3. Consider the following statistics: almost 28,000 international students studied in the United States in 2006, while more than 2,600 U.S. students studied abroad that year. What can you conclude?

4. Explain whether or not you are an authority on learning in a global classroom.

Writing Skills Focus
Think as a Reader/Writer

In Chapter 7, you will read more persuasive texts. Writing Skills Focus activities will give you practice in evaluating evidence and making assertions.

Academic Vocabulary for Chapter 7

Talking and Writing About Persuasion

Academic Vocabulary is the language you use to talk and write about texts. Use these words to discuss the informational texts you read in this chapter. The words will be underlined throughout the chapter.

adequacy (AD uh kwiht) *n.*: quality of being enough to meet a need or requirement. *An argument's strength depends, in part, on the adequacy of the evidence.*

authority (uh THAWR uh tee) *n.*: someone who is respected because of his or her knowledge about a subject. *Writers of persuasion will often quote a person who is an authority.*

conclude (kuhn KLOOD) *v.*: form an opinion or make a judgment after considering all the information you have. *You need to conclude whether a writer provides enough evidence.*

crucial (KROO shuhl) *adj.*: very important. *It is crucial that you evaluate a writer's opinion before accepting it.*

Your Turn

Copy the Academic Vocabulary words into your *Reader/Writer Notebook.* Then, use each word in a sentence about an issue or cause that is important to you.

INFORMATIONAL TEXT FOCUS
Persuasion

CONTENTS

What Do You Think? Why is education important in efforts to make the world a better place?

QuickWrite
How has education improved you, your friends and family, or your community? Write a paragraph explaining at least one way education has changed *your* world.

Reading Standard 2.6 Determine the adequacy and appropriateness of the evidence for an author's conclusions.

A Surprising Secret to a Long Life: Stay in School

Informational Text Focus

Persuasion It's everywhere. Advertisements urge us to buy things, politicians ask for votes, and editorial writers try to influence our thinking on issues. **Persuasion** is the use of language to get us to *believe* or *do* something. In persuasive texts, writers present an opinion or claim and then use reasons and evidence to build an argument. As you read this article, identify the writer's claim, and consider whether she is presenting a convincing argument based on evidence.

Reading Skills Focus

Evaluating Evidence An argument is only as strong as its evidence. **Evidence** is information that supports or proves a point or a <u>conclusion</u>. To create a convincing argument, a writer must present evidence that is appropriate and adequate. To evaluate a writer's evidence as you read, ask yourself: Has the writer presented evidence that is *directly related* to the point and truly supports it? Has the writer provided *enough* evidence, or has the writer only partially supported the point?

Into Action As you read, record the writer's evidence in a chart like the one below. After you read, you will be asked to determine the <u>adequacy</u> and appropriateness of the evidence.

Writer's Opinion or Claim	Evidence
	1.
	2.
	[etc.]

Writing Skills Focus

Preparing for Timed ∟Writing This article explores a connection between staying in school and living a longer life. Pay attention to the way the writer organizes evidence to support her claim and <u>conclusion</u>.

Reader/Writer
Notebook

Use your **RWN** to complete the activities for this selection.

Vocabulary

dispute (dihs PYOOT) *n.:* disagreement; argument. *There's no dispute that education is important.*

isolated (Y suh LAY tihd) *adj.:* apart from others; separate. *Living an isolated life can lead to poor health.*

declined (dih KLYND) *v.:* dropped; went down. *When people became sick, their income declined.*

Language Coach

Word Families The writer of this article uses the Vocabulary word *isolated* and a related word that's in the same word family: *isolation.* The suffix (a word part added to the end of a word or root) *–ion* tells you that *isolation* is a noun. The word means "the state of being apart from others."

Disputable and *disputation* are in the same word family as the Vocabulary word *dispute.* What do the suffixes *–able* and *–ion* tell you about the parts of speech of *disputable* and *disputation?* What do you think each word means? Use a dictionary to check your answers.

Learn It Online
Explore the use of persuasion in advertisements online at MediaScope:

go.hrw.com   H6-687   **Go**

A Surprising Secret to a Long Life:
STAY IN SCHOOL

by GINA KOLATA

adapted from a *New York Times* article, January 3, 2007

Read with a Purpose
Read this article to learn why education might help you to live longer.

James Smith, a health economist at RAND Corporation, has heard many ideas about what it takes to live a long life. The theories include money, lack of stress, a loving family, and lots of friends. It has been Smith's job to question these beliefs. Clearly, some people live longer than others. The rich live longer than the poor in the United States, for instance. But what is cause and what is effect?

In every country, there is an average life span for the nation as a whole, and there are average life spans for groups within, based on race, geography, education, and even churchgoing. Smith and other researchers find that the one factor linked to longer lives in every country studied is education. In study after study, says Richard Hodes, director of the National Institute on Aging, education "keeps coming up."

Education is not the only factor, of course. There is smoking, which curtails life span. There is a connection between having a network of friends and family and living a long and healthy life. But there is little dispute about education's importance. **Ⓐ**

"If you were to ask me what affects health and longevity,"[1] says Michael Grossman, a health economist at the City University of New York, "I would put education at the top of my list." **Ⓑ**

Graduate Student Finds Answer

In 1999, Adriana Lleras-Muney was a graduate student at Columbia University. She found a 1969 research paper noting the correlation[2] between education and health. It concluded: You can improve health more by investing in education than by investing in medical care. These findings could be true only if education caused good health, she thought. But there were other possibilities.

Maybe sick children did not go to school or dropped out early. Or maybe education was a part of wealth, and wealth led to health. Perhaps richer parents provided better nutrition, medical care, and education—and their children lived longer.

How, she asked herself, could she sort out causes and effects? Then she read that, about 100 years ago, different states started passing laws forcing children to go to school for longer periods. She knew she had to study those results and see if she could find a difference in life spans.

When she finished, Lleras-Muney says, "I was surprised; I was really surprised." It turned out that life expectancy at age 35 was extended by as much as one and a half years simply by going to school for one extra year.

Lessons Learned

Lleras-Muney has since become an assistant professor at Princeton,[3] and other papers on the subject have appeared in Sweden, Denmark, England, and Wales. In every country studied, forcing children to spend a longer time in school led to better health.

She and others pose this possible reason why education helps people live longer: As a group, less-educated people are less able to plan for the future. They are not as able to delay gratification.[4]

How might that difference in outlook change life spans? Consider smoking. Smokers are at least twice as likely to die as people who never smoked, says Samuel Preston, a researcher at the University of Pennsylvania. And poorly educated people are more likely

---

1. **longevity** (lahn JEHV uh tee): length of life.
2. **correlation** (kawr uh LAY shuhn): relationship between two ideas, facts, etc.

3. **Princeton:** highly respected ivy-league college in New Jersey.
4. **gratification** (grat uh fuh KAY shuhn): satisfaction or pleasure; a source of satisfaction and pleasure.

Ⓐ **Informational Focus** Persuasion What does the writer want you to believe? How can you tell?

Ⓑ **Reading Focus** Evaluating Evidence What kind of evidence has the writer presented so far?

Vocabulary **dispute** (dihs PYOOT) *n.*: disagreement; argument.

to smoke, he says, even though "everybody [including the poorly educated] knows that smoking can be deadly."

In one large federal study of middle-aged people, Smith reports, those with less education were less able to think ahead. And living for the day, says Smith, can be "the worst thing for your health." **C**

Other Factors at Work

In the late 1970s, Lisa Berkman, now a professor of public policy at the Harvard School of Public Health, worked at a San Francisco health care center. And she noticed something. "In Chinatown and North Beach, there were these tightly bound social networks," Berkman recalls. "You saw old people with young people. In the Tenderloin[5] people were just sort of dumped. People were really isolated."

The risks of being socially isolated are "phenomenal,"[6] Berkman says. Isolation was associated with twofold to fivefold increases in mortality rates. These associations emerged in study after study and in country after country.

> In one large federal study of middle-aged people, Smith reports, those with less education were less able to think ahead.

She asked herself: Does social isolation shorten lives? Or are people isolated when sick and frail? Berkman says the more she investigated, the more she found that social isolation might lead to poor health and shorter lives. Isolation can, for example, increase stress and make it harder to get assistance. **D**

Researchers at Dartmouth College find that the lowest death rates are in the wealthiest places. An obvious explanation for this is that wealth buys health. Poorer people, at least in the United States, are less likely to have health insurance. But the differences between rich and poor do not shrink in countries where everyone has health care. In fact, says Smith, it is not that lower incomes lead to poor health so much as that poor health leads to lower incomes.

Smith notes that sick people often are unable to work or unable to work full time. He analyzed data from a National Institute on Aging sample of U.S. households with at least one person aged 51 to 61. When someone developed cancer, heart disease, or lung disease, that person's household income declined an average of more than $37,000.

---

5. **the Tenderloin:** poor area in downtown San Francisco.

6. **phenomenal** (fuh NOM uh nuhl): out of the ordinary; surprising; rare.

C **Reading Focus** Evaluating Evidence What evidence is there for Lleras-Muney's opinion about education and planning for the future?

D **Reading Focus** Evaluating Evidence Why can Berkman be considered an authority?

Vocabulary **isolated** (y suh LAY tihd) *adj.*: apart from others; separate.
declined (dih KLYND) *v.*: dropped; went down.

Analyzing Visuals **Connecting to the Text** What are these people doing that might increase their life spans?

Connecting to the Text In what ways might this young man be improving the long-term quality of his life?

Smith asked whether getting richer made people healthier, an effect that could lengthen life. It did not, he concluded after studying increases in income during the stock market surge of the 1990s. "I find almost no role of financial anything in the onset of disease," Smith says.

There are some important findings about factors other than education that make a difference in life span. Health and nutrition in early life can affect adult health and longevity.

For the most part, genes have little effect on life spans. But controlling risk factors for heart disease, such as smoking, cholesterol, blood pressure, and diabetes, pays off in a more vigorous old age and a longer life. It seems increasingly likely that education plays a major role in health and life spans. **E**

Read with a Purpose

How can getting a good education help you live longer?

E **Read and Discuss** What did you learn about factors other than education that help to lengthen life span?

Applying Your Skills

A Surprising Secret to a Long Life: Stay in School

Standards Review

Informational Text and Vocabulary

1. Which factor is *not* mentioned in the article as affecting length of life?

 A smoking

 B number of years of education

 C being isolated

 D region of the U.S. where a person lives

2. Which statement *best* expresses the writer's **conclusion**?

 A Education is the only factor that can accurately determine a person's potential life span.

 B Education plays a major role in helping people to live a long life.

 C It's impossible to figure out why some people live longer than others.

 D People are healthier now than they were one hundred years ago.

3. Evidence for the writer's **conclusion** could take the form of statistics that show

 A which countries have health care for all.

 B how many doctors practice in the countries with the healthiest populations.

 C the average amount of education people have in the countries with the healthiest populations.

 D the number of elderly smokers in different countries.

4. *Dispute* is *most* similar in meaning to which of the following words?

 A reputation

 B argument

 C correction

 D insult

5. An *isolated* person *most likely*

 A gets lost frequently.

 B feels lonely.

 C expects the best.

 D has many friends.

6. If something has *declined*, its value has

 A gone up.

 C stayed the same.

 B gone down.

 D doubled.

Writing Skills Focus

Timed └Writing Does the writer present adequate and appropriate evidence to create a convincing argument? Does she organize the evidence effectively? Critique the article by writing a paragraph in which you make an assertion, or claim, about the text. Support your assertion with accurate citations, or evidence, from the article.

What Do You Think Now

This article discusses one major benefit of education. What other benefits are there?

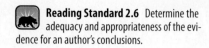

Reading Standard 2.6 Determine the adequacy and appropriateness of the evidence for an author's conclusions.

Oprah Talks About Her South African "Dreamgirls"

Informational Text Focus

Logical and Emotional Appeals To persuade us, writers use **logical appeals,** such as facts and statistics, that appeal to our sense of reason. They also use **emotional appeals,** such as anecdotes and loaded words (words that have strong emotions associated with them), to affect our feelings. This article focuses on a school that Oprah Winfrey founded in South Africa. The writer quotes Winfrey responding to critics and explaining her reasons for establishing the school. As you read, ask yourself: Are the writer and Winfrey convincing me to take Winfrey's side? Is my opinion influenced by logical appeals, emotional appeals, or both?

Reading Skills Focus

Evaluating Evidence Before you accept people's opinions and con-clusions, you need to determine the adequacy and appropriateness of their evidence. Ask yourself these questions: Have they presented *enough* evidence? Are they relying too much on emotional appeals and not enough on logical appeals? Does the evidence *directly support* the points? What other evidence would have provided stronger support?

Into Action As you read, fill in a chart like the one below to help you evaluate the evidence in the article.

Opinion or Conclusion	Evidence
girls "bring history of . . . suffering"	half of South African population lives in poverty

Writing Skills Focus

Preparing for **Timed └Writing** As you read, note how the logical and emotional appeals affect how you think and feel about the school.

Reader/Writer
Notebook

Use your **RWN** to complete the activities for this selection.

Vocabulary

criticism (KRIHT uh sihz uhm) *n.:* unfavorable remarks. *Oprah Winfrey believes in her school, despite the criticism it has received.*

circumstance (SUR kuhm stans) *n.:* fact or condition that affects a situation, action, or event. *Poverty is a circumstance that some people endure.*

yearning (YUR nihng) *n.:* feeling of wanting something badly. *The girls in the school had a yearning to succeed.*

```
        ( Dreamgirls )
              |
attend school that receives criticism
              |
affected by circumstance of poverty
              |
have a yearning to become educated
```

Language Coach

Word Families The Vocabulary word *criticism* is a member of a word family, or group of related words. One word in the same word family is *criticize.* List some other words that are in the word family.

Learn It Online
Check out the *PowerNotes* introduction to this article on:

go.hrw.com | H6-694 | **Go**

Some of the first students at the Oprah Winfrey Leadership Academy for Girls in South Africa

Oprah Talks About Her South African
"Dreamgirls"

ABC News Report

Read with a Purpose
Read the following news story to find out who the South African "dreamgirls" are—and why they have been given that name.

In South Africa on Tuesday, the curtain for the Oprah Winfrey Leadership Academy for Girls parted for 152 girls in ankle socks.

They bring a history of so much suffering and so much hope for the future.

"You want dream girls? Take a look at these," said Oprah Winfrey, who made good on her pledge six years ago to Nelson Mandela to build the school. **A**

Half the population of South Africa lives in poverty, a quarter of the people have HIV, and there is an epidemic of violence among girls. **B**

A **Read and Discuss** What have you learned so far about the Oprah Winfrey Leadership Academy for Girls?

B **Informational Focus** **Logical and Emotional Appeals** What kind of evidence is used here?

Still, for some in the country, Winfrey's school, with its amazing theater, beautiful library and African art everywhere, seems "too much."

Critics inside and outside the country have asked, in a land with this kind of poverty, how can you spend more than $40 million on one school?

"I did love that the minister of education for this entire country stood up and said, 'I'm going to address the criticism. Is it too much? No, it isn't,'" Winfrey said in an exclusive interview with Diane Sawyer for "Good Morning America."

Winfrey said she got resistance from the very beginning, even from the school's architects.

"The resistance was too much," Winfrey said. "'What are you doing? What do they need all that room for? Why does a girl need all that closet space when she has no clothes?' That's what they first said to me."

"And my idea was to understand, yes, you come from nothing, but oh, what a something you will become, if given the opportunity," Winfrey said.

Most of the girls who were admitted to the school have come from very little—no running water, no electricity, many of them studying by candlelight.

They are still the best in their class.

At Tuesday's opening ceremony, one irrepressible girl named Losego said, "I went to a lot of effort to come to this school." **C**

Diamonds and Dreams

Winfrey, who will stay very involved with the school and even teach leadership classes, said she believed the future was unimaginably bright for all of the girls.

"Somebody asked me, what do I think will happen or what do I imagine for them. I don't. I don't imagine . . . I can't imagine what it's like to have a miracle like this. It's just a miracle," Winfrey said.

And the girls already have big dreams. Losego had a suggested question for Winfrey: "What did you do with your first million?" **D**

Nelson Mandela and Oprah Winfrey at the groundbreaking for Winfrey's Leadership Academy

C Reading Focus Evaluating Evidence What reasons and evidence have Winfrey and the writer presented to prove that the school is not "too much"? Is the evidence adequate and appropriate?

D Read and Discuss What is Losego thinking here?

Vocabulary criticism (KRIHT uh sihz uhm) n.: unfavorable remarks.

Oprah Winfrey and students cut the ribbon at the opening of the Oprah Winfrey Leadership Academy for Girls in South Africa.

Analyzing Visuals **Connecting to the Text** How does this photograph appeal to your emotions? How does it affect your view of the school?

Winfrey dressed up for the school's opening ceremony, diamonds and all. The girls had seen them in pictures, and Winfrey said she had worn them as a signal that this was an important celebration.

"One of the things that's very important for me is for the girls to be proud of themselves and to be proud of the way they look and where they come from, and a lot of them in the beginning were very embarrassed about being poor," Winfrey said.

When Winfrey asked some of the girls why they wanted to come to the school, many said they wanted to take care of their families.

"And some of them would say, 'I want to come to this school because I am a poor girl,' and then they would drop their heads," Winfrey said. "I was a poor girl, too. So there's no shame in being a poor girl because being poor is just a circumstance. It's not who you are. It's not what can be possible for you." **E**

The school's curriculum and standards of behavior are high. This is a school for leaders, Winfrey says.

"I said to the girls, 'I'm going to take care of you. I'm going to do everything in my power to make sure you now have a good life and the best opportunity to go to the best schools in the world so when you leave this school you will choose universities all over the world,'" she said.

E Read and Discuss What did you find out about the girls attending the academy?

Vocabulary **circumstance** (SUR kuhm stans) *n.:* fact or condition that affects a situation, action, or event.

A Responsibility to Her New Daughters

One question that has been asked of Winfrey is why not build a school like this in the United States?

"What is different about this country is that there is this sort of desperate yearning to know better and do better that you just don't have in the United States," she said. "You don't have it because the opportunity's always been there."

The parents of the South African girls are also grateful for the opportunity.

"And I don't know a South African mother or father who didn't understand what a value, what a gift, what an opportunity an education is," Winfrey said. **(F)**

Winfrey admits that putting such a big stake into this school and these girls is a huge responsibility.

"It's not just about using your money wisely and making the best investment possible by investing in the future of young girls, but now I have a lot of responsibility," she said. "I feel it."

Winfrey has vowed to care for the new students at her school as if they were her own daughters.

"I said to the mothers, the family members, the aunts, the grannies—because most of these girls have lost their families, their parents—I said to them, 'Your daughters are now my daughters and I promise you I'm going to take care of your daughters. I promise you.'"

Read with a Purpose

Why are Oprah's students called "dreamgirls"? Explain why you do or do not think this is a good name for them.

Analyzing Visuals **Connecting to the Text**
How does this photograph serve as an emotional appeal?

Oprah Winfrey hugs Loyiswa Sibekoat, a student at Winfrey's Leadership Academy for Girls.

(F) Reading Focus **Evaluating Evidence** Explain whether you think Winfrey has provided <u>adequate</u> and appropriate evidence to support her decision to build the school in South Africa and not in the United States.

Vocabulary **yearning** (YUR nihng) *n.*: feeling of wanting something badly.

Applying Your Skills

Oprah Talks About Her South African "Dreamgirls"

Standards Review

Informational Text and Vocabulary

1. Winfrey's statement to the relatives of the girls, "Your daughters are now my daughters," can *best* be described as
   A a fact.
   B a statistic.
   C an emotional appeal.
   D an example.

2. Which of the following **statements** is supported by information in this article?
   A All of the students in the Leadership Academy will go on to do great things.
   B If the students have pride, they will become leaders.
   C Oprah Winfrey's students have more opportunities than do American students.
   D Oprah Winfrey is hopeful about the students' futures.

3. Which of the following statements *best* supports the opinion that a school like Oprah's is more necessary in South Africa than in the United States?
   A Educational opportunities have long been available in the United States but not in South Africa.
   B Forty million dollars is not much money to someone like Oprah Winfrey.
   C Many of the girls in Oprah's school are poor and don't have families.
   D There is an epidemic of violence among girls in South Africa but not among those in the United States.

4. When people give *criticism*, they are
   A praising something.
   B giving assignments to someone.
   C saying what they think is wrong with something.
   D giving reports to support an opinion.

5. Having a *yearning* means
   A wanting something badly.
   B feeling disgusted by something.
   C having hunger pangs.
   D holding a discussion.

6. A *circumstance* has to do with
   A the measurement around a globe.
   B the condition that affects a situation.
   C evidence that is not fully convincing.
   D people keeping things to themselves.

Writing Skills Focus

Timed Writing Have Winfrey and the writer presented a strong case for Winfrey's school? Write a paragraph explaining your opinion. Be sure to determine whether the evidence in the article is <u>adequate</u> and appropriate. Consider, too, whether Winfrey and the writer rely more heavily on logical appeals or emotional appeals to try to win you over.

What Do **You Think Now**

In what ways could a school like Oprah Winfrey's Leadership Academy help to change the world?

Preparing to Read

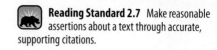
Reading Standard 2.7 Make reasonable assertions about a text through accurate, supporting citations.

Peace Parks Help Environment and Communities

Informational Text Focus

Assertions and Citations Writers use evidence, such as facts and expert opinions (statements by <u>authorities</u>), to support their opinions and <u>conclusions</u>. It's equally important for *you* to use evidence when you critique, or evaluate, a text. When you make an **assertion**—a statement or claim—about a text, you should always support it with **citations,** or evidence, from the work. Make sure that your assertions are reasonable—that they make sense based on evidence from the text. Check that your citations are accurate and truly support your assertion.

Reading Skills Focus

Distinguishing Between Fact and Opinion **Facts** are pieces of information that can be proved true. In contrast, **opinions** are personal beliefs or attitudes. Facts are reliable evidence. Opinions can be reliable, too, when they are those of experts or are supported by facts.

Into Action As you read, fill in a chart like the one below to help you distinguish between facts and opinions.

Facts	Opinions
People are creating "parks that cross country borders."	

Writing Skills Focus

Preparing for Timed Writing As you read, pay attention to the types of evidence that the writer presents. Which type do you think is the most persuasive?

Reader/Writer
Notebook
Use your **RWN** to complete the activities for this selection.

Vocabulary

cooperation (koh op uh RAY shuhn) *n.:* support; act of working together. *Cooperation between nations may lead to the creation of peace parks.*

conservation (kon suhr VAY shuhn) *n.:* protection of natural things, such as animals, plants, and forests. *The society protects wildlife through its efforts in conservation.*

confinement (kuhn FYN muhnt) *n.:* condition of being kept from moving around; lack of freedom. *Confinement to a small area has a bad effect on animals' health.*

pollution (puh LOO shuhn) *n.:* something that makes air, water, and soil dangerously dirty. *Pollution is a major threat to the environment.*

Language Coach

Suffixes Three of the Vocabulary words above contain the suffix *–ion*, which means "state or condition." List three other words that end with this suffix. Use a dictionary if you need help.

Learn It Online
Polish your vocabulary skills with Word Watch at:

| go.hrw.com | H6-700 | Go |

Read with a Purpose

Read this article to learn what peace parks are and why they have been given this unusual name.

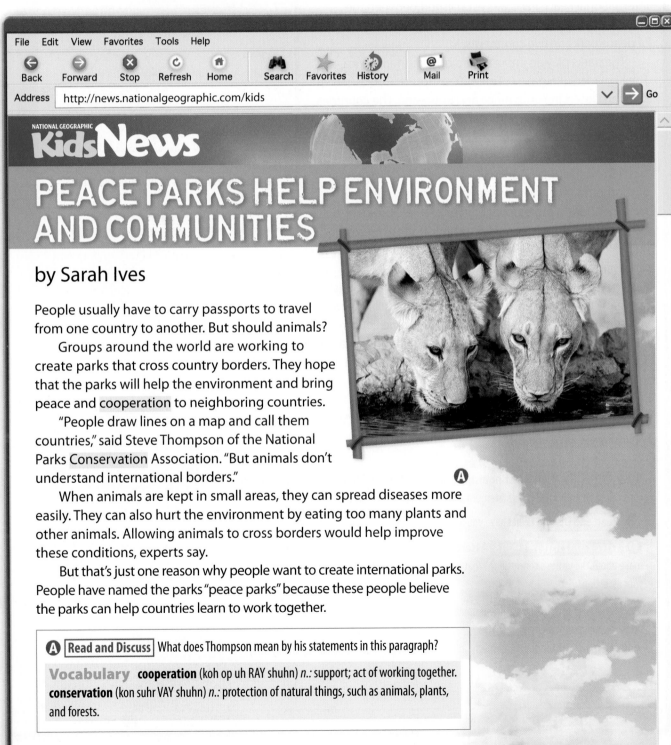

File   Edit   View   Favorites   Tools   Help

Back   Forward   Stop   Refresh   Home   Search   Favorites   History   Mail   Print

Address   http://news.nationalgeographic.com/kids   Go

NATIONAL GEOGRAPHIC
KidsNews

PEACE PARKS HELP ENVIRONMENT AND COMMUNITIES

by Sarah Ives

People usually have to carry passports to travel from one country to another. But should animals?

Groups around the world are working to create parks that cross country borders. They hope that the parks will help the environment and bring peace and cooperation to neighboring countries.

"People draw lines on a map and call them countries," said Steve Thompson of the National Parks Conservation Association. "But animals don't understand international borders."

🅐

When animals are kept in small areas, they can spread diseases more easily. They can also hurt the environment by eating too many plants and other animals. Allowing animals to cross borders would help improve these conditions, experts say.

But that's just one reason why people want to create international parks. People have named the parks "peace parks" because these people believe the parks can help countries learn to work together.

🅐 Read and Discuss   What does Thompson mean by his statements in this paragraph?

Vocabulary   **cooperation** (koh op uh RAY shuhn) *n.*: support; act of working together.
conservation (kon suhr VAY shuhn) *n.*: protection of natural things, such as animals, plants, and forests.

"[The parks create] a link between communities and a common desire to learn more about one another," said Anushka Bangara of the International Institute for Peace Through Tourism.

According to Steve Thompson, the parks can "help nations resolve international conflict or even war." **B**

The first international peace park, Waterton-Glacier International Peace Park, was established between the United States and Canada in 1932. Today there are dozens of peace parks on five continents.

The parks play an important role in southern Africa. The Kgalagadi (ka-gal-a-GA-dee) Transfrontier Park is in the Kalahari Desert in South Africa and Botswana. The countries work together to manage the land and the animals that live there. Other countries, such as Zimbabwe, Mozambique, Namibia, and Lesotho, are also forming parks. **C**

"[The parks] will let animals wander over larger parts of southern Africa, much as they did centuries ago," said Jack Shepherd, a professor of Environmental Studies at Dartmouth College in New Hampshire. "It should really help expand elephant and lion populations, which are now damaged by confinement in smaller parks."

The parks can also help countries by attracting tourists and creating jobs. But many issues still remain, such as the illegal killing of animals, pollution, and population pressure on the land. Plus, some countries have different ideas about how they want to manage their parks and animals.

Countries are trying to solve those problems—and learning to work together in the process. **D**

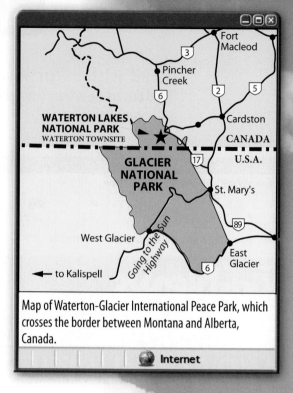

Map of Waterton-Glacier International Peace Park, which crosses the border between Montana and Alberta, Canada.

Read with a Purpose
Explain whether you think "peace parks" is a good name for these international parks.

B **Reading Focus** **Distinguishing Between Fact and Opinion** Can Thompson be considered an authority? Is his statement a fact or an opinion? How do you know?

C **Read and Discuss** What have you learned about peace parks so far?

D **Informational Focus** **Assertions and Citations** What assertion can you make about the writer's conclusion? What evidence in the article can you find to support your assertion?

Vocabulary **confinement** (kuhn FYN muhnt) *n.*: condition of being kept from moving around; lack of freedom.
pollution (puh LOO shuhn) *n.*: something that makes air, water, and soil dangerously dirty.

Applying Your Skills

Peace Parks Help Environment and Communities

Standards Review

Informational Text and Vocabulary

1. Which of the following is an **opinion**?

  A "Animals don't understand international borders."

  B Peace parks can "help nations resolve international conflict or even war."

  C Waterton-Glacier International Peace Park was established in 1932.

  D "The Kgalagadi . . . Transfrontier Park is in the Kalahari Desert."

2. Which of the following **facts** is *not* mentioned in the article?

  A The first peace park borders the United States and Canada.

  B There are now peace parks in Africa.

  C Peace parks helped gray wolves.

  D More peace parks are being developed.

3. The writer provides reasons or **evidence** to support all of the conclusions *except* which of the following?

  A Peace parks might help nations work together.

  B Peace parks are good for the environment.

  C Peace parks have solved the problem of animals being killed illegally.

  D Peace parks should help animals.

4. *Cooperation* is *most* similar in meaning to

  A competition.

  B teamwork.

  C war.

  D education.

5. *Conservation* is *most* similar in meaning to

  A information.

  B protection.

  C revolution.

  D suspension.

6. Animals would *most likely* have a sense of *confinement*

  A in the jungle.

  B in a peace park.

  C on an open plain.

  D in a zoo.

7. When humans cause *pollution*, they are

  A helping the environment.

  B making air, water, or soil dirty.

  C establishing borders.

  D creating solutions.

Writing Skills Focus

Timed └Writing Do you think the writer uses facts and opinions effectively to make her points? Write a paragraph in which you evaluate the article. Make an assertion (a statement or claim), and use citations, or evidence, from the text to support it. Be sure to check that your assertion is reasonable and that your citations are accurate.

What Do You Think Now

How could educating people and nations about peace parks improve the world in long-lasting ways?

COMPARING TEXTS

Comparing Persuasion and Propaganda

CONTENTS

 What Do You Think? How does advertising appeal to our desire to improve ourselves and our lives?

 QuickWrite
What ad, commercial, or poster have you seen lately that was especially clever? Describe it, and explain why you remember it.

Preparing to Read

Reading Standard 2.6 Determine the adequacy and appropriateness of the evidence for an author's conclusions. **2.8 Note instances of** unsupported inferences, fallacious reasoning, **persuasion**, and propaganda **in text.**

Start the Day Right!

Informational Text Focus

Persuasive Techniques **Persuasion** is the use of language or visual images to get you to believe or do something. Writers use such **persuasive techniques** as logical appeals and emotional appeals to convince their audience. **Logical appeals,** such as reasons and facts, are aimed at an audience's judgment. **Emotional appeals** stir the feelings of an audience, usually through the use of **loaded words**—words with positive or negative connotations, or associations.

Reading Skills Focus

Evaluating Evidence Public service announcements and advertisements are aimed at our minds and our hearts, so they depend on both logical appeals and emotional appeals to get their messages across. To decide whether you should accept their claims, you need to evaluate the evidence: Are the logical appeals <u>adequate</u>, appropriate, and accurate? Do the announcements or ads rely too heavily on emotional appeals to sway your feelings instead of supporting their messages with facts?

Into Action As you read, record examples of logical and emotional appeals in a chart like the one below.

Logical Appeals	Emotional Appeals
	Loaded word: "Every morning, in every classroom . . ."

Vocabulary

engaged (ehn GAYJD) *adj.:* busy and interested; absorbed in something. *Most of the students are engaged by the teacher's explanation.*

nutritious (noo TRIHSH uhs) *adj.:* full of nourishment; healthful. *Cereal and fruit can make a nutritious breakfast.*

irritable (IHR uh tuh buhl) *adj.:* in a bad mood; short-tempered. *Tired students are often irritable and unhappy in class.*

Language Coach

Multiple-Meaning Words Some words have multiple—and very different—meanings. The adjective *engaged* can mean "being interested in something," but *engaged* can also be used to describe two people who have pledged to marry each other. As a class, brainstorm at least four other words that have two or more very different meanings.

Writing Skills Focus

Preparing for **Timed** Writing As you read, think about whether the creators of this announcement have convinced you to accept their claim. What questions do you have? What more do you want to know?

Reader/Writer
Notebook

Use your **RWN** to complete the activities for this selection.

Learn It Online
To learn more about analyzing persuasive messages on television, visit MediaScope at:

go.hrw.com	H6-705	Go

CAMPAIGN: **START THE DAY RIGHT!**

FOR: Health for Kids and Other Important People

TV: 30-second spot

Read with a Purpose
Read this storyboard to decide if the televised public service announcement it represents would convince you that eating breakfast is important.

VIDEO

Camera opens on sunlit classroom with middle school students at desks. Most of them seem engaged, listening to a teacher at the front of the room, out of frame. The camera starts to focus on one boy, who looks like he is about to fall asleep.

AUDIO

Announcer: Every morning, in every classroom in America, students come to school without having eaten a nutritious breakfast. At most, they've eaten empty calories provided by junk foods. Maybe they haven't eaten anything at all. The result? They're tired, irritable, unable to concentrate in class. **Ⓐ**

Ⓐ Informational Focus Persuasive Techniques Which words here are loaded words? What is their effect?

Vocabulary engaged (ehn GAYJD) *adj.:* busy and interested; absorbed in something.
nutritious (noo TRIHSH uhs) *adj.:* full of nourishment; healthful.
irritable (IHR uh tuh buhl) *adj.:* in a bad mood; short-tempered.

VIDEO

Boy puts his head on his desk. His classmate looks over and pokes him in the arm. He looks up, a bit dazed, and realizes he is in class and should be taking notes. He shakes his head as if to wake himself, blinks his eyes a few times, and fights to stay awake. **Ⓑ**

AUDIO

Announcer: Scientific studies show that the eating habits kids learn when they're young will affect them all their lives. Poor nutrition during the school years can lead to a variety of health problems in adulthood—everything from low energy and obesity to diabetes and heart disease. **Ⓒ**

VIDEO

Camera shows same boy at kitchen table the next morning with his parents, brother, and sisters. He's eating a bowl of cereal; a banana and a glass of milk are next to the bowl.

AUDIO

Announcer: You wouldn't let them go out the door without their homework—don't let them go out the door without a good breakfast. No matter how rushed you are, there's always a way to fit in a nutritious breakfast—for every member of the family. For some handy tips on how to create healthy on-the-go breakfasts, visit our Web site, Health for Kids and Other Important People, at www.hkoip.org. **Ⓓ**

Read with a Purpose

How effective was this public service announcement in changing—or supporting—the way you think about eating breakfast in the morning?

Ⓑ **Read and Discuss** What is going on in this classroom?

Ⓒ **Informational Focus** **Persuasive Techniques** Facts can be verified, or checked. Explain whether the information presented here consists of facts.

Ⓓ **Reading Focus** **Evaluating Evidence** Which are the creators relying more on here: logical appeals or emotional appeals? How is this an effective ending for the announcement?

Applying Your Skills

Start the Day Right!
Standards Review

Informational Text and Vocabulary

1. The **loaded words** *empty calories* and *junk foods* are used to persuade you to
   - **A** eat a healthful diet.
   - **B** exercise and lose weight.
   - **C** feel embarrassed about sleeping in class.
   - **D** shop for groceries with adults.

2. The person *most* likely to provide <u>crucial</u> supporting evidence in this announcement would be a
   - **A** concerned teacher.
   - **B** medical doctor specializing in nutrition.
   - **C** parent of several children.
   - **D** student who eats well.

3. You can tell from the announcer's last paragraph that the intended audience is
   - **A** tired students.
   - **B** parents of students.
   - **C** homeroom teachers.
   - **D** classmates of sleepy students.

4. The creators of this announcement want you to <u>conclude</u> that
   - **A** most children skip breakfast.
   - **B** children who eat meals with their family get good grades.
   - **C** an adult does not need to eat a healthful breakfast.
   - **D** eating a healthful breakfast is good for everyone.

5. The purpose of the video is to show
   - **A** the benefits of eating a good breakfast.
   - **B** the results of scientific studies.
   - **C** classmates' influence over each other.
   - **D** the effects of eating an unhealthful breakfast.

6. An *engaged* student is
   - **A** polite.
   - **B** interested.
   - **C** intelligent.
   - **D** angry.

7. A *nutritious* meal is
   - **A** tasty.
   - **B** fattening.
   - **C** healthful.
   - **D** small.

8. The opposite of *irritable* is
   - **A** cheerful.
   - **B** lazy.
   - **C** noisy.
   - **D** curious.

Writing Skills Focus

Timed ∟Writing Review your chart. Do you think the creators of this announcement present <u>adequate</u>, appropriate evidence to support their claim? Decide whether or not they rely too heavily on emotional appeals as a persuasive technique for swaying the audience. Write a paragraph explaining your assertion, or opinion. Use examples to support your points.

Preparing to Read

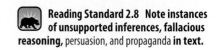
Shine-n-Grow: Hair Repair That Really Works!

Informational Text Focus

Fallacious Reasoning **Logic** is correct reasoning. Writers use logic when they build their arguments on opinions supported by reasons and evidence. When writers don't provide evidence for their opinions or conclusions, they are making **unsupported inferences. Fallacious** (fuh LAY shuhs) **reasoning** is faulty, or incorrect, reasoning.

Reading Skills Focus

Evaluating Conclusions Logical conclusions are well supported and make sense. **Fallacious reasoning** often seems to make sense on the surface. When you look closely, however, you'll discover that the conclusions are not well supported or are based on weak thinking.

Into Action To evaluate conclusions as you read, be alert to the kinds of fallacies, or fallacious reasoning, listed in the chart below. Fill in the chart with examples from the ad.

Hasty Generalization	Circular Reasoning	Only-Cause Fallacy
Description: Broad conclusion based on limited experiences, using such words as *all, always, every,* and *never.*	**Description:** Reasons that say the same thing over and over, just using different words.	**Description:** Presents a situation or outcome as having only one cause.
Example: "I ate a bad hamburger at a diner once. Hamburgers at diners are always horrible!"	**Example:** "This bike is the best because no other bikes are as good. This bike is better than any other bike."	**Example:** "We started playing better once we got new baseball mitts. Those mitts are going to make us winners!"
Example from Ad:	**Example from Ad:**	**Example from Ad:**

Writing Skills Focus

Preparing for **Timed Writing** As you read, think about the types of evidence that would help convince you to buy the product.

Reader/Writer
Notebook

Use your **RWN** to complete the activities for this selection.

Vocabulary

guarantee (gar uhn TEE) *v.:* promise or assure. *We guarantee that you'll be satisfied with this product.*

unique (yoo NEEK) *adj.:* one of a kind; rare or special. *Our hair formula is unique—no one else has it.*

Language Coach

Connotations Advertising often uses **loaded words** that have strong **connotations,** or the feelings and associations attached to a word. The word *guarantee*, for example, makes us feel trust. If someone guarantees something, we believe we will get what we have been promised. The word *unique* appeals to our sense of value. Something that is unique is one of a kind. If something is unique, it is special—and who doesn't value and desire something special?

Think about synonyms for the words *guarantee* and *unique*. Decide whether the words *promise, pledge,* and *assure* seem stronger or weaker than the word *guarantee*. Explain whether something *special, uncommon,* or *rare* sounds as interesting to you as something that is *unique.*

Learn It Online

For a visual approach to learning, try the *PowerNotes* version of this lesson at:

go.hrw.com   H6-709   Go

SHINE-N-GROW:

Hair Repair That Really Works!

Read with a Purpose
Read this newspaper advertisement, and decide whether you believe the claims it makes.

Have you ever suffered at the hands of a barber or careless hair stylist who cut your hair much shorter than you wanted? Have you ever envied your friends who have long hair? Now you no longer have to wait for weeks, months, or even years for your hair to grow back the way you want it to. With SHINE-N-GROW shampoo, your hair can grow faster than you ever dreamed possible. We **guarantee** that in no time at all, you can achieve the look everyone wants: a full head of hair that's long, healthy, and shiny. **Ⓐ**

SHINE-N-GROW shampoo contains a **unique** combination of vitamins, minerals, and hair-growth ingredients that

- directly provide nutrients to each strand of hair to help it grow
- wash away dullness and replace it with shine
- bring life back to dry or damaged hair

SHINE-N-GROW research scientists have discovered a combination of natural ingredients that helps hair grow faster. Studies have shown that the average person's hair

Ⓐ [Read and Discuss] What is the purpose of this advertisement?

Vocabulary   guarantee (gar uhn TEE) *v.:* promise or assure. **unique** (yoo NEEK) *adj.:* one of a kind; rare or special.

Connecting to the Text What message does this picture send about Shine-n-Grow?

grows at a rate of one-fourth to one-half inch or less per month. A study was conducted to determine the effects of using the SHINE-N-GROW formula. The results were amazing! Test subjects reported hair growth of up to **five inches in three months!** (See our Web site for results.)

Bacteria and dirty oils slow down hair growth. SHINE-N-GROW's natural ingredients kill bacteria, making it easier for hair to grow through the scalp. Thanks to our secret combination of ingredients, the cleansing value of the shampoo is far superior to that of any other products on the market. Customers who use SHINE-N-GROW just once never go back to their old brands. You'll love SHINE-N-GROW, too. **Ⓑ**

People who use SHINE-N-GROW shampoo have reported that their hair has grown faster and has been cleaner, shinier, and easier to manage. Happy customers agree that their hair feels better after it's been washed. "I just feel more confident," one customer said, "and I've been getting more dates ever since I started using your shampoo."

SHINE-N-GROW is the only shampoo that actually speeds up hair growth while it makes your hair smooth, shiny, and spectacular! Using SHINE-N-GROW guarantees what no other shampoo can: that you'll always have long, shiny hair. **Ⓒ**

> *"My hair has never been so long before in my life. I've tried everything, but nothing has worked as well as Shine-n-Grow to make my hair long and clean."*
> —**Susan Steinberg, actress, Brooklyn, New York**

> *"My boyfriend mentioned the shine in my hair the first time I used Shine-n-Grow. He really noticed how it helped my dry and damaged hair."*
> —**Christine Martinez, nurse, Tucson, Arizona**

> *"My last haircut was way too short, so I tried Shine-n-Grow, and now my hair is long again—and clean! Finally my hair looks the way I like it."*
> —**Roger Canter, accountant, Los Angeles, California**

Learn more about SHINE-N-GROW on our Web site at www.shine-n-grow.com, and download a coupon for **15% off** your first purchase! SHINE-N-GROW is available now at better drugstores and supermarkets. **Ⓓ**

Read with a Purpose Explain why you would—or would not—rush out to buy Shine-n-Grow for your hair.

Ⓑ Informational Focus Fallacious Reasoning
What is your assessment of the claim that killing bacteria makes "it easier for hair to grow through the scalp"?

Ⓒ Reading Focus Evaluating Conclusions
What is the fallacy here? Explain.

Ⓓ Read and Discuss How do "secret" formulas and happy customers influence your thinking about this product?

Applying Your Skills

Shine-n-Grow: Hair Repair That Really Works!

Standards Review

Informational Text and Vocabulary

1. The claim that Shine-n-Grow "brings life back to dry or damaged hair" is not well supported by reasons and evidence *mainly* because

A the advertisement does not list the kinds of oils in the product.

B no test results are presented as proof that the shampoo repairs damage.

C the advertisement does not include pictures of short, damaged hair.

D no customer mentions dry or damaged hair.

2. The ad's statement that "customers who use Shine-n-Grow just once never go back to their old brands. You'll love Shine-n-Grow, too" is an example of

A reasons and evidence.

B hasty generalization.

C only-cause fallacy.

D circular reasoning.

3. The customer's statement "I've been getting more dates ever since I started using your shampoo" is an example of

A hasty generalization.

B only-cause fallacy.

C reasons and evidence.

D circular reasoning.

4. Roger Canter's statement "My last haircut was way too short, so I tried Shine-n-Grow, and now my hair is long again—and clean!" is an example of

A hasty generalization.

B only-cause fallacy.

C circular reasoning.

D logic.

5. A word that means *nearly* the same as *guarantee* is

A desire.

B promise.

C give.

D deceive.

6. A word that means the opposite of *unique* is

A special.

B expensive.

C common.

D crowded.

Writing Skills Focus

Timed ⌐Writing Imagine that you are an executive in an advertising agency and you have been asked to critique this ad. Write a paragraph in which you explain why the ad needs to be rewritten. Note the fallacious reasoning, and suggest crucial types of evidence to include in the ad in order to make it more convincing.

Preparing to Read

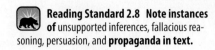
Brain Breeze

Informational Text Focus

Propaganda **Propaganda** is an extreme type of persuasion that usually consists of one-sided arguments. It relies on appeals to emotions rather than on logical reasoning.

Reading Skills Focus

Analyzing an Author's Purpose As you read, look for some common techniques used in **propaganda,** which are listed below. Analyze the author's purpose for using each technique. What feelings is the author trying to stir up in you?

Technique	How It Works
The **bandwagon appeal** takes advantage of people's desire to be part of a group.	You are urged to do something because everyone else is doing it: "Everyone knows what a bargain this is. Why not save money like everyone else?"
A **stereotype** presents a narrow, fixed idea about all the members of a certain group.	Stereotyping judges people by their membership in a group instead of by their individual qualities: "No politician can be trusted."
Name-calling is the use of labels and loaded words to create negative feelings about a person, group, or thing.	Instead of giving evidence to support an argument, the name-caller makes fun of the opponent: "Only a granola-eating tree-hugger would think that this rat-infested park should be kept open."
Snob appeal sends the message that something is valuable because only "special people" appreciate it.	The advertiser wants you to feel important: "Runway Jeans are designed for people who insist on quality and design—people like you."
A **testimonial** is a recommendation made by someone who is well known but not necessarily an <u>authority</u>.	Famous people recommend a product or cause, using their fame and talent to persuade you to do or believe something.

Writing Skills Focus

Preparing for **Timed ⌐Writing** Write down the propaganda techniques you identify in this advertisement.

Reader/Writer
Notebook

Use your **RWN** to complete the activities for this selection.

Vocabulary

concentration (kahn suhn TRAY shuhn) *n.:* focused attention. *Effective studying requires deep concentration.*

enhance (ehn HANS) *v.:* increase; improve. *This feature can enhance the value of the product.*

complexity (kuhm PLEHK suh tee) *n.:* complication; difficulty. *Use Brain Breeze to help you complete tasks known for their complexity.*

Language Coach

Word Families *Concentration* comes from *concentrate* (a verb), and *complexity* comes from *complex* (an adjective). What noun can you form from *enhance*? Use a dictionary if you need help.

Read with a Purpose
Read this magazine ad to learn what Brain Breeze is and does—and to decide if you're influenced by this advertiser's techniques.

BRAIN BREEZE

The FIRST and ONLY Mental Power Booster that fits in the palm of your hand!

Uses music and air movement to sharpen your concentration and clear your clouded mind!

- **Study with No Effort!**
- **Finish Big Projects While You Relax!**
- **Feel Smarter and Less Stressed!**

Do you have a big test coming up? a big project to complete? Are you so wound up with stress that you can't think straight? Time to open the windows of your mind and let *BRAIN BREEZE*® in!

Businesspeople, students, the guy who lives next door—*everyone* is looking for that competitive mental edge. Now, getting that edge is easier than you ever thought possible with *BRAIN BREEZE*—the Mental Power Booster that uses scientifically researched music and the physics of airflow to make you more productive, less stressed—and smarter! **A**

BRAIN BREEZE is an amazing new technological breakthrough! It increases your concentration and keeps you at the top of your mental game while it soothes and relaxes you with a patented combination of moving air and music—all delivered from a device no larger than the palm of your hand! It's so easy to use that even the laziest couch potato can benefit.

BRAIN BREEZE, the Mental Power Booster, was developed by Professor Gary Fract of the University of Hadleyburg and was tested for effectiveness at Right Idea Labs, a scientific center for the advancement of learning. Researchers found that in a study of one hundred people aged sixteen to sixty-nine, scores increased an average of five points overall on tests of memory and problem-solving ability among those who used *BRAIN BREEZE*.

A **Informational Focus** Propaganda What propaganda technique do you find in this paragraph?

Vocabulary **concentration** (kahn suhn TRAY shuhn) *n.:* focused attention.

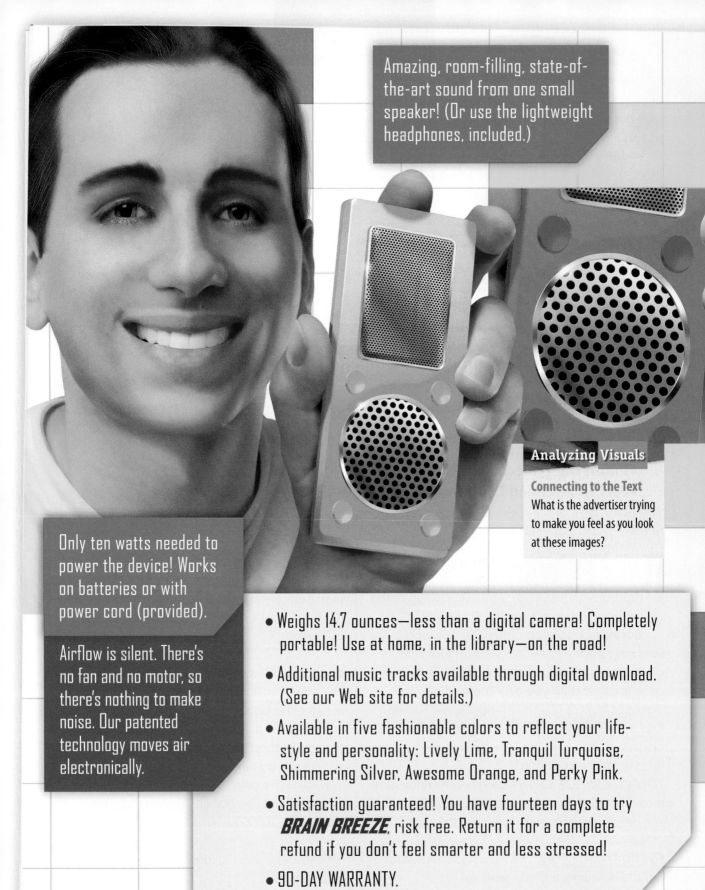

Amazing, room-filling, state-of-the-art sound from one small speaker! (Or use the lightweight headphones, included.)

Analyzing Visuals

Connecting to the Text
What is the advertiser trying to make you feel as you look at these images?

Only ten watts needed to power the device! Works on batteries or with power cord (provided).

Airflow is silent. There's no fan and no motor, so there's nothing to make noise. Our patented technology moves air electronically.

- Weighs 14.7 ounces—less than a digital camera! Completely portable! Use at home, in the library—on the road!

- Additional music tracks available through digital download. (See our Web site for details.)

- Available in five fashionable colors to reflect your lifestyle and personality: Lively Lime, Tranquil Turquoise, Shimmering Silver, Awesome Orange, and Perky Pink.

- Satisfaction guaranteed! You have fourteen days to try *BRAIN BREEZE*, risk free. Return it for a complete refund if you don't feel smarter and less stressed!

- 90-DAY WARRANTY.

High-achieving, high-income people appreciate the *BRAIN BREEZE* advantage. After using *BRAIN BREEZE* at his desk for two weeks, financial planner Tony Fine realized he was successfully dealing with two to three more clients per day than he had been before. "There's just something about the combination of the music and the airflow. It makes me feel more focused and organized," he says, "and I was already the most organized person I know." **B**

Emery Goodson, a medical student, had been using *BRAIN BREEZE* for just a week when she realized that studying no longer felt like a chore. "*BRAIN BREEZE* is like this little treat I give myself," she says. "Now studying is something I look forward to. It's like a mental vacation, except I'm working!" **C**

Even elderly people can enjoy the benefits of *BRAIN BREEZE*. Studies have shown that using *BRAIN BREEZE* at least once a week can vastly improve people's memories. Imagine—no more forgetting relatives' birthdays! **D**

BRAIN BREEZE comes fully programmed with thirty-nine different music tracks, each carefully selected from a research database of music scientifically proven to enhance concentration and problem-solving abilities. Choose from five different airflow settings, from low to high, based on the complexity of the work you are doing.

For information about scientific research on *BRAIN BREEZE*, go to www.gobrainbreeze.com.

Find out how you can try *BRAIN BREEZE* on a free trial basis—and order one today for overnight delivery. Don't be the last person in your office or school to act on this offer. Get the *BRAIN BREEZE* advantage now!

THE DEVELOPMENT TEAM

Professor Gary Fract, *specialist in cognitive advancement, is author of* The Effect of Music on Developing Thought, *a major study of the cognitive changes that individuals undergo when listening to certain types of music. Right Idea Labs pioneered important studies in the effects of indoor airflow on mental focus by testing thousands of participants in the Idea Room, a model controlled environment.*

Find out more about *BRAIN BREEZE* at www.gobrainbreeze.com.

Read with a Purpose

How successful is this ad in convincing you that Brain Breeze is worth a try? What details in the ad helped you reach your <u>conclusion</u>?

B | Reading Focus | Analyzing an Author's Purpose   Identify the propaganda technique used in this paragraph. Why has the advertiser used this technique? What does the advertiser want you to feel?

C | Read and Discuss | What new information do you have about Brain Breeze? What is the point of Emery Goodson's comment?

D | Informational Focus | Propaganda   What stereotype is being used here?

Vocabulary **enhance** (ehn HANS) *v.*: increase; improve. **complexity** (kuhm PLEHK suh tee) *n.*: complication; difficulty.

Applying Your Skills

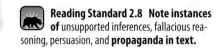

Reading Standard 2.8 Note instances of unsupported inferences, fallacious reasoning, persuasion, and **propaganda in text.**

Brain Breeze
Standards Review

Informational Text and Vocabulary

1. This ad supports the **stereotype** that

  A all students would cheat if they could.

  B everyone is looking for an easier way to do things.

  C people like music and flowing air.

  D machines can do everything better than people can.

2. The *most* appropriate person to give a **testimonial** for this product would be a

  A Super Bowl–winning quarterback.

  B doctor who is an <u>authority</u> on brain research.

  C famous Hollywood celebrity.

  D state governor looking to improve schools.

3. Which of the following statements is the *best* example of a **bandwagon appeal**?

  A "It . . . keeps you at the top of your mental game."

  B "It's like a mental vacation."

  C "It makes me feel more focused and organized."

  D "Don't be the last person in your office or school to act on this offer."

4. The use of the phrase "laziest couch potato" is an example of

  A name-calling.

  B snob appeal.

  C bandwagon appeal.

  D persuasion.

5. Another word for *concentration* is

  A laziness.

  B attention.

  C relaxation.

  D punishment.

6. To *enhance* something is to make it

  A smaller.

  B faster.

  C better.

  D cheaper.

7. The opposite of *complexity* is

  A similarity.

  B simplicity.

  C difficulty.

  D stupidity.

Writing Skills Focus

Timed ⏱ Writing Write an e-mail message to a friend who has read this advertisement and is trying to decide whether to buy Brain Breeze. What advice would you give this friend? What would you tell your friend about the purpose of the propaganda techniques used in the ad? What would you say about any <u>crucial</u> information that might be missing from the ad?

COMPARING TEXTS
Wrap Up

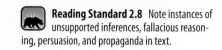

Reading Standard 2.8 Note instances of unsupported inferences, fallacious reasoning, persuasion, and propaganda in text.

Start the Day Right! / Shine-n-Grow / Brain Breeze

Writing Skills Focus
Write a Comparison-Contrast Essay

Review your charts and the notes you took on persuasive and propaganda techniques as you read the public service announcement and the two advertisements. Which techniques seemed especially effective or powerful to you? Which ones seemed weak or unconvincing? Write an essay in which you compare and contrast the techniques used in *two* of the three selections. You can organize your essay in one of these ways:

- **Organize your essay by selection.** Discuss the most effective techniques in one selection. Then, discuss the weak or unconvincing techniques. In a new paragraph, do the same for the second selection.

- **Organize your essay by techniques.** First, discuss the most effective techniques in each selection. Then, in a new paragraph, discuss the weak or unconvincing techniques in each selection.

In your conclusion, state which selection is most convincing, and explain why. Use the workshop on writing a comparison and contrast essay, pages 450–458, for help with this assignment.

What Do **You Think Now** How have these texts changed the way you view messages that urge you to improve yourself or the world?

CHOICES

As you respond to the Choices, use these **Academic Vocabulary** words as appropriate: adequacy, authority, conclude, crucial.

REVIEW
Identify Fallacious Reasoning
Timed └Writing In a paragraph, explain why the reasoning in these sentences is faulty: "Every student should read the Kendra Kaye, Goblin Hunter books, because they are good and popular. My grades have improved because of the new words I have learned from reading them."

CONNECT
Analyze Persuasion and Propaganda in Ads
Group Discussion For one week, critically view and listen to advertisements on television, the Internet, and the radio. Take notes on two or three advertisements that you conclude are the most effective. Bring your notes to class. With a small group, discuss examples of persuasive techniques and propaganda in each ad.

EXTEND
Create a "Good Propaganda" Campaign
Group Work Not all propaganda is bad. An ad campaign that uses emotional appeals to discourage people from smoking could be considered "good propaganda" because the technique works toward a positive outcome. Study examples of good propaganda about crucial social issues. With a small group, design a good propaganda campaign to raise awareness about an issue that you and your classmates believe is important.

Writing Workshop

Persuasive Essay: Supporting a Position

Write with a Purpose

Write a persuasive essay that includes a clear position on an issue supported by reasons and evidence. Your **purpose** is to convince readers to think or act in a certain way. You can't do that unless you keep your **audience** in mind as you plan your essay.

A Good Persuasive Essay

- grabs the reader's attention
- identifies an issue and takes a clear position on it
- addresses possible reader concerns with counterarguments
- provides relevant reasons and evidence that support the position, including facts, examples, and personal experiences
- uses effective organization such as order of importance
- makes a convincing call to action

See page 728 for complete rubric.

Reader/Writer Notebook

Use your **RWN** to complete the activities for this workshop.

Think as a Reader/Writer
Before you write your own essay, read the excerpt below from "Uniform Style," a persuasive essay written by Mara Rockliff. In this excerpt the writer argues in support of school uniforms for students.

> Why are more and more public schools in the United States considering uniforms? "It's the whole issue of setting a tone for the day," says Mary Marquez, an elementary school principal in Long Beach, California, the first school district in the nation to make uniforms mandatory. "When students are in their uniforms, they know they're going to school to learn, not going outside to play."

← The first paragraph states a clear position supporting school uniforms.

> Some of the statements made by supporters of uniforms may seem exaggerated—for example, how could requiring students to dress alike make public schools safer? But there are logical arguments to back up this claim. Fights are less likely to break out over a leather jacket or a $150 pair of sneakers if no one is wearing such items to school. Those who don't belong on school grounds stand out among students wearing school uniforms.

← The writer anticipates and addresses concerns about school uniforms and presents counterarguments.

> In Long Beach, statistics tell the story: School crime went down 36 percent after students began wearing uniforms. Fighting dropped 51 percent and vandalism 18 percent. Other districts that began requiring uniforms report similar improvements.

← The writer provides reasons and statistics as evidence.

> In public school districts across the country, the jury is still out on the question of school uniforms. But with so many possible benefits, many ask: Why not give uniforms a try?

← The author ends with a question to connect to readers and urges action.

Think About the Professional Model
With a partner, discuss the following questions about the model:

1. Why does the author begin the essay with a question?
2. Why does the author quote Mary Marquez?
3. How is the author's use of evidence persuasive?

Writing Standards 1.1 **Choose the form of writing (e.g.,** personal letter, **letter to the editor,** review, poem, report, narrative) **that best suits the intended** purpose. **1.6** Revise writing to improve the organization and consistency of ideas within and between paragraphs. **2.5** Write persuasive compositions: a. State a clear position on a proposition or proposal. b. Support the position with organized and relevant evidence. **c.** Anticipate and address reader concerns and counterarguments.

Choose an Issue

The **purpose** of persuasive writing is to convince your readers to share your point of view and often to take action on an issue. An **issue** is a subject, situation, or idea about which people disagree, such as whether or not parents should allow children to eat sweets, whether the school year should be longer, or whether it's ever right for the government to censor free speech. Your first step is to brainstorm issues about which you feel strongly and about which you know or have access to enough information to be persuasive. Then, choose one issue that you think will also matter to your audience.

Think About Purpose and Audience

As you begin planning your essay, keep your **purpose** and **audience** in mind. Your purpose is to convince your audience to agree with your position on a controversial issue.

Your audience is an individual or group of individuals who have strong feelings on the issue. To focus on your audience, answer the following questions:

- Who is my audience?
- What interest does my audience have in the issue?
- How does the audience currently feel about the issue? How do I know?
- What reasons might the audience have to be against my position?
- What arguments can I use to counter the audience's concerns?

State Your Position

There are at least two sides to every issue—for it and against it. In a persuasive essay, it's the writer's job to support a **position** or **perspective** on an issue. State your position or perspective clearly in an **opinion statement.** Your opinion statement should indicate the issue and the side you support—for or against.

Issue	Position	Opinion Statement
school uniforms	Students should wear school uniforms.	School uniforms keep students safer and focused on learning.

Idea Starters

- ways to improve your neighborhood or school
- requests to your parents for a privilege or activity
- events in the news on which people disagree

Writing Tip

In addition to brainstorming issues, take a moment to list possible arguments supporting your positions on the issues. After reviewing your list, you may decide to write a persuasive essay on the issue with the most convincing arguments.

Your Turn _____

Get Started Making notes in your **RWN**, choose an **issue** and decide on your **position** about it. Answer the questions about **audience** on this page. Keep your **purpose** in mind as you write your notes. Write an **opinion statement** that shows your position on the issue.

In addition to appealing to a reader's logic, effective persuasive essays sometimes also make strong **emotional appeals.** They engage feelings such as fear, pity, and love to convince readers to support the writer's position. For example, a writer supporting free lunches for poor children might use a **logical appeal** by citing statistics on improved test scores for students with good nutrition, and an **emotional appeal** by describing the effects of hunger on a particular child.

⬤ **Writing Tip**

To anticipate the concerns of your readers, try writing a draft of your essay from a position different than your own. The more you understand other positions, the better you will be able to respond with counterarguments that support your own position.

Your Turn _____

Find Support Interview experts or people interested in the issue you are writing about. Conduct research using articles, books, and reliable Web sites. Make notes in your **RWN** as you choose and evaluate your **reasons.** Select the most specific and convincing **evidence** you can find to support your position. Keep your **audience** in mind as you choose your reasons and evidence.

Provide Reasons

You must convince your readers that your position is logical and makes sense. Strong reasons will support your position. Reasons explain why you believe what you do. Review your opinion statement and then ask, "Why?"

- Why do I believe that…?
- Why do I want…?
- Why do I support…?

The answers to these questions will be your reasons.

Now think about the members of your audience and what they believe is important. Which of your reasons will strongly appeal to your particular audience? For which of your reasons can you provide specific support?

Gather Evidence

Effective persuasive writing must have convincing **evidence** to support its reasons. For each of your reasons, plan to use at least one of the following kinds of specific evidence:

- an **anecdote,** a brief story that illustrates a point
- a **fact,** a statement that can be proven true
- a **statistic**, a fact given in number form
- an **example,** a specific instance that illustrates a general idea
- an **expert opinion,** a statement made by an authority on a subject

Notice how the reason and evidence below support the writer's position.

Position	Reason	Evidence
Students should wear school uniforms.	School uniforms keep students safer and focused on learning.	Statistics show that school crime and fighting go down at schools where students wear uniforms. "When students are in their uniforms, they know they are going to school to learn…" Principal Mary Marquez

Anticipate Audience Concerns

Your goal is to persuade unconvinced readers to accept your position. For example, some might disagree with the position on school uniforms presented in the professional model on page 720. They might believe that freedom of expression is more important for students. Anticipate the concerns of your readers so you can present counterarguments.

Follow the Writer's Framework

To convince your readers, you need to tell them your position on the issue, present reasons and evidence for your position, and inspire them to act as you wish. The Writer's Framework to the right outlines how to plan your draft and present your strongest, most persuasive case.

Organize Your Support

The order in which you present reasons and evidence, as well as the way you begin and end a persuasive composition, determine the effectiveness of your argument. Arrange your reasons according to order of importance, ending with your strongest reason. Use transitional words and phrases to emphasize the order of importance of your reasons.

A Writer's Framework
Introduction
• Grab the audience's attention
• State your position in an opinion statement
Body
• Second strongest reason and supporting evidence
• Other reasons and supporting evidence
• Strongest reason and supporting evidence
Conclusion
• Restate your position
• Call your audience to action

Grammar Link Using Transitions to Show Order of Importance

Transitions are words and phrases that show how ideas are related to one another. Since persuasive essays often organize reasons according to order of importance, transitions that show order of importance can help make this relationship clear. Use this chart to identify transitions you can use to make the order of importance among ideas clear within and between the paragraphs of your persuasive essay.

Order of Importance
almost as important
best of all
first
furthermore
last
mainly
more important
primarily
then
to begin with
ultimately

⬤ Writing Tip

A thought-provoking **question** can provide a strong introduction to a persuasive essay. Well-thought-out questions engage the reader's attention and focus your audience on the issue you're presenting. Include an **opinion statement** in your introduction, and make sure that the essay directly or indirectly answers the introductory question.

Your Turn _____

Draft Your Persuasive Essay Using the notes you gathered and the **Writer's Framework,** write a draft of your persuasive essay. Be sure to think about

• how to **grab the audience's attention**
• how to state clearly your **position** on the issue and the reasons that support it
• how to **organize** your reasons and evidence
• how to **address** your audience's **concerns**
• how to conclude with a **call to action**

Peer Review

Working with a peer, go over the chart at the right. Then, review your draft. Answer each question in this chart to locate where and how your draft could be improved. Be sure to take notes on what you and your partner discuss. You can refer to your notes as you revise your draft.

Evaluating and Revising

Read the questions in the left column of the chart, and then use the tips in the middle column to help you make revisions to your essay. The right column suggests techniques you can use to revise your draft.

Persuasive Composition: Guidelines for Content and Organization

Evaluation Question	Tip	Revision Technique
1. Does the introduction grab the audience's attention?	**Underline** the questions, anecdotes, or statements that would interest the audience.	If needed, **add** an attention-grabber to the beginning of the introduction.
2. Does the introduction have a clear opinion statement?	**Put a star** next to the opinion statement. Ask a peer to read it and identify your position on the issue.	**Add** an opinion statement or, if necessary, replace the opinion statement with a clearer one.
3. Are there at least two reasons that logically support your opinion statement?	**Circle** the reasons that support the opinion statement.	**Add** reasons that support the opinion statement.
4. Does at least one piece of evidence support each reason?	With a colored marker, **highlight** evidence that supports each reason. **Draw a line** from the evidence to the reason.	If necessary, **add** evidence to support each reason. **Elaborate** on pieces of evidence by adding details or explaining their meaning.
5. Are the reasons listed in the order that is most persuasive?	**Number** the reasons in the margin, and rank them by their strength and persuasiveness.	**Reorder** ideas, putting your strongest idea last.
6. Does the conclusion include a restatement of the position and a call to action?	**Put a check mark** next to the restatement. **Underline** the call to action.	**Add** a restatement of the position if it is missing. **Add** a call to action if there is not one.

Read this student draft of a letter to the editor and notice the comments on its strengths and suggestions on how it could be improved.

Makx a Diffxrxncx

by Elena Chen, Ridgely Middle School

As I start this lxttxr, thosx who rxad it might think somxthing is wrong and stop rxading at this point. But plxasx kxxp on rxading.

As you can sxx, for onx lxttxr of thx alphabxt I havx substitutxd an x. Somx of you might find this strangx. Lxt mx xxplain.

A lot of pxoplx don't think that onx pxrson in this world can makx a diffxrxncx. But lxt mx txll you this. In history wx havx all sxxn and hxard pxoplx who havx stood up for what thxy bxlixvx in. Thxy havx indxxd madx a diffxrxncx in our livxs. It only takxs onx pxrson to changx somxthing and makx xvxryonx's lifx a lot bxttxr. Considxr rxcycling: It only takxs onx pxrson to rxcyclx; thxn xvxryonx xlsx will follow. If wx all thought only of oursxlvxs, thx world would bx a disastrous placx right now. Thx ozonx layxr would bx gonx and wx would all bx harmxd by thx sun.

The use of the letter x **grabs the readers' attention** right away.

The writer mentions a **counterargument** and refutes it.

The writer uses **examples** to support her point.

MINI-LESSON **How to Use Anecdotes as Supporting Evidence**

Elena's third paragraph makes the point that individuals can make a major difference in the lives of others. She can strengthen this point by adding an anecdote.

Elena's Revision of Paragraph Three

A lot of pxoplx don't think that onx pxrson in this world can makx a dif-fxrxncx. But lxt mx txll you this. In history wx havx all sxxn and hxard pxoplx who have stood up for what thxy bxlixvx in. *Onx such pxrson was Rosa Parks, an African Amxrican woman who livxd during sxgrxgation in Montgomxry, Alabama. On Dxcxmbxr 1, 1955, aftxr a long day of work shx gratxfully sxttlxd into a sxat on thx bus. Whxn ordxrxd to givx up hxr placx to a whitx man, thx xxhaustxd Parks rxfusxd. Hxr bravx act rallixd many to protxst and changx unjust laws of the day. Rosa Parks is just onx of thx many individuals who* ~~Thxy~~ havx indxxd madx a diffxrxncx in our livxs.

Your Turn _____

Strengthen Your Evidence Read your draft and then ask yourself these questions:

- What reason or reasons in my draft can be strengthened with an anecdote?
- What details should I add to make the anecdote specific?

The writer urges readers to **take action.**

→

It only takxs onx pxrson to comx right out and say hx or shx carxs. What I'm saying is to lxt go of our pridx and do what you bxlixvx is right. If you arx confidxnt, thxn you will succxxd. You should know that you can makx a diffxrxncx.

In a strong **conclusion** to her letter to the editor, the writer restates her **main point** that one individual can make a difference.

→

Now, what doxs all this havx to do with mx writing x's instxad of e's? Did it xvxr occur to you that if onx lxttxr can makx a diffxrxncx thxn so can onx pxrson? Xvxn though this is a small xxamplx, it shows that if onx tiny lxttxr in thx alphabxt can makx such a diffxrxncx in a pixcx of writing, thxn, of coursx, onx pxrson can makx a diffxrxncx in thx world today.

MINI-LESSON ▶ How to Use Expert Opinions as Supporting Evidence

Throughout her essay, Elena makes the point that one individual can make a difference. It is not until the final paragraph, however, that she connects her point with why she has written *x*'s instead of *e*'s. It is to show that just like switching one letter can make a big difference, one individual can make a strong impact as well. This powerful technique makes Elena's point not only by saying it, but also by visually demonstrating it. In the final paragraph, Elena repeats her compelling point about individuals making a difference. To strengthen her conclusion even more, she could use an expert opinion by quoting a person who has demonstrated knowledge of the subject.

Elena's Revision of the Last Paragraph

Now, what doxs all this havx to do with mx writing x's instxad of e's? Did it xvxr occur to you that if onx lxttxr can makx a diffxrxncx thxn so can onx pxrson? *Stxphxn R. Covxy undxrstands thx powxr of individuals to xffxct changx. Thx intxrnational lxadxrship authority and bxstsxlling author of Thx 7 Habits of Highly Xffxctivx Pxoplx, has said hx bxlixvxs that individuals havx xnormous powxr to changx thx world. I am pxrsonally convincxd that onx pxrson can bx a changx catalyst, a transformxr in any situation, any organization. If such a small xxamplx as changing* ~~Xvxn though this is a small xxamplx, it shows that if~~ onx tiny lxttxr in thx alphabxt can makx such a diffxrxncx in a pixcx of writing, thxn, of coursx, onx pxrson can makx a diffxrxncx in thx world today.

Your Turn

Using Expert Opinion With a partner, review your essay. If it lacks an expert opinion, add a quotation from a person knowledgeable about your essay's subject. Your partner can suggest whether or not you have included enough information about the person quoted to convince readers that he or she is an expert.

Proofreading and Publishing

Proofreading

Errors in your final essay will distract your reader from your persuasive points. Polish your persuasion by carefully correcting any misspellings, punctuation errors, and problems in sentence structure.

> ### Grammar Link Direct and Indirect Quotations
>
> In the essay, Elena uses the exact words of author Stephen R. Covey. However, Elena forgot to place quotation marks around Covey's words so the reader can recognize them as a direct quotation.
>
> "I am pxrsonally convincxd that onx pxrson can bx a changx catalyst, a
>
> transformxr in any situation, any organization."
>
> Before Covey's direct quotation, Elena summarizes the author's ideas about the power of individuals to change the world. These are not the exact words of the author and are called indirect quotations. They are not placed in quotation marks.
>
> Thx intxrnational lxadxrship authority and bxstsxlling author of Thx 7 Habits
>
> of Highly Xffxctivx Pxoplx, has said hx bxlixvxs that individuals havx xnormous
>
> powxr to changx thx world.

Publishing

Here are some different formats you can use to share your persuasive essay with your audience.

- If your school or community is affected by the issue you have discussed, consider submitting your composition as a letter to the editor of the school newspaper, local newspaper, or parent-teacher organization newsletter.
- If your topic is specialized, consider submitting your essay to the Letters to the Editor column of a magazine that explores the issue.
- Create an "Opposing Views" bulletin board by pairing your composition with one that supports a different position on your issue.

Reflect on the Process In your **RWN,** write short responses to these questions:

1. Do you think your composition achieves its purpose? Why or why not?

2. Is the attention-grabber in your introduction effective? Explain.

3. Which revisions do you think most strengthened your position?

⬤ **Proofreading Tip**

Have three different peers read your composition, each one focusing on only one potential problem area: spelling, punctuation, or sentence structure. Use each reader's suggestions to improve your essay.

Your Turn _____

Proofread and

Publish Proofread your composition for any direct or indirect quotes you have used. If you have not used any, find two places where you can add them. Find an effective direct or indirect quote for each spot. Remember to use quotation marks around direct quotes only. In addition, proofread your essay for any additional errors in punctuation, spelling, and sentence structure. Make the corrections on your final draft. Then, publish your essay so that others can read it.

Scoring Rubric

You can use the rubric below to evaluate your persuasive essay.

	Persuasive Writing	Organization and Focus	Sentence Structure	Conventions
4	• Provides a *thoroughly developed* argument with a *clearly* stated position, *fully* elaborated reasons, and *compelling* evidence (facts, statistics, expert opinions). • Includes *consistently appropriate* strategies (e.g., attention-grabbing introduction, anecdotes, quotations, call to action).	• *Clearly* addresses all of the writing tasks. • Demonstrates a *clear* understanding of purpose and audience. • Maintains a *consistent* point of view and *smooth transitions, skillfully* indicating order of importance of ideas. • Includes a *clearly presented* central idea with relevant details.	• Includes sentence *variety*.	• Contains *few, if any,* errors in the conventions of the English language (grammar, punctuation, capitalization, spelling). These errors do **not** interfere with the reader's understanding of the writing.
3	• Provides an *adequately developed* argument with a *clearly* stated position, *mostly* elaborated reasons, and *convincing* evidence (facts, statistics, expert opinions). • Includes *appropriate* strategies (e.g., attention-grabbing introduction, anecdotes, quotations, call to action).	• Addresses *most* of the writing task. • Demonstrates a *general* understanding of purpose and audience. • Maintains a *mostly consistent* point of view and *relatively smooth* transitions, *mostly skillfully* indicating order of importance of ideas. • *Presents* a central idea with relevant details.	• Includes *some* sentence *variety.*	• Contains *some errors* in the conventions of the English language (grammar, punctuation, capitalization, spelling). These errors do **not** interfere with the reader's understanding of the writing.
2	• Provides a *minimally developed* argument with a *vaguely* stated position, and *non-compelling* reasons, and evidence. • *Attempts* to use strategies but with *minimal* effectiveness.	• Addresses *some* of the writing task. • Demonstrates *little* understanding of purpose and audience. • Maintains an *inconsistent* point of view and *awkward* transitions that do not indicate order of importance of ideas. • *Suggests* a central idea with limited details.	• Includes *little* sentence variety.	• Contains *several errors* in the conventions of the English language (grammar, punctuation, capitalization, spelling). These errors **may** interfere with the reader's understanding of the writing.
1	• *Lacks* an argument, position, reasons, and evidence. • *Fails* to use strategies.	• Addresses *only one* part of the writing task. • Demonstrates *no* understanding of purpose and audience. • *Lacks* a point of view and transitions that indicate order of importance of ideas. • *Lacks* a central idea but may contain *marginally related* details.	• Includes *no* sentence variety.	• Contains *serious errors* in the conventions of the English language (grammar, punctuation, capitalization, spelling). These errors interfere with the reader's understanding of the writing.

Persuasive Essay

When responding to an on-demand persuasive prompt, use models you've read, what you've learned by writing your own persuasive essay, the rubric on page 728, and the steps below.

Writing Standard 2.5 Write persuasive compositions: a. State a clear position on a proposition or proposal. b. Support the position with organized and relevant evidence. c. Anticipate and address reader concerns and counterarguments.

Writing Prompt

You want your parents to raise your weekly allowance. They aren't sure it's a good idea, since they raised it only eight months ago. Write a persuasive essay in the form of a letter convincing your parents to support your request. Give your parents an account of what the money would be spent on (perhaps school expenses) as well as examples of why you deserve the raise (perhaps you've taken on new chores and responsibilities). Use specific reasons and examples as you write your persuasive letter.

Study the Prompt

Begin by reading the prompt carefully. Notice that the **position** is determined for you. Underline "convincing your parents to support your request." Circle the proposal: "raise your weekly allowance." Now circle the next sentence "They aren't sure it's a good idea, since they raised it only eight months ago." That is the **counterargument** you must address. Note and underline any additional information in the prompt, such as references to school expenses and new chores and responsibilities. Your audience is your parents.

Tip: Spend about five minute studying the prompt.

Plan Your Response

Reasons Persuasive writing requires that you ask and answer the question *Why?* in relation to your position. **Ask,** "Why do I want/need a raise in my allowance?" Your answers become your reasons. Brainstorm convincing reasons that will also appeal to your audience.

Evidence Next, answer the question *How?* **Ask,** "How can I show that I deserve a raise?" Your answers will lead to supporting evidence. Include an **example** or **anecdote** supporting each reason.

Organization Once you have decided on two to three reasons, plan their order in your essay. Put your strongest reason last to be most convincing.

Tip: Spend about ten minutes planning your response.

Respond to the Prompt

Drafting One way to begin your persuasive essay is to address the **counterargument** in your lead. Then, the rest of the essay concentrates on supporting your **position**.

Tip: Spend about twenty minutes writing your essay.

Improve Your Response

Revising Go back to the key aspects of the prompt. Add any missing information.

- Do you state your position clearly?
- Do you offer good reasons and evidence?
- Does your composition have an introduction, a body, and a conclusion with a call to action?
- Have you consistently organized your ideas within and between paragraphs?

Proofreading Take a few minutes to edit your response to correct errors in grammar, spelling, punctuation, and capitalization.

Checking Your Final Copy Read your essay one more time to catch any errors you may have missed and to make any finishing touches.

Tip: Save five or ten minutes to read and improve your draft.

Delivering a Persuasive Speech

Speak with a Purpose

Adapt your persuasive essay into a persuasive presentation. Practice your presentation, and then present it to your class.

Think as a Reader/Writer Adapting your essay into an oral presentation will still require you to think as a writer. However, in your oral presentation, you may need to pay more attention to your audience (the listeners) than you did in your essay. You've already written a persuasive essay. Now you will deliver it as an oral presentation.

Adapt Your Essay

Giving a persuasive presentation may seem as simple as reading aloud the persuasive essay you wrote in the Writing Workshop, but there is much more to it. You need to begin by adapting your essay.

Make It Engaging

Your presentation will address the same topic as the one in your essay. However, you have only one chance to persuade your audience when giving an oral presentation. Listeners cannot go back and re-read your words. Therefore, it is especially important to engage your audience and make them care about the issue as much as you do. Answer the following questions to make sure your presentation will engage your audience. If you answer no to any of these questions, make adjustments in the text you will use for your presentation.

- Do you begin by grabbing your listeners' attention?
- Do you address possible objections your audience may have to your solution?
- Does each piece of evidence that you use to support your position appeal to your listeners' interests and backgrounds?
- Do you use rhetorical devices to emphasize major points and deliver a memorable message? Specifically, do you repeat words or phrases to stress their importance and help your audience remember main ideas?

Check for Clear Transitions

To help listeners follow your presentation, you might need to add words that clarify the connections between ideas. Help your listeners by adding **transitions** such as *however, therefore, for this reason,* and *finally.*

Reader/Writer Notebook

Use your **RWN** to complete the activities for this workshop.

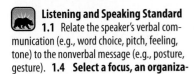

Listening and Speaking Standard 1.1 Relate the speaker's verbal communication (e.g., word choice, pitch, feeling, tone) to the nonverbal message (e.g., posture, gesture). **1.4 Select a focus, an organizational structure, a point of view, matching the purpose,** message, occasion, **and vocal modulation to the audience. 1.8 Analyze the use of rhetorical devices (e.g., cadence, repetitive patterns, use of onomatopoeia)** for intent and effect. **2.4** Deliver persuasive presentations: a. Provide a clear statement of the position. b. Include relevant evidence. c. Offer a logical sequence of information. d. Engage the listener and foster acceptance of the proposition or proposal.

Deliver Your Persuasive Speech

Even the most persuasive ideas can fall flat if they aren't delivered well. For example, if you get rattled by distractions, mumble, or speak in a dull monotone, your listeners are probably not going to have much confidence in you or pay much attention to your message. Practice your speech to make sure you don't fall into any of these bad speaking habits. As you practice, concentrate on using **verbal elements** (what your voice does as you speak) and **nonverbal elements** (what your face and body do as you speak).

Use Verbal Elements

When you give a persuasive speech, it is important to speak at a slow **rate** so your audience can keep up with what you are saying. You should also speak at a loud enough **volume** so the people in the back of the room can hear you. Varying your **vocal modulation,** or **pitch**—the rise and fall of your speaking voice—can help keep your audience interested. Adjusting the **tone,** or attitude, of your voice to match your message will help the audience understand your feelings about the issue. When giving a persuasive speech, use an enthusiastic and believable tone to help convince your audience to agree with your position.

Use Nonverbal Elements

Your **posture, eye contact** with the audience, **gestures,** and **facial expressions** are examples of nonverbal elements. Standing tall while looking directly at your audience shows that you are confident, and using appropriate gestures and facial expressions can help **emphasize** important ideas. For example, you might raise your eyebrows to show your disapproval of a possible objection to your position.

Deal with Distractions

Try not to let noises or unexpected events distract you. For example, if your presentation is interrupted by continuous or recurring background noise, ignore it and speak louder. If you are interrupted by a more noticeable but temporary noise, pause until the noise stops and then continue. Similarly, if you realize you accidentally skipped a minor point in your speech, go on as if nothing happened. If you skip an important point, explain the point to your listeners, and then resume your presentation.

A Good Persuasive Speech

- clearly presents the speaker's position on an important issue and stays focused on that issue
- employs a positive tone
- includes relevant evidence that supports the speaker's position
- is well organized and uses logical transitions that help listeners follow from one idea to the next
- makes effective use of verbal and nonverbal techniques

⬤ Listening Tip

A very important part of persuasive speaking is nonverbal communication. Various techniques, such as gestures and facial expressions, are often used to emphasize the points of the speech and the speaker's attitude toward the subject. The speaker is counting on you to watch as well as to listen, so be sure to do so to get the most out of the speech.

 Learn It Online
A media display can help persuade your listeners. Check out *MediaScope* on:

| go.hrw.com | H6-731 | **Go** |

Informational Skills Review

Persuasive Texts   **Directions:** Read the article. Then, answer the questions that follow.

Too Much TV Can Equal Too Much Weight

from **Children's Express** by **Jamie Rodgers, 12 years old**

In 1970, only 10 percent of kids in America were overweight. In the 1980s, it was 30 percent, and in the 1990s, it was 60 percent. Studies show that obesity is linked to watching TV and using the Internet.

Children's Express interviewed two professors from Johns Hopkins University School of Medicine about the link. Ross Andersen, M.D., is with the weight management center, and Carlos Crespo, M.D., is an assistant professor of health and fitness.

"Dr. Crespo and I have published a study that appeared in the *Journal of the American Medical Association*. We looked at how fat kids were in relation to the number of hours of television they watch per day," said Andersen. "We found that kids who are low TV watchers were much leaner. The kids who were the fattest were those who watched a lot of TV. We defined a lot as four or more hours per day. Roughly, one in three kids in America is watching four or more hours per day. I would estimate sitting in front of a computer would be just as great a risk factor for being overweight."

Andersen and Crespo say the blame is not just on the parents. Sometimes it's a lack of places to play.

"[It's a] lack of facilities, services for the children to be able to go out and play basketball or go to a swimming pool. The community should have open spaces and safe spaces for girls and boys to be active," said Crespo.

"The thing is not that it's bad to watch TV; it's just that you need to have a balance. There [is] a certain number of hours in the day you're supposed to sleep, do your homework, . . . [and] go to school, and then there is a certain [number] of hours that you're free to do whatever you want. If you spend that time watching TV, then you spend less time doing physical activity." . . .

"Kids and parents need to look for opportunities to remain physically active. So instead of sitting down to watch *Who Wants to Be a Millionaire*, it may be that the whole family could get up and go for a walk." . . .

Reading Standard 2.6 Determine the
adequacy and appropriateness of the
evidence for an author's conclusions. **2.7** Make
reasonable assertions about a text through accurate,
supporting citations.

1. What evidence supports the conclusion that obesity is linked to watching TV?
   A a study published in the *Journal of the American Medical Association*
   B the opinion that communities should have swimming pools
   C the fact that 30 percent of kids in America were overweight in the 1980s
   D the fact that Andersen and Crespo are both doctors

2. Which of the following statements is a fact?
   A Kids and parents need to exercise together.
   B Lack of places to play is the main reason kids watch too much TV.
   C About one third of kids in America watch TV for more than four hours per day.
   D Kids waste their time by spending free time watching TV.

3. When the author states that in 1970, only 10 percent of kids were overweight, but by the 1990s, 60 percent of kids were overweight, what type of evidence is she using?
   A quotations
   B statistics
   C case study
   D anecdote

4. Andersen and Crespo place part of the blame for obesity in children on
   A a lack of safe open spaces.
   B poor health education.
   C a lack of medical attention.
   D fast foods.

5. Andersen and Crespo believe that children and parents should
   A prepare meals together.
   B remain physically active.
   C limit their free time.
   D work on a computer four hours a day.

6. Which statement *best* expresses the author's conclusion?
   A Watching TV is more common today than ever before.
   B Obesity is linked to watching TV and using the Internet.
   C Families need to watch TV and surf the Internet together.
   D Doctors say that parents are the real cause of childhood obesity.

Timed Writing

7. Does the author present adequate and appropriate evidence for her conclusion? Write an essay expressing your evaluation of the article. Support your assertion with citations from the text.

Vocabulary Skills Review

Synonyms **Directions:** Choose the word that is closest in meaning to the italicized Vocabulary word in each item.

1. If you are having a *dispute* with a friend, you are having
   A a party.
   B an argument.
   C a contest.
   D a discussion.

2. An *isolated* tree is one that is
   A different.
   B ordinary.
   C noticeable.
   D separate.

3. If standards in a business *declined,* they
   A improved.
   B changed.
   C dropped.
   D increased.

4. A *nutritious* snack is
   A healthful.
   B inexpensive.
   C large.
   D unappealing.

5. An *irritable* child is
   A friendly.
   B mature.
   C dangerous.
   D short-tempered.

6. A *unique* gift is
   A rare.
   B worthless.
   C appropriate.
   D beautiful.

7. If you are discussing the *complexity* of a problem, you are talking about its
   A outcome.
   B seriousness.
   C difficulty.
   D cause.

Academic Vocabulary

Directions: Use context clues to determine the meaning of the italicized Academic Vocabulary words below.

8. To improve their lives, it is *crucial* for poor girls in South Africa to gain an education.
   A not allowed
   B very important
   C optional
   D difficult

9. From what he told me, I was able to *conclude* that the accident was minor.
   A judge
   B guess
   C predict
   D imagine

Writing Skills Review

Writing Standard 2.5 Write persuasive compositions. a. State a clear position on a proposition or proposal. b. Support the position with organized and relevant evidence. c. Anticipate and address reader concerns and counterarguments.

Persuasive Text **Directions:** Read the following paragraph from a student's persuasive letter. Then, answer each question that follows.

(1) The Helping Hands Community Assistance Program needs our school's help. (2) The supplies of clothing, shoes, and blankets are very low and will not be enough to help everyone who seeks assistance. (3) Only four coats, six blankets, and one pair of shoes are available. (4) Also, winter is coming soon. (5) The cooler winter temperatures always bring a higher demand for warm clothing. (6) Last winter some families were left without supplies because the supplies were gone.

1. Which of the following sentences, if added to the paragraph, would provide details showing how low the supplies are?

   A Helping Hands is a nonprofit organization.

   B The Helping Hands Community Assistance Program has low supplies.

   C You can tell winter is approaching because the temperatures are cooler.

   D The program needs clothing for twenty adults and ten children.

2. This paragraph presents the problem. The next paragraph will present the writer's proposed solution. Which of these sentences would you expect to see in that paragraph as a *reasonable* and *specific* call to action?

   A Everyone should call the governor of our state and tell her about the problem.

   B The Helping Hands Community Assistance Program needs help now!

   C Our school should organize a clothing and blanket drive to help the program gather supplies.

   D The people of our community should do something to help.

3. Which of these would be the *most* effective way for the writer to address the concern of some readers that helping the program may cost money they do not have?

   A Suggest that they donate used clothing and blankets that are in good condition instead of buying new ones.

   B Tell them to borrow money from someone to purchase clothing and blankets.

   C Provide them with a list of stores that have nice blankets, boots, and coats.

   D Ignore this concern because not all readers may share it.

4. Which sentence below *best* summarizes the writer's opinion about this issue?

   A Last year, some people were not able to get supplies.

   B The school is in a good position to help collect supplies for the Helping Hands Program.

   C During cold weather, many people need coats, shoes, and blankets.

   D The program has four coats, six blankets, and one pair of shoes.

Read On

For Independent Reading

Nonfiction

Media Madness:
An Insider's Guide to Media

This humorously illustrated book, written by Dominic Ali, offers you a lesson in how to read media. In *Media Madness,* Ali shares many secrets and tells about the influence of television, music, magazines, video games, and the Internet. Ali urges readers to approach media with a critical eye by asking such questions as "What is the message, and who is the sender?" "How does it grab my attention?" and "What does it *not* tell me?"

Oprah Winfrey

Learn details about Oprah Winfrey's childhood, education, and career in this biography written by Heather Hudak. The biography also includes self-improvement tools for readers, such as tips on improving public-speaking skills and suggestions for starting a book club similar to Oprah's. Read *Oprah Winfrey* for an introduction to one of the most influential people in the United States.

My Life with the Chimpanzees

As a young girl, Jane Goodall spent hours observing the animals all around her. She dreamed of spending her life working with them. At age twenty-six, she got her wish: She went to the forests of Tanzania to observe chimpanzees living in the wild. She came to know a group of wild chimpanzees, whose lives, in work, play, and family relationships, bear a surprising resemblance to our own. Her adventures gained her worldwide recognition, and in this book she tells her story in her own words.

At the Controls: Questioning Video and Computer Games

Play smart! Analyze the messages directed at you by the games you're playing. Neil Andersen gives you the information you need to take a critical look at video and computer games. After reading *At the Controls: Questioning Video and Computer Games,* you'll be able to challenge the content in popular games and better understand its effects on you.

Explorers Wanted! On Safari

Would you like to take an exciting and educational excursion to Africa? Author Simon Chapman tells you how to prepare for the trip and what you'll find once you arrive. You'll track elephants, escape hungry insects, and even speak some Swahili. In *Explorers Wanted! On Safari,* you'll take a fact-filled adventure and learn all about the people and animals of the African savanna.

Advertising

In this book, Bess Milton investigates the effects of advertising on America's past, present, and future. She discusses how advertisements convey the American Dream and how they've united people behind patriotic causes. *Advertising* also explores the psychology behind many common marketing tactics.

Internet: Electronic Global Village

In this brightly illustrated book by David Jefferis, you'll be introduced to the Internet's history, its workings, and the changes it has brought about in society. *Internet: Electronic Global Village* reveals the many tasks forever altered by the Internet revolution, such as communicating, researching, shopping, and publishing.

Television and Movies

Television shows and movies shape our lives perhaps more than any other art form does. In *Television and Movies,* Philip Abraham examines the invention of these entertaining technologies and probes the ways they have affected American pop culture. You'll be a more knowledgeable viewer after reading this informative book.

Learn It Online
Learn to analyze novels. Get tips to help in your study at *NovelWise:*

go.hrw.com | H6-737 | **Go**

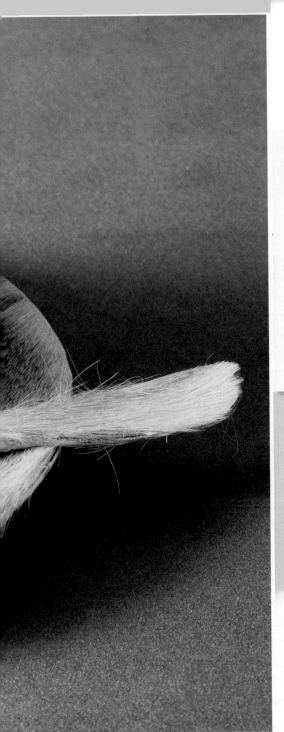

CHAPTER **8**

Literary Criticism

Reading Standards

Here are the Grade 6 standards you will work toward mastering in Chapter 8.

Word Analysis, Fluency, and Systematic Vocabulary Development
1.2 Identify and interpret figurative language and words with multiple meanings.

Literary Response and Analysis
3.8 Critique the credibility of characterization and the degree to which a plot is contrived or realistic (e.g., compare use of fact and fantasy in historical fiction).

Writing Applications (Genres and Their Characteristics)
2.4 Write responses to literature:
  a. Develop an interpretation exhibiting careful reading, understanding, and insight.
  b. Organize the interpretation around several clear ideas, premises, or images.
  c. Develop and justify the interpretation through sustained use of examples and textual evidence.

"Fiction is Truth in another shape."

—**Leigh Hunt**

What Do
You
Think

How does fiction express truths about our lives?

Learn It Online
Can you read pictures? Let *PowerNotes* show you how at:

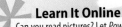
go.hrw.com   H6-739   **Go**

Literary Skills Focus

by **Linda Rief**

What Is Literary Criticism?

You ask a friend if she liked a story. She responds, "No, I really didn't like it." Her answer doesn't tell you much, so you ask her to explain *why* she didn't like it. This time, she says, "The characters were not believable; they did things real people would never do. The plot was not realistic at all." Now your friend is talking like a real literary critic!

Literary Criticism

Literary Criticism is the practice of evaluating the qualities of a literary work in order to make a judgment about it. Good literary critics explain what they like or don't like about a text. They go beyond "It's really good" or "It's boring" to offer specifics. Which of these statements about Christopher Paul Curtis's novel *Bud, Not Buddy* offer opinions that are supported with specific explanations?

> 1. "I liked this book a lot. It was really good. Other people will like it too."
> 2. "This is a great book. It is fun in parts and sad in parts, and the plot has a lot of exciting action."
> 3. "I didn't like this book very much. It wasn't good, and so I didn't like it."
> 4. "I didn't like this book. I didn't think it was realistic that a little kid would travel all over the country. The ending was disappointing because he doesn't find his real father."

If you picked statements 2 and 4, you chose the best answers. Statements 1 and 3 certainly offer opinions, but those opinions are not supported.

Critiquing Characters' Credibility

When evaluating a literary work, critics often focus on the **credibility** of the characterization. *Credible* means "believable." When you read fiction, you expect, above all, that the characters will be credible, that they will act the way real people do. Even if you're reading a story in which the characters are animals, you still want to believe in the characters. How believable is this description of Zlateh, a goat?

> Zlateh stood as patiently and good-naturedly as ever. She licked Reuven's hand. She shook her small white beard. Zlateh trusted human beings.
>
> from "Zlateh the Goat"
> by Isaac Bashevis Singer

To decide whether characters are credible, ask yourself these questions:

- Do the characters have weaknesses as well as strengths? Is a character too good to be true? too strong? too unselfish? too evil?
- Do the characters talk and act like real people?
- Do the characters grow and change as a result of the events in the story?

Critiquing a Plot: Believable or Not?

A credible plot is just as important as credible characters in a literary work. Critics often evaluate the degree to which a plot is realistic or contrived. A **contrived** plot is artificial and includes events that are not believable. Such a plot may contain too many coincidences, like chance meetings, and major conflicts in the plot may be quickly overcome. If you read a story in which two lovers on a sinking ship struggle through icy water up to their waists, hack through chains holding the hero captive, kill a gunman, leap onto an ice floe, and survive, you know you're dealing with a contrived plot.

In this chapter, you'll critique a plot in which a blind boy named Tito is taken care of and fed by a dog named Bimbo.

> As long as people could remember seeing Tito—about twelve or thirteen years—they had seen Bimbo. Bimbo had never left his side. He was not only dog but nurse, pillow, playmate, mother, and father to Tito.
>
> from "The Dog of Pompeii"
> by Louis Untermeyer

To test the credibility of a plot, ask yourself questions like these:

- Do the events in the plot grow naturally out of the characters' decisions and actions?
- Do many of the events result from chance or luck, or are there believable causes and effects?
- Do events unfold the way they would in real life?

The Language of Literary Criticism

The charts below show some of the words and phrases critics use when they critique characterization and plot. Using these words will help you present specific opinions and support.

Literary Criticism: A Glossary

Words and Phrases Used to Describe Plot

Positive	Negative
realistic *or* credible	unrealistic *or* contrived *or* not credible
well-paced	plodding
suspenseful	predictable
satisfying ending	disappointing ending

Words and Phrases Used to Describe Characters

Positive	Negative
original	stereotyped
believable *or* credible *or* convincing	unbelievable *or* not credible *or* unconvincing
well-rounded	flat
dynamic—*refers to characters who change and grow*	static—*refers to characters who remain the same*

Your Turn Evaluate Credibility

1. Using words from the charts above, write a paragraph critiquing the credibility of the characterization and plot in a story or novel. Be sure to support your opinions with examples from the text.

2. Write three tips for filmmakers about how to make sure the characters and plots in their movies are credible.

Learn It Online
Try the *PowerNotes* version of this lesson at:

go.hrw.com   H6-741   **Go**

Reading Skills Focus

by **Kylene Beers**

What Skills Help You Critique a Literary Work?

Your teacher asks if you think the characterization and plot in a story are credible. "Uh-oh," you think to yourself. "I don't know. I don't really remember the story that well." Reading for details and making generalizations as you read will help you focus on specifics and draw conclusions—important steps in critiquing a literary work.

Reading for Details

You might have learned that scanning a text (looking for something specific in the work) and skimming it (reading it quickly) can be very useful when you're previewing a text or searching for specific information. There's an old saying, though, that the truth lies in the details. When you read a work of fiction, it's important to read it carefully and to pay attention to key details.

Characterization Reading for details will help you critique the credibility of characters in a story. For example, if a six-year-old child in a story speaks like an adult, then the child probably won't seem like a credible character. As you read, look for details related to characters' qualities, thoughts, words, and actions, and ask yourself the following:

- Do these details make the characters seem believable?
- Has the writer provided enough details to bring the characters to life on the page, or do the characters seem like flat cardboard figures?

Plot Reading for details will also help you critique the degree to which a story's plot is contrived or realistic. Imagine, for example, that you're reading a story in which a character escapes his or her enemy by leaping over a building in a single bound. If the character is a superhero, then that plot detail would probably seem credible. If the character is just an ordinary person, however, then that detail would seem terribly unrealistic. As you read, ask yourself the following questions:

- Are plot details based on facts?
- If plot details are not based on facts, do they still seem believable within the context of the world the writer has created in the story?

When you're reading for details, you might find it helpful to re-read key passages or even a whole story in order to identify telling details.

Reading Standard 3.8 Critique the credibility of characterization and the degree to which a plot is contrived or realistic (e.g., compare use of fact and fantasy in historical fiction).

Making Generalizations

A **generalization** is a general conclusion based on several examples or pieces of evidence. When you make a generalization as you read, you combine your own knowledge with evidence from the text to make a broad, universal statement about a topic.

For example, after reading "The Bracelet" by Yoshiko Uchida, you might want to make a generalization about the treatment of Japanese Americans during World War II. Look at how one reader makes a generalization based on the short story "The Dog of Pompeii":

Evidence in Text	My Knowledge	Generalization
Bimbo, the dog, takes care of Tito, a boy who is blind.	Guide dogs help people who are visually impaired.	Dogs can serve as valuable companions and helpers for people.

Making generalizations as you read can help you critique a story's credibility. Ask yourself, "What conclusions can I draw about people or life based on the story?" in order to test whether the characters and plot seem believable and realistic. For example, the reader who created the chart about "The Dog of Pompeii," above, might determine that the character of Bimbo is credible based on her generalization about dogs.

"I thought it was pretty good, for a book."

Your Turn   Apply Reading Skills

1. Re-read a passage in a favorite short story or novel that contains important information about a character or the plot. Identify details that make the character or the plot event seem credible or realistic.

2. Make a generalization about people or life based on your knowledge and evidence from a movie you've seen. How does this generalization help you critique the credibility of the movie?

Now go to the Skills in Action: Reading Model

Learn It Online
Try the *PowerNotes* version of this lesson at:

go.hrw.com   H6-743   **Go**

Build Background

This fantasy was written in 1951. At that time, computers were huge machines humming day and night in refrigerated buildings. These mainframe computers had wires, gears, dials, and circuit boards mounted on frames in cabinets. They were used only by specialists who stored information in them by creating patterns of holes on cards or tape. (That's why in this story a character writes for the computer in punch code.)

Twenty years after Asimov wrote this story, the silicon chip transformed computers. Computers became smaller, more powerful, and cheaper. They left their refrigerated buildings and entered our everyday lives.

Literary Focus

Credibility: Character Whether authors are writing historical fiction or science fiction, they make their characters credible by having them behave as real people do. Asimov establishes Margie's credibility by making her reactions to doing poorly and her attitude toward school seem realistic.

Read with a Purpose Read this story to explore the writer's vision of what schools might be like in the distant future.

The Fun They Had

by **Isaac Asimov**

Margie even wrote about it that night in her diary. On the page headed May 17, 2155, she wrote, "Today Tommy found a real book!"

It was a very old book. Margie's grandfather once said that when he was a little boy, *his* grandfather told him that there was a time when all stories were printed on paper.

They turned the pages, which were yellow and crinkly, and it was awfully funny to read words that stood still instead of moving the way they were supposed to—on a screen, you know. And then, when they turned back to the page before, it had the same words on it that it had had when they read it the first time.

"Gee," said Tommy, "what a waste. When you're through with the book, you just throw it away, I guess. Our television screen must have had a million books on it and it's good for plenty more. I wouldn't throw *it* away."

"Same with mine," said Margie. She was eleven and hadn't seen as many telebooks as Tommy had. He was thirteen.

She said, "Where did you find it?"

"In my house." He pointed without looking, because he was busy reading. "In the attic."

"What's it about?"

"School."

Margie was scornful. "School? What's there to write about school? I hate school." Margie always hated school, but now she hated it more than ever. The mechanical teacher had been giving her test after test in geography, and she had been doing worse and worse until her mother had shaken her head sorrowfully and sent for the county inspector.

He was a round little man with a red face and a whole box of tools with dials and wires. He smiled at her and gave her an apple, then took the teacher apart. Margie had hoped he wouldn't know how to put it together again, but he knew how all right, and after an hour or so, there it was again, large and ugly, with a big screen on which all the lessons were shown and the questions were asked. That wasn't so bad. The part she hated most was the slot where she had to put homework and test papers. She always had to write them out in a punch code they made her learn when she was six years old, and the mechanical teacher calculated the mark in no time.

The inspector had smiled after he was finished and patted her head. He said to her mother, "It's not the little girl's fault, Mrs. Jones. I think the geography sector was geared a little too quick. Those things happen sometimes. I've slowed it up to an average ten-year level. Actually, the overall pattern of her progress is quite satisfactory." And he patted Margie's head again.

Margie was disappointed. She had been hoping they would take the teacher away altogether. They had once taken Tommy's teacher away for nearly a month because the history sector had blanked out completely.

Reading Focus

Reading for Details When this story was written, people used punch code to write computer documents. By including such factual details, writers make their stories realistic. As you read, look for other details that help make the story believable.

Reading Model

So she said to Tommy, "Why would anyone write about school?"

Tommy looked at her with very superior eyes. "Because it's not our kind of school, stupid. This is the old kind of school that they had hundreds and hundreds of years ago." He added loftily, pronouncing the word carefully, "*Centuries* ago."

Margie was hurt. "Well, I don't know what kind of school they had all that time ago." She read the book over his shoulder for a while, then said, "Anyway, they had a teacher."

"Sure they had a teacher, but it wasn't a *regular* teacher. It was a man."

"A man? How could a man be a teacher?"

"Well, he just told the boys and girls things and gave them homework and asked them questions."

"A man isn't smart enough."

"Sure he is. My father knows as much as my teacher."

"He can't. A man can't know as much as a teacher."

"He knows almost as much I betcha."

Margie wasn't prepared to dispute that. She said, "I wouldn't want a strange man in my house to teach me."

Tommy screamed with laughter. "You don't know much, Margie. The teachers didn't live in the house. They had a special building and all the kids went there."

"And all the kids learned the same thing?"

"Sure, if they were the same age."

"But my mother says a teacher has to be adjusted to fit the mind of each boy and girl it teaches and that each kid has to be taught differently."

"Just the same, they didn't do it that way then. If you don't like it, you don't have to read the book."

"I didn't say I didn't like it," Margie said quickly. She wanted to read about those funny schools.

They weren't even half finished when Margie's mother called, "Margie! School!"

Margie looked up. "Not yet, Mamma."

"Now," said Mrs. Jones. "And it's probably time for Tommy, too."

Margie said to Tommy, "Can I read the book some more with you after school?"

Literary Focus

Credibility: Character Like Tommy, real children don't always treat each other with respect. Credible characters have weaknesses as well as strengths, just as real people do. When you read, evaluate whether characters' interactions make them seem like real people or make them seem too good to be true.

Reading Focus

Making Generalizations A generalization is a broad conclusion. Based on your knowledge, you might make the generalization "Great changes have taken place in education over the centuries." Such a generalization can help you determine whether it's credible that education would change so dramatically in the distant future.

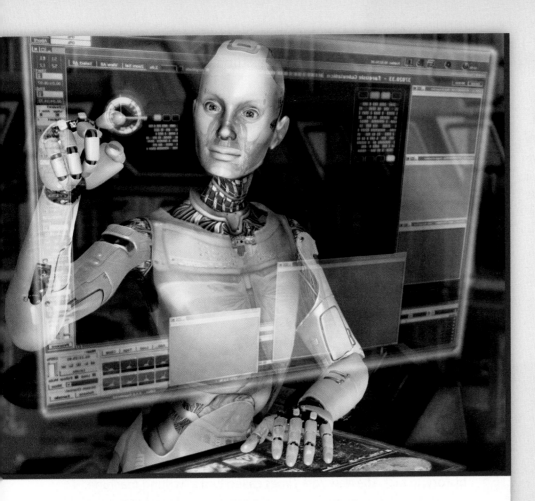

"Maybe," he said, nonchalantly. He walked away whistling, the dusty old book tucked beneath his arm.

Margie went into the schoolroom. It was right next to her bedroom, and the mechanical teacher was on and waiting for her. It was always on at the same time every day except Saturday and Sunday, because her mother said little girls learned better if they learned at regular hours.

The screen was lit up, and it said: "Today's arithmetic lesson is on the addition of proper fractions. Please insert yesterday's homework in the proper slot."

Margie did so with a sigh. She was thinking about the old schools they had when her grandfather's grandfather was a little boy. All the kids from the whole neighborhood came, laughing and shouting in the schoolyard, sitting together in the schoolroom, going home together at the end of the day. They learned the same things so they could help one another on the homework and talk about it.

And the teachers were people. . . .

Reading Focus

Reading for Details Use your knowledge of the world to evaluate whether details seem realistic. You might think this detail is credible based on your knowledge of the kinds of computer programs used by students in school or at home today.

The mechanical teacher was flashing on the screen: "When we add the fractions 1/2 and 1/4 . . ."

Margie was thinking about how the kids must have loved it in the old days. She was thinking about the fun they had.

Literary Focus

Credibility: Plot A plot's resolution will be realistic, not contrived, if it develops naturally from events in the story. Margie's thoughts at the end of the story are a logical outcome of the plot.

Read with a Purpose Do you think there will ever be a time when students will be taught solely by computers? Why or why not?

MEET THE WRITER

Isaac Asimov
(1920–1992)

A "Writing Machine"

Isaac Asimov wrote or edited more than 470 books, as well as many short stories and scholarly articles. That's more books than any other American writer has written. Asimov also holds the unofficial record for writing about more nonfiction subjects than any other writer in history. In fact, *The New York Times* called him a "writing machine."

Asimov was born in Russia and came to the United States with his parents when he was three years old. He submitted his first story to a science fiction magazine when he was only fourteen. The story was rejected, but the editor encouraged Asimov and helped him improve his writing.

Asimov talked about "The Fun They Had" in the first volume of his autobiography. A friend of his had asked him to write a short story for young readers. Asimov said:

"I thought about it and decided to write a little story about school. What could interest children more? It would be about a school of the future, by way of teaching machines, with children longing for the good old days when there were old-fashioned schools that children loved. I thought the kids would get a bang out of the irony."

He wrote the story in one sitting and earned ten dollars for it—"a penny a word," Asimov said.

Think About the Writer

Was Asimov right that students would find the story's ending ironic and entertaining?

Reading Standard 3.8 Critique the credibility of characterization and the degree to which a plot is contrived or realistic (e.g., compare use of fact and fantasy in historical fiction).

Into Action: Reading for Details

Record details in the story in a chart like this one, and determine whether each detail is credible. How do you think the details as a whole contribute to the story's credibility? Do some details prevent the story from being fully believable? Explain.

Details	Credibility
"yellow and crinkly" pages	I've seen old books that look like that.

Talk About . . .

1. With a partner, critique the story's credibility. Do you think the characters are believable? To what degree is the plot <u>contrived</u> or realistic? Try to use each Academic Vocabulary word listed at the right at least once in your discussion.

Write About . . .

Answer the following questions about "The Fun They Had." For definitions of the underlined Academic Vocabulary words, see the column at the right.

2. Is the story's opening, in which Margie writes in her diary, <u>contrived</u>? Explain.

3. Do any aspects of this story <u>correspond</u> to your view of the future? Did this story give you <u>insight</u> into what the future might be like?

4. How do you <u>perceive</u> the role of computers in our lives? What are the benefits and drawbacks of their use?

Writing Skills Focus
Think as a Reader/Writer

In Chapter 8, you will have the opportunity to critique the credibility of other stories. Writing Skills Focus activities will give you practice in using credible details.

Academic Vocabulary for Chapter 8

Talking and Writing About Credibility

Academic Vocabulary is the language you use to write and talk about literature. Use these words to discuss the stories you read in this chapter. The words are underlined throughout the chapter.

contrived (kuhn TRYVD) *adj.*: unnatural; artificial. *Critics evaluate whether a story's plot is contrived or realistic.*

correspond (kawr uh SPOND) *v.*: be similar to. *In credible stories, characters' reactions correspond to those of real people.*

insight (IHN syt) *n.*: clear understanding of the true nature of something. *Stories can give you insight into aspects of life.*

perceive (puhr SEEV) *v.*: grasp mentally; understand. *You might perceive a character differently than a friend does.*

Your Turn

Copy the Academic Vocabulary words into your *Reader/Writer Notebook*. Use each word in a sentence about another science fiction story or a science fiction movie you know.

Eruption of Mount Vesuvius in 1790 by Pietro Fabris.

THE DOG OF POMPEII
by **Louis Untermeyer**

POMPEII
by **Robert Silverberg**

What Do You Think? What is the role of facts in works of fiction?

QuickWrite

How does reading a social studies textbook or a history book differ from reading a short story or a novel? Are there any similarities? Write down your thoughts.

Reader/Writer
Notebook

Use your **RWN** to complete the
activities for these selections.

Reading Standard 3.8 Critique the
credibility of characterization and the degree
to which a plot is contrived or realistic (e.g., compare
use of fact and fantasy in historical fiction).

The Dog of Pompeii / Pompeii

Literary Skills Focus

Credibility and Historical Fiction "The Dog of Pompeii" is **historical fiction.** The author, Louis Untermeyer, mixes fantasy—fictional characters and events—with facts about an actual historical event. Writers
of historical fiction face a great challenge. The fictional elements of their
stories must seem as **credible,** or believable, and realistic as the historical events they describe. As you read this story and the nonfiction work
that follows it, think about whether Untermeyer succeeds in creating
credible characters and a realistic plot.

Reading Skills Focus

Reading for Details Writers use details to turn their ideas into stories. Reading for details will help you critique the credibility of a story
because the details determine, to a large extent, whether we <u>perceive</u>
the characters and plot as believable and realistic.

Into Action As you read "The Dog of Pompeii," record in a chart like
the one below key details about the eruption of Mount Vesuvius and
the events that follow it. Then, record any details in "Pompeii" that <u>cor-
respond</u> to details you noted in the story.

"The Dog of Pompeii"	"Pompeii"
"falling buildings," p. 760	"buildings were collapsing," p. 762

TechFocus Imagine that you were recording an audiobook of the
story that would include sound effects. As you read, think about the
sound effects you would use to make the action seem real.

Writing Skills Focus

Think as a Reader/Writer

Find It in Your Reading As you read, record in your *Reader/Writer
Notebook* examples of **personification** (the giving of human qual-
ities to something that is not human) used to characterize Bimbo.
Think about the effects of this personification.

Vocabulary

The Dog of Pompeii

ambitious (am BIHSH uhs) *adj.*: eager
to succeed or to achieve something.
*The ambitious citizens wanted to
make their city famous.*

proverb (PRAHV urb) *n.*: short traditional saying that expresses a truth.
"Haste makes waste" is a proverb.

revived (rih VYVD) *v.*: awakened;
brought back to life. *The splash of
water revived him, and he opened
his eyes.*

Language Coach

Word Origins The word *revived*
comes from the Latin prefix *re–*,
meaning "again," and the Latin root
word *vivere*, meaning "to live." From
its origin, you can easily see why
revived means "brought back to
life." The word has other meanings
as well: "brought back into use";
"brought to mind again"; "presented
a play or movie that hasn't been
seen for a long time." Explain how
each of these three meanings is
related to the word's origin.

Learn It Online
Check out the *PowerNotes* introduction to these
selections at:

go.hrw.com   H6-751   Go

Louis Untermeyer
(1885–1977)

Reviving an Old World

Louis Untermeyer could have been thinking of this story when he described the writer's job as the "struggle somehow to revive an old world, or create a new one."

As a child, Untermeyer loved to read, but he disliked school, especially math. His parents expected him to go to college, but he dropped out of high school when he was sixteen. For the next twenty-two years he worked in his family's jewelry business. He said he did not become serious about working or writing until he met the poet Robert Frost in 1915. Frost became Untermeyer's lifelong friend. It was Frost who encouraged Untermeyer to quit his day job and become a full-time writer.

Today Untermeyer is best known not for his own writing but for the very popular collections of poetry he put together, some for children and some for adults. In his autobiography *From Another World* he describes himself as a friend to three generations of poets.

Robert Silverberg
(1935–   )

The Future and the Past

Robert Silverberg has written hundreds of works in many different genres. One of the world's most famous science fiction writers, Silverberg has also written nonfiction about archaeology and history—especially the history of people and places long vanished.

Think About the Writers

Why might authors like these two write about people and places of the past?

Build Background

"The Dog of Pompeii" is **historical fiction.** Louis Untermeyer combined a fictional story with facts about actual historical events. The story's setting is Pompeii, an ancient Roman city that was buried by a volcanic eruption in A.D. 79.

The volcano that destroyed the city of Pompeii also preserved it. Beginning in the eighteenth century, archaeologists brought the past to life as they excavated buildings, furniture, food, paintings, and tools. They found about two thousand hollow forms of humans, dogs, and other animals that had been frozen in place by the ash that buried them.

An Italian archaeologist named Giuseppe Fiorelli found a way to make molds of the bodies, by pumping plaster into the hollows they had left in the ashes. When the plaster hardened, the ash around it was chipped off, leaving a cast in the shape of the body.

Today three quarters of old Pompeii has been unearthed. You can visit Pompeii as a tourist, walk the same streets, look at the same buildings, and gaze at the same volcano that the unsuspecting residents of Pompeii saw for the last time on that day nearly two thousand years ago.

Preview the Selections

In the short story "The Dog of Pompeii," you'll meet **Tito,** a boy who is blind, and his faithful dog **Bimbo.** Both characters live in ancient Pompeii, the Roman city that was buried by the eruption of Mount Vesuvius in A.D. 79.

Next, you'll read "Pompeii," a nonfiction historical account of the same event—the eruption of Vesuvius.

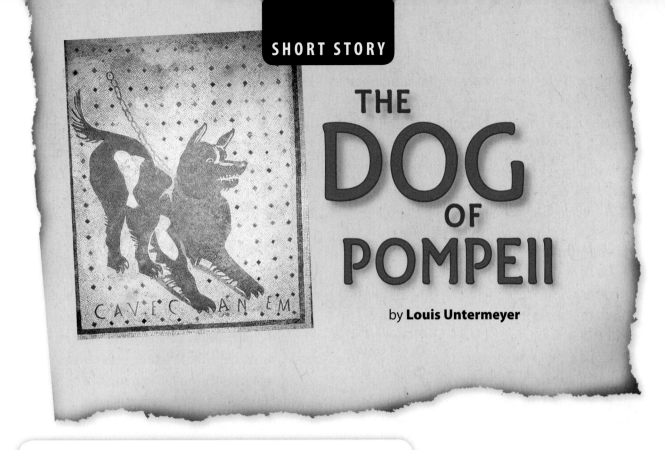

THE DOG OF POMPEII

by **Louis Untermeyer**

Read with a Purpose
Read "The Dog of Pompeii" to learn how the bond between a boy and his dog is tested during one of the greatest natural disasters in history.

Tito and his dog Bimbo lived (if you could call it living) under the wall where it joined the inner gate. They really didn't live there; they just slept there. They lived anywhere. Pompeii was one of the gayest of the old Latin towns, but although Tito was never an unhappy boy, he was not exactly a merry one. The streets were always lively with shining chariots and bright red trappings; the open-air theaters rocked with laughing crowds; sham[1] battles and athletic sports were free for the asking in the great stadium. Once a year the Caesar[2] visited the pleasure city and the fireworks lasted for days; the sacrifices[3] in the forum were better than a show.

But Tito saw none of these things. He was blind—had been blind from birth. He was known to everyone in the poorer quarters. But no one could say how old he was, no one remembered his parents, no one could tell

---

1. **sham:** make-believe.

2. **Caesar** (SEE zuhr): Roman emperor. The word *Caesar* comes from the family name of Julius Caesar, a great general who ruled Rome as dictator from 49 B.C. to 44 B.C.

3. **sacrifices:** offerings (especially of slaughtered animals) to the gods.

where he came from. Bimbo was another mystery. As long as people could remember seeing Tito—about twelve or thirteen years—they had seen Bimbo. Bimbo had never left his side. He was not only dog but nurse, pillow, playmate, mother, and father to Tito. **Ⓐ**

Did I say Bimbo never left his master? (Perhaps I had better say comrade, for if anyone was the master, it was Bimbo.) I was wrong. Bimbo did trust Tito alone exactly three times a day. It was a fixed routine, a custom understood between boy and dog since the beginning of their friendship, and the way it worked was this: Early in the morning, shortly after dawn, while Tito was still dreaming, Bimbo would disappear. When Tito awoke, Bimbo would be sitting quietly at his side, his ears cocked, his stump of a tail tapping the ground, and a fresh-baked bread—more like a large round roll—at his feet. Tito would stretch himself; Bimbo would yawn; then they would breakfast. At noon, no matter where they happened to be, Bimbo would put his paw on Tito's knee and the two of them would return to the inner gate. Tito would curl up in the corner (almost like a dog) and go to sleep, while Bimbo, looking quite important (almost like a boy), would disappear again. In half an hour he'd be back with their lunch. Sometimes it would be a piece of fruit or a scrap of meat, often it was nothing but a dry crust. But sometimes there would be one of those flat rich cakes, sprinkled with raisins and sugar, that Tito liked so much. At suppertime the same thing happened, although there was a little

less of everything, for things were hard to snatch in the evening, with the streets full of people. Besides, Bimbo didn't approve of too much food before going to sleep. A heavy supper made boys too restless and dogs too stodgy[4]—and it was the business of a dog to sleep lightly with one ear open and muscles ready for action. **Ⓑ**

But, whether there was much or little, hot or cold, fresh or dry, food was always there. Tito never asked where it came from and Bimbo never told him. There was plenty of rainwater in the hollows of soft stones; the old egg woman at the corner sometimes gave him a cupful of strong goat's milk; in the grape season the fat winemaker let him have drippings of the mild juice. So there was no danger of going hungry or thirsty. There was plenty of everything in Pompeii—if you knew where to find it—and if you had a dog like Bimbo.

As I said before, Tito was not the merriest boy in Pompeii. He could not romp with the other youngsters and play "hare and hounds" and "I spy" and "follow your master" and "ball against the building" and "jackstones" and "kings and robbers" with them. But that did not make him sorry for himself. If he could not see the sights that delighted the lads of Pompeii, he could hear and smell things they never noticed. He could really see more with his ears and nose than they could with their eyes. When he and Bimbo went out walking, he knew just where they were going and exactly what was happening.

4. **stodgy** (STAH jee): heavy and slow in movement.

Ⓐ Read and Discuss | What is the author telling you in the opening paragraphs? What's his attitude toward his characters?

Ⓑ Literary Focus | Historical Fiction | Are the characters in this story—Tito and Bimbo—credible so far? Why or why not?

"Ah," he'd sniff and say, as they passed a handsome villa,[5] "Glaucus Pansa is giving a grand dinner tonight. They're going to have three kinds of bread, and roast pigling, and stuffed goose, and a great stew—I think bear stew—and a fig pie." And Bimbo would note that this would be a good place to visit tomorrow. **C**

Or, "H'm," Tito would murmur, half through his lips, half through his nostrils. "The wife of Marcus Lucretius is expecting her mother. She's shaking out every piece of goods in the house; she's going to use the best clothes—the ones she's been keeping in pine needles and camphor[6]—and there's an extra girl in the kitchen. Come, Bimbo, let's get out of the dust!"

Or, as they passed a small but elegant dwelling opposite the public baths, "Too bad! The tragic poet is ill again. It must be a bad fever this time, for they're trying smoke fumes instead of medicine. Whew! I'm glad I'm not a tragic poet!"

Or, as they neared the forum, "Mm-m! What good things they have in the macellum[7] today!" (It really was a sort of butcher-grocer-marketplace, but Tito didn't know any better. He called it the macellum.) "Dates from Africa, and salt oysters from sea caves, and

Analyzing Visuals **Connecting to the Text**
What does this illustration show about the relationship between Tito and Bimbo?

cuttlefish, and new honey, and sweet onions, and—ugh!—water-buffalo steaks. Come, let's see what's what in the forum." And Bimbo, just as curious as his comrade, hurried on. Being a dog, he trusted his ears and nose (like Tito) more than his eyes. And so the two of them entered the center of Pompeii. **D**

The forum was the part of the town to which everybody came at least once during the day. It was the central square, and everything happened here. There were no private houses; all was public—the chief temples, the gold and red bazaars, the silk shops, the town hall, the booths belonging to the weavers and jewel merchants, the wealthy woolen market,

---

5. **villa:** large house.
6. **camphor** (KAM fuhr): strong-smelling substance used to keep moths away from clothing. Camphor is still used for this purpose.
7. **macellum** (MUH sehl uhm): market, especially a meat market.

C Read and Discuss Why does Bimbo think this villa would be a good place to visit tomorrow?

D Literary Focus Historical Fiction Do Tito's observations during his walk with Bimbo seem credible to you? Why or why not?

Analyzing Visuals   Connecting to the Text   What scene in the story
does this picture illustrate?

the shrine of the household gods. Everything glittered here. The buildings looked as if they were new—which, in a sense, they were. The earthquake of twelve years ago had brought down all the old structures and, since the citizens of Pompeii were ambitious to rival Naples and even Rome, they had seized the opportunity to rebuild the whole town. And they had done it all within a dozen years. There was scarcely a building that was older than Tito.

Tito had heard a great deal about the earthquake, though being about a year old at the time, he could scarcely remember it. This particular quake had been a light one—as

🄴

earthquakes go. The weaker houses had been shaken down, parts of the outworn wall had been wrecked; but there was little loss of life, and the brilliant new Pompeii had taken the place of the old. No one knew what caused these earthquakes. Records showed they had happened in the neighborhood since the beginning of time. Sailors said that it was to teach the lazy city folk a lesson and make them appreciate those who risked the dangers of the sea to bring them luxuries and protect their town from invaders. The priests said that the gods took this way of showing their anger to those who refused to worship properly and who failed to bring enough sacrifices

🄴 Read and Discuss What insights have you gained about life in Pompeii from this account of Tito's and Bimbo's walk through the city?

Vocabulary   **ambitious** (am BIHSH uhs) *adj.:* eager to succeed or to achieve something.

to the altars and (though they didn't say it in so many words) presents to the priests. The tradesmen said that the foreign merchants had corrupted the ground and it was no longer safe to traffic in imported goods that came from strange places and carried a curse with them. Everyone had a different explanation and everyone's explanation was louder and sillier than his neighbor's. **(F)**

They were talking about it this afternoon as Tito and Bimbo came out of the side street into the public square. The forum was the favorite promenade[8] for rich and poor. What with the priests arguing with the politicians, servants doing the day's shopping, tradesmen crying their wares, women displaying the latest fashions from Greece and Egypt, children playing hide-and-seek among the marble columns, knots of soldiers, sailors, peasants from the provinces[9]—to say nothing of those who merely came to lounge and look on—the square was crowded to its last inch. His ears even more than his nose guided Tito to the place where the talk was loudest. It was in front of the shrine of the household gods that, naturally enough, the householders were arguing.

"I tell you," rumbled a voice which Tito recognized as bath master Rufus's, "there won't be another earthquake in my lifetime or yours. There may be a tremble or two, but earthquakes, like lightnings, never strike twice in the same place."

---

8. **promenade** (prahm uh NAYD): public place where people stroll.

9. **provinces**: places far from the capital, under Roman control.

"Do they not?" asked a thin voice Tito had never heard. It had a high, sharp ring to it and Tito knew it as the accent of a stranger. "How about the two towns of Sicily that have been ruined three times within fifteen years by the eruptions of Mount Etna? And were they not warned? And does that column of smoke above Vesuvius mean nothing?"

"That?" Tito could hear the grunt with which one question answered another. "That's always there. We use it for our weather guide. When the smoke stands up straight, we know we'll have fair weather; when it flattens out, it's sure to be foggy; when it drifts to the east—"

"Yes, yes," cut in the edged voice. "I've heard about your mountain barometer.[10] But the column of smoke seems hundreds of feet higher than usual and it's thickening and spreading like a shadowy tree. They say in Naples—"

"Oh, Naples!" Tito knew this voice by the little squeak that went with it. It was Attilio the cameo cutter.[11] "They talk while we suffer. Little help we got from them last time. Naples commits the crimes and Pompeii pays the price. It's become a proverb with us. Let them mind their own business."

"Yes," grumbled Rufus, "and others', too."

"Very well, my confident friends," responded the thin voice, which now sounded curiously flat. "We also have a proverb—and

---

10. **barometer** (buh RAHM uh tuhr): instrument for measuring atmospheric pressure. Barometers are used in forecasting changes in the weather.

11. **cameo cutter**: artist who carves small, delicate pictures on gems or shells.

(F) Read and Discuss | What didn't people at this time understand about earthquakes?

Vocabulary **proverb** (PRAHV urb) *n.:* short traditional saying that expresses a truth.

The Dog of Pompeii **757**

it is this: *Those who will not listen to men must be taught by the gods.* I say no more. But I leave a last warning. Remember the holy ones. Look to your temples. And when the smoke tree above Vesuvius grows to the shape of an umbrella pine, look to your lives." **G**

Tito could hear the air whistle as the speaker drew his toga about him, and the quick shuffle of feet told him the stranger had gone.

"Now what," said the cameo cutter, "did he mean by that?"

"I wonder," grunted Rufus. "I wonder."

Tito wondered, too. And Bimbo, his head at a thoughtful angle, looked as if he had been doing a heavy piece of pondering. By nightfall the argument had been forgotten. If the smoke had increased, no one saw it in the dark. Besides, it was Caesar's birthday and the town was in a holiday mood. Tito and Bimbo were among the merrymakers, dodging the charioteers who shouted at them. A dozen times they almost upset baskets of sweets and jars of Vesuvian wine, said to be as fiery as the streams inside the volcano, and a dozen times they were cursed and cuffed. But Tito never missed his footing. He was thankful for his keen ears and quick instinct—most thankful of all for Bimbo.

They visited the uncovered theater, and though Tito could not see the faces of the actors, he could follow the play better than most of the audience, for their attention wandered—they were distracted by the scenery, the costumes, the byplay,[12] even by themselves—while Tito's whole attention was centered in what he heard. Then to the city walls, where the people of Pompeii watched a mock naval battle in which the city was attacked by the sea and saved after thousands of flaming arrows had been exchanged and countless colored torches had been burned. Though the thrill of flaring ships and lighted skies was lost to Tito, the shouts and cheers excited him as much as any, and he cried out with the loudest of them.

The next morning there were two of the beloved raisin-and-sugar cakes for his breakfast. Bimbo was unusually active and thumped his bit of a tail until Tito was afraid he would wear it out. The boy could not imagine whether Bimbo was urging him to some sort of game or was trying to tell him something. After a while, he ceased to notice Bimbo. He felt drowsy. Last night's late hours had tired him. Besides, there was a heavy mist in the air—no, a thick fog rather than a mist—a fog that got into his throat and scraped it and made him cough. He walked as far as the marine gate[13] to get a breath of the sea. But the blanket of haze had spread all over the bay and even the salt air seemed smoky. **H**

He went to bed before dusk and slept. But he did not sleep well. He had too many dreams—dreams of ships lurching in the forum, of losing his way in a screaming crowd,

---

12. **byplay:** action taking place outside the main action of a play.

13. **marine gate:** gate in a city wall leading to the sea.

G **Reading Focus** **Read and Discuss** Explain the stranger's warning. How does his attitude in this conversation differ from that of the other men?

H **Reading Focus** **Reading for Details** Which details about the setting seem important in this paragraph? Why? What do they tell you?

of armies marching across his chest, of being pulled over every rough pavement of Pompeii.

He woke early. Or, rather, he was pulled awake. Bimbo was doing the pulling. The dog had dragged Tito to his feet and was urging the boy along. Somewhere. Where, Tito did not know. His feet stumbled uncertainly; he was still half asleep. For a while he noticed nothing except the fact that it was hard to breathe. The air was hot. And heavy. So heavy that he could taste it. The air, it seemed, had turned to powder—a warm powder that stung his nostrils and burned his sightless eyes.

Then he began to hear sounds. Peculiar sounds. Like animals under the earth. Hissings and groanings and muffled cries that a dying creature might make dislodging the stones of his underground cave. There was no doubt of it now. The noises came from underneath. He not only heard them—he could feel them. The earth twitched; the twitching changed to an uneven shrugging of the soil. Then, as Bimbo half pulled, half coaxed him across, the ground jerked away from his feet and he was thrown against a stone fountain. **❶**

The water—hot water—splashing in his face revived him. He got to his feet, Bimbo steadying him, helping him on again. The noises grew louder; they came closer. The cries were even more animal-like than before, but now they came from human throats. A few people, quicker of foot and more hurried by fear, began to rush by. A family or two—then a section—then, it seemed, an army

broken out of bounds. Tito, bewildered though he was, could recognize Rufus as he bellowed past him, like a water buffalo gone mad. Time was lost in a nightmare.

It was then the crashing began. First a sharp crackling, like a monstrous snapping of twigs; then a roar like the fall of a whole forest of trees; then an explosion that tore earth and sky. The heavens, though Tito could not see them, were shot through with continual flickerings of fire. Lightnings above were answered by thunders beneath. A house fell. Then another. By a miracle the two companions had escaped the dangerous side streets and were in a more open space. It was the forum. They rested here awhile—how long, he did not know. **❿**

Tito had no idea of the time of day. He could feel it was black—an unnatural blackness. Something inside—perhaps the lack of breakfast and lunch—told him it was past noon. But it didn't matter. Nothing seemed to matter. He was getting drowsy, too drowsy to walk. But walk he must. He knew it. And Bimbo knew it; the sharp tugs told him so. Nor was it a moment too soon. The sacred ground of the forum was safe no longer. It was beginning to rock, then to pitch, then to split. As they stumbled out of the square, the earth wriggled like a caught snake and all the columns of the temple of Jupiter[14] came down. It was the end of the world—or so it seemed.

14. **Jupiter:** the supreme god in the religion of the Romans.

---

❶ Read and Discuss | What is causing these peculiar sounds?

Vocabulary **revived** (rih VYVD) *v.*: awakened; brought back to life.

❿ Reading Focus **Reading for Details** Which details in the last two paragraphs make the effects of the volcanic eruption seem most real to you?

To walk was not enough now. They must run. Tito was too frightened to know what to do or where to go. He had lost all sense of direction. He started to go back to the inner gate; but Bimbo, straining his back to the last inch, almost pulled his clothes from him. What did the creature want? Had the dog gone mad?

Then suddenly he understood. Bimbo was telling him the way out—urging him there. The sea gate, of course. The sea gate—and then the sea. Far from falling buildings, heaving ground. He turned, Bimbo guiding him across open pits and dangerous pools of bubbling mud, away from buildings that had caught fire and were dropping their burning beams. Tito could no longer tell whether the noises were made by the shrieking sky or the agonized people. He and Bimbo ran on—the only silent beings in a howling world.

New dangers threatened. All Pompeii seemed to be thronging toward the marine gate and, squeezing among the crowds, there was the chance of being trampled to death. But the chance had to be taken. It was growing harder and harder to breathe. What air there was choked him. It was all dust now—dust and pebbles, pebbles as large as beans. They fell on his head, his hands—pumice stones from the black heart of Vesuvius. The mountain was turning itself inside out. Tito remembered a phrase that the stranger had said in the forum two days ago: "Those who will not listen to men must be taught by the gods." The people of Pompeii had refused to heed the warnings; they were being taught now—if it was not too late. **Ⓚ**

Suddenly it seemed too late for Tito. The red-hot ashes blistered his skin, the sting-ing vapors tore his throat. He could not go on. He staggered toward a small tree at the side of the road and fell. In a moment Bimbo was beside him. He coaxed. But there was no answer. He licked Tito's hands, his feet, his face. The boy did not stir. Then Bimbo did the last thing he could—the last thing he wanted to do. He bit his comrade, bit him deep in the arm. With a cry of pain, Tito jumped to his feet, Bimbo after him. Tito was in despair, but Bimbo was determined. He drove the boy on, snapping at his heels, wor-rying his way through the crowd, barking, baring his teeth, heedless of kicks or falling stones. Sick with hunger, half dead with fear and sulfur fumes, Tito pounded on, pursued by Bimbo. How long, he never knew. At last he staggered through the marine gate and felt soft sand under him. Then Tito fainted. . . . **Ⓛ**

Someone was dashing seawater over him. Someone was carrying him toward a boat.

"Bimbo," he called. And then louder, "Bimbo!" But Bimbo had disappeared.

Voices jarred against each other. "Hurry—hurry!" "To the boats!" "Can't you see the child's frightened and starving!" "He keeps calling for someone!" "Poor boy, he's out of his mind." "Here, child—take this!"

They tucked him in among them. The oarlocks creaked; the oars splashed; the boat rode over toppling waves. Tito was safe. But he wept continually.

"Bimbo!" he wailed. "Bimbo! Bimbo!" He could not be comforted.

Ⓚ **Reading Focus** **Reading for Details** What dangers does Tito face, as described in the last two paragraphs?

Ⓛ **Literary Focus** **Historical Fiction** Does this part of the plot, in which Bimbo tries to save Tito, seem realistic or contrived to you? Explain.

Eighteen hundred years passed. Scientists were restoring the ancient city; excavators[15] were working their way through the stones and trash that had buried the entire town. Much had already been brought to light—statues, bronze instruments, bright mosaics,[16] household articles; even delicate paintings had been preserved by the fall of ashes that had taken over two thousand lives. Columns were dug up, and the forum was beginning to emerge.

It was at a place where the ruins lay deepest that the director paused.

"Come here," he called to his assistant. "I think we've discovered the remains of a building in good shape. Here are four huge millstones that were most likely turned by slaves or mules—and here is a whole wall standing with shelves inside it. Why! It must have been a bakery. And here's a curious thing. What do you think I found under this heap where the ashes were thickest? The skeleton of a dog!"

"Amazing!" gasped his assistant. "You'd think a dog would have had sense enough to run away at the time. And what is that flat thing he's holding between his teeth? It can't be a stone."

---

15. **excavators** (EHKS kuh vay tuhrz): diggers; here, archaeologists.
16. **mosaics** (moh ZAY ihks): pictures or designs made by inlaying small bits of stone, glass, tile, or other materials in mortar.

Analyzing Visuals   **Connecting to the Text**
What is happening to Tito here? How does this illustration show the chaos that follows after the volcano's eruption?

"No. It must have come from this bakery. You know it looks to me like some sort of cake hardened with the years. And, bless me, if those little black pebbles aren't raisins. A raisin cake almost two thousand years old! I wonder what made him want it at such a moment."

"I wonder," murmured the assistant.

 Read and Discuss What solution can you offer to the mystery of why the dog would want a raisin cake at such a dangerous time?

POMPEII

by **Robert Silverberg**

Read with a Purpose
Read this selection to compare a fictional and nonfiction account of the eruption of Mount Vesuvius.

Preparing to Read for the selection is on page 751.

Build Background
In his nonfiction book *Lost Cities and Vanished Civilizations*, Robert Silverberg describes Pompeii in A.D. 79 and tells about the eruption of Mount Vesuvius. In writing his book, Silverberg drew on the findings of archaeologists who conducted excavations of Pompeii and Herculaneum, another ancient city destroyed by the volcanic eruption.

The people of Pompeii knew that doom was on hand, now. Their fears were doubled when an enormous rain of hot ashes began to fall on them, along with more lapilli.[1] Pelted with stones, half smothered by ashes, the Pompeiians cried to the gods for mercy. The wooden roofs of some of the houses began to catch fire as the heat of the ashes reached them. Other buildings were collapsing under the weight of the pumice stones that had fallen on them.

In those first few hours, only the quick-witted managed to escape. Vesonius Primus,

---
1. **lapilli** (luh PIHL y): small pieces of hardened lava.

the wealthy wool merchant, called his family together and piled jewelry and money into a sack. Lighting a torch, Vesonius led his little band out into the nightmare of the streets. Overlooked in the confusion was Vesonius' black watchdog, chained in the courtyard. The terrified dog barked wildly as lapilli struck and drifting white ash settled around him. The animal struggled with his chain, battling fiercely to get free, but the chain held, and no one heard the dog's cries. The humans were too busy saving themselves.

Many hundreds of Pompeiians fled in those first few dark hours. Stumbling in the darkness, they made their way to the city gates, then out, down to the harbor. They boarded boats and got away, living to tell the tale of their city's destruction. Others preferred to remain within the city, huddling inside the temples, or in the public baths, or in the cellars of their homes. They still hoped that the nightmare would end—that the tranquility of a few hours ago would return. . . . **Ⓐ**

It was evening, now. And new woe was in store for Pompeii. The earth trembled and quaked! Roofs that had somehow withstood the rain of lapilli went crashing in ruin, burying hundreds who had hoped to survive the eruption. In the forum, tall columns toppled as they had in 63.[2] Those who remembered that great earthquake screamed in new terror as the entire city seemed to shake in the grip of a giant fist.

Three feet of lapilli now covered the ground. Ash floated in the air. Gusts of poisonous gas came drifting from the belching crater, though people could still breathe. Roofs were collapsing everywhere. Rushing throngs, blinded by the darkness and the smoke, hurtled madly up one street and down the next, trampling the fallen in a crazy, fruitless dash toward safety. Dozens of people plunged into dead-end streets and found themselves trapped by crashing buildings. They waited there, too frightened to run farther, expecting the end. **Ⓑ**

The rich man Diomedes was another of those who decided not to flee at the first sign of alarm. Rather than risk being crushed by the screaming mobs, Diomedes calmly led the members of his household into the solidly built basement of his villa. Sixteen people altogether, as well as his daughter's dog and her beloved little goat. They took enough food and water to last for several days.

But for all his shrewdness and foresight, Diomedes was undone anyway. Poison gas was creeping slowly into the underground shelter! He watched his daughter begin to cough and struggle for breath. Vesuvius was giving off vast quantities of deadly carbon monoxide that was now settling like a blanket over the dying city.

"We can't stay here!" Diomedes gasped. Better to risk the uncertainties outside than to remain here and suffocate.

---

2. There had been an earthquake in Pompeii sixteen years before Vesuvius erupted.

Ⓐ Reading Focus Reading for Details Which facts in this paragraph <u>correspond</u> to details in "The Dog of Pompeii"?

Ⓑ Reading Focus Reading for Details Which events in the last two paragraphs <u>correspond</u> to events in Untermeyer's story?

"I'll open the door," he told them. "Wait for me here."

Accompanied only by an old and faithful servant, who carried a lantern to light Diomedes' way in the inky blackness, the nobleman stumbled toward the door. He held the silver key in his hand. Another few steps and he would have been at the door, he could have opened it, they could have fled into the air—but a shroud of gas swooped down on him. He fell, still clutching the key, dying within minutes. Beneath the porch, fourteen people waited hopefully for him, their lives ticking away with each second. Diomedes did not return. At the last moment, all fourteen embraced each other, servants and masters alike, as death took them. **C**

The poison gas thickened as the terrible night continued. It was possible to hide from the lapilli, but not from the gas, and Pompeiians died by the hundreds. Carbon monoxide gas keeps the body from absorbing oxygen. Victims of carbon monoxide poisoning get sleepier and sleepier, until they lose consciousness, never to regain it. All over Pompeii, people lay down in the beds of lapilli, overwhelmed by the gas, and death came quietly to them. Even those who had made their way outside the city now fell victim to the spreading clouds of gas. It covered the entire countryside.

In a lane near the forum, a hundred people were trapped by a blind-alley wall. Others hid in the stoutly built public bathhouses, protected against collapsing roofs but not against the deadly gas. Near the house of Diomedes, a beggar and his little goat sought shelter. The man fell dead a few feet from Diomedes' door; the faithful goat remained by his side, its silver bell tinkling, until its turn came.

All through the endless night, Pompeiians wandered about the streets or crouched in their ruined homes or clustered in the temples to pray. By morning, few remained alive. Not once had Vesuvius stopped hurling lapilli and ash into the air, and the streets of Pompeii were filling quickly. At midday on August 25, exactly twenty-four hours after the beginning of the holocaust,[3] a second eruption racked the volcano. A second cloud of ashes rose above Vesuvius' summit. The wind blew ash as far as Rome and Egypt. But most of the new ashes descended on Pompeii.

The deadly shower of stone and ashes went unslackening into its second day. But it no longer mattered to Pompeii whether the eruption continued another day or another year. For by midday on August 25, Pompeii was a city of the dead. **D**

3. **holocaust:** great destruction of life.

C Read and Discuss How does the story of Diomedes help you imagine what people experienced during the volcanic eruption?

D Read and Discuss Why didn't it matter that the eruption continued? What does the author mean when he describes Pompeii as "a city of the dead"?

Applying Your Skills

Reading Standard 3.8 Critique the credibility of characterization and the degree to which a plot is contrived or realistic (e.g., compare use of fact and fantasy in historical fiction).

The Dog of Pompeii / Pompeii
Literary Response and Analysis

Reading Skills Focus
Quick Check

1. In the short story, what sign does the volcano give before it erupts?
2. What happens to Bimbo in the end?

Read with a Purpose

3. What does "The Dog of Pompeii" illustrate about the bond between dogs and humans?
4. Which selection—"The Dog of Pompeii" or "Pompeii"—gave you more <u>insight</u> into the effects of the volcanic eruption? Explain.

Reading Skills: Reading for Details

5. Review your chart and the <u>corresponding</u> details in the two selections. How does reading "Pompeii" help you evaluate the **credibility** of "The Dog of Pompeii"? Record your response in a new row in your chart.

"The Dog of Pompeii"	"Pompeii"
"falling buildings," p. 760	"buildings were collapsing," p. 762

Evaluation:

Literary Skills Focus
Literary Analysis

6. **Analyze** Many people read historical fiction to learn about history. What did you learn from this story about the way people lived in Pompeii—their religious beliefs, leisure activities, diet, attitudes toward nature?

7. **Identify** What did you learn about history from the nonfiction "Pompeii" that you didn't learn from the short story "The Dog of Pompeii"?

Literary Skills: Historical Fiction

8. **Evaluate** Are Tito and Bimbo **credible** characters—that is, do they behave like real boys and real dogs? Support your answer with details about their characters that you found believable or unbelievable.

9. **Evaluate** To what degree is the plot of "The Dog of Pompeii" realistic or <u>contrived</u>? To answer, consider the author's use of facts (be sure to review your Reading Skills chart) and fantasy—the events that are products of the author's imagination.

Literary Skills Review: Setting

10. **Analyze** In this story the **setting** plays an essential role. How does the setting create a problem for the characters? How does it influence the problem's resolution?

Writing Skills Focus
Think as a Reader/Writer

Use It in Your Writing Write a paragraph about an animal that faces a natural disaster. Use personification, but make the animal credible.

What Do You Think Now

How can fiction help bring the past to life?

Applying Your Skills

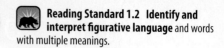
The Dog of Pompeii / Pompeii

Vocabulary Development

Figurative Language

In "The Dog of Pompeii," Louis Untermeyer uses figurative language to create vivid descriptions. **Figurative language** is not meant to be taken literally. **Similes,** one type of figurative language, are comparisons between two unlike things using words such as *like* or *as*.

Your Turn

Interpreting Similes Interpret the meaning of each simile from the story by explaining what the two items being compared have in common.

1. "Tito . . . could recognize Rufus as he bellowed past him, like a water buffalo gone mad."
2. "The earth wriggled like a caught snake."

Interpreting Comparisons
Answer each question to clarify the meaning of the italicized Vocabulary word.

> ambitious
> proverb
> revived

3. Why might an *ambitious* person be compared to an ant?
4. How can a *proverb* be like a trusted friend?
5. If doctors *revived* a man, why might he feel like a newborn baby?

Academic Vocabulary

Talk About . . .
Think of movies about disasters that you've seen. Do you usually <u>perceive</u> the characters as credible? What makes the plots seem <u>contrived</u> or realistic? What <u>insights</u> can you offer to explain why such movies are so popular?

Language Coach

Prefixes Sometimes you can figure out the meaning of an unfamiliar word if you analyze the meanings of its parts. The more prefixes you know, the more words you'll be able to figure out.

A **prefix** is a word part added to the beginning of a word or root. The chart below lists common prefixes.

1. Identify the **prefix** in each of the words listed just below. In the chart, find the meaning of the prefix; then, define the whole word.
   discomfort   incapable
   nonstop   unhappy
2. Used each word from item 1 in a sentence or two about Bimbo and Tito.

Common Prefixes		
Prefix	**Meaning**	**Examples**
dis–	opposing; away	dishonor, dislike
in–	not	incomplete, incorrect
non–	not	nonhuman, nonprofit
un–	not	unwise

Learn It Online
For action-packed vocabulary lessons, visit:
go.hrw.com   H6-766   **Go**

Reading Standard 3.8 Critique the credibility of characterization and the degree to which a plot is contrived or realistic (e.g., compare use of fact and fantasy in historical fiction).

Grammar Link

Types of Adjectives

A **comparative** is an adjective or adverb used to compare two things. A **superlative** is an adjective or adverb used to compare three or more things. Watch out for these two common mistakes:

Don't use a superlative to compare only two people or things.

> **smarter**
> A sighted boy was smart, but Tito was ~~smartest~~.

> **more**
> Of the dog and his master, the dog was ~~most~~ daring.

Don't use both *more* and *–er* to form a comparative. Don't use both *most* and *–est* to form a superlative.

> There were few buildings that were ~~more~~ older than Tito.

> Mrs. Lucretius is wearing her ~~most~~ nicest clothes during her mother's visit.

Your Turn

Correct these comparisons:

1. There was no one with a more better sense of smell than Tito.
2. Between Tito and Bimbo, Bimbo was fastest.
3. Tito is not the merrier boy in all Pompeii.
4. Tito had the most keenest hearing of all.
5. Some of the people in the square are more activer than others.

CHOICES

As you respond to the Choices, use these **Academic Vocabulary** words as appropriate: <u>contrived</u>, <u>correspond</u>, <u>insight</u>, <u>perceive</u>.

REVIEW
Write a Critique

Imagine that you were a publisher, and Untermeyer submitted "The Dog of Pompeii" to you for publication. What feedback would you give him about the story? Is the characterization credible? Is the plot <u>contrived</u> or realistic? What revisions would you suggest he make? Write a brief critique of the story.

CONNECT
Make an Audio Recording

TechFocus With a partner, make a recording of one scene in "The Dog of Pompeii." First, decide which parts you will each read, and practice reading the scene with expression. Choose sound effects that will help your audience picture events and that will make the action seem real. Play your recording for your classmates.

EXTEND
Write Historical Fiction

Write your own work of historical fiction. Choose a past historical event or time period (perhaps one that you've studied) for your story's setting. Then, create credible characters and a realistic plot. Be sure to create a balance between fact and fantasy in your story.

Learn It Online
Tell your story in a whole new way. Try digital storytelling at:

go.hrw.com   H6-767   **Go**

Zlateh the Goat

by **Isaac Bashevis Singer**

TRIAL BY FIRE

from *People Magazine*

What Do **You** Think?
How can stories set in the past have meaning for us today?

Reader/Writer
Notebook
Use your **RWN** to complete the
activities for these selections.

Reading Standard 3.8 Critique the
credibility of characterization and the
degree to which a plot is contrived or realistic
(e.g., compare use of fact and fantasy in historical
fiction).

Zlateh the Goat / Trial by Fire

Literary Skills Focus

Credibility of Plot and Characters One of the main tasks of a literary critic is to evaluate whether the characters and plot in a story are **credible,** or believable. Readers expect a story's characters to act the way real people do. Even if the characters are aliens or young wizards, the characters' actions should make sense. A plot should also be credible, developing naturally from the actions of the characters. If a plot has too many coincidences or if the chain of causes and effects is weak, then the plot is <u>contrived</u>, instead of being realistic, and it won't hold readers' interest. As you read this story and the article that follows it, think about whether the story's characters and plot are credible.

Reading Skills Focus

Making Generalizations A **generalization** is a conclusion drawn from several examples or pieces of evidence. To make a generalization, you combine evidence in a text with what you already know to come up with a broad statement that expresses a truth. Making generalizations can help you test a story's credibility.

Into Action As you read, use a chart like the one below to record generalizations about animals based on evidence in the texts.

Evidence in Texts	My Knowledge	Generalizations
"Zlateh the Goat": Zlateh "trusted" people, p. 772.	My dog trusts me.	Animals and people develop relationships based on trust.
"Trial by Fire":		

Vocabulary

Zlateh the Goat

penetrated (PEHN uh tray tihd) *v.:* pierced; made a way through. *Sunlight penetrated the clouds.*

cleft (klehft) *adj.:* split; divided. *Goats have cleft hooves.*

chaos (KAY ahs) *n.:* total confusion or disorder. *The storm created chaos outside Aaron's shelter.*

exuded (ehg ZOO dihd) *v.:* gave off. *The hay exuded warmth.*

Language Coach

Word Origins The word *exuded* comes from the Latin prefix *ex–*, meaning "out," and the Latin root word *sudare*, meaning "to sweat." One meaning of *exuded* is "flowed out of a cut or pores"—as in the way sweat is released through the pores of your skin. How is the meaning of *exuded* that is used in this story—"gave off"—related to the word's origin?

Writing Skills Focus
Think as a Reader/Writer
Find It in Your Reading "Zlateh the Goat" contains realistic details. As you read, list in your *Reader/Writer Notebook* the details that add to the credibility of the characters and the plot.

Learn It Online
For a preview of "The Dog of Pompeii," see the video introduction on:

go.hrw.com   H6-769   **Go**

Isaac Bashevis Singer

(1904–1991)

"Time Does Not Vanish"

Nobel Prize WINNER

Isaac Bashevis Singer was born in a village like the one in this story and grew up in Warsaw, Poland, where his father was a rabbi. As a boy he read constantly and was curious about everything. Both of Singer's parents were skilled storytellers.

Singer listened and watched carefully, storing in his memory scenes, people, and incidents he would write about later in his life. His stories won him the Nobel Prize for Literature in 1978.

In "Zlateh the Goat" and many other stories, Singer recalls a way of life that no longer exists. He wrote:

> "Children are as puzzled by passing time as grown-ups. What happens to a day once it is gone? Where are all our yesterdays with their joys and sorrows? Literature helps us remember the past with its many moods. To the storyteller yesterday is still here as are the years and the decades gone by.
>
> In stories time does not vanish. Neither do men and animals. For the writer and his readers all creatures go on living forever. What happened long ago is still present. . . ."

Think About the Writer How do you think stories ensure that "time does not vanish"?

Preview the Selections

In "Zlateh the Goat," you'll read about a boy, **Aaron,** and his adventures when he takes the family goat, **Zlateh,** to town to be sold.

"Trial by Fire" tells the true story of a brave mother cat, **Scarlett,** who saves her kittens from a fire.

Zlateh the Goat

by **Isaac Bashevis Singer**
pictures by **Maurice Sendak**

Read with a Purpose
Read this story to explore the bond between a boy and the family's goat.

Build Background
"Zlateh the Goat" takes place around Hanukkah (HAH nuh kah), a Jewish religious festival usually observed in December. Hanukkah is an eight-day-long celebration of the rededication of the Temple in Jerusalem in 165 B.C., following the victory of Jewish fighters over a huge Syrian army. The Temple, which had been taken over by Antiochus, ruler of the Syrians, had been violated and damaged. While the Jews were purifying and repairing the Temple, a miracle occurred. A tiny bit of oil for the holy lamp—barely enough for one day—lasted eight days.

At Hanukkah time the road from the village to the town is usually covered with snow, but this year the winter had been a mild one. Hanukkah had almost come, yet little snow had fallen. The sun shone most of the time. The peasants complained that because of the dry weather there would be a poor harvest of winter grain. New grass sprouted, and the peasants sent their cattle out to pasture. **A**

For Reuven the furrier[1] it was a bad year, and after long hesitation he decided to sell Zlateh the goat. She was old and gave little milk. Feyvel the town butcher had offered eight gulden[2] for her. Such a sum would buy Hanukkah candles, potatoes and oil for pancakes, gifts for the children, and other holiday necessaries for the house. Reuven told his oldest boy, Aaron, to take the goat to town.

Aaron understood what taking the goat to Feyvel meant, but he had to obey his father. Leah, his mother, wiped the tears from her eyes when she heard the

---

1. **furrier** (FUR ee uhr): someone who makes and repairs fur garments.

2. **gulden** (GUL duhn): coins formerly used in several European countries.

A | Read and Discuss | What do you learn in this paragraph?

news. Aaron's younger sisters, Anna and Miriam, cried loudly. Aaron put on his quilted jacket and a cap with earmuffs, bound a rope around Zlateh's neck, and took along two slices of bread with cheese to eat on the road. Aaron was supposed to deliver the goat by evening, spend the night at the butcher's, and return the next day with the money. **B**

While the family said goodbye to the goat, and Aaron placed the rope around her neck, Zlateh stood as patiently and good-naturedly as ever. She licked Reuven's hand. She shook her small white beard. Zlateh

trusted human beings. She knew that they always fed her and never did her any harm.

When Aaron brought her out on the road to town, she seemed somewhat astonished. She'd never been led in that direction before. She looked back at him questioningly, as if to say, "Where are you taking me?" But after a while she seemed to come to the conclusion that a goat shouldn't ask questions. Still, the road was different. They passed new fields, pastures, and huts with thatched roofs. Here and there a dog barked and came running after them, but Aaron chased it away with his stick. **C**

The sun was shining when Aaron left the village. Suddenly the weather changed. A large black cloud with a bluish center appeared in the east and spread itself rapidly over the sky. A cold wind blew in with it. The crows flew low, croaking. At first it looked as if it would rain, but instead it began to hail as in summer. It was early in the day, but it became dark as dusk. After a while the hail turned to snow.

In his twelve years Aaron had seen all kinds of weather, but he had never experienced a snow like this one. It was so dense it shut out the light of the day. In a short time their path was completely covered. The wind became as cold as ice. The road to town was narrow and winding. Aaron no longer knew where he was. He could not see

---

B **Read and Discuss** What is on the father's mind, and what is he planning to do? How does his plan affect the family?

C **Literary Focus** **Credibility** Singer suggests that Zlateh can think—that she can question and draw conclusions. Explain why this makes her a more or less believable character.

through the snow. The cold soon penetrated his quilted jacket.

At first Zlateh didn't seem to mind the change in weather. She too was twelve years old and knew what winter meant. But when her legs sank deeper and deeper into the snow, she began to turn her head and look at Aaron in wonderment. Her mild eyes seemed to ask, "Why are we out in such a storm?" Aaron hoped that a peasant would come along with his cart, but no one passed by.

The snow grew thicker, falling to the ground in large, whirling flakes. Beneath it Aaron's boots touched the softness of a plowed field. He realized that he was no longer on the road. He had gone astray. He could no longer figure out which was east or west, which way was the village, the town. The wind whistled, howled, whirled the snow about in eddies. It looked as if white imps were playing tag on the fields. A white dust rose above the ground. Zlateh stopped. She could walk no longer. Stubbornly she

anchored her cleft hooves in the earth and bleated as if pleading to be taken home. Icicles hung from her white beard, and her horns were glazed with frost. **D**

Aaron did not want to admit the danger, but he knew just the same that if they did not find shelter, they would freeze to death. This was no ordinary storm. It was a mighty blizzard. The snowfall had reached his knees. His hands were numb, and he could no longer feel his toes. He choked when he breathed. His nose felt like wood, and he rubbed it with snow. Zlateh's bleating began to sound like crying. Those humans in whom she had so much confidence had dragged her into a trap. Aaron began to pray to God for himself and for the innocent animal. **E**

Suddenly he made out the shape of a hill. He wondered what it could be. Who had piled snow into such a huge heap? He moved toward it, dragging Zlateh after him. When he came near it, he realized that it was a large haystack which the snow had blanketed.

> **Aaron did not want to admit the danger, but he knew just the same that if they did not find shelter, they would freeze to death.**

D Literary Focus Credibility What details make this situation seem credible?

E Read and Discuss What is happening now? What is the author trying to tell us about Zlateh's and Aaron's thoughts?

Aaron realized immediately that they were saved. With great effort he dug his way through the snow. He was a village boy and knew what to do. When he reached the hay, he hollowed out a nest for himself and the goat. No matter how cold it may be outside, in the hay it is always warm. And hay was food for Zlateh. The moment she smelled it, she became contented and began to eat. Outside, the snow continued to fall. It quickly covered the passageway Aaron had dug. But a boy and an animal need to breathe, and there was hardly any air in their hide-out. Aaron bored a kind of a window through the hay and snow and carefully kept the passage clear.

Zlateh, having eaten her fill, sat down on her hind legs and seemed to have regained her confidence in man. Aaron ate his two slices of bread and cheese, but after the difficult journey he was still hungry. He looked at Zlateh and noticed her udders were full. He lay down next to her, placing himself so that when he milked her, he could squirt the milk into his mouth. It was rich and sweet. Zlateh was not accustomed to being milked that way, but she did not resist. On the contrary, she seemed eager to reward Aaron for bringing her to a shelter whose very walls, floor, and ceiling were made of food. **ⓕ**

Analyzing Visuals   **Connecting to the Text**
What scene in the story does this picture illustrate?

ⓕ [Read and Discuss] What does the author mean when he says that Zlateh "seemed eager to reward Aaron"? How does this fit with what you've already learned about Zlateh?

Through the window Aaron could catch a glimpse of the chaos outside. The wind carried before it whole drifts of snow. It was completely dark, and he did not know whether night had already come or whether it was the darkness of the storm. Thank God that in the hay it was not cold. The

Vocabulary chaos (KAY ahs) *n.*: total confusion or disorder.

Connecting to the Text

How does this illustration compare with the image of Aaron and Zlateh's shelter in the haystack that you picture in your mind?

dried hay, grass, and field flowers exuded the warmth of the summer sun. Zlateh ate frequently; she nibbled from above, below, from the left and right. Her body gave forth an animal warmth, and Aaron cuddled up to her. He had always loved Zlateh, but

now she was like a sister. He was alone, cut off from his family, and wanted to talk. He began to talk to Zlateh. "Zlateh, what do you think about what has happened to us?" he asked.

"Maaaa," Zlateh answered.

"If we hadn't found this stack of hay, we would both be frozen stiff by now," Aaron said.

"Maaaa," was the goat's reply.

"If the snow keeps on falling like this, we may have to stay here for days," Aaron explained.

"Maaaa," Zlateh bleated.

"What does 'Maaaa' mean?" Aaron asked. "You'd better speak up clearly."

"Maaaa. Maaaa," Zlateh tried.

"Well, let it be 'Maaaa' then," Aaron said patiently. "You can't speak, but I know you understand. I need you and you need me. Isn't that right?"

"Maaaa." **G**

Aaron became sleepy. He made a pillow out of some hay, leaned his head on it, and dozed off. Zlateh too fell asleep.

When Aaron opened his eyes, he didn't know whether it was morning or night. The snow had blocked up his window. He tried to clear it, but when he had bored through to the length of his arm, he still hadn't reached the outside. Luckily he had his stick with him and was able to break through to the open

G **Reading Focus** Making Generalizations What generalization can you make about animals from the way Aaron and Zlateh communicate?

Vocabulary exuded (ehg ZOO dihd) *v.*: gave off.

air. It was still dark outside. The snow continued to fall and the wind wailed, first with one voice and then with many. Sometimes it had the sound of devilish laughter. Zlateh too awoke, and when Aaron greeted her, she answered, "Maaaa." Yes, Zlateh's language consisted of only one word, but it meant many things. Now she was saying, "We must accept all that God gives us—heat, cold, hunger, satisfaction, light, and darkness."

Aaron had awakened hungry. He had eaten up his food, but Zlateh had plenty of milk.

For three days Aaron and Zlateh stayed in the haystack. Aaron had always loved Zlateh, but in these three days he loved her more and more. She fed him with her milk and helped him keep warm. She comforted him with her patience. He told her many stories, and she always cocked her ears and listened. When he patted her, she licked his hand and his face. Then she said, "Maaaa," and he knew it meant, I love you too. **(H)**

The snow fell for three days, though after the first day it was not as thick and the wind quieted down. Sometimes Aaron felt that there could never have been a summer, that the snow had always fallen, ever since he could remember. He, Aaron, never had a father or mother or sisters. He was a snow child, born of the snow, and so was Zlateh. It was so quiet in the hay that his ears rang in the stillness. Aaron and Zlateh slept all night and a good part of the day. As for Aaron's dreams, they were all about warm weather. He dreamed of green fields, trees covered with blossoms, clear brooks, and singing birds. By the third night the snow had stopped, but Aaron did not dare to find his way home in the darkness. The sky became clear and the moon shone, casting silvery nets on the snow. Aaron dug his way out and looked at the world. It was all white, quiet, dreaming dreams of heavenly splendor. The stars were large and close. The moon swam in the sky as in a sea. **(I)**

On the morning of the fourth day, Aaron heard the ringing of sleigh bells. The haystack was not far from the road. The

> **Sometimes Aaron felt that there could never have been a summer, that the snow had always fallen, ever since he could remember.**

(H) Literary Focus Credibility How do the characters of Aaron and Zlateh change and develop during the time they are together in the haystack? How do their attitudes change? Explain whether the changes make them more or less credible.

(I) Read and Discuss How do you know that the writer's statement that Aaron "never had a father or mother or sisters" is not literal? What is the writer trying to say here?

peasant who drove the sleigh pointed out the way to him—not to the town and Feyvel the butcher, but home to the village. Aaron had decided in the haystack that he would never part with Zlateh.

Aaron's family and their neighbors had searched for the boy and the goat but had found no trace of them during the storm. They feared they were lost. Aaron's mother and sisters cried for him; his father remained silent and gloomy. Suddenly one of the neighbors came running to their house with the news that Aaron and Zlateh were coming up the road.

There was great joy in the family. Aaron told them how he had found the stack of hay and how Zlateh had fed him with her milk. Aaron's sisters kissed and hugged Zlateh and gave her a special treat of chopped carrots and potato peels, which Zlateh gobbled up hungrily.

Nobody ever again thought of selling Zlateh, and now that the cold weather had finally set in, the villagers needed the services of Reuven the furrier once more. When Hanukkah came, Aaron's mother was able to fry pancakes every evening, and Zlateh got her portion too. Even though Zlateh had her own pen, she often came to the kitchen, knocking on the door with her horns to indicate that she was ready to visit, and she was always admitted. In the evening, Aaron, Miriam, and Anna played dreidel.[3] Zlateh sat near the stove, watching the children and the flickering of the Hanukkah candles. **J**

Once in a while Aaron would ask her, "Zlateh, do you remember the three days we spent together?"

And Zlateh would scratch her neck with a horn, shake her white bearded head, and come out with the single sound which expressed all her thoughts, and all her love. **K**

> Even though Zlateh had her own pen, she often came to the kitchen, knocking on the door with her horns to indicate that she was ready to visit.

---

3. **dreidel** (DRAY duhl): spinning top played with at Hanukkah. Its four sides display Hebrew letters that stand for "A great miracle happened there."

J Reading Focus **Making Generalizations** How have things changed from the way they were at the beginning of the story? What generalization can you make about the bond between humans and animals based on what has happened in the story?

K Read and Discuss How have events turned out for Zlateh, Aaron, and his family?

TRIAL BY FIRE

from *People* **Magazine**

Read with a Purpose

Read this true story to learn about the heroic act of a mother cat.

Preparing to Read for the selection is on page 769.

Build Background

This article reports on an event that actually occurred in New York City on March 29, 1996. The article appeared in *People* magazine, July 14, 1997.

After battling a blaze in an abandoned auto shop on March 29 last year, New York City firefighters were startled to hear meowing. There, amid the smoke, sat three crying kittens; across the street were two more. Within moments, their mother, a badly injured calico,[1] was found nearby. "She had done her job and pulled them out one by one," says firefighter David Giannelli, who placed the animals in a box. "Her eyes were burnt shut, but she touched every one of those babies with the tip of her nose." Ⓐ

Taken to Long Island's North Shore Animal League, the kittens and their mother—named Scarlett at the shelter— were treated for smoke inhalation and burns. "The instinct to save your young is very strong," says Dr. Bonnie Brown, North Shore's medical director. "This was just an extraordinary example." Sifting through 2,000 adoption applications, administrators finally sent Scarlett home with Karen Wellen, a New York City writer, and her parents. (One kitten died from a viral infection; the others were placed in area homes.) Now three times a day, Scarlett—a plump 15 pounds—receives eye cream to counter damage to her lids but otherwise is healthy and loving. Karen can't believe her own luck: "This cat risked her life to save her kittens. To come out of it with such a sweet personality is amazing." Ⓑ

---

1. **calico** (KAL uh koh): cat with spots and markings of several colors.

Ⓐ **Read and Discuss** What has the author told you so far? What do the mother cat's actions tell you about her?

Ⓑ **Reading Focus** **Making Generalizations** What generalization about animals can you make based on this article?

Applying Your Skills

Reading Standard 3.8 Critique the credibility of characterization and the degree to which a plot is contrived or realistic (e.g., compare use of fact and fantasy in historical fiction).

Zlateh the Goat / Trial by Fire

Literary Response and Analysis

Reading Skills Focus

Quick Check

1. Why does the father want to sell Zlateh?
2. What changes occur in Aaron's family as a result of events in the story?

Read with a Purpose

3. How does the story illustrate the bonds that can exist between humans and animals?
4. Explain whether you were surprised by the heroic actions of Scarlett, the cat.

Reading Skills: Making Generalizations

5. Singer once said, "I believe men can learn a lot from God's creatures." Review the generalizations in your chart. What did you learn about animals from the story? What do the characters learn from Zlateh? Explain whether "Trial by Fire" helps make these lessons seem **credible.** Record your responses in your chart.

Evidence in Texts	My Knowledge	Generalizations
"Zlateh the Goat": Zlateh "trusted" people, p. 772.	My dog trusts me.	Animals and people develop relationships based on trust.
"Trial by Fire":		

Literary Skills Focus

Literary Analysis

6. **Analyze** Hanukkah celebrates a rebirth: the rededication of the Temple in Jerusalem. Why do you suppose Singer set the story during Hanukkah?

Literary Skills: Credibility

7. **Evaluate** Where in the story does Zlateh express her thoughts and feelings? Did you find her methods of communication **credible?** Why or why not?
8. **Evaluate** To what degree is the story's plot realistic or <u>contrived</u>? Support your critique with details from the story.

Literary Skills Review: Suspense

9. **Evaluate** Do you think the story contains **suspense?** Were there points where you worried about what would happen next? Support your evaluation with details from the story.

Writing Skills Focus

Think as a Reader/Writer

Use It in Your Writing Using credible details from the story, write a one-page article about Zlateh, similar to "Trial by Fire."

What Do You Think Now

What <u>insight</u> into the power of love did you gain from this story? How did the article contribute to this insight?

Applying Your Skills

Zlateh the Goat / Trial by Fire

Vocabulary Development

Figurative Language

A **simile** is a comparison between two unlike things using a word such as *like* or *as*. A **metaphor** is a comparison between two unlike things in which one thing becomes another thing. In "Zlateh the Goat," Singer uses these two types of **figurative language**—language that is not meant to be taken literally—to help you imagine the scene and the storm's effects.

Your Turn

Interpreting Figurative Language Identify the type of figurative language used in each example from the story, and interpret its meaning.

1. "His nose felt like wood."
2. "The moon swam in the sky as in a sea."

Using Figurative Language
Create your own metaphors and similes by completing the items below using the italicized Vocabulary words.

> penetrated
> cleft
> chaos
> exuded

1. The heat *penetrated* the room, making it seem like _____.
2. The goat's *cleft* hooves were like _____.
3. The *chaos* in the streets was a(n) _____.
4. The bakery *exuded* a smell that was like _____.

Language Coach

Word Origins The prefix *ex–*, meaning "out," forms part of the Latin origin of *exuded*. This specific prefix can be found in many other words as well. List two or three other words that contain this prefix. How does the meaning of this prefix relate to the definition of each word? How can knowing the meanings of common prefixes help you determine the meanings of unfamiliar words?

Academic Vocabulary

Talk About . . .
Singer wrote, "Literature helps us remember the past." What <u>insights</u> did you gain into Aaron's family's way of life in the story? Do you <u>perceive</u> the characters' lives as completely different from people's lives today? What details about their family life, struggles, or concerns <u>correspond</u> to aspects of your life or the lives of people you know?

Learn It Online
Sharpen your word skills at:

go.hrw.com | H6-780 | **Go**

Reading Standard 3.8 Critique the credibility of characterization and the degree to which a plot is contrived or realistic (e.g., compare use of fact and fantasy in historical fiction).

Grammar Link

Modifiers

To work well, modifiers have to be in the right place. Here's an example of a **misplaced modifier:**

> Aaron wished that he didn't have to sell the goat like his mother.

Is Aaron saying that his mother was sold like the goat? Or that the goat is like his mother? No, the phrase *like his mother* has been misplaced in the sentence. To fix the sentence, place the modifier as close as possible to the word it modifies—*wished*.

> Aaron wished <u>like his mother</u> that he didn't have to sell the goat.

Your Turn

Move the misplaced modifier in each sentence to the right place. If you are uncertain of the correct placement, draw an arrow from the modifier to the word it modifies. Then, place the modifier next to that word.

1. Aaron hoped that someone would come along in a cart with all his heart.
2. He moved toward the haystack with Zlateh.
3. He hollowed out the hay for himself and Zlateh into a nest.

CHOICES

As you respond to the Choices, use these **Academic Vocabulary** words as appropriate: <u>contrived</u>, <u>correspond</u>, <u>insight</u>, <u>perceive</u>.

REVIEW
Write a Critique

Timed ∟Writing Critique the credibility of "Zlateh the Goat" as compared with another story or movie featuring an animal. Do you think Zlateh is more or less credible than this other animal? Is the plot of Singer's story more realistic or more <u>contrived</u> than the other story's plot?

CONNECT
Pitch a Screenplay Idea

Partner Work With a partner, write a "pitch" for a film based on the story of Aaron and Zlateh or of Scarlett and her kittens. Summarize the story, and then describe how you imagine the film. Will it be live action or animated? Will you make any changes to the original story? Why is it a story audiences would pay to see?

EXTEND
Write a Comparison-Contrast Essay

"Zlateh the Goat" and "The Dog of Pompeii" (page 753) have many similarities, even though their settings are so different. Write a brief essay comparing the stories' plots, characters, and themes. Conclude by explaining which story you <u>perceive</u> as more credible.

Learn It Online
Tell your story in a whole new way. Try digital storytelling at:

go.hrw.com | H6-781 | **Go**

Writing Workshop

Response to Literature

Write with a Purpose

Analyze an aspect of a literary work by writing a response to literature. Use evidence from the text to support your thesis. Your **audience** includes your classmates and teacher, and your **purpose** is to persuade them that your interpretation of the work is well-reasoned, based on careful reading and understanding.

Think as a Reader/Writer Whether you realize it or not, when you read a literary work, you are also interpreting it—developing your own understanding of its meaning. Writing a response to literature gives you the chance to explain your interpretation of a literary work and to convince others that your interpretation is valid. You choose an element of the work that is central to your interpretation, make a statement about that element (called a thesis), and support your interpretation with details, examples, and quotations from the text.

Before you write your own response to literature, read the following excerpt from an essay by the writer Louise Sherman. In this excerpt, Sherman discusses the main character in a Lois Lowry novel called *Number the Stars*. Notice how Sherman uses evidence from the text to support the idea that the character Annemarie is central to the story's meaning.

A Good Response to Literature

- identifies the work by title and author
- clearly states the thesis
- develops an interpretation exhibiting careful reading, understanding, and insight
- supports the thesis with evidence from the text, such as details, examples, and quotations.
- is organized clearly
- restates or reinforces the thesis in a strong conclusion

See page 790 for complete rubric.

Reader/Writer Notebook

Use your **RWN** to complete the activities for this workshop.

When an important packet must be taken to the captain of one of the ships smuggling Jews to neutral Sweden, Annemarie finds the courage needed to deliver it despite grave danger to herself. Later her Uncle Hendrick tells her that *brave* means "not thinking about the dangers. Just thinking about what you must do." Lowry's story is not just of Annemarie; it is also of Denmark and the Danish people, whose Resistance was so effective in saving their Jews. Annemarie is not just a symbol, however. She is a very real child who is equally involved in playing with a new kitten and running races at school as in the danger of the occupation.

← Important **background** information is provided.

← A direct **quotation** is used as supporting evidence.

← **Details** provide further evidence that Annemarie is a believable character.

Think About the Professional Model

With a partner, discuss the following questions about the model.

1. Based on this excerpt, how would you state the writer's thesis?
2. Which piece of evidence do you feel is the strongest? Why?
3. How does Sherman let readers know that she thinks the character Annemarie is realistic?

Writing Standards 1.3 **Use a variety of effective and coherent organizational patterns, including** comparison and contrast; organization by categories; and **arrangement by** spatial order, **order of importance,** or climactic order. **1.6** Revise writing to improve the organization and consistency of ideas within and between paragraphs. **2.4** Write responses to literature: a. Develop an interpretation exhibiting careful reading, understanding, and insight. b. Organize the interpretation around several clear ideas, premises, or images. c. Develop and justify the interpretation through sustained use of examples and textual evidence.

Prewriting

Choose a Topic

First, choose a literary work—one that interests you and that you remember well. You will want to re-read the work, studying it closely for details. Try to choose a work with at least one literary element that is important to your understanding of the work as a whole. The Idea Starters at right list different literary elements you could consider.

Develop a Thesis

Once you have chosen a literary work, you will need to draft a **thesis statement,** or **opinion statement,** which sums up the main point that you will make in your response. Your thesis statement should clearly identify your purpose for writing and explain the importance of one element of the literary work, such as character or theme. To help you decide on a thesis statement, consider the following questions about the work.

- **Main Character:** Who or what is the main character? How does that character affect the events of the story? How does the author bring that character to life? Does the author use that character to illustrate a main idea?

- **Plot:** What are the main events in the literary work? What is the main conflict, and is it mainly internal or external? What complications arise? How is the conflict resolved? Does the resolution express a theme?

- **Setting:** Where and when does the story take place? Does the setting affect the characters and the plot? Could the work take place elsewhere?

- **Theme:** What is the theme of the literary work? How do the characters' actions and the chain of events in the work illustrate the theme?

Decide which element of the literary work stands out more than others. Then, determine what your main point is about that element. Here is a sample thesis statement to guide you:

Selection: "All Summer in a Day" (page 29)

> **Thesis:** The setting of this short story is otherworldly, but the interactions between the characters are something every reader has seen and experienced.

Notice how this thesis states the literary element (setting) and the writer's point about it.

Idea Starters
- setting
- characters
- plot events
- conflict
- theme

⦿ Writing Tip

Your **thesis statement** should clearly signal to your readers what you are going to say about your topic. Get together with a partner and exchange thesis statements. Can your partner tell by reading your thesis statement what your literary response is going to be about? If not, keep revising your statement until it is clear.

Your Turn _____

Get Started Making notes in your **RWN,** decide on a literary work and literary element you'll write about in your essay. Then, write a thesis statement that indicates the element and your main point about it.

Learn It Online
An interactive graphic organizer can help you generate and organize ideas. Try one at:

go.hrw.com | H6-783 | Go

Writing Tip

If your thesis is about the importance of character in a literary work, your main points of **evidence** may be things like a character's words, a character's actions, and how other characters relate to him or her. Your evidence will include specific details, examples, and quotations from the work.

Gather Evidence

In order to persuade your readers that your interpretation of the literary work is well reasoned, you must use **evidence** from the selection to support your insights and ideas. After you have decided on your thesis statement, re-read any notes you took while reading the literary work, and identify two to four strong points from the text that support your thesis.

To gather evidence, look more closely at the text to identify details, examples, and quotations that you can use to **support** your thesis statement. Your interpretation will be more convincing if you include various kinds of support. Here are the kinds of support you may include:

• direct quotations
• paraphrased lines or short passages
• details, such as images and dialogue
• examples, such as actions

Choose the evidence that best supports your thesis. For each piece of evidence, include a brief explanation to show how the evidence supports your thesis.

You can use a simple chart like the one below to organize and analyze the evidence you gather. Keeping track of where you find evidence will help you write your draft. This example is a partially completed evidence chart for the model on page 782.

Thesis: The character Annemarie is central to *Number the Stars*.

Evidence	What it shows	Page numbers
Annemarie takes the packet to the ship's captain.	Annemarie is brave.	

Your Turn

Gather Evidence To help plan your response to literature, create a graphic organizer like the one at right. As you find more **evidence** to support your thesis, you can fill in the blanks of your chart. Keep your audience and purpose in mind as you plan.

Think About Purpose and Audience

Keeping your purpose and audience in mind will help you write an effective response to literature. Your **purpose** is to explain your interpretation of a literary work by discussing an important element of the work. Additionally, you want to help your **audience**—your teacher and classmates—understand the literary work and to persuade them that your interpretation is a good one. Since your readers may not have read the work that you are interpreting, it is important to provide any background information that might help them better understand your interpretation.

Drafting

Follow the Writer's Framework

The **Writer's Framework** at right outlines how to plan your draft to create an effective response to literature. Remember to include the complete **title** of the literary work and the **author's name** in your introduction.

Organize Evidence

The main organizational pattern for your essay will be **order of importance.** Follow these steps to organize the evidence in your response to literature.

- Number your evidence in order of importance. What is the strongest evidence in support of your thesis?

- Decide how many and what kinds of details to include as evidence supporting your examples, paraphrases, or quotations.

- Decide where to present your most important evidence. If you place your strongest evidence first, readers will easily be able to follow the rest of your essay. If you place your strongest evidence last, readers will be left with a strong, memorable impression.

> ### A Writer's Framework
>
> **Introduction**
> - Complete title and author of the work
> - Clear thesis and necessary background
>
> **Body**
> - First piece of evidence from the text and what it shows
> - Second piece of evidence from the text and what it shows
> - Other evidence from the text and what it shows
>
> **Conclusion**
> - Restatement of thesis
> - Brief summary of supporting evidence
> - Overall impression or insight into the work

○ Writing Tip

Your **thesis** is the most important part of your introduction, so you want the thesis to be easy for readers to identify. Writers often build toward the thesis and then state it in the last sentence of the introduction.

Grammar Link Capitalizing Proper Nouns

When you write a response to literature, you include the title of a literary work, the author of the work, and other proper nouns such as characters' names and place names. Study the example below from the model on page 782, and remember to follow the rules for capitalizing proper nouns as you write your essay.

> When an important packet must be taken to the captain of one of the ships smuggling **Jews** to neutral **Sweden**, **Annemarie** finds the courage needed to deliver it despite grave danger to herself.

- Proper nouns name a particular person, place, thing, or idea, such as *Jews, Sweden,* and *Annemarie.* Proper nouns always begin with a capital letter.

Your Turn _____

Write Your Draft Follow your plan to write a draft of your essay. Be sure to think about these points:
- What is the most effective way to arrange your evidence?
- What proper nouns do you need to capitalize?

Peer Review

Sometimes an idea seems clear in your head when it is not clear on your paper. Work with one or more of your classmates to review each other's drafts and the guidelines at right. If your partner has difficulty identifying the main idea of a paragraph, the idea might not be clearly stated. Take notes about your partner's suggestions to help you improve your essay, and check the chart for revision suggestions.

Evaluating and Revising

Now that you've written your draft, re-read it carefully and use the chart below to help identify areas that can be improved.

Response to Literature: Guidelines for Content and Organization

Evaluation Question	Tip	Revision Technique
1. Are the author and title of the literary work included in your introduction?	**Highlight** the author and title.	**Add** a sentence or phrase naming the author and the title.
2. Does your introduction have a clear thesis that states the literary element and your main point about it?	**Underline** the thesis, the main point you are making. **Circle** the literary element and your main point about it.	**Add** a sentence that clearly states the thesis.
3. Is the main idea of each paragraph clear, and does each main idea support the thesis?	**Bracket** the main idea discussed in each paragraph of the body.	**Revise** the body paragraphs so that each one has a clearly stated main idea.
4. Is the main idea of each body paragraph supported by evidence?	**Draw a box** around each supporting detail, example, or quotation. **Draw a wavy line** under elaborations, or explanations.	**Add** details, examples, or quotations to support your thesis. **Elaborate** on details, examples, or quotations with commentary.
5. Are ideas well organized and consistent within and between paragraphs?	**Circle** transition words and phrases that show how ideas are related to one another.	**Revise** writing to add transition words and phrases as needed.
6. Does the essay end with a restatement of the thesis?	**Put a star** above the restatement.	**Add** a restatement of the thesis, if necessary.

Read this student's draft with comments on its structure and suggestions for how the response could be made even stronger.

Student Draft

Literary Review of the Novel *Iqbal*

by Reid Cline, Murchison Middle School

When children are abused, the only way their lives can be saved is if someone intervenes and fights for their rights. *Iqbal,* a novel by Francesco D'Adamo, is based on the true story of a young boy living in Pakistan.

Iqbal Masih was forced to work twelve hours a day at a carpet factory, chained to his loom in unimaginable conditions. His parents bonded him into child labor to pay off a debt they owed to moneylenders, a fate shared by more than 700,000 children at that time in Pakistan.

Courageous and unwilling to accept his situation, Iqbal once took a knife and sliced down the middle of a beautiful carpet he had just completed. For his defiance, he was imprisoned in the "tomb," an underground cistern filled with snakes, scorpions, and suffocating heat. The other children were also brutally punished for Iqbal's rebellion. Iqbal's bravery, however, showed the other children that they could fight back.

← The work is identified by **title** and **author.**

← **Details** and **examples** are used as **evidence.**

← An **example** supports the idea that Iqbal was courageous.

MINI-LESSON ▶ **How to Create a Thesis Statement**

In the draft of his essay, Reid has identified the title and author of the work he is writing about, but he has not stated his thesis. Without a thesis statement, the essay lacks focus. Readers will not fully understand the purpose of the evidence that Reid presents. Reid revised his introduction by answering these questions and then rewriting the first paragraph:

What does this novel show about how a person can affect others? It shows that one person can help improve other people's lives. *How can I support this idea in my interpretation?* I can use evidence of Iqbal's acts of courage.

Reid's Revision of Paragraph One

One person's act of courage can improve the lives of many other people. Iqbal, the main character in Francesco D'Adamo's novel of the same name, is a perfect example of this. As a young boy living in Pakistan, Iqbal showed selfless courage that helped free thousands of children from slavery.

Writing Tip

Use transitions between sentences and paragraphs to lead readers from one idea to the next. To emphasize ideas, you might use transitions such as *mainly, lastly,* and *most important.* To contrast ideas, you might use transitions like *on the other hand, another,* and *however.*

Your Turn _____

Create a Thesis Statement

Read your draft. Have you clearly stated your thesis? To write a draft of a thesis statement, complete the following sentence: *In my essay, I will show that the (character, plot, setting, or conflict) of (title of work) by (author's name) is (believable or unbelievable).*

Student Draft *continues*

The narrator of the novel is Fatima, a ten-year-old girl imprisoned with Iqbal and hundreds of other children by their cruel master, Hussain Khan. It is through her voice that we learn how Iqbal's courage affected the other children. They learned the master was tricking them with lies. Iqbal convinced the children that the master was cheating them by changing the marks counting their debt payment.

Iqbal vowed never to give up the fight for the children of Pakistan. He eventually escaped from the carpet factory and returned with the Bonded Liberation Front of Pakistan to rescue his friends. He continued to work with the Bonded Liberation Front to free children from slave labor. He became the voice and face for the liberation of bonded child laborers working in the factories, fields, kilns, and mines of Pakistan. Iqbal was gunned down by the "carpet mafia" on April 16, 1995.

Iqbal's example encouraged other oppressed children to stand up against the wrong done to them. He showed them that if they stood together, they could influence change in the society, they could bring this terrible injustice to the attention of the world.

*Here is another **example** of how Iqbal's courage affects the other children.*

*Reid uses historical **facts** to support his thesis.*

*A strong **conclusion** restates the **thesis** in a fresh way.*

MINI-LESSON ▸ **How to Add Evidence from the Text**

Direct quotations can provide strong and specific evidence to support your thesis. Reid decides to add a direct quotation from the text to the fourth paragraph of his essay to show, rather than tell about, Iqbal's effect on Fatima and the other children.

Reid's Revision to Paragraph Four

The narrator of the novel is Fatima, a ten-year-old girl imprisoned with Iqbal and hundreds of other children by their cruel master, Hussain Khan. It is through her voice that we learn how Iqbal's courage affected the other children. They learned the master was tricking them with lies. Iqbal convinced the children that the master was cheating them by changing the marks counting their debt payment. ∧ *Fatima remembers "Iqbal had been the first brave enough to say loud and clear that the debt is never cancelled. And he was the only one to talk concretely about the future."*

Your Turn _____

Add Evidence from the Text

Have you provided your readers with enough evidence to support your thesis? Review the literary work, and make a list of three more pieces of evidence that you could include. Choose the strongest, and add it to your draft.

Proofreading and Publishing

Proofreading

Re-read your essay for errors in punctuation, spelling, grammar, and usage. Make sure you have followed the rules of capitalization for proper nouns and that you do not have any run-on sentences. Trade papers with a partner to proofread each other's work. Then, prepare your final copy to share with your audience.

Grammar Link Correcting Run-on Sentences

Sometimes when you write, your pencil or typing cannot keep up with your thoughts. When this happens, you may write run-on sentences. A **run-on sentence** is really two or more sentences incorrectly written as one. As Reid was proofreading his draft, he noticed a run-on sentence in the last paragraph. To correct it, he broke the run-on sentence into two sentences.

> He showed them that if they stood together, they could influence change in
>
> the society, they could bring this terrible injustice to the attention of the world.

Another way to revise a run-on sentence is to make it into a **compound sentence** by adding a comma and a conjunction, such as *and, but,* or *or*: "... they could influence change in the society, *and* they could bring this terrible injustice to the attention of the world."

Publishing

Now it's time to publish your response to literature to a wider audience. Think about where you have seen essays about literature or reviews of movies or plays.

- Ask the school librarian if you may post a copy of your essay on a bulletin board in the library.
- If your class has a Web page, see if you can post it there.
- Submit your essay to your school newspaper.

Reflect on the Process In your **RWN,** write a short response to each of these questions:

1. What process did you use to develop a thesis statement?
2. How did you decide which evidence to include? How did you decide how to organize your evidence?
3. What did you learn about the work of literature by writing the essay?

● Proofreading Tip

As you proofread your draft, circle every proper noun. Have you followed the rules of capitalization? Draw three lines under any lowercase letter that should be capitalized. This is the proofreading symbol for capitalization, and it will remind you to correct the capitalization when you prepare your final copy.

Your Turn _____

Proofread and Publish As you proofread, look for run-on sentences. Before you publish your response to literature, remember to **revise run-ons** by breaking them into two or more separate sentences. You can also use a comma and conjunction—such as *and, but,* or *or*—to make them compound sentences.

Scoring Rubric

You can use the rubric below to evaluate your response to literature.

Response to Literature Writing	Organization and Focus	Sentence Structure	Conventions
4 • Exhibits *careful* reading and includes *insightful* interpretations. • Organizes the interpretation around *very clear* ideas, premises, or images. • *Strongly* develops and justifies the interpretation through sustained use of examples and textual evidence.	• *Clearly* addresses all parts of the writing task. • Demonstrates a *clear* understanding of purpose and audience. • Shows *effective* organization *throughout,* with *smooth* transitions. • Focuses *consistently* on a *coherent* thesis. • Provides a clear introduction and a *well-supported* conclusion.	• Includes sentence *variety* (e.g., simple, complex, compound-complex).	• Contains *few, if any,* errors in the conventions of the English language (grammar, punctuation, capitalization, spelling). These errors do **not** interfere with the reader's understanding of the writing.
3 • Exhibits *mostly careful* reading and includes *relatively insightful* interpretations. • Organizes the interpretation around *clear* ideas, premises, or images. • Develops and justifies the interpretation through sustained use of examples and textual evidence.	• Addresses *most* of the writing task. • Demonstrates a *general* understanding of purpose and audience. • Shows *effective* organization throughout, with minor lapses. • Focuses on a coherent thesis, with *minor* distractions. • Provides a *relatively* clear introduction and a *partially supported* conclusion.	• Includes *some* sentence variety (e.g., simple, complex, compound-complex).	• Contains *some errors* in the conventions of the English language (grammar, punctuation, capitalization, spelling). These errors do **not** interfere with the reader's understanding of the writing.
2 • Exhibits *some attention* to reading and includes *few* interpretations. • Organizes the interpretation around *somewhat clear* ideas, premises, or images. • *Partially* develops and justifies the interpretation through *inconsistent* use of examples and textual evidence.	• Addresses *some* of the writing task. • Demonstrates *little* understanding of purpose and audience. • Shows *some* organization, with *noticeable gaps* in the logical flow of ideas. • Includes some *loosely related* ideas that *distract* from the writer's focus. • *Suggests* an introduction and conclusion.	• Includes *little* sentence variety.	• Contains *several errors* in the conventions of the English language (grammar, punctuation, capitalization, spelling). These errors **may** interfere with the reader's understanding of the writing.
1 • Exhibits *no* attention to reading and includes *unclear* interpretations. • *Lacks* organization and offers *unclear* ideas, premises, or images, if at all. • *Fails* to develop the interpretation and provide examples and/or textual evidence.	• Addresses *only one or no* part of the writing task. • Demonstrates *no* understanding of purpose and audience. • *Lacks* focus and organization. • *Lacks* an introduction, and/or conclusion.	• Includes *no* sentence variety.	• Contains *serious errors* in the conventions of the English language (grammar, punctuation, capitalization, spelling). These errors interfere with the reader's understanding of the writing.

Preparing for Timed Writing

Response to Literature

When responding to an on-demand prompt requiring a response to literature, use models you have read, what you've learned from writing your own response to literature, the rubric on page 790, and the steps below.

Writing Standard 2.4 Write responses to literature: **a.** Develop an interpretation exhibiting careful reading, understanding, and insight. **b.** Organize the interpretation around several clear ideas, premises, or images. **c.** Develop and justify the interpretation through sustained use of examples and textual evidence.

Writing Prompt

Write a response to literature in which you analyze an element of a short story you have read. Select a story that you know well, and support a thesis about a literary element with evidence.

Study the Prompt

Begin by reading the prompt carefully. Note what is required in your essay: an analysis of and opinion on an element of a short story that is supported with relevant **evidence.** Your **audience** is your teacher. Your **purpose** is to convince your teacher that your analysis is correct. Your **topic** could be the setting, characters, plot, conflict, theme, or other element of the story. Your **thesis** will express an opinion concerning one of those elements. **Tip:** Spend about five minutes studying the prompt.

Plan Your Response

Think of some short stories that you have read recently, and choose the story that you know best. Once you have settled on your subject,

- write down the **title** and **author**
- consider any **background** information your readers might need to know
- write down the element that you will analyze (characters, setting, or plot, for example)
- write down your opinion of the work
- write down the main points that support your opinion.

Tip: Spend about ten minutes planning your response.

Respond to the Prompt

Using the notes you've just made, draft your essay. Follow these guidelines:

- In the introduction, get your readers' attention with an engaging opening. Provide the **title** and **author** of the story, along with a clear **thesis** statement.
- In the body, present the main points that support your thesis, and include **evidence** (facts, actions, and examples) for each main point.
- In the conclusion, restate your thesis, including your opinion of the work.

    As you are writing, remember to present only one main point in each paragraph. Write as neatly as you can. If your essay can't be read easily, it may lose points.

Tip: Spend about twenty minutes writing your draft.

Improve Your Response

Revising Go back over the key aspects of the essay. Did you state your thesis clearly? Did you provide supporting evidence for your thesis points?

Proofreading Take a few minutes to proofread your essay to correct any errors in grammar, spelling, punctuation, and capitalization. Make sure all your edits are neat, and erase any stray marks.

Checking Your Final Copy Before you turn in your essay, read it one more time to catch any errors you may have missed. You'll be glad that you took the extra time for one final review.

Tip: Save five to ten minutes to improve your essay.

Listening & Speaking Workshop

Giving an Oral Response to Literature

Think as a Reader/Writer You believe that your thesis is solid and that you have supported it well in your written response to literature. Can you make it equally clear to a listening audience that your ideas are valid? To be an effective speaker, you will probably need to adapt your written response to literature instead of just reading it aloud. Listeners cannot re-read spoken words as they can written words. Therefore, it is especially important that you present the key points of your response clearly so your audience can follow and understand them.

Adapt Your Essay

Read with New Eyes

The first step in organizing an oral response to literature is to find the most important points in your written response. Read over your essay. As you read, highlight the most important ideas in every paragraph. Remember to include enough **evidence** to support each main idea. Then, using a note card for each paragraph in your essay, write the points you will include in your speech.

Once you have your ideas on the note cards, you can organize them in a logical order. Remember that **order of importance** works well. In this type of organization, you either start or end with the most important idea. Also remember that you should begin and end your speech with a clear statement of your **thesis.**

Consider Audience and Purpose

Since the occasion, or the situation that prompts you to speak, is a class assignment, your **audience** will be your teacher and classmates. They are probably familiar with the literary work that is the subject of your speech, so that is helpful. You will not have to provide much **background information** to make sure they know the basics.

Remember that the **purpose** of your speech is to share information (your response to the literary work) and to persuade the audience that your **thesis** is valid. Remembering your purpose will help you maintain the right **tone** and include the right information.

Listening and Speaking Standard
1.2 Identify the tone, mood, and emotion conveyed in the oral communication. **1.7** Use effective rate, volume, pitch, and tone and align nonverbal elements to sustain audience interest and attention. **2.3** Deliver oral responses to literature: a. Develop an interpretation exhibiting careful reading, understanding, and insight. b. Organize the selected interpretation around several clear ideas, premises, or images. c. Develop and justify the selected interpretation through sustained use of examples and textual evidence.

Deliver Your Oral Response

Use Nonverbal Elements

To become a good public speaker, you must use more than just words. **Nonverbal** communication, or body language, adds to your message. Here are some ways to include nonverbal elements in your oral response:

Eye Contact Look audience members in the eyes to keep their attention.

Facial Expression Smile, frown, or raise an eyebrow to show your feelings or to emphasize parts of your message.

Gestures Give a thumbs up, shrug, nod, or shake your head to emphasize a point or to add meaning to your speech.

Use Verbal Elements

How you use your voice can also affect the message you send. Consider these **verbal elements** as you practice and deliver your speech.

Feeling Don't speak in a **monotone**, a dull voice with no change in expression. Instead, show enthusiasm through your voice so your audience will become enthusiastic about your response.

Pitch Your voice rises and falls naturally when you speak. If you are nervous, your voice may get higher. Control your pitch by taking deep breaths. Stay calm as you give your speech. Grab the audience's attention by using the pitch of your voice to emphasize key points.

Rate In conversations you may speak at a fast rate, or speed. When you deliver a speech, speak more slowly to help listeners understand you. Pause now and then so that important points can sink in.

Tone Strive to maintain a reasonable and informed tone. You should sound as if you know what you're talking about. That will go a long way toward supporting your point of view about the story.

Volume Even if you normally speak quietly, you will need to speak loudly when giving your oral response. You shouldn't yell, but the listeners at the back of the room should be able to hear you clearly.

Take Note

On your note cards, you can write cues about the verbal and the nonverbal elements you plan to use in presenting your main ideas.

A Good Oral Response to Literature

- includes a clear thesis statement
- provides background information
- provides a variety of evidence to support the thesis
- uses convincing nonverbal support
- ends by restating the thesis

Speaking Tip

Make sure the nonverbal elements you use make sense with the verbal elements you use. For example, if you are explaining how a character is always doing something crazy or unexpected in a story, you might raise your eyebrows or shake your head (nonverbal element) and speak with humor in your voice (verbal element) at the same time.

Learn It Online

Find out how you can get and keep your audience's attention. Visit *MediaScope* at:

go.hrw.com   H6-793   **Go**

Literary Skills Review

Literary Criticism   **Directions:** Read the following story. Then, answer each question that follows.

The Story of the Owl a Hmong folk tale,

retold by **Norma J. Livo and Dia Cha**

Long ago, the owl could see during the day as well as other animals could. One day, the owl was sitting by himself on the branch of a huge tree without much to do. He saw a monkey eating corn in the field and wanted to make fun of the monkey, so he suddenly made a very loud noise. "Hoot!" the owl cried.

The monkey was frightened and immediately ran away as fast as he could. As he ran, he accidentally stepped on the stem of the pumpkin vine, which caused the pumpkin to drop and roll very fast down the field until it hit a nat plant (sesame). The nat plant had very tiny seeds, and they all fell to the ground. In fact, some of the tiny seeds fell into a rooster's eyes, and the rooster was blinded.

The rooster ran aimlessly, pecking the ground, and unintentionally picked up a few ants from a group of worker ants. The other ants started rushing around and then dug into their anthill to hide themselves.

This caused the anthill to collapse, and it crushed and killed a mother chicken's two chicks. The mother chicken was very angry because, of course, she loved her babies very much.

The mother chicken decided to investigate what had killed her babies. She first started to question the anthill. "Why did you kill my babies?"

The anthill told her, "I was standing in my place and did not do anything wrong. But the ants started digging into me, and I collapsed and fell down and squashed your chicks. I never meant to do it."

Then she went to the ants. "Why were you digging in the anthill? It fell down and killed my babies," she said.

"It was not our fault. We were busy working and the rooster pecked a few of our workers, so we dug into the anthill to hide ourselves. We did not want the rooster to catch us," snapped the ants.

So the hen went to the rooster and demanded, "Why did you peck the worker ants? They started to dig into the anthill to hide from you, and it collapsed on my two chicks and killed them!"

"I did not intend to peck the ants," the rooster answered. "I was on my way to look for food and some seeds suddenly fell into my eyes and blinded me. I could not see anything. I pecked around with my beak trying to figure out where I was and I accidentally pecked the ants."

The mother hen waddled straight to the nat plant to find out why its seeds had fallen down and into the eyes of the rooster. The nat plant told her, "I was holding all my seeds in place, but the pumpkin rolled down the hill and hit me. It hit me so hard I could not hold on to my seeds, so I lost them."

Now the mother hen half-flew and half-hopped to the pumpkin plant. "Why did you roll down the hill and hit the nat plant? It lost all of its seeds and some fell into the eyes of the rooster, so he pecked some worker ants who started digging at the anthill to hide from him. The anthill fell down and killed my two chicks!"

The bruised pumpkin plant answered, "I was hanging on my vine when the clumsy monkey stepped on my stem so I fell down. I rolled down the hill and hit the nat plant. I did not want to do it."

Clucking and squawking, the mother hen ran to the monkey to find out why he had stepped on the pumpkin vine. The monkey chattered, "It was the owl! He made a sudden loud noise and scared me. I was afraid that someone was going to shoot me, so I ran as fast as I could and mistakenly stepped on the stem of the pumpkin vine. I am sorry."

Furiously the hen went straight to the owl and demanded, "Why did you make the loud noise that scared the monkey and made him step on the pumpkin vine? The pumpkin fell off and rolled down the hill and hit the nat plant and made all of its tiny seeds fall. Some seeds fell into the rooster's eyes and blinded him, so he pecked some worker ants and the other ants dug into the anthill to hide from him. When they did that, the anthill collapsed and killed my two chicks. Why did you make that noise?"

The owl just stared at the mother hen with his eyes wide open. Finally, she angrily grabbed the owl's neck and twisted his head back and forth. "You are a wretch. From now on you will see only at night because you are not like the other animals."

And that is why the owl can see only at night, and why he is able to turn his head all the way around.

Literary Skills Review CONTINUED

Reading Standard 3.8 Critique the credibility of characterization and the degree to which a plot is contrived or realistic (e.g., compare use of fact and fantasy in historical fiction).

1. Which character is responsible for starting the chain of causes and effects in the folk tale?

   A the rooster

   B the owl

   C the monkey

   D the mother chicken

2. Why does the anthill collapse?

   A The pumpkin hits it.

   B The monkey steps on it.

   C The rooster pecks at it.

   D Ants dig into it.

3. The mother chicken can *best* be characterized as

   A angry.

   B sad.

   C frightened.

   D confused.

4. The purpose of this folk tale is to explain

   A the dangers posed by the natural world.

   B how the two chicks were killed.

   C why the owl can see only at night and turn its head all the way around.

   D how animals' actions and reactions can be similar to those of humans.

5. Which of the following statements *best* expresses the moral, or message, of the folk tale?

   A People should not let their emotions get out of control.

   B Our actions can have unintended consequences for others.

   C The punishment should fit the crime.

   D A community must protect those members who cannot take care of themselves.

6. Folk tales often use talking animals to

   A make the story seem credible.

   B make the story seem unrealistic.

   C appeal to animal lovers.

   D represent human behaviors.

Timed Writing

7. To what degree is the plot of this folk tale believable? To answer, consider whether the chain of causes and effects seems contrived and whether any elements of the plot seem realistic. Use details from the tale to support your answer.

Vocabulary Skills Review

Reading Standard 1.5 Understand and explain "shades of meaning" in related words (e.g., *softly* and *quietly*).

Synonyms **Directions:** Choose the word or phrase that is closest in meaning to the italicized Vocabulary word in each item.

1. An *ambitious* person is
   A curious.
   B selfish.
   C eager.
   D talented.

2. A *proverb* is a
   A promise.
   B saying.
   C question.
   D fact.

3. A person who has been *revived* has been
   A fed.
   B awakened.
   C changed.
   D educated.

4. *Penetrated* means the same as
   A pierced.
   B committed.
   C destroyed.
   D tempted.

5. When something is *cleft,* it is
   A split.
   B clean.
   C rough.
   D heavy.

6. When there is *chaos* during a protest, there is great
   A distrust.
   B unity.
   C success.
   D confusion.

7. *Exuded* means
   A departed.
   B admitted.
   C thrown out.
   D gave off.

Academic Vocabulary

Directions: Use context clues to determine the meaning of the italicized Academic Vocabulary words in the following sentences.

8. Since the details in the article *corresponded* to those in other sources, I decided that the article was a reliable source.
   A were older than
   B were similar to
   C were different from
   D were greater than

Vocabulary Skills Review CONTINUED

9. My friend *perceived* that I was worried, so she tried to comfort me.

A teased

B ignored

C understood

D criticized

10. The ending of the movie was so *contrived* that we decided to make up a more realistic resolution.

A complicated

B troublesome

C imaginative

D artificial

11. My work as a volunteer in the nursing home gave me greater *insight* into the feelings of elderly people.

A clear understanding

B far-sighted vision

C wide experience

D sense of connection

Writing Skills Review

Response to Literature **Directions:** Read the following paragraph from an essay that gives an interpretation of a short story. Then, answer each question that follows.

Writing Standard 2.4 Write responses to literature: a. Develop an interpretation exhibiting careful reading, understanding, and insight. b. Organize the interpretation around several clear ideas, premises, or images. c. Develop and justify the interpretation through sustained use of examples and textual evidence.

(1) In Cynthia Rylant's short story "Boar Out There," she uses her main character, Jenny, to help readers see how the power of sympathy and understanding can overcome fear. (2) In the story the character Jenny shows these emotions in a very believable way. (3) Jenny is a pretty average girl in terms of looks and intelligence. (4) When she hears the boar rushing toward her, Jenny is truly afraid. (5) She forgets to breathe, she chokes and coughs, and she even cries. (6) However, she is brave enough to fight her fear. (7) In fact, she seems to want to test her courage. (8) She does not run or scream. (9) Instead, she stands silently, looking at the boar's scars and "ragged ears, caked with blood." (10) All at once, Jenny is not afraid. (11) Her fear is replaced with sympathy when she realizes that the boar is afraid and alone. (12) Jenny's emotions are revealed clearly through this sequence of events. (13) Through a clear description of Jenny's feelings, Rylant shows us the power of sympathy.

1. Which sentence expresses the thesis, or main idea, of the essay by giving an interpretation of the short story?
   A Sentence 1
   B Sentence 3
   C Sentence 4
   D Sentence 7

2. Which sentence justifies the interpretation in the form of a quotation from the short story?
   A Sentence 5
   B Sentence 9
   C Sentence 11
   D Sentence 13

3. Which of these sentences does *not* contain a transitional word or phrase?
   A Sentence 6
   B Sentence 9
   C Sentence 10
   D Sentence 12

4. If you were revising this paragraph, which sentence would you delete because it does not exhibit understanding of the interpretation?
   A Sentence 3
   B Sentence 6
   C Sentence 7
   D Sentence 10

5. Why is the final sentence a strong ending?
   A It uses a formal tone.
   B It presents plenty of evidence.
   C It introduces a new idea.
   D It sums up the main idea of the paragraph.

Read On

Fiction

The Buried City of Pompeii

The eruption of Mount Vesuvius and destruction of Pompeii continue to intrigue people centuries later. In *The Buried City of Pompeii,* Shelly Tanaka looks at the disaster through the eyes of Eros, a steward. Following Eros's tale, Tanaka presents a scientific explanation for the eruption of the volcano.

The True Confessions of Charlotte Doyle

When she boards an English ship bound for Rhode Island, Charlotte Doyle has no idea that she'll be the only female passenger on board. She soon finds herself caught up in a conflict between a power-mad captain and his bitter, rebellious crew. When Charlotte is given an unusual gift, events take a shocking turn in Avi's *The True Confessions of Charlotte Doyle.*

Outcast

When a Roman trading ship is destroyed, Beric is the only survivor. A British tribe takes Beric in and raises him as one of their own. As Beric reaches manhood, the tribe suffers through bad times. Beric is blamed for their troubles and banished from his home. In Rosemary Sutcliff's *Outcast,* Beric lives in fear of his life until he finds a home at last.

The Arkadians

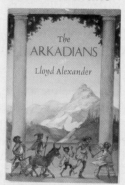

When charming bean counter Lucian witnesses corruption by the local palace officials, he unfortunately reports the crimes to the wrong people. He narrowly escapes a tragic fate and flees to the Greek countryside. Wandering through Arkadia, Lucian is joined by several unique companions, such as a hotheaded girl and a donkey-poet. You'll find romance, magic, and wisdom in *The Arkadians* by Lloyd Alexander.

Nonfiction

Pompeii: City of Ashes

Read along with Sarah Pitt Kaplan as she describes the destruction of Pompeii in A.D. 79 by an eruption of Mount Vesuvius. Then learn how the rediscovery and excavation of this buried city have helped us unlock the mysteries of ancient Roman life. Filled with illustrations, photos, and maps, *Pompeii: City of Ashes* gives you a clear look at the past and present of the lost city.

Volcano: The Eruption and Healing of Mount St. Helens

In this chapter you read about a devastating volcanic eruption that took place hundreds of years ago. In *Volcano: The Eruption and Healing of Mount St. Helens,* Patricia Lauber examines a recent eruption in the state of Washington. Lauber's text, accompanied by stunning photographs, gives you an up-close look at the eruption and the destruction it caused, as well as the recovery period that followed.

Ancient Rome

In *Ancient Rome,* Simon James takes you on a tour of Rome in the days of the empire. James shows you what Roman forts, theaters, and townhouses looked like, and his transparent cutaways give you a glimpse of what went on inside them. You'll also learn about structures like forums and aqueducts. If you enjoy this book, you may want to read other titles in the See Through History series.

How Would You Survive as an Ancient Greek?

Have you ever wondered what it would be like to live in the past? Fiona MacDonald shows you in *How Would You Survive as an Ancient Greek?* This interactive book, packed with useful information and colorful illustrations, tells you how you would eat, work, and travel in ancient Greece.

Learn It Online
Explore other novels—and find tips for choosing, reading, and studying words—at:

go.hrw.com   H6-801   Go

Resource Center

Reading Matters Strategy Lessons by Kylene Beers

 **Reading Standard 3.3** Analyze the influence of setting on the problem and its resolution.

Strategy Lesson 1

How Do I Analyze the Impact of Setting?

Somebody Wanted But So

I asked my students to think about how the folk tale "Goldilocks and the Three Bears" would be different if it had taken place underwater instead of in the forest. One student said, "They'd all get wet." Someone else said that the bears would be fish. Another said that Goldilocks would be a mermaid. Then someone said, "The bears, which would be fish, wouldn't have gone out for a walk but instead would have gone to school!" She paused, then asked, "Get it? School . . . fish . . . fish travel in schools!" The whole class moaned when they got it. Then they came up with other ways in which the story would be different if it were set underwater (beds would be clam beds; porridge would be seaweed soup; fish wouldn't walk to school but would ride sea horses).

Change Setting, Change Story

Those students understood that changing the setting—when and where the story takes place—affects other elements of the story.

Think about . . .	and change the setting . . .
The Narnia books	from England to the United States
The Watsons Go to Birmingham—1963	from 1963 to 1863 and then to 2003
The Flintstones	from prehistoric times to the year 2010

Somebody Wanted But So . . .

Just how much of an impact does setting have on a story's problem and its resolution? To figure this out, you can use a strategy called **Somebody Wanted But So** (SWBS). Jot down those words on your paper, like this:

Somebody	Wanted	But	So

Next, think of a story you are familiar with. Under "Somebody," name the "somebody" in the story. Under "Wanted," state what he or she wanted. In the "But" column, describe the problem that arose. Under "So," explain how the problem was resolved. When you're done, your SWBS chart will look something like this:

Somebody	Wanted	But	So
Goldilocks	food and a place to rest in the forest since night was coming on,	there was no one in the lonely house she found,	she entered, ate the food, and ruined some things, then got scared when the bears came home.

Your Turn   Identify the Impact of Setting

1. What happens in the "Wanted" column if the location of the story changes? (Set the story in a place other than forest, and see what happens.)

2. What happens in the "Wanted" column if the time of the story is changed (to early morning, for example)?

3. How might changing that column affect the "But" and "So" columns?

4. How much of a difference do the changes in setting make to the outcome of the story?

Your Turn   Analyze the Influence of Setting on the Problem and Its Resolution

In the story "All Summer in a Day" (page 29), setting is especially important. Make an SWBS chart for Margot, the other children, and the teacher. Next, think about what changes would occur in the "Wanted," "But," and "So" columns if the story were set in the Sahara, rather than on Venus. Are the changes in the outcome column—the "So" column—significant?

Reading Standard 3.2 Analyze the effect of the qualities of the character (e.g., courage or cowardice, ambition or laziness) on the plot and the resolution of the conflict.

Strategy Lesson 2

How Does Character Affect Plot?

If . . . Then . . .

Take a Close Look!

Is the runner in this picture

- confident or fearful?
- strong or weak?

The outcome of this runner's leap depends on how you interpret the drawing. Without any information about the character, it's hard to know what he is going to do. In the same way, know-

ing something about a character helps you understand the development of a story's plot and the resolution of the conflict.

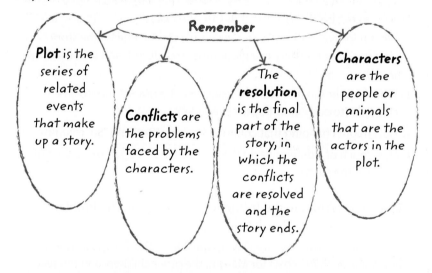

Remember

Plot is the series of related events that make up a story.

Conflicts are the problems faced by the characters.

The **resolution** is the final part of the story, in which the conflicts are resolved and the story ends.

Characters are the people or animals that are the actors in the plot.

If . . . Then . . .

It is not difficult to identify the characters in a story or describe the events of the plot, but sometimes it is hard to explain how a character's qualities or traits affect the outcome of the plot. To do this, use the **If . . . Then . . .** strategy.

If . . . Then . . . at Work: "Three Little Pigs"

If Pig Number Three is smart and hardworking, *then* he'll live in a brick house, outwit the wolf when the wolf comes knocking at his door, and live happily ever after. On the other hand, *if* Pig Number Three is as careless and lazy as his brothers, *then* he'll live in a house made of flimsy materials, be outwitted by the wolf, and find himself the wolf's next meal.

Character Traits
bold/shy
brave/cowardly
careful/careless
expert/unskilled
fair/unfair
faithful/disloyal
friendly/unfriendly
gentle/fierce
genuine/fake
happy/sad
hardworking/lazy
honest/sneaky
kind/cruel
obedient/disobedient
patient/impatient
reliable/unreliable
respectful/rude
wise/foolish

Your Turn   Analyzing the Way a Character's Qualities Affect Plot

After you read "Ta-Na-E-Ka" (page 243), think about the main character, Mary. Look at the list of character traits on the right, and find four qualities that *best* describe Mary.

Then, think about how the story would be different if Mary had the opposite qualities. How would the plot be different? How would the conflict be resolved? How would the story end?

Set up your exercise like this:

If	Then
Mary had been . . .	[this probably would have happened]

Your Turn   Analyzing the Way a Character's Qualities Affect an Event

Sometimes characters surprise us. A weak character who is put to the test becomes extraordinarily brave. An honest character who faces a difficult situation cheats. That is one of the joys of reading: In a well-written story, characters can surprise us—just as people do in real life.

The "If" column of the chart below presents three versions of a character named Sam. In the "Then" column, write a few lines describing what would happen if each "Sam" were faced with the following situation:

Sam has just found a wallet with two hundred dollars inside. There is no identification in the wallet. What will Sam do?

If	Then
Sam is stingy but honest,	
Sam is generous but lazy,	
Sam is ambitious but unfriendly,	

Reading Standard 3.6 Identify and analyze features of themes conveyed through characters, actions, and images.

Strategy Lesson 3

How Do I Identify and Analyze Theme?

Most Important Word

If finding the **theme** of a story or novel is difficult for you, read on. Help is on the way!

Theme Isn't Topic or Plot

Theme—what a story reveals about life—emerges as you read the story or novel. Don't confuse theme with topic or plot.

- The **topic** of the poem "Casey at the Bat" is a baseball game.
- The **plot** involves a mighty baseball player who tries to save a game but instead strikes out.
- Some might say the **theme** shows us that in life many things are uncertain; others might say the theme shows us that even the mightiest sometimes meet with failure.

In other words, the same story or novel might reveal different themes to different people.

Most Important Word

To find the theme of a piece of literature, try a strategy called **Most Important Word.** Ask yourself what the most important word in a story is, and why that word is so important. Thinking about these questions will help you focus on the theme of the work. After you decide on the word, consider how it relates to the setting, characters, plot, and conflict of the story.

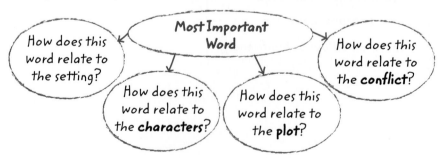

Most Important Word

How does this word relate to the setting?

How does this word relate to the **characters**?

How does this word relate to the **plot**?

How does this word relate to the **conflict**?

Your Turn Identify and Analyze Theme: "The All-American Slurp"

After reading "The All-American Slurp" (page 257), one student stated the theme as "Embarrassing things sometimes happen to all people." She decided that that was the theme after choosing *embarrassed* as the most important word and thinking about how the idea of being embarrassed related to the characters, plot, setting, and conflict of the story.

embarrassed

Characters: The Lins are embarrassed because they don't know American table customs.

Plot: The story starts when the Lins eat at a neighbors' house and embarrass themselves when they eat. Later the main character is embarrassed by her family's behavior when they eat at a fancy restaurant.

Setting: The Lins are embarrassed because they are in an unfamiliar setting with unfamiliar customs.

Conflict: The conflict is mostly inside the daughter. She is often embarrassed because she thinks she doesn't fit in.

How would the information in these boxes change if you thought the most important word in "The All-American Slurp" was *family* or *American* or even *slurp*?

Your Turn Identify and Analyze Theme: "The King of Mazy May"

After you read "The King of Mazy May" (page 123), choose what you think is the most important word from this list: *courageous, fair, mature.* Then, complete the chart. Use the information in the chart to figure out the story's theme. (You can usually state a story's theme in one sentence.)

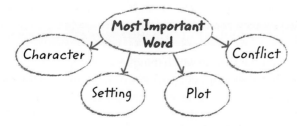

Most Important Word

Character

Setting

Plot

Conflict

Reading Standard 2.2 Analyze text that uses the compare-and-contrast organizational pattern.

Strategy Lesson 4

How Do I Identify and Analyze Text Structures?

Study these two pictures. Find at least five ways in which the two pictures differ. Then, with a partner, compare your findings.

Think about how you went about comparing those two pictures. You probably compared part of one picture with a similar part in the other picture. In this way, you found contrasts between the two pictures.

You can do something similar when you read a text. You can compare characters, ideas, settings, and events by looking at one part of a text and comparing it with another part. Sometimes writers help us by using a text structure called **comparison and contrast.**

Comparison and Contrast

When writers point out ways in which things are alike, they are making a **comparison.** When they point out ways in which things are different, they are making a **contrast.** Here are some words and phrases that signal comparisons and contrasts:

Comparison:	Contrast:
additionally, also, by the same token, equally, in the same manner, just as, like, likewise, similarly, too	although, but, by contrast, different from, however, in spite of, nevertheless, on the other hand, unlike, yet

Writers of informational texts often use comparison and contrast. Such texts might be organized by the point-by-point method or by the block method. You'll find models of these organizational structures on page 202.

Sequencing and Chronological Order

Writers use a **sequence structure** when the order of events is important. *Sequence* refers to the order in which events occur. **Chronological order,** the time order in which events occur, is one kind of sequence structure.

Which of these would you write using a sequence structure?

1 a description of what you did at school yesterday
2. an essay explaining why you believe the age for getting a driver's license should be lowered or raised
3. instructions for dealing with a flash fire in your area
4. instructions for making pizza at home

If you aren't sure which of these require a sequence structure, try discussing each topic without using words like *first, second, third, next, later, after, then,* and *finally.* If you find that you don't need these words, the sequence, or order of events, probably isn't important.

Informational texts in which sequencing is often used include science articles, history texts, and instruction manuals.

Cause and Effect

Another text structure writers use is called **cause and effect.** This structure is often used in informational texts, such as social studies books, which focus on the causes and effects of wars or discoveries or political movements. The following sentences illustrate the cause-and-effect structure:

1. Because the temperature fell below 32 degrees, the water froze.
2. Jonas stopped smiling when he got braces on his teeth.
3. The dinosaurs were wiped out when a huge meteorite smashed into the earth.
4. The wind from the volcanic eruption carried rocks that flattened whole forests of 180-foot trees.

Here's how that information might be presented in a cause-and-effect chart:

Cause	Effect
Temperature fell below 32 degrees.	The water froze.
Jonas got braces.	Jonas stopped smiling.
Meteorite smashed into the earth.	Dinosaurs disappeared.
Wind carried rocks as big as cars.	Rocks flattened forests.

When you read a text that discusses cause and effect, keep track of **causal relationships** (causes and effects) by making a chart like the one on page 811. As you read, ask yourself what caused various outcomes. Give it a try with this passage. (Hint: Two of the sentences don't contain a causal relationship.)

(1) In 1803, the United States bought the Louisiana Territory from the French dictator Napoleon.

(2) Settlers moved into the Louisiana Territory, forcing American Indians off the land.

(3) The Indians responded by fighting for what they believed was theirs.

(4) Most settlers saw no need to ask the Indians to share the land or sell the land to them.

Your Turn Analyze Text Structures

What text structure (**comparison and contrast, sequencing,** or **cause and effect**) is used in each of the following sentences?

1. Blood that travels to the heart through veins carries carbon dioxide; blood that travels from the heart through arteries carries oxygen.

2. After blood passes through the lungs, it returns to the heart through the pulmonary veins.

3. If the heart's mitral valve is blocked, blood can't flow from the upper left chamber of the heart to the lower left chamber. If it can't flow to that chamber, it can't get to the aorta, and problems arise.

4. The heart moves blood through the circulatory system the way a tire pump forces air through a hose.

5. Exercise helps strengthen the heart.

6. People who eat right and exercise help their hearts stay healthy; people who eat a lot of fatty foods and get little exercise generally have less healthy hearts.

Strategy Lesson 5

How Do I Find the Main Idea?

Using a Little TLC

Look at the "text" below. Then, answer these questions:

XXXXXXXXX

xxxxx

xx xxxxx xxxxx xx xxxx xxx xxxx xxx
1) xxxxx xx xxxxxxx xx xx
2) xxxx xxxxx xxxxx xxxxxxx xx
xxxxxxxx xxxx xxxxx xxxx

xxxxxx

xxxxx xxxxx xxxxxxx xxxxxxx xxx
xxxxx xxxx xxxx xxxxxxx xxxx x
xxx xxxxxx **xxxxx** xxx xxxx xxxxx
xxxxxxx xxxxx xxxxxx xxxxxx xx
xxxxxxxx xxxx xxxxx xxx xxx
xxxxxxxx xxxx xxxxx xxxxxx
xxxxx xxxx xxxxx xx xxxx xxx
x xxxx xxx.

1. Is the "text" fiction or nonfiction?

2. Does it have a title?

3. How many topics does it cover? At which point does the topic change?

4. What do the numbers in the first paragraph indicate?

5. Why is one of the "words" in the second paragraph set in boldface?

Now, look at the "text" again. Even though you can't read it, you can still figure out a number of things about it. You may have guessed that it is nonfiction (fiction doesn't usually include numbered lists, as this text does). You may have noticed that it deals with two topics and that the first paragraph includes a list of two items. You may have spotted a boldface term in the second paragraph (another feature rarely seen in fiction). That's a lot to learn from a "text" that's made up of *x*'s!

Previewing the Text

Experienced readers can get information from a text even before they begin to read it. For instance, when you pick up a novel, you know you'll be reading a story that has characters trying to resolve a conflict. When you pick up an informational text—like a textbook, a magazine, or a computer manual—you know you'll be looking at topics and main ideas.

Cracking the Code

Identifying the characters in a novel or story is easy—they're the people taking part in the action. Identifying the main idea in an informational text can be a bit trickier.

Tips for Finding the Main Idea

Here are some tips to keep in mind as you look for the main idea in an informational text:

1. Remember that the topic and the main idea are not the same. The **topic** is what the text is all about. The **main idea** is the most important thing said about that topic.

2. Remember that writers sometimes state the main idea directly, often near the beginning or the end of the text.

3. Keep in mind that if the main idea isn't stated directly, you must **infer** it from the information in the text.

   As you read, ask yourself, "What's the most important point being made about the topic of this text?"

4. Try using a little TLC. *TLC* in another context means "tender loving care." Here it means find the **T**opic; **L**ook for the least important sentences, and set them aside; **C**onnect the other ideas to the topic to come up with the main idea.

Your Turn Find the Main Idea

Read the following paragraph. Identify the topic; then, use the **TLC strategy** to identify the main idea. The questions below will help you apply the strategy.

> Most texts do not state the main idea directly. It's up to you to figure out the main idea yourself. As you read a text, think about its topic. Then, decide which details of this topic are the most important. Once you've done that, ask yourself, "What do these details say about the topic?" Using this method will help you find the main idea of the text.

1. What is the topic of this paragraph?

2. Which sentence or sentences are the least important in explaining that topic?

3. Which sentence or sentences are the most important in explaining that topic?

4. Restate the most important sentences in your own words to come up with the main idea.

Find the Topic. → Look for the least important sentences, and set them aside. → Connect the other ideas in the remaining sentences to the topic.

Strategy Lesson 6

How Do I Understand and Explain Shades of Meaning?

Becoming Word-Wise

Your best friend whispers to you, "That is the coolest thing, don't you think?" Later, another friend says, "Did you hear what she said to him? That was so cold." When you're angry about something, another friend tells you, "Chill."

Cool, cold, chill—three words that are usually weather related but in these conversations are not. Words often mean different things in different contexts. Using the right word at the right time is important if you want to make a point. If you don't believe that, the next time you want to say, "That is so cool," instead say, "That is so chill!" You'll get a strange look and a quick lesson on the importance of using the right word at the right time.

Practice with "OK"

- Your mom says, "How was your day?" You say, "OK."
- A teacher asks, "How'd you do on the test?" You answer, "OK."
- Your friend says, "You want to go to the mall?" You say, "OK!"

  1. In which situation do you think *OK* really means "great"?

  2. What might it mean in the other situations?

  3. Why do people use a word like *OK* in situations in which they don't really mean *OK*?

Your answer to the third question may have been that it's simply easier to say "OK." Using the same word over and over takes very little effort. Using the right word can help you communicate your thoughts clearly.

Get Specific

Read these two sentences, and discuss the differences between them:

- Ben walked quietly down the hallway.
- Ben walked softly down the hallway.

Even though both sentences tell you that Ben isn't making much noise as he walks down the hallway, there is a difference. The first sentence suggests that Ben is walking quietly by simply not talking. The second sentence creates a picture of Ben carefully placing one foot in front of the other so that he makes as little noise as possible. *Quietly* and *softly* are related—both have to do with noise level—but their meanings are slightly different.

Recognizing shades of meaning between words helps you pick the right word when you're writing. It also helps you understand exactly what a writer means when you're reading.

Your Turn   Explain Shades of Meaning

Read each of the following pairs of words. Then, ask yourself how the words in each pair are related and how they differ.

stop/pause   annoyed/angry   forgetful/neglectful
grimace/frown   shrink/shrivel   hot/scalding
sad/depressing   complex/hard   happy/overjoyed

Working with a partner, make a diagram for each pair to show how the words are both alike and different in meaning. Here is an example for *stop* and *pause*:

Your Turn   Identify and Explain Shades of Meaning

Read each of the following sentences. Choose a word from the under-lined pair to complete each sentence. Be prepared to explain why you chose that word. (You may find that in some sentences either word could be used, depending on what is meant.)

1. After the rain stopped, we suddenly/quickly ran to the car.

2. The grimace/frown on her face told me that she was not only disappointed but also in pain.

3. My watch stopped/paused after it fell into the bathtub.

4. The mechanism of the watch, with all its tiny moving parts, was very hard/complex.

5. After sitting in the hot sun for a week, the plums looked as shriveled/shrunken as raisins.

6. When he took the shirt out of the dryer, Jay saw that it had shriveled/shrunk.

Becoming Word-Wise

You can increase your word-wisdom by remembering **FDR**—not President Franklin Delano Roosevelt, but the other FDR: **F**ocus, **D**ouble-check, **R**e-read!

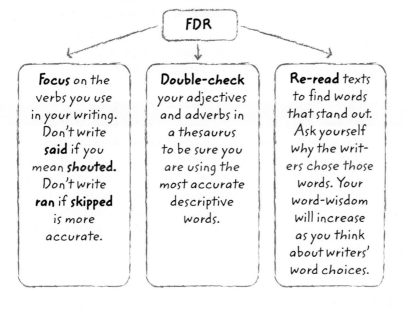

FDR

Focus on the verbs you use in your writing. Don't write **said** if you mean **shouted.** Don't write **ran** if **skipped** is more accurate.

Double-check your adjectives and adverbs in a thesaurus to be sure you are using the most accurate descriptive words.

Re-read texts to find words that stand out. Ask yourself why the writers chose those words. Your word-wisdom will increase as you think about writers' word choices.

Reading Standard 2.8 Note instances of unsupported inferences, fallacious reasoning, persuasion, and propaganda in text.

Strategy Lesson 7

How Do I Recognize Faulty Reasoning?

Bandwagon Appeal

Have you ever used one of these arguments in hopes of getting your way?

- "But everybody else is going."
- "Everyone has one but me."
- "Nobody else has to do that."

You may have gotten a response like "Well, you aren't everyone" or "If everybody jumped off a bridge, would you jump too?" or "Just who is everybody?" If you were asked to name "everybody," you may have realized that you had only five or six names—or even fewer. Your argument—the "everyone else is doing it" argument—suddenly fell apart, revealed as what it really is: an argument with no valid support.

This argument, called the **bandwagon appeal,** is a type of faulty reasoning. Card stacking, testimonial, and faulty generalization are three others.

Card Stacking

This kind of argument presents only one side of an issue, leaving out any information favorable to the other side. Here is an illustration of card stacking: A student tries to explain a bad grade to her parents by claiming that the teacher is too tough, the test covered too much material, and everyone in the class did poorly. She doesn't mention that she skipped the teacher's after-school review sessions, waited until the night before the test to study, and didn't keep up with the homework.

Another example is an advertisement stating, "Summit Outerwear's double-stitched seams, titanium zippers and snaps, and breathable nylon-composite shell offer comfort and protection. Try finding these features in our competitors' products; you'll be looking for a long time." (What desirable features of the competition aren't we told about?)

Testimonial

When advertisers use a testimonial, they try to persuade you to do something by using a respected or popular person to endorse their message. They might pay a famous athlete a lot of money to say something nice about their product. A testimonial might proclaim, "Golf great Don Kelley wears these running shoes. Shouldn't you?" or "You may know me as the commander of the space shuttle, but on weekends you'll find me at the wheel of the Gopher 200 riding mower. Great for doing the big jobs right here on earth." Endorsement by a famous person doesn't mean that a product is right for you.

Faulty Generalization

Faulty generalizations are false or unsound, or do not apply in all cases. A person who says, "Since all teenagers are careless drivers, the driving age should be raised to twenty-one" is using a faulty generalization. Every teenager is *not* a careless driver.

Your Turn Recognize Faulty Reasoning

Choose one of the five scenarios listed below. Prepare an argument, using one or more of the techniques discussed above. Then, exchange responses with a classmate, and see if you can spot the faulty reasoning in your partner's argument.

1. You need to explain why you didn't make the honor roll.
2. You want your parents to buy you an expensive new computer game.
3. You want your own phone and phone line.
4. You're trying to persuade your neighbors to buy candy you're selling for your school.
5. You want your parents to let you get an after-school job.

Reading Standard 1.1 Read aloud narrative and expository text fluently and accurately and with appropriate pacing, intonation, and expression.

Strategy Lesson 8

Improving Fluency and Reading Rate

If people read too quickly, they may miss important information; if they read too slowly, they may have trouble making sense of what they're reading.

How Can I Improve?

Reading fluency (how easily and well you read) and **reading rate** (how fast you read) are related. If you are a fluent reader, you read with expression, know when to pause, read by phrases or thought groups instead of word by word, know when you don't understand what you've read, and know how to adjust your rate to what you are reading.

If you think you need to improve your fluency, practice reading aloud, either alone (use a tape recorder so that you can listen to yourself) or with a buddy. Choose a passage or paragraph that's 150–200 words long. Read it to yourself silently a few times; then, read it aloud. Afterward, fill out the checklist below. Keep practicing; you'll soon see that your score is going down—which means that your fluency is going up.

Name _____ Date _____
Listener's Name _____

Oral Fluency	Often (5 points)	Sometimes (3 points)	Never (0 points)
Reads word by word			
Stops and starts			
Re-reads words or sentences			
Ignores			
• periods			
• commas			
• question marks			
Reads too fast			
Reads too slow			
Slurs words			
Guesses at pronunciations			
Seems nervous			
Loses place in text			

Final Score: _____

What's My Reading Rate?

If fluency is tied to reading rate, then what rate is right? Remember that different rates are right for different kinds of texts. You might zip through a comic book, but you need to move more slowly through your social studies textbook. In other words, your reading rate depends on what you're reading and why you're reading it.

If you think you read too slowly all the time, you can improve your reading rate. Follow these steps:

1. Choose something you want to read. (Don't choose something that's too easy.)
2. Ask a friend to time you as you read aloud for one minute.
3. Count the words you read in that one minute.
4. Repeat this process two more times, with different passages.
5. Add the three numbers, and divide the total by three.

That number is your oral reading rate. The chart below shows average reading rates for students in grades 3–6.

If you think your rate is too low, practice reading aloud every week, having someone time you as you read for one minute. Use the same passages to practice fluency. Use new passages to check your reading rate.

Grade Level	Average Words per Minute
3	110
4	140
5	160
6	180

Don't Forget . . .

If you don't understand what you read, you aren't reading fluently. As you read, keep asking yourself if what you're reading makes sense. If you get confused at any point, stop and re-read. From time to time, pause and think about what you've read. Sum up the main events or ideas. Be sure you understand what causes events to happen. Compare what actually happens with what you expected. If you still don't understand what you're reading, try reading more slowly.

Handbook of Literary Terms

For more information about a topic, turn to the page(s) in this book indicated on a separate line at the end of the entries.

On another line are cross-references to entries in this Handbook that provide closely related information. For instance, *Autobiography* contains a cross-reference to *Biography*.

ALLITERATION **The repetition of the same or very similar consonant sounds in words that are close together.** Alliteration usually occurs at the beginning of words, as in the phrase "*busy as a bee.*" It can also occur within or at the end of words.

Alliteration can establish a mood and emphasize words. If you've ever twisted your tongue around a line like "She sells seashells by the seashore" or "How much wood could a woodchuck chuck if a woodchuck could chuck wood?" you have already had some experience with alliteration.

ALLUSION **A reference to a statement, a person, a place, or an event from literature, history, religion, mythology, politics, sports, or science.** Writers expect readers to recognize an allusion and to think, almost at the same time, about the literary work, person, place, or event that it refers to. The cartoon at the top of the next column makes an allusion you will recognize right away.

"Someone's been sleeping in my bed, too, and there she is on Screen Nine!"

AUTOBIOGRAPHY **The story of a person's life, written or told by that person.** Maya Angelou's account of her childhood experiences, called "Brother" (page 569), is taken from her autobiography *I Know Why the Caged Bird Sings*.

See pages 567, 575.
See also *Biography*.

BIOGRAPHY **The story of a real person's life, written or told by another person.** A classic American biography is Carl Sandburg's life of Abraham Lincoln. A biography popular with young adults is Russell Freedman's *Lincoln: A Photobiography* (see excerpt on page 614). Movie stars, television personalities, politicians, sports figures, self-made millionaires, and artists are frequent subjects of biographies. Today biographies are among the most popular forms of literature.

See page 589.
See also *Autobiography*.

CHARACTER **A person or an animal in a story, play, or other literary work.** In some works, such as folk tales, animals are characters (see "He Lion, Bruh Bear, and Bruh Rabbit" on page 387). In other works, such as fairy tales, fantastic creatures, like dragons, are characters. In still other works, characters are gods or heroes (see "Medusa's Head" on page 169). Most often characters are ordinary human beings, as in "The All-American Slurp" (page 257).

The way in which a writer reveals the personality of a character is called **characterization.** A writer can reveal character in six ways:

1. by describing how the character looks and dresses
2. by letting the reader hear the character speak
3. by showing the reader how the character acts
4. by letting the reader know the character's inner thoughts and feelings
5. by revealing what other people in the story think or say about the character
6. by telling the reader directly what the character's personality is like (cruel, kind, sneaky, brave, and so on)

See pages 100, 102, 111, 121, 137, 147, 167.

CONFLICT **A struggle or clash between opposing characters or opposing forces.** An **external conflict** is a struggle between a character and some outside force. This outside force may be another character, a society as a whole, or a natural force, like bitter-cold weather or a ferocious shark. An **internal conflict,** on the other hand, is a struggle between opposing desires or emotions within a person. A character with an internal conflict may be struggling against fear or loneliness or even being a sore loser.

See pages 39, 137, 167.

CONNOTATIONS **The feelings and associations that have come to be attached to a word.** For example, the words *inexpensive* and *cheap* are used to describe something that is not costly. The dictionary definitions, or **denotations,** of these words are roughly the same. A manufacturer of DVD players, however, would not use *cheap* in advertising its latest model, since the word *cheap* is associated with something that is not made well. *Inexpensive* would be a better choice. Connotations can be especially important in poetry.

DESCRIPTION **The kind of writing that creates a clear image of something, usually by using details that appeal to one or more of the senses: sight, hearing, smell, taste, and touch.** Description works through **images,** words that appeal to the five senses. Writers use description in all forms of writing—in fiction, nonfiction, and poetry. Here is a description of a famous character who has found a place in the hearts of readers everywhere. The writer's description appeals to the sense of sight, but it also hints at the girl's character. Viewing this lone figure in a deserted train station, an "ordinary observer" would see

> a child of about eleven, garbed in a very short, very tight, very ugly dress of yellowish gray wincey. She wore a faded brown sailor hat and beneath the hat, extending down her back, were two braids of very thick, decidedly red hair. Her face was small, white, and thin, also much freckled; her mouth was large and so were her eyes, that looked green in some lights and moods and gray in others.
>
> —L. M. Montgomery,
> *from* Anne of Green Gables

See pages 536, 545.

DIALECT **A way of speaking that is characteristic of a particular region or of a particular group of people.** A dialect may have a distinct vocabulary, pronunciation system, and grammar. In a sense, we all speak dialects. The dialect that is dominant in a country or culture becomes accepted as the standard way of speaking. Writers often reproduce regional dialects or dialects that reveal a person's economic or social class. For example, the animal characters in "He Lion, Bruh Bear, and Bruh Rabbit" (page 387) use an African American dialect spoken in the rural South. In the passage below, a spunky young girl gets up the courage to ask her uncle a hard question (she is speaking an African American urban dialect).

> So there I am in the navigator seat. And I turn to him and just plain ole ax him. I mean I come right on out with it. . . . And like my mama say, Hazel—which is my real name and what she remembers to call me when she bein serious—when you got somethin on your mind, speak up and let the chips fall where they may. And if anybody don't like it, tell em to come see your mama. And Daddy look up from the paper and say, You hear your mama good, Hazel. And tell em to come see me first. Like that. That's how I was raised. So I turn clear round in the navigator seat and say, "Look here, . . . you gonna marry this girl?"
>
> —Toni Cade Bambara,
> from "Gorilla, My Love"

DIALOGUE **Conversation between two or more characters.** Most plays consist entirely of dialogue. Dialogue is also an important element in most stories and novels. It is very effective in revealing character and can add realism and humor to a story.

In the written form of a play, such as *Blanca Flor* (page 149), dialogue appears without quotation marks. In prose or poetry, however, dialogue is usually enclosed in quotation marks.

DRAMA **A story written to be acted in front of an audience.** A drama, such as *Blanca Flor* (page 149), can also be appreciated and enjoyed in written form. The related events that take place within a drama are often separated into **acts.** Each act is often made up of shorter sections, or **scenes.** Many plays have two or three acts, but there are many variations. The elements of drama are often described as **introduction** or **exposition, complications, conflict, climax,** and **resolution.**

See also *Dialogue.*

ESSAY **A short piece of nonfiction prose.** An essay usually examines a subject from a personal point of view. The French writer Michel de Montaigne (1533–1592) is credited with creating the essay. Robert Fulghum, a popular essayist, is represented in this book (page 222).

FABLE **A very brief story in prose or verse that teaches a moral, a practical lesson about how to succeed in life.** The characters of most fables are animals who behave and speak like human beings. Some of the most popular fables are those thought to have been told by Aesop, who was a slave in ancient Greece. You may be familiar with his fable about the sly fox who praises the crow for her beautiful voice and begs her to sing for him. When the crow opens her mouth to sing, she lets fall from her beak the piece of cheese that the fox had been after the whole time.

See page 385.
See also *Folk Tale, Myth.*

FANTASY **Imaginative writing that carries the reader into an invented world where the laws of nature as we know them do not operate.** In fantasy worlds, fantastic forces are often at play. Characters wave magic wands, cast spells, or appear and disappear at will. These characters may be ordinary human beings—or they may be Martians, elves, giants, or fairies. Some of the oldest fantasy stories are called **fairy tales.** A newer type of fantasy, one that deals with a future world changed by science, is called **science fiction.** "All Summer in a Day" (page 29) is Ray Bradbury's science fiction story about life as he imagines it on the planet Venus.

FICTION **A prose account that is made up rather than true.** The term *fiction* usually refers to novels and short stories.

See pages 343, 344, 346, 355, 367, 385, 399.
See also *Fantasy, Nonfiction*.

FIGURATIVE LANGUAGE **Language that describes one thing in terms of something else and is not literally true.** Figures of speech always involve some sort of imaginative comparison between seemingly unlike things. The most common forms are **simile** ("My heart is like a singing bird"), **metaphor** ("The road was a ribbon of moonlight"), and **personification** ("The leaves were whispering to the night").

See pages 474, 603, 605, 613.
See also *Metaphor, Personification, Simile*.

FLASHBACK **A scene that breaks the normal time order of the plot to show a past event.** A flashback can be placed anywhere in a story, even at the beginning. There, it usually gives background information. Most of the play *The Diary of Anne Frank* is a flashback.

FOLK TALE **A story with no known author, originally passed on from one generation to another by word of mouth.** Folk tales generally differ from myths in that they are not about gods and they were never connected with religion. The folk tales in this book include "Little Mangy One" (page 462) and "He Lion, Bruh Bear, and Bruh Rabbit" (page 387). Sometimes similar folk tales appear in many cultures. For example, stories similar to the old European folk tale of Cinderella have turned up in hundreds of cultures.

See page 385.
See also *Fable, Myth, Oral Tradition*.

FORESHADOWING **The use of clues or hints to suggest events that will occur later in the plot.** Foreshadowing builds suspense or anxiety in the reader or viewer. In a movie, for example, strange, alien creatures glimpsed among the trees may foreshadow danger for the exploring astronauts.

See also *Suspense*.

FREE VERSE **Poetry that is "free" of a regular meter and rhyme scheme.** Poets writing in free verse try to capture the natural rhythms of ordinary speech. The following poem is written in free verse:

> **The City**
> If flowers want to grow
> right out of the concrete sidewalk cracks
> I'm going to bend down to smell them.
>
> —David Ignatow

See also *Poetry, Rhyme, Rhythm*.

IMAGERY **Language that appeals to the senses— sight, hearing, touch, taste, and smell.** Most images are visual—that is, they create pictures in the mind by appealing to the sense of sight. Images can also appeal to the senses of hearing, touch, taste, and smell. They can appeal to several senses at once. Though imagery is an element in all types of writing, it is especially important in poetry. The following poem is full of images about rain:

> **The Storm**
> In fury and terror
> the tempest broke,
> it tore up the pine
> and shattered the oak,
> yet the hummingbird hovered
> within the hour
> sipping clear rain
> from a trumpet flower.
>
> —Elizabeth Coatsworth

See pages 474, 605.

IRONY **A contrast between what is expected and what really happens.** Irony can create powerful effects, from humor to horror. Here are some examples of situations that would make us feel a sense of irony:

- A shoemaker wears shoes with holes in them.
- The children of a famous dancer trip over their own feet.
- It rains on the day a group of weather forecasters have scheduled a picnic.
- Someone asks, "How's my driving?" after going through a stop sign.
- A Great Dane runs away from a mouse.
- Someone living in the desert keeps a boat in her yard.
- The child of a police officer robs a bank.
- Someone walks out in the midst of a hurricane and says, "Nice day."

LEGEND **A story, usually based on some historical fact, that has been handed down from one generation to the next.** Legends often grow up around famous figures or events. For example, legend has it that Abraham Lincoln was a simple, ordinary man. In reality, Lincoln was a complicated man of unusual ability and ambition. The stories about King Arthur and his knights are legends based on the exploits of an actual warrior-king who probably lived in Wales in the 500s. Legends often make use of fantastic details.

LIMERICK **A humorous five-line verse that has a regular meter and the rhyme scheme** *aabba.* Limericks often have place names in their rhymes. The following limerick was published in Edward Lear's *Book of Nonsense* in 1846, when limericks were at the height of their popularity:

There was an old man of Peru
Who dreamt he was eating a shoe.
He awoke in the night
With a terrible fright
And found it was perfectly true!

MAIN IDEA **The most important idea expressed in a piece of writing.** Sometimes the main idea is stated directly by the writer; at other times the reader must infer it.

See page 633.

METAPHOR **A comparison between two unlike things in which one thing becomes another thing.** An **extended metaphor** carries the comparison through an entire work. A metaphor is an important type of figure of speech. Metaphors are used in all forms of writing and are common in ordinary speech. When you say about your grumpy friend, "He's such a bear today," you do not mean that he is growing bushy black fur. You mean that he is in a bad mood and is ready to attack, just the way a bear might be.

Metaphors differ from **similes,** which use specific words, such as *like, as, than,* and *resembles,* to make their comparisons. "He is behaving like a bear" is a simile.

The following famous poem compares fame to an insect:

Fame is a bee.
It has a song—
It has a sting—
Ah, too, it has a wing.

—Emily Dickinson

See also *Figurative Language, Personification, Simile.*

MOOD **The overall emotion created by a work of literature.** Mood can often be described in one or two adjectives, such as *eerie, dreamy, mysterious, depressing.* The mood created by the poem below is sad and lonely:

> **Since Hanna Moved Away**
> The tires on my bike are flat.
> The sky is grouchy gray.
> At least it sure feels like that
> Since Hanna moved away.
>
> Chocolate ice cream tastes like prunes.
> December's come to stay.
> They've taken back the Mays and Junes
> Since Hanna moved away.
>
> Flowers smell like halibut.
> Velvet feels like hay.
> Every handsome dog's a mutt
> Since Hanna moved away.
>
> Nothing's fun to laugh about.
> Nothing's fun to play.
> They call me, but I won't come out
> Since Hanna moved away.
>
> —Judith Viorst

MYTH **A story that usually explains something about the world and involves gods and superheroes.** Myths are deeply connected to the traditions and religious beliefs of the cultures that produced them. Myths often explain certain aspects of life, such as what thunder is or where sunlight comes from or why people die. **Origin myths,** or **creation myths,** explain how something in the world began or was created. Most myths are very old and were handed down orally for many centuries before being put in writing. The story of the hero Perseus (page 179) is a famous Greek myth.

See page 399.
See also *Fable, Folk Tale, Oral Tradition.*

NARRATION **The kind of writing that relates a series of connected events to tell "what happened."** Narration (also called **narrative**) is the form of writing storytellers use to tell stories. Narration can be used to relate both fictional and true-life events.

See pages 556, 567, 589.

NONFICTION **Prose writing that deals with real people, events, and places without changing any facts.** Popular forms of nonfiction are the autobiography, the biography, and the essay. Other examples of nonfiction are newspaper stories, magazine articles, historical writing, travel writing, science reports, and personal diaries and letters.

See also *Fiction.*

NOVEL **A long fictional story that is usually more than one hundred book pages in length.** A novel includes all the elements of storytelling—**plot, character, setting, theme,** and **point of view.** Because of its length, a novel usually has a more complex plot, subplots, and more characters, settings, and themes than a short story.

ONOMATOPOEIA **The use of a word whose sound imitates or suggests its meaning.** Onomatopoeia (ahn uh mat uh PEE uh) is so natural to us that we begin to use it at a very early age. *Boom, bang, sniffle, rumble, hush, ding,* and *snort* are all examples of onomatopoeia. Onomatopoeia helps create the music of poetry. The following poem uses onomatopoeia:

> **Our Washing Machine**
> Our washing machine went whisity whirr
> Whisity whisity whisity whirr
> One day at noon it went whisity click
> Whisity whisity whisity click
> click grr click grr click grr click
>   Call the repairman
>   Fix it . . . quick.
>
> —Patricia Hubbell

See also *Alliteration.*

ORAL TRADITION **A collection of folk tales, songs, and poems that have been passed on orally from generation to generation.**

See also *Folk Tale.*

PARAPHRASE **A restatement of a written work in which the meaning is expressed in other words.** A paraphrase of a poem should tell what the poem says, line by line, but in the paraphraser's own words. A paraphrase of a work of prose should briefly summarize the major events or ideas. Here is the first stanza of a famous poem, followed by a paraphrase:

> Once upon a midnight dreary, while I
>   pondered, weak and weary,
> Over many a quaint and curious volume of
>   forgotten lore—
> While I nodded, nearly napping, suddenly
>   there came a tapping,
> As of someone gently rapping, rapping at my
>   chamber door.
> "'Tis some visitor," I muttered, "tapping at
> my chamber door—
>   Only this, and nothing more."
>
> —Edgar Allan Poe,
>   from "The Raven"
>
> **Paraphrase:** One midnight, when I was tired, I was reading some interesting old books that contain information no one learns anymore. As I was dozing off, I suddenly heard what sounded like someone tapping at the door to the room. "It is someone coming to see me," I said to myself, "knocking at the door. That's all it is."

Notice that the paraphrase is neither as eerie nor as elegant as the poem.

PERSONIFICATION **A special kind of metaphor in which a nonhuman or nonliving thing or quality is talked about as if it were human or alive.** You would be using personification if you said, "The leaves danced along the sidewalk." Of course, leaves don't dance—only people do. The poem at the top of the next column personifies the night wind:

> **Rags**
> The night wind
> rips a cloud sheet
> into rags,
> then rubs, rubs
> the October moon
> until it shines
> like a brass doorknob.
>
> —Judith Thurman

In the cartoon below, history and fame are talked about as though they were human.

"While you were out for lunch, History passed by and Fame came knocking."

See also *Figurative Language, Metaphor, Simile.*

PLOT **The series of related events that make up a story.** Plot tells "what happens" in a short story, novel, play, or narrative poem. Most plots are built on these bare bones: An **introduction** tells who the characters are and what their **conflict,** or problem, is. **Complications** arise as the characters take steps to resolve the conflict. When the outcome of the conflict is decided one way or another, the plot reaches a **climax,** the most exciting moment in the story. The final part of the story is the **resolution,** when the characters' problems are solved and the story ends.

See pages 4, 6, 15, 51, 283.
See also *Conflict.*

POETRY A kind of rhythmic, compressed language that uses figures of speech and imagery to appeal to emotion and imagination. Poetry often has a regular pattern of rhythm, and it may have a regular pattern of rhyme. **Free verse** is poetry that has no regular pattern of rhythm or rhyme.

See pages 472, 476, 483, 498.
See also *Free Verse, Imagery, Refrain, Rhyme, Rhythm, Speaker, Stanza.*

POINT OF VIEW The vantage point from which a story is told. Two common points of view are the omniscient (ahm NIHSH uhnt) and the first person.

1. In the **omniscient,** or all-knowing, **third-person point of view,** the narrator knows everything about the characters and their problems. This all-knowing narrator can tell us about the past, the present, and the future. Below is part of a familiar story told from the omniscient point of view:

> Once upon a time in a small village, there were three houses built by three brother pigs. One house was made of straw, one was made of twigs, and one was made of brick. Each pig thought his house was the best and the strongest. A wolf—a very hungry wolf—lived just outside the town. He was practicing house-destroying techniques and was trying to decide which pig's house was the weakest.

2. In the **first-person point of view,** one of the characters, using the personal pronoun *I*, is telling the story. The reader becomes familiar with this narrator and can know only what he or she knows and can observe only what he or she observes. All information about the story must come from this one narrator. In some cases, as in the example at the top of the next column, the information this narrator gives may not be correct:

> As soon as I found out some new pigs had moved into the neighborhood, I started to practice my house-destroying techniques. I like to blow down houses and eat whoever is inside. The little pigs have built their houses of different materials—but I know I can blow 'em down in no time. That brick house looks especially weak.

See pages 556, 567, 589.

PROSE Any writing that is not poetry. Essays, short stories, novels, news articles, and letters are written in prose.

REFRAIN A repeated word, phrase, line, or group of lines in a poem or song or even in a speech. Refrains are usually associated with songs and poems, but they are also used in speeches and some other forms of literature. Refrains are often used to create rhythm. They are also used for emphasis and emotional effects.

See page 491.

RHYME The repetition of accented vowel sounds and all sounds following them. *Trouble* and *bubble* are rhymes, as are *clown* and *noun*. Rhymes in poetry help create rhythm and lend a songlike quality to a poem. They can also emphasize ideas and provide humor or delight.

End rhymes are rhymes at the ends of lines. **Internal rhymes** are rhymes within lines. Here is an example of a poem with both kinds of rhymes:

> In days of *old* when knights caught *cold*,
> They were not quickly *cured*;
> No aspirin *pill* would check the *ill*,
> Which had to be *endured*.
>
> —David Daiches,
> from "Thoughts on Progress,"
> from *The New Yorker*

Rhyme scheme is the pattern of rhyming sounds at the ends of lines in a poem. Notice the pattern of end rhymes in the poem in the cartoon at the bottom of the next page.

See page 483.

RHYTHM **A musical quality produced by the repetition of stressed and unstressed syllables or by the repetition of other sound patterns.** Rhythm occurs in all language—written and spoken—but is particularly important in poetry. The most obvious kind of rhythm is the repeated pattern of stressed and unstressed syllables, called **meter.** Finding this pattern is called **scanning.** If you scan or say the following lines aloud, you'll hear a strong, regular rhythm. (Crowns, pounds, and guineas are British currency.)

> When I was one-and-twenty
>   I heard a wise man say,
> "Give crowns and pounds and guineas
>   But not your heart away."
>
>   —A. E. Housman, from
>   "When I Was One-and-Twenty"

See page 483.
See also *Free Verse, Poetry.*

SETTING **The time and place of a story, a poem, or a play.** The setting can help create mood or atmosphere. The setting can also affect the events of the plot. In some stories the conflict is provided by the setting. This happens in "The Dog of Pompeii" (page 753) when the characters' lives are threatened by a volcano. Some examples of vivid settings are the gloomy planet where it rains for seven years in "All Summer in a Day" (page 29), the snow-covered countryside in "Zlateh the Goat" (page 771), and Ernie's Riverside restaurant in "Ta-Na-E-Ka" (page 243).

See pages 4, 6, 15, 27, 39, 51.

SHORT STORY **A fictional prose narrative that is about five to twenty book pages long.** Short stories are usually built on a **plot** that consists of these elements: **introduction, conflict, complications, climax,** and **resolution.** Short stories are more limited than novels. They usually have only one or two major characters and one setting.

See page 355.
See also *Conflict, Fiction, Novel, Plot.*

SIMILE **A comparison between two unlike things using a word such as** *like, as, than,* **or** *resembles.* The simile (SIHM uh lee) is an important figure of speech. "His voice is as loud as a trumpet" and "Her eyes are like the blue sky" are similes. In the following poem the poet uses a simile to help us see a winter scene in a new way:

> Scene
> Little trees like pencil strokes
> black and still
> etched forever in my mind
> on that snowy hill.
>
>   —Charlotte Zolotow

See also *Figurative Language, Metaphor.*

Calvin and Hobbes
by Bill Watterson

CALVIN AND HOBBES © Watterson. Reprinted with permission of UNIVERSAL PRESS SYNDICATE. All Rights Reserved.

SPEAKER **The voice talking to us in a poem.** Sometimes the speaker is identical to the poet, but often the speaker and the poet are not the same. A poet may speak as a child, a woman, a man, an animal, or even an object. The speaker of "Things to Do If You Are a Subway" asks the reader to imagine that he or she is a subway train and to act like one.

Things to Do If You Are a Subway
Pretend you are a dragon.
Live in underground caves.
Roar about underneath the city.
Swallow piles of people.
Spit them out at the next station.
Zoom through the darkness.
Be an express.
Go fast.
Make as much noise as you please.
—Bobbi Katz

See page 527.

STANZA **In a poem, a group of lines that form a unit.** A stanza in a poem is something like a paragraph in prose; it often expresses a unit of thought.

SUSPENSE **The anxious curiosity the reader feels about what will happen next in a story.** Any kind of writing that has a plot evokes some degree of suspense. Our sense of suspense is awakened in *The Gold Cadillac* (page 369), for example, when the narrator and her family begin their trip to Mississippi. The anxious and fearful warnings of the family's friends and relatives make us eager to read on to see if the journey will prove dangerous.

See also *Foreshadowing, Plot.*

SYMBOL **A person, a place, a thing, or an event that has its own meaning and stands for something beyond itself as well.** Examples of symbols are all around us—in music, on television, and in everyday conversation. The skull and crossbones, for example, is a symbol of danger; the dove is a symbol of peace; and the red rose stands for true love. In literature, symbols are often more personal. For example, in *The Gold Cadillac,* the Cadillac stands for success in the eyes of Wilbert.

See page 621.

TALL TALE **An exaggerated, fanciful story that gets "taller and taller," or more and more far-fetched, the more it is told and retold.** The tall tale is an American story form. John Henry (page 493) is a famous tall-tale character. Here is a short tall tale:

When the temperature reached 118 degrees, a whole field of corn popped. White flakes filled the air and covered the ground six inches deep and drifted across roads and collected on tree limbs.

A mule that saw all this thought it was snowing and lay down and quietly froze to death.

THEME **A truth about life revealed in a work of literature.** A theme is not the same as a subject. A subject can usually be expressed in a word or two—*love, childhood, death.* A theme is the idea the writer wishes to reveal about that subject. A theme has to be expressed in a full sentence. A work can have more than one theme. A theme is usually not stated directly in the work. Instead, the reader has to think about the elements of the work and then make an inference, or educated guess, about what they all mean. One theme of "The All-American Slurp" (page 257) can be stated this way: Different cultures are similar in some ways.

See pages 230, 232, 241, 255, 269, 413.

TONE **The attitude a writer takes toward an audience, a subject, or a character.** Tone is conveyed through the writer's choice of words and details. The tone can be light and humorous, serious and sad, friendly or hostile toward a character, and so forth. The poem "The Sneetches" (page 485) is light and humorous in tone. In contrast, Francisco X. Alarcón's "In a Neighborhood in Los Angeles" (page 511) has a loving and respectful tone.

See pages 474, 476, 527.

Handbook of Reading and Informational Terms

For more information about a topic, turn to the page(s) in this book indicated on a separate line at the end of the entry. To learn more about *Cause and Effect,* for example, turn to page 233.

On another line there are cross-references to entries in this Handbook that provide closely related information. For instance, *Chronological Order* contains a cross-reference to *Text Structures.*

AUTHOR'S PURPOSE The author's purpose may be to **inform,** to **persuade,** to **express feelings,** or to **entertain.** An author may create a **text,** which is any written work, with more than one purpose in mind. One of the purposes is usually more important than the others. Once you've identified the author's purpose, you'll have a pretty good idea of how to read the text. If you're reading an **informational text,** you may need to read slowly and carefully. You may also want to complete a think sheet like the one below or take notes. If you're reading a text that the author wrote mostly for you to enjoy, you can read at your own pace—any way you want.

> **Question Sheet for Informational Texts**
> 1. What is the topic? _____
> 2. Do I understand what I'm reading? _____
> 3. What parts should I re-read? _____
> _____
> 4. What are the main ideas and details?
>
> Main idea: _____ Details: _____
> Main idea: _____ Details: _____
> Main idea: _____ Details: _____
> Main idea: _____ Details: _____
> 5. Summary of what I learned:
> _____
> _____

See pages 575, 605, 714.
See also *Note Taking; Reading Rate.*

CAUSE AND EFFECT A **cause** is the reason something happens. An **effect** is *what happens* as a result of the cause. The cause happens first in time. The *later* event is the effect. In most stories, events in the plot are connected by cause and effect. Look for a **cause-and-effect text structure** in informational materials. Watch out! Sometimes writers put the effect first even though that event happened as a result of (and after) the cause. For instance, consider the following sentence:

> Bears come out of their dens when the winter snow melts.

The *cause* is the melting snow. The *effect* is that bears come out of their dens. Some of the clue words that signal cause-and-effect relationships are *because, since, so that, therefore,* and *as a result.*

See pages 233, 269, 283.
See also *Text Structures.*

CHRONOLOGICAL ORDER Most narratives are written in **chronological** or **time order,** the order in which events happen in time. When you read a story, look for time clues— words and phrases like *next, then, finally,* and *the following night.* Writers use time clues as signals to help you follow the **sequence,** or order, of events. Sometimes writers break the sequence with a **flashback,** an event that happened earlier. Look for chronological order in any kind of text where the order of events is important. For instance, in an article explaining how to make something, the steps are usually listed in chronological order.

See also *Text Structures.*

COMPARISON AND CONTRAST When you **compare,** you look for **similarities,** ways in which things are alike. When you **contrast,** you look for **differences.** In a comparison-contrast text, the features looked at are called **points of comparison.** The points of comparison are usually organized in either a **block pattern** or a **point-by-point pattern.** When you read a comparison organized in a block pattern, you find the points of comparison about each subject presented separately, first one, then the other. Here is a **block-pattern** paragraph comparing Mary's and Roger's ways of surviving Ta-Na-E-Ka (page 243):

> Mary survived by getting help from other people. She borrowed money from a teacher and used it to pay for food at Ernie's restaurant. Ernie gave her warm clothes to wear and a place to stay at night. In contrast, Roger survived on his own in the traditional Kaw way. He ate berries and maybe even grasshoppers. He lost weight during Ta-Na-E-Ka and was never warm and comfortable.

A writer who uses the **point-by-point pattern** goes back and forth between the two subjects being compared, like this:

> Mary ate well, but Roger lost weight. Mary ate good food at a restaurant while Roger lived on berries. Mary got help from others, but Roger survived by himself.
>
> Both passed the test; however, Roger survived in the traditional way. Mary found a new way of surviving.

Some of the clue words that signal comparison and contrast are *although*, *but*, *either . . . or*, *however*, and *yet*.

See page 195.
See also *Text Structures*.

CONTEXT CLUES You can often find clues to the meaning of a word you don't know by looking at its **context,** the words and sentences around it. Here is the beginning of a paragraph from "The Dog of Pompeii" (page 753):

> The water—hot water—splashing in his face <u>revived</u> him. He got to his feet, Bimbo steadying him, helping him on again.

If you don't know the meaning of *revived* in the first sentence, look at the context. The beginning of the second sentence, "He got to his feet," helps you figure out that *revived* means "brought back to life."

See pages 24, 36, 266, 586, 600.

EVALUATING EVIDENCE When you read informational and persuasive texts, you need to weigh the **evidence** that writers use to support their ideas. That means you need to read carefully and decide whether the writer has presented evidence that's **adequate, appropriate,** and **accurate.** *Adequate* means "sufficient" or "enough." You make sure there's enough evidence to prove the writer's points. Sometimes one example or one fact may be adequate. Other times the writer may need to provide several facts and maybe even statistics. A direct quotation from a well-respected expert in the field can often be convincing. Make sure that the writer chooses *appropriate* evidence that relates directly to the writer's idea. To be sure that evidence is *accurate*, or correct, make sure it comes from a source you can trust. Don't assume that everything you see in print is accurate. If a fact, example, or quotation doesn't sound right, check out the magazine or book that it came from. Is the magazine or book a trustworthy and reliable source? What is the author's background?

See pages 687, 694, 705.
See also *Fact and Opinion*.

EVIDENCE **Evidence** is the support or proof that backs up an idea, conclusion, or opinion. When you're reading an informational or persuasive text, you look for evidence in the form of examples, quotations from experts, statistics (information expressed as numbers), and personal experiences.

FACT AND OPINION A **fact** is something that can be proved true.

> **Fact:** Abraham Lincoln was the sixteenth president of the United States.

An **opinion** expresses a personal belief or feeling. An opinion cannot be proved true or false.

> **Opinion:** Abraham Lincoln was the best president the United States has ever had.

A **valid opinion** is a personal belief that is strongly supported by facts. When you read "The Mysterious Mr. Lincoln" (page 614), look for the facts that Russell Freedman uses to back up his opinions.

See pages 567, 613, 700.
See also Evidence.

GENERALIZATION A **generalization** is a broad statement based on several particular situations. When you make a generalization, you combine evidence in a text with what you already know to make a broad, universal statement about some topic. For example, after reading "Wartime Mistakes, Peacetime Apologies" (page 66), you might want to make a generalization about the treatment of Japanese Americans during World War II.

See pages 255, 769.
See also Evidence.

GRAPHIC FEATURES Headings, design features, maps, charts, tables, diagrams, and illustrations are all **graphic features.** They present information visually. Shapes, lines, and colors combine with words to help you understand a text.

A **heading** is a kind of title for the information that follows it. Size and color set off the heading from the rest of the text. A repeated heading like "Literary Focus" in this textbook is always followed by the same type of material.

Some of the **design features** you may find in a text are colors, borders, boldface and italic type, type in different styles (fonts) and sizes, bullets (the dots that set off items in a list), and logos (like computer icons). The Timed Writing heading always appears with the clock logo, for instance. Design features make a text look more attractive. They steer

your eyes to different types of information and make the text easier to read.

Graphic features such as **maps, charts, diagrams, graphs,** and **tables** communicate complex information with lines, drawings, and symbols. The following elements help to make them effective:

1. A **title** identifies the subject or main idea of the graphic.
2. **Labels** identify specific information.
3. A **caption** is the text (usually under a photo or another kind of illustration) that explains what you're looking at.
4. A **legend** or **key** helps you interpret symbols and colors. Look for a **scale,** which helps you relate the size or distance of something on the graphic to real-life sizes and distances.
5. The **source** tells where the information in the graphic came from. Knowing the source helps you evaluate the graphic's accuracy.

Charts and **diagrams** use symbols, lines, and numbers to explain or to display information. They are used to compare ideas, show steps in a process, illustrate the way something is made, or show how the parts of something relate to the whole thing. A **pie graph,** for instance, shows proportions. It's a circle divided into different-size sections, like slices of pie.

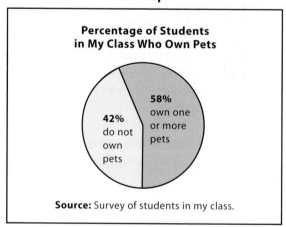

Pie Graph

Percentage of Students in My Class Who Own Pets

58% own one or more pets

42% do not own pets

Source: Survey of students in my class.

A **flowchart** shows you the steps in a process, a sequence of events, or cause-and-effect relationships.

Graphs, including bar graphs and line graphs, show changes or trends over time. Notice that the same information is presented in the following bar graph and line graph:

Bar Graph

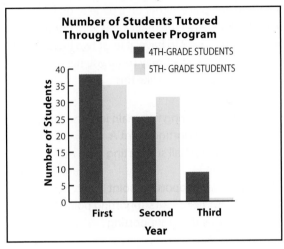

Line Graph

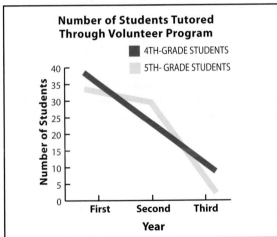

A **table** presents facts and details arranged in rows and columns. It simplifies information to make it easy to understand.

Table

Number of Volunteers in the Peer-Tutoring Program	
First year	15
Second year	10
Third year	8

Viewing Tips: When you come across graphic features, use the tips below:

1. Read the title, labels, and legend before you try to analyze the information.
2. Read numbers carefully. Note increases or decreases. Look for the direction or order of events and for trends and relationships.
3. Draw your own conclusions from the graphic, and compare them with the conclusions the writer makes.

INFERENCE An **inference** is an educated guess. You make inferences all the time in real life. For instance, if you see pawprints crossing the snow, you can **infer** that an animal walked there. The pawprints are the **evidence.** On the basis of your experience with animal tracks, you might be able to infer that the animal was a rabbit, a cat, a dog, or a raccoon.

Readers **make inferences** on the basis of clues writers give them and experiences from their own lives. When you make inferences, you read between the lines to figure out what the writer suggests but does not state directly.

Read this passage from Avi's story "What Do Fish Have to Do with Anything?"(page 622).

> During the twenty minutes that Willie watched, no one who passed looked in the beggar's direction. Willie wondered if they even saw the man. Certainly no one put any money into his open hand.
>
> A lady leading a dog by a leash went by. The dog strained in the direction of the man sitting on the crate. The dog's tail wagged. The lady pulled the dog away. "Heel!" she commanded.

Here are some **inferences** you might draw from the passage: People don't want to look at the man who is begging. It's as if he doesn't exist for them. The dog is friendlier than the people.

See page 111.

MAIN IDEA The most important idea in a piece of nonfiction writing is the **main idea.** There may be more than one main idea in a nonfiction story or article. Sometimes the writer states a main idea directly; at other times the writer only **implies,** or suggests, the main idea. Then the reader must **infer** or guess what it is.

To infer the main idea, look at the **key details** or **important events** in the text. See whether you can create a statement that expresses the idea that these details or events develop or support. In a nonfiction text the writer may state the main idea more than once and use different words for each statement. Look especially for a **key passage** near the end of the piece. That's where the writer often emphasizes or sums up a main idea.

See page 633.
See also *Outlining.*

NOTE TAKING Taking notes is important for readers who want to remember ideas and facts. It's especially useful when you read **informational texts.** You can jot down notes in a notebook or on note cards. Notes don't have to be written in complete sentences. Put them in your own words; use phrases that will help you recall the text. You may want to put each important idea at the top of its own page or note card. As you read, add details that relate to that idea. Put related ideas on the same page or card as the main idea they support.

Whenever you copy a writer's exact words, put quotation marks around them. Write down the number of the page that was the source of each note. Even though no one but you may see your notes, try to write clearly so that you'll be able to read them later. When you finish taking notes, review them to make sure they make sense to you.

See page 65.
See also *Author's Purpose.*

OUTLINING **Outlining** an informational text helps you identify important ideas and understand how they are connected or related to each other. Once you've made an outline, you have a quick visual summary of the information. Start with the notes you've taken on an article. (See *Note Taking.*) You should have each **main idea** with **supporting details** in one place, either on a page or on a card. Many outlines label the main ideas with Roman numerals. You need to have at least two headings at each level. Three levels may be all you need. A four-level outline is arranged like this:

I. First main idea
   A. Detail supporting first main idea
      1. Detail supporting point A
      2. Another detail supporting point A
         a. Detail supporting point 2
         b. Another detail supporting point 2
      3. Another detail supporting point A
   B. Another detail supporting first main idea
II. Second main idea

See page 73.
See also *Main Idea.*

PARAPHRASING When you **paraphrase** a text, you put it into your own words. You can check how well you understand a poem, for instance, by paraphrasing it, line by line. When you paraphrase, you follow the author's sequence of ideas. You carefully reword each line or sentence without changing the author's meaning or leaving anything out.

PERSUASION **Persuasion** is the use of language or visual images to get you to *believe* or *do* something. Writers who want to change your mind about an issue use **persuasive techniques.** Learning about these techniques will help you evaluate persuasion.

Emotional appeals get the reader's feelings involved in the argument. Some writers use vivid language and give reasons, examples, and anecdotes (personal-experience stories) that appeal to basic feelings such as fear, pity, jealousy, and love.

Logical appeals make sense because they're based on correct reasoning. They appeal to your brain with reasons and evidence. (See *Evidence*.) When you're reading a persuasive text, make sure that the writer has good reasons to support each opinion or conclusion. Evidence such as facts, personal experiences, examples, statistics, and statements by experts on the issue should back up each reason.

Logical fallacies are mistakes in reasoning. If you're reading a text quickly, an argument based on **fallacious reasoning** may look as if it made sense. Watch out for these fallacies:

1. **Hasty generalizations.** Valid generalizations are based on solid evidence. (See *Generalization*.) Not all generalizations are valid. Here's an example of a hasty generalization, one made on the basis of too little evidence.

> "The Sneetches" is a poem that rhymes.
> "John Henry" is a poem that rhymes.
> **Hasty generalization:** All poems rhyme.

Sometimes hasty generalizations can be corrected by the use of **qualifying words,** such as *most, usually, some, many,* and *often.* After you've read all the poems in this textbook and considered all the evidence, you could make this generalization:

> **Valid generalization:** Some poems rhyme.

2. **Circular reasoning.** This example illustrates circular reasoning, another kind of logical fallacy:

> We have the greatest football team because no other school has a team that's as fantastic as ours.

Someone using circular reasoning simply repeats an argument instead of backing it up with reasons and evidence.

3. **Only-cause fallacy.** This fallacy assumes that a problem has only one cause. It conveniently ignores the fact that most situations are the result of many causes. The **either-or fallacy** is related to the only-cause fallacy. The either-or fallacy assumes that there are only two sides to an issue.

> **Only-cause fallacy:** I didn't do well on the test because it wasn't fair.
> **Either-or fallacy:** If your parents don't buy this set of encyclopedias for you, they don't care about your education.

Persuasion tends to be most interesting—and effective—when it appeals to both head and heart. However, it's important to be able to recognize logical fallacies and emotional appeals—and to be aware of how they can mislead you.

See pages 687, 694, 705, 709.

PREDICTING Making **predictions** as you read helps you think about and understand what you're reading. To make predictions, look for clues that the writer gives you. Connect those clues with other things you've read, as well as your own experience. You'll probably find yourself **adjusting predictions** as you read.

See page 367.

PRIOR KNOWLEDGE *Prior* means "earlier" or "previous." **Prior knowledge** is what you know about a subject when you're at the starting line—before you read a selection. **Using prior knowledge** is a reading skill that starts with recalling experiences you've had, as well as what you've learned about the subject of the text. Glancing through the text, looking at the pictures, and reading subtitles and captions will help you recall what you already know. As you focus on the subject, you'll come up with questions that the text may answer. Making a **KWL chart** is one way to record your reading process. Here is part of a KWL chart for Mildred D. Taylor's *The Gold Cadillac* (page 369).

K	W	L
What I **Know**	What I **Want** to Know	What I **Learned**
A Cadillac is an expensive car.	How would someone feel riding in a gold Cadillac?	

PROPAGANDA **Propaganda** is an organized attempt to persuade people to accept certain ideas or to take certain actions. Writers sometimes use propaganda to advance a good cause. However, most writers of propaganda use emotional appeals to confuse readers and convince them that the writers' opinions are the only ones worth considering. Propaganda relies on emotional appeals rather than on logical reasons and evidence.

Here are some common propaganda techniques:

1. The **bandwagon appeal** suggests that you need something or should believe something because everyone else already has it or believes it. It's an appeal to "join the crowd, climb on the bandwagon, and join the parade."

2. A **testimonial** uses a famous person, such as an actor or an athlete, to promote an idea or a product.

3. People who use **snob appeal** associate the product or idea they're promoting with power, wealth, or membership in a special group.

4. Writers who use **stereotypes** refer to members of a group as if they were all the same. For instance, an article stating that all professional wrestlers have limited intelligence unfairly stereotypes wrestlers. Stereotyping often leads to prejudice, or the formation of unfavorable opinions with complete disregard for the facts.

5. People who engage in **name-calling** offer no reasons or evidence to support their position. Instead, they attack opponents by calling them names, such as "busy bodies," "nitpickers," or "rumormongers."

See page 714.

READING RATE Readers adjust the rate at which they read depending on their purpose for reading and the difficulty of the material. The following chart shows how you can adjust your reading rate for different purposes.

Reading Rates According to Purpose

Reading Rate	Purpose	Example
Scanning	Reading quickly for specific details	Finding the age of a character
Skimming	Reading quickly for main points	Previewing a science chapter by reading the headings
Reading slowly and carefully	Reading for mastery (reading to learn)	Reading and taking notes from an article for a research report
Reading at a comfortable speed	Reading for enjoyment	Reading a novel by your favorite writer

See page 515.
See also *Author's Purpose.*

RETELLING **Retelling** is a reading strategy that helps you recall and understand the major events in a story. From time to time in your reading—for instance, after something important has happened—stop for a few moments. Review what has just taken place before you go ahead. Focus on the major events. Think about them, and retell them briefly in your own words.

See pages 6, 15.

SUMMARIZING When you **summarize** a text, you restate the author's main points in your own words. You include only the important ideas and details. A **summary** of a text is much shorter than the original, while a paraphrase may be the same length as, or even longer than, the original text.

When you're summarizing, stop after each paragraph you read. Try to restate in one sentence what the author wrote. If you're summarizing a story, look for the major events in the **plot,** the ones that lead to the **climax.** If you're summarizing an **essay,** look for the important ideas. Here is a summary of Maya Angelou's "Brother" (page 569):

> Bailey was the person who was most important to the writer when she was a child. She loved Bailey because he was smart, generous, kind, and full of life. He always defended her whenever anyone insulted her. He always came up with ideas to have fun. The author says that Bailey was someone she trusted and loved with all her heart.

See pages 39, 51.

TEXT STRUCTURES Understanding the way a text is structured, or organized, can help you follow the writer's ideas. **Analyzing text structures** will help you understand the information you're reading. The five patterns of organization that writers use most often are **cause and effect, chronological order, comparison and contrast, listing,** and **problem solution.** Some texts contain just one pattern; others combine two or more patterns. The following guidelines can help you analyze text structure:

1. Look for words that hint at a specific pattern of organization. (See *Cause and Effect, Chronological Order,* and *Comparison* and *Contrast.*)
2. Look for important ideas. See whether these ideas are connected in an obvious pattern.
3. Draw a graphic organizer that shows how the text is structured. Compare your graphic organizer with the following five diagrams, which illustrate the most common text structures.

A **cause-and-effect pattern** focuses on the relationship between causes and effects. The **causal chain** below shows how the city of Pompeii was destroyed.

Causal Chain

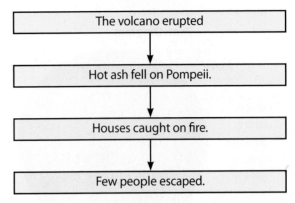

Chronological order shows events in the order in which they happen. The **sequence chain** below is a list of steps for making salsa.

Sequence Chain

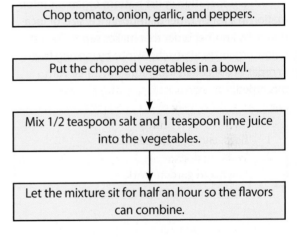

A **comparison-and-contrast** pattern focuses on similarities and differences between things. The Venn diagram below compares and contrasts Mary's and Roger's experiences during Ta-Na-E-Ka (page 243).

Venn Diagram

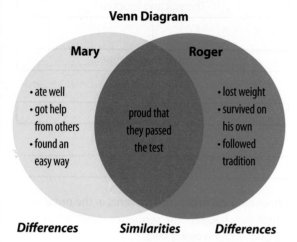

Differences   *Similarities*   *Differences*

An **enumeration** or **list pattern** organizes information in a list by order of importance, size, or location or by another order that makes sense. The list below organizes after-school jobs by ranking them in order of difficulty. (You might not agree with this order!)

List
1. Baby-sitting (most difficult)
2. Walking dogs
3. Lawn and garden work

A **problem-solution pattern** focuses on a problem and solutions to the problem. The cluster below shows a problem and some possible solutions:

Cluster

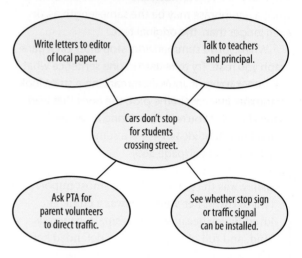

See also *Cause and Effect, Chronological Order, Comparison and Contrast*.

Glossary

The glossary that follows is an alphabetical list of words defined in the selections in this book. Use this glossary just as you would use a dictionary—to find out the meaning of unfamiliar words. (Some technical, foreign, and more obscure words in this book are defined for you in the footnotes that accompany many of the selections.)

This glossary gives the meanings that apply to the words as they are used in the selections in this book.

The following abbreviations are used:

adj.	adjective
adv.	adverb
n.	noun
v.	verb

Each word's pronunciation is in parentheses. For more information about the words in this glossary or for information about words not listed here, consult a dictionary.

A

abandoned (uh BAN duhnd) *adj.* not used or taken care of any longer.

acquaintance (uh KWAYN tuhns) *n.* friend; someone known casually.

acquainted (uh KWAYNT ihd) *v.* know someone but not know him or her well.

adjoining (uh JOY nihng) *adj.* next to.

aggressive (uh GREHS ihv) *adj.* ready to attack.

amateurs (AM uh churz) *n.* people who participate in sports or other activities for fun rather than money; not professionals.

ambitious (am BIHSH uhs) *adj.* eager to achieve something; very much wanting success.

amiably (AY mee uh blee) *adv.* in a friendly way.

anonymous (uh NAHN uh muhs) *adj.* unknown; unidentified.

apprehensively (ap rih HEHN sihv lee) *adv.* fearfully; uneasily.

apprentice (uh PREHN tihs) *n.* beginner; someone who is just starting to learn a craft or job.

apt (apt) *adj.* skilled; capable.

arrogant (AR uh guhnt) *adj.* unpleasantly proud; thinking one is more important than others.

ashamed (uh SHAYMD) *adj.* embarrassed.

audacity (aw DAS uh tee) *n.* boldness; daring.

authorities (uh THAWR uh teez) *n.* people with the official responsibility for something.

avenge (uh VEHNJ) *v.* get even for; get revenge for.

B

balmy (BAH mee) *adj.* weather or air that is warm and pleasant.

barren (BAR uhn) *adj.* unable to bear crops or fruit.

befriended (bih FREHND ihd) *v.* helped out or encouraged.

behold (bih HOHLD) *v.* look at; see.

C

cast (kast) *n.* group of performers in a play or event.

cautious (KAW shuhs) *adj.* careful.

cautiously (KAW shuhs lee) *adv.* safely; carefully.

chaos (KAY ahs) *n.* total confusion or disorder.

circumstance (SUR kuhm stans) *n.* fact or condition that affects a situation, action, or event.

civilizations (sihv uh luh ZAY shuhnz) *n.* advanced cultures characteristic of particular times and places.

claim (klaym) *n.* piece of land a prospector takes as his or her own.

cleft (klehft) *adj.* split; divided.

clenched (klehnchd) *v.* closed tightly.

clutch (kluhch) *v.* hold something tightly.

coincidence (koh IHN suh duhns) *n.* accidental happening of events that seem connected.

compensation (kahm puhn SAY shuhn) *n.* payment given to make up for a loss or injury.

competition (kahm puh TISH uhn) *n.* contest; struggle to see who is better.

complexity (kuhm PLEHK suh tee) *n.* complication; difficulty.

concentration (kahn suhn TRAY shuhn) *n.* focused attention.

confinement (kuhn FYN muhnt) *n.* condition of being kept from moving around; lack of freedom.

consequence (KAHN suh kwehns) *n.* importance.

conservation (kahn suhr VAY shuhn) *n.* protection of natural things such as animals, plants, and forests.

consoled (kuhn SOHLD) *v.* comforted when sad or disappointed.

conspicuous (kuhn SPIHK yu uhs) *adj.* attracting attention.

contemporary (kuhn TEHM puh rehr ee) *adj.* relating to the present time; modern.

contented (kuhn TEHN tihd) *adj.* happy or satisfied.

contribution (kahn truh BYOO shuhn) *n.* payment given for a specific purpose.

cooperation (koh ahp uh RAY shuhn) *n.* support; working together.

craned (kraynd) *v.* stretched (the neck) in order to see better.

criticism (KRIHT uh sihz uhm) *n.* unfavorable remarks.

cropped (krahpt) *v.* bit or cut off the top.

D

dangled (DANG guhld) *v.* held something or swung it loosely.

declined (dih KLYND) *v.* dropped; went down.

defense (dih FEHNS) *n.* team acting to keep the opposing team from scoring points.

defiant (dih FY uhnt) *adj.* disobedient; boldly resistant.

defy (dih FY) *v.* resist.

depressed (dih PREST) *adj.* very sad.

desperate (DEHS puhr iht) *adj.* having a great and urgent need.

devastating (DEHV uh STAY tihng) *adj.* causing great damage.

devour (dih VOWR) *v.* eat in a greedy way.

diligence (DIHL uh juhns) *n.* steady effort.

discretion (dihs KREHSH uhn) *n.* authority to make decisions.

dismal (DIHZ muhl) *adj.* cheerless; depressing.

dispute (dihs PYOOT) *n.* disagreement; argument.

downpour (DOWN pawr) *n.* great amount of rain that falls in a short time.

dribble (DRIHB uhl) *n.* irregular drops that flow slowly.

duplicate (DOO pluh kayt) *v.* copy.

dusk (duhsk) *n.* period of time when the sky darkens as the sun goes down.

E

eccentric (ehk SEHN trihk) *adj.* peculiar; unusual.

elude (ih LOOD) *v.* escape the notice of; avoid detection by.

endured (ehn DURD) *v.* withstood or held out.

engaged (ehn GAYJD) *adj.* busy and interested; absorbed in something.

enhance (ehn HANS) *v.* increase; improve.

erupt (ih RUHPT) *v.* release suddenly or violently.

etiquette (EHT uh keht) *n.* acceptable manners and behavior.

evacuated (ih VAK yoo ayt uhd) *v.* removed from an area.

evident (EHV uh duhnt) *adj.* easily seen or understood; obvious.

express (ehk SPREHS) *n.* train that travels from one point to another without making stops.

exterior (ehk STIHR ee uhr) *adj.* outdoor.

extinct (ehk STIHNGKT) *adj.* no longer existing.

exuded (ehg ZOO dihd) *v.* gave off.

F

fascinated (FAS uh nayt ihd) *v.* charmed by something.

feat (feet) *n.* accomplishment; daring act.

finality (fy NAL uh tee) *n.* feeling that something is finished and can't be changed.

flattery (FLAT uhr ee) *n.* praise that is false or pretended.

flourish (FLUR ihsh) *n.* sweeping movement.

forsaken (fawr SAY kuhn) *adj.* abandoned.

frail (frayl) *adj.* not very strong; easily broken.

fraud (frawd) *n.* someone who pretends to be what he or she is not.

G

gesture (JEHS chuhr) *n.* action performed to show feelings.

gorging (GAWRJ ihng) *v.* filling up; stuffing.

grimaced (GRIHM ihsd) *v.* twist the face to express pain, anger, or disgust.

groove (groov) *n.* state of being comfortable.

guarantee (gar uhn TEE) *v.* promise or assure.

guaranteed (gar uhn TEED) *adj.* condition of being promised or pledged to pay or do something if another fails to do it.

H

hallucination (huh loo suh NAY shuhn) *n.* sight or sound of something that isn't really there.
hazardous (HAZ uhr duhs) *adj.* dangerous; risky.
hovered (HUHV uhrd) *v.* floated; remained still in the air.

I

ignorance (IHG nuhr uhns) *n.* lack of knowledge.
impressing (ihm PREHS ihng) *v.* making someone feel admiration.
improbable (ihm PRAHB uh buhl) *adj.* unlikely to be true.
indifference (ihn DIHF uhr uhns) *n.* state of being unconcerned about something.
indignant (ihn DIHG nuhnt) *adj.* offended; angry.
infested (ihn FEHST ihd) *v.* inhabited in large numbers (said of something harmful).
instrumental (ihn struh MEHN tuhl) *adj.* helping to make something happen.
interned (ihn TURND) *v.* imprisoned or confined.
intriguing (ihn TREE gihng) *adj.* causing great interest.
investigate (ihn VEHS tuh gayt) *v.* look into; examine.
invincible (ihn VIHN suh buhl) *adj.* unable to be defeated.
invisible (ihn VIHZ uh buhl) *adj.* not able to be seen.
irritable (IHR uh tuh buhl) *adj.* in a bad mood; short-tempered.
isolated (y suh LAY tihd) *adj.* apart from others; separate.
isolation (y suh LAY shun) *n.* condition of being apart from others; removed.

J

jammed (jamd) *v.* got stuck and became unworkable.
jubilant (JOO buh luhnt) *adj.* joyful.

K

keen (keen) *adj.* eager; enthusiastic.

L

lair (lair) *n.* home of a wild animal; den.
lavishly (LAV ihsh lee) *adv.* abundantly; plentifully.
legacy (LEHG uh see) *n.* something handed down or left for others.
legitimate (luh JIHT uh miht) *adj.* reasonable; justified.
linen (LIHN uhn) *n.* fine-quality writing paper.
literally (LIHT uhr uh lee) *adv.* actually; in truth.
loftiest (LAWF tee ihst) *adj.* noblest; highest.
lunged (luhnjd) *v.* moved suddenly forward.

M

maneuvered (muh NOO vuhrd) *v.* moved, as a group, into position.
manipulate (muh NIHP yuh layt) *v.* manage or control, often in an unfair way.
marvel (MAHR vuhl) *v.* wonder at.
menacing (MEHN uh sihng) *adj.* threatening.
montage (mahn TAHZH) *n.* combination of pictures.
mortified (MAWR tuh fyd) *v.* used as *adj.* ashamed; embarrassed.
motto (MAHT oh) *n.* short statement that expresses the aims or beliefs of a person or institution.

N

nurturing (NUR chuhr ihng) *v.* keeping alive.
nutritious (noo TRIHSH uhs) *adj.* full of nourishment; healthful.

O

occupation (ahk yuh PAY shuhn) *n.* work a person does regularly.
outrageous (owt RAY juhs) *adj.* extreme; shocking.

P-Q

peculiar (pih KYOOL yuhr) *adj.* strange.
penetrated (PEHN uh tray tihd) *v.* pierced; made a way through.
permanent (PUR muh nuhnt) *adj.* lasting; unchanging.

perplexed (puhr PLEHKST) *adj.* puzzled.

persistent (puhr SIHS tuhnt) *adj.* repeated or continuing.

plunged (pluhnjd) *v.* dived down suddenly.

pollution (puh LOO shuhn) *n.* something that makes air, water, and soil dangerously dirty.

ponder (PAHN duhr) *v.* think over carefully.

precision (prih SIHZH uhn) *n.* exactness; accuracy.

prehistoric (pree hihs TAWR ihk) *adj.* relating to the time before written history.

prescribe (prih SKRYB) *v.* define officially.

previously (PREE vee uhs lee) *adv.* before now.

primary (PRY mehr ee) *adj.* first in importance.

privilege (PRIHV uh lihj) *n.* special right or benefit.

projection (proh JEHK shuhn) *n.* display of an image made by shining light through a small version of the image.

protective (pruh TEHK tihv) *adj.* preventing injury.

proverb (PRAHV urb) *n.* short wise saying.

prudent (PROO duhnt) *adj.* wise; sensible.

R

raggedy (RAG uh dee) *adj.* torn; in bad condition.

rash (rash) *adj.* impatient; reacting quickly.

rattling (RAT lihng) *v.* shaking and hitting together.

ravaged (RAV ihjd) *v.* damaged greatly.

recall (rih KAWL) *v.* remember; bring to mind.

recovered (rih KUHV uhrd) *v.* got back something lost.

rectify (REHK tuh fy) *v.* correct.

remedy (REHM uh dee) *n.* cure; solution.

resembled (rih ZEHM buhld) *v.* was similar to.

resumed (rih ZOOMD) *v.* began again.

revived (rih VYVD) *v.* awakened; brought back to life.

rival (RY vul) *adj.* competing.

rural (RUR uhl) *adj.* having to do with country life.

S

savored (SAY vuhrd) *v.* delighted in.

shrewdest (SHROOD ihst) *adj.* sharpest; most clever.

sift (sihft) *v.* strain or filter through something.

sinister (SIHN uh stuhr) *adj.* creepy; threatening.

snatched (snatchd) *v.* grabbed; ran off with.

spectacle (SPEHK tuh kuhl) *n.* strange or impressive sight.

splendor (SPLEHN duhr) *n.* brightness; glory.

stampede (stam PEED) *n.* sudden rush.

structure (STRUHK chuhr) *n.* something built or constructed.

supervisor (SOO puhr vy zuhr) *n.* person in charge.

surged (surjd) *v.* moved forward, as if in a wave.

surveyed (suhr VAYD) *v.* looked over and examined closely.

suspicion (suh SPIHSH uhn) *n.* feeling that someone is guilty of something.

T

tangles (TANG guhlz) *v.* becomes twisted into knots.

techniques (tehk NEEKS) *n.* ways of doing complex activities.

thrashing (THRASH ihng) *v.* moving from side to side in an uncontrolled way.

thrust (thruhst) *v.* shoved; pushed.

timid (TIHM ihd) *adj.* shy; lacking self-confidence.

tolerant (TAHL uhr uhnt) *adj.* patient; accepting of others.

torrents (TAWR uhnts) *n.* rushing streams of water.

treacherous (TREHCH uhr uhs) *adj.* dangerous.

tumult (TOO muhlt) *n.* violent disturbance.

U

unique (yoo NEEK) *adj.* one of a kind; rare or special.

urgency (UR juhn see) *n.* pressure; insistence.

V

valiant (VAL yuhnt) *adj.* determined; brave.

victorious (vihk TAWR ee uhs) *adj.* having won.

vigor (VIHG uhr) *n.* energy; physical or mental strength.

vital (VY tuhl) *adj.* necessary for life; very important.

vivid (VIHV ihd) *adj.* producing strong, clear images.

W-Z

wily (WY lee) *adj.* sly; clever in a sneaky way.

yearning (YUR nihng) *n.* feeling of wanting something badly.

Spanish Glossary

A-B

ademán *sust.* gesto que demuestra lo que uno siente.

adulación *sust.* alabanza o elogio que es falso o fingido.

afablemente *v.* de manera amigable; amablemente.

aferrar *v.* agarrar algo con firmeza.

aficionado *sust.* persona que participa en deportes u otras actividades por diversión y no por dinero; persona que no es un profesional.

agresivo *adj.* listo para atacar.

aguacero *sust.* lluvia abundante y repentina de poca duración.

aislado *adj.* apartado, separado.

aislamiento *sust.* estado de incomunicación con otras personas; soledad.

alucinación *sust.* percepción de un sonido o una imagen que en realidad no existe.

ambicioso *adj.* que tiene deseos y entusiasmo por lograr algo.

ambicioso *adj.* que tiene deseos y entusiasmo por lograr algo.

anhelo *sust.* sensación de desear mucho algo.

anónimo *adj.* desconocido; que no está identificado con un nombre.

apremio *sust.* urgencia; insistencia.

aprendiz *sust.* principiante; alguien que empieza a aprender un arte o un oficio.

aprensivamente *adv.* temerosamente; con preocupación.

apto *adj.* capaz.

arrastrar *v.* mover hacia adelante.

arrebatar *v.* agarrar de un manotazo.

arriesgado *adj.* peligroso.

arrogante *adj.* orgulloso de un modo desagradable.

artero *adj.* astuto; inteligente y engañoso.

asemejarse *v.* ser parecido a alguien o a algo.

asomarse *v.* estirar (el cuello) para ver mejor.

aspaviento *sust.* movimiento amplio.

atardecer *sust.* momento del día en el que se oscurece el cielo a medida que el sol se pone.

atascar *v.* atorar y hacer que algo ya no funcione.

atiborrar *v.* llenar; atestar.

audacia *sust.* atrevimiento.

autoridad *sust.* persona que tiene la responsabilidad oficial para hacer algo.

auxiliar *v.* ayudar.

bienestar *sust.* sensación de comodidad y agrado.

C-E

caos *sust.* desorden o confusión total.

cautelosamente *adv.* con cuidado.

cauteloso *adj.* cuidadoso.

cavilar *v.* pensar detenidamente en algo.

cercenar *v.* cortar la punta de algo.

cimbrar *v.* hacer vibrar algo.

circunstancia *sust.* hecho o condición que afecta a una situación, una acción o un suceso.

civilización *sust.* cultura avanzada característica de un tiempo y un lugar determinados.

cohibido *adj.* tímido; que no tiene seguridad en sí mismo.

coincidencia *sust.* hechos que suceden de forma accidental y parecen estar relacionados.

competencia *sust.* concurso; lucha por ver quién es mejor en algo.

complacido *adj.* feliz o satisfecho.

complejidad *sust.* complicación; dificultad.

comprometido *adj.* interesado por algo y ocupado en eso.

concentración *sust.* atención profunda en algo.

confinamiento *sust.* condición de estar retenido en un lugar; falta de libertad.

conocido *sust.* persona que se conoce pero con quien no hay mucha confianza.

conservación *sust.* protección de la naturaleza, como los animales, las plantas y los bosques.

consolar *v.* confortar o aliviar cuando uno está triste o desilusionado.

contemplar *v.* mirar algo detenidamente.

contemporáneo *adj.* relativo al tiempo presente; moderno.

contribución *sust.* pago que se hace con un propósito determinado.

cooperación *sust.* apoyo; trabajo en conjunto.

criterio *sust.* capacidad para tomar decisiones con responsabilidad.

crítica *sust.* comentario desfavorable.

decrecer *v.* disminuir; descender.

defensa *sust.* acción de equipo para evitar que el equipo contrario anote puntos.

deprimido *adj.* muy triste.

desafiante *adj.* desobediente; que se resiste.

desafiar *v.* resistir.

desatendido *adj.* que ya no se usa o no se cuida.

desesperado *adj.* que tiene una necesidad grande y urgente.

desolado *adj.* abandonado.

devastador *adj.* que causa mucho daño.

devastar *v.* causar destrucción, daño.

devorar *v.* comer con glotonería.

dictar *v.* establecer oficialmente.

diligencia *sust.* cuidado y empeño al hacer algo.

disputa *sust.* desacuerdo; discusión.

duplicar *v.* hacer una copia.

elenco *sust.* grupo de actores de una obra de teatro o espectáculo.

eludir *v.* evitar; esquivar.

embestir *v.* empujar de repente hacia adelante.

enmarañar *v.* enredar.

entusiasta *adj.* que tiene mucho interés en algo o muchas ganas de hacer algo.

escandaloso *adj.* vergonzoso.

espectáculo *sust.* algo que se ve y produce extrañeza o asombro.

esplendor *sust.* brillo; gloria.

estampida *sust.* huida repentina.

estéril *adj.* que no da frutos o no produce cosecha.

estructura *sust.* algo construido.

estrujar *v.* apretar con fuerza.

etiqueta *sust.* comportamiento y modales aceptables.

evacuar *v.* desocupar un área.

evidente *adj.* fácil de ver o entender; claro.

evocar *v.* recordar; traer a la memoria.

excéntrico *adj.* raro; extravagante.

exclusivo *adj.* único; raro o especial.

expreso *sust.* tren que viaja de u punto a otro sin hacer paradas.

expulsar *v.* liberar de repente o violentamente.

exterior *adj.* al aire libre.

extinto *adj.* que ya no existe.

exultante *adj.* lleno de alegría.

F-K

fascinar *v.* provocar atracción.

flotar *v.* mantenerse quieto en el aire.

frágil *adj.* débil; que se rompe fácilmente.

garantizado *adj.* que se prometió hacer o se aseguró que se haría si otra persona no lo hacía.

garantizar *v.* prometer o asegurar.

generosamente *adv.* mucho; en abundancia.

gesticular *v.* retorcer la cara para expresar algo, como dolor, enojo o disgusto.

goteo *sust.* cantidades pequeñas de un líquido que caen lentamente.

guarida *sust.* lugar donde vive un animal salvaje; refugio.

harapiento adj. roto y en malas condiciones.

ignorancia *sust.* falta de conocimiento.

impeler *v.* empujar; impulsar.

impostor *sust.* alguien que finge ser lo que no es.

impresionar *v.* hacer que alguien sienta admiración.

improbable *adj.* que no parece que pueda ser cierto.

indemnización *sust.* pago que se da como compensación por una pérdida o un daño.

indiferencia *sust.* estado de ánimo en que no se siente interés por algo.

indignado *adj.* ofendido; enojado.

inspeccionar *v.* observar o examinar de cerca.

instrumental *adj.* que sirve como medio para que algo suceda.

intimidante *adj.* amenazante.

intrigante *adj.* que causa gran curiosidad o interés.

invencible *adj.* que no puede ser derrotado.

invisible *adj.* que no se puede ver.

irascible *adj.* de mal humor; irritable.

irrevocabilidad *sust.* sensación de que algo es definitivo y no se puede cambiar.

L-Q

legado *sust.* algo que se deja o se transmite a otros.

legítimo *adj.* razonable; conforme a las leyes.

lema *sust.* frase breve que expresa los objetivos o las creencias de una persona, una escuela o una institución.

lindante *adj.* que está próximo a algo.

literalmente *adv.* realmente; en verdad.

llamativo *adj.* que atrae la atención.

lúgubre *adj.* sombrío; deprimente.

maniobrar *v.* mover algo.

manipular *v.* manejar o controlar, a menudo de manera injusta.

montaje *sust.* combinación de imágenes.

nutrir *v.* alimentar.

nutritivo *adj.* que tiene las sustancias alimenticias necesarias; saludable.

ocupación *sust.* trabajo que realiza una persona de forma regular.

paladear *v.* saborear.

papel tela *sust.* papel para escribir de muy buena calidad que antiguamente se hacía con trapos de lino.

parcela *sust.* porción de tierra.

partido *adj.* dividido; separado.

pasmar *v.* asombrar; maravillar.

peculiar *adj.* extraño.

pender *v.* estar algo colgado o suspendido.

perforar *v.* agujerear; atravesar.

permanente *adj.* definitivo; duradero.

perplejo *adj.* desconcertado.

persistente *adj.* que se repite o continúa.

picor *sust.* sensación en la piel que provoca ganas de frotarse o rascarse.

plagar *v.* habitar en gran número (algo dañino).

polución *sust.* algo que hace que el aire, el agua y el suelo se ensucien de manera peligrosa.

precipitado *adj.* impaciente.

precisión *sust.* exactitud.

prehistórico *adj.* relacionado con la época anterior a la historia escrita.

previamente *adv.* antes de ahora.

primordial *adj.* principal; primero en importancia.

privilegio *sust.* derecho o beneficio especial.

proeza *sust.* logro; acción valerosa.

protector *adj.* que impide que se produzcan lesiones.

proverbio *sust.* dicho corto y sabio.

proyección *sust.* imagen que, por medio de un foco luminoso, se fija temporalmente sobre una superficie plana.

prudente *adj.* sensato.

R-Z

realzar *v.* mejorar.

reanimar *v.* despertar; revivir.

reanudar *v.* comenzar de nuevo; continuar.

recluir *v.* encarcelar o encerrar.

recobrar *v.* recuperar algo perdido.

rectificar *v.* corregir.

remedio *sust.* cura; solución.

rezumar *v.* liberar, despedir algo.

riesgoso *adj.* peligroso; arriesgado.

rival *adj.* que compite; que trata de igualar o sobrepasar a otro.

rural *adj.* del campo o relacionado con él.

sagaz *adj.* astuto; inteligente.

siniestro *adj.* escalofriante; amenazante.

soportar *v.* resistir o aguantar.

sospecha *sust.* sensación de que alguien es culpable de algo.

sublime *adj.* noble; muy elevado.

supervisor *sust.* persona a cargo.

tamizar *v.* pasar por un filtro.

técnica *sust.* modo de llevar a cado actividades complejas.

templado *adj.* relativo al clima o al aire, cálido y agradable.

tolerante *adj.* paciente; que acepta a los demás.

torrente *sust.* corriente brusca de agua.

trascendencia *sust.* importancia.

tumulto *sust.* alboroto o agitaciún violenta.

turbado *adj.* avergonzado.

turbar *v.* avergonzar; abochornar.

valeroso *adj.* valiente; decidido.

vengar *v.* hacer un mal a alguien que le hizo mal a uno; tomar represalias.

victorioso *adj.* que obtuvo un triunfo.

vigor *sust.* energía; fuerza física o mental.

vital *adj.* necesario para la vida; muy importante.

vívido *adj.* que produce imágenes claras y fuertes.

zambullirse *v.* sumergirse de repente.

zarandear *v.* mover de un lado a otro de manera incontrolada.

Academic Vocabulary Glossary

The Academic Vocabulary Glossary is an alphabetical list of the Academic Vocabulary words defined in this textbook. Use this glossary just as you would use a dictionary—to find out the meanings of words used in your literature class. For each word, the glossary includes the pronunciation, part of speech, and meaning. A Spanish version of the glossary immediately follows the English version. For more information about the words in the Academic Vocabulary Glossary, please consult a dictionary.

ENGLISH

A-C

achieve (uh CHEEV) *v.* succeed in getting a good result or in doing something you want.

adapt (uh DAPT) *v.* change ideas or behavior to fit a new situation.

adequacy (AD uh kwuh see): *n.* quality of being enough to meet a need or requirement.

appreciate (uh PREE shee ayt) *v.* understand and enjoy the good qualities or value of something.

attitude (AT uh tood) *n.* opinions and feelings about someone or something.

authority (uh THAWR uh tee) *n.* someone who is respected because of his or her knowledge about a subject.

characteristics (kar ihk tuh RIHS tihks) *n.* important, typical parts or features.

circumstance (SUR kuhm stans) *n.* event or condition that affects a person.

communicate (kuh MYOO nuh kayt) *v.* express thoughts or feelings clearly so that other people understand them.

concept (KAHN sehpt) *n.* idea of how something is or could be.

conclude (kuh KLOOD) *v.* decide something after considering all the information.

contribute (kuh TRIHB yut) *v.* give or add something, such as resources or ideas.

contrived (kuh TRYVD) *adj.* unnatural; artificial.

conveyed (kuh VAYD) *v.* made known.

correspond (kawr uh SPOND) *v.* be similar to.

crucial (KROO shuhl) *adj.* very important.

D-G

detect (dih TEHKT) *v.* notice or discover, especially something that is not easy to see, hear, and so on.

device (dih VYS) *n.* way of achieving a particular purpose.

display (dihs PLAY) *v.* show clearly; reveal.

distinct (dihs TIHNGKT) *adj.* distinguishable; clearly different or of a different type.

H-O

illustrate (IHL uh strayt) *v.* explain or make something clear by giving examples.

indicate (IHN duh kayt) *v.* show; express; suggest.

influence (IHN flu uhns) *n.* ability or power to affect thought, behavior, or development.

insight (IHN syt) *n.* clear understanding of the true nature of something.

interact (ihn tuhr AKT) *v.* talk to and deal with others.

interpret (ihn TUR priht) *v.* decide on the meaning of something.

major (MAY juhr) *adj.* very large and important, especially compared with other things of a similar kind.

obvious (AHB vee uhs) *adj.* easy to notice or understand.

P-Z

perceive (puhr SEEV) *v.* grasp mentally; understand.

perspective (puhr SPEHK tihv) *n.* mental view or outlook; way of thinking.

qualities (KWAHL uh teez) *n.* traits; distinguishing characteristics.

U-V

uniform (YOO nuh fawrm) *adj.* having the same shape, size, quality, or other characteristics.

visual (VIHZH oo uhl) *adj.* related to seeing or to sight.

SPANISH

A-C

actitud *sust.* opiniones que uno toma y sentimientos que uno tiene con respecto a alguien o a algo.

adaptarse *v.* cambiar las ideas o la conducta para amoldarse a una situación nueva.

adecuación *sust.* adaptado para cumplir una necesidad o requisito.

apreciar *v.* comprender y disfrutar de la calidad o el valor de algo.

artificial *adj.* no natural.

autoridad *sust.* alguien que es respetado por su conocimiento acerca de un tema.

característica sust. rasgo importante o típico.

circunstancia *sust.* suceso o situación que rodea a una persona y la afecta.

complejo *adj.* que no es sencillo; complicado, difícil.

comunicar *v.* expresar los pensamientos o sentimientos claramente para que otras personas los entiendan.

concepto *sust.* idea de cómo es o cómo podría ser algo.

concluir *v.* decidir algo después de considerar toda la información disponible.

contraste *sust.* diferencia entre dos personas, situaciones, ideas, etc. al compararlas.

contribuir *v.* dar o agregar algo, como recursos o ideas.

corresponder *v.* ser parecido a algo.

crear *v.* hacer que suceda o que exista algo nuevo.

crucial *adj.* muy importante.

cualidades *sust.* atributos, características típicas

D-G

dato *sust.* hecho o cifra; información.

detectar *v.* notar o descubrir, especialmente algo que no es fácil de ver, oír, etc.

dinámico *adj.* que se caracteriza por la acción; enérgico.

distinto *adj.* diferente; claramente diferenciado o de otro tipo.

entendimiento *sust.* razonar y entender claramente la verdadera naturaleza de algo.

estrategia *sust.* modo de alcanzar un objetivo determinado.

exteriorizar *v.* mostrar claramente los sentimientos o cualidades.

fundamental *adj.* muy importante, especialmente en comparación con otras cosas del mismo tipo.

género *sust.* hecho de que algo o alguien sea femenino o masculino.

H-O

ilustrar *v.* demostrar o explicar algo mediante ejemplos.

indicar *v.* mostrar; expresar; sugerir.

influencia *sust.* capacidad o poder para aftectar el pensamiento o el comportamiento de otro.

interactuar *v.* hablar con otras personas y trabajar con ellas.

interpretar *v.* decidir sobre el significado de algo.

lograr *v.* tener éxito en algo que uno quiere.

obvio *adj.* fácil de notar o entender.

P-Z

percivir *v.* advertir, apreciar, comprender algo.

perspectiva *sust.* punto de vista; modo de pensar.

uniforme *adj.* que tiene la misma forma, tamaño, calidad u otras características.

visual *adj.* de la vista o relacionado con ella.

ACKNOWLEDGMENTS

For permission to reprint copyrighted material, grateful acknowledgment is made to the following sources:

"Oprah Talks About Her South African 'Dreamgirls'" from *ABC News* Web site, accessed October 1, 2007, at http://abcnews. go.com/GMA/story?id=2767103&page=1&CMP=OTC-RSSFeeds0312. Copyright © 2007 by **ABC News.** Reproduced by permission of the copyright holder.

From *Two in the Far North* by Margaret E. Murie. Copyright © 1978 by Margaret E. Murie. Reproduced by permission of **Alaska Northwest Books®, an imprint of Graphic Arts Center Publishing Company.**

From "Letters to Rev. Phillips Brooks" from *The Story of My Life* by Helen Keller. Copyright © 2005 by **The American Foundation for the Blind.** Reproduced by permission of the copyright holder.

"A Balmy Spring Wind" from *Haiku: This Other World* by Richard Wright. Copyright © 1998 by Ellen Wright. Reproduced by permission of **Arcade Publishing, New York, New York.**

"In the Blood" from *Chants* by Pat Mora, www.patmora.com. Copyright © 1985 by Pat Mora. Reproduced by permission of **Arte Público Press/University of Houston.**

"En la Sangre" from *Chants* by Pat Mora, www.patmora.com. Copyright © 1985 by Pat Mora. Reproduced by permission of **Arte Público Press/University of Houston.**

"The Bracelet" by Yoshiko Uchida from *The Scribner Anthology for Young People,* edited by Anne Diven. Copyright © 1976 by Yoshiko Uchida. Reproduced by permission of **Atheneum Books for Young Readers, an imprint of Simon & Schuster Children's Publishing Division.**

"Stray" from *Every Living Thing* by Cynthia Rylant. Copyright © 1985 by Cynthia Rylant. Reproduced by permission of **Atheneum Books for Young Readers, an imprint of Simon & Schuster Children's Publishing Division.**

From *Desert Exile: The Uprooting of a Japanese American Family* by Yoshiko Uchida. Copyright © 1982 by Yoshiko Uchida. Reproduced by permission of **Bancroft Library, University of California, Berkeley.**

"Eleven" from *Woman Hollering Creek* by Sandra Cisneros. Copyright © 1991 by Sandra Cisneros. Published by Vintage Books, a division of Random House, Inc., New York, and originally in hardcover by Random House, Inc. All rights reserved. Reproduced by permission of **Susan Bergholz Literary Services, New York.**

"Good Hot Dogs" from *My Wicked, Wicked Ways* by Sandra Cisneros. Copyright © 1987 by Sandra Cisneros. Published by Third Woman Press and in hardcover by Alfred A. Knopf. All rights reserved. Reproduced by permission of **Susan Bergholz Literary Services, New York.**

"Straw into Gold" by Sandra Cisneros from *The Texas Observer,* September 1987. Copyright © 1987 by Sandra Cisneros.

Reproduced by permission of **Susan Bergholz Literary Services, Inc., New York.**

"Dragon, Dragon" from *Dragon, Dragon and Other Tales* by John Gardner. Copyright © 1975 by Boskydell Artists Ltd. Reproduced by permission of **Georges Borchardt, Inc., for The Estate of John Gardner.**

"Winter Rain" by Nozawa Bonchō from *The Penguin Book of Japanese Verse,* translated by Geoffrey Bownas and Anthony Thwaite, Penguin Books, 1964. Translation copyright © 1964 by **Geoffrey Bownas and Anthony Thwaite.** Reproduced by permission of the translators.

"Bad-tempered, I got back" by Ōshima Ryōta from *The Penguin Book of Japanese Verse,* translated by Geoffrey Bownas and Anthony Thwaite, Penguin Books, 1964. Translation copyright © 1964 by **Geoffrey Bownas and Anthony Thwaite.** Reproduced by permission of the translators.

"Cynthia in the Snow" from *Bronzeville Boys and Girls* by Gwendolyn Brooks. Copyright © 1956 by Gwendolyn Brooks. Reproduced by permission of **Brooks Permissions.**

"A Caution to Everybody," "The Camel," "The Duck," "The Octopus," and "The Panther" from *Verses From 1929 On* by Ogden Nash. Copyright © 1953, 1935, 1940, 1942, 1940 by Ogden Nash. Reproduced by permission of **Curtis Brown, Ltd.**

Quote by Ogden Nash. Reproduced by permission of **Curtis Brown, Ltd.**

From *What Do Fish Have to Do With Anything?* by Avi, illustrated by Tracy Mitchell. Copyright © 1997 by Avi. Reproduced by permission of **Candlewick Press, Inc., Cambridge, MA.**

"Perseus and the Gorgon's Head" from *Greek Myths for Young Children* by Marcia Williams. Copyright © 1991 by Marcia Williams. Reproduced by permission of **Candlewick Press, Inc., Cambridge, MA, on behalf of Walker Books Ltd., London.**

Quote about comic books by Marcia Williams from *Candlewick Press* Web site, accessed October 1, 2007, at http://www. candlewick.com/authill.asp?b=Author&m=bio&id=1779&pix=y. Reproduced by permission of **Candlewick Press, Inc., Cambridge, MA.**

"Wartime Mistakes, Peacetime Apologies" by Nancy Day from *Cobblestone: Japanese Americans,* April 1996. Copyright © 1996 by Cobblestone Publishing, 30 Grove Street, Suite C, Peterborough, NH 03458. All rights reserved. Reproduced by permission of **Carus Publishing Company.**

"Making a Flying Fish" by Paula Morrow, adapted from *FACES: Happy Holidays,* vol. 7, no. 4, December 1990. Copyright © 1990 by Cobblestone Publishing, 30 Grove Street, Suite C, Peterborough, NH 03458. All rights reserved. Reproduced by permission of **Carus Publishing Company.**

PICTURE CREDITS

The illustrations and photographs on the Contents pages are picked up from pages in the textbook.
Credits for those can be found either on the textbook page on which they appear or in the listing below.

NY; (b), ©Tim Platt/Getty Images; **245,** ©Worldwide Picture Library/Alamy; **246** (t), ©Jonathan Kantor/Getty Images; (b), ©image100/CORBIS; **247,** ©Portraits Now Expressions; **249,** ©Pam Ingalls/CORBIS; **254,** ©Westend 61/Alamy; **256,** Courtesy of Lensey Namioka; **259,** ©Royalty-Free/CORBIS; **260,** ©Kevin Dodge/CORBIS; **263,** ©Sean Justice/Getty Images; **268,** ©Annie Griffiths Belt/CORBIS; **270** (tr), Hulton Archive/Getty Images; (bl), Courtesy of Myron Levoy; (br), ©Rudy Sulgan/CORBIS; **271,** ©Patrick Byrd/Alamy; **272,** ©Robert Brenner/Photo Edit; **274,** ©Neil Snape/Getty Images; **277,** ©Time & Life Pictures/Getty Images; **278,** ©DK Limited/CORBIS; **282,** ©Allan Davey/Masterfile; **284** (cr), ©Bettmann/CORBIS; **285,** ©Photowood Inc./CORBIS; **291,** ©Zac Macaulay/Getty Images; **292,** ©Chris E. Heisey/Place Photography; **293,** ©Steppenwolf/Alamy; **295,** ©Raymond K Gehman/Getty Images; **297,** ©Lake County Museum/CORBIS; **298,** ©Patrick Strattner/Getty Images; **299,** ©Dale OÕDell/Alamy; **301,** ©Hallmark Institute/Index Stock Imagery; **303, 304,** ©Patrick Strattner/Getty Images; **307,** Art Resource, NY; **308,** ©Ingram Publishing (Superstock Limited)/Alamy; **312,** ©The Cats' House; **314,** ©Rena Durham/ZUMA/newscom; **317** (bkgd), ©Co Rentmeester Inc./Getty Images; (inset), HRW Photo/Scott B. Rosen; **318, 319** (all), HRW Photo/Scott B. Rosen; **320,** ©Royalty-Free/CORBIS; **326,** HRW Photo; **340** (br), Cover image from *A Dog's Life: The Autobiography of a Stray* by Ann M. Martin. Copyright ©2005 by Matt Mahurin. Reproduced by permission of Scholastic, Inc.; (tl), Cover image from *The Heart of a Chief* by Joseph Bruchac. Copyright ©1998 by Joseph Bruchac. Reproduced by permission of Dial Books for Young Readers, a division of Penguin Group (USA) Inc., www.penguin.com; **341** (tr), Cover image from *Endangered Bats* by Bobbie Kalman. Copyright ©2006 by Crabtree Publishing Company. Reproduced by permission of the publisher; **342-343,** Courtesy of Agra-Art S. A.; **343,** ©Gerard Fritz/Getty Images; **349,** ©Hans Strand/CORBIS; **351,** ©Catherine Karnow/CORBIS; **352** (t), ©Jim Cooper/Getty Images; (b), Courtesy of John Cech; **354,** ©Stuart Cohen/The Image Works; **356** (l), Courtesy of Gary Soto; (r), ©Royalty-Free/CORBIS; **359,** ©Bettmann/CORBIS; **360,** ©Royalty-Free/CORBIS; **362,** ©Randy Faris/CORBIS; **366** (bkgd), ©Map Resources; (inset), National Motor Museum, Beaulieu; **368** (r), ©Michael Nelson/Getty Images; **371,** ©Connie Hayes; **373,** ©Map Resources; **377,** ©Lake County Museum/CORBIS; **380,** ©Map Resources; **384,** Courtesy of William Wegman; **386** (t), ©Arnold Adoff, used by permission; (b), ©Bettmann/CORBIS; **388,** ©Steve Maslowski/Getty Images; **389,** ©David Cole/Alamy; **390,** ©age fotostock/SuperStock; **391** (l), ©Royalty-Free/CORBIS; (r), ©Phyllis Greenberg/Animals Animals; **400,** The Daily Telegraph, London; **405** (all), ©Araldo de Luca/CORBIS; **412** (tl), ©Nancy Kaszerman/Zuma Press; (tr), Courtesy of the Walter Dean Myers Collection; (c), ©Brian Heath; (cr), Courtesy of the Walter Dean Myers Collection; **414,** ©Hugh Grannum/Knight Ridder/Tribune/Newscom; **415,** ©Brian Heath; **416,** Courtesy of the Walter Dean Myers Collection; **417,** Courtesy of Constance Myers; **419,** ©Anne-Marie Weber/Getty Images; **421,** ©Photodisc/Getty Images; **429** (border), Photodisc/Getty Images; (inset), ©Jim Erickson/CORBIS; **434,** ©Richard Hutchings/PhotoEdit, Inc.; **435,** ©Private Collection/©Look and Learn/The Bridgeman Art Library; **437,** ©Catherine Karnow/CORBIS; **446,** ©Gianni Dagli Orti/CORBIS; **447,** ©Petit Philippe/Paris-Match/GAMMA/Newscom; **448,** ©Sisse Brimberg/National Geographic Images/Getty Images; **454,** HRW Photo; **468** (tr), Cover image from *Regarding the Sink* by Kate Klise. Copyright ©2004 by Kate Klise. Reproduced by permission of

Harcourt, Inc.; **469** (bl), Cover image from *Ancient Mesopotamia: The Sumerians, Babylonians, and Assyrians* by Virginia Schomp. Copyright ©2004 by Scholastic, Inc. Reproduced by permission of the publisher; (br), Cover image from *But That's Another Story: Famous Authors Introduce Popular Genres,* edited by Sandy Asher. Copyright ©1996 by Sandy Asher. Reproduced by permission of Walker and Company, Inc.; **470-471,** ©Greg Pease/Getty Images; **471** (br), ©John Foxx/Getty Images; **478-479,** ©Kim Westerskov/Getty Images; **482,** Everett Collection, Inc.; **484** (bl), ©James L. Amos/CORBIS; (br), AFP PHOTOS/USPS/Newscom; **487** (t), ©Randy Duchaine; **492,** John Henry Stamp Design c 1996 United States Postal Service. All Rights Reserved. Used with Permission.; **494-495,** ©Martin Diebel/Getty Images; **496,** ©John Kelly/Getty Images; **499** (b), ©Hulton Archive/Getty Images; **500,** ©Geoff Manasse/Getty Images; **501** (bkgd), ©John Foxx/Getty Images; (inset), ©Christie's Images/CORBIS; **502** (t), ©Geoff Brightling/Getty Images; (b), ©Dave King/Getty Images; **503** (t), ©blickwinkel/Meyers/Alamy; (b), ©Christopher Scott/Alamy; **504,** cBettmann/CORBIS; **506,** ©blickwinkel/Alamy; **508** (t), Courtesy of Gary Soto; (c), ©Neil Michael/Axiom; (b), ©Anne Lindsay Photograpy; **509,** ©Leana Alagia/Getty Images; **510,** ©SuperStock, Inc.; **511** (inset), ©Frank Conaway/Getty Images; (bkgd), ©Peter Dazeley/Getty Images; **512** (bkgd), ©Peter Dazeley/Getty Images; (l), ©Larry Brownstein/Getty Images; (r), ©Jeff Foott/Getty Images; **513,** ©Dave & Les Jacobs/Alamy; **516** (bl), Hulton Archive/Getty Images; (br), ©Stewart Smith/Illustration Works/Getty Images; **517,** Veer; **518,** ©Gilbert Mayers/SuperStock; **521** (t), ©Snark/Art Resource, NY; (b), ©Robert Kradin/AP Photos; **522-523,** ©Christie's Images/SuperStock; **526,** Collection of Aaron & Marion Borenstein, Miami, Florida. ©1995 Carmen Lomas Garza; **528** (c), ©Cheron Bayna; (b), Courtesy of David Kherdian; **529,** ©FLILET Patrick/Hemis/Alamy; **530** (bkgd), ©ZenShui/Michele Constantini/Getty Images; (l), Collection of Aaron & Marion Borenstein, Miami, Florida. ©1995 Carmen Lomas Garza; **532,** ©LWA-Dann Tardif/CORBIS; **533** (bkgd), ©LWA-Dann Tardif/CORBIS; (inset), Courtesy of David Kherdian; **540,** HRW Photo; **548,** ©George Diebold/Getty Images; **552** (tl), Cover image from *Rimshots* by Charles R. Smith. Copyright ©1999 by Charles R. Smith Jr. Reproduced by permission of Penguin Books for Young Readers, a division of Penguin Group (USA) Inc., www.penguin.com; (tr), Cover image by Leticia Tarrago from *The Tree Is Older Than You Are* by Naomi Shihab Nye. Copyright ©1995 by Naomi Shihab Nye. Reproduced by permission of Simon & Schuster Children's Publishing Division; (br), Cover image from *Langston Hughes: Young Black Poet* by Montrew Dunham. Copyright ©1972 by the Bobbs-Merrill Company, Inc. Reproduced by permission of Simon & Schuster Children's Publishing Division; **553** (tl), Cover image from *Whisked Away* by Richard Brown. Copyright ©1993 by Cambridge University Press. Reproduced by permission of the publisher.; (tr), Cover image from *Poetry Matters: Writing a Poem from the Inside Out* by Ralph Fletcher. Copyright ©2002 by Ralph Fletcher. Reproduced by permission of HarperCollins Publishers, Inc.; (bl), Cover image from *Home: A Journey Through America* by Thomas Locker. Copyright ©1998 by Thomas Locker. Reproduced by permission of Harcourt, Inc.; **563,** ©Steve Smith/Getty Images; **588,** ©Gulliver Books; Harcourt, Inc.; New York, N.Y.; **695** (inset), ©Fani Mahuntsi/Images24; (bkgd), Photos.com; **736** (br), Cover image for *At the Controls: Questioning Video and Computer Games* by Neil Anderson. Copyright ©2007 by Capstone Press. Reproduced by permission of the publisher. Cover photos ©David Hsu/Shutterstock; **554-555,** ©Stephen

Chernin/Getty Images; **555,** (r) ©Travel Ink/Getty Images; **560,** ©Goodshoot/CORBIS; **561,** ©Mike Greenslade/Alamy; **563,** ©Steve Smith/Getty Images; **564** (t), ©Arthur S Aubry/Stockbyte/Getty Images; (b), Courtesy of Gary Soto; **566,** ©Hyancinth Manning/SuperStock; **568** (tr), ©David Sanger Photography/Alamy; (bl), ©Syracuse Newspapers/Frank Ordonez/The Image Works; (br), Photo Courtesy of the National Endowment for the Arts; **569,** ©Michele Salmieri/Masterfile; **574,** ©John William Banagan/Getty Images; **576,** ©2005 Antonia Deutsch/Getty Images; **577,** ©Owen Franken/Getty Images; **579,** ©Bertrand Gardel/Getty Images; **581,** ©Tim Page/CORBIS; **582-583,** ©Randy Olson/Getty Images; **588,** Illustration from LET IT SHINE: STORIES OF BLACK WOMEN FREEDOM FIGHTERS by Andrea Davis Pinkney, illustrations copyright ©2000 by Stephen Alcorn, reproduced by permission of Harcourt, Inc. this material may not be reproduced in any form or by any means without prior written permission of the publisher; **590** (l), Jacob Harris/AP/Wide World Photos; (r), ©Bettmann/CORBIS; **593,** ©Bridgeman Art Library; **597** (bkgd), ©Stanley Walker/Syracuse Newspapers/The Image Works; (inset), ©North Wind Picture Archives/Alamy; **602,** Private Collection/Bridgeman Art Library; **604** (t), Random House; (c), Houghton Mifflin Company; (b), ©Jim Shea/AP/Wide World Photos; **606-611** (all), Courtesy of Scott Kennedy; **615** (bkgd), ©Morton Beebe/CORBIS; (inset), ©The Corcoran Gallery of Art/CORBIS; **617** (bkgd), ©Hugh Talman/Smithsonian Images; (inset), ©Bettmann/CORBIS; **618,** ©Alan Schein Photography/CORBIS; **622** (all), Mark Preston/HRW Photo; **623,** ©Dante Fenolio/Photo Researchers, Inc.; **625-628** (all), Mark Preston/HRW Photo; **634** (l), ©Folio Inc/Alamy; (r bkgd), ©Jeremy Woodhouse/Getty Images; (r), Courtesy of the Historical Society of Delaware; **635** (bkgd), ©Louie Psihoyos/CORBIS; (inset), Courtesy of the Historical Society of Delaware; **638,** Private Collection, Photo ©Christie's Images/The Bridgeman Art Library; **640,** ©Louie Psihoyos/CORBIS; **643** (l), ©age fotostock/SuperStock; (r), ©Folio Inc/Alamy; **644,** ©Stockbyte/Getty Images; **645,** Photo: The Jacob and Gwendolyn Lawrence Foundation/Art Resource, NY; **646,** Photo: The Jacob and Gwendolyn Lawrence Foundation/Art Resource, NY; **647,** Photo: The Jacob and Gwendolyn Lawrence Foundation/Art Resource, NY; **648,** Photo: The Jacob and Gwendolyn Lawrence Foundation/Art Resource, NY; **654,** HRW Photo; **673** (tl), ©Getty Images; (tr), Cover image from *Faces: People, Places, and Cultures,* April 2007. Cover copyright ©2007 by Thinkstock/Alamy. Reproduced by permission of Cobblestone Publishing, Inc; (bl), ©Getty Images; (br), ©Adriana Zehbrauskas/Polaris Images; **674-675,** ©Todd Gipstein/CORBIS; **675** (br), ©Peter Dazeley/Getty Images; **680-681** (bkgd), ©Artifacts Images/Getty Images; **681,** ©Will & Deni McIntyre/CORBIS; **682** (bkgd), ©Artifacts Images/Getty Images; (inset), ©Robin Nelson/Zuma/CORBIS; **684** (bkgd), ©Artifacts Images/Getty Images; (inset), ©blue jean images/Getty Images; **686,** ©David Deas/Getty Images; **688,** ©Hans Neleman/Getty Images; **691** (tl), ©Brad Wrobleski/Masterfile; (tr), ©Nick White/Getty Images; (b), ©Sylvain Grandadam/Getty Images; **692,** ©Tim Pannell/CORBIS; **695** (bkgd), Photos.com; (inset), ©Fani Mahuntsi/Images24; **696,** ©Louise Gubb/CORBIS; **697,** ©Denis Farell/AP Photo; **698,** ©AFP PHOTO/Joe Alexander/Newscom; **701** (bkgd), ©Timothy Hearsum/Getty Images; (inset), ©Steve & Ann Toon/Robert Harding World Imagery/CORBIS; **702** (bkgd), ©Timothy Hearsum/Getty Images; (map), Courtesy of Parks Canada; (t), ©Gregor Schuster/Getty Images; **706-707** (bkgd), ©UntitledOne productions inc./Getty Images; **706** (tr), ©David Toase/Getty Images; (c), ©Digital Vision/Getty Images; **707** (tc, br), ©David Toase/Getty Images; **710-711** (bkgd), ©Allana Wesley White/CORBIS; **724,** Victoria Smith/HRW Photo; **736** (tr), Cover image by National Geographic from *My Life with the Chimpanzees* by Jane Goodall. Copyright 1988, 1996 by Byron Preiss Visual Publications, Inc. Reproduced by permission of National Geographic Society; (tl), Cover image for *Media Madness: An Insider's Guide to Media* by Dominic Ali. Illustrations copyright ©2005 by Michael Cho. Reproduced by permission of Kids Can Press Ltd.; (bl), Cover image from *Oprah Winfrey* by Heather Hudak. Copyright ©2006 by Weigl Publishers Inc. Reproduced by permission of the publishers; (br), Cover image for *At the Controls: Questioning Video and Computer Games* by Neil Anderson. Copyright ©2007 by Capstone Press. Reproduced by permission of the publisher. Cover photos ©David Hsu/Shutterstock; **737** (tl), Cover image from *Explorers Wanted! On Safari* by Simon Chapman. Copyright ©2003 by Simon Chapman. Reproduced by permission of Little, Brown and Company; (tr), Cover image from *Advertising* by Bess Milton. Cover copyright ©2004 by Lester Lefkowitz/Corbis. Reproduced by permission of Children's Press, an imprint of Scholastic Library Publishing; (bl), Cover image from *Internet: Electronic Global Village* by David Jefferis. Copyright ©2002 by David Jefferis and Alpha Communications. Reproduced by permission of Crabtree Publishing Company; (br), Cover image from *Television and Movies* by Philip Abraham. Copyright ©2004 by Rosen Book Works, Inc. Reproduced by permission of Children's Press, an imprint of Scholastic Library Publishing; **738-739,** Digital Image ©The Museum of Modern Art/Licensed by SCALA/Art Resource, NY. The Museum of Modern Art, New York, NY, U.S. A. ©2008 Artists Rights Society (ARS), New York/ProLitteris, Zürich, Switzerland; **739** (br), ©Bloomimage/CORBIS; **745, 747,** ©William Whitehurst/CORBIS; **748,** ©Deborah Feingold/CORBIS; **750,** ©Stapleton Collection/CORBIS; **752** (t), ©Bettmann/CORBIS; (b), ©Miriam Berkley; **753,** ©Scala/Art Resource, NY; **762,** ©Roger Ressmeyer/CORBIS; **768,** ©Andrew Parrish/Illustration Works/CORBIS; **770,** ©Robert Maass/CORBIS; **771** (t), ©VisionsofAmerica/Joe Sohm/Getty Images; **772-777** (t), ©VisionsofAmerica/Joe Sohm/Getty Images; **778** (tl), ©Taro Yamasaki/Time & Life Pictures/Getty Images; **801** (tl), Cover image from *Pompeii: City of Ashes* by Sarah Pitt Kaplan. Copyright ©2005 by Rosen Book Works, Inc. Cover art copyright by Roger Ressmeyer/Corbis. Reproduced by permission of Children's Press, an imprint of Scholastic Library Publishing.

INDEX OF SKILLS

The boldface page numbers indicate an extensive treatment of the topic.

INDEX OF AUTHORS AND TITLES

Page numbers in italics indicate author biographies.

Aaron's Gift, 268, 271–278
ABC News Report, 686, 695–698
About "That Day," 533
Aesop, 384, *386,* 392, 393
Alarcón, Francisco X., 506, *508,* 511–512
All Aboard with Thomas Garrett, 632, 635–640
All I Really Needed to Know, I Learned in Kindergarten, from, 222–223
All Summer in a Day, 26, 29–34
All-American Slurp, The, 254, 257–264
Angelou, Maya, 566, *568,* 569
Anonymous African American, 482, 492, 493
Anthony, Michael, 136, *138,* 139
Asimov, Issac, 744, *748*
Avi, 602, *604,* 622

Bailey, Pearl, 3
Bakowski, Barbara, 432, 440
Bashō, Matsuo, *521,* 522
Blanca Flor, 146, 149–162
Bonchō, Nozawa, *521,* 522
Bracelet, The, 38, 41–46
Bradbury, Ray, 26, *28,* 29
Bradford, Sarah, 632, 642
Brain Breeze, 704, 715–717
Brooks, Gwendolyn, 482, *499,* 500
Brother, from *I Know Why the Caged Bird Sings,* 566, 569–570
Brown, Claude, 334
Bruchac, Joseph, 343
Bushnaq, Inea, 462
Bud, Not Buddy, from, 104–108

CAVE Online, 432, 446–448
Cech, John, 348, *352*
Celebrating the Quinceañera, 92–93
Cha, Dia, 794
Cisneros, Sandra, 110, *112,* 113
Concha, 50, 58–61
Coolidge, Olivia, 166, *168,* 169
Cricket in the Road, 136, 139–142
Curtis, Christopher Paul, 104, *108*
Cynthia in the Snow, 482, 500

Day, Nancy, 64, 66
Do or Die from *Gilgamesh the Hero,* 398, 401–408
Dog of Pompeii, The, 750, 753–761

Dragon, Dragon, 166, 184–191
Dudley, William, 322
Dygard, Thomas, 14, *16,* 17

Eleven, 110, 113–116
Everett, Gwen, 662

Fletcher, Lucille, 282, *284,* 295
Forty-one Seconds on a Sunday in June, in Salt Lake City, Utah, 548–549
Fox and the Crow, The, 384, 392
Frank, Anne, 675
Freedman, Russell, 602, *604,* 614
Fulghum, Robert, 222
Full Fathom Five, from *The Tempest,* 482, 501
Fun They Had, The, 744–748

Game, The, 412, 419–422
Gardner, John, 166, *168,* 184
Geiger, Milton, 282, *284,* 285
Geisel, Theodor (Dr. Seuss), 482, *484,* 485
George, Jean Craighead, 220
Global Classroom, The, 680–684
Glory over Everything, A, 588, 591–598
Going Batty! How to Build a Bat House, 312, 317–320
Going to Bat for Baseball and Cricket, 194, 203–206
Gold Cadillac, The, 366, 369–380
Golden Serpent, The, 412, 424–428

Haiku, 522–523
Haley, Alex, 229
Hamilton, Virginia, 384, *386,* 387
Hard on the Gas, 506, 513
Harriet Tubman: Conductor on the Underground Railroad, from, 664–665
Harriet Tubman: The Moses of Her People, from, 632, 642–643
He Lion, Bruh Bear, and Bruh Rabbit, 384, 387–391
Hitchhiker, The, 282, 295–309
Hoffman, Barbara, 412, 415
Hughes, Langston, 506, *516,* 517, 518
Hunt, Leigh, 739
In a Neighborhood in Los Angeles, 506, 511–512

In the Blood/En la Sangre, 526, 530
In the Fog, 282, 285–293
Interview with Walter Dean Myers, An, 412, 415–417
Iraqi Treasures Hunted, 432, 440–443
Ives, Sarah, 686, 701

Jacket, The, 560–564
John Brown: One Man Against Slavery, from, 662–663
John Henry, 482, 492, 493–496
Julie of the Wolves, from, 220–221
Just Once, 14, 17–22

Keller, Helen, 471
King of Mazy May, The, 120, 123–132
Kherdian, David, 526, *528,* 532, 533
Kolata, Gina, 686, 688–692
Kroll, Jennifer, 432, 434

La Bamba, 354, 357–362
Land I Lost, The, from, 574, 577–584
Lawrence, Jacob, 632, 644
Levoy, Myron, 268, *270,* 271
Life of Harriet Tubman, The, from, 632, 644–648
Little Mangy One, 462
Livo, Norma J., 794
London, Jack, 120, *122,* 123
Love That Boy, 412, 429

Making a Flying Fish, 208
Making It Up as We Go: The History of Storytelling, 432, 434–437
McCaughrean, Geraldine, 398, *400,* 401
Medusa's Head, 166, 169–178
Miller, Alice P., 632, 635
Mora, Pat, 526, *528,* 530
Morrow, Paula, 208
Motto, 506, 518
Myers, Walter Dean, 412, *414,* 419, 424, 429
Mysterious Mr. Lincoln, The, 602, 614–618

Namioka, Lensey, 254, *256,* 257
Nash Menagerie, A, 482, 502–504
Nash, Ogden, 482, *499,* 502–504
National Geographic Kids News, 686, 701–702
New York Times, The, 686, 688–692
Nhuong, Huynh Quang, 574, *576,* 577

868 Index of Authors and Titles

RESOURCE CENTER

Index of Authors and Titles